Dictionary of Literary Biography

Dictionary of Literary Biography Documentary Series

9 *American Writers of the Vietnam War: W. D. Ehrhart, Larry Heinemann, Tim O'Brien, Walter McDonald, John M. Del Vecchio,* edited by Ronald Baughman (1991)

10 *The Bloomsbury Group,* edited by Edward L. Bishop (1992)

11 *American Proletarian Culture: The Twenties and The Thirties,* edited by Jon Christian Suggs (1993)

12 *Southern Women Writers: Flannery O'Connor, Katherine Anne Porter, Eudora Welty,* edited by Mary Ann Wimsatt and Karen L. Rood (1994)

13 *The House of Scribner, 1846–1904,* edited by John Delaney (1996)

14 *Four Women Writers for Children, 1868–1918,* edited by Caroline C. Hunt (1996)

15 *American Expatriate Writers: Paris in the Twenties,* edited by Matthew J. Bruccoli and Robert W. Trogdon (1997)

16 *The House of Scribner, 1905–1930,* edited by John Delaney (1997)

17 *The House of Scribner, 1931–1984,* edited by John Delaney (1998)

18 *British Poets of The Great War: Sassoon, Graves, Owen,* edited by Patrick Quinn (1999)

19 *James Dickey,* edited by Judith S. Baughman (1999)

See also DLB 210, 216, 219, 222, 224, 229, 237, 247, 253, 254, 263, 269, 273, 274, 280, 284, 288, 291, 294, 298, 301, 304, 308, 309, 315, 316, 320, 324, 338, 340

Dictionary of Literary Biography Yearbooks

1980 edited by Karen L. Rood, Jean W. Ross, and Richard Ziegfeld (1981)

1981 edited by Karen L. Rood, Jean W. Ross, and Richard Ziegfeld (1982)

1982 edited by Richard Ziegfeld; associate editors: Jean W. Ross and Lynne C. Zeigler (1983)

1983 edited by Mary Bruccoli and Jean W. Ross; associate editor Richard Ziegfeld (1984)

1984 edited by Jean W. Ross (1985)

1985 edited by Jean W. Ross (1986)

1986 edited by J. M. Brook (1987)

1987 edited by J. M. Brook (1988)

1988 edited by J. M. Brook (1989)

1989 edited by J. M. Brook (1990)

1990 edited by James W. Hipp (1991)

1991 edited by James W. Hipp (1992)

1992 edited by James W. Hipp (1993)

1993 edited by James W. Hipp, contributing editor George Garrett (1994)

1994 edited by James W. Hipp, contributing editor George Garrett (1995)

1995 edited by James W. Hipp, contributing editor George Garrett (1996)

1996 edited by Samuel W. Bruce and L. Kay Webster, contributing editor George Garrett (1997)

1997 edited by Matthew J. Bruccoli and George Garrett, with the assistance of L. Kay Webster (1998)

1998 edited by Matthew J. Bruccoli, contributing editor George Garrett, with the assistance of D. W. Thomas (1999)

1999 edited by Matthew J. Bruccoli, contributing editor George Garrett, with the assistance of D. W. Thomas (2000)

2000 edited by Matthew J. Bruccoli, contributing editor George Garrett, with the assistance of George Parker Anderson (2001)

2001 edited by Matthew J. Bruccoli, contributing editor George Garrett, with the assistance of George Parker Anderson (2002)

2002 edited by Matthew J. Bruccoli and George Garrett; George Parker Anderson, Assistant Editor (2003)

Concise Series

Concise Dictionary of American Literary Biography, 7 volumes (1988–1999): *The New Consciousness, 1941–1968; Colonization to the American Renaissance, 1640–1865; Realism, Naturalism, and Local Color, 1865–1917; The Twenties, 1917–1929; The Age of Maturity, 1929–1941; Broadening Views, 1968–1988; Supplement: Modern Writers, 1900–1998.*

Concise Dictionary of British Literary Biography, 8 volumes (1991–1992): *Writers of the Middle Ages and Renaissance Before 1660; Writers of the Restoration and Eighteenth Century, 1660–1789; Writers of the Romantic Period, 1789–1832; Victorian Writers, 1832–1890; Late-Victorian and Edwardian Writers, 1890–1914; Modern Writers, 1914–1945; Writers After World War II, 1945–1960; Contemporary Writers, 1960 to Present.*

Concise Dictionary of World Literary Biography, 4 volumes (1999–2000): *Ancient Greek and Roman Writers; German Writers; African, Caribbean, and Latin American Writers; South Slavic and Eastern European Writers.*

Dictionary of Literary Biography® • Volume Three Hundred Forty

The Brontës:
A Documentary Volume

Dictionary of Literary Biography® • Volume Three Hundred Forty

The Brontës:
A Documentary Volume

Edited by

Susan B. Taylor

University of Colorado, Colorado Springs

A Bruccoli Clark Layman Book

GALE
CENGAGE Learning™

Detroit • New York • San Francisco • New Haven, Conn • Waterville, Maine • London

**Dictionary of Literary Biography,
Volume 340: The Brontës:
A Documentary Volume**
Susan B. Taylor

Advisory Board: John Baker,
William Cagle, Patrick O'Connor,
George Garrett, Trudier Harris,
Alvin Kernan

Editorial Directors: Matthew J. Bruccoli and
Richard Layman

For product information and technology assistance, contact us at
Gale Customer Support, 1-800-877-4253.

For permission to use material from this text or product,
submit all requests online at **www.cengage.com/permissions**
Further permissions questions can be emailed to
permissionrequest@cengage.com

LIBRARY OF CONGRESS CATALOGING-IN-PUBLICATION DATA

The Brontës : a documentary volume / edited by Susan B. Taylor.
     p. cm. — (Dictionary of literary biography ; v. 340)
"A Bruccoli Clark Layman book."
Includes bibliographical references and index.
ISBN-13: 978-0-7876-8158-6 (hardcover)
    1. Brontë family—Biography—Dictionaries. 2. Brontë family—Bio-bibliography—Dictionaries. 3. Authors, English—19th century—Bio-bibliography—Dictionaries. 4. Brontë, Charlotte, 1816-1855—Bio-bibliography—Dictionaries.
5. Brontë, Emily, 1818-1848—Bio-bibliography—Dictionaries. 6. Brontë, Anne,1820-1849—Bio-bibliography—Dictionaries. 7. Brontë, Patrick Branwell, 1817-1848—Bio-bibliography—Dictionaries. I. Taylor, Susan B.

PR4168.B762 2008
823'809—dc22

ISBN-13: 978-0-7876-8158-6   ISBN-10: 0-7876-8158-X

Gale
27500 Drake Rd.
Farmington Hills, MI 48331-3535

Printed in the United States of America
1 2 3 4 5 6 7 12 11 10 09 08

*This work is dedicated to my husband Stephen Getty and our children Kevin, Drew,
and Julia, who made it possible.*

Contents

Contents

Plan of the Series

. . . Almost the most prodigious asset of a country, and perhaps its most precious possession, is its native literary product—when that product is fine and noble and enduring.

Mark Twain*

The advisory board, the editors, and the publisher of the *Dictionary of Literary Biography* are joined in endorsing Mark Twain's declaration. The literature of a nation provides an inexhaustible resource of permanent worth. Our purpose is to make literature and its creators better understood and more accessible to students and the reading public, while satisfying the needs of teachers and researchers.

To meet these requirements, *literary biography* has been construed in terms of the author's achievement. The most important thing about a writer is his writing. Accordingly, the entries in *DLB* are career biographies, tracing the development of the author's canon and the evolution of his reputation.

The purpose of *DLB* is not only to provide reliable information in a usable format but also to place the figures in the larger perspective of literary history and to offer appraisals of their accomplishments by qualified scholars.

The publication plan for *DLB* resulted from two years of preparation. The project was proposed to Bruccoli Clark by Frederick G. Ruffner, president of the Gale Research Company, in November 1975. After specimen entries were prepared and typeset, an advisory board was formed to refine the entry format and develop the series rationale. In meetings held during 1976, the publisher, series editors, and advisory board approved the scheme for a comprehensive biographical dictionary of persons who contributed to literature. Editorial work on the first volume began in January 1977, and it was published in 1978. In order to make *DLB* more than a dictionary and to compile volumes that individually have claim to status as literary history, it was decided to organize volumes by topic, period, or genre. Each of these freestanding volumes provides a

*From an unpublished section of Mark Twain's autobiography, copyright by the Mark Twain Company

biographical-bibliographical guide and overview for a particular area of literature. We are convinced that this organization—as opposed to a single alphabet method—constitutes a valuable innovation in the presentation of reference material. The volume plan necessarily requires many decisions for the placement and treatment of authors. Certain figures will be included in separate volumes, but with different entries emphasizing the aspect of his career appropriate to each volume. Ernest Hemingway, for example, is represented in *American Writers in Paris, 1920–1939* by an entry focusing on his expatriate apprenticeship; he is also in *American Novelists, 1910–1945* with an entry surveying his entire career, as well as in *American Short-Story Writers, 1910–1945, Second Series* with an entry concentrating on his short fiction. Each volume includes a cumulative index of the subject authors and articles.

Between 1981 and 2002 the series was augmented and updated by the *DLB Yearbooks*. There have also been nineteen *DLB Documentary Series* volumes, which provide illustrations, facsimiles, and biographical and critical source materials for figures, works, or groups judged to have particular interest for students. In 1999 the *Documentary Series* was incorporated into the *DLB* volume numbering system beginning with *DLB 210: Ernest Hemingway*.

We define literature as the *intellectual commerce of a nation:* not merely as belles lettres but as that ample and complex process by which ideas are generated, shaped, and transmitted. *DLB* entries are not limited to "creative writers" but extend to other figures who in their time and in their way influenced the mind of a people. Thus the series encompasses historians, journalists, publishers, book collectors, and screenwriters. By this means readers of *DLB* may be aided to perceive literature not as cult scripture in the keeping of intellectual high priests but firmly positioned at the center of a nation's life.

DLB includes the major writers appropriate to each volume and those standing in the ranks behind them. Scholarly and critical counsel has been sought in deciding which minor figures to include and how full their entries should be. Wherever possible, useful references are made to figures who do not warrant separate entries.

Each *DLB* volume has an expert volume editor responsible for planning the volume, selecting the figures for inclusion, and assigning the entries. Volume editors are also responsible for preparing, where appropriate, appendices surveying the major periodicals and literary and intellectual movements for their volumes, as well as lists of further readings. Work on the series as a whole is coordinated at the Bruccoli Clark Layman editorial center in Columbia, South Carolina, where the editorial staff is responsible for accuracy and utility of the published volumes.

One feature that distinguishes *DLB* is the illustration policy—its concern with the iconography of literature. Just as an author is influenced by his surroundings, so is the reader's understanding of the author enhanced by a knowledge of his environment. Therefore *DLB* volumes include not only drawings, paintings, and photographs of authors, often depicting them at various stages in their careers, but also illustrations of their families and places where they lived. Title pages are regularly reproduced in facsimile along with dust jackets for modern authors. The dust jackets are a special feature of *DLB* because they often document better than anything else the way in which an author's work was perceived in its own time. Specimens of the writers' manuscripts and letters are included when feasible.

Samuel Johnson rightly decreed that "The chief glory of every people arises from its authors." The purpose of the *Dictionary of Literary Biography* is to compile literary history in the surest way available to us—by accurate and comprehensive treatment of the lives and work of those who contributed to it.

The *DLB* Advisory Board

Introduction

When the census was taken in England on 30 March 1851 Charlotte Brontë's occupation was listed as "none."* By that time, Brontë had not only collaborated with her sisters Emily and Anne on a collection of verse, *Poems by Currer, Ellis and Acton Bell* (1846), but also had written and published two novels, *Jane Eyre* (1847) and *Shirley* (1849). By November 1851 she was at work on *Villette,* published in early 1853. This datum from the 1851 census becomes understandable when one studies the lives of Charlotte Brontë and her family, especially the challenges faced by educated and enterprising women in the mid nineteenth century who needed to support themselves. The search for a fulfilling life within society's bounds echoes throughout the letters, diaries, novels, and poems of the Brontë sisters, as is illustrated by the materials in *Dictionary of Literary Biography 340: The Brontës: A Documentary Volume.*

This collection of documents and images has been selected to give readers access to a range of contexts germane to the Brontës' lives and work. Placing written texts together with a selection of photographs, drawings, and facsimiles is especially appropriate for the Brontës, since they all were drawn to visual as well as verbal expression. The six chapters of this book are arranged to focus separately on the four children of Maria and Patrick Brontë who survived into adulthood—Branwell (1817–1848), Anne (1820–1849), Emily (1818–1848), and Charlotte (1816–1855)—with additional introductory and summary chapters elaborating the biographical and cultural contexts of their work. Branwell used pseudonyms to publish eighteen poems and one essay in Yorkshire area newspapers, and it is not clear whether his sisters knew the extent of his success. However, he played an important role in the lives of his sisters, each of whom made lasting contributions to literature, Charlotte with her four novels, including *The Professor,* posthumously published in 1857; Anne with *Agnes Grey* (1847) and *The Tenant of Wildfell Hall* (1848), and Emily with her powerful novel *Wuthering Heights* (1847) and her poetry.

* I am indebted to David Annal, Development Manager of the Family Records Centre, London, for supplying me with a transcription of the census returns.

The connections between their lives and work have fascinated critics and readers from the beginning of their publishing endeavors, when Charlotte, Emily, and Anne masked the Brontës' identities in the pen names of Currer, Ellis, and Acton Bell, respectively. The subtitle for *Jane Eyre* suggested by Charlotte's publisher—"An Autobiography"—may have fueled this curiosity. Charlotte Brontë's "Biographical Notice of Ellis and Acton Bell" (1850), written after Emily's and Anne's deaths and revealing their identities, added to the interest in the Brontës' lives. The Brontës as writers and individuals and the reception of their work over the past 160 years provide an opportunity to examine the parallels that are drawn between literature and biography. Many of the documents in this volume exemplify how supposed knowledge of a writer's life may influence an understanding of her work, whether appropriate or not.

The first important biography of a Brontë, Elizabeth Gaskell's *The Life of Charlotte Brontë* (1857), demonstrates how details from Charlotte's life chosen to emphasize her qualities as devoted daughter, loyal friend, and proper woman obscured fundamental aspects of Charlotte's personality, such as those revealed in the journal entries she wrote as a teacher at Roe Head School, in which she expressed her frustration with her students, her longing to continue writing the adventures of the characters from her juvenilia, and her sense of being confined by her teaching duties. Gaskell's portrayal of Charlotte as a virtuous, domestically centered woman (as well as an accomplished writer) persisted and was taken up by reviewers and biographers in the nineteenth and twentieth centuries. Only gradually, several decades after Gaskell's *Life* was published, did scholars begin to expand the story of the Brontës to focus on other family members and in greater detail upon the psychology and social position of the siblings.

One of the influences on the Brontës' literary work was their early and continuing interests in politics, art, and literature. The stimulating atmosphere of the Haworth Parsonage, the home for the family during the important years of the children's development, is evident in the manuscript books and magazines the children created. Their drawings and writings were influenced by artists such as the painter Sir Edwin Landseer (1802–1873), the painter/engraver

John Martin (1789–1854), the engraver Thomas Bewick (1753–1828), and the contemporary engravers the Finden brothers, William (1787–1852) and Edward (1791–1857)– whose work appeared in novels, magazines, and literary annuals such as the *Literary Souvenir, Friendship's Offering,* and the *Forget me Not,* of which the Brontës owned occasional issues. Writers such as George Gordon Lord Byron (1788– 1824), Thomas Moore (1779–1852), Sir Walter Scott (1771–1832), William Wordsworth (1770–1850), John Milton (1608–1674), Samuel Taylor Coleridge (1772–1834), William Cowper (1731–1800), Madame Germaine de Staël (1766–1817), and William Shakespeare (1564–1616) were read by the Brontës and influenced the characters, plot, and tone of their stories. The children included a range of contemporary events in their tales and booklets, such as the explorations of the west coast of Africa reported in *Blackwood's Edinburgh Magazine,* which shaped the invented kingdom that provided a backdrop for their writings. Other periodicals the family read included *Fraser's Magazine* and *The Lady's Magazine* and newspapers such as the *Leeds Mercury,* the *Leeds Intelligencer,* and the *Bradford Observer.* Satire, political intrigue, revolution, and power struggles among competing rulers feature in the Brontës' juvenilia, as reported by their imaginary journalists and literary figures in their tiny books and journals. The children imagined adventures for important historical and contemporary figures–including Napoleon (1769–1821), the Duke of Wellington (1769–1852) and his family, and the explorers Sir William Edward Parry (1790–1855), Sir John Ross (1777–1856), and Sir James Clark Ross (1800–1862)–that were rooted in some of their actual circumstances and accomplishments.

The children's academic pursuits were encouraged by their father, Reverend Patrick Brontë (1777– 1861), whose ambitions had carried him from a modest background in Ireland to St. John's College, Cambridge, where he earned his A.B. in 1806 and prepared for his ordination as minister in the Church of England. By the time the Brontë family settled in the parsonage in Haworth in 1820, Reverend Brontë had published two collections of poems as well as two narrative works. The mother of the family, Maria Branwell Brontë (1783–1821), who died in 1821 when Anne, the youngest of the six Brontë children was twenty-one months old, wrote at least one essay intended for publication. The letters she wrote to Patrick Brontë before their marriage reveal an engaging writer.

The Brontë children's educations also are a factor in understanding their works. Reverend Brontë hoped to provide his five daughters with schooling that would qualify them to support themselves through work as governesses or teachers, two of the few professions suited to women of their background. With these intentions, in 1824 he enrolled the four eldest girls, Maria (1814?–1825), Elizabeth (1815–1825), Charlotte, and Emily, at the recently opened Clergy Daughters' School, Cowan Bridge. Unsanitary living conditions and poor food at the school contributed to the deaths of Maria and Elizabeth in early summer 1825, events that Charlotte re-created in *Jane Eyre's* Lowood School. Following this disastrous experience at Cowan Bridge, Reverend Brontë and his sister-in-law, the unmarried "Aunt Branwell," taught the surviving children at home, including Anne and the only boy, Patrick Branwell (known as Branwell). Charlotte and Anne finished their educations with several terms of institutional education at Miss Wooler's excellent school at Roe Head, Mirfield.

Although the Brontë children experienced great loss with the deaths of their mother and two eldest sisters, their childhood writings suggest a life filled with imagination, humor, and physical and intellectual energy. The children created entire societies of imaginary characters and recorded their adventures, politics, battles, and literary endeavors in their miniature books; Charlotte and Branwell worked together on sagas about "Glass Town" and "Angria" while Emily and Anne focused on a kingdom they called "Gondal." The juvenilia illustrate their thematic preoccupations with important figures and events of the early nineteenth century, such as the Duke of Wellington (Charlotte's favorite hero) and famous explorers and statesmen of the day. Branwell's literary creation, Northangerland, served as his alter ego even into his adulthood.

The juvenilia appears to foreshadow that the Brontës were destined to become writers, but, as Juliet Barker notes in *The Brontës* (1994), it is important to realize that the sisters' careers as writers were launched in large measure because they found the occupations of teacher and governess uncongenial. Charlotte, working as a teacher at Miss Wooler's School from July 1835 to December 1838 described her employment as "wretched bondage." Especially challenging was spending time with students whose interests and abilities were mundane; furthermore, even in a well-run school like Miss Wooler's, teachers were expected to put in long hours, working well into the evenings. Anne's five-year post as governess to the three daughters of the Reverend and Mrs. Edmund Robinson entailed its own difficulties, including the poor salary, long hours, and being faced with the at-times corrupt behavior of the gentry.

As documents in this volume demonstrate, the difficulty of finding agreeable employment was to trouble all four grown Brontë children for much of their brief adult lives. Branwell tried working as a portrait painter, being a tutor to gentlemen's sons, and working for the new railroad line in the area. Although the first of the siblings to publish poems, he was unsuccessful in supporting himself through writing. Charlotte, Emily, and Anne decided that by starting their own school they might achieve the autonomy and community they lacked as employees. With funds from Aunt Branwell, Charlotte and Emily went to study in Brussels at a school run by Mme. Claire Zoë Héger and her husband, Constantin, hoping that more impressive credentials would enable them to open their own school.

Charlotte and Emily's experiences in Brussels contributed to the Brontës' finding a career—but not as schoolmistresses. Under the teaching of M. Héger, Charlotte and Emily improved their French composition skills in addition to other areas of study. M. Héger's guidance on Charlotte's writing helped her continue developing what became the mature style of her novels. After one term as students, Charlotte and Emily were invited by Mme. Héger to stay on as teachers in exchange for some further lessons—Charlotte to teach English and Emily music. This arrangement lasted until Aunt Branwell died in October of 1842, and Emily remained home after the funeral. Charlotte returned to Brussels for one more year as a teacher, probably motivated in part by her attraction to M. Héger, who did not reciprocate. More important, Charlotte's experiences influenced the novels she later wrote, including her depictions of unconventional heroes and heroines.

In contrast to the wealth of biographical detail for Charlotte's life (supplied by her letters especially) is the relative paucity of primary source materials for studying Emily's and Anne's lives. Much of what is known about Emily and Anne, especially their personalities, comes from Charlotte. For example, according to Charlotte, it was Emily's writing that inspired Charlotte to initiate the sisters' careers as writers. In "Biographical Notice of Ellis and Acton Bell," Charlotte indicates that she found Emily's poetry notebooks (one titled "Gondal Poems," the other just marked with her initials "E.J.B.") and eventually persuaded her sisters to collaborate with her on the volume of *Poems,* which they published at the cost of £36 10s.—money left to them by Aunt Branwell upon her death—under the pseudonyms of Currer, Ellis, and Acton Bell in 1846. It was Charlotte's descriptions of her sisters—the exceptional Emily in whose "nature the extremes of vigour and simplicity seemed to meet" and the milder Anne who "wanted the power, the fire, the originality of her sister"—that first introduced them to the public. Readers of the Brontës' works must decide to what extent biographical information about the sisters is useful in understanding and appreciating their fiction.

Almost from the moment Currer, Ellis, and Acton Bell published their first novels in 1847, questions concerning the relationship of biography and literature were raised by critics and readers. *Jane Eyre,* published in London by Smith, Elder in October 1847, caused a sensation, drawing condemnation as well as praise. When *Wuthering Heights* and *Agnes Grey* were published in December 1847, the mysterious Bells and the power and boldness of their works perplexed many critics. Underlying the critical response were all sorts of assumptions—including that writers write about what they know (and therefore that there was something "coarse" about the Bells who wrote such "coarse" books); that the gender of the writer would be obvious from the text; that women could not or should not write books about such topics as married men's affairs and destructive relationships; and that the writer's morality could be deduced from the work of fiction. In "Biographical Notice of Ellis and Acton Bell," where she hoped to rebut those who criticized the Bells' morality and choice of topics, Charlotte relies upon some of the same assumptions. With her revelations about her sisters, Charlotte determined how the "genius" Emily and "gentle" Anne would be viewed for much of the last century and a half.

The publication of Elizabeth Gaskell's *Life of Charlotte Brontë,* two years after Charlotte's death, further emphasized the idea that to understand the Brontës' novels one must understand their lives. Gaskell's biography portrayed as fact many points that were clearly matters of interpretation (such as Reverend Brontë's seemingly erratic and violent behavior and what she regarded as the deplorable conduct of Mrs. Robinson, the woman with whom Branwell may have had an affair). Although later interpreters of the Brontës' work often perpetuated Gaskell's occasionally erroneous assumptions, her biography remains an important text for understanding the Brontës' lives and works and the ways they were viewed by their contemporaries; intertwined with its inaccuracies are compelling narratives of influential moments in the family's experiences and of Charlotte's career as a nineteenth-century woman writer. As scholars in succeeding years have read the correspondence and private papers of the Brontës and their contemporaries, a much more complex portrait of the family has emerged, based in greater part in fact rather than speculation, myth, and idealization. As Gaskell's book suggests, there are important connections that can be drawn between the Brontës' biography and their writings. *DLB 340: The Brontës* integrates some of the important images, texts, and documents so that readers of the Brontës' works can make their own connections.

—*Susan B. Taylor*

Acknowledgments

This book was produced by Bruccoli Clark Layman, Inc. George Parker Anderson was the in-house editor.

Production manager is Philip B. Dematteis.

Administrative support was provided by Carol A. Cheschi.

Accountant is Ann-Marie Holland.

Copyediting supervisor is Sally R. Evans. The copyediting staff includes Phyllis A. Avant, Caryl Brown, and Rebecca Mayo. Freelance copyeditors are Brenda L. Cabra, Jennifer E. Cooper, and David C. King.

Pipeline manager is James F. Tidd Jr.

Editorial associates are Elizabeth Leverton and Dickson Monk.

Permissions editor is Kourtnay King.

Office manager is Kathy Lawler Merlette.

Photography editor is Kourtnay King.

Digital photographic copy work was performed by Kourtnay King.

Systems manager is James Sellers.

Typesetting supervisor is Kathleen M. Flanagan. The typesetting staff includes Patricia M. Flanagan.

Library research was facilitated by the following librarians at the Thomas Cooper Library of the University of South Carolina: Elizabeth Sudduth and the rare-book department; Jo Cottingham, interlibrary loan department; circulation department head Tucker Taylor; reference department head Virginia W. Weathers; reference department staff Marilee Birchfield, Karen Brown, Mary Bull, Gerri Corson, Joshua Garris, Beki Gettys, Laura Ladwig, Tom Marcil, Anthony Diana McKissick, Bob Skinder, and Sharon Verba; interlibrary loan department head Marna Hostetler; and interlibrary loan staff Robert Amerson and Timothy Simmons.

Many people and institutions made this project feasible. The University of Colorado at Colorado Springs granted me a research sabbatical in spring 2004 for this work. The Women's Committee of the Faculty Assembly assisted with travel expenses. My sincere thanks go to Joan Ray for her wisdom and encouragement and to the faculty of the Department of English who offered advice and support, as has Ashley Cross. Students in my Senior Seminar: The Brontës have inspired me with their questions and insights. For help finding sources, I thank librarian Christina Martinez; Laurie Williams and the interlibrary loan staff; and Liz Taylor, Carol Pacheco, and others at the Kraemer Family Library. I am grateful for archival research help from Malcolm Davis and the staff of the Brotherton Collection, University of Leeds; Sarah Carrat the Brontë Parsonage Museum Research Library; staff at the British Library; and David Annal of the Family Records Centre, London. Kathy Andrus, director, and staff at the university Teaching and Learning Center assisted with document scanning. Scott Bauer provided generous help with photographs for this volume. I am indebted to editor George Parker Anderson and the staff at Bruccoli Clark Layman for their work on this book. The encouragement and support of family and friends have made this project enjoyable, especially William and Barbara Taylor, Nancy and Jack Alves, Gene Getty and Sally Dunn, Beth Taylor Quirk and Gerald Quirk, Bill Taylor and Mark Noble, Sarah Mozelle and Ken Karakotsios, Matthew and Carrie Getty, and Rebecca Tucker.

—Susan B. Taylor

Permissions

The Atlantic Monthly. Excerpt from W. Somerset Maugham, "The Ten Best Novels: Wuthering Heights," *The Atlantic Monthly,* February 1948.

Auckland University Press. Excerpts from *Mary Taylor: Friend of Charlotte Brontë: Letters from New Zealand & Elsewhere,* edited by Joan Stevens. Auckland, New Zealand: Auckland University Press, 1972.

Blackwell. Excerpt from *The Brontës: Their Lives, Friendships and Correspondence,* volume 14 in *The Shakespeare Head Brontë.* Oxford: Blackwell, 1932.

The British Library. Illustrations on pages 42, 51, 148, 183, 185, 187, 209.

British Museum. Illustrations on pages 184.

Brontë Parsonage Museum/The Brontë Society. Illustrations on pages 14, 22, 23, 46, 48, 53, 59, 85, 91, 99, 101, 124, 127, 129, 180.

The Brotherton Collection, Leeds University Library. Illustrations on pages 81, 96.

Greening & Co. Illustration on page 306.

Harcourt, Brace. Virginia Woolf, "Jane Eyre and *Wuthering Heights,*" in her *The Common Reader.* New York: Harcourt, Brace, 1925.

Knopf. Excerpts from Lucasta Miller, *The Brontë Myth.* New York: Knopf, 2003.

Morgan Library & Museum. Illustration on page 126.

National Portrait Gallery. Illustrations on pages 14, 122.

Norton. Excerpts from *Jane Eyre,* by Charlotte Brontë, Norton Critical Edition, edited by Richard J. Dunn. New York: Norton, 2001.

Oxford University Press. Selections and excerpts from *The Letters of Charlotte Brontë,* 3 volumes, edited by Margaret Smith. Oxford: Oxford University Press, 1995, 2000, 2004. Illustration on page 42.

Pacific Film Archive Library. Illustration on page 308.

Penguin. Excerpt from *Charlotte Brontë: Juvenilia 1829–1835,* edited by Juliet Barker. London: Penguin, 1996.

Smithsonian Institution. Excerpt from an interview with illustrator Fritz Eichenberg conducted by Robert Brown, 14 May 1979 and 7 December 1979, Archives of American Art, Smithsonian Institution.

St. Martin's Press. Excerpts from Juliet Barker, *The Brontës.* New York: St. Martin's Press, 1995. Illustrations on pages 93, 202.

Thomas Cooper Library, University of South Carolina. Illustrations on pages 103, 137, 269, 270–271.

Thomas Nelson. Excerpt from Winifred Gérin, *Branwell Brontë.* London & New York: Thomas Nelson, 1961.

University of Missouri, Special Collections. Illustration on page 162. Courtesy of the Special Collections & Rare Books Department, University of Missouri-Columbia.

University of Virginia. Illustration on page 312.

Yale University Press. Translated essay by Sue Lonoff from *The Belgian Essays: Charlotte Brontë and Emily Brontë, A Critical Edition,* edited by Sue Lonoff. New Haven and London: Yale University Press, 1996.4

Dictionary of Literary Biography® • Volume Three Hundred Forty

The Brontës:
A Documentary Volume

Dictionary of Literary Biography

Works by the Brontës

Branwell Brontë

"And the Weary Are at Rest" (London: Privately printed, 1924).

Patrick Branwell Brontë: A Complete Transcript of the Leyland Manuscripts Showing the Unpublished Portions from the Original Documents in the Collection of Col. Sir Edward Brotherton, Bart., LLD, edited by Alex J. Symington and C. W. Hatfield (Leeds: Privately printed, 1925; republished, Folcroft, Pa.: Folcroft, 1969).

The Miscellaneous and Unpublished Writings of Charlotte and Patrick Brontë, 2 volumes, edited by Thomas James Wise and John Alexander Symington (Oxford: Blackwell, 1936, 1938).

The Poems of Patrick Branwell Brontë, edited by Victor A. Neufeldt (New York: Garland, 1990).

The Works of Patrick Branwell Brontë, 3 volumes, edited by Neufeldt (New York: Garland, 1997, 1999).

OTHER: *The Odes of Quintus Horatius Flaccus,* translated by Branwell Brontë, introduction by John Drinkwater (London: Privately printed, 1923).

Anne Brontë

See also the Anne Brontë entries in *DLB 21: Victorian Novelists Before 1885* and *DLB 199: Victorian Women Poets.*

BOOKS: *Poems by Currer, Ellis, and Acton Bell* (London: Alyott & Jones, 1846; Philadelphia: Lea & Blanchard, 1848)—includes twenty-one poems by Anne Brontë: "A Reminiscence," "The Arbour," "Home," "Vanitas Vanitatum, Omnia Vanitas," "The Penitent," "Music on Christmas Morning," "Stanzas," "If this be all," "Memory," "To Cowper," "The Doubter's Prayer," "A Word to the Elect," "Past Days," "The Consolation," "Lines Composed in a Wood on a Windy Day," "Views of Life," "Appeal," "The Student's Serenade," "The Captive Dove," "Self-Congratulation," and "Fluctuations."

Agnes Grey, as Acton Bell (London: Newby, 1847; Philadelphia: Peterson, 1850).

The Tenant of Wildfell Hall, as Acton Bell (3 volumes, London: Newby, 1848; 1 volume, New York: Harper, 1848).

Anne Brontë's Song Book (Clarabricken, Ireland: Boethius Press Limited, 1980).

COLLECTION: *The Poems of Anne Brontë: A New Text and Commentary,* edited by Edward Chitham (London: Macmillan, 1979; Totowa, N.J.: Rowman & Littlefield, 1979).

Emily Brontë

See also the Emily Brontë entries in *DLB 21: Victorian Novelists Before 1885; DLB 32: Victorian Poets Before 1850;* and *DLB 199: Victorian Women Poets.*

BOOKS: *Poems by Currer, Ellis, and Acton Bell* (London: Aylott & Jones, 1846; Philadelphia: Lea & Blanchard, 1848)—includes twenty-one poems by Emily Brontë: "Faith and Despondency," "Stars," "The Philosopher," "Remembrance," "A Death Scene," "Song," "Anticipation," "The Prisoner," "Hope," "A Day-Dream," "To Imagination," "How clear she shines," "Sympathy," "Plead for Me," "Self-Interrogation," "Death," "Stanzas to –," "Honour's Martyr," "Stanzas," "My Comforter," and "The Old Stoic."

Wuthering Heights: A Novel, as Ellis Bell (2 volumes, London: Newby, 1847; republished as 1 volume, Boston: Coolidge & Wiley, 1848).

The Complete Poems of Emily Jane Brontë, edited by C. W. Hatfield (New York: Columbia University Press, 1941; London: Oxford University Press, 1941).

Five Essays Written in French by Emily Jane Brontë, translated by Lorine White Nagel, edited by Fannie E. Ratchford (Austin: University of Texas Press, 1948).

The Belgian Essays: Charlotte and Emily Brontë, edited and translated by Sue Lonoff (New Haven: Yale University Press, 1996)—includes nine essays by Emily Brontë.

EDITIONS & COLLECTIONS: *Wuthering Heights,* with wood engravings by Fritz Eichenberg (New York: Random House, 1943).

Emily Jane Brontë: The Complete Poems, edited by Janet Gezari (London: Penguin, 1992).

The Poems of Emily Brontë, edited by Derek Roper and Edward Chitham (Oxford: Clarendon Press, 1995).

Wuthering Heights, edited by Pauline Nestor (London: Penguin, 2003).

Charlotte Brontë

See also the Charlotte Brontë entries in *DLB 21: Victorian Novelists Before 1885; DLB 159: British Short-Fiction Writers, 1800–1880;* and *DLB 199: Victorian Women Poets.*

BOOKS: *Poems by Currer, Ellis and Acton Bell* (London: Aylott & Jones, 1846; Philadelphia: Lea & Blanchard, 1848)—includes nineteen poems by Charlotte Brontë: "Pilate's Wife's Dream," "Mementos," "The Wife's Will," "The Wood," "Frances," "Gilbert," "Life," "The Letter," "Regret," "Presentiment," "The Teacher's Monologue," "Passion," "Preference," "Evening Solace," "Stanzas," "Parting," "Apostasy," "Winter Stores," and "The Missionary."

Jane Eyre. An Autobiography, as Currer Bell (3 volumes, London: Smith, Elder, 1847; 1 volume, New York: Harper, 1847).

Shirley: A Tale, as Currer Bell (3 volumes, London: Smith, Elder, 1849; 1 volume, New York: Harper, 1850).

Villette, as Currer Bell (3 volumes, London: Smith, Elder, 1853; 1 volume, New York: Harper, 1853).

The Professor: A Tale, as Currer Bell (2 volumes, London: Smith, Elder, 1857; 1 volume, New York: Harper, 1857).

The Twelve Adventurers and Other Stories, edited by C. K. Shorter and C. W. Hatfield (London: Hodder & Stoughton, 1925).

Legends of Angria: Compiled from the Early Writings of Charlotte Brontë, edited by Fannie E. Ratchford and William Clyde DeVane (New Haven: Yale University Press, 1933).

Charlotte Brontë: Five Novelettes, edited by Winifred Gérin (London: Folio Press, 1971).

The Secret & Lily Hart: Two Tales by Charlotte Brontë, edited by William Holtz (Columbia: University of Missouri Press, 1979).

The Poems of Charlotte Brontë: A New Annotated and Enlarged Edition of the Shakespeare Head Brontë, edited by Tom Winnifrith (Oxford & New York: Blackwell, 1984).

The Poems of Charlotte Brontë: A New Text and Commentary, edited by Victor A. Neufeldt (New York: Garland, 1985).

An Edition of the Early Writings of Charlotte Brontë, 3 volumes, edited by Christine Alexander (Oxford & New York: Blackwell, 1987, 1991)–comprises volume 1, *The Glass Town Saga 1826–1832* (1987); volume 2, *The Rise of Angria, 1833–1835, part 1: 1833–1834* (1991); volume 3, *The Rise of Angria, 1833–1835, part 2: 1834–1835* (1991).

The Belgian Essays: Charlotte and Emily Brontë, edited and translated by Sue Lonoff (New Haven: Yale University Press, 1996)–includes twenty-one essays by Charlotte Brontë.

EDITIONS: *Jane Eyre,* third edition (London: Smith, Elder, 1848).

Jane Eyre, with wood engravings by Fritz Eichenberg (New York: Random House, 1943).

Charlotte Brontë: Juvenilia 1829–1835, edited by Juliet Barker (London: Penguin, 1996).

Jane Eyre, Norton Critical Edition, edited by Richard J. Dunn (New York: Norton, 2001).

Stancliffe's Hotel, edited by Heather Glen (London: Penguin 2003).

OTHER: "Biographical Notice of Ellis and Acton Bell," in *Wuthering Heights, Agnes Grey,* together with a selection of poems by Ellis and Acton Bell, as Currer Bell (London: Smith, Elder, 1850).

LETTERS: *The Letters of Charlotte Brontë,* 3 volumes, edited by Margaret Smith (Oxford: Oxford University Press, 1995, 2000, 2004).

General Collections

The Life and Works of Charlotte Brontë and her Sisters, Haworth Edition, 7 volumes, edited by Mrs. Humphry Ward and C. K. Shorter (London: Smith, Elder, 1899–1900); republished as *Life and Works of the Sisters Brontë* (New York & London: Harper, 1899–1903)–comprises volume 1, *Jane Eyre;* volume 2, *Shirley;* volume 3, *Villette;* volume 4, *The Professor, Poems by Charlotte, Emily, and Anne Brontë and the Rev. Patrick Brontë;* volume 5,

Wuthering Heights and *Agnes Grey;* volume 6, *The Tenant of Wildfell Hall;* and volume 7, Gaskell, *The Life of Charlotte Brontë.*

The Complete Works of Charlotte Brontë and Her Sisters, 7 volumes (London: Gresham [1905])—comprises volume 1, *Jane Eyre;* volume 2, *The Professor,* "Emma" & Poems; volume 3, *Shirley;* volume 4, *Villette;* volume 5, *Tenant of Wildfell Hall;* volume 6, *Wuthering Heights* and *Agnes Gray;* volume 7, *The Life of Charlotte Brontë.*

Brontë Poems: Selections from the Poetry of Charlotte, Emily, Anne and Branwell Brontë, edited by Arthur C. Benson (New York & London: Putnam, 1915).

The Shakespeare Head Brontë, 19 volumes, edited by T. J. Wise and John Alexander Symington (Oxford: Blackwell, 1931–1938)—comprises volumes 1 and 2, *Jane Eyre* (1931); volume 3, *The Professor* (1931); volumes 4 and 5, *Shirley* (1931); volumes 6 and 7, *Villette* (1931); volume 8, *Wuthering Heights* (1931); volume 9, *Agnes Grey* (1931); volumes 10 and 11, *The Tenant of Wildfell Hall* (1931); volumes 12, 13, 14, and 15, *The Brontës: Their Lives, Friendships and Correspondence,* in four volumes (1932) [volume 1, 1777–1843; volume 2, 1844–1849; volume 3, 1849–1852; volume 4, 1852–1928]; volume 16, *The Poems of Emily Jane Brontë and Anne Brontë* (1834); volume 17, *The Poems of Charlotte Brontë and Patrick Branwell Brontë* (1934); volumes 18 and 19, *The Miscellaneous and Unpublished Writings of Charlotte and Patrick Branwell Brontë,* in two volumes (volume 1, 1936; volume 2, 1938).

The Brontë Letters, edited by Muriel Spark (London: Peter Nevill, 1954); republished as *The Letters of the Brontës* (Norman: University of Oklahoma Press, 1954).

Chronology of the Brontë Family

1777

17 March   Patrick Brunty (later Brontë), father of the Brontës, born at Emdale, County Down, Northern Ireland, the first of ten children.

1783

15 April   Maria Branwell, mother of the Brontës, born at Penzance, eighth of eleven children.

1802

1 October   Patrick Brunty enrolls at St. John's College, Cambridge, spelling his last name as Bronte in the register.

1806

23 April   Patrick Brontë graduates from St. John's College with a bachelor of arts degree.

1807

21 December   Patrick Brontë ordained as priest.

1811   Reverend Brontë's *Cottage Poems* published by P. K. Holden, Halifax.

1812

29 December   Patrick Brontë and Maria Branwell marry at Guiseley Parish Church, Yorkshire.

1813   Reverend Brontë's *The Rural Minstrel: A Miscellany of Descriptive Poems* published by P. K. Holden, Halifax.

1814

23 April   Maria Brontë baptized, first child of Patrick and Maria; birthdate in Hartshead, Yorkshire, unknown.

1815

8 February   Elizabeth Brontë born at Hartshead, Yorkshire.

19 May   Reverend Brontë becomes perpetual curate at Thornton, Yorkshire. Family moves into the parsonage on Market Street, Thornton.

1816

21 April   Charlotte Brontë born at Thornton.

1817

26 June   Patrick Branwell Brontë born at Thornton.

1818	Reverend Brontë's *The Maid of Killarney* is published in London by Baldwin, Cradock, and Joy.
30 July	Emily Jane Brontë born at Thornton.
1820	
17 January	Anne Brontë born at Thornton.
25 February	Reverend Brontë becomes perpetual curate of the Church of St. Michael and All Angels, Haworth, in the Parish of Bradford, Yorkshire. Annual income £170.
April	The Brontës move to the parsonage at Haworth.
1821	
Summer	Aunt Branwell comes to help at Haworth; she stays for twenty-one years, until her death.
15 September	Maria Branwell Brontë dies of cancer after seven and a half months of illness, Haworth. Buried 22 September.
1824	
21 July	Maria and Elizabeth sent to Clergy Daughters' School, Cowan Bridge, north of Haworth.
10 August	Charlotte enrolls at Cowan Bridge.
25 November	Emily enrolls at Cowan Bridge.
1825	
14 February	Maria diagnosed with pulmonary tuberculosis and sent home from Cowan Bridge; she dies on 6 May.
31 May	Elizabeth brought home ill with pulmonary tuberculosis from Cowan Bridge; she dies on 15 June.
1 June	Reverend Brontë takes Charlotte and Emily home from Cowan Bridge.
1826	
5 June	Branwell receives toy soldiers (called The Twelves in the juvenilia) from Leeds.
1826–1830	The Brontë children's "Plays" begin, as indicated in extant juvenile writings. These writings include Charlotte and Branwell's Young Men's Plays, Our Fellows Play, Plays of the Islanders, and Charlotte and Emily's "bed plays." By 1829/1830 Charlotte and Branwell are working on variations of "Branwell's Blackwood's Magazine" and "Blackwood's Young Men's Magazine." The children record their stories of Glass Town, Angria, and Gondal in tiny manuscript books.
1831	
17 January	Charlotte begins studies at Miss Wooler's school at Roe Head, Mirfield, Yorkshire. Becomes friends with Ellen Nussey and Mary Taylor.
1832	
June	Charlotte leaves Roe Head; that summer she becomes first superintendent of Haworth National Sunday School.
1835	Branwell begins art lessons with William Robinson of Leeds that end in mid September.
29 July	Charlotte and Emily go to Roe Head, Charlotte to teach and Emily to study.
October	Anne takes Emily's place as student at Roe Head because Emily's health has declined there.

1836

Emily and Anne are writing their earliest poetry that survives.

29 December

Charlotte writes to Robert Southey for advice on her writing, enclosing some poetry for his evaluation.

1837

10 January

Branwell writes to William Wordsworth, enclosing a poem for his evaluation.

December

Anne becomes ill at Roe Head.

1838

30 January

Charlotte returns to Roe Head without Anne, who convalesces at home. She teaches till May, when she resigns, only to return in August and teach until December.

Summer

Branwell moves to Bradford to set up a portrait studio, which he keeps until late winter 1839, when he returns to Haworth.

September

Emily begins as teacher at Law Hill School, Halifax. She stays until late March 1839.

1839

8 April

Anne begins as governess to the Ingham family, Blake Hall, Mirfield; she keeps the post until December, when she is dismissed.

May

Charlotte begins as temporary governess to the Sidgwick family, Stonegappe, Lothersdale, Yorkshire; the position ends mid July.

August

Charlotte and Ellen Nussey travel to Bridlington area for a month, and Charlotte sees the ocean for the first time.

31 December

Branwell becomes tutor to the Postlethwaites, staying in Broughton-in-Furness, Lancashire; he is dismissed in mid summer 1840 and returns to Haworth.

1840

May

Anne begins as governess to children of Reverend Edmund Robinson, Thorp Green, near York, a position she holds for five years.

31 August

Branwell appointed assistant clerk at Sowerby Bridge Railway Station at £75 per year.

1841

2 March

Charlotte becomes governess to John White's family, Upperwood House, Rawdon, near Leeds at £20 per year minus £4 for laundry; she resigns in December.

1 April

Branwell appointed clerk in charge of Luddenden Foot Station at £130 per year; he is dismissed from the post in March 1842 because of money missing from the railway accounts he managed.

5 June

Halifax Guardian publishes Branwell's poem "Heaven and Earth" under his pseudonym "Northangerland"; it is the first of more than twenty poems he published in area newspapers, including the *Bradford Herald, Leeds Intelligencer,* and *Yorkshire Gazette.*

Summer

Charlotte, Anne, and Emily consider starting their own school. Charlotte decides she and Emily must first study abroad in Belgium.

1842

8 February

Charlotte and Emily leave for Brussels, traveling to London with Reverend Brontë and Mary and Joe Taylor, reaching Pensionnat Héger on 15 February.

August–September

Charlotte begins teaching English and Emily begins teaching music at the Pensionnat Héger in exchange for tuition and board.

29 October	Aunt Branwell dies in Haworth. Anne returns from Thorp Green to attend the funeral. Charlotte and Emily arrive in Haworth from Brussels on 8 November. Aunt Branwell's will leaves a legacy of approximately £300 each for Charlotte, Emily, and Anne, invested mostly in railway shares.

1843

January	Branwell begins as tutor to Robinson's son at Thorp Green with Anne.
27 January	Charlotte returns without Emily to teach at Pensionnat Héger in Brussels; her salary is £16 per year, minus the cost of German lessons and laundry. During the year she falls in love with Constantin Héger, a married man, and suffers from loneliness. She leaves on 31 December to return to Haworth, where she occasionally writes to Héger; he does not write back.

1844

February	Emily copies poems from earlier writings into two notebooks labeled "Gondal Poems" and "E.J.B."; she continues to use these notebooks until May 1848.
July	Charlotte, Emily, and Anne plan to set up school in the parsonage at Haworth; they write to various acquaintances to solicit students and have advertising cards printed. The project is abandoned in the fall.

1845

12 March	Mary Taylor immigrates to New Zealand.
24 March	Charlotte writes to Ellen Nussey from Haworth: "I feel as if we were all buried here—I long to travel—to work to live a life of action."
11 June	Anne resigns as the Robinsons' governess.
17 July	Branwell claims he is dismissed as tutor (perhaps as early as June) by Mr. Robinson, possibly because he is suspected of having an affair with Mrs. Robinson.
31 July	Anne and Emily open their diary papers of 1841. Charlotte writes to Ellen Nussey about Branwell's drinking, which she calls his "illness."
September	Charlotte finds Emily's poetry manuscripts and decides that all three sisters should publish their poetry together.

1846

6 February	Charlotte sends the publishing house Aylott and Jones the manuscript of poems by "Currer, Ellis, and Acton Bell"—the pseudonyms for Charlotte, Emily, and Anne.
3 March	Charlotte pays Aylott and Jones £31.10s. to print their volume of poetry.
7 May	Copies of *Poems by Currer, Ellis, and Acton Bell* are delivered to the Brontës; only two copies of the book, priced 4s., are sold.
June	Branwell hopes to marry Mrs. Robinson after the death of her husband in May but is told by her coachman that he cannot see her or contact her.
4 July	Charlotte sends the manuscript for her novel *The Professor* along with Emily's *Wuthering Heights* and Anne's *Agnes Grey* to the publisher H. Colburn. The works are rejected, the first of several rejections the Brontës' work will garner during the next year.
19 August	Charlotte takes Reverend Brontë to Manchester for cataract surgery; the operation is successful, and Charlotte and her father remain for five weeks in Manchester, where Charlotte begins writing *Jane Eyre*.
Fall	Branwell's drinking and physical decline intensify; he spends time in Halifax with his friend J. B. Leyland.

1847

3 April — Mrs. Collins, the abused wife of a clergyman in Keighley, visits the parsonage, and describes how she has supported herself since her alcoholic husband abandoned her and their children; her story may have inspired Anne's depiction of Arthur and Helen Huntingdon in Anne's novel *The Tenant of Wildfell Hall*.

July — T. C. Newby accepts *Wuthering Heights* and *Agnes Grey* for publication. He requires £50 that he claims will be returned when the books' profits exceed that amount. The sisters' investment is not returned.

15 July — Charlotte sends *The Professor* to the publisher Smith, Elder; the house rejects the manuscript but express interest in another work by the author.

12 September — Smith, Elder accepts *Jane Eyre*.

19 October — *Jane Eyre: An Autobiography* is published in three volumes to favorable reviews. The first printing sells out in three months; subsequent editions are published in January and April 1848.

December — *Wuthering Heights* and *Agnes Grey* published in a three-volume edition by T. C. Newby. The book has errors that Emily and Anne had corrected. Reviewers are disturbed and intrigued by *Wuthering Heights*; *Agnes Grey* receives little critical attention.

21 December — Charlotte writes a revised preface dedicated to William Makepeace Thackeray for the second edition of *Jane Eyre*.

1848

January — Charlotte reveals to her father that she is a published author.

February — A dramatic version of the popular *Jane Eyre* is staged at the Victoria Theatre, London, titled *Jane Eyre: The Secrets of Thornfield Manor*.

13 March — To deny rumors that Currer Bell is the author of all the Brontë novels, Charlotte writes a note for the third edition of *Jane Eyre,* to be published in April, insisting as Currer Bell "that my claim to the title of novelist rests on this one work alone."

June — T. C. Newby publishes *The Tenant of Wildfell Hall,* by Acton Bell. Newby deceitfully claims that Currer Bell has written all of the Bells' books.

7–12 July — Charlotte and Anne go to London to prove their identities, insisting that their publishers keep the secret of their identities.

August — The second edition of *The Tenant of Wildfell Hall* is published with a preface by Anne in which she responds to critics who have found the work too coarse.

24 September — Branwell, age thirty-one, dies of "chronic bronchitis and marasmus (wasting)"—possibly pulmonary tuberculosis. Buried 28 September in Haworth Church.

October — Smith, Elder publishes a new edition of *Poems by Currer, Ellis, and Acton Bell*.
Emily shows signs of illness, with coughing and weight loss; she refuses medical treatment.

19 December — Emily dies of "Consumption—2 months duration" at 2 P.M.; she is buried 22 December in Haworth Church.

1849

5 January — Anne's persistent illness diagnosed as consumption. Anne tries medicines and a "respirator."

4 February — Charlotte sends Smith, Elder the first volume of *Shirley* manuscript.

24 May — Although Anne is very ill, Charlotte and Ellen Nussey acquiesce to her desire to travel to Scarborough, staying overnight in York en route and visiting York Minster the next morning.

28 May — Anne dies in Scarborough and is buried in St. Mary's Churchyard on 30 May.

21 June	Charlotte returns to Haworth and resumes work on *Shirley*. The manuscript is completed by 8 September, when a clerk from Smith, Elder picks it up at the parsonage. She receives £500 for the work.
26 October	*Shirley* is published and receives mixed reviews.
November	Charlotte corresponds with novelist Elizabeth Gaskell and asks to have a copy of *Shirley* sent from Smith, Elder to Harriet Martineau.
4 December	Charlotte, who has traveled to London and is staying with the family of publisher George Smith, meets Thackeray at dinner with the Smiths. She stays in the city until 14 December, also meeting Martineau and various critics.

1850

28 February	The *Bradford Observer* reports that "Currer Bell" is actually the daughter of Reverend Brontë of Haworth.
30 May–25 June	Charlotte stays with George Smith's family in London at their new house in Hyde Park Gardens. She visits the opera, the Royal Academy, the Zoological Gardens, the Ladies' Gallery in the House of Commons, and sees the duke of Wellington at the Chapel Royal. Her portrait is drawn by George Richmond.
7 December	A new edition of *Wuthering Heights* and *Agnes Grey,* edited by Currer Bell, is published by Smith, Elder. Charlotte includes a "Biographical Notice" about her sisters, selects poetry by Emily and Anne to include, and provides a preface for *Wuthering Heights*.

1851

28 May–27 June	Charlotte visits the Smiths in London. During her visit she attends the Great Exhibition at the Crystal Palace five times, sees plays at the French Theatre, and hears Thackeray lecture.
December	Charlotte is prescribed mercury pills for a liver condition and develops mercury poisoning.

1852

29 March	Charlotte finishes first draft of volume one of *Villette*. She begins writing the second volume in June.
26 October	Charlotte finishes volume two of *Villette* and sends it to Smith, Elder, and tells them volume three will be ready soon.
20 November	Charlotte sends the completed volume three of *Villette* to Smith, Elder.
December	Charlotte is paid £500 for *Villette*.
13 December	Reverend Arthur Bell Nicholls, who became Reverend Brontë's curate in May 1845, asks Charlotte to marry him. Charlotte's father strongly opposes the match, and Charlotte refuses Nicholls.

1853

5 January	Charlotte visits the Smiths in London; she corrects the proofs of *Villette* and visits Pentonville and Newgate prisons, the Bank of England, *The Times* offices, the General Post Office, the Foundling Hospital for orphans, and "Bedlam," Bethlehem Hospital for the insane.
28 January	*Villette* is published, to favorable reviews overall. Charlotte is offended by Martineau's review of the novel.
26 May	Reverend Nicholls leaves Haworth, moving to a post as curate in Kirk Smeaton in August.
Summer	Charlotte corresponds with Reverend Nicholls, without her father's knowledge. Charlotte and Ellen Nussey quarrel.
December	Charlotte tells her father that she has been corresponding with Reverend Nicholls for six months. Reverend Brontë gives permission for them to see each other.

1854

January	Reverend Nicholls visits the Haworth area for ten days and sees Charlotte at the parsonage.
3 April	Reverend Nicholls visits Haworth, and Charlotte and he become engaged, with Reverend Brontë's agreement.
29 June	Charlotte and Arthur marry; they honeymoon in Wales and Ireland, returning to Haworth to live with Reverend Brontë at the parsonage on 1 August.

1855

January	Charlotte and Arthur visit the Kay-Shuttleworths at Gawthorpe Hall. Charlotte feels unwell. By late January, Charlotte cannot travel and rests in bed.
17 February	Charlotte writes her will, leaving everything to Arthur Bell Nicholls. She continues to decline, suffering from extreme nausea probably caused by pregnancy.
31 March	Charlotte dies, official cause "pthisis" (tuberculosis/progressive wasting disease); she is buried on 4 April in the family vault in Haworth church.
16 June	Reverend Brontë asks Elizabeth Gaskell to write a biography of Charlotte. She begins writing by February of the following year, having gathered letters and anecdotes from Charlotte's friends and correspondents.

1857

25 March	Mrs. Gaskell's *Life of Charlotte Brontë* is published by Smith, Elder.
Early June	*The Professor,* prepared by Arthur Bell Nicholls, is published by Smith, Elder.

1860

March	*The Cornhill Magazine,* George Smith's new publication, publishes the first two chapters of Charlotte's unfinished novel as "The Last Sketch," with an introduction by Thackeray. *The Cornhill Magazine* also publishes one of Emily's poems and two of Charlotte's in later issues.

1861

7 June	Reverend Patrick Brontë dies at age eighty-four, having outlived his wife and all of his children; he is buried 12 June in the family vault.

Portrait of Charlotte, Emily, and Anne by their brother, Branwell Brontë, circa 1834 (National Portrait Gallery, London)

Branwell Brontë's self-portrait, circa 1840 (Brontë Parsonage Museum, Bonnell 18v)

Overview of the Brontë Family

A Family of Writers

The story of the family that produced the extraordinary siblings Charlotte (1816–1855), Branwell (1817–1848), Emily (1818–1848), and Anne (1820–1849) begins with their parents, Maria Branwell (1783–1821) and Patrick Brontë (1777–1861). Reverend Patrick Brontë, a graduate of St. John's College, Cambridge, had been ordained as a minister in the Church of England in 1807. Maria was from a comfortable home in Penzance, Cornwall, and had been left a £50 annuity on her father's death in 1808. In 1812 she was working for her aunt Jane Branwell Fennell and uncle John Fennell at Woodhouse Grove, a school near Bradford, Yorkshire. The couple met through their mutual friend Reverend William Morgan and the Fennells. During their courtship, begun in summer 1812 and culminating with their marriage on 29 December 1812, Maria Branwell wrote Patrick Brontë nine letters that survive; no letters survive from Patrick Brontë to Maria Branwell.

This letter was written after the couple's engagement and was sent from Woodhouse Grove to Hartshead, Yorkshire, where the Reverend Brontë was minister at the church of St. Peter. It shows the affectionate tone of her letters to Patrick, mixed with her emphasis on religious faith and the role of the divine in shaping their lives. Her teasing nickname for her future husband—"My Dear Saucy Pat"—contrasts with later depictions of Patrick as a rigid, austere man. Maria refers here to a box of her belongings that was almost entirely destroyed in a shipwreck en route from her home in Penzance to her at Woodhouse Grove.

Maria Branwell to Patrick Brontë, 18 November 1812

MY DEAR SAUCY PAT,—Now don't you think you deserve this epithet, far more, than I do that which you have given me? I really know not what to make of the beginning of your last; the winds, waves, and rocks almost stunned me. I thought you were giving me the account of some terrible dream, or that you had had a presentiment of the fate of my poor box, having no idea that your lively imagination could make so much of the slight reproof conveyed in my last. What will you say then when you get a *real, downright scolding?* Since you shew such a readiness to atone for your offences, after receiving a mild rebuke, I am inclined to hope, you will seldom deserve a severe one. I accept—with pleasure your atonement, and send you a free

and full forgiveness—But I cannot allow that your affection is more deeply rooted than mine. However we will dispute no more about this—but rather embrace every opportunity to prove its sincerity and strength, by acting, in every respect, as friends and fellow-pilgrims, travelling the same road, actuated by the same motives, and having in view the same end. I think, if our lives are spared twenty years hence, I shall then pray for you with the same, if not greater, fervour and delight that I do now.

I am pleased that you are so fully convinced of my candour, for, to know that you suspected me of a deficiency in this virtue, would grieve and mortify me beyond expression. I do not derive any merit from the possession of it, for in me it is constitutional. Yet I think, where it is possessed, it will rarely exist alone, and where it is wanted, there is reason to doubt the existence of almost every other virtue. As to the other qualities which your partiality attributes to me, although I rejoice to know that I stand so

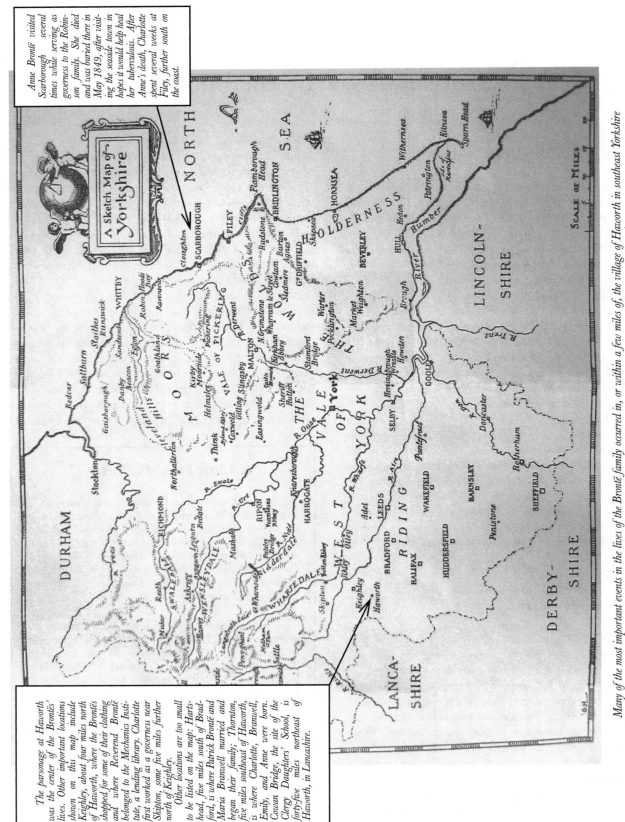

Anne Brontë visited Scarborough several times while serving as governess to the Robinson family. She died and was buried there in May 1849, after visiting the seaside town in hopes it would help heal her tuberculosis. After Anne's death, Charlotte spent several weeks at Filey, further south on the coast.

The parsonage at Haworth was the center of the Brontës' lives. Other important locations shown on this map include Keighley, about four miles north of Haworth, where the Brontës shopped for some of their clothing and where Reverend Brontë belonged to the Mechanics Institute, a lending library. Charlotte first worked as a governess near Skipton, some five miles further north of Keighley.

Other locations are too small to be listed on the map: Hartshead, five miles south of Bradford, is where Patrick Brontë and Maria Branwell married and began their family; Thornton, five miles southeast of Haworth, is where Charlotte, Branwell, Emily, and Anne were born. Cowan Bridge, the site of the Clergy Daughters' School, is forty-five miles northeast of Haworth, in Lancashire.

Many of the most important events in the lives of the Brontë family occurred in, or within a few miles of, the village of Haworth in southeast Yorkshire (from Gordon Home, Yorkshire: Painted & Described, University of Colorado Libraries).

Mrs. Brontë's Mother at the age of 55.
(Reproduced from "The Sketch," by kind permission of the London Electrotype Agency.)

Mrs. Brontë's Father at the age of 53.
(Reproduced from "The Sketch," by kind permission of the London Electrotype Agency.)

Photo J. J. Stead.

Maria Branwell (afterwards Mrs. Brontë)
at the age of 15.

Maria Branwell with her parents Anne Carne Branwell (1744–1809) and Thomas Branwell (1746–1809). Her father was a wealthy tea merchant and grocer (from The Bookman, *October 1904, Colorado College Library).*

The Reverend Patrick Brontë circa 1809 (Brontë Parsonage Museum; from J. Horsfall Turner, Brontëana: The Rev. Patrick Brontë, A.B., His Collected Works and Life, *University of Colorado Libraries)*

The Rise of Patrick Brontë

William Wright in The Brontës in Ireland; or Facts Stranger Than Fiction *(1893) asserts that "few men have ever emerged from humbler circumstances than Patrick Brontë." The cottage in which he was born "consisted of two rooms. That over which the roof still stands was without chimney, and was used as bedroom and parlour; and the outer room, from which the roof has fallen, was used as a corn-kiln and also as kitchen and reception room." He became a schoolteacher and then with the aide of a patron studied the classics and was admitted to St. John's College.*

The Reverend Brontë's birthplace, Emdale, Drumballyroney, County Down, Ireland (from The Bookman, *October 1904)*

St. John's College, Cambridge, where the Reverend Brontë studied from October 1802 to April 1806 (from J. A. Erskine Stuart,
The Brontë Country: Its Topography, Antiquities, and History, *Sam Houston State University)*

The Hartshead church where Reverend Brontë was curate from 1811 to 1815, during which time he met and married Maria Branwell.
Elizabeth Gaskell in The Life of Charlotte Brontë *describes Hartshead as "a very small village, lying to the east of Huddersfield*
and Halifax; and from its high situation—on a mound as it were, surrounded by a circular basin—commanding a
magnificent view" (from The Bookman, *October 1904).*

high in your good opinion, yet I blush to think in how small a degree I possess them. But it shall be the pleasing study of my future life, to gain such an increase of grace and wisdom as shall enable me to act up to your highest expectations and prove to you a helpmeet. I firmly believe the Almighty has set us apart for each other; may we by earnest, frequent prayer, and every possible exertion, endeavour to fulfil His will in all things! I do not, cannot, doubt your love, and here I freely declare I love you above all the world besides! I feel very, very grateful to the great Author of all our mercies, for His unspeakable love and condescension towards us, and desire 'to shew forth my gratitude not only with my lips, but by my life and conversation.' I indulge a hope that our mutual prayers will be answered, and that our intimacy will tend much to promote our temporal and eternal interest.

I suppose you never expected to be much the richer for me, but I am sorry to inform you that I am still poorer than I thought myself. I mentioned having sent for my books, clothes, etc. On Saturday evening about the time you were writing the description of your imaginary shipwreck, I was reading and feeling the effects of a real one, having then received a letter from my sister giving me an account of the vessel, in which she had sent my box, being stranded on the coast of Devonshire, in consequence of which the box was dashed to pieces with the violence of the sea and all my little property, with the exception of a very few articles, swallowed up in the mighty deep. If this should not prove the prelude to something worse, I shall think little of it, as it is the first disastrous circumstance which has occurred since I left my home, and having been so highly favoured it would be highly ungrateful in me were I to suffer this to dwell much on my mind.

Mr Morgan was here yesterday, indeed he only left this morning. He mentioned having written to invite you to Bierley on Sunday next, and if you complied with his request it is likely that we shall see you both here on Sunday evening.—As we intend going to Leeds next week, we should be happy if you would accompany us on Monday or Tuesday. I mention this by desire of Miss F[ennell], who begs to be remembered affectionately to you—Notwithstanding Mr F[ennell']s complaints and threats, I doubt not but he will give you a cordial reception whenever you think fit to make your appearance at the Grove—Which you may likewise be assured of receiving from your ever truly affectionate   MARIA.

Both the Dr and his lady very much wish to know what kind of address we make use of in our letters to each other—I think they would scarcely hit on *this*!!

— The Brontës: Their Lives, Friendships and Correspondence, in *The Shakespeare Head Brontë*, v. 1, pp. 20–22

* * *

Maria was twenty-nine when she married Patrick Brontë, six years her senior. In the following eight years she gave birth to six children—four of whom survived to adulthood—before her death at age thirty-eight of cancer.

Reverend Brontë set an example for his children by publishing four books—two collections of verse, Cottage Poems *(1811) and* The Rural Minstrel: A Miscellany of Descriptive Poems *(1813), and two didactic narratives,* The Cottage in the Wood or the Art of Becoming Rich and Happy *(1815) and* The Maid of Killarney *(1818)—as well as a few pamphlets and sermons.*

This excerpt (lines 72–99) is from a 164-line poem originally published by Patrick Brontë in his second collection of poetry, The Rural Minstrel. *The ruined Kirkstall Abbey held sentimental significance for the Brontës because it was a spot that Reverend Brontë and Maria Branwell visited several times during their courtship in September and October 1812.*

An Excerpt from "Kirkstall Abbey"
Patrick Brontë

> Hail ruined tower! that like a learned sage,
> With lofty brow, looks thoughtful on the night;
> The sable ebony, and silver white,
>   Thy ragged sides from age to age,
> With charming art inlays,
> When Luna's lovely rays,
> Fall trembling on the night,
>   And round the smiling landscape, throw,
>   And on the ruined walls below,
> Their mild uncertain light.
>
> How heavenly fair, the arches ivy-crowned,
> Look forth on all around!
>   Enchant the heart, and charm the sight,
> And give the soul serene delight!
> Whilst here, and there,
> The shapeless openings spread a solemn gloom,
> Recal the thoughtful mind, down to the silent tomb,
> And bid us for another world prepare.
>
> Who would be solemn, and not sad,
> Who would be cheerful, and not glad,
> Who would have all his heart's desire,
> And yet, feel all his soul on fire,
> To gain the realms of his eternal rest,
> Who would be happy, yet not truly blest,
> Who in the world, would yet forget his worldly care,
>   With hope fast anchored in the sands above,
>   And heart attuned by sacred love,
> Let him by moonlight pale, to this sweet scene repair.

— The Rural Minstrel: A Miscellany of Descriptive Poems, pp. 25–27

* * *

COTTAGE POEMS,

BY THE

REV. PATRICK BRONTË, B. A.

MINISTER
OF
HARTSHEAD-CUM-CLIFTON,

NEAR LEEDS, YORKSHIRE.

All you who turn the sturdy soil,
Or ply the loom with daily toil,
And lowly on, through life turmoil
  For scanty fare:
Attend: and gather richest spoil,
  To sooth your care.

Halifax:

Printed and sold by P. K. Holden, for the Author.

Sold also by Mr. Crosby and Co. Stationers'-Court, London;
Mr. Houlston and Son, Wellington;
and by the Booksellers of Halifax, Leeds, York, &c.

1811.

THE
RURAL MINSTREL:
A MISCELLANY
OF
DESCRIPTIVE POEMS.

BY THE REV. P. BRONTË, A. B.
MINISTER
OF
HARTSHEAD-CUM-CLIFTON,

NEAR LEEDS, YORKSHIRE.

The smile of spring, the fragrant summer's breeze,
The fields of autumn, and the naked trees,
Hoarse, braying through stern winter's doubling storms;
E'en rural scenery, in all its forms,
When pure religion rules the feeling heart,
Compose the soul, and sweetest joys impart.

HALIFAX:
PRINTED AND SOLD BY P. K. HOLDEN, FOR THE AUTHOR.

SOLD ALSO BY
B. AND R. CROSBY & Co. STATIONERS'-COURT, LONDON;
And by all other Booksellers.

1813.

Title pages for the Reverend Patrick Brontë's first collections of poetry (National Library of Scotland; British Library)

Although Maria did not publish any work during her lifetime, her interest in writing for an audience beyond her family is shown by an essay she wrote that is preserved as a manuscript in the Brotherton Collection at the University of Leeds (Ms 19c Brontë F1). At the end of Maria's manuscript, below a hand-drawn line, a note was added by Reverend Brontë: "The above was written by my dear Wife, and sent for insertion in one of the periodical publications__Keep it, as a memorial of her__." The last sentence is written in lighter and smaller writing—perhaps at a later point in time, perhaps after her death. Excerpts.

The Advantages of Poverty in Religious Concerns
Maria Branwell Brontë

Poverty is generally, if not universally, considered an evil; and not only an evil in itself, but attended with a train of innumerable other evils. But is not this a mistaken notion—one of those prevailing errors, which are so frequently to be met with in the world, & are received as uncontroverted truths? Let the understanding be enlightened by divine grace, the judgment improved and corrected by an acquaintance with the holy Scriptures, the spirit of the world subdued, and the heart filled with the earnest desires for heavenly attainments, & heavenly enjoyments, & then, what is poverty? Nothing—or rather a something, which, with the assistance and blessing of our Gracious Master, will greatly promote our spiritual welfare, & tend to increase, & strengthen our efforts to gain that Land of pure delight, where neither our souls nor bodies can possibly know pain or want.—Perhaps, some, who are daily, & hourly sinking under the distresses, & privations, which attend extreme poverty, should this paper fall in the way of any such, may be ready to say, that the writer never experienced its horrors, & is, therefore, unqualified to judge of its effects—they may indignantly exclaim, 'Is it not an evil to be deprived of the necessaries of life? Can there be any anguish equal to that, occasioned by the sight of objects, dear as your own soul, famishing

The ruins of Kirkstall Abbey, near Leeds, the subject of one of Reverend Brontë's descriptive poems for The Rural Minstrel
(from Gordon Home, Yorkshire: Painted & Described, *University of Colorado Libraries)*

*One of several pencil drawings of Kirkstall Abbey by Charlotte Brontë. In 1834 it was accepted to the summer
exhibition of the Royal Northern Society for the Encouragement of the
Fine Arts in Leeds (Brontë Parsonage Museum, C72).*

with cold & hunger? Is it no evil, to hear the heartrending cries of your children, craving for that, which you have it not in your power to give them? And, as an aggrava[tio]n of this distress to know, that some are surfeited by abundance, at the same time, that you, & yours are perishing for want?['] Yes, these are evils indeed of peculiar bitterness; & he must be less than man, that can behold them without sympathy, & an active desire to relieve them. But these sufferers possess not the qualifications described above; which alone can enable any human being, to consider poverty, in any other light, than, an evil–They have not had their hearts, understandings, & judgments, changed by divine grace; nor are these the characters, who can look forward to another life, wh [*sic*] the pleasing, invigorating hope, of finding it to be a life, of perfect, unchanging, & everlasting bliss. Such a wretched extremity of poverty is seldom experienced in this land of general benevolence. When a case of this kind occurs, it is to be feared, the sufferers bring it on themselves by their own excess, & imprudent folly–but, even, when they reap the fruit of their doings, they are not permitted long, to suffer– The penetrating eye of christian charity, soon discovers, & its hand is as soon, stretched out for their relief–The poor, but honest, & industrious christian, for whose benefit this humble attempt is made, is scarcely ever suffered to languish in extreme want, yet he may be exposed to great distresses, which, at times, he is tempted to consider evils hard to be endured: almost repines at his lot, &, thinks, that the God, who is declared to be <u>merciful to all</u>, &, whose <u>tender mercies</u> are said to be <u>over all his works</u>–has forgotten to be gracious to him–Dismiss these unworthy thoughts, my christian frien[ds;] they come from the enemy of your immortal interests, &, the father of lies.– Rather, consider, that though you have now [no] visible supply, & know not, from whence the wants of tom[orro]w are to meet with relief, there is one above, in whose hands all the riches of the earth, who sees your necessities, & has faithfully promised, that all things shall work together for your good. . . . Being prevented from sharing in the luxuries of life, you are less liable to be assailed by the corrupt dispositions, & disorderly passions, which, an enjoyment of these luxuries, tend to produce. You think, now, perhaps, that you could be temperate in the midst of plenty, but the human heart is not to be trusted, we are assured, from the sacred writings, that 'it is deceitful above all things, & desperately wicked.' Possessing the means of gratifying every perverse, idle, & inordinate, inclination– who dares say, he would not be led into those vain, & sinful excesses, which would infallibly lead to unhappiness in this world & to endless misery in the world to come? That poverty which is sanctified by true religion, is perhaps, the state most free from care, & discontent; the farthest removed from pride, & ambition; & the most calculated to promote scriptural views, & feelings, & the universal wel-

Charlotte Brontë copied this portrait of her mother in October 1830 (Brontë Parsonage Museum, C10.5).

fare of the soul. The man who possesses little of this world [has] consequently but little to attach him to it; he is not so much tempted to be attracted by its riches, nor its pleasures:–he can not experimentally love that, which he does not possess; he cannot delight in that, which he has no opportunity of enjoying.–Having nothing to lose, he fears not the approach of the spoiler. Neither oppression, nor violence, can add to his wants, or deprive him of his riches. As he has no property to improve, or secure, he is free from the anxious inquietude, & perplexing care, of the man of business. If his days are spent in honest labour, his nights afford the sweet refreshment of peaceful slumbers.– His coarse, but wholesome meal, eaten with relish, and followed by thankfulness, & contentment; invigorates the active body, & fits it for the exertions, necessary, to earn another. Content with his lot, he envies not his more prosperous neighbour: unless, perhaps, in seasons of peculiar distress, when he has been relieved by the bounty of another, a wish has been excited in his breast, that it were in his power to shew his gratitude to his Heavenly Benefactor, by contributing to the necessities of others. But this wish is quickly repressed, by, the conviction, that God knows what is best; & has given to each, that portion which will tend most to his glory, & the lasting good of his children.

Far removed, from the ensnaring, & tumultuous scenes of a vain, unthinking world, he is not ambitious of its honours, nor proud of its fame—He does not, even, understand its principles, nor its language—It may be said, that, though the poor man is not liable to the temptations which peculiarly assail the rich; yet he is liable to others, which commonly prevail among the poor; such as envy, murmuring ingratitude, & covetousness—But it is [necessary] to remind the reader, that poverty is here considered, as united with religion; &, that so united, it is exposed to fewer temptations, than a state of prosperity, & attended with greater religious advantages. The poor need not fear incurring contempt by making a religious proffession [sic]—A religious, & orderly conduct will insure him commendation, rather than censure. And, if his habitual practice is found to agree with his proffession [sic], he will meet with that confidence, respect, & attention, which, he could never have experienced on any other ground—Free from the pride, & prejudice, of learning, & philosophy, his mind is prepared to receive the truths which the Bible inculcates. He yields to the inward workings of the Spirit of truth; with simplicity receives, the various, & unspeakable blessings, purchased for him by the Saviours blood; nor once thinks of opposing the weakness of human reason, to divine Revelation. He may have less leisure for reading, but he has little call his thoughts from devout meditation, & [mental] prayer; the practice of which, tends more to keep up the life of God in the soul, than the closest study & most enlarged acquaintance, with human learning, independant [sic] of these. Having no worldly ties, he contemplates with holy joy, the inheritance laid up for the saints; &, with a hope full of assurance, through the alone merits of his Redeemer, expects, ere long, to be made a partaker of that inheritance, & to join the heavenly throng in eternal Bliss—

Taking this view of Poverty—where are the evils attending it? Do they not appear to be imaginary? But, O, what words can express, the great misery of those, who suffer all the evils of poverty here, & that, too, by their own bad conduct, & have no hope of happiness hereafter: but rather have cause to fear, that the end of this miserable life, will be the beginning of another, infinitely more miserable, never, never to have an end!!

It surely is the duty of all christians, to exert themselves, in every possible way, to promote the instruction, & conversion of the Poor; &, above all, to pray with all the ardor of Christian faith, & love, that every poor man, may be a religious man—

M.

—transcribed by Susan B. Taylor

Childhood and Cowan Bridge School

Before the Brontës moved to the parsonage at Haworth in April 1820, they lived at Thornton, five miles southeast of Haworth, from 1815 to 1820. The Reverend Brontë remembered fondly the friends his family made in the area, including Elizabeth Firth, later Franks (1797–1837), godmother to Elizabeth and Anne Brontë. After the death of his wife, Reverend Brontë asked Firth to marry him. Although she refused his proposal and later married the Reverend James Clarke Franks, she remained a friend of the family. This unsigned article was written by Firth descendant C. C. Moore Smith. In the diary entries, F. O. was Fannie Outhwaite, a close friend of Elizabeth Firth. Excerpts.

The Brontës at Thornton

My grandmother, Elizabeth Firth, was born on January 2nd, 1797. She was the only child of John Scholefield Firth, of Kipping House, Thornton, near Bradford, the house which, a century earlier, was the home of his ancestor, Dr. John Hall, a stalwart Independent, whose name is well known to the readers of Joseph Lister's Autobiography and Oliver Heywood's diaries. As a girl of eighteen she was keeping house for her father when in 1815 the

Birthplace of Charlotte, Branwell, Emily, and Anne Brontë, Market Street, Thornton, where the Brontës lived from 1815 to 1820 (from The Complete Works of Charlotte Brontë and Her Sisters, *Denver Public Library)*

Rev. Patrick Brontë removed from Hartshead to succeed the Rev. Thos. Atkinson as Incumbent of Thornton Chapel. Mr. Brontë had married at Hartshead (Dec. 29th, 1812) Miss Maria Branwell, of Penzance, and two daughters, Maria and a second infant, had been born to him before his removal to Thornton on 19th May, 1815. My grandmother naturally made speedy acquaintance with the new clergyman and his wife, and when the baby daughter (born at Hartshead on Feb. 8th) was christened at Thornton on August 26th, Mr. Firth was its godfather and Miss Firth was godmother, together with Miss Branwell, the child's aunt. . . .

During all the years from 1812 to 1820, my grandmother put down in the briefest and barest form in a pocket-book some fact for almost each day of her uneventful life. They are in a sense very insignificant entries; but such is the interest felt in that strange Brontë household that it seems almost worth while to put into print even the number of times that the Rev. Patrick Brontë went out to tea, if only to show that Mrs. Gaskell's picture of the stern man, unsocial in his habits, however true of the Haworth time, is not true of the years spent at Thornton. . . .

I append a few extracts from Miss Firth's diary which illustrate the life led by the Brontës at Thornton.

1815.

May 19 –Mr. Brontë came to reside at Thornton.

June   7 –I called at Mr. Brontë's.

"   9 –We met Mr. Brontë's family at Mr. Kay's.

"   11 –See St. Matthew, c. 13, vs. 3–9; The Parable of the Sower. The first time I heard Mr. Brontë preach.

"   12 –Mrs. Brontë and Miss Branwell called.

"   14 –Drank tea at Mrs. Brontë's.

"   20 –We had the Outhwaites, Brontës, and Miss M. Ibbotson to dinner.

Aug. 26 –Sun. Mr. Brontë's second daughter was christened Elizabeth by Mr. Fennel. My papa was Godfather, Miss Branwell and I were Godmothers.

Sep. 6 –My papa was married to Miss Greame at Bradford Church by Mr. Morgan. The bridal party dined at Exley and came here in the evening.

"   20 –Mr. Brontë and Mrs. Morgan drank tea here.

Oct. 25 –We drank tea at Mr. Brontë's.

Dec. 12 –Mr. Brontë took tea here.

1816.

Feb. 8 –Elizabeth Brontë was a year old this day.

April 2 –Sun. C. Brontë was born.

May 25 –Mr. Brontë went to prayer with my papa.

"   27 –Mr. Brontë again. My papa was very ill.

July 17 –We drank tea at Mr. Brontë's.

"   18 –The ladies assisted me in altering a gown.

"   25 –Mrs. Brontë and Miss Branwell drank tea here the last time.

"   28 –I took leave of Miss Branwell. She kissed me, and was much affected. She left Thornton that evening.

(In a Cash Account for Sept., 1816, occurs the entry, "Frock for one of the Brontës, 16s.")

1817.

May 9 –Mr. Horsfall and Mr. and Mrs. Brontë's family dined here.

"   13 –My papa and Mr. Brontë went to Wakefield to vote for Mr. Scott. Stopped all night at Longlands.

June 26 –Went to see Mrs. Brontë. Branwell Patrick was born early in the morning.

Nov. 6 –I went to Bradford with Mr. Brontë.

1818.

April 20 –We walked to Bradford with Mr. Brontë and returned the same evening.

May 19 –Mr. Brontë, F. O., and I went to Agden Kirk.

June 29 –F. O., Mr. Brontë, and I took tea at Mr. J. Ibbotson's.

July 30 –Emily Jane Brontë was born.

Dec. 10 –Mr. Brontë's to tea.

"   11 –We drank tea at Mr. Brontë's.

"   17 –I went to Bradford with Mr. Brontë.

"   19 –Came home with Mr. Brontë.

1819.

Jan. 8 –M. E. and C. Brontë to tea.

Sep. 30 –Mr. Brontë to breakfast. He and Mrs. Brontë to tea.

Oct. 4 –The little Brontës called.

1820.

Jan. 17 –Anne Brontë born. The other children spent the day here. (The Cash Account for Jan., 1820, contained the entry, "Gave at A. Brontë's christening, £1.")

Feb. 25 –Mr. Brontë was licensed to Haworth.

Mar. 25 –Anne Brontë was christened by Mr. Morgan. F. Outhwaite and I were Godmothers.

Mar. 31 –Good Friday. No service. We sat up expecting the Radicals.

[Smith adds a note of explanation for this entry: "I have been told that Mr. Brontë, who had seen the Irish Rebellion, by his prophecies of what was coming in England almost frightened Mr. Firth to death, so that he had all his windows barred up in consequence of Mr. Brontë's warnings."]

                –*The Bookman*, 27 (October 1904): 18–19

* * *

The ruins of the chapel at Thornton in which Mr. Brontë preached, 1815–1820 (from The Bookman, *October 1904)*

After the death of Maria Branwell Brontë in 1821, Reverend Brontë raised his six children with the help of Maria's sister Elizabeth Branwell, who came to the Haworth Parsonage from Penzance to assist during Maria's illness and stayed until her own death in 1842. In this excerpt from the first biography about Charlotte Brontë, Elizabeth Gaskell quotes and comments upon a letter written by Reverend Brontë after Charlotte's death in 1855.

"From Under Cover of the Mask"
Elizabeth Gaskell

The servants of the household appear to have been much impressed with the little Brontës' extraordinary cleverness. In a letter which I had from him on the subject, their father writes:–"The servants often said that they had never seen such a clever little child" (as Charlotte), "and that they were obliged to be on their guard as to what they said and did before her. Yet she and the servants always lived on good terms with each other." . . .

I return to the father's letter. He says:–

"When mere children, as soon as they could read and write, Charlotte and her brother and sisters used to invent and act little plays of their own, in which the Duke of Wellington, my daughter Charlotte's hero, was sure to come off conqueror; when a dispute would not unfrequently arise amongst them regarding the comparative merits of him, Buonaparte, Hannibal, and Caesar. When the argument got warm, and rose to its height, as their mother was then dead, I had sometimes to come in as arbitrator, and settle the dispute according to the best of my judgment. Generally, in the management of these concerns, I frequently thought that I discovered signs of rising talent, which I had seldom or never before seen in any of their age. . . . A circumstance now occurs to my mind which I may as well mention. When my children were very young, when, as far as I can remember, the oldest was about ten years of age, and the youngest about four, thinking that they knew more than I had yet discovered, in order to make them speak with less timidity, I deemed that if they were put under a sort of cover I might gain my end; and happening to have a mask in the house, I told them all to stand and speak boldly from under cover of the mask.

"I began with the youngest (Anne, afterwards Acton Bell), and asked what a child like her most wanted; she answered, 'Age and experience.' I asked the next (Emily, afterwards Ellis Bell), what I had best do with her brother Branwell, who was sometimes a naughty boy; she answered, 'Reason with him, and when he won't listen to reason, whip him.' I asked Branwell what was the best way of knowing the difference between the intellects of men and women; he answered, 'By considering the difference between them as to their bodies.' I then asked Charlotte what was the best book in the world; she answered, 'The Bible.' And what was the next best; she answered, 'The Book of Nature.' I then asked the next what was the best mode of education for a woman; she answered, 'That which would make her rule her house well.' Lastly, I asked the oldest what was the best mode of spending time; she answered, 'By laying it out in preparation for a happy eternity.' I may not have given precisely their words, but I have nearly done so, as they made a deep and lasting impression on my memory. The substance, however, was exactly what I have stated."

The strange and quaint simplicity of the mode taken by the father to ascertain the hidden characters of his children, and the tone and character of these questions and answers, show the curious education which was made by the circumstances sur-

Haworth Village. The parsonage and church tower are visible on the last line of hills; a chimney for a textile mill is prominent in the foreground (from Scribner's Monthly, *May 1871, Colorado College Library).*

rounding the Brontës. They knew no other children. They knew no other modes of thought than what were suggested to them by the fragments of clerical conversation which they overheard in the parlour, or the subjects of village and local interest which they heard discussed in the kitchen. Each had their own strong characteristic flavour.

They took a vivid interest in the public characters, and the local and foreign politics discussed in the newspapers. Long before Maria Brontë died, at the age of eleven, her father used to say he could converse with her on any of the leading topics of the day with as much freedom and pleasure as with any grown-up person.

–*The Life of Charlotte Brontë*, v. 1, pp. 57–60

* * *

In 1824 Reverend Brontë decided to send his four eldest daughters to the recently established Clergy Daughters' School at Cowan Bridge, north of Haworth. Fees for the school were partially subsidized by a respectable list of subscribers; nevertheless, Reverend Brontë spent nearly half of his annual salary on less than one full year of education for Maria, Elizabeth, Charlotte, and Emily. While at the Clergy Daughters' School, Maria and Elizabeth fell ill; they each died at home of pulmonary tuberculosis, on 6 May 1825 and 15 June 1825, respectively. Reverend Brontë brought Charlotte and Emily home on 1 June. Charlotte later turned the experience into fiction in her novel Jane Eyre *(1847).*

Main Street, Haworth. Visitors often remarked on the steepness of this street, which leads to the church and the parsonage. In The Life of Charlotte Brontë *Elizabeth Gaskell observed that the flagstones "are placed endways, that the horses' feet may have something to cling to" (from* The Bookman, *October 1904).*

The Haworth parsonage, the home in which the Brontë children grew up
(*from* The Bookman, *October 1904*)

The following two printed documents were associated with the origins of Clergy Daughters' School at Cowan Bridge, which was founded by the Reverend W. Carus Wilson. They were discovered at the front of a bound volume of Annual Reports of the School and, according to Dame Myra Curtis, the author of the article in which they were republished, "were evidently intended for issue to subscribers."

School for Clergymen's Daughters

It has long been a subject of regret among the friends of the established Church, that the provision for a considerable portion of the Clergy is inadequate to their support; and whether we consider the happiness of individuals, or the welfare of parishes and congregations, few projects can more strongly recommend themselves to our benevolence, than those which aim at the alleviation of this evil. Efforts of this nature have long been made with considerable success. The salutary effects of Queen Anne's Bounty are felt throughout the kingdom. The Corporation of the Sons of the Clergy, and the Clergy Orphan Society, are the means of relieving much misery; while in most of our dioceses, Clerical Charities have been established, and are in successful operation.

In addition to the means already adopted, of administering to the wants of the poorer Clergy, a School is now opened for the education of their Daughters, at Cowen Bridge in the parish of Tunstall; and on the turnpike road from Leeds to Kendall; between which towns a Coach runs daily. The property is transferred to Trustees; thereby to guard against the uncertainties of the life of the projector; and to perpetuate the establishment for the benefit of those for whom it is designed.

The house is enlarged and altered for the accommodation of sixty or seventy pupils; each pupil pays £14 a year (half in advance) for clothing, lodging, boarding, and educating; and £1 entrance towards the expense of books &c. The education is directed according to the capacities of the pupils, and the wishes of their friends. In all cases, the great object in view is their intellectual and religious improvement; and to give that plain and useful education, which may best fit them to return with respectability and advantage to their own homes, or to maintain themselves in the different stations of life to which Providence may call them.

In cases where the parents are unable to pay the whole of the annual sum of £14, (which unhappily must frequently occur) it is hoped that more affluent parishioners, and other friends, who are locally interested in a Clergyman, will gladly avail themselves of this method of administering to his wants.

It is calculated, that the sum of £14 will so far defray the whole annual expenditure, as not to require more than £200, or £250 a year, to be raised by subscription.

The school is open to the whole kingdom. Donors and Subscribers will gain the first attention in the recommendation of pupils; and every effort will be made to confine the benefits of the school to the *really* necessitous clergy.

Several additions have been made to the original plan; but it is expected that about £500 more will cover the first expenditure.

The undertaking is an arduous and responsible one; but it has been ventured upon in a confident expectation, that the plan will recommend itself to the benevolent members of our Church, and ensure their liberal assistance. It were indeed to be wished, that the Clergy could be relieved from the necessity of accepting such aid as is now proposed to them; but until that object is effected, it is clearly incumbent on the friends of religion, to do what they can on behalf of a class of persons, on whose welfare so much depends that of the community at large.

Donations and subscriptions are received by the Rev. Wm. Carus Wilson, M.A., Vicar of Tunstall, near Kirkby Lonsdale, who will be happy to give further particulars; and to receive recommendations of proper pupils. He may be addressed under cover to W. W. Carus Wilson, Esq., M.P., Casterton Hall, Kirkby Lonsdale. Contributions will also be received by Messrs. Hatchard, 187 Piccadilly, London; George Thorne, Esq., Bristol; the Rev. J. Scholefield, Fellow of Trinity College, Cambridge; John Ingleby, Esq., Walthamstow; and Messrs. Heywood and Co. Bankers, Manchester.

Tunstall Vicarage, August 1824

Entrance Rules, &c.

I. The terms for clothing, lodging, boarding, and educating are £14 a year; half to be paid in advance when the pupils are sent: and also £1 entrance money for the use of books &c. The system of education comprehends History, Geography, the Use of the Globes, Grammar, Writing and Arithmetic; all kinds of Needlework, and the nicer kinds of household-work, such as getting up fine linen, &c. If Accomplishments are required, an additional charge is made, for French, Music, or Drawing, of £3 a year each.

II. It is particularly requested that the wishes of the friends may be stated regarding the line of education for each pupil; as it will be desirable to give it that direction, which will best suit their future prospects, as well as their respective dispositions and abilities.

III. Each pupil must bring with her, a Bible and Prayer Book, a Workbag, with necessary Sewing Implements, &c., Combs, Brushes, Pair of Pattens, Gloves, and the following Articles of clothing, &c.

4 Day Shifts	2 Pair of Pockets
3 Night do.	4 Pair of White Cotton Stockings
3 Night Caps	3 Pair of Black worsted do.
2 Pair of Stays	1 Nankeen Spencer
2 Flannel Petticoats	4 Brown Holland Pinafores
3 White Upper Petticoats	2 White do.
1 Grey Stuff do.	1 Short coloured Dressing Gown.
2 Pair of Shoes	

[do. *is an abbreviation for ditto.*]

The pupils all appear in the same dress. They wear plain straw cottage bonnets; in summer, white frocks on Sundays, and nankeen on other days. In winter, purple stuff frocks and purple cloth pelisses. For the sake of uniformity, therefore, it is requested that each pupil may bring £3 in lieu of frocks, pelisse, bonnet, tippet, and frills. They may however bring with them such bonnet, spencer or pelisse, as they may happen to be wearing at the time of their coming: as they will answer for walking out and playing.

IV. There are five weeks holiday at Midsummer; but any of the pupils may remain at the school during the holidays, for which £1 1s. is to be paid.

V. The parents are requested to state what diseases incidental to children each girl has had.

VI. A quarter's notice is requested previous to the removal of a pupil.

VII. All letters and parcels will be inspected by the Governess.

–Dame Myra Curtis, "Cowan Bridge School: An Old Prospectus Re-examined," *Brontë Society Transactions*, 12, no. 63 (1953): 190–192

* * *

In Charlotte Brontë's novel the fictional Reverend Brocklehurst presents to Jane Eyre, who has been falsely accused of "a tendency to deceit" by her Aunt Reed, "a thin pamphlet sewn in a cover": "Little girl, here is a book entitled the 'Child's Guide;' read it with prayer, especially that part containing 'an account of the awfully sudden death of Martha G——, a naughty child addicted to falsehood and deceit."

Like Brocklehurst, the Reverend Wilson collected memoirs of pious children in a small volume, with most of the narratives in the collection featuring children whose professions of growing Christian beliefs culminate in their deathbed scenes. This is the conclusion of Wilson's book.

An Address to Children

W. Carus Wilson

Dear Children,

The work in which your teachers are engaged, is of that nature, which renders it impossible that it should be done rightly without your *diligent attention.* If you desire to have the wants of your precious souls supplied, you must be punctual at school: early and constant attendance is of great importance to yourselves, and it is also a mark of that respect that your teachers wish you to show them. A girl, about thirteen years of age, after being in a Sunday school a short time became so very fond of it, that at times, though prevented attending through the want of clothes and food, she would often go without food, rather than be absent from school. At length her father dying, she and her mother were obliged to go to the poor-house. With many tears, the poor girl said to her teacher, "This will be the last time I shall have the privilege of attending this Sunday school, as to-morrow we are going to the poor-house;" adding at the same time, "though it is my unhappy lot frequently to want the necessities of life, yet I would rather stay out of the poor-house, and almost starve, if, by that means, I could have the opportunity of attending the school." Now, the love which this little girl felt to her school and to her teachers, is just that love which *you* ought to feel to your school, and to your teachers; and then, nothing of a vain and trifling nature would keep you at home on the Sabbath day, and no idle companion, no foolish play, would cause you to be late in your attendance at school.

But, diligent attention to the instructions of your teachers, is a part of the duty which you owe to them as well as to yourselves. You should listen to the things they say, with the same fixedness of thought, as Mary did, when she sat at the feet of Jesus and heard him preach; and with the same eagerness of mind, as if they were speaking to you on your dying bed.

As it may not be long before you are removed from your school to your chamber; from the bench of instruction to the bed of death; they are desirous to teach you the way that leads to life, and how you may enter in at the strait gate, that you may be happy in the season of affliction, and safe in the hour of death. Surely then, your hearts should rejoice when you see your teachers enter the door of the school, and be ready to say, when they sit down by your side,—"Now, teachers, tell me something about Jesus!" This would greatly delight their souls, and abundantly encourage them to go on in their work.

Remember, children, the precious Saviour who bare our sins in his own body on the tree. Behold the cross of Christ, it is the most wonderful object that was ever beheld! On it hung the Creator of all worlds! The Lord of angels! The King of kings! The Judge of all. How wonderful that he, who made men, and could in a moment destroy them, should allow them to lead him as a lamb to the slaughter, to nail him to a tree, to pierce his side, to draw forth his blood! Did you ever see or hear any thing, dear children, so wonderful as the cross of Christ? And why was there ever such a scene as the cross of Christ to look at? Because man became a guilty sinner—because Adam destroyed himself and all his children—because the curse of God fell upon our race—because we are exposed to the everlasting punishment of hell—and because God so loved the world, that he gave his only begotten Son, that whosoever believeth in him should not perish, but have everlasting life! These are the reasons why the Son of God became a man of sorrows, and why the Lord of Life and Glory died upon the cross. How much does Jesus deserve our love! But is he loved by every one of you? No. Then you are his enemies; the enemies of him who suffered for sin, and who alone can save you from hell! Do you wish to sing in heaven? Fall down before him and seek him as your only Saviour. For unless you make him your friend, unless you come to him, and love him, and obey him, you will perish for ever in hell. O pray for the Holy Spirit to change your hearts, and to lead you to Christ.

–Youthful Memoirs, pp. 141–144

* * *

Cowan Bridge, (from the Bridge).

Two views of the school that Maria, Elizabeth, Charlotte, and Emily Brontë attended. Charlotte in her novel Jane Eyre *wrote about the school in the guise of Lowood Institution (top, from J. A. Erskine Stuart,* The Brontë Country, *Sam Houston State University; bottom, from* The Bookman, *October 1904).*

In Jane Eyre *Charlotte Brontë depicted the Clergy Daughters' School as Lowood Institution; the character of Helen Burns is described by Charlotte as being closely based on her eldest sister Maria.*

Elizabeth Gaskell described the Brontës' experiences at the Clergy Daughters' School in The Life of Charlotte Brontë, *clearly intending to balance reports of the Reverend Wilson's mismanagement of the Clergy Daughters' School by noting the challenges he faced in running a charity school. Nevertheless, controversy flared over what conditions were like at the school in the Brontës' era and what responsibility should be ascribed to Reverend Wilson for the school environment.*

As is the case in other passages in her biography of Charlotte, Gaskell misstates some factual details, claiming, for example, that Maria died a few days after she was brought home, when in fact she died 6 May 1825, almost three months after Reverend Brontë brought her home on 14 February 1825. Elizabeth was brought home from the Clergy Daughters' School 31 May 1825 and died two weeks later on 15 June 1825.

The Brontës at Mr. Wilson's School
Elizabeth Gaskell

The house is still remaining that formed part of that occupied by the school. It is a long, low bow-windowed cottage, now divided into two dwellings. It stands facing the Leck, between which and it intervenes a space, about seventy yards deep, that was once the school garden. Running from this building, at right angles with what now remains of the school-house, there was formerly a bobbin-mill connected with the stream, where wooden reels were made out of the alders which grow profusely in such ground as that surrounding Cowan's Bridge. Mr. Wilson adapted this mill to his purpose; there were school-rooms on the lower floor, and dormitories on the upper. The present cottage was occupied by the teachers' rooms, the dining-room and kitchens, and some smaller bedrooms. On going into this building, I found one part, that nearest to the high road, converted into a poor kind of public-house, then to let, and having all the squalid appearance of a deserted place, which rendered it difficult to judge what it would look like when neatly kept up, the broken panes replaced in the windows, and the rough-cast (now cracked and discoloured) made white and whole. The other end forms a cottage, with the low ceilings and stone floors of a hundred years ago; the windows do not open freely and widely; and the passage up-stairs, leading to the bed-rooms, is narrow and tortuous; altogether, smells would linger about the house, and damp cling to it. But sanitary matters were little understood thirty years ago; and it was a great thing to get a roomy building close to the high road, and not too far from the habitation of Mr. Wilson, the originator of the educational scheme.

There was much need of such an institution; numbers of ill-paid clergymen hailed the prospect with joy, and eagerly put down the names of their children as pupils when the establishment should be ready to receive them. Mr. Wilson was, no doubt, pleased by the impatience with which the realization of his idea was anticipated, and opened the school with less than a hundred pounds in hand, and, as far as I can make out, from seventy to eighty pupils.

Mr. Wilson felt, most probably, that the responsibility of the whole plan rested upon him. The payment made by the parents was barely enough for food and lodging; the subscriptions did not flow very freely into an untried scheme; and great economy was necessary in all the domestic arrangements. He determined to enforce this by frequent personal inspection; and his love of authority seems to have led to a great deal of unnecessary and irritating meddling with little matters. Yet, although there was economy in providing for the household, there does not appear to have been any parsimony. The meat, flour, milk, &c., were contracted for, but were of very fair quality; and the dietary, which has been shown to me in manuscript, was neither bad nor unwholesome; nor, on the whole, was it wanting in variety. Oatmeal porridge for breakfast; a piece of oat-cake for those who required luncheon; baked and boiled beef, and mutton, potato-pie, and plain homely puddings of different kinds for dinner. At five o'clock, bread and milk for the younger ones; and one piece of bread (this was the only time at which the food was limited) for the elder pupils, who sat up till a later meal of the same description. Mr. Wilson himself ordered in the food, and was anxious that it should be of good quality. But the cook, who had much of his confidence, and against whom for a long time no one durst utter a complaint, was careless, dirty, and wasteful. To some children oatmeal porridge is distasteful, and consequently unwholesome, even when properly made; at Cowan's Bridge School it was too often sent up, not merely burnt, but with offensive fragments of other substances discoverable in it. The beef, that should have been carefully salted before it was dressed, had often become tainted from neglect; and girls, who were schoolfellows with the Brontës, during the reign of the cook of whom I am speaking, tell me that the house seemed to be pervaded, morning, noon, and night, by the odour of rancid fat that steamed out of the oven in which much of their food was prepared. There was the same carelessness in making the puddings; one of those ordered was rice boiled in water, and eaten with a sauce of treacle and sugar; but it was often uneatable, because the water had been taken out of the rain-tub, and was strongly impregnated with the dust lodging on the roof, whence it had trickled down into the old wooden cask, which also added its own flavour to that of the original rain water. The milk, too, was often "bingy," to use a country expression for a kind of taint that is far worse than sourness, and suggests the idea that it is caused by want of cleanliness about the milk pans, rather than by the heat of the weather. On Saturdays, a kind of pie, or mixture of potatoes and meat, was served up, which was made of all the fragments accumulated during the week. Scraps of meat from a dirty and disorderly larder, could never be very appetizing; and, I believe, that this dinner was more loathed than any in the early days of Cowan's Bridge School. One may fancy how repulsive such fare would be to children whose appetites were small, and who had been accustomed to food, far simpler perhaps, but prepared with a delicate cleanliness that made it both tempting and wholesome. Many a meal the little Brontës went without food, although craving with hunger. They were not strong when they came, having only just recovered from a complication of measles and hooping-cough; indeed, I suspect they had scarcely recovered; for there was some consultation on the part of the school authorities whether Maria and Elizabeth should be received or not, in July 1824. Mr. Brontë came again, in the September of that year, bringing with him Charlotte and Emily to be admitted as pupils. . . .

There was another trial of health common to all the girls. The path from Cowan's Bridge to Tunstall Church, where Mr. Wilson preached, and where they all attended on the Sunday, is more than two miles in length, and goes sweeping along the rise and fall of the unsheltered country, in a way to make it a fresh and exhilarating walk in summer, but a bitter cold one in winter, especially to children whose blood flowed languidly in consequence of their half-starved condition. The church was not warmed, there being no means for this purpose. It stands in the midst of fields, and the damp mists must have gathered round the walls, and crept in at the windows. The girls took their cold dinner with them, and ate it between the services, in a chamber over the entrance, opening out of the former galleries. The arrangements for this day were peculiarly trying to delicate children, particularly to those who were spiritless, and longing for home, as poor Maria Brontë must have been. For her ill health was increasing; the old cough, the remains of the hooping-cough, lingered about her; she was far superior in mind to any of her play-fellows and companions, and was lonely amongst them from that very cause; and yet she had faults so annoying that she was in constant disgrace with her teachers, and an object of merciless dislike to one of them, who is depicted as "Miss Scatcherd" in "Jane Eyre," and whose real name I will be merciful enough not to disclose. I need hardly say, that Helen

---

Burns is as exact a transcript of Maria Brontë as Charlotte's wonderful power of reproducing character could give. Her heart, to the latest day on which we met, still beat with unavailing indignation at the worrying and the cruelty to which her gentle, patient, dying sister had been subjected by this woman. Not a word of that part of "Jane Eyre" but is a literal repetition of scenes between the pupil and the teacher. Those who had been pupils at the same time knew who must have written the book, from the force with which Helen Burns' sufferings are described. They had, before that, recognised the description of the sweet dignity and benevolence of Miss Temple as only a just tribute to the merits of one whom all that knew her appear to hold in honour; but when Miss Scatcherd was held up to opprobrium they also recognised in the writer of "Jane Eyre" an unconsciously avenging sister of the sufferer.

One of these fellow-pupils of Charlotte and Maria Brontë's, among other statements even worse, gives me the following:–The dormitory in which Maria slept was a long room, holding a row of narrow little beds on each side, occupied by the pupils; and at the end of this dormitory there was a small bed-chamber opening out of it, appropriated to the use of Miss Scatcherd. Maria's bed stood nearest to the door of this room. One morning, after she had become so seriously unwell as to have had a blister applied to her side (the sore from which was not perfectly healed), when the getting-up bell was heard, poor Maria moaned out that she was so ill, so very ill, she wished she might stop in bed; and some of the girls urged her to do so, and said they would explain it all to Miss Temple, the superintendent. But Miss Scatcherd was close at hand, and her anger would have to be faced before Miss Temple's kind thoughtfulness could interfere; so the sick child began to dress, shivering with cold, as, without leaving her bed, she slowly put on her black worsted stockings over her thin white legs (my informant spoke as if she saw it yet, and her whole face flashed out undying indignation). Just then Miss Scatcherd issued from her room, and, without asking for a word of explanation from the sick and frightened girl, she took her by the arm, on the side to which the blister had been applied, and by one vigorous movement whirled her out into the middle of the floor, abusing her all the time for dirty and untidy habits. There she left her. My informant says, Maria hardly spoke, except to beg some of the more indignant girls to be calm; but, in slow, trembling movements, with many a pause, she went down stairs at last,–and was punished for being late. . . .

Before Maria Brontë's death, that low fever broke out, in the spring of 1825, which is spoken of in "Jane Eyre." Mr. Wilson was extremely alarmed at the first symptoms of this; his self-confidence was shaken; he did not understand what kind of illness it could be, that made the girls too dull and heavy to understand remonstrances, or be roused by texts and spiritual exhortation; but caused them to sink away into dull stupor, and half-unconscious listlessness. He went to a kind motherly woman, who had had some connection with the school— as laundress, I believe—and asked her to come and tell him what was the matter with them. She made herself ready, and drove with him in his gig. When she entered the school-room, she saw from twelve to fifteen girls lying about; some resting their aching heads on the table, others on the ground; all heavy-eyed, flushed, indifferent, and weary, with pains in every limb. Some peculiar odour, she says, made her recognise that they were sickening for "the fever;" and she told Mr. Wilson so, and that she could not stay there for fear of conveying the infection to her own children; but he half commanded, and half intreated her to remain and nurse them; and finally mounted his gig and drove away, while she was still urging that she must return to her own house, and to her domestic duties, for which she had provided no substitute. However, when she was left in this unceremonious manner, she determined to make the best of it; and a most efficient nurse she proved, although, as she says, it was a

dreary time. Mr. Wilson supplied everything ordered by the doctors of the best quality, and in the most liberal manner; he even sent for additional advice, in the person of his own brother-in-law, a very clever medical man in Kirby, with whom he had not been on good terms for some time previously; and it was this doctor who tasted and condemned the daily food of the girls by the expressive action of spitting out a portion which he had taken in order to taste it. About forty of the girls suffered from this fever, but none of them died at Cowan's Bridge, though one died at her own home, sinking under the state of health which followed it. None of the Brontës had the fever. But the same causes, which affected the health of the other pupils through typhus, told more slowly, but not less surely, upon their constitutions. The principal of these causes was the food.

The bad management of the cook was chiefly to be blamed for this; she was dismissed, and the woman who had been forced against her will to serve as head nurse, took the place of housekeeper; and henceforward the food was so well prepared that no one could ever reasonably complain of it. Of course it cannot be expected that a new institution, comprising domestic and educational arrangements for nearly a hundred persons, should work quite smoothly at the beginning, and all this occurred during the first two years of the establishment. But Mr. Wilson seems to have had the unlucky gift of irritating even those to whom he meant kindly, and for whom he was making perpetual sacrifices of time and money, by never showing any respect for their independence of opinion and action. . . . The pictures, ideas, and conceptions of character received into the mind of the child of eight years old, were destined to be reproduced in fiery words a quarter of a century afterwards. She saw only one side, and that the unfavourable side of Mr. Wilson; but many of those who knew him, assure me of the wonderful fidelity with which his disagreeable qualities, his spiritual pride, his love of power, his ignorance of human nature and consequent want of tenderness are represented; while, at the same time, they regret that the delineation of these should have obliterated, as it were, nearly all that was noble and conscientious.

The recollections left of the four Brontë sisters at this period of their lives, on the minds of those who associated with them, are not very distinct. Wild, strong hearts, and powerful minds, were hidden under an enforced propriety and regularity of demeanour and expression, just as their faces had been concealed by their father, under his stiff, unchanging mask. Maria was delicate, unusually clever and thoughtful for her age, gentle, and untidy. Of her frequent disgrace from this last fault—of her sufferings, so patiently borne—I have already spoken. The only glimpse we get of Eliza-

BRONTË WATERFALL.
When "Summer suns are glowing."
(*Photo by J. J. Stead, Heckmondwike*).

BRONTË BRIDGE.

Two sites on the moors around Haworth associated with the Brontës (from Whiteley Turner, A Spring-Time Saunter:
Round and About Brontë Land, *Sam Houston State University Library)*

beth, through the few years of her short life, is contained in a letter which I have received from Miss "Temple." "The second, Elizabeth, is the only one of the family of whom I have a vivid recollection, from her meeting with a somewhat alarming accident, in consequence of which I had her for some days and nights in my bed-room, not only for the sake of greater quiet, but that I might watch over her myself. Her head was severely cut, but she bore all the consequent suffering with exemplary patience, and by it won much upon my esteem. Of the two younger ones (if two there were) I have very slight recollections, save that one, a darling child, under five years of age, was quite the pet nursling of the school." This last would be Emily. Charlotte was considered the most talkative of the sisters—a "bright, clever little child." Her great friend was a certain "Mellany Hane" (so Mr. Brontë spells the name), a West Indian, whose brother paid for her schooling, and who had no remarkable talent except for music, which her brother's circumstances forbade her to cultivate. She was "a hungry, good-natured, ordinary girl;" older than Charlotte, and ever ready to protect her from any petty tyranny or encroachments on the part of the elder girls. Charlotte always remembered her with affection and gratitude.

I have quoted the word "bright" in the account of Charlotte. I suspect that this year of 1825 was the last time it could ever be applied to her. In this spring, Maria became so rapidly worse that Mr. Brontë was sent for. He had not previously been aware of her illness, and the condition in which he found her was a terrible shock to him. He took her home by the Leeds coach, the girls crowding out into the road to follow her with their eyes over the bridge, past the cottages, and then out of sight for ever. She died a very few days after her arrival at home. Perhaps the news of her death, falling suddenly into the life of which her patient existence had formed a part, only a little week or so before, made those who remained at Cowan's Bridge look with more anxiety on Elizabeth's symptoms, which also turned out to be consumptive. She was sent home in charge of a confidential servant of the establishment; and she, too, died in the early summer of that year. Charlotte was thus suddenly called into the responsibilities of eldest sister in a motherless family. She remembered how anxiously her dear sister Maria had striven, in her grave earnest way, to be a tender helper and a counsellor to them all; and the duties that now fell upon her seemed almost like a legacy from the gentle little sufferer so lately dead.

–*The Life of Charlotte Brontë*, v. 1, pp. 67–80

Juvenilia

Most of the extant juvenile writings of the surviving Brontë children is based upon the "plays" they developed around sets of toy soldiers Branwell received from Reverend Brontë. They created entire societies of characters in distinct geographical settings; as the children matured, their imaginary worlds—replete with literature, political power struggles, military conflicts, and romantic relationships—became even more sophisticated.

In her 1961 biography of Branwell Brontë, Winifred Gérin describes the Brontë children's growing interest in their imagined literary worlds with a focus on the origins and development of Branwell's creations. Gérin notes especially the literary context of the children's writings found in Blackwood's Edinburgh Magazine *of the 1820s and 1830s. In this excerpt Gérin quotes the first part of Branwell's "The History of the Young Men" (1831) in which he summarizes the events that started the children's plays.*

Branwell's "Young Men"
Winifred Gérin

"It was sometime in a summer of the year A.D. 1824 when I, being desirous to possess a box of soldiers, asked papa to buy me one, which shortly afterwards he procured me from Bradford. They were 12 in number, price 1s. 6d., and were the best I ever have had. Soon after this I got from Keighley another set of the same number. These soldiers I kept for about a year until either maimed, lost, burnt, or destroyed by various casualties they

departed and left not a wrack behind!

Now, therefore, not satisfied with what I had formerly got, I purchased at Keighley a band of Turkish musicians which I continued to keep till the summer of A.D. 1825, when Charlotte and Emily returned from school, where they had been during the days of my former sets. I remained for 10 months after they had returned without any soldiers, when on June 5th A.D. 1826 papa procured me from Leeds another set (these were the 12s) which I kept for 2 years, though 2 or 3 of them are in being at the time of my writing this (Dec 15, A.D. 1830). Sometime in 1827 I bought another set of Turkish Musicians at Halifax, and in 1828 I purchased the Last Box, a band of Indians, at Haworth. Both these I still keep. Here now ends the catalogue of soldiers bought by or for me. . . . "

The "catalogue" formed part of the "Introduction" to a work entitled by Branwell "The History of the Young Men" who were, in effect, none other than the toy soldiers brought to life. But to what a life—and

The History of the Year

Even as an adult Charlotte Brontë's spelling and punctuation were erratic. She was not yet thirteen when she wrote this account of the beginning of the children's plays. Her juvenilia was typically written in a miniscule printed script on pieces of paper that measured five by three centimeters.

Once papa lent my Sister Maria A book it was an old Geography and she wrote on it[s] Blank leaf papa lent me this Book. the Book is an hundred and twenty years old[.] it is at this moment lying Before me while I write this[.] I am in the kitchen of the parsonage house Hawarth[.] Taby the servent is washing up after Breakfast and Anne my youngest Sister (Maria was my eldest) is kneeling on a chair looking at some cakes whiche Tabby has been Baking for us. Emily is in the parlour brushing it papa and Branwell are gone to Keighly Aunt is up stairs in her Room and I am siting by the table writing this in the kitchen. Keighly is a small twon four miles from here[.] papa and Branwell are gone for the newspaper the Leeds Intelligencer—a most excellent Tory news paper edited by Mr [Edwa]rd Wood the proprieter Mr Hernaman[.] we take 2 and see three Newspapers as such we take the Leeds Inteligencer [par?]ty Tory and the Leeds Mercury Whig Edited by Mr Bains and His Brother Soninlaw and his 2 sons Edward and Talbot— We see the Jhon Bull it is a High Tory very violent[:] Mr Driver Lends us it as Likewise Blackwoods Magazine the most able periodical there is[.] the editor is Mr Christopher North an old man 74 years of age the 1st of April is his Birthday[.] his company are Timothy Ticklar Morgan Odoherty Macrabin Mordecai Mullion Warrell and James Hogg a man of most extraordinary genius a Scottish Sheppherd.

Our plays were established Young Men June 1826 Our fellows July 1827 islanders December 1827. those are our thre[e] great plays that are not kept secret. Emily's and my Bed play's where Established the 1st December 1827 the other March 1828–Bed plays means secret plays they are very nice ones[.] all our plays are very strange ones there nature I need not write on paper for I think I shall always remember them. the young man play took its rise from some wooden soldier's Branwell had Our fellows from Esops fables and the Islanders from several events whi[c]h happened[.] I will skecth out the origin of our plays more explicit[l]y if I can[.]

papa bought Branwell some soldiers at Leeds[.] when papa came home it was night and we where in Bed so next morning Branwell came to our Door with a Box of soldiers[.] Emily and I jumped out of Bed and I snat[c]hed up one and exclaimed this is the Duke of Wellington it shall be mine!! when I said this Emily likewise took one and said it should be hers[;] when Anne came down she took one also. Mine was the prettiest of the whole and perfect in every part[.] Emilys was a Grave looking ferllow we called him Gravey[.] Anne's was a queer litle thing very much like herself he was called waiting Boy[.] Branwell chose Bonaparte[.] March 12 1829

the origin of the ODears was as follows[.] we pretended we had each a large Island inhabited by people 6 miles high[.] the people we took out of Esops fables[:] Hay Man was my chief Man Boaster Branwells Hunter Annes and Clown Emily's[.] our Cheif Men where 10 miles high except Emilys who was only 4. March 12 1829.

—*Charlotte Brontë: Juvenilia 1829–1835*, pp. 2–3

what an immortality—their earnest young historian had not even then an inkling.

". . . I must now conclude this Introduction," proceeds Branwell, "already too long with saying, that what is contained in this History is a statement of what Myself, Charlotte, Emily and Anne really pretended did happen among the 'Young Men' (that being the name we gave them) during the period of nearly 6 years, though in some places slightly altered according to the form and taste of the aforesaid Young Men. It is written by Captain John Bud the greatest prose writer they have among them."

"When I first saw them," Branwell further wrote about the incident in a footnote to his "History of the Young Men", "in the morning after they were bought, I carried them to Emily, Charlotte and Anne. They each took up a soldier, gave them names, which I consented to, and I gave Charlotte Twemy (i.e. Wellington), to Emily, Pare (Parry), to Anne, Trott (Ross) to take care

of them, though they were to be mine and I to have the disposal of them as I would—shortly after this I gave them to them as their own."

On something more than nodding terms as they might be with the illustrious figures of the day—the obvious giants, Wellington and Napoleon—it gives one pause to hear this nursery party bandying the names of Parry and Ross, even if somewhat mangled, as though they equally were household words.

The fact, of course, is that they were. Reference has but to be made to the pages of *Blackwood's Magazine* for the eighteen-twenties, to find the exploits of both these explorers constantly to the fore in reviews of their "Travels".

That the little Brontës had access to *Blackwood's Magazine* has been known ever since Mrs Gaskell quoted Charlotte's statement to that effect, written in March 1829 when she was barely thirteen. There is, moreover, an important letter of Branwell's written as a

*The warriors and explorers chosen by the Brontë children as their original champions: top left, Charlotte's Duke of Wellington
(from Elizabeth Wormeley Latimer,* England in the Nineteenth Century, *Colorado College Library); top right, Branwell's
Napoleon Bonaparte (Hermitage Museum, St. Petersburg); bottom right, Emily's William Edward Parry
(The Mariner's Museum); and bottom left, Anne's John Ross (from* Finding the North Pole)

young man of eighteen to the editor of *Blackwood's*, which shows that the children were reading and revelling in its monthly issues even at the time of the death of Maria. But what neither statement can give is the direct proof of the influence exercised by *Blackwood's* on their earliest creative writing which a close comparison with the numbers for the eighteen-twenties and early eighteen-thirties alone can do. In article after article, in year after year, one finds the sources of their phenomenally precocious knowledge on matters of history, literature, politics, travel and art; and, more striking still, of the very shape and direction their imaginative writings took.

Both the promise and the pathos of Branwell's early passion for the journal is reflected in the above-mentioned letter written on 7th December 1835. The immediate occasion of his writing was the death of the famous Ettrick Shepherd (James Hogg) who, from the magazine's inception in October 1817, had been, with Wilson and Lockhart, a chief contributor. On hearing of his death Branwell wrote to solicit the reversion of his post. ". . . It is not from affected hypocrisy," he writes, "that I commence my letter with the name of James Hogg; for the writings of that man in your numbers, his speeches in your 'Noctes' [the celebrated symposium of wits which figured almost monthly in the journal from 1822 to 1835] when I was a child, laid a hold on my mind which succeeding years have consecrated into a most sacred feeling. I cannot express . . . the heavenliness of associations connected with such articles as Professor Wilson's, read and re-read while a little child, with all their poetry of language and divine flight into that visionary region of imagination which one very young would believe reality. . . . I speak so, Sir, because while a child 'Blackwood' formed my chief delight, and, I feel certain that no child before enjoyed reading as I did, because none ever had such works as 'The Noctes', 'Christmas Dreams', 'Christopher in his Sporting Jacket', to read."

"Even now," continued Branwell, quoting favourite passages from those old numbers of the magazine, "'Millions o' reasonable creatures at this hour'–. . . etc. or 'Long, long ago, seems the time when we danced hand in hand with our golden-haired sister, . . . Long, long ago, the day on which she died. That hour, so far more dreadful than any hour that now can darken us on this earth, when she, her coffin and that velvet pall descended–and descended–slowly–slowly into the horrid clay, and we were borne death-like, and wishing to die, out of the churchyard. . . .' Passages like these, Sir, (and when the last was written my sister died)–passages like these, read then and remembered now, afford feelings which, I repeat, I cannot describe."

The familiarity such reading bred with figures in all walks of public life can be measured only when viewed in the light of the children's unselfconscious statements, meant for no eyes but their own.

Wishing to record how their principal "plays"–as they called their games–arose, Charlotte wrote on 31st June [*sic*] 1829,

> The Play of the Islanders was formed in December 1827, in the following manner.
> One night about the time when the cold sleet and dreary fogs of November are succeeded by the snow storms, and high peircing night winds of confirmed winter, we where all sitting round the warm blazing kitchen fire having just concluded a quarel with Taby concerning the propriety of lighting a candle from which she came of victorious, no candle having been produced. a long pause suceeded, which was at last broken by Bany saying, in a lazy maner, I don't know what to do. This was re-echoed by E & A.
> T.: Wha ya may go t'bed.
> B.: I'd rather do anything than that.
> C.: Why are you so glum to-night? supose we had each an island.
> B.: If we had I would choose the Island of Man.
> C.: And I would choose the Isle of Wight.
> E.: The Isle of Aran for me.
> A.: And mine should be Guernsey.
> We then chose who should be chief men in our islands: Branwell chose John Bull, Astley Cooper, and Leigh Hunt; Emily, Walter Scott, Mr Lockhart, Johnny Lockhart; Anne, Michael Sadler, Lord Bentinck, Sir Henry Halford. I chose the Duke of Wellington and sons, Christopher North and Co Mr Abernathy. Here our conversation was interrupted by the, to us, dismal sound of the clock striking seven, and we where sumoned of to bed.

The names of Sir Walter Scott, "Mr" Lockhart and "Johnny" Lockhart, chosen by Emily for her chief islanders, though of general interest no doubt in that day and age, refer in particular to closer contacts the little Brontës had with them. On 1st January 1828, Miss Branwell made a very welcome New Year's present to the children, in the shape of Scott's *Tales of a Grandfather* in three volumes, and wrote in the fly-leaf:

> A New Year's Gift by Miss E. B. to her dear little nephew and nieces, Patrick, Charlotte, Emily and Anne Brontë. 1828.

Less obvious were the personalities chosen by Branwell and Anne, "Astley Cooper" and "Sir Henry Halford", the court physicians. Reference to *Blackwood's Magazine* for May 1827, however, shows that in an article on "The Last Illness and Death of H.R.H. The Duke of York", particular mention is made of

"H.R.H.'s gratitude to his physicians"—the Duke of York was shortly to play a major role in the children's secret games.

Though not his earliest literary composition, Branwell's "History of the Young Men" was the most ambitious to date (1830) and is the keystone to the whole future edifice of his and Charlotte's "Glasstown" creation, the absorbing occupation of their childhood and adolescence.

Sprung originally out of the acquisition of the twelve soldiers (the "Twelves" as they became), the plot was equally based upon the children's early readings of *The Arabian Nights* and *Aesop's Fables,* with its insistence on Giants Ten Miles High and Genii dispensing the powers of life and death and the restoration of life, and upon the practical lessons of geography received from studies with their father and the stirring reports—constantly echoed in the pages of *Blackwood's,* of the explorations of John Ross and William Edward Parry and Mungo Park.

The directions taken by genius are impossible to track, but there would appear to have occurred a strange converging of forces at a given moment in the Brontës' childhood, upon a given point: in their case the point was the west coast of Africa and the Gulf of Guinea.

The travels of Mungo Park, lost in 1806 while exploring the upper reaches of the Niger, had brought the interior of the African west coast into the news. His own account of his first voyages of discovery had been published in 1799 and it is significant that a copy of the book, in its edition of 1800, existed in the library of Ponden House—a source of reading open to the children of Haworth Parsonage possibly even before *Blackwood's Magazine* came their way.

Frequent references to Mungo Park occur in Branwell's juvenilia. More contemporary still were the explorations in northern and central Africa of Major Denham in 1822, 1823 and 1824, of which a detailed report appeared in the June issue of *Blackwood's* in 1826, accompanied by a map of the district—so far as it had yet been charted—which may indeed be said to be the deciding factor in *locating* the "Young Men's Play" for, as examination of the original manuscript of Branwell's "History of the Young Men" shows, he very closely *copied* the map from *Blackwood's.*

It has hitherto been supposed that the choice of the west coast of Africa for the setting of the "Kingdom of the Twelves" and later of the "Great Glass Town Confederacy" as it became, arose from the children's study of the map of Africa in the old geography book—still to be seen at the Brontë Parsonage—Goldsmith's *Grammar of General Geography,* which was

the great delight of their childhood. A comparison of Branwell's map with that appearing in *Blackwood's* and with the map of Africa in Goldsmith, reveals two things: firstly, that Goldsmith's map, which is on a very small scale, represents the whole continent of Africa, while the Blackwood map, which is on a large scale, represents only the west coast from the Gulf of Guinea northwards. It is this map that Branwell copied. Names in the Blackwood map, i.e. the province of Ardrah and the rivers Calabar and Etrei, became household words in the history of the Young Men and later throughout the chronicles of "Angria", into which the Young Men's kingdom evolved, but these names do not appear in Goldsmith's map of Africa. Nevertheless Goldsmith's map played a very large part in the children's creation of their African make-believe kingdom.

In Goldsmith's map of Africa, as in the Blackwood map, the Kingdom of the Ashantee figured. This tribe became in the children's play of the "Young Men" the inveterate enemy who, from the very outset, opposed their disembarkation on African territory and years later in the last phase of Branwell's sanguinary campaigns, supported the traitor in the Angrian Wars—the Earl of Northangerland—against the elected monarch, Arthur Augustus Adrien Wellesley, Duke of Zamorna and King of Angria. The long tale, branching out over the nine years of its creation into countless ramifications and complexities, retained constant factors which were the country, as first mapped by Branwell, and the "Twelves" who, starting as teen-agers in the "History of the Young Men", grew up with their creators and assumed the main roles in the evolving tale.

The names bestowed on the four chief soldiers of the children's choice—Wellington, Parry, Ross and Bonaparte—also supplied the names for the principal geographical divisions of the African Kingdom of the Twelves, shortly to be conquered by the intrepid warriors. On Branwell's Map of the West Coast of Africa, in place of the divisions shown on the Blackwood map, we find the divisions "Wellington's Land, Parry's Land, Ross's Land"—and, Bonaparte being voted a sneak by the time the "play" was thus far evolved, "Sneaky's Land" figures instead.

Islands charted in neither Blackwood's nor any geographer's map, figure large in Branwell's Gulf of Guinea—"Stumps Land", "Monkey's Land" (later "Donkey's Isle") and "Frenchy Land"— derived from names gradually bestowed on the rank and file of the twelve soldiers. . . .

In renewed hostilities against the Ashantees, mention is made for the first time of the Ashantee Prince—Quashia Quamina—the black devil who, through various evolutions, would go right through Branwell's juvenilia and on into his adult writing, appearing in his last attempt at fiction, "And the Weary are at Rest", as late as 1845.

The very name "Quashia" was probably taken from *Blackwood's Magazine,* appearing under the variant "Quashee" in the September serialisation of the novel *The Man-of-War's-Man.* He is described by his messmates as a "little silly blackamoor boy", a "little black majesty", who has, in fact, just died and must be conveyed overboard for burial. Dead, he is the source of terror to his messmates as the agent of evil overtaking their ship.

The figure of an orphaned, abandoned black boy occurs and recurs not only in the Brontë juvenilia but in their mature works. Charlotte introduces him both in her "Green Dwarf", 1829, and in the "African Queen's Lament" of 1833, as found by the Duke of Wellington lying under a tree by the dead body of his mother. The Duke takes the boy home and adopts him, thus causing bad blood with his own sons—a theme which Emily was to develop to its ultimate limits when in *Wuthering Heights* Mr Earnshaw brought home the black changeling from Liverpool. Throughout Branwell and Charlotte's "Glasstown" fiction, Quashia, Prince of the Ashantees, plays the villain's part in ceaseless warfare against the British, finally leaguing himself with the traitor "Earl of Northangerland" against Arthur Wellesley, "Marquis of Douro, The Duke of Zamorna and King of Angria".

Thus early in the children's corporate games were the seeds sown of their ultimate achievements.

In pitched battle against Quashia and the Ashantees, King Frederick was killed in the region of Coomasie (Kumasi, the capital of the Ashantees) at the battle of Rossendale Hill, a mountain described by Branwell as "shaped like Pendle Hill".

A local landmark to the Brontë children, and visible to them every time their walks took them from home across the Lancashire border, Pendle Hill has a very characteristic flat top and sides reminiscent of Table Mountain. Like Quashia, it would appear constantly in Angrian literature and figure in Branwell's last novel, "And the Weary are at Rest", where the setting is recognisably that of the district round Haworth. . . .

In successive campaigns where always, in spite of enormous enemy superiority of numbers, the Twelves were victorious, several feats of prowess are recorded by Branwell as reminiscent of, but superior to, similar exploits performed by Homeric heroes. Passages are frequent showing the young author's

acquaintance with Greek history and literature, confined so far to the translation of Pope. "Now indeed there ensued a scene utterly unparalleled in the annals of the world," writes the historian of the Young Men; ". . . the battle of Marathon and the conflict at the pass of Thermopylae are not to be compared to this. . . ." The battle to regain the dead body of Frederick I killed at Rossendale Hill is compared to "the conflict for the dead body of Patroclus on the shores of Troy . . . which must sink to nothing before the actions of this memorable day. . . ." The bravery of the Twelves was in all circumstances, their historian claimed, "superior to that of Leonidas the Spartan".

Charlotte, in the meantime, had been writing on matters closely allied to the central subject of the Young Men—she had written her own account of their voyage in the *Invincible* and their landing in the Country of the Genii, in a tale written in April 1829 called "The Twelve Adventurers". Her stories, unlike Branwell's, were little concerned with the military aspect of these events, but with the fabulous, the human and the romantic. By introducing the Duke of Wellington and his two sons, the Marquis of Douro (Arthur Augustus Adrien Wellesley) and Lord Charles Wellesley into every story, always as heroes and sometimes as narrators (a habit of projecting herself into a male protagonist, which she carried over into her adult novel *The Professor*), Charlotte rapidly and radically altered the essentially *epic* character of Branwell's Young Men sequel, and converted it into a commentary on the social and political world of their day. The chief pastime of the Wellesleys, "père et fils", in her pages was no longer war but courtship, and their fabulous Glass Town was hardly erected before she had peopled it with a society of wits and beautiful women.

The scene set, the chief and subsidiary actors in place, chroniclers were not wanting to record their doings. Charlotte was soon director of policy of the organ of "Glass Town" society, the monthly journal which, it is hardly surprising to learn, had for title: "Blackwood's Young Men's Magazine".

Running almost concurrently with the "History of the Young Men," from January 1829 to December 1830, these amazing replicas of the children's favourite reading permitted them to deal in a variety of matter and style that was invaluable to them as a literary apprenticeship.

—Branwell Brontë, pp. 27–39

* * *

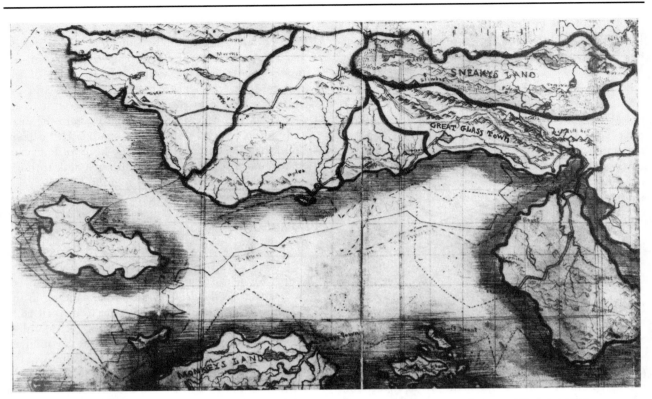

*Branwell Brontë's map of the Glass Town Federation, based on the west coast of Africa, drawn between 15 December 1830
and 7 May 1831 (British Library, Ashley 2468)*

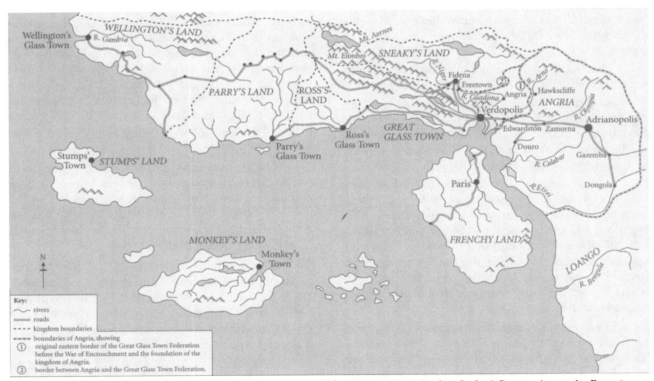

Enhancement of Branwell's map showing the Brontës' imaginary world (by Christine Alexander, from Oxford Companion to the Brontës,
Thomas Cooper Library, University of South Carolina)

In January 1831, Charlotte left Haworth for Miss Wooler's School at Roe Head, Mirfield. Her success as a student—she completed her studies in June 1832 and was awarded the honor of a silver medal—prepared the way for her later return to the school as a teacher. In "The Brontës' Web of Dreams" (1931), the first serious study of the Brontë juvenilia, Fannie Ratchford argues that time away from Haworth and her siblings was especially difficult for Charlotte because it meant her absence from the imaginary world they had created. Ratchford used unpublished Brontë manuscripts to deepen the understanding of the sisters' lives and later adult writing, introducing many of the topics later scholars of the juvenilia have explored. She expanded her research into The Brontës' Web of Childhood *(1941). Excerpts.*

The Brontës' Web of Dreams
Fannie E. Ratchford

On July 29, 1835, Charlotte Brontë exchanged the freedom of Haworth parsonage and moors for the drudgery of a teacher's life in Miss Wooler's school, Roe Head, Mirfield, which she had left as an honor student three years before. She was then nineteen. With her, as a pupil, went her sister Emily, two years younger. Emily's stay was of short duration. She fell ill of homesickness and was allowed, through Charlotte's intervention, to return home, thus establishing a tradition for devotion to her native environs that overshadowed all her other characteristics. More enduring Charlotte remained with Miss Wooler for almost three years and gave her biographers, from Mrs. Gaskell to the latest psychoanalyst, excuse for innumerable chapters on her "ill health," "despondency," and "nervous terrors" of these months. No one seems to have suspected that she, too, might have been homesick, or that behind the nostalgia of the girls lay something far more deeply interfused with their spirits than home and moors.

Charlotte's account of Emily's homesickness is almost as familiar as the Brontë name, but the story of her own sufferings has been known to fewer, perhaps, than half a dozen persons. It has remained hidden for almost a century under the microscopic script of her youthful "books" and manuscripts scattered among the libraries of England and America, valued as literary curiosities but deemed worthless in content. These juvenile writings form the formative period between Charlotte's fourteenth and twenty-fourth years—more than fifty in number and aggregating more pages than her printed works—tell, when read in chronological order, an astonishing story.

In June, 1826, the four little Brontës, Charlotte, then aged ten, Branwell, nine, Emily, eight, and Anne, seven, inaugurated a game which they called "The

Young Men's Play," centering around a set of wooden soldiers brought by their father to Branwell from Leeds. In the course of the innumerable and varied adventures assigned to the Young Men by the active imaginations of their small owners, the Twelve Heroes were shipwrecked on the coast of Guinea, where, by the help of their guardian genii, Talli (Charlotte), Branni (Branwell), Emmi (Emily), and Anni (Anne), they erected a magic city, called at first Glasstown, later Verdopolis. As the play progressed, this city became a marvel of magnificence, the unrivalled capital of a confederacy of kingdoms ruled by the original "Twelves," as the toy adventurers came to be called, all under the general leadership of the Duke of Wellington.

Thus far, with many amusing details, the play had progressed when it was interrupted by Charlotte's first departure for Roe Head, in January, 1831. It was not forgotten in her absence, and on her return after eighteen months, it was revived with renewed interest by herself and her brother, though the toys which were its original inspiration, to quote Branwell, "had departed and left not a wrack behind." There is no evidence that the two younger girls took any further part in this game; it may be that they did, but it is more probable that they had already launched their separate play, "The Gondals," which absorbed them in later years.

In the third year of its existence, that is, in 1829, when Charlotte was thirteen years old, the play of "The Young Men" attained the dignity of a written literature. By August 3, 1830, it had produced the twenty-two "books" listed by Charlotte in her "catalogue" of that date, and one very long volume by Branwell, called "The History of the Young Men," besides six or more numbers of "The Young Men's Backwood Magazine," written some by Charlotte, some by Branwell. Most of these "books" were miniatures, made in scale to the wooden soldiers, their supposed authors—not, as has been thought, to save paper. The magazines were hardly more than 1 1/2 by 1 1/4 inches, and all were executed in minute hand printing, with elaborate title-pages and colophons. The subject matter, stories, poems, dramas, and advertisements, was drawn exclusively from the play-world of the children.

Regarding their absorbing pastime, the little Brontës were consistently silent to the outside world, even to their father and aunt. Only one time, so far as the records tell, was their secret in danger. Then fortunately, the significance of Charlotte's impulsive confidence was not understood by her auditors, or by her biographer Mrs. Gaskell, to whom it was repeated many years later. In answer to Mrs. Gaskell's request for information concerning Charlotte Brontë's school days, Mary Taylor, who shared with Ellen Nussey the

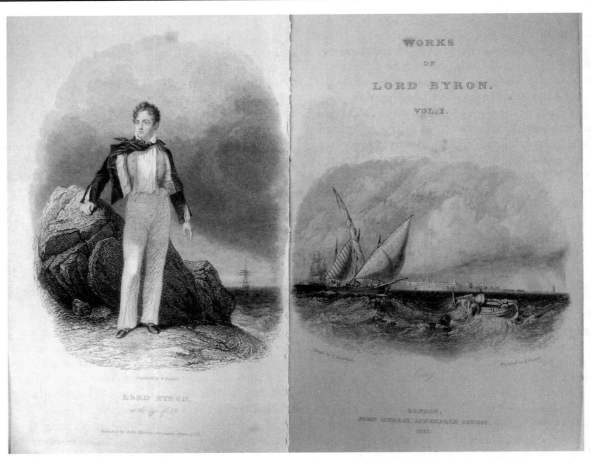

Frontispiece and title page for the first volume of a fourteen-volume edition of the works of George Gordon, Lord Byron (1788–1824), edited by Thomas Moore. Byron as a figure and as a writer was an influence on the Brontës' juvenilia as well as their later fiction. The Brontës read Moore's biography of Byron, and critics have noted Rochester's and Heathcliff's connections to Byron's heroes and to Byron's biography (The University of Colorado at Boulder Libraries).

honor of being her closest friend, wrote: "She had a habit of writing in italics (printing characters), and said she had learnt it by writing in their magazine. They brought out a 'magazine' once a month, and wished it to look as like print as possible. She told us a tale out of it, No one wrote in it, and no one read it, but herself, her brother, and two sisters. She promised to show me some of these magazines, but retracted it afterwards, and would never be persuaded to do so."

Not once in all her apparently confidential letters to Ellen Nussey following her return from school did Charlotte give the slightest hint of the play which colored all her thoughts. Rather she tacitly denied it at the time that it absorbed her: "An account of one day is an account of all. In the morning, from 9 o'clock to half past 12, I instruct my sisters, and draw; then we walk out till dinner-time. After dinner I sew till tea-time, and after tea I either write, read, do a little fancy work, or draw, as I please. Thus in one delightful, though somewhat monotonous course, my life is passed."

Years later, Charlotte told Mrs. Gaskell that at the period in question, drawing and walking out with her sisters formed the two great pleasures and relaxations of the day. Not one word to anybody of "that divine, silent, unseen land of thought," whose landscape she knew "in every variety of shade and light" as she knew her own moors! Never a mention of its people, whom to herself she called "my friends and my intimate acquaintances . . . who people my thoughts by day and not seldom steal strangely into my dreams at night"! Not one hint of "that bright, darling dream," whose magic transported her to strange lands to walk as an equal with other "transcendently high and inaccessibly sacred beings whose fates are interwoven with the highest of the high"!

Notwithstanding her implied denial, Charlotte, during the three years between her school days and teaching days at Roe Head, was living a life of golden romance, walking with kings, guiding the destinies of a mighty empire, and receiving the plaudits due genius from an admiring world. As a visible evidence of this unseen life, she produced with astonishing facility and rapidity innumerable novels and poems of the so-called "Angrian" society and politics. Her earlier hero, the Duke of Wellington, had receded into the background, and in the centre of the stage was now his elder son, Arthur Augustus Adrian Wellesley, Marquis of Douro, an unrestrained Byronic hero, possessing in a highly exaggerated degree the characteristics of Rochester of "Jane Eyre." She herself, in the person of his younger brother, Lord Charles Albert Florian Wellesley, was the omnipresent, all-observing recorder of his doings and misdoings. Branwell, under the pseudonym, first, of Captain John Flower, later, of Lord John Flower, Viscount Richton, introduced revolutionary changes with a suddenness and rapidity that would have bewildered a collaborator less adaptable than Charlotte.

Early in the game she had married her arch-hero to Florence Marian Hume, a gentle green-and-white maiden of snowdrop purity and sweetness. Their union had been violently opposed by the mad jealousy of Lady Zenobia Ellrington, the most brilliant and learned lady of all Verdopolis, whose strong mind had been temporarily upset by her hopeless but enduring passion for the Marquis. While Charlotte was picturing Marian as an adored and adoring wife and happy mother, Branwell was preparing her death blow. He brought forward from wooden-soldier days a Luciferian pirate called Rogue, with the more aristocratic name Alexander Percy now added, whom he married, after an astonishing courtship, to Lady Zenobia. He then introduced Percy's daughter by an earlier marriage, Mary Henrietta, to court, where she instantly won the interest and admiration of the Marquis of Douro. Charlotte, delightfully adaptable as always, accepted this new situation and obligingly allowed Marian to die the romantic death of a brokenhearted and devoted wife so that the Marquis might marry the more regal Mary Percy.

The Marquis and Percy now entered into a political coalition for their mutual aggrandizement. Douro, having saved his country from an invasion of allied French and Negroes, demanded of the Verdopolitan parliament, through his father-in-law, the cession of a large and fertile, but unpopulated province to the east, called Angria, which he received, after a bitter fight, in full sovereignty, though it was to remain, like Wellingtonland and the other original kingdoms, "part and parcel of the Glasstown Confederacy." In keeping with his elevation in rank, the Marquis assumed in rapid succession the titles Duke of Zamorna, King of Angria, and Emperor Adrian, showing with each a corresponding change in character which made him in the end a compound in about equal parts of an Oriental despot, Napoleon, and Byron. The first and last were, appar-

"Offspring of the Moors"

Gaskell's descriptions of the Brontë children's childhood were accepted as authoritative. This excerpt is from John Skelton's unsigned review of The Life of Charlotte Brontë.

But from the youngest up to Charlotte, they are all sedate and precocious. They write plays and act them. They publish a magazine for themselves every month; and they give, as *Blackwood* used to do in those days, 'a double number for December.' Charlotte's favourite hero is the Duke of Wellington. He and his sons, the Marquis of Douro and Lord Charles Wellesley, appear in a hundred romances which she wrote in those invisible microscopic characters before she was fourteen. The little creatures are fierce politicians—Tories to the backbone, every one of them. They read the *John Bull* and *Blackwood's Magazine.* 'The editor,' says Charlotte, solemnly, in a paper written at the time, 'is Mr. Christopher North, an old man, seventy-four years of age; the first of April is his birthday: his company are Timothy Tickler, Morgan O'Doherty, Macrabin Mordecai, and James Hogg, a man of most extraordinary genius, a Scottish shepherd.' One of their plays is entitled *The Islanders.* In it each of the children takes possession of a favourite island, and selects 'chief men' to carry on the government. 'Bramwell,' in Charlotte's contemporary account, 'chose John Bull, Astley Cooper, and Leigh Hunt; Emily, Walter Scott, Mr. Lockhart, Johnny Lockhart; Anne, Michael Sadler, Lord Bentinck, and Sir Henry Halford. I chose the Duke of Wellington and two sons, Christopher North and Co., and Mr. Abernethy.' Little sister Annie, who is seven, and has to be lifted upon her chair, chooses Sir Henry Halford and Mr. Sadler!

A strange childhood!—out of which, through various schools and other harsh experiences, the Brontës grew up to man and woman's estate, and which explains a good deal in their subsequent history. They are the offspring of the moors; and after the sea—whose authority is supreme—the moorland has perhaps the strongest influence in forming and determining the character. All their lives the Brontës love these moors intensely. They look down from their bleak 'hills of Judea,' and wonder how the dwellers contrive to exist in the 'Philistine flats' beneath. The turbid waters of their 'beck' are more sacred than the Jordan's. In dreams, at Brussels they hear the Haworth harebells rustle in the wind. Emily cannot live away from them. She pines and sickens, and would die if she were not brought back and restored to their wild companionship. Everything they say or write is consecrated by this bleak communion. Their honey has the taste of the heath. The scent of the heather is as clearly traceable in their works as the smack of the salt sea in the architecture of the lagoons.

—*Fraser's Magazine*, 55 (May 1857): 569–570

A selection of the miniature books and magazines created by the Brontë children. The ten-pence coin shown is approximately the size of an American half-dollar (Brontë Parsonage Museum).

ently, Charlotte's conceptions, the second Branwell's patchwork.

From each new complication Charlotte drew themes for her "books." While her brother was fixing the boundaries of the new nation, laying out its cities and rearing its buildings, she was peopling them with human beings, breathing the breath of genius into his crude absurdities.

Percy, with the title of Earl of Northangerland, by Branwell's dispensation, was prime minister of the new nation, Zamorna's ablest lieutenant. But Percy could not long support a subordinate part in any affair, or keep faith with any friend. Nor could Branwell long endure the monotony of peace. The play which had its beginning in a set of wooden soldiers remained to its end, in his mind, a game of war.

Percy joined with Zamorna's enemies in criticism of his private life and public acts; the newspapers of Angria and Verdopolis were full of the threatened break. Zamorna hurled down the gauntlet in his melodramatic "Address to the Angrians," and Percy defiantly took it up in "Northangerland's Famous Letter." Zamorna, despite the protest of other kings, dragged his quarrel into the general parliament. On the opening night of the new session, he publicly charged his father-in-law with disloyalty to himself and declared he would have his revenge, even if he must take it through his own wife, the only person in the world whom Percy loved. He threatened that unless Percy broke immediately and finally with his, Zamorna's, enemies and returned to his former attitude of unquestioning loyalty,

he would put away his wife, Percy's daughter; this, all knew, would mean her death.

Such was the exciting and eventful life that Charlotte was living during the months designated by Mrs. Gaskell as "A Dreary Season at Haworth," and such was the uncertain and threatening state of Angrian politics when Charlotte set out to teach at Roe Head. To the pain of leaving her family was added intense anxiety for Angria as Branwell launched simultaneously civil war and foreign invasion, wasting the land, desolating the magnificent capital, Adrianopolis, killing the Duchess by breaking her heart, and sending the mighty Duke of Zamorna into Napoleonic captivity. Something of what she suffered may be read in her secret outpourings of the next three years, in which she voiced her heart-breaking grief at her exile and her poignant longing for Angria. Haworth and the parsonage signified little more to her than the portals of her lost paradise. It was the land of her imagination for which she pined because that was the only outlet she had ever known for her creative impulse, strong in her as life itself. Thus she wrote:

"Once more on a dull Saturday afternoon I sit down to try to summon around me the dim shadows . . . of incidents long departed, of feelings, of pleasures whose exquisite relish I sometimes fear it will never be my lot again to taste. How few would believe that from sources purely imaginary such happiness could be derived! Pen cannot portray the deep interests of the scenes, of the continued train of events, I have witnessed in that little room with the low, narrow bed and bare, white-washed walls twenty miles away. . . . There have I sat on the low bedstead, my eye fixed on the window, through which appeared no other landscape than a monotonous stretch of moorland, a gray church tower rising from the center of a churchyard so filled with graves that the rank weeds and coarse grass scarce had room to shoot tip between the monuments. . . . Such was the picture that threw its reflections upon my eye but communicated no impression on my heart. . . . A long tale was perhaps then evolving itself in my mind, the history of an ancient and aristocratic family . . . young lords and ladies . . . dazzled with the brilliancy of courts, happy with the ambition of senates.

"As I saw them stately and handsome, gliding through these salons, where many well known forms crossed my sight, where there were faces looking up, eyes smiling and lips moving in audible speech, that I knew better almost than my brother and sisters, yet whose voices never woke an echo in this world, what glorious associations crowded upon me! Far from home I cannot write of them; . . . except in total solitude I scarce dare think of them."

Again she confides her secrets to her journals—"Haworth and home wakes sensations which lie dormant elsewhere. Last night I did indeed lean upon the thunder-wakening wings of such a stormy blast as I have seldom heard blow, and it whirled me away like heath in the wilderness for five seconds of ecstasy; and as I sat by myself in the dining room, while all the rest were at tea, the trance seemed to descend on a sudden. Verily this foot trod the war-shaken shores of the Calabar, and these eyes saw the defiled and violated Adrianopolis shedding its lights on the river from lattices whence the invader looked out."

Roe Head and her duties there she hated because they held her spirit in bondage. "All this day," she writes, "I have been in a dream, half-miserable; half-ecstatic,—miserable because I could not follow it out uninterruptedly, ecstatic because it showed almost in the vivid light of reality the ongoings of the infernal world." And at another time: "I now resume my own thoughts; my mind relaxes from the stretch on which it has been for the last twelve hours and falls back on to the rest which nobody in this house knows of but myself. . . . I fulfil my duties strictly and well. . . . As God was not in the fire nor the wind nor the earthquake, so neither is my heart in the task, the theme, or the exercise. It is the still small voice always that comes to me at eventide, that—like a breeze with a voice in it over the deeply blue hills and out of the now leafless forests and from cities on distant river banks—of a far and bright continent; it is that which takes up my spirit and engrosses all my living feelings, all my energies which are not merely mechanical."

The howl of winter wind reminded her of Haworth, but Haworth was but a link with Angria. The sound of Huddersfield Parish Church wafted her away to Verdopolis:

"That wind, pouring in impetuous currents through the air, sounding wildly, unremittingly from hour to hour, deepening its tone as the night advances, coming not in gusts, but with a rapid gathering, storm swell—that wind, I know, is heard at this moment far away on the moors of Haworth. Branwell and Emily hear it, and, as it sweeps over our house down the churchyard and round the old church, they think, perhaps, of me and Anne. Glorious! That blast was mighty; it reminded me of Northangerland; there was something so merciless in the heavier rush that made the very house groan, as if it could scarce bear this acceleration of impulse. . . .

"I listened—the sound sailed full and liquid down the descent: it was the bells of Huddersfield Parish Church. I shut the window and went back to my seat. Then came on me, rushing impetuously, all the mighty phantasm that this had conjured from nothing,—from nothing to a system strange as some religious creed. I felt as if I could have written gloriously. The spirit of all Verdopolis—of all the mountainous North—of all the woodland West—of all the river-watered East, came crowding into my mind. If I had had time to indulge it I felt that the vague suggestions of that moment would have settled down into some narrative better at least than anything I ever produced before. But just then a dolt came up with a lesson."

Even her letters from home were prized chiefly because they brought her news of war-torn Angria and the exiled and dying Duchess of Zamorna:

"About a week since I got a letter from Branwell containing a most exquisitely characteristic epistle from Northangerland to his daughter. . . . I lived on its contents for days. In every pause of employment it came chiming in like some sweet bar of music, bringing with it agreeable thoughts such as I had for many weeks been a stranger to. . . . A curtain seemed to rise and discover to me the Duchess as she might appear when newly risen and lightly dressed for the morning, discovering her father's letter in the mail which lies on her breakfast table."

Again:

"I wonder if Branwell has really killed the Duchess. Is she dead? Is she buried? Is she alone in the cold earth on this dreary night? . . . I hope she's alive still, partly because I can't abide to think how hopelessly and cheerlessly she must have died, and partly because her removal, if it has taken place, must have been to Northangerland like the quenching of the last spark that averted utter darkness."

2   The Goshawk

Thomas Bewick's engravings of a cormorant on rocky coast and a goshawk for his History of British Birds *(from Robert Hutchinson,*
1800 Woodcuts by Thomas Bewick and His School, *Colorado College Library)*

Thomas Bewick and the Brontës

*Among the Brontës' favorite books as children was Thomas
Bewick's* History of British Birds, *2 volumes (1816).
Bewick (1753–1828) was an engraver who wrote and illustrated a series of books on natural history, as well as editions of
Aesop's fables and other works. The Brontës all copied pictures
from his works, especially the volumes of* A History of British
Birds. *Charlotte Brontë refers to Bewick's work at the start of
her novel* Jane Eyre *(1847), when Jane escapes into the window seat to read* History of British Birds.

*Pencil drawings of Bewick's engravings by Charlotte, left, 24 January 1829; and Branwell, right, 1833 (Brontë Parsonage Museum;
from Christine Alexander and Jane Sellars,* The Art of the Brontës, *University of Colorado Libraries)*

Not once in the many pages of microscopic script that have survived from her Roe Head days does she voice any direct homesickness for Haworth; all her longing was for Angria, the land of her spirit's freedom. Even her Christmas and summer vacations, as the dates of numerous manuscripts attest, were spent in the palaces of Angria and Verdopolis rather than in the parsonage and on the moors of Haworth.

Her "otherworldliness" and her tendency to withdraw herself from companionship were noted by those about her and discussed as "ill health," "despondency," and "irritability," terms which Charlotte admitted herself in her letters to Ellen Nussey. But to her diary she poured out a different story.

Mary Taylor, the most understanding and discerning of Charlotte's friends, visited her at Roe Head, and wrote Mrs. Gaskell, more than ten years later, of her visit:

"She seemed to have no interest or pleasure beyond the feeling of duty, and, when she could get the opportunity, used to sit alone and 'make out.' She told me . . . that one evening she had sat in the dressing-room until it was quite dark, and then observing it all at once, she had taken sudden fright. . . . She told me that one night, sitting alone, about this time, she heard a voice repeat these lines:

Come thou high and holy feeling,
Shine o'er mountain, flit o'er wave,
Gleam like light o'er dome and shieling.

There were eight or ten lines which I forget. She insisted that she had not made them, that she had heard a voice repeat them."

Yet even Mary Taylor had no intimation that Charlotte's "making out" was the calling up of realistic spirits from her imagination, or that the lines which she quoted were the cry of genius in travail. In one of her diary-like fragments of this period, Charlotte recounts this incident, or one similar to it:

"Miss Wooler tried to make me talk at tea-time and was exceedingly kind to me, but I could not have roused if she had offered me worlds. After tea we took a long weary walk. I came back fatigued to the last degree. . . . The ladies went into the schoolroom to do their exercises, and I crept up to the bed-room to be alone for the first time that day. Delicious, to be sure, was the sensation I experienced as I lay down on the spare bed and resigned myself to the luxury of twilight and solitude. The stream of thought, checked all day, came flowing free and calm along the channel. My ideas were too shattered to form any defined picture, as they would have done in such circumstances at home, but detached thoughts soothingly flitted round me and unconnected scenes occurred, then vanished, producing an effect cer-

tainly strange but to me very pleasing. The toil of the day, succeeded by this moment of divine leisure, had acted on me like opium and was coiling about me a disturbed but fascinating spell such as I had never felt before. What I imagined grew morbidly vivid. I remember I quite seemed to see with my bodily eyes a lady standing in the hall of a gentleman's house as if waiting for someone. It was dusk, and there was the dim outline of antlers, with a hat and a rough great-coat upon them. She had a flat candlestick in her hand and seemed coming from the kitchen or some such place. . . .

"I grew frightened at the vivid glow of the candle, at the reality of the lady's erect and symmetrical figure, of her spirited and handsome face, of her anxious eye. . . . I felt confounded and annoyed I scarcely knew by what. . . . A horrid apprehension quickened every pulse I had. I must get up, I thought, and did so on a start. I had had enough of morbidly vivid realizations. Every advantage has its corresponding disadvantage. Tea's real. Miss Wooler is impatient." The picture that had frightened her was an Angrian scene strongly foreshadowing one in "Villette."

A more connected story of what the Angrian dream meant to Charlotte as an escape from her schoolroom surroundings is found in a long narrative poem written at Haworth, in the course of her Christmas vacation, in 1836. The first three stanzas are familiar, but separated from the rest of the poem, they lose their significance. They were probably copied out from the original manuscript, now in the Huntington Library, by Charlotte in 1846 when she was preparing "Poems by Currer, Ellis, and Acton Bell" for publication. The "web of sunny air," the "spring in infancy," the "mustard seed," and the "almond rod" are fitting figures for the childish play which had spread and swelled and towered to transcendent proportions.

We wove a web in childhood,
    A web of sunny air;
We dug a spring in infancy
    Of water pure and fair.

We sowed in youth a mustard seed;
    We cut an almond rod.
We are now grown up to riper age:
    Are they withered in the sod?

Are they blighted, failed, and faded?
    Are they mouldered back to clay?
For life is darkly shaded,
    And Its joys fleet fast away.

Faded! the web is still of air,
    But now its folds are spread!
And from its tints of crimson clear,
    How deep a glow is shed!
The light of an Italian sky,

Where clouds of sunset lingering lie,
Is not more ruby-red.

But the spring was under a mossy stone,
  Its jet may gush no more.
Hark, sceptic, bid thy doubts be gone;
  Is that a feeble roar?
Rushing around thee, lo! the tide
  Of waves where armed fleets may ride,
Sinking and swelling, frowns and smiles,
  An ocean with a thousand Isles
And scarce a glimpse of shore.

The mustard seed in distant land
  Bends down a mighty tree;
The dry and budding almond wand
  Has touched eternity.

The poem, in another meter, goes on to tell how when the writer "sat 'neath a strange roof-tree," in the black hour of twilight, "longing for her own dear home and the sight of old familiar faces," the dream by its magic bore her away to scenes of joy and excitement:

Where was I ere an hour had passed?
  Still listening to that dreary blast?
Still in that mirthless room,
  Cramped, chilled, and deadened by its gloom?

No! thanks to that bright, darling dream!
Its power had shot one kindling gleam,
Its voice had sent one wakening cry
And bade me lay my sorrows by,
And called me earnestly to come,
And borne me to my moorland home.
I heard no more the senseless sound
Of task and chat that hummed around;
I saw no more that grisly night
Closing the day's sepulchral light.
The vision's spell had deepened o'er me,
Its lands, its scenes were spread before me.
In one short hour a hundred homes
Had roofed me with their lordly domes,
And I had sat by fires whose lights
Flashed wide o'er halls of regal height,
And I had seen those come and go
Whose forms gave radiance to the glow,
And I had heard the matted floor
Of ante-room and corridor
Shake to some half-remembered tread,
Whose haughty firmness woke even dread,
As through the curtained portal strode
Some spurred and fur-wrapped demi-god,
Whose ride through that tempestuous night
Had added somewhat of a frown
To brows that shadowed eyes of light
Fit to flash fire from Scythian crown
Till sweet salute from lady gay
Chased that unconscious scowl away.

After painting a detailed picture of the Duke of Zamorna in his drawing-room, the poem shifts the scene to a heath on a moonlit summer's night, as the Duke and a companion have come to sound a requiem for a kinsman who has fallen in battle:

It was Camalia's ancient field.
I knew the desert well,
For traced around a sculptured shield
These words the summer moon revealed,
  "Here brave Macarthy fell,
The men of Keswick leading on,
Their first, their best, their noblest one
  He did his duty well."

Never shall I, Charlotte Brontë, forget what a voice of wild and wailing music now came thrillingly to my mind's, almost to my body's, ear, nor how distinctly I, sitting in the school-room at Roe Head, saw the Duke of Zamorna leaning against that obelisk with the mute marble Victory above him, the fern waving at his feet, his black horse turned loose grazing among the heather, the moonlight so mild, so exquisitely tranquil, sleeping upon that vast and vacant road, and the African sky quivering and shaking with stars, expanded above all. I was quite gone. I had really utterly forgot where I was and all the gloom and cheerlessness of my situation. I felt myself breathing quick and short, as I beheld the Duke lifting up his sable crest which undulated as the plume of a hearse waves to the wind, and I knew that music which sprung as mournfully triumphant as the scriptural verse,

O Grave, where is thy sting? O Death, where is thy victory?

was exciting him and quickening his ever rapid pulse. 'Miss Brontë, what are you thinking about?' said a voice that dissipated all the charm, and Miss Lister thrust her little, rough black head into my face. *Sic transit &c*

In an undated fragment, written . . . in 1837, Charlotte took at twenty-one a formal farewell of Angria in one of the most emotional passages that she ever wrote:

"I have now written a great many books, and for a long time have dwelt upon the same characters and scenes and subjects. I have shewn my landscapes in every variety of shades and light which morning, noon, and evening—the rising, the meridian, and the setting sun can bestow upon them . . . So it is with persons. My readers have been habituated to one set of features which they have seen, now in profile, now in full face, now in outline, and again in finished painting—varied but by the thought or feeling or temper or age; lit with love, flushed with passion, shaded with grief, kindled with ecstasy; in meditation and mirth, in sorrow and scorn and rapture; with the round outlines of child-hood, the beauty and freshness of youth, the strength of manhood and the furrows of thoughtful decline;—But we must change, for the eye is tired of the picture so oft recurring and now so familiar.

"Yet do not urge me too fast, reader; it is not easy to dismiss from my imagination the images which have filled it for so long; they were my friends and intimate acquaintances, and I could with little labor describe to you the faces, the voices, the actions of those who peo-ple my thoughts by day and not seldom stole strangely into my dreams by night. When I depart from these, I feel almost as if I stood on the threshold of a home and were bidding farewell to its inmates. . . . Still, I long to quit for awhile that burning clime where we have sojourned too long—its skies flame—the glow of sunset is always upon it—the mind would cease from excitement and turn now to a cooler region where the dawn breaks gray and sober, and the coming day, for a time at least, is subdued by clouds."

If the date assigned to this passage is correct, Charlotte broke her resolution by more than one journey back to Angria, for her novels of that coun-try continued well into 1839, after she had passed her twenty-third birthday. For the rest of her life, her literary efforts were spent in an attempt to European-ize her Africans. Her success is attested by the cer-tainty with which Mr Yorke, Paul Emanuel, Shirley, and others have been identified as portraits of real persons. As late as 1843, she wrote Branwell from Brussels that in the evenings, when she was alone in the great dormitory of the Héger *Pensionnat* she recurred as "fanatically as ever to the old ideas, the old faces, and the old scenes."

If Emily Brontë ever poured out her homesick-ness on paper, the precious document has been lost. But Charlotte's confessions give new meaning to her own explanation of her sister's early return to Haworth.

"Every morning when she woke, the vision of home and the moors rushed on her and darkened and saddened the day that lay before her. Nobody knew what ailed her but me. . . . I felt in my heart that she would die, if she did not go home, and with this conviction obtained her recall. . . .

"My sister Emily loved the moors. Flowers brighter than the rose bloomed in the blackest of the heath for her;—out of a sullen hollow in a livid hill-side, her mind could make an Eden. She found in the bleak solitude many dear delights; not the least and best-loved was—liberty. Liberty was the breath of Emily's nostrils; without it she perished."

Were the flowers that bloomed on the heath for Emily the halls of Gondal? Was the Eden which she

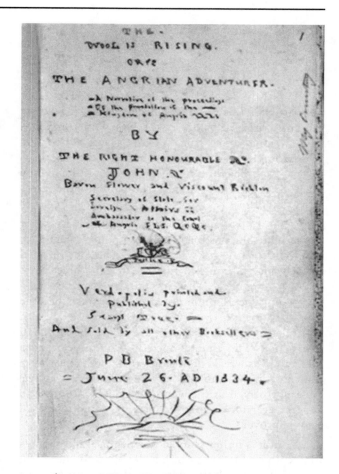

The title page for a tale by Branwell (The British Library, record number 10271, Shelfmark Ashley 2469)

conjured from the bleak hillside the land of King Julius? Was the liberty that was as the breath of life to her the freedom to worship without interruption her "God of Visions"?

Analogy need not be strained; the facts, few as they are, are suggestive enough. Of the great mass of prose written by Emily and Anne in their childhood and early girlhood, there remain but five short frag-ments, four of these being notes exchanged between the two on Emily's birthday, to be opened four years from that date. All of these five bits speak of Gondal as an inherent part of their lives. On November 24, 1834, Emily chronicled along with other events of family importance, "The Gondals are exploring the interior of Gaaldine." Anne's pencilled notes in the family geography explain that Gondal was a large island in the Northern Pacific, and the Gaaldine was an island newly discovered in the South Pacific. In her birthday note of July 30, 1841, Emily says, "The

Gondals are at present in a threatening state, but there is no open rupture as yet," and Anne, on the same day looking forward four years, wonders "whether the Gondolians will still be flourishing."

On July 30, 1845, Emily answers, "The Gondals are still flourishing as bright as ever. I am at present writing a history of the First War. Anne has been writing some articles on this and a book by Henry Sophona. We intend to stick by the rascals as long as they delight us, which I am glad to say they do at the present." Anne's companion note gives more details:

"Emily is engaged in writing the Emperor Julius's life. She has read some of it, and I want very much to hear the rest. . . . We have not yet finished our Gondal Chronicles that we began three years and a half ago. . . . The Gondals are at present in a sad state. The Republicans are uppermost, but the Royalists are not overcome. The young sovereigns, with their brothers and sister, are still at the Palace of Instruction. The Unique Society, about a year and a half ago, was wrecked on a desert island as they were returning from Gaul. They are still there, but we have not played at them much yet. The Gondals in general are not in firstrate playing condition. Will they improve?"

But it is in her Gondal poems that Emily voices the depth and intensity of her devotion to "her own, her spirit's home!" In them the childish tone of the birthday journals falls away before elemental passions rising to sublime heights of joy and tragedy. It may be that these, like Charlotte's Angrian poems, were originally incorporated in prose tales as songs and emotional outbursts of her favorite characters, or it may be that they are but fragments of a long epic. However they were composed, she had copied them out in the volume "accidentally lighted upon" by Charlotte in the autumn of 1845, when their vigor and sincerity and their "peculiar music, wild, melancholy, and elevating" so pleased the discoverer that she persuaded their author to join in the famous publication of 1846.

The qualities which impressed Charlotte have been felt by all who have read Emily's poems, but the obscurity of their background has denied them the popularity that their merits deserve. Only from other sources, such as Anne's notes in the family geography, could one learn that Alexandra, Almedore, Zelona, and Elseraden—names of frequent occurrence—were kingdoms of Gaaldine, together with "Ula, . . . governed by four sovereigns," and "Zendora, . . . governed by a viceroy." And without careful and repeated reading one would never guess that

the greater number of Emily's poems recount the fortunes of King Julius (who for the love of his proud and ambitious wife, Rosina, usurped the throne of Gondal in violation of his oath, and for his perfidy fell by an avenger's dagger) and the fate of his daughter Augusta who succeeded him, with many ramifications inspired always by the elemental passions of love, hate, and revenge.

To inherent obscurity has been added the misconception spread abroad by biographers who have persisted in interpreting autobiographically poems reflecting experiences and feelings of purely imaginary characters in a purely imaginary world. The tradition of a mysterious lover who died in Emily's early youth is based on the magnificent poem of intense and lofty passion which begins,

Cold in the earth—and the deep snow piled above thee,

which Emily's own manuscript tells us is the lament of Rosina for her murdered husband.

Yet Emily has spoken with startling plainness to those who have ears to hear. Her poem "Plead for Me" is hardly less explicit than Charlotte's "We Wove a Web in Childhood." She is calling her dream to defend her before the "scornful brow" of "Stern judgment":

. . . Radiant angel, speak and say
Why I did cast the world away,–
Why I have persevered to shun
The common paths that others run;
And on a strange road journey on. . . .

As earnestly and devoutly as Charlotte invoked her "high and holy feeling" to lighten her days at Roe Head, Emily, at Haworth, worshipped her "God of Visions":

Am I wrong to worship where
Faith cannot doubt, nor hope despair,
Since my own soul can grant my prayer?
Speak, God of Visions, plead for me,
And tell why I have chosen thee.

Was the face of her god turned from her at Roe Head?

Against the background of Gondal "Wuthering Heights" is no more of a mystery than "Jane Eyre" and "Villette" to one who knows the Angrian stories.

–*The Yale Review,* 21 (September 1931): 139–157

The Brontës at Home and the Plan for a School

This excerpt is from an article, "Reminiscences of Charlotte Brontë," by Ellen Nussey, Charlotte's lifelong friend from her student days at Miss Wooler's School. The selection provides her memories of the Brontë family at Haworth, which she first visited in July 1833.

Impressions of the Brontës
Ellen Nussey

My first visit to Haworth was full of novelty and freshness. The scenery for some miles before we reached Haworth was wild and uncultivated, with hardly any population; at last we came to what seemed a terrific hill, such a steep declivity no one thought of riding down it; the horse had to be carefully led. We no sooner reached the foot of this hill than we had to begin to mount again, over a narrow, rough, stone-paved road; the horses' feet seemed to catch at boulders, as if climbing. When we reached the top of the village there was apparently no outlet, but we were directed to drive into an entry which just admitted the gig; we wound round in this entry and then saw the church close at hand, and we entered on the short lane which led to the parsonage gate-way. Here Charlotte was waiting, having caught the sound of the approaching gig. When greetings and introductions were over, Miss Branwell (the aunt of the Brontës) took possession of their guest and treated her with the care and solicitude due to a weary traveler. Mr. Brontë, also, was stirred out of his usual retirement by his own kind consideration, for not only the guest but the man-servant and the horse were to be made comfortable. He made inquiries about the man, of his length of service, &c., with the kind purpose of making a few moments of conversation agreeable to him.

Even at this time, Mr. Brontë struck me as looking very venerable, with his snow-white hair and powdered coat-collar. His manner and mode of speech always had the tone of high-bred courtesy. He was considered somewhat of an invalid, and always lived in the most abstemious and simple manner. His white cravat was not then so remarkable as it grew to be afterwards. He was in the habit of covering this cravat himself. We never saw the operation, but we always had to wind for him the white sewing-silk which he used. Charlotte said it was her father's one extravagance—he cut up yards and yards of white lutestring (silk) in covering his cravat; and, like Dr. Joseph Woolffe (the renowned and learned traveler), who, when on a visit and in a long fit of absence, "went into a clean shirt every day for a week, without taking one off," so Mr. Brontë's cravat went into new silk and new size without taking any off,

Anne Brontë's drawing of Miss Margaret Wooler's school at Roe Head, a hamlet some eighteen miles southeast of Haworth. The school opened in 1830 and had just ten pupils when Charlotte arrived in January 1831. Emily attended the school in 1835 and Anne from 1835 to 1837 (from Christine Alexander and Jane Sellars, The Art of the Brontës, *University of Colorado Libraries).*

till at length nearly half his head was enveloped in cravat. His liability to bronchial attacks, no doubt, attached him to this increasing growth of cravat.

Miss Branwell was a very small, antiquated little lady. She wore caps large enough for half a dozen of the present fashion, and a front of light auburn curls over her forehead. She always dressed in silk. She had a horror of the climate so far north, and of the stone floors in the parsonage. She amused us by clicking about in pattens whenever she had to go into the kitchen or look after household operations.

She talked a great deal of her younger days; the gayeties of her dear native town, Penzance, in Cornwall; the soft, warm climate, etc. The social life of her younger days she used to recall with regret; she gave one the idea that she had been a belle among her own home acquaintances. She took snuff out of a very pretty gold snuff-box, which she sometimes presented to you with a little laugh, as if she enjoyed the slight shock and astonishment visible in your countenance. In summer she spent part of the afternoon in reading aloud to Mr. Brontë. In the winter evenings she must have enjoyed this; for she and Mr. Brontë had often to finish their dis-

"This Land of Probation"

This excerpt is from a 6 July 1835 letter the Reverend Brontë wrote when Charlotte returned to Miss Wooler's School as a teacher, accompanied by Emily as student. His correspondent was his former neighbor at Thornton, Elizabeth Firth Franks, who had married and lived near Roe Head.

My Dear Madam,—As two of my dear children are soon to be placed near you, I take the liberty of writing to you a few lines in order to request both you and Mr. Franks to be so kind as to interpose with your advice and counsel to them in any case of necessity, and if expedient to write to Miss Branwell or me if our interference should be requisite. I will charge them strictly to attend to what you may advise, though it is not my intention to speak to them of this letter. They both have good abilities, and as far as I can judge their principles are good also, but they are very young, and unacquainted with the ways of this delusive and ensnaring world, and though they will be placed under the superintendence of Miss Wooler, who will, I doubt not, do what she can for their good, yet I am well aware that neither they nor any other can ever, in this land of probation, lie beyond the reach of temptation. It is my design to send my son—for whom, as you may remember, my kind and true friends Mr. Firth and Mrs. Firth were sponsors—to the Royal Academy for Artists in London, and my dear little Anne I intend to keep at home for another year, under her aunt's tuition and my own. For their dispositions I feel indebted, under God, to you, and Miss Outhwaite, and

Mrs. Firth, and other kind friends, and for every act of kindness I feel truly grateful. It has given us all unfeigned pleasure to learn that your health is nearly restored, and that Mr. Franks and your dear little children are all well. [. . .] My own health is generally but *very* delicate, yet through gracious providence, and with great care, I am for the most part able to perform my various ministerial duties. Indeed, I have never been very well since I left Thornton. My happiest days were spent there. In this place I have received civilities, and have, I trust, been civil to all, but I have not tried to make any friends, nor have I met with any whose mind was congenial with my own. I have not been at Thornton or Kipping for many years. The last time I was there I travelled over some of my ancient paths, and thought of my dear wife and children whom death had removed, and when I was in the church, and reflected that my beloved friend, with whom I was wont to take sweet counsel, was beneath my feet, sadness came over my heart, and afterwards, as I walked round your garden, I called to mind *all* my dear friends who were removed from thence by the vicissitudes of life, and I soon found the *whole* aspect of affairs to be entirely changed, and so I returned home, fully intending to visit Thornton and Kipping no more, unless I should be in a great measure forced by reason of circumstances.

—"The Brontës at Thornton," *The Bookman*, 27 (October 1904): 20–21

cussions on what she had read when we all met for tea. She would be very lively and intelligent, and tilt arguments against Mr. Brontë without fear.

"Tabby," the faithful, trustworthy old servant, was very quaint in appearance—very active, and, in these days, the general servant and factotum. We were all "childer" and "bairns," in her estimation. She still kept to her duty of walking out with the "childer," if they went any distance from home, unless Branwell were sent by his father as a protector. Poor "Tabby," in later days, after she had been attacked with paralysis, would most anxiously look out for such duties as she was still capable of. The post-man was her special point of attention. She did not approve of the inspection which the younger eyes of her fellow-servant bestowed on his deliveries. She jealously seized them when she could, and carried them off with hobbling step, and shaking head and hand, to the safe custody of Charlotte.

Emily Brontë had by this time acquired a lithesome, graceful figure. She was the tallest person in the house, except her father. Her hair, which was naturally as beautiful as Charlotte's, was in the same unbecoming tight curl and frizz, and there was the same want of complexion. She had very beautiful eyes—kind, kindling, liquid eyes; but

she did not often look at you: she was too reserved. Their color might be said to be dark gray, at other times dark blue, they varied so. She talked very little. She and Anne were like twins—inseparable companions, and in the very closest sympathy, which never had any interruption.

Anne—dear, gentle Anne—was quite different in appearance from the others. She was her aunt's favorite. Her hair was a very pretty light brown, and fell on her neck in graceful curls. She had lovely violet-blue eyes, fine penciled eyebrows, and clear, almost transparent complexion. She still pursued her studies, and especially her sewing, under the surveillance of her aunt. Emily had now begun to have the disposal of her own time.

Branwell studied regularly with his father, and used to paint in oils, which was regarded as study for what might be eventually his profession. All the household entertained the idea of his becoming an artist, and hoped he would be a distinguished one.

In fine and suitable weather delightful rambles were made over the moors, and down into the glens and ravines that here and there broke the monotony of the moorland. The rugged bank and rippling brook were treasures of delight. Emily, Anne, and Branwell used to ford the streams, and sometimes placed stepping-stones for the other two; there was always a lingering delight in these spots,—every moss, every flower, every tint and form, were noted and enjoyed. Emily especially had a gleesome delight in these nooks of beauty,—her reserve for the time vanished. One long ramble made in these early days was far away over the moors, to a spot familiar to Emily and Anne, which they called "The Meeting of the Waters." It was a small oasis of emerald green turf, broken here and there by small clear springs; a few large stones served as resting-places; seated here, we were hidden from all the world, nothing appearing in view but miles and miles of heather, a glorious blue sky, and brightening sun. A fresh breeze wafted on us its exhilarating influence; we laughed and made mirth of each other, and settled we would call ourselves the quartette. Emily, half reclining on a slab of stone, played like a young child with the tadpoles in the water, making them swim about, and then fell to moralizing on the strong and the weak, the brave and the cowardly, as she chased them with her hand. No serious care or sorrow had so far cast its gloom on nature's youth and buoyancy, and nature's simplest offerings were fountains of pleasure and enjoyment.

The interior of the now far-famed parsonage lacked drapery of all kinds. Mr. Brontë's horror of fire forbade curtains to the windows; they never had these accessories to comfort and appearance till long after Charlotte was the only inmate of the family sitting-room,—she then ventured on the innovation when her friend was with her; it did not please her father, but it was not forbidden.

There was not much carpet anywhere except in the sitting-room, and on the study floor. The hall floor and stairs were done with sand-stone, always beautifully clean, as everything was about the house; the walls were not papered, but stained in a pretty dove-colored tint; hair-seated chairs and mahogany tables, book-shelves in the study, but not many of these elsewhere. Scant and bare indeed, many will say, yet it was not a scantness that made itself felt. Mind and thought, I had almost said elegance, but certainly refinement, diffused themselves over all, and made nothing really wanting.

A little later on, there was the addition of a piano. Emily, after some application, played with precision and brilliancy. Anne played also, but she preferred soft harmonies and vocal music. She sang a little; her voice was weak, but very sweet in tone.

Mr. Brontë's health caused him to retire early. He assembled his household for family worship at eight o'clock; at nine he locked and barred the front door, always giving, as he passed the sitting-room door, a kindly admonition to the "children" not to be late; half way up the stairs he stayed his steps to wind up the clock, the clock that in after days seemed to click like a

Martha Brown (1828–1880), daughter of Haworth sexton John Brown, who worked for the Brontës from 1841 until Reverend Brontë's death in 1861 (from The Bookman, *October 1904)*

dirge in the refrain of Longfellow's poem, "The old Clock on the Stairs:"—

"Forever—never!
Never—forever!"

Every morning was heard the firing of a pistol from Mr. Brontë's room window,—it was the discharging of the loading which was made every night. Mr. Brontë's tastes led him to delight in the perusal of battle-scenes, and in following the artifice of war; had he entered on military service instead of ecclesiastical, he would probably have had a very distinguished career. The self-denials and privations of camp-life would have agreed entirely with his nature, for he was remarkably independent of the luxuries and comforts of life. The only dread he had was of *fire,* and this dread was so intense it caused him to prohibit all but silk or woollen dresses for his daughters; indeed, for any one to wear any other kind of fabric was almost to forfeit his respect.

Mr. Brontë at times would relate strange stories, which had been told to him by some of the oldest inhabitants of the parish, of the extraordinary lives and doings of people who had resided in far-off, out-of-the-way places, but in contiguity with Haworth,—stories which made one shiver and shrink from hearing; but they were full of grim humor and interest to Mr. Brontë and his children, as revealing the characteristics of a class in the human race, and as such Emily Brontë has stereotyped them in her *Wuthering Heights*.

During Miss Branwell's reign at the parsonage, the love of animals had to be kept in due subjection. There was then but one dog which was admitted to the parlor at stated times. Emily and Anne always gave him a portion of their breakfast, which was, by their own choice, the old north country diet of oatmeal porridge. Later on, there were three household pets—the tawny, strong-limbed "Keeper," Emily's favorite: he was so completely under her control, she could quite easily make him spring and roar like a lion. She taught him this kind of occasional play without any coercion. "Flossy"—long, silky-haired, black and white "Flossy"—was Anne's favorite; and black "Tom," the tabby, was everybody's favorite. It received such gentle treatment it seemed to have lost cat's nature, and subsided into luxurious amiability and contentment. The Brontës' love of dumb creatures made them very sensitive of the treatment bestowed upon them. For any one to offend in this respect was with them an infallible bad sign, and a blot on the disposition.

The services in church in these days were such as can only be seen (if ever seen again) in localities like Haworth. The people assembled, but it was apparently to *listen*. Any part beyond that was quite out of their reckoning. All through the prayers, a stolid look of apathy was fixed on the generality of their faces. There they sat, or leaned, in their pews; some few, perhaps, were resting, after a long walk over the moors. The children, many of them in clogs (or sabots), pattered in from the school after service had commenced, and pattered out again before the sermon. The sexton, with a long staff, continually walked round in the aisles, "knobbing" sleepers when he dare, shaking his head at and threatening unruly children; but when the sermon began there was a change. Attitudes took the listening forms, eyes were turned on the preacher. It was curious, now, to note the expression. A rustic, untaught intelligence, gleamed in their faces; in some, a daring, doubting, questioning look, as if they would like to offer some defiant objection. Mr. Brontë always addressed his hearers in extempore style. Very often he selected a parable from one of the Gospels, which he explained in the simplest manner—sometimes going over his own words and explaining them also, so as to be perfectly intelligible to the lowest comprehension.

A re-creation of the Brontë sisters' advertising cards for the school they hoped to start in the parsonage (from Whiteley Turner,
A Spring-Time Saunter: Round and About Brontë Land, *Sam Houston State University Library)*

The parishioners respected Mr. Brontë because, as one of them said, "he's a grand man; he lets other folks' business alone." No doubt Mr. Brontë's knowledge of human nature made him aware that this was the best course to pursue, till their independence had acquired a more civilized standard. There were exceptions, however, among them. Two or three individuals deserve particular note—they were men remarkable for self-culture and intelligence. One, it was said, vied with Mr. Brontë himself in his knowledge of the dead languages. He and another had, in addition to their mental stamina, such stalwart frames and stature they looked capable of doing duty as guards to the whole village. The third individual was an ailing, suffering man; but he wrote such a critique on Charlotte's writings, when they became known, that it was valued more than any other coming from such a source. The villagers would have liked Tabby to talk to them about the family in the parsonage; but Tabby was invincible and impenetrable. When they asked her "if they were not fearfully larn'd," she left them in a "huff;" but she did not deny her "childer" the laugh she knew they would have if she told them the village query.

Haworth of the present day, like many other secluded, places, has made a step onwards, in that it has now its railway station, and its institutions for the easy acquirement of learning, politics, and literature. The parsonage is quite another habitation from the parsonage of former days. The garden, which was nearly all grass, and possessed only a few stunted thorns and shrubs, and a few currant bushes which Emily and Anne treasured as their own bit of fruit-garden, is now a perfect Arcadia of floral culture and beauty. At first the alteration, in spite of its improvement, strikes one with heart-ache and regret; for it is quite impossible, even in imagination, to people those rooms with their former inhabitants. But after-thought shows one the folly of such regret; for what the Brontës cared for and *lived* in most were the surroundings of nature, the free expanse of hill and mountain, the purple heather, the dells, and glens, and brooks, the broad sky view, the whistling winds, the snowy expanse, the starry heavens, and the charm of that solitude and seclusion which sees things from a distance without the disturbing atmosphere which lesser minds are apt to create. For it was not the seclusion of a *solitary* person, such as Charlotte endured in after days, and which in time becomes awfully

---

A First Visit to London

On the first leg of their journey to Brussels, Charlotte and Emily were accompanied by their father, Charlotte's friend Mary Taylor, and Mary's brother Joe. In London the group stayed at the Chapter Coffee House, adjacent to St. Paul's Cathedral, where Reverend Brontë had stayed in the early years of the century. On this initial visit to the city, the sisters saw such sights as Westminster Abbey, the British Museum, and the National Gallery.

A decade later Charlotte created an episode for her novel Villette *(1853), in which her protagonist, Lucy Snowe, arrives for the first time in London, friendless, on "a dark, raw, and rainy evening." As she tries to sleep, Lucy listens as "a deep, low, mighty tone swung through the night. At first I knew it not; but it was uttered twelve times, and at the twelfth colossal hum and trembling knell, I said: 'I lie in the shadow of St. Paul's.'" The next chapter opens with an evocation of the cathedral.*

The next day was the first of March, and when I awoke, rose, and opened my curtain, I saw the risen sun struggling through fog. Above my head, above the house-tops, co-elevate almost with the clouds, I saw a solemn, orbed mass, dark blue and dim—THE DOME. While I looked, my inner self moved; my spirit shook its always-fettered wings half loose; I had a sudden feeling as if I, who never yet truly lived, were at last about to taste life. In that morning my soul grew as fast as Jonah's gourd.

"I did well to come," I said, proceeding to dress with speed and care. "I like the spirit of this great London which I feel around me. Who but a coward would pass his whole life in hamlets; and for ever abandon his faculties to the eating rust of obscurity?"

—Vilette, volume 1, chapter 6

The dome of St. Paul's Cathedral, as seen from near the Chapter Coffee House, where Charlotte Brontë stayed on London visits (photograph by Susan B. Taylor)

oppressive and injurious. It was solitude and seclusion shared and enjoyed with intelligent companionship, and intense family affection.

—*Scribner's Magazine*, 2 (May 1871): 18–31; pp. 24–31

* * *

Each of the Brontë sisters in early adulthood worked as a governess or teacher. Anne held the longest post, staying with the Robinson family for five years (1840–1845). Charlotte and Emily each worked shorter periods in different situations. By summer 1841, the sisters were imagining how they might open their own school at the Haworth Parsonage and attain the autonomy they lacked when working for others.

In this letter to her Aunt Branwell, which was written from Upperwood House in Rawdon, where she was serving as a governess to the Whites, Charlotte suggests a plan to better the chances of their proposed school becoming a success.

Charlotte Brontë to Elizabeth Branwell, 29 September 1841

Dear Aunt,—I have heard nothing of Miss Wooler yet since I wrote to her intimating that I would accept her offer. I cannot conjecture the reason of this long silence, unless some unforeseen impediment has occurred in concluding the bargain. Meantime, a plan has been suggested and approved by Mr. and Mrs. White, and others, which I wish now to impart to you. My friends recommend me, if I desire to secure permanent success, to delay commencing the school for six months longer, and by all means to contrive, by hook or by crook, to spend the intervening time in some school on the continent. They say schools in England are so numerous, competition so great, that without some such step towards attaining superiority we shall probably have a very hard struggle, and may fail in the end. They say, moreover, that the loan of £100, which you have been so kind as to offer us, will, perhaps, not be all required now, as Miss Wooler will lend us the furniture; and that, if the speculation is intended to be a good and successful one, half the sum, at least, ought to be laid out in the manner I have mentioned, thereby insuring a more speedy repayment both of interest and principal.

I would not go to France or to Paris. I would go to Brussels, in Belgium. The cost of the journey there, at the dearest rate of travelling, would be £5; living is there little more than half as dear as it is in England, and the facilities for education are equal or superior to any other place in Europe. In half a year, I could acquire a thorough familiarity with French. I could improve greatly in Italian, and even get a dash of German, *i.e.,* providing my health continued as good as it is now. Martha Taylor is now staying in Brussels, at a first-rate establishment there. I should not think of

going to the Château de Kockleberg, where she is resident, as the terms are much too high; but if I wrote to her, she, with the assistance of Mrs. Jenkins, the wife of the British Consul, would be able to secure me a cheap and decent residence and respectable protection. I should have the opportunity of seeing her frequently, she would make me acquainted with the city; and, with the assistance of her cousins, I should probably in time be introduced to connections far more improving, polished, and cultivated, than any I have yet known.

These are advantages which would turn to vast account, when we actually commenced a school—and, if Emily could share them with me, only for a single half-year, we could take a footing in the world afterwards which we can never do now. I say Emily instead of Anne; for Anne might take her turn at some future period, if our school answered. I feel certain, while I am writing, that you will see the propriety of what I say; you always like to use your money to the best advantage; you are not fond of making shabby purchases; when you do confer a favour, it is often done in style; and depend upon it £50, or £100, thus laid out, would be well employed. Of course, I know no other friend in the world to whom I could apply on this subject except yourself. I feel an absolute conviction that, if this advantage were allowed us, it would be the making of us for life. Papa will perhaps think it a wild and ambitious scheme; but who ever rose in the world without ambition? When he left Ireland to go to Cambridge University, he was as ambitious as I am now. I want us *all* to go on. I know we have talents, and I want them to be turned to account. I look to you, aunt, to help us. I think you will not refuse. I know, if you consent, it shall not be my fault if you ever repent your kindness. With love to all, and the hope that you are all well,—Believe me, dear aunt, your affectionate niece,

MISS BRANWELL.   C. BRONTË

—Clement K. Shorter, *Charlotte Brontë and Her Circle*, pp. 96–97

* * *

With Aunt Branwell's financial assistance Charlotte and Emily began as students in the Pensionnat Héger in Brussels in February 1842; they studied there for a term and then were hired as teachers while they continued their studies in autumn 1842. Aunt Branwell's death 29 October 1842 after an illness of several weeks brought Emily and Charlotte back to Haworth. Emily took over running the household for Reverend Brontë, and Charlotte returned alone to Brussels to teach and continue studies in January 1843. At the end of December 1843, Charlotte returned to Haworth and, having given up the idea of a school, began once again to search for a livelihood.

A First Publication

When the sisters realized their school scheme would not succeed, Charlotte decided they should try their hand at writing for publication. She persuaded Emily and Anne to contribute poems to a volume they had published by Aylott and Jones at a cost of £31.10s, with further charges for advertising. The sisters adopted pseudonyms to mask their identities: Currer, Ellis, and Acton Bell. Poems by Currer, Ellis, and Acton Bell *was published in May 1846 and sold only two copies. Four periodicals reviewed the volume when it was published; others reviewed it later when the Bells' novels were published.*

William Archer Butler reviewed the Brontës poems in his unsigned article titled "Evenings with Our Younger Poets."

"Unaffected and Sincere"
Review of *Poems by Currer, Ellis, and Acton Bell*

Of the triad of versemen, who style themselves "CURRER, ELLIS, and ACTON BELL," we know nothing beyond the little volume in which, without preface or comment, they assume the grave simplicity of title, voice of *prænomen* or *agnomen,* which belongs to established fame, and thus calmly anticipate their own immortality. Whether—as the Irish Cleon was wont, in his "physical force" days, to say so often and ferociously of his repeal shillings—there be indeed a "man behind" each of these representative titles; or whether it be in truth but one master spirit—for the book is, after all, not beyond the utmost powers of a single human intelligence—that has been pleased to project itself into three imaginary poets,—we are wholly unable to conjecture; but we are bound, of course, in default of all evidence to the contrary, to accept the former hypothesis. The tone of all these little poems is certainly uniform; this, however, is no unpardonable offence, if they be, as in truth they are, uniform in a sort of Cowperian amiability and sweetness, no-wise unfragrant to our critical nostrils. The fairest course may, perhaps, be, to present a little specimen from each of the three.

The following pretty stanzas are from Currer's pen.

"THE WIFE'S WILL.

"Sit still—a word—a breath may break
(As light airs stir a sleeping lake)
The glassy calm that soothes my woes,
The sweet, the deep, the full repose.
O leave me not! for ever be
Thus, more than life itself to me!

"Yes, close beside thee let me kneel—
Give me thy hand, that I may feel
The friend so true—so tried—so dear—
My heart's own chosen—indeed is near;
And check me not—this hour divine
Belongs to me—is fully mine.

"'Tis thy own hearth thou sitt'st beside,
After long absence—wandering wide;
'Tis thy own wife reads in thine eyes
A promise clear of stormless skies,
For faith and true love light the rays
Which shine responsive to her gaze.

"Ay—well that single tear may fall;
Ten thousand might mine eyes recall,
Which from their lids ran blinding fast,
In hours of grief, yet scarcely past,
Well may'st thou speak of love to me;
For oh! most truly I love thee!

"Yet smile, for we are happy now.
Whence, then, that sadness on thy brow?
What say'st thou? 'We must once again,
Ere long, be severed by the main.'
I knew not this—I deemed no more
Thy step would err from Britain's shore.

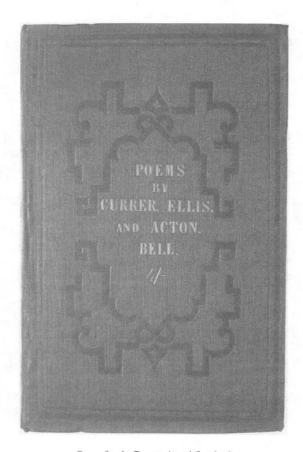

Cover for the Brontë sisters' first book
(Brontë Parsonage Museum)

"'Duty commands!' 'Tis true—'tis just;
Thy slightest word I wholly trust;
Nor by request, nor faintest sigh,
Would I, to turn thy purpose, try;
But, William, hear my solemn vow—
Hear and confirm—with thee I go!

"'Distance and suffering,' didst thou say?
'Danger by night, and toil by day?'
Oh, idle words, and vain are these—
Hear me—I cross with thee the seas!
Such risk as thou must meet and dare,
I—thy true wife—will duly share.

"Passive, at home, I will not pine—
Thy toils—thy perils shall be mine.
Grant this, and be hereafter paid
By a warm heart's devoted aid.'
'Tis granted—with that yielding kiss
Entered my soul unmingled bliss.

"Thanks, William—thanks! thy love has joy,
Pure—undefiled with base alloy;
'Tis not a passion, false and blind,
Inspired, enchains, absorbs my mind;
Worthy, I feel, art thou to be
Loved with my perfect energy.

"This evening now shall sweetly flow,
Lit by our clear fire's happy glow;
And parting's peace-embittering fear
Is warned our hearts to come not near;
For fate admits my soul's decree,
In bliss or bale, to go with thee!"

Ellis contributes this touching "Death-Scene."

"'O Day! he cannot die,
When thou so fair art shining!
O Sun, in such a glorious sky,
So tranquilly declining.

"He cannot leave thee now,
While fresh west winds are blowing,
And all around his youthful brow
Thy cheerful light is glowing!

"Edward, awake, awake—
Thy golden evening gleams
Warm and bright on Arden's lake—
Arouse thee from thy dreams!

"Beside thee, on my knee,
My dearest friend! I pray
That thou to cross the eternal sea,
Wouldst yet one hour delay.

"I hear its billows roar—
I see them foaming high;
But no glimpse of a further shore
Has blest my straining eye.

"Believe not what they urge
Of Eden isles beyond;
Turn back, from that tempestuous surge,
To thy own native land.

"It is not death, but pain
That struggles in thy breast;
Nay, rally, Edward, rouse again—
I cannot let thee rest!'

"One long look, that sore reproved me
For the woe I could not bear—
One mute look of suffering moved me
To repent my useless prayer;

"And, with sudden check, the heaving
Of distraction passed away;
Not a sign of further grieving
Stirred my soul that awful day.

"Paled at length, the sweet sun setting;
Sunk to peace the twilight breeze;
Summer dews fell softly, wetting
Glen, and glade, and silent trees.

"Then his eyes began to weary,
Weighed beneath a mortal sleep;
And their orbs grew strangely dreary,
Clouded, even as they would weep.

"But they wept not—but they changed not—
Never moved, and never closed;
Troubled still, and still they ranged not—
Wandered not, nor yet reposed!

So I knew that he was dying—
Stooped, and raised his languid head;
Felt no breath, and heard no sighing—
So I knew that he was dead."

And now *loquitur* Acton Bell.

"Yes, thou art gone! and never more
Thy sunny smile shall gladden me;
But I may pass the old church door,
And pace the floor that covers thee;

"May stand upon the cold, damp stone,
And think that, frozen, lies below
The lightest heart that I have known,
The kindest I shall ever know.

"Yet, though I cannot see thee more,
'Tis still a comfort to *have* seen;
And though thy transient life is o'er,
'Tis sweet to think that thou hast been;

"To think a soul so near divine,
Within a form so angel fair,
United to a heart like thine,
Has gladdened once our humble sphere."

THE DUBLIN
UNIVERSITY MAGAZINE.

No. CLXVI.   OCTOBER, 1846.   Vol. XXVIII.

EVENINGS WITH OUR YOUNGER POETS—THE FIRST EVENING.

CURRER, ELLIS AND ACTON BELL—CAMILLA TOULMIN—R. H. HORNE.*

OH, ye young Poets! What are the feelings with which we regard ye? what is the temper with which we sit down to peruse ye, and undertake the needful task of pruning your pinions that they may fly the swifter, and by this criticism, which you so abominate, narrowing at times the rush of your fountain, that the jet may be loftier and the curve more graceful? Believe us, in no ungenial spirit. The immortalizing gift is rare; the power of ennobling man by showing him a hallowed and purified image of himself, till gazing he grows like the glorious thing he contemplates; the art to weave a spell in which the marvellous music of verse, and the deeper harmony of symphonious thought shall unite to charm mankind for ages with a magic old yet ever new,—these are endowments we are not so idle as to demand of all; well content if each generation of articulate-speaking men can club together from all the families of the earth, one half dozen of such miracles of mind. But long and gradual is the flower-besprent slope that leads to the awful summits of our English "double-peaked Parnassus;" where, each in sole and unapproached majesty, sit—the myriad-minded man of Avon, and He who, midway between man and angel, heard the infernal parley by the fiery lake, and caught the whispers of the heavenly host in paradise. Many are they who at various points of elevation (but we have no time now for taking their critical altitudes), and with each

his own point of prospect, gloomy, gentle, grave, or gay, people the sides of the mighty ascent. And where, upon the *lower* slopes, stretch out those vales of ever-blooming green, where the shade lies thick and the sun rests lovingly—where, in nature's own gardens, crowd her wild flowers (stray children of her summer loves), dog rose and broom, lily and meadow-sweet, harebell, and fox-glove, and sundew, and the rest of these *gipsies* of the floral realm—*there*, think you, we fail to find aught to please, or that, even though with eyes shaded from the day-beam we look *upward* in awful joy, those eyes are never by any chance to droop upon the pretty things about our feet? Poor justice ye do us, if you deem our taste so sublimely narrow, so magnificently exclusive. In truth, we are in heart too hospitably Irish for such unmerciful canons of criticism; we have never without severe violence to our charitable nature, turned altogether from our door any poor dog of a poet, barked he never so whiningly. We respect his ambition when it is not wholly preposterous; when he can furnish *any* sign or token of the genuine gift; for (we confess it) while we do not demand a Prometheus hot with the fiery theft from heaven, we will not put up with puffs of unmingled smoke. Give us but one twinkling spark of the real illumination—give us but one drop of the native still of Hippocrene, the genuine distillation of the heart, and we will en-

---

* "Poems by Currer, Ellis, and Acton Bell." Small 8vo. London. 1846.
"Poems; by Camilla Toulmin." Small 8vo. London. 1846.
"Orion; an Epic Poem," by R. H. Horne. Sixth Edition, small 8vo. 1843.

VOL. XXVIII.—No. 166.   2 D

First page of a review article that includes a positive notice of the Brontë sisters'
collaboration, Poems by Currer, Ellis, and Acton Bell
(University of Colorado Libraries)

There are pleasing thoughts, too, in Ellis's poem about the "Stars," p. 21; and his "Prisoner," p. 76; and Currer's "Gilbert" is impressively told. Altogether, we are disposed to approve of the efforts of "these three gentlemen aforesaid" (to adopt the old clergyman's substitution in the unpronounceable chapter of the fiery furnace); their verses are full of unobtrusive feeling; and their tone of thought seems unaffected and sincere.

—*The Dublin University Magazine,* 28 (October 1846): 392–393

* * *

Charlotte Brontë to the Editor of the *Dublin University Magazine,* 6 October 1846

Sir

I thank you in my own name and that of my brothers, Ellis and Acton, for the indulgent notice that appeared in your last number of our first, humble efforts in literature; but I thank you far more for the essay on Modern poetry which preceded that Notice—an essay in which seems to me to be condensed the very spirit of truth and beauty: if all or half your other readers shall have derived from its perusal the delight it afforded to myself and my brothers your labours have produced a rich result.

After such criticism an author may indeed be smitten at first by a sense of his own insignificance—as we were—but on a second and a third perusal he finds a power and beauty therein which stirs him to a desire to do more and better things—it fulfils the right end of criticism—without absolutely crushing—it corrects and rouses—I again thank you heartily and beg to subscribe myself

Your Constant and grateful reader
Currer Bell.
—*The Letters of Charlotte Brontë,* v. 1, p. 501

* * *

Branwell Brontë had sent some of his verse to the poet Thomas De Quincey in 1840. De Quincey was also among several prominent authors to whom Charlotte sent a copy of Poems. *In* De Quincey Memorials, *editor Alexander H. Japp writes, "It was told by Miss de Quincey in her father's Memoir that he received many letters from the Brontës while yet they were merely to the world Currer, Ellis, and Acton Bell, as well as afterwards with copies of their works. These letters, unfortunately, have been lost or given to autograph collectors, with the sole exception of the first."*

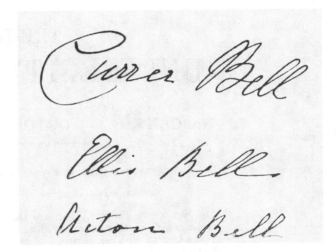

Pseudonymous autographs sent to Frederick Enoch, one of the two persons who purchased Poems *(from* The Bookman, *October 1904)*

Charlotte Brontë to Thomas De Quincey, 16 June 1847

Sir,—My relations, Ellis and Acton Bell, and myself, heedless of the repeated warnings of various respectable publishers, have committed the rash act of printing a volume of poems.

The consequences predicted have, of course, overtaken us; our book is found to be a drug; no man needs it or heeds it; in the space of a year our publisher has disposed but of two copies, and by what painful efforts he succeeded in getting rid of those two, himself only knows.

Before transferring the edition to the trunkmakers we have decided on distributing as presents a few copies of what we cannot sell: and we beg to offer you one in acknowledgment of the pleasure and profit we have often and long derived from your works.—I am, Sir, yours very respectfully,

Currer Bell
—*De Quincey Memorials,* v. 2, pp. 207–208

* * *

This excerpt is from John Skelton's unsigned review of Gaskell's Life of Charlotte Brontë.

"Simple, Genuine, and Characteristic" A Look Back at the Brontës' First Book

For the poems are perfectly genuine—veritable utterances of the women who wrote them. There is no poetic exaggeration, no false sentiment, nor study of theatrical effect. They do not wanton with the flowers of rhetoric. I do not believe that more than half a dozen metaphors occur throughout the volume. A Puritan could not be more conscientious in his intercourse with his crop-eared brethren, than these girls are in their poetic talk. The imagination is taken to task. The estimate of life is strictly subdued. They have worked out an experience for themselves, and with God's help they will stick to it. Their gravity of thought and chasteness of language contrast strikingly with the florid and exuberant ornamentation of our younger poets—the poets of the *Renaissance*.

And because of this entire genuineness they never imitate. There is no foreign music in their melody. One does not detect the influence of any other writer. Young poets are habitual plagiarists: but with this volume neither Byron, nor Scott, nor Tennyson, nor Browning has anything to do. The writers speak out plainly and calmly what they have felt themselves, and their thoughts assume without effort the poetic form to which they are most adapted.

They speak calmly, I say, yet we feel sometimes that this composure is enforced. There are deeps of passion underneath the passionless face. The estimate of life is studiously grave and sombre: but at times an intoxicating sense of liberty thrills their blood, and the wild gladness of a Bacchante sparkles in their eyes:—

I'd die when all the foam is up,
 The bright wine sparkling high,
Nor wait till in the exhausted cup
 Life's dull dregs only lie.

There is the martyr's spirit, but there is the hero's too. They *will* not love nor hate over-much: but the throbbing of the wounded heart cannot be always restrained, and at times they are intensely bitter:—

They named him mad and laid his bones
 Where holier ashes lie,
But doubt not that his spirit groans
 In hell's eternity.

Three Novels by the Bells

The Brontë sisters realized that publishing poetry would not provide them with the income they needed to be self-sufficient. Even before Poems *was published, the sisters decided to try publishing novels. This 11 April 1846 letter Charlotte wrote to the publisher Aylott and Jones initiated a hunt for a publisher for the sisters' novels that took more than a year.*

Gentlemen

I beg to thank you in the name of C. E. & A Bell for your obliging offer of advice; I will avail myself of it to request information on two or three points.

It is evident that unknown authors have great difficulties to contend with before they can succeed in bringing their works before the public, can you give me any hint as to the way in which these difficulties are best met. For instance, in the present case, where a work of fiction is in question, in what form would a publisher be most likely to accept the M.S.—? whether offered as a work of 3 vols or as tales which might be published in numbers or as contributions to a periodical?

What publishers would be most likely to receive favourably a proposal of this nature?

Would it suffice to <u>write</u> to a publisher on the subject or would it be necessary to have recourse to a personal interview?

Your opinion and advice on these three points or on any other which your experience may suggest as important—would be esteemed by us a favour

I am Gentlemen
Yrs truly
C Brontë

—*The Letters of Charlotte Brontë*, v. 1, p. 462

In this 4 July 1846 letter, Charlotte Brontë writes to publisher Henry Colburn about the three novel manuscripts by the "Bells": The Professor *by Currer Bell,* Wuthering Heights *by Ellis Bell, and* Agnes Grey *by Acton Bell.*

Sir

I request permission to send for your inspection the M.S of a work of fiction in 3 vols. It consists of three tales, each occupying a volume and capable of being published together or separately, as thought most advisable. The authors of these tales have already appeared before the public.

Should you consent to examine the work, would you, in your reply, state at what period after transmission of the M.S. to you, the authors may expect to receive your decision upon its merits—

I am Sir
Yours respectfully
C Bell

Colburn was one of several publishers to reject the manuscript. It was not until summer 1847 that Thomas Newby accepted Wuthering Heights *and* Agnes Grey *for publication. Newby rejected* The Professor, *as did the publisher Smith, Elder; however, Smith, Elder accepted Charlotte's* Jane Eyre, *which became the first novel by the sisters to actually be published, on 19 October 1847.* Wuthering Heights *and* Agnes Grey *were published in December 1847. The appearance of three novels by the mysterious Bells so closely together piqued the interest of critics and the reading public.*

—*The Letters of Charlotte Brontë*, v. 1,
pp. 481

There are indications in Currer's contributions of that amazing intellectual force which a year afterwards was to move painfully every English heart: but as yet she has not learnt her strength. Her steps are restrained and embarrassed. She does not move freely. She touches life with the tips of her fingers, so to speak: her whole heart and soul have not yet been cast into her work.

Yet most of the subjects are strangely chosen for girls, and such as a very marked and decided idioscyncrasy alone would have selected. In Acton's, indeed, there is more of the ordinary woman, mild, patient, devout, loving; and her poetry has little to distinguish it from the poetry of many women who acquire 'the faculty of verse.' But those of the other two are very different. In them there is none of the ordinary romance of girlhood. Their heroes are not the heroes of the ball-room, but of the covenant and the stake,—the warrior priest who can die for his faith; the patriot who, if it be for his country's gain, will steadfastly allow his honour to be soiled, and

> wait securely
> For the atoning hour to come;

the worker who in his loneliness achieves the redemption of his people; the martyr with the thorny crown upon his brow, but with the peace of God and the hope of immortality in his heart. Success, the usual gauge applied by youth, is not with them the test of worth.

> The long war closing in defeat;
> Defeat serenely borne,

is in their eyes the noblest fate that can be reserved for any man. So they do not pray for happiness, but for inward control, and the patience which endures to the end.

> Of God alone, and self-reliance,
> I ask for solace,—hope for aid.

Praise, fame, friendship, the good word of the world, they do not covet; they can live without them; nay, resign them cheerfully if need be.

> There's such a thing as dwelling
> On the thought ourselves have nursed,
> And with scorn and courage telling,
> The world to do its worst.

And these are the feelings expressed, not by strong men, but by two delicate women in their girlhood! The stern spirit of their northern hills and of the bleak Yorkshire moorland haunted their birthplace, and must have entered early into their souls.

Yet the book does not altogether lack the gentler graces of poetry. In the concise realism of Currer there is little indeed of that abstract and ethereal spirit men call the imagination; but it inspires the wild and plaintive music of many of Ellis's songs. Some of these are so perfect that we cannot understand why they are not widely known; certainly modern poetry has produced few lyrics more felicitous either in sentiment or expression than 'Remembrance.' How quaint and composed, and yet how plaintive, it is! The bereaved speaks calmly, but there is a passion of tears below:—

REMEMBRANCE.

Cold in the earth—and the deep snow piled above thee,
    Far, far removed, cold in the dreary grave!
Have I forgot, my only love, to love thee,
    Severed at last by Time's all-severing wave?

Now, when alone do my thoughts no longer hover
    Over the mountains, on that northern shore,
Resting their wings where heath and fern-leaves cover
    Thy noble heart for ever, ever more?

Cold in the earth—and fifteen wild Decembers,
    From those brown hills, have melted into spring:
Faithful, indeed, is the spirit that remembers
    After such years of change and suffering!

Sweet love of youth, forgive, if I forget thee,
    While the world's tide is bearing me along;
Other desires and other hopes beset me,
    Hopes which obscure, but cannot do thee wrong!

No later light has lightened up my heaven,
    No second morn has ever shone for me;
All my life's bliss from thy dear life was given,
    All my life's bliss is in the grave with thee.

But when the days of golden dreams had perished,
    And even despair was powerless to destroy,
Then did I learn how existence could be cherished,
    Strengthened, and fed without the aid of joy.

Then did I check the tears of useless passion—
    Weaned my young soul from yearning after thine;
Sternly denied its burning wish to hasten
    Down to that tomb already more than mine.

And, even yet, I dare not let it languish,
    Dare not indulge in memory's rapturous pain;
Once drinking deep of that divinest anguish,
    How could I seek the empty world again?

. . . .

Here is a song which reminds us of one sung in the *Princess;* but this was written before *her* time:–

SYMPATHY.

There should be no despair for you
  While nightly stars are burning:
While evening pours its silent dew,
  And sunshine gilds the morning.
There should be no despair–though tears
  May flow down like a river:
Are not the best beloved of years
  Around your heart for ever?

They weep, you weep, it must be so:
  Winds sigh as you are sighing,
And Winter sheds his grief in snow
  Where Autumn's leaves are lying:
Yet these revive, and from their fate
  Your fate cannot be parted:
Then journey on, if not elate,
  Still, *never* broken-hearted!

Though I do not think Currer's contributions quite equal to Ellis's, yet in some of them much sympathy for natural beauty is manifested. The wealth of affection which was so jealously watched in her intercourse with men and women, was permitted in the lonely presence of the hills to lavish itself unchecked. Here are Dawn, Twilight, and Night:–

And oh! how slow that keen-eyed star
  Has tracked the chilly grey!
What watching yet! how very far
  The morning lies away!

That sunset! Look beneath the boughs
  Over the copse,–beyond the hills;
How soft yet deep and warm it glows,
  And heaven with rich suffusion fills
With hues where still the opal's tint
Its gleam of prisoned fire is blent;
  Where flame through azure thrills!

Pause in the lane, returning home;
  'Tis dusk it will be still:
Pause near the elm, a sacred gloom
  Its breezeless boughs will fill.
Look at that soft and golden light
  High in the unclouded sky;
Watch the last bird's belated flight
  As it flits silent by.
Nor would she leave that hill till night
Trembled from pole to pole with light.

I have spoken at length of this first volume, because we find in it, I think, the germ of much in their later and more mature works. It is little known; but the poems are so simple, genuine, and characteristic, that they must some time become popular.

–*Fraser's Magazine,* 55, no. 329 (May 1857): 569–582

The Bells Make Themselves Known

After the publication of Currer, Ellis, and Acton Bell's novels in late 1847, the following year seemed to promise great things for the three authors. Anne was the first to place a second novel, The Tenant of Wildfell Hall, *published in June 1848 by Thomas Newby.*

In this excerpt from his reminiscence, Currer Bell's publisher recounts the circumstances that led Charlotte and Anne Brontë to travel to London in July 1848 to make themselves known to their publishers.

"A Serious Expedition"
George Smith

The works of Ellis and Acton Bell had been published by a Mr. Newby, on terms which rather depleted the scanty purses of the authors. When we were about to publish 'Shirley'–the work which, in the summer of 1848, succeeded 'Jane Eyre'–we endeavoured to make an arrangement with an American publisher to sell him advance sheets of the book, in order to give him an advantage in regard to time over other American publishers. There was, of course, no copyright with America in those days. We were met during the negotiations with our American correspondents by the statement that Mr. Newby had informed them that he was about to publish the next book by the author of 'Jane Eyre,' under her other *nom de plume* of Acton Bell–Currer, Ellis, and Acton Bell being in fact, according to him, one person. We wrote to 'Currer Bell' to say that we should be glad to be in a position to contradict the statement, adding at the same time we were quite sure Mr. Newby's assertion was untrue. Charlotte Brontë has related how the letter affected her. She was persuaded that her honour was impugned. 'With rapid decision,' says Mrs. Gaskell in her 'Life of Charlotte Brontë,' 'Charlotte and her sister Anne resolved that they should start for London that very day in order to prove their separate identity to Messrs. Smith, Elder, & Co.'

With what haste and energy the sisters plunged into what was, for them, a serious expedition, how they reached London at eight o'clock on a Saturday morning, took lodgings in the 'Chapter' coffee-house in Paternoster Row, and, after an agitated breakfast, set out on a pilgrimage to my office in Cornhill, is told at length in Mrs. Gaskell's 'Life of Charlotte Brontë.'

–*The Cornhill Magazine,* new series 9 (December 1900): 778–795

* * *

THE CHAPTER COFFEE HOUSE

Chapter Coffee House, 50 Paternoster Row, London, where Emily and Charlotte stayed in 1842 and Charlotte and Anne stayed in 1848 (from Life and Works of the Sisters Brontë, *University of Colorado Libraries)*

Charlotte described their London expedition in this letter to her friend Mary Taylor.

Charlotte Brontë to Mary Taylor, 4 September 1848

Dear Polly

I write to you a great many more letters than you write to me—though whether they all reach you or not, Heaven knows. I daresay you will not be without a certain desire to know how our affairs get on—I will give you therefore a notion—as briefly as may be.

"Acton Bell" has published another book—it is in 3. vols. but I do not like it quite as well as "Agnes Grey" the subject not being such as the author had pleasure in handling—it has been praised by some reviews and blamed by others—as yet only £25 have been realized for the copyright—and as "Acton Bell's" publisher is a shuffling scamp—I expect no more.

About 2 months since, I had a letter from my publishers, Smith & Elder—saying that "Jane Eyre" had had a great run in America—and that a publisher there had consequently bid high for the first sheets of the next work by "Currer Bell", which they had promised to let him have.

Presently after came a second missive from Smith & Elder—all in alarm, suspicion and wrath—their American correspondent had written to them complaining that the first sheets of a new work by "Currer Bell" had been already received and not by their house but by a rival publisher—and asking the meaning of such false play—it inclosed an extract from a letter from Mr. Newby (A & E. Bell's publisher) affirming that "to the best of his belief" "Jane Eyre" "Wuthering Heights"–Agnes Grey"—and the "Tenant of Wildfell Hall" (the new work) were all the production of one writer"

This was a lie, as Newby had been told repeatedly that they were the productions of 3 different authors—but the fact was he wanted to make a dishonest move in the game—to make the Public & "the Trade" believe that he had got hold of "Currer Bell" & thus cheat Smith & Elder—by securing the American publishers' bid.

The upshot of it was that on the very day I received Smith & Elder's letter—Anne & I packed up a small box, sent it down to Keighley—set out ourselves after tea—walked through a thunderstorm to the station, got to Leeds and whirled up by the Night train to London—with the view of proving our separate identity to Smith & Elder and confronting Newby with his lie—

We arrived at the Chapter Coffee House—(our old place Polly—we did not well know where else to go) about eight o'clock in the morning—We washed ourselves—had some breakfast—sat a few minutes and then set of[f] in queer, inward excitement, to 65. Cornhill. Neither Mr. Smith nor Mr. Williams knew we were coming they had never seen us—they did not know whether we were men or women—but had always written to us as men.

We found 65—to be a large bookseller's shop in a street almost as bustling as the Strand—we went in—walked up to the counter—there were a great many young men and lads here and there—I said to the first I could accost "May I see Mr. Smith—?" he hesitated, looked a little surprised—but went to fetch him—We sat down and waited awhile—looking a[t] some books on the counter—publications of theirs well known to us—of many of which they had sent us copies as presents. At last somebody came up and said dubiously

"Two Rather Quaintly Dressed Little Ladies"

George Smith's recollection of his meeting with the Bells differs in some details from Charlotte's.

That particular Saturday morning I was at work in my room, when a clerk reported that two ladies wished to see me. I was very busy and sent out to ask their names. The clerk returned to say that the ladies declined to give their names, but wished to see me on a private matter. After a moment's hesitation I told him to show them in. I was in the midst of my correspondence, and my thoughts were far away from 'Currer Bell' and 'Jane Eyre.' Two rather quaintly dressed little ladies, pale-faced and anxious-looking, walked into my room; one of them came forward and presented me with a letter addressed, in my own handwriting, to 'Currer Bell, Esq.' I noticed that the letter had been opened, and said, with some sharpness, 'Where did you get this from?' 'From the post-office,' was the reply; 'it was addressed to me. We have both come that you might have ocular proof that there are at least two of us.' This then was 'Currer Bell' in person. I need hardly say that I was at once keenly interested, not to say excited. Mr. Williams was called down and introduced, and I began to plan all sorts of attentions to our visitors. . . .

This is the only occasion on which I saw Anne Brontë. She was a gentle, quiet, rather subdued person, by no means pretty, yet of a pleasing appearance. Her manner was curiously expressive of a wish for protection and encouragement, a kind of constant appeal which invited sympathy.

I must confess that my first impression of Charlotte Brontë's personal appearance was that it was interesting rather than attractive. She was very small, and had a quaint old-fashioned look. Her head seemed too large for her body. She had fine eyes, but her face was marred by the shape of the mouth and by the complexion. There was but little feminine charm about her; and of this fact she herself was uneasily and perpetually conscious. It may seem strange that the possession of genius did not lift her above the weakness of an excessive anxiety about her personal appearance. But I believe that she would have given all her genius and her fame to have been beautiful. Perhaps few women ever existed more anxious to be pretty than she, or more angrily conscious of the circumstance that she was *not* pretty.

– *The Cornhill Magazine,* new series 9
(December 1900): 778–795

"Did you wish to see me, Ma'am?"

"Is it Mr. Smith?" I said looking up through my spectacles at a young, tall, gentlemanly man

"It is."

I then put his own letter into his hand directed to "Currer Bell." He looked at it—then at me—again—yet again—I laughed at his queer perplexity—A recognition took place—. I gave my real name—"Miss Brontë—" We were both hurried from the shop into a little back room—ceiled with a great skylight and only large enough to hold 3 chairs and a desk—and there explanations were rapidly gone into—Mr. Newby being anathematized, I fear with undue vehemence. Smith hurried out and returned quickly with one whom he introduced as Mr. Williams—a pale, mild, stooping man of fifty—very much like a faded Tom Dixon—Another recognition—a long, nervous shaking of hands—Then followed talk—talk—talk—Mr. Williams being silent—Mr. Smith loquacious—

"Allow me to introduce you to my mother & sisters—How long do you stay in Town.? You must make the most of the time—to-night you must go to the Italian opera—you must see the Exhibition—Mr. Thackeray would be pleased to see you—If Mr. Lewes knew "Currer Bell" was in town he would have to be shut up—I

will ask them both to dinner at my house &c." I stopped his projects and discourse by a grave explanation—that though I should very much like to see both Mr. Lewes and still more Mr. Thackeray—we were as resolved as ever to preserve our incognito—We had only confessed ourselves to our publisher—in order to do away with the inconveniences that had arisen from our too well preserved mystery—to all the rest of the world we must be "gentlemen" as heretofore.

Williams understood me directly—Smith comprehended by slower degrees—he did not like the quiet plan—he would have liked some excitement, eclat &c.

He then urged us to meet a literary party incognito—he would introduce us a[s] "country cousins" The desire to see some of the personages whose names he mentioned—kindled in me very strongly—but when I found on further examination that he could not venture to ask such men as Thackeray &c. at a short notice, without giving them a hint as to whom they were to meet, I declined even this—I felt it would have ended in our being made a show of—a thing I have ever resolved to avoid.

Then he said we must come and stay at his house—but we were not prepared for a long stay & declined this also—as we took leave—he told us he should bring his sisters to call on us that evening—We returned to our Inn—and I paid for the excitement of the interview by a thundering head-ache & harrassing sickness—towards evening as I got not better & expected the Smiths to call—I took a strong dose of sal volatile—it roused me a little—still I was in grievous bodily case when they were announced—They came in two elegant, young ladies in full dress—prepared for the Opera—Smith himself in evening costume white gloves &c. a distinguished, handsome fellow enough—We had by no means understood that it was settled that we were to go to the Opera—and were not ready—Moreover we had no fine, elegant dresses either with us or in the world. however on brief rumination, I though[t] it would be wise to make no objections—I put my headache in my pocket we attired ourselves in the plain—high-made, country garments we possessed—and went with them to their carriage—where we found Williams likewise in full dress. They must have thought us queer, quizzical looking beings—especially me with my spectacles—I smiled inwardly at the contrast which must have been apparent between me and Mr. Smith as I walked with him up the crimson carpeted staircase of the Opera House and stood amongst a brilliant throng at the box-door which was not yet open. Fine ladies & gentlemen glanced at us with a slight, graceful superciliousness quite warranted by the circumstances—Still I felt pleasurably excited—in spite of headache sickness & conscious clownishness; and I saw Anne was calm and gentle which she always is—

The Performance was Ros[s]ini's opera of the "Barber of Seville—" very brilliant though I fancy there are things I should like better—We got home after one o'clock—We had never been in bed the night before—had been in constant excitement for 24 hours—you may imagine we were tired.

The next day—(Sunday) Mr. Williams came early to take us to church—he was so quiet but so sincere in his attentions—one could not but have a most friendly leaning towards him—he has a nervous hesitation in speech and a difficulty in finding appropriate language in which to express himself—which throws him into the background in conversation—but I had been his correspondent—and therefore knew with what intelligence he could write—so that I was not in danger of underrating him.

In the afternoon—Mr. Smith came in his carriage with his Mother—to take us to his house to dine—I should mention by the way that neither his Mother nor his Sisters knew who we were—and their strange perplexity would have been ludicrous if one had dared to laugh—To be brought down to a part of the city into whose obscure, narrow streets they said they had never penetrated before—to an old, dark strange-looking Inn—

to take up in their fine carriage a couple of odd-looking country-women—to see their elegant, handsome son & brother treating with scrupulous politeness these insignificant spinsters—must have puzzled them thoroughly Mr. Smith's residence is at Bayswater, 6 miles from Cornhill—a very fine place—the rooms—the drawing-room especially looked splendid to us—There was no company—only his mother his two grown up sisters—and his brother a lad of 12–13 and a little sister—the youngest of the family—very like himself—they are all dark-eyed—dark-haired and have clear & pale faces—the Mother is a portly, handsome woman of her age—and all her children more or less well-looking—one of the daughters decidedly pretty—except that the expression of her countenance—is not equal to the beauty of her features.—We had a fine dinner—which neither Anne nor I had appetite to eat—and were glad when it was over—I always feel under awkward constraint at table. Dining-out would be a hideous bore to me.

Mr. Smith made himself very pleasant,—he is a firm, intelligent man of business though so young—bent on getting on—and I think desirous to make his way by fair, honourable means—he is enterprising—but likewise cool & cautious. Mr. Smith is <u>practical</u> man—I wish Mr. Williams were more so—but he is altogether of the contemplative, theorizing order—Mr. Williams lives too much in abstractions—

On Monday we went to the Exhibition of the Royal Academy—the National Gallery, dined again at Mr. Smith's—then went home with Mr. Williams to tea—and saw his comparatively humble but neat residence and his fine family of eight children—his wife was ill. A daughter of Leigh Hunts' was there—she sung some little Italian airs which she had picked up amongst the peasantry in Tuscany, in a manner that charmed me—For herself she was a rattling good-natured personage enough—

On Tuesday Morning we left London—laden with books Mr. Smith had given us—and got safely home. A more jaded wretch than I looked when I returned, it would be difficult to conceive—I was thin when I went but was meagre indeed when I returned, my face looked grey & very old—with strange, deep lines plough[ed] in it—my eyes stared unnaturally—I was weak and yet restless. In a while however these bad effects of excitement went off and I regained my normal condition—

We saw Newby—but of him more another [time]

Good by—God bless you—
write CB

—*The Letters of Charlotte Brontë,* v. 2, pp. 111–115

Early Deaths and Lasting Fame

By September 1848 it became apparent that Branwell, who had been drinking heavily for several years, was very ill. His death at age thirty-one on 24 September 1848 of "chronic bronchitis and marasmus (wasting)" occurred as Smith, Elder was preparing to reprint Poems by Currer, Ellis, and Acton Bell. *Following Branwell's death, Emily became increasingly ill with pulmonary tuberculosis. She refused to see a doctor until the day of her death at age thirty of "Consumption—2 months duration" on 19 December 1848. By January 1849 Anne had developed pulmonary tuberculosis; she underwent various treatments but died at the coastal town of Scarborough on 28 May 1849, age twenty-nine. In little more than eight months, Charlotte was left as the only surviving sibling.*

In 1850 Charlotte brought out a new edition of her sisters' first novels, including with them a selection of their poetry, and provided the first public account of the sisters' career. In discussing the reception of Wuthering Heights, *she praises a particular critic of "keen vision and fine sympathies"—using a footnote to direct her reader to the review in the September 1850 issue of the* Palladium, *which is printed in the chapter on Emily Brontë in this volume.*

Biographical Notice of Ellis and Acton Bell
Currer Bell

It has been thought that all the works published under the names of Currer, Ellis, and Acton Bell, were, in reality, the production of one person. This mistake I endeavoured to rectify by a few words of disclaimer prefixed to the third edition of *Jane Eyre*. These, too, it appears, failed to gain general credence, and now, on the occasion of a reprint of *Wuthering Heights* and *Agnes Grey,* I am advised distinctly to state how the case really stands.

Indeed, I feel myself that it is time the obscurity attending those two names—Ellis and Acton—was done away. The little mystery, which formerly yielded some harmless pleasure, has lost its interest; circumstances are changed. It becomes, then, my duty to explain briefly the origin and authorship of the books written by Currer, Ellis, and Acton Bell.

About five years ago, my two sisters and myself, after a somewhat prolonged period of separation, found ourselves reunited, and at home. Resident in a remote district where education had made little progress, and where, consequently, there was no inducement to seek social intercourse beyond our own domestic circle, we were wholly dependent on ourselves and each other, on books and study, for the enjoyments and occupations of life. The highest stimulus, as well as the liveliest pleasure we had known from childhood upwards, lay in

attempts at literary composition; formerly we used to show each other what we wrote, but of late years this habit of communication and consultation had been discontinued; hence it ensued, that we were mutually ignorant of the progress we might respectively have made.

One day, in the autumn of 1845, 1 accidentally lighted on a MS. volume of verse in my sister Emily's handwriting. Of course, I was not surprised, knowing that she could and did write verse: I looked it over, and something more than surprise seized me,—a deep conviction that these were not common effusions, nor at all like the poetry women generally write. I thought them condensed and terse, vigorous and genuine. To my ear, they had also a peculiar music—wild, melancholy, and elevating.

My sister Emily was not a person of demonstrative character, nor one, on the recesses of whose mind and feelings, even those nearest and dearest to her could, with impunity, intrude unlicensed; it took hours to reconcile her to the discovery I had made, and days to persuade her that such poems merited publication. I knew, however, that a mind like hers could not be without some latent spark of honourable ambition, and

The Reverend Patrick Brontë (from The Bookman, *October 1904)*

refused to be discouraged in my attempts to fan that spark to flame.

Meantime, my younger sister quietly produced some of her own compositions, intimating that since Emily's had given me pleasure, I might like to look at hers. I could not but be a partial judge, yet I thought that these verses too had a sweet sincere pathos of their own.

We had very early cherished the dream of one day becoming authors. This dream, never relinquished even when distance divided and absorbing tasks occupied us, now suddenly acquired strength and consistency: it took the character of a resolve. We agreed to arrange a small selection of our poems, and, if possible, get them printed. Averse to personal publicity, we veiled our own names under those of Currer, Ellis, and Acton Bell; the ambiguous choice being dictated by a sort of conscientious scruple at assuming Christian names positively masculine, while we did not like to declare ourselves women, because—without at that time suspecting that our mode of writing and thinking was not what is called 'feminine'—we had a vague impression that authoresses are liable to be looked on with prejudice; we had noticed how critics sometimes use for their chastisement the weapon of personality, and for them reward, a flattery, which is not true praise.

The bringing out of our little book was hard work. As was to be expected, neither we nor our poems were at all wanted; but for this we had been prepared at the outset; though inexperienced ourselves, we had read the experience of others. The great puzzle lay in the difficulty of getting answers of any kind from the publishers to whom we applied. Being greatly harassed by this obstacle, I ventured to apply to the Messrs Chambers, of Edinburgh, for a word of advice; *they* may have forgotten the circumstance, but *I* have not, for from them I received a brief and business-like, but civil and sensible reply, on which we acted, and at last made a way.

The book was printed: it is scarcely known, and all of it that merits to be known are the poems of Ellis Bell. The fixed conviction I held, and hold, of the worth of these poems has not indeed received the confirmation of much favourable criticism; but I must retain it notwithstanding.

Ill-success failed to crush us: the mere effort to succeed had given a wonderful zest to existence; it must be pursued. We each set to work on a prose tale: Ellis Bell produced *Wuthering Heights*, Acton Bell, *Agnes Grey*, and Currer Bell also wrote a narrative in one volume. These MSS. were perseveringly obtruded upon various publishers for the space of a year and a half; usually, their fate was an ignominious and abrupt dismissal.

At last *Wuthering Heights* and *Agnes Grey* were accepted on terms somewhat impoverishing to the two authors; Currer Bell's book found acceptance nowhere, nor any acknowledgment of merit, so that something like the chill of despair began to invade his heart. As a forlorn hope, he tried one publishing house more—Messrs Smith and Elder. Ere long, in a much shorter space than that on which experience had taught him to calculate—there came a letter, which he opened in the dreary expectation of finding two hard hopeless lines, intimating that Messrs Smith and Elder 'were not disposed to publish the MS.,' and, instead, he took out of the envelope a letter of two pages. He read it trembling. It declined, indeed, to publish that tale, for business reasons, but it discussed its merits and demerits so courteously, so considerately, in a spirit so rational, with a discrimination so enlightened, that this very refusal cheered the author better than a vulgarly-expressed acceptance would have done. It was added, that a work in three volumes would meet with careful attention.

I was then just completing *Jane Eyre,* at which I had been working while the one volume tale was plodding its weary round in London: in three weeks I sent it off; friendly and skilful hands took it in. This was in the commencement of September 1847; it came out before the close of October following, while *Wuthering Heights* and *Agnes Grey,* my sisters' works, which had already been in the press for months, still lingered under a different management.

They appeared at last. Critics failed to do them justice. The immature but very real powers revealed in *Wuthering Heights* were scarcely recognized; its import and nature were misunderstood; the identity of its author was misrepresented; it was said that this was an earlier and ruder attempt of the same pen which had produced *Jane Eyre*. Unjust and grievous error! We laughed at it at first, but I deeply lament it now. Hence, I fear, arose a prejudice against the book. That writer who could attempt to palm off an inferior and immature production under cover of one successful effort, must indeed be unduly eager after the secondary and sordid result of authorship, and pitiably indifferent to its true and honourable meed. If reviewers and the public truly believed this, no wonder that they looked darkly on the cheat.

Yet I must not be understood to make these things subject for reproach or complaint; I dare not do so; respect for my sister's memory forbids me. By her any such querulous manifestation would have been regarded as an unworthy, and offensive weakness.

It is my duty, as well as my pleasure, to acknowledge one exception to the general rule of criticism. One writer, endowed with the keen vision and fine sympathies of genius, has discerned the real nature of *Wuther-*

ing Heights, and has, with equal accuracy, noted its beauties and touched on its faults. Too often do reviewers remind us of the mob of Astrologers, Chaldeans, and Soothsayers gathered before the 'writing on the wall,' and unable to read the characters or make known the interpretation. We have a right to rejoice when a true seer comes at last, some man in whom is an excellent spirit, to whom have been given light, wisdom, and understanding; who can accurately read the 'Mene, Mene, Tekel, Upharsin' of an original mind (however unripe, however inefficiently cultured and partially expanded that mind may be); and who can say with confidence, 'This is the interpretation thereof.'

Yet even the writer to whom I allude shares the mistake about the authorship, and does me the injustice to suppose that there was equivoque in my former rejection of this honour (as an honour, I regard it). May I assure him that I would scorn in this and in every case to deal in equivoque; I believe language to have been given us to make our meaning clear, and not to wrap it in dishonest doubt.

The Tenant of Wildfell Hall by Acton Bell, had likewise an unfavourable reception. At this I cannot wonder. The choice of subject was an entire mistake. Nothing less congruous with the writer's nature could be conceived. The motives which dictated this choice were pure, but, I think, slightly morbid. She had, in the course of her life, been called on to contemplate, near at hand and for a long time, the terrible effects of talents misused and faculties abused; hers was naturally a sensitive, reserved, and dejected nature; what she saw sank very deeply into her mind; it did her harm. She brooded over it till she believed it to be a duty to reproduce every detail (of course with fictitious characters, incidents, and situations) as a warning to others. She hated her work, but would pursue it. When reasoned with on the subject, she regarded such reasonings as a temptation to self-indulgence. She must be honest; she must not varnish, soften, or conceal. This well-meant resolution brought on her misconstruction and some abuse; which she bore, as it was her custom to bear whatever was unpleasant, with mild, steady patience. She was a very sincere and practical Christian, but the tinge of religious melancholy communicated a sad shade to her brief, blameless life.

Neither Ellis nor Acton allowed herself for one moment to sink under want of encouragement; energy nerved the one, and endurance held the other. They were both prepared to try again; I would fain think that hope and the sense of power was yet strong within them. But a great change approached: affliction came in that shape which to anticipate is dread; to look back on, grief. In the very heat and burden of the day, the labourers failed over their work.

My sister Emily first declined. The details of her illness are deep-branded in my memory, but to dwell on them, either in thought or narrative, is not in my power. Never in all her life had she lingered over any task that lay before her, and she did not linger now. She sank rapidly. She made haste to leave us. Yet, while physically she perished, mentally, she grew stronger than we had yet known her. Day by day, when I saw with what a front she met suffering, I looked on her with an anguish of wonder and love. I have seen nothing like it; but, indeed, I have never seen her parallel in anything. Stronger than a man, simpler than a child, her nature stood alone. The awful point was, that, while full of ruth for others, on herself she had no pity; the spirit was inexorable to the flesh; from the trembling hand, the unnerved limbs, the faded eyes, the same service was exacted as they had rendered in health. To stand by and witness this, and not dare to remonstrate, was a pain no words can render.

Two cruel months of hope and fear passed painfully by, and the day came at last when the terrors and pains of death were to be undergone by this treasure, which had grown dearer and dearer to our hearts as it wasted before our eyes. Towards the decline of that day, we had nothing left of Emily but her mortal remains as consumption left them. She died December 19, 1848.

We thought this enough: but we were utterly and presumptuously wrong. She was not buried ere Anne fell ill. She had not been committed to the grave a fortnight, before we received distinct intimation that it was necessary to prepare our minds to see the younger sister go after the elder. Accordingly, she followed in the same path with slower steps, and with a patience that equalled the other's fortitude. I have said that she was religious, and it was by leaning on those Christian doctrines in which she firmly believed, that she found support through her most painful journey. I witnessed their efficacy in her latest hour and greatest trial, and must bear my testimony to the calm triumph with which they brought her through. She died May 28, 1849.

What more shall I say about them? I cannot and need not say much more. In externals, they were two unobtrusive women; a perfectly secluded life gave them retiring manners and habits. In Emily's nature the extremes of vigour and simplicity seemed to meet. Under an unsophisticated culture, inartificial tastes, and an unpretending outside, lay a secret power and fire that might have informed the brain and kindled the veins of a hero; but she had no worldly wisdom; her powers were unadapted to the practical business of life; she would fail to defend her most manifest rights, to consult her most legitimate advantage. An interpreter ought always to have stood between her and the world. Her will was not very flexible, and it generally opposed her interest. Her temper was magnanimous, but warm and sudden; her spirit altogether unbending.

Anne's character was milder and more subdued; she wanted the power, the fire, the originality of her sister, but was well-endowed with quiet virtues of her own. Long-suffering, self-denying, reflective, and intelligent, a constitutional reserve and taciturnity placed and kept her in the shade, and covered her mind, and especially her feeling, with a sort of nun-like veil, which was rarely lifted. Neither Emily nor Anne was learned; they had no thought of filling their pitchers at the well-spring of other minds; they always wrote from the impulse of nature, the dictates of intuition, and from such stores of observation as their limited experience had enabled them to amass. I may sum up all by saying, that for strangers they were nothing, for superficial observers less than nothing; but for those who had known them all their lives in the intimacy of close relationship, they were genuinely good and truly great.

This notice has been written, because I felt it a sacred duty to wipe the dust off their gravestones, and leave their dear names free from soil.

                                                CURRER BELL

September 19, 1850

* * *

The brief glimpses Charlotte provided in 1850 of life at the parsonage in Haworth and the personalities of the women who had written these novels simply increased the public's desire to know more. Her account set the tone and assumptions later critics adopted when analyzing the works of her sisters.

This excerpt is from an unsigned review that may have been written by music and literature critic H. F. Chorley.

"English Female Genius"
Review of *Wuthering Heights* and *Agnes Grey*

Female genius and female authorship may be said to present some peculiarities of aspect and circumstance in England, which we find associated with them in no other country. Among the most daring and original manifestations of invention by Englishwomen,—some of the most daring and original have owed their parentage, not to defying *Britomarts* at war with society, who choose to make their literature match with their lives,—not to brilliant women figuring in the world, in whom every gift and faculty has been enriched, and whetted sharp, and encouraged into creative utterance, by perpetual communication with the most distinguished men of the time,—but to writers living retired lives in retired places, stimu-

lated to activity by no outward influence, driven to confession by no history that demands apologetic parable or subtle plea. This, as a characteristic of English female genius, we have long noticed:—but it has rarely been more simply, more strongly, some will add more strangely, illustrated than in the volume before us.

The lifting of that veil which for a while concealed the authorship of 'Jane Eyre' and its sister-novels, excites in us no surprise. It seemed evident from the first prose pages bearing the signatures of Currer, Ellis, and Acton Bell, that these were *Rosalinds*—or a *Rosalind*—in masquerade:—some doubt as to the plurality of persons being engendered by a certain uniformity of local colour and resemblance in choice of subject, which might have arisen either from identity, or from joint peculiarities of situation and of circumstance.

                        —*The Athenæum* (28 December 1850): 1368

* * *

This excerpt is from an unsigned review by George Henry Lewes.

"Haunted by the Same Experience"
Review of *Wuthering Heights* and *Agnes Grey*

There are various points of interest in this republication, some arising from the intrinsic excellence of the works themselves, others from the lustre reflected on them by *Jane Eyre*. The biographical notice of her two sisters is plainly and touchingly written by Currer Bell. With their early struggles in authorship thousands will sympathize. . . .

Critics, we are told, failed to do them justice. But to judge from the extracts given of articles in the *Britannia* and *Atlas,* the critics were excessively indulgent, and we take it the great public was the most recalcitrant, and would *not* be amused with these strange wild pictures of incult humanity, painted as if by lurid torchlight, though painted with unmistakeable power—the very power only heightening their repulsiveness. The visions of madmen are not more savage, or more remote from ordinary life. The error committed is an error in art—the excessive predominance of shadows darkening the picture. One cannot dine off condiments, nor sup off horrors without an indigestion.

And yet, although there is a want of air and light in the picture we cannot deny its truth; sombre, rude, brutal, yet true. The fierce ungoverned instincts of powerful organizations, bred up amidst violence, revolt, and moral apathy, are here seen in operation;

such brutes we should all be, or the most of us, were our lives as insubordinate to law; were our affections and sympathies as little cultivated, our imaginations as undirected. And herein lies the moral of the book, though most people will fail to draw the moral from very irritation at it.

Curious enough it is to read *Wuthering Heights* and *The Tenant of Wildfell Hall,* and remember that the writers were two retiring, solitary, consumptive girls! Books, coarse even for men, coarse in language and coarse in conception, the coarseness apparently of violent and uncultivated men—turn out to be the productions of two girls living almost alone, filling their loneliness with quiet studies, and writing these books from a sense of duty, hating the pictures they drew, yet drawing them with austere conscientiousness! There is matter here for the moralist or critic to speculate on.

That it was no caprice of a poor imagination wandering in search of an "exciting" subject we are most thoroughly convinced. The three sisters have been haunted by the same experience. Currer Bell throws more humanity into her picture; but Rochester belongs to the Earnshaw and Heathcliff family. Currer Bell's riper mind enables her to paint with a freer hand; nor can we doubt but that her two sisters, had they lived, would also have risen into greater strength and clearness, retaining the extraordinary power of vigorous delineation which makes their writings so remarkable.

The power, indeed, is wonderful. Heathcliff, devil though he be, is drawn with a sort of dusky splendour which fascinates, and we feel the truth of his burning and impassioned love for Catherine, and of her inextinguishable love for him. It was a happy thought to make her love the kind, weak, elegant Edgar, and yet without lessening her passion for Heathcliff. Edgar appeals to her love of refinement, and goodness, and culture; Heathcliff clutches her soul in his passionate embrace. Edgar is the husband she has chosen, the man who alone is fit to call her wife; but although she is ashamed of her early playmate she loves him with a passionate abandonment which sets culture, education, the world, at defiance. It is in the treatment of this subject that Ellis Bell shows real mastery, and it shows more genius, in the highest sense of the word, than you will find in a thousand novels.

Creative power is so rare and so valuable that we should accept even its caprices with gratitude. Currer Bell, in a passage on this question, doubts whether the artist can control his power; she seems to think with Plato (see his argument in the *Ion*), that the artist does not possess, but is possessed. . . .

This is so true that we suppose every writer will easily recall his sensation of being "carried away" by the thoughts which in moments of exaltation possessed his soul—will recal the headlong feeling of letting the reins slip—being himself as much astonished at the result as any reader can be. There is at such time a *momentum* which propels the mind into regions inaccessible to calculation, unsuspected in our calmer moods.

The present publication is decidedly an interesting one. Besides the two novels of *Wuthering Heights* and *Agnes Grey* it contains the biographical notices already spoken of, and a selection from the poems left by both sisters. We cannot share Currer Bell's partiality for them; in no one quality distinguishing poetry from prose are they remarkable; but although their poetic interest is next to nought they have a biographical interest which justifies their publication. The volume is compact, and may be slipped into a coat pocket for the railway, so that the traveller may wile away with it the long hours of his journey in grim pleasure.

—*The Leader* (18 December 1850): 953

* * *

Marker in Haworth Church. Anne is buried at Scarborough, where she died (photograph by Susan B. Taylor).

Tales for "Iron Nerves"

Charlotte did not long outlive her sisters, dying of tuberculosis on 31 March 1855, a month shy of her thirty-ninth birthday. In her 1855 memoir of Charlotte, Harriet Martineau commented on the works of Emily and Anne, as well as that of Charlotte.

. . . In her obituary notice of her two sisters Currer reveals something of their process of authorship and their experience of failure and success. How terrible some of their experience of life was, in the midst of the domestic freedom and indulgence afforded them by their studious father, may be seen by the fearful representations of masculine nature and character found in the novels and tales of Emily and Ann. They considered it their duty, they told us, to present life as they knew it; and they gave us "Wuthering Heights," and "The Tenant of Wildfiell [sic] Hall." Such an experience as this indicates is really perplexing to English people in general; and all that we have to do with it is to bear it in mind when disposed to pass criticism on the coarseness which to a certain degree pervades the works of all the sisters, and the repulsiveness which makes the tales by Emily and Ann really horrible to people who have not iron nerves.

—*Daily News*, 6 April 1855, p. 5

In the early 1850s Brontë admirers were beginning to travel to Haworth to seek out Charlotte. Jane Forster, sister of Matthew Arnold, was among those who traveled to Haworth and recorded her impressions.

"Our Long-Planned Excursion"
Jane Forster

Though the weather was drizzly, we resolved to make our long-planned excursion to Haworth; so we packed ourselves into the buffalo-skin, and that into the gig and set off about eleven. The rain ceased, and the day was just suited to the scenery,—wild and chill,—with great masses of cloud glooming over the moors, and here and there a ray of sunshine covertly stealing through, and resting with a dim magical light upon some high bleak village; or darting down into some deep glen, lighting up the tall chimney, or glistening on the windows and wet roof of the mill which lies couching in the bottom. The country got wilder and wilder as we approached Haworth; for the last four miles we were ascending a huge moor, at the very top of which lies the dreary black-looking village of Haworth. The village-street itself is one of the steepest hills I have ever seen, and the stones are so horribly jolting that I should have

got out and walked with W[illiam], if possible, but, having once begun the ascent, to stop was out of the question. At the top was the Inn where we put up, close by the Church; and the clergyman's house, we were told, was at the top of the church-yard. So through that we went,—a dreary, dreary place, literally <u>paved</u> with rain-blackened tombstones, and all on the slope, for at Haworth there is on the highest heighth a higher still, and Mr. Brontë's house stands considerably above the church. There was the house before us, a small oblong stone house, with not a tree to screen it from the cutting wind; but how were we to get at it from the churchyard we could not see! There was an old man in the Church-yard, brooding like a Ghoul over the graves, with a sort of grim hilarity on his face. I thought he looked hardly human; however, he was human enough to tell us the way; and presently we found ourselves in the little bare parlour. . . . Presently the door opened, and in came a superannuated mastiff, followed by an old gentleman very like Miss Brontë, who shook hands with us, and then went to call his daughter. A long interval during which we coaxed the old dog and looked at a picture of Miss Brontë, by Richmond, the solitary ornament of the room, looking strangely out of place on the bare walls, and at the books on the little shelves, most of them evidently the gift of the authors since Miss Brontë's celebrity. Presently she came in, and welcomed us very kindly, and took me upstairs to take off my bonnet, and herself brought me water and towels. The uncarpeted stone stairs and floors, the old drawers propped on wood, were all scrupulously clean and neat. When we went into the parlour again, we began talking very comfortably, when the door opened and Mr. Brontë looked in; seeing his daughter there, 'I suppose' he thought it was all right, and he retreated to his study on the opposite side of the passage; presently emerging again to bring W. a country newspaper; this was his last appearance till we went. Miss Brontë spoke with the greatest warmth of Miss Martineau, and of the good she had gained from her. Well! we talked about various things; the character of the people,—about her solitude &c., till she left the room to help about dinner, I suppose, for she did not return for an age. The old dog had vanished; a fat curly-haired dog honoured us with his company for some time, but finally manifested a wish to get out, so we were left alone. At last she returned, followed by the maid and dinner, which made us all more comfortable; and we had some very pleasant conversation, in the midst of which time passed quicker than we supposed, for at last W found that it was half-past three, and we had fourteen or fifteen miles before us. So

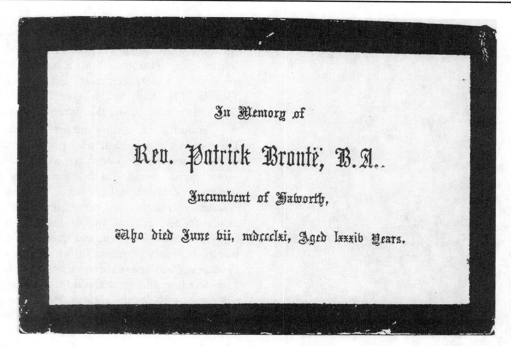

Funeral card for the Reverend Patrick Brontë, who died having outlived his wife and six children (from Whiteley Turner,
A Spring-Time Saunter: Round and About Brontë Land, Sam Houston State University Library)

we hurried off, having obtained from her a promise to pay us a visit in the spring; and the old gentleman having issued once more from his study to say good-bye, we returned to the inn, and made the best of our way homewards.

Miss Brontë put me so in mind of her own 'Jane Eyre.' She looked smaller than ever, and moved about so quietly, and noiselessly, just like a little bird, as Rochester called her, barring that all birds are joyous, and that joy can never have entered that house since it was first built; and yet, perhaps, when that old man married, and took home his bride, and children's voices and feet were heard about the house, even that desolate crowded grave-yard, and biting blast could not quench cheerfulness and hope. Now there is something touching in the sight of that little creature entombed in such a place, and moving about herself like a spirit, especially when you think that the slight still frame encloses a force of strong fiery life, which nothing has been able to freeze or extinguish.
– *The Letters of Charlotte Brontë,* edited by Margaret Smith (Oxford: Oxford University Press, 2000), v. 2, pp. 568–569

* * *

With the death of Charlotte, the only remnant of the Brontë family were her her father and her widowed husband, Arthur Bell Nicholls. The two men continued to live and work together at the parsonage until the Reverend Brontë's death at age eighty-four on 7 June 1861. Walter White, a visitor in the late 1850s, describes how the village was becoming accustomed to literary tourists.

"The Family Who Made Haworth Famous"
Walter White

An hour of ascent and you come to a cross-road, where, turning to the right for about a furlong, you see Haworth, piled from base to summit of a steep hill, the highest point crowned by the church. The road makes a long bend in approaching the acclivity, which, if you choose, may be avoided by a cut-off; but coming as a pilgrim you will perhaps at first desire to see all. You pass a board which notifies *Haworth Town,* and then begins the ascent painfully steep, bounded on one side by houses, on the other—where you look into the valley—by little gardens and a line of ragged little sheds and hutches. What a wearisome hill; you will half doubt whether horses can draw a load up it. Presently we have houses on both sides, and shops with plate-glass and mahogany mouldings, contrasting strongly with the general rustic aspect, and the primitive shop of the *Clogger.* Some of the windows denote an expectation of visitors; the apothecary exhibits photographs of the church, the parsonage, and Mr. Brontë; and no one seems surprised at your arrival.

The *Black Bull* stands invitingly on the hill-top. I was ready for breakfast, and the hostess quite ready to

Patrick Brontë's sister Alice (1795?–1891) who served as a source for biographers of the family (J. Horsfall Turner, Brontëana: The Rev. Patrick Brontë, A.B., His Collected Works and Life, *University of Colorado Libraries)*

serve; and while I ate she talked of the family who made Haworth famous. She knew them all, brother and sisters: Mr. Nicholls had preached the day before in the morning; Mr. Brontë in the afternoon. It was mostly in the afternoon that the old gentleman preached, and he delivered his sermon without a book. The people felt sorry for his bereavements; and they all liked Mr. Nicholls. She had had a good many visitors, but expected "a vast" before the summer was over.

From the inn to the churchyard is but a few paces. The church is ugly enough to have had a Puritan for architect; and there, just beyond the crowded graves, stands the parsonage, as unsmiling as the church. After I had looked at it from a distance, and around on the landscape, which, in summer dress, is not dreary, though bounded by dark moors; the sexton came and admitted me to the church. He points to the low roof, and quotes Milton, and leads you to the family pew, and shows you the corner where *she*—that is, Charlotte—used to sit; and against the wall, but a few feet from this corner, you see the long plain memorial stone, with its melancholy list of names. As they descend, the inscriptions crowd close together; and beneath the lowest, that which records the decease of her who wrote *Jane Eyre,* there remains but a narrow blank for those which are to follow.

Then the sexton, turning away to the vestry, showed me in the marriage register the signatures of Charlotte Brontë, her husband, and father; and next, his collection of photographs, with an intimation that they were for sale. When he saw that I had not the slightest inclination to become a purchaser, to have seen the place was quite enough; he said, that if I had a card to send in the old gentleman would see me. It seemed to me, I replied, that the greatest kindness a stranger could show to the venerable pastor, would be, not to intrude upon him.

— *A Month in Yorkshire,* pp. 334–336

Branwell Brontë

Patrick Branwell Brontë (1817–1848), known as Branwell, was the fourth child and only boy in the Brontë family. As children and into their youth, Branwell and Charlotte were particularly close; they collaborated extensively on their juvenile writings, and the humorous rivalry they often express in these pieces demonstrates their familiarity with each other's literary styles and preoccupations. As a young man Branwell showed exceptional promise, but his achievements in his brief life did not match those of his sisters. He remained an influential intellectual and artistic presence in his sisters' lives. Brontë biographers debate to what extent Branwell is the model for dissolute characters in the sisters' novels, such as Heathcliff and Hindley Earnshaw in Wuthering Heights, and Arthur Huntingdon in The Tenant of Wildfell Hall. In the last three years of his life, his sisters' feelings toward him reflected their love, concern, anger, and distress at the destructive course of his life.

Early Promise

Branwell was interested in both art and literature; he studied art with William Robinson of Leeds in 1835. In summer 1835 Branwell contemplated applying to the Royal Academy in London. He may have traveled to London in fall 1835 or spring 1836; however, no record of such a trip exists.

Elizabeth Gaskell in The Life of Charlotte Brontë (1857) comments on Branwell's interest in art and the portrait of

A drawing from a painting by Branwell showing him with his sisters: left to right, Charlotte, Emily, and Anne. The "Gun Group," which was painted by Branwell in 1833–1834, was inherited by Arthur Bell Nicholls, who is believed to have saved only the portion that included Emily's portrait—a fragment that now hangs in the National Portrait Gallery (frontispiece for The Complete Works of Charlotte Brontë and Her Sisters, *British Library).*

Black Bull Inn, Haworth, where Branwell enjoyed spending time. The steps leading up to the church next door are visible to the right
(from J. A. Erskine Stuart, The Brontë Country: Its Topography, Antiquities, and History,
Sam Houston State University Library).

his sisters that she saw—the now-famous image of the three sisters that hangs in the National Portrait Gallery in London. Excerpts.

"The Pride of the Village"
Elizabeth Gaskell

In the middle of the summer of 1835, a great family plan was mooted at the parsonage. The question was, to what trade or profession should Branwell be brought up? He was now nearly eighteen; it was time to decide. He was very clever, no doubt; perhaps, to begin with, the greatest genius in this rare family. The sisters hardly recognised their own, or each others' powers, but they knew *his*. The father, ignorant of many failings in moral conduct, did proud homage to the great gifts of his son; for Branwell's talents were readily and willingly brought out for the entertainment of others. Popular admira-

tion was sweet to him. And this led to his presence being sought at "arvills" [funeral feasts] and all the great village gatherings, for the Yorkshire men have a keen relish for intellect; and it likewise procured him the undesirable distinction of having his company recommended by the landlord of the Black Bull to any chance traveller who might happen to feel solitary or dull over his liquor. "Do you want someone to help you with your bottle, sir? If you do, I'll send up for Patrick" (so the villagers called him till the day of his death). And while the messenger went, the landlord entertained his guest with accounts of the wonderful talents of the boy, whose precocious cleverness, and great conversational powers, were the pride of the village. . . .

It is singular how strong a yearning the whole family had towards the art of drawing. Mr. Brontë had been very solicitous to get them good instruction; the girls themselves loved everything connected with it—all descriptions or engravings of great pictures; and, in default of good ones, they would take and analyse any print or drawing which came in their way, and find out how much thought had gone to its composition, what ideas it was intended to suggest, and what it *did* suggest. In the same spirit, they laboured to design imaginations of their own; they lacked the power of execution, not of conception. At one time, Charlotte had the notion of making her living as an artist, and wearied her eyes in drawing with pre-Raphaelite minuteness, but not with pre-Raphaelite accuracy, for she drew from fancy rather than from nature.

But they all thought there could be no doubt about Branwell's talent for drawing. I have seen an oil painting of his, done I know not when, but probably about this time. It was a group of his sisters, life size, three-quarters' length; not much better than sign-painting, as to manipulation; but the likenesses were, I should think, admirable. I could only judge of the fidelity with which the other two were depicted, from the striking resemblance which Charlotte, upholding the great frame of canvas, and consequently standing right behind it, bore to her own representation, though it must have been ten years and more since the portraits were taken. The picture was divided, almost in the middle, by a great pillar. On the side of the column which was lighted by the sun, stood Charlotte, in the womanly dress of that day of jigot sleeves and large collars. On the deeply shadowed side, was Emily, with Anne's gentle face resting on her shoulder. Emily's countenance struck me as full of power; Charlotte's of solicitude; Anne's of tenderness. The two younger seemed hardly to have attained their full growth, though Emily was taller than Charlotte; they had cropped hair, and a more girlish dress. I remember looking on those two sad, earnest, shadowed faces, and wondering whether I could trace the mysterious expression which is said to foretell an early death. I had some fond superstitious hope that the column divided their fates from hers, who stood apart in the canvas, as in life she survived. I liked to see that the bright side of the pillar was towards *her*—that the light in the picture fell on *her*. I might more truly have sought in her presentment—nay, in her living face—for the sign of death in her prime. They were good likenesses, however badly executed. From thence I should guess his family augured truly that, if Branwell had but the opportunity, and, alas! had but the moral qualities, he might turn out a great painter.

The best way of preparing him to become so appeared to be to send him as a pupil to the Royal Academy. I dare say, he longed and yearned to follow this path, principally because it would lead him to that mysterious London—that Babylon the great—which seems to have filled the imaginations and haunted the minds of all the younger members of this recluse family. To Branwell it was more than a vivid imagination, it was an impressed reality. By dint of studying maps, he was as well acquainted with it, even down to its by-ways, as if he had lived there. Poor misguided fellow! this craving to see and know London, and that stronger craving after fame, were never to be satisfied. He was to die at the end of a short and blighted life. But in this year of 1835, all his home kindred were thinking how they could best forward his views, and how help him up to the pinnacle where he desired to be.

—*The Life of Charlotte Brontë*, v. 2, pp. 143–148

* * *

In 1838 Branwell moved to Bradford, near Haworth, to set up a portrait studio. For a while he enjoyed some success, as his portraits of Bradford and Haworth citizens indicate, but he closed the studio in winter 1839. Although Branwell had talent as a painter, his need for more extensive training and the competitive market for portrait painting frustrated his ambition.

Branwell had been given a classical education by Reverend Brontë, as his writing demonstrates. His facility with the classics also enabled him to offer himself as a tutor. At the end of December 1839, Branwell began his first post, moving to Broughton-in-Furness, Lancashire, to work for the Postlethwaite family.

While with the Postlethwaites, Branwell spent time on his own poetry. From age eleven or earlier, he had been writing poetry using various pseudonyms and characters' identities within the Glass Town/Angria sagas he created with Charlotte. In his later teens, he began signing his poems as himself, "P. B. Brontë," or as "Northangerland"— the pen name he used in his adulthood that was based on a character from the juvenilia. Although his sisters may not have been aware of it, Branwell was the first of his generation in the family to become published; his poem "Heaven and Earth" was printed in the Halifax Guardian *newspaper on 5 June 1841 as by "Northangerland." By the time of his death in 1848, Branwell had published poems in several area newspapers including the* Halifax Guardian *(twelve poems total; three of which were also published in the* Bradford Herald*),* Bradford Herald *(eight poems total),* Leeds Intelligencer *(one poem), and* Yorkshire Gazette *(four poems). Branwell's essay "Thomas Bewick," on the engraver whose work the Brontë siblings enjoyed, was published in the* Halifax Guardian *on 1 October 1842.*

Branwell approached several prominent writers to ascertain the merits of his compositions. One of the first he

The chair in which Branwell often sat at the Black Bull Inn (from Whiteley Turner, A Spring-Time Saunter: Round and About Brontë Land, *Sam Houston State University Library)*

wrote to was William Wordsworth, enclosing with his letter a portion of a longer poem, "The Struggles of flesh with Spirit / Scene I–Infancy." Wordsworth never wrote back.

Branwell Brontë to William Wordsworth, 10 January 1837

Sir

I most earnestly entreat you to read and pass your judgement upon what I have sent you, because from the day of my birth to this the nineteenth year of my life I have lived among wild and secluded hills where I could neither know what I was or what I could do.—I read for the same reason that I eat or drank,—because it was a real craving of Nature. I wrote on the same principle as I spoke,—out of the impulse and feelings of the mind;—nor could I help it, for what came, came out and there was the end of it, for as to self conceit, that could not receive food from flattery, since to this hour Not half a dozen people in the world know that I have ever penned a line.—

But a change has taken place now, Sir and I am arrived at an age wherein I must do something for myself—the powers I possess must be exercised to a definite end, and as I dont know them myself I must ask of others what they are worth—yet there is not one here to tell me, and still, if they are worthless, time will henceforth be too precious to be wasted on them.

Do pardon me, Sir, that I have ventured to come before one whose works I have most loved in our Literature and who most has been with me a divinity of the mind—laying before him one of my writings, and asking of him a Judgement of its contents,—I must come before some one from whose sentence there is no appeal, and such an one he is who has developed the theory of poetry as well as its practice, and both in such a way as to claim a place in the memory of a thousand years to come.

My aim, Sir, is to push out into the open world and for this I trust not poetry alone that might launch the vessel but could not bear her on—sensible and scientific prose, bold and vigorous efforts in my walk in Life would give a further title to the notice of the world and <u>then</u> again poetry ought to brighten and crown that name with glory—but nothing of all this can be even begun without <u>means</u> and as I dont possess these I must in every shape strive to gain them; Surely, in this day, when there is not a <u>writing</u> poet worth a sixpence the field must be open if a better man can step forward

What I send to you is the prefatory scene of a much longer Subject in which I have striven to develope strong passions and weak principles struggling with a high imagination and acute feelings till as youth hardens towards age evil deeds and short enjoyments end in mental misery and bodily ruin—Now to send you the whole of this would be a mock upon your patience; what you see, does not even <u>pretend</u> to be more than the description of an Imaginative child—But read it Sir and as you would hold a light to one in utter darkness as you value your own kind heartedness <u>return</u> me an <u>Answer</u> if but one word telling me whether I should write on or write no more—

Forgive undue warmth because my feelings in this matter cannot be cool and believe me to be Sir

with deep respect
Your really humble Servant
P B Brontë.

—The Letters of Charlotte Brontë, v. 1, pp. 160–161

* * *

In April 1840 Branwell sent some of his poems to Thomas De Quincey, famous for his work Confessions of an English Opium Eater *(1822), and Hartley Coleridge, the son of Samuel Taylor Coleridge. Included with his letter to De Quincey were his poems "Sir Henry Tunstall" and some translations of Horace's odes. When Alexander Japp edited De Quincey's letters, he published Branwell's poem and translations. In these excerpts, Japp refers to Francis A. Leyland's* The Brontë Family with Special Reference to Patrick Branwell Brontë *(1886), as well as Gaskell's* The Life of Charlotte Brontë *and Mary F. Robinson's* Emily Brontë *(1883).*

"High Aspirings"
Alexander Japp

That remarkable brother, Patrick Branwell Brontë, a genius, but in his last days, at all events, a mournful wreck, round whom, as we know from Charlotte's letters, the thoughts and anxieties of the sisters so long painfully circled, seems also to have written frequently to the Opium-Eater—letters which, so far as they can now be remembered, were full of confessions, of regrets, of hopes, and aspirations mingled together in the most affecting and striking manner. That correspondence has left tokens of itself in some copies of poems, which, as we are not aware that they have been preserved elsewhere, we here venture partially to give, in memory of that weak, wayward, unfortunate man, but singular genius—so singular that Mr. Leyland, indeed, essays to prove that the leading idea of one at least of the sisters' stories was due to him; and that, in fact, he had written a novel with the same plot, characters, and incidents as "Wuthering Heights," quoting Mr. Grundy to this effect: "Patrick declared to me, and what his sister said bore out the assertion, that he wrote a great portion of 'Wuthering Heights' himself." Mr. Leyland, with full knowledge and refined sympathy, abundantly establishes the fact that much misknowledge and exaggeration characterised the writing of Mrs. Gaskell in her Memoir of Charlotte Brontë, so far as it related to Patrick, and that she has been only too closely followed in many of her misrepresentations by Mr. Swinburne, Miss Mary F. Robinson, and other writers of more recent date. Patrick Brontë has enough to bear in his inherited constitution, his tendency to disease, his morbid predisposition to melancholy, and the reactions from it favouring out bursts of excess in many directions, without having fables fathered upon him. "The defects of faith, and taints of blood," of which the Laureate sings, were very strong in him; and great allowance should be made for a man of such a temperament and such inheritances. But it is clear, from Mr. Leyland's volumes, that there must have been great exaggeration with regard to many things in the career of Patrick Brontë. Mr. Leyland, in his picture up to the last few years, would

Branwell Brontë's drawing "Northangerland./Alexander Percy Esq.," circa 1835. Northangerland figures repeatedly in Branwell Brontë's juvenilia, where he is also called Alexander Percy, Rogue, Percy, and Ellrington (The Brotherton Collection, Leeds University Library, University of Colorado Libraries; from Christine Alexander and Jane Sellars, The Art of the Brontës*).*

have us to regard him as a shy, sensitive, fanciful, excitable creature, with high aspirings, but without steadiness or will to adhere to fixed resolutions, and finally losing his balance, and surrendering himself to hallucinations of many kinds. This, at all events, is at once the more charitable and the more grateful view to take; and certainly in Mr. Leyland, Patrick Brontë has found a very thoughtful and well-informed apologist, if not a defender. His portrait of Branwell, at all events, is not that of a half-madman, half-fiend, half-poet, half-reprobate; rather that of a man with many fine impulses, but without ballast, and finally surrendering himself to indulgences that did much to wreck his career and shorten his life.

While disproving wholly the truth of the assertion of Miss Mary Robinson that Patrick Brontë was an opium-eater at twenty, he goes on to speak of the attraction of De Quincey's writings for the whole family, and is fain to admit that when, later, Branwell betook himself to opium, he may have *in some degree* been led thereto by study of De Quincey's "Confessions." He writes:

"There is no reliable evidence whatever that Branwell at this period of his life [his twentieth year] was an opium-eater; and, considering the fact that the biographer of Emily has assigned the art-practice at Bradford to a period subsequent to tutorship at Broughton-in-Furness, one may, perhaps, be permitted to suspect that she is equally in error in her assertions as to his opium-eating so young. Branwell did, indeed, later fall into the baneful habit, and suffered at times in consequence; but there is no reason to believe that he became wholly subject to it, or was greatly injured by the practice either in mind or body. We can only surmise as to the original cause of his use of opium; but, when we consider the extraordinary fascination which De Quincey's wonderful book had for the younger generation of literary men of his day, we shall recognise that Branwell, who read the book, in all probability fell under its influence. Let us remember, moreover, that the young man's two sisters had died of consumption, and that De Quincey declares the use of the drug had saved him from the fate of his father, who had fallen a victim to the same scourge. De Quincey had used the drug intermittently, and we have reason to believe that Branwell, who followed him, did the same. Let us, then, imagine the young Brontë revelling in the realm of the dreamy and impassioned, and hoping fondly that consumption might be driven away, resolving to try the effect of the 'dread agent of unimaginable pleasure and pain,' a proceeding from which many less brave would have shrunk. Branwell had doubtless read in the 'Confessions of an English Opium-Eater' that the drug does not disorder the system, but gives tone, a sort of health, that might be natural, if it were not for the means by which it is procured."

Mr. Leyland has devoted a good deal of space to Patrick Brontë's poetical efforts, and cites extracts from many of them, but of those which are before us it does not seem that he had any knowledge. Probably they were written at a time when neither he nor his friends were in personal association or correspondence with Brontë—and it is certain that they reached De Quincey at a time of sickness and great prostration, which may account for their having been swallowed up in his vast piles of papers and never recovered till his death. We give the most striking passages of the poem—together with the translations of Horace's Odes, which accompanied it:—

SIR HENRY TUNSTALL.

'Tis only afternoon—but midnight's gloom
Could scarce seem stiller, in the darkest room,
Than does this ancient mansion's strange repose,
So long ere common cares of daylight close.
I hear the clock slow ticking in the Hall;
And—far away—the woodland waterfall
Sounds, lost, like stars from out the noon-day skies—
And seldom heard until those stars arise.

The parlour group are seated all together,
With long looks turned toward the threat'ning weather,
Whose grey clouds, gathering o'er the moveless trees,
Nor break nor brighten with the passing breeze.
Why seems that group attired with such a care?
And who's the visitor they watch for there?
The aged Father, on his customed seat,
With cushioned stool to prop his crippled feet,
Averting from the rest his forehead high
To hide the drop that quivers in his eye;
And strange the pang which bids that drop to start;
For hope and sadness mingle in his heart;
A trembling hope for what may come to-day—
A sadness sent from what has passed away!
Fast by the window sits his daughter fair;
Who, gazing earnest on the clouded air,
Clasps close her mother's hand, and paler grows
With every leaf that falls, or breeze that blows:
Sickened with long hope bursting into morn
Too bright for her, with longer pining worn!
Even those young children o'er the table bent;
And on that map with childish eyes intent,
Are guiding fancied ships through ocean's foam,
And wondering—"what he's like"—and "when he'll come."

. . . .

Japp quotes large portions of the long poem that tells of the homecoming of Sir Henry after an absence of sixteen years spent achieving glory as a soldier in India. Although his father, mother, and sister Mary live, he finds little sense of belonging in his former home, especially as he remembers his sister, Caroline, who has died in the interim. The poem concludes with Sir Henry alone in his darkening room, looking on the "pictured wall" that first inspired his dreams of adventure.

"Well—world, oh world!—as I have bowed to thee,
I must consent to suffer thy decree;
I asked—Thou'st given me my destiny;
I asked—when gazing on that pictured wall,
Like England's Hero to command or fall;
I asked when wandering over mountains lone,
Some day to wander over lands unknown;
I asked for gain and glory—place and power;
Thou gavest them all—I have them all this hour;
But I forgot to ask for youthful blood,
The thrill divine of feelings unsubdued,
The nerves that quivered to the sound of fame,
The tongue that trembled o'er a lover's name,
The eye that glistened with delightful tears,
The Hope that gladdened past and gilded future years;
So—I have rigid nerves and ready tongue,
Fit to subdue the weak and serve the strong;
And eyes that look on all things as the same,
And Hope—no, callousness, that thinks all things *a name!*
So, Caroline—I'll bid farewell once more,
Nor mourn, lost shade; for though thou'rt gone before,
Gone is *thy* Henry too—and didst not thou, While just
 departing from this world below,
Say thou no longer wert a guileless child,

That all old things were altered or despoiled?—
And—hadst thou lived—thine angel heart, like mine,
Would soon have hardened with thy youth's decline—
Cold, perhaps, to me, if beating, as when laid
Beneath its grave-stone 'neath the churchyard shade.
. . . .
      "I home returned for rest—but feel to-day
Home is no rest—and long to be away,
To play life's game out where my soldiers are,
Returned from India to a wilder war
Upon the hills of Spain—again to ride
Before their bayonets at Wellesley's side,
Again to sleep with horses trampling round,
In watch-cloak wrapped, and on a battle-ground; To
    waken with the loud commencing gun,
And feed life's failing flame and drive the moments on—
There is our aim—to *that* our labours tend—
Strange we should love to hurry on our end!
But so it is, and nowhere can I speed
So swift through life as on my battle-steed!"

He ceased—unconsciously declined his head,
And stealingly the sense of waking fled,
Wafting his spirit into weeping Spain:

Till—starting momently—he gazed again,
But all looked strange to his beclouded brain:
And all was strange—for, though the scenes were known,
The thoughts that should have cherished them were gone,
Gone like the sunshine—and none others came
To shake the encroaching slumbers from his frame.
So, while he lay there, twilight deepened fast,
And silent, but resistless, hours swept past,
Till chairs and pictures lost themselves in gloom,
And but a window glimmered through the room,
With one pale star above the sombre trees,
Listening from Heaven to earth's repining breeze.
      That Star looked down with cold and quiet eye,
While all else darkened, brightening up the sky,
And though his eye scarce saw it, yet his mind,
As, half awake and half to dreams resigned,
Could scarce help feeling in its holy shine
The solemn look of sainted Caroline,
With mute reproachfulness reminding him
That faith and fondness were not all a dream;
That form, not feeling, should be changed by clime;
That looks, not love, should suffer hurt by time;
That o'er life's waters, guiding us from far,
And brightening with life's night, should glisten Memory's
Star.   P. B. B.

Boughton-in-Furkess, *April 15,* 1840.

HORACE.
ODE XV. BOOK I.

'Twas when the treacherous shepherd bore
    His Royal prize away,
In Phrygian ship—from Spartan shore—
    Across the Ægean Sea,

That Nereus raised his awful brow,
    And hushed each favouring breeze,
Till not a ship its path could plough
    Upon the slumbering seas;

And thus did that old Sea-god sing
    His prophecy of doom—
"Vain Man! ill-omened thou dost bring
    Thine hostess to thy home,

Whom Greece shall seek with mighty host,
    Conjured to overwhelm
Thy pleasures, bought at such a cost,
    And thy ancestral realm.

Alas! what strife round Xanthus' wave
    Thy treachery shall bring!
What fiery funerals o'er the grave
    Of Ilion and her king!

Now Pallas lays her olive by,
    And grasps her shield and spear,
And mounts her chariot in the sky,
    And wakes her rage for war.

In vain thy guardian goddess' care
    Thy spirit may inspire;
In vain thou comb'st thy curling hair,
    Or wakest thy wanton lyre;

In vain the shouts—the lances' thrust—
    Or Ajax,—thou may'st fly,
For, with thy long locks trailed in dust,
    Adulterer! thou shalt die!

Ulysses see, and Nestor grave—
    Thy hapless people scourge;
And Sthenelus and Teucer brave
    Thy flying footsteps urge:

'Tis Sthenelus the reins can guide,
    While noble Diomede,
Greater than Tydeus, at his side
    Hunts for the adulterer's head;

Whom thou shalt fly as flies the wind
    In vale or woodland lone,
From the deep death-bark, heard behind,
    Of wild wolf hastening on;

With beating heart and bated breath,
    O'er mountain and through grove—
Was this the victory—this the death
    Thou promisedst thy love?

Peclides' ships, Pelides' arm
    O'er Phrygia's fated shore
For these thy deeds, the avenging storm
    Resistlessly shall pour;

And after years of weary wars,
    Shall wrap in funeral flame,
Unquenched by all her blood and tears,
    My Ilion's very name."

BOOK I. ODE XI.

    Leuconæ, seek no more
    By magic arts t' explore
How long a life our God has given to thee or me.
    If we've winters yet in store;
    Or if this whose tempests roar
Across the Tyrrhene deep, is the *last* that we shall see.

    Be cheerful wisdom thine;
    My goblet fill with wine;
And shape thy hopes to suit the hour that hastes away;
    For while we speak, that hour
    Is past beyond our power;
So do not trust to-morrow, *but seize upon to-day.*

BOOK I. ODE IX.

See'st thou not amid the skies
White with snow Soracte rise;
While the forests on the plain
Scarce their hoary weight sustain;
And congealed the waters stand
'Neath the frost's arresting hand.

    Drive away the winter wild;
On the hearths be fuel piled;
And from out its sacred cell–
Kept in Sabine vase so well–
Generous–bring thy four years' wine,
Wakener of the song divine.
    Wisely leave the rest to Heaven,
Who, when warring winds have striven
With the forests or the main,
Bids their raging rest again.
    Be not ever pondering
Over what the morn may bring.
Whether it be joy or pain
Wisely count it all as gain,
And, while age upon thy brow
Shall forbear to shed his snow,
Do not shun the dancers' feet,
Nor thy loved one's dear retreat.
Hasten to the plain or square;
List the whisper, telling where,
When the calm night rules above,
Thou may'st meet thy dearest love:
When the laugh round corner sly
Shall instruct thee where to spy:
When the wanton's feigned retreating
Still shall leave some pledge of meeting:
Perhaps a ring or bracelet bright,
Snatched from arm or finger white.

BOOK I. ODE X.

For what does the poet to Phoebus pray–
    With new wine from his vessels flowing?
Not for the flocks o'er Calabria that stray;
    Nor for corn in Sardinia growing;

Nor prays he for ivory, or gold, or land
    Which the Liris, gently gliding,
Would crumble away into fugitive sand
    Down its silent waters sliding.

Let *him* gather the grapes who has planted the vine;
    Let the Merchant whom Jupiter favours,
His Syrian treasures exchange for wine
    Which a golden goblet flavours:

Thrice in a season o'erpassing the sea,
    Nor by waters or winds prevented,
While olives and mallows shall satisfy me,
    With the lot fortune gives me contented.

Son of Satona! oh grant me to taste
    The goods thou hast placed before me;
And a spirit undimmed, and an age undisgraced,
    And a Harp with whose strains to adore thee!

BOOK I. ODE XIX.

The mother of love and the father of wine
    And passion resuming its throne,
Backward command me my mind to incline
    And kindle the flame that seemed gone.
      For Glycera warms
      My heart with her charms
    Whiter than Parian stone.

Her sweet arts inflame me, her countenance beams
    Too bright to be gazed upon,
Till Venus, departing from Cyprus, seems
    To rush upon me alone:
      And no longer my verse
      The deeds can rehearse
    By Scythian or Parthian done.

Raise me an altar of living sod,
    And crown it with garlands and bear
Wine undiluted, a drink for a god,
    That Glycera, hearing my prayer,
      May know I adore,
      And be cruel no more,
    But an answering passion declare.

    There are doubtless many mistakes of sense and language – except the first. I had not, when I translated them, a Horace at hand, so was forced to rely on memory. – P. B. Brontë.

        –*De Quincey Memorials*, v. 2, pp. 208–212

* * *

Branwell Brontë's oil portrait of his close friend John Brown, the Haworth sexton, circa 1835–1839 (Brontë Parsonage Museum; from Christine Alexander and Jane Sellars, The Art of the Brontës, *University of Colorado Libraries).*

"Clerk on the Leeds and Manchester Railroad"

Branwell's search for steady employment took him in August 1840 to the newly opened Leeds and Manchester railway line. As Assistant Clerk in Charge at the new Sowerby Bridge railway station, Branwell received a salary of £75 a year. Charlotte reports Branwell's employment in this late September letter to Ellen Nussey.

A distant relation of mine, one Patrick Boanerges, has set off to seek his fortune, in the wild, wandering, adventurous, romantic, knight-errant-like capacity of clerk on the Leeds and Manchester Railroad. Leeds and Manchester, where are they? Cities in the wilderness—like Tadmor, alias Palmyra—are they not?

–*The Letters of Charlotte Brontë,* v. 1, p. 228

In April 1841, Branwell was promoted to Clerk in Charge of Luddenden Foot station with a salary raise to £130 a year—a comfortable living when one considers that Charlotte at the time was serving as governess to John White's family for £20 per year, minus £4 for her laundry. Branwell's interests in poetry, music, art, and the cultural life of the towns he lived in may have undermined his focus on his clerk post, and he kept the position less than a year. Although he was not suspected of embezzlement, Branwell was discharged from the railway in March 1842 because accounts he managed were missing money.

Poet, critic, and playwright John Drinkwater (1882–1937) prepared a limited edition of Branwell's translations of Horace's odes in 1923 and praised Branwell's poetry, in particular his translations. Excerpts.

Patrick Branwell Brontë and His "Horace"
John Drinkwater

Patrick Branwell Brontë died in 1848, at the age of thirty-one. Little celebrated for any achievement of his own, he is a not unfamiliar figure to students of the ever-increasing volume of Brontë literature. Through the life-story of his more famous sisters, already sufficiently tragic in itself, his failure of character sounds, perhaps, the most unhappy note of all. The scourge of disease that destroyed the family, and the incessant problem of ways and means, could be faced with a greater fortitude than the constant betrayal of the hopes that were centred in a brother at once highly gifted, beloved, and incurably weak in fibre. Most of the biographers and critics have been agreed upon the matter, and the evidence is plain enough. Branwell made a mess of his life, and he was a cause of great suffering to three brave and devoted women. When drink and opium made an end—or hastened it, since by the latter he died of consumption like the others—natural affection can but have been conscious of a deep anxiety gone. But, while bad remains bad, there are aspects of the badness in this case that have, perhaps, been overlooked by Branwell's detractors.

Formal acknowledgment has generally been made of his gifts; they have even been allowed to have been brilliant. Mrs. Gaskell tells us how among the children, all pretty much of an age, busily writing their poems and romances, it was the brother who by common consent was to bring fame to the family; she adds, on her own account: "He was very clever, no doubt; perhaps to begin with, the greatest genius in this rare family." We are told that his wit and talent were sought for the entertainment of strangers by the landlord of the "Black Bull" at Haworth, in return for a share in the bottle. Other writers, speaking in censure, have nevertheless allowed that the disaster of Branwell's life was the more miserable because of the promise betrayed. What this promise actually was we are not so clearly told. Mrs. Gaskell quotes only one fragment of his juvenile verse. It is not notable, but the poor opinion that the biographer expresses of it would be more convincing if she had not already given an equally indifferent specimen of Charlotte's writing as showing "remarkable poetical talent." When the sisters published their book of poems in 1846, Branwell's work was not included, though it almost certainly must have been known to them, and was, in flashes, better than anything that the book contained with the exception of Emily's best poems. Francis A. Leyland, in *The Brontë Family* gave several examples of

Hartley Coleridge (1796–1849), son of Samuel Taylor Coleridge, who invited Branwell to visit him and encouraged Branwell to keep working on his translations of Horace's odes (from Eleanor A. Towle, A Poet's Children: Hartley and Sara Coleridge, Thomas Cooper Library, University of South Carolina)

his work, which did not reappear in book form until Mr. A. C. Benson included a very clumsily edited selection in his *Brontë Poems* of 1915. Mr. Benson's Introduction pays a qualified tribute to Branwell's "instinct for poetry," and a yet more qualified one to his expression. This was, perhaps, all that could be asked; it was, in any case, nearer justice than the merely uncritical petulance of Mary F. Robinson and some other writers. The poems recovered, carelessly enough, by Mr. Benson, had no more than traces of genius. But they had that. *Noah's Warning over Methuselah's Grave* and some twenty lines scattered among the other poems, were not enough to call up more than the ghost of a reputation for Branwell. But they are very good in themselves, and they have this interest: they are tokens of the something in him that gave rise to the tradition of his rare gifts that survives from the family records. . . .

The extant poems of Branwell Brontë, with three exceptions, are to be found in Leyland, and in various manuscripts. Of the last the most considerable is that printed for the first time in 1924. It consists of a complete translation, written out entirely in Branwell's own hand, of the first book of Horace's Odes, omitting the last, of which he says: " This Ode I have no heart to attempt, after having heard Mr. H. Coleridge's translation, on May Day, at Ambleside." The manuscript is signed at the end, "P. B. Brontë," and dated "Haworth, Nr. Bradford, Yorks, June 27, 1840." On New Year's Day of that year, he had gone to Broughton-in-Furness, on the edge of the Lake District, as tutor in the family of a Mr. Postlethwaite, and he returned to Haworth in June, so that most of the translations were presumably made while he held that appointment. He was twenty-three years of age at the time. Just as the portrait of Emily is the most convincing proof of his gifts as a painter, so these translations seem to me to be his best achievement, so far as we can judge, as a poet. They are unequal, and they have many of the bad tricks of writing that come out of some deeply rooted defect of character. But they also have a great many passages of clear lyrical beauty, and they have something of the style that comes from a spiritual understanding, as apart from merely formal knowledge, of great models.

Horace has been a favourite mark for English translators, including many of our more considerable poets. Jonson, Cowley, Milton, Dryden, Pope, Prior, Congreve, Calverley—these and others have done occasionally what less famous writers have done systematically, and it cannot be said that on the whole they have done it any better. Cowley may bring off a line like

And trusts the faithless April of thy May,

Or Dryden—

The half unwilling willing kiss,

but they are no surer of making a good poem in translation than the Creeches and the Sewells. And that is the only test. If you know Latin, you don't want an English translation of Horace unless into the bargain you get a good English poem; if you don't know Latin (as I don't), still you want the translation only on the same terms. Horace has been responsible for some good English poems, and a great many dull ones. Even Ben Jonson, in his translation *The Art of Poetry* (1640), in spite of a few splendid phrases, such as "The deeds of Kings, great Captains, and sad wars," strangely demonstrates for the most part what poetry is not, and, as a later translator, Henry Ames, protests in 1727, "has trod so close upon the Heels of Horace, that he has not only crampt, but made him halt in (almost) every line." The Earl of Roscommon's translation (1680) in blank verse gives the sense but little else. And so also it is generally with the Odes. Among the more or less complete translations are those of Sir Thomas Hawkins (1625, with later enlarged editions), Thomas Creech (1684), and miscellanies such as Alexander Brome's (1666), and Jacob Tomson's (1715), containing translations by various hands. In later days we have W. Sewell (1850), John Conington (1863–1869), and Sir Theodore Martin (1860). Scattered about these volumes are several beautiful versions of different poems, reasonably faithful to the original, and many more striking passages or stanzas. Now we get Hawkins with

> no lot shall gaine
> Thee a King's Title in a Taverne-raigne;

and then Richard Fanshawe with

> What Stripling now thee discomposes
> In Woodbine Rooms, on Beds of Roses,

and again Creech, mildly, with

> But now I do repent the wrong
> And now compose a softer Song
>   To make Thee just amends.
> Recant the errors of my Youth
> And swear those scandals were not Truth;
>   So You and I be friends.

Conington is, perhaps, the most consistently attractive of them all, and he does make many of the Odes into charming English verse. He often strikes the note as surely as in

> O lovelier than the lovely dame
>   That bore you, sentence as you please
> Those scurril verses, be it flame
>   Your vengeance craves, or Hadrian seas;

and no less an authority than Mr. A. E. Housman tells me that he considers Conington's to be the best English translations that he knows of Horace, and as among the best verse translations in the language.

Branwell Brontë's translations of the *First Book of Odes* need, at their best, fear comparison with none. They are not so uniformly good as Conington's, and there are the ugly blemishes here and there of which I have spoken. "Than thee" (XXIV.) is a lapse of a less unpleasant kind than "gushing gore " (II.), "swells my liver" and "boisterous bite " (XIII.). Also, I think he occasionally mistranslates, as in XIX. and XX., in the one of which he seems to be confused as to the women and in the other as to the wines. Sometimes, too, he chooses a bad measure, as in XII. and XXXII., sometimes he is unexpectedly halting, as in XXXI., and again flat or dull or heavy as in XXVI., XXIX., XXXV., and XXXVII. Then there are other cases where he just manages good average verse, making it more interesting on the whole than most of his competitors; XXVIII. is an instance. There remain more than half the Odes, of which it may be said that they are excellent in themselves, and as good as any English versions that I know, including Conington's. In a few instances I should say that they are decidedly the best of all. It is not only in frequent passages that Branwell sings with the right lyric ease, as in

> Yet – shuddering too at poverty
>   Again he seeks that very sea –

and

> If but Euterpe yield to me
> Her thrilling pipe of melody,
> If Polyhymnia but inspire
> My spirit with her Lesbian lyre.
>   Oh ! Give thy friend a poet's name
> And heaven shall hardly bound his fame;

and

> O! brightest of his phalanx bright!
> With shining shoulders veiled from sight,
>   Descend, Apollo Thou!

and many others (e.g., the opening lines of the last stanza of IV.), but in some whole poems, as in the lovely rendering of XXI., there is hardly a flaw from beginning to end. At his best he has melody and phrase, and he builds his stanzas well. Further, he was happier in verse with Horace's subject-matter than he generally was with the experience of his own confused and frustrated life. I do not wish to advance any extravagant claim for this little book, but I think it adds appreciably to the evidence that Branwell Brontë was the second poet in his family, and a very good second at that, and that it leaves no justification for anyone again to say that he "composed nothing which gives him the slightest claim to the most inconsiderable niche in the temple of literature."

> –*A Book for Bookmen: Being Edited Manuscripts &*
> *Marginalia with Essays on Several Occasions,*
> pp. 43–45, 53–59

The Leylands and the Literary Legacy of Branwell Brontë

One of Branwell's closest friends was a talented Halifax sculptor named Joseph Leyland (1811–1851). Leyland and his younger brother Francis A. Leyland (1813–1894), who published the Halifax Guardian *for a period, were active in the artistic and literary community in the Halifax area where Branwell worked on the railways 1840–1842. Branwell's letters to Joseph, including several poems, were saved by Francis after Joseph's death in 1851, and were later published in* The Brontë Family with Special Reference to Patrick Branwell Brontë, *a version of the Brontë story that he hoped would correct the depiction of Branwell as alcoholic ne'er-do-well in* Elizabeth Gaskell's Life of Charlotte Brontë *and Mary F. Robinson's* Emily Brontë. *Branwell's letters and poems to Leyland were later edited and printed in* Patrick Branwell Brontë: A Complete Transcript of the Leyland Manuscripts *(1925), following Edward Brotherton's purchase of the collection from Francis Leyland.*

Branwell and Lydia Robinson

In January 1843 Branwell was hired as tutor to the son of Reverend Edmund Robinson, whose family Anne Brontë had been serving as a governess since May 1840. At some point during the two-and-a-half years Branwell worked at Thorp Green he fell in love with Reverend Robinson's wife, Lydia Robinson (1799–1859), who when they met was forty-four years old, seventeen years his senior. The attraction between Branwell and Mrs. Robinson became known within the household, but it is unclear if it evolved into an affair. In any event, Branwell was dismissed by Reverend Robinson in June or July 1845, soon after Anne resigned from her post as governess.

From 1845 to his death in September 1848, Branwell became increasingly addicted to alcohol and probably opiates as well. His psychological deterioration—which Charlotte refers to as his "illness" in letters to Ellen Nussey—deeply disturbed his sisters and father. During this period Branwell continued to write and was working on a novel, "And the Weary are at Rest," of which portions survive. The novel featured Alexander Percy and Maria Thurston, characters from Branwell's earlier writings. In this excerpt from The Brontë Family, *Francis Leyland comments upon and quotes a letter Branwell wrote to his friend Joseph Leyland in the aftermath of his dismissal from Thorp Green. In the beginning of his letter Branwell refers to a mishap that had occurred to the monument Joseph was working on.*

Branwell's Projected Novel
Francis A. Leyland

Branwell . . . resolved, soon after a visit to his friend Leyland,—whom he found engaged upon a tomb and recumbent statue of the late Doctor Stephen Beckwith, a benefactor to several public institutions in York, to be erected in the Minster there,—to make an effort to arouse himself. With the desire, then, of finding an absorbing occupation for his mind, by which he might be able to lay the tempest of the heart, the whirlwind of wounded vanity, of injured self-esteem, and of blighted hope, which swept through his mind in hours of reflection, and drove him to distraction of desperation, he turned, with the resolution of a new-born energy, engendered of despair, to literary composition. He proposed to himself to depict, as best he could, in a fictitious form, and as an ordinary novel, which should extend to three volumes, the different feelings that work in the human soul. The necessary labour which this undertaking involved, gave a stimulus to his ambition, which for a time was sustained; and he evidently hoped that he might yet be able to make a place for himself in the busy world of letters. At this time the novels of his sisters were not in existence, and probably had scarcely been dreamed of. Char-

Silhouette of Branwell Brontë (from Clement K. Shorter, Charlotte Brontë and Her Circle, *University of Colorado at Boulder Library)*

lotte had not yet lighted on the volume of verse in the handwriting of Emily, and the literary future of the sisters had still to dawn upon them. Yet Branwell, whose behaviour had given them cause enough for disquietude, and whose sorrows were embittering his mind, had now braced himself up for an object which they had not attempted, and to the accomplishment of which he looked forward with something like confidence. In the following letter to his friend Leyland, he discloses his design; and it is probably that in this we have almost all the direct light upon it which can be found:

'Haworth, Sept. 10th, 1845.
'My dear Sir,

'I was certainly sadly disappointed at not having seen you on the Friday you named for your visit, but the cause you allege for not arriving was justifiable with a vengeance. I should have been as cracked as my cast had I entered a room and seen the labour of weeks or months destroyed (apparently—not, I trust, really) in a moment.

'That vexation is, I hope, over; and I build upon your renewed promise of a visit; for no thing cheers me so much as the company of one whom I believe to be a *man,* and who has known care well enough to be able to appreciate the discomfort of another who knows it *too* well.

'Never mind the lines I put into your hands, but come hither with them, and, if they should have been lost out of your pocket on the way, I won't grumble, provided you are present to apologize for the accident.

'I have, since I saw you at Halifax, devoted my hours of time, snatched from downright illness, to the composition of a three-volume *novel,* one volume of which is completed, and, along with the two forthcoming ones, has been really the result of half-a-dozen by-past years of thoughts about, and experience in, this crooked path of life.

'I felt that I must rouse myself to attempt something while roasting daily and nightly over a slow fire, to while away my torments; and I knew that, in the present state of the publishing and reading world, a novel is the most saleable article, so that—where ten pounds would be offered for a work, the production of which would require the utmost stretch of a man's intellect— two hundred pounds would be a refused offer for three volumes, whose composition would require the smoking of a cigar and the humming of a tune.

'My novel is the result of years of thought; and, if it gives a vivid picture of human feelings for good and evil, veiled by the cloak of deceit which must enwrap man and woman; if it records, as faithfully as the pages that unveil man's heart in "Hamlet" or "Lear," the conflicting feelings and clashing pursuits in our uncertain path through life, I shall be as much gratified (and as much astonished) as I should be if, in betting that I could jump over the Mersey, I jumped over the Irish Sea. It would not be more pleasant to light on Dublin instead of Birkenhead, than to leap from the present bathos of fictitious literature to the firmly-fixed rock honoured by the foot of a Smollett or a Fielding.

'That jump I expect to take when I can model a rival to your noble Theseus, who haunted my dreams when I slept after seeing him. But, meanwhile, I can try my utmost to rouse myself from almost killing cares, and that alone will be its own reward.

'Tell me when I may hope to see you, and believe me, dear sir,

'Yours,

'P. B. Brontë'

A spirited sketch in pen-and-ink concludes this letter; it represents a bust of himself thrown down, and the lady of his admiration holding forth her hands towards it with an air of pity, while underneath it is the sentence: 'A cast, cast down, but not cast away!'

We have in this letter an instance of Branwell's general coherency under his disappointment, in which the elegance and freedom of his style of composition are combined with a consequent and logical arrangement of the various parts of his subject; but he cannot help concluding his letter with a direct allusion to the lady, whom he believes,—all evidence to the contrary not withstanding,—to love him with undiminished devotion. Under this fascination he still hopes for the prosperity and happiness of which he had before spoken to his friends.

—*The Brontë Family with Special Reference to Patrick Branwell Brontë,* v. 2, pp. 80–85

* * *

Branwell gave various accounts of what had happened with Mrs. Robinson. This excerpt is from a letter to a civil engineer and railway surveyor whom Branwell had met when he worked at Sowerby Bridge. Branwell's claim that Reverend Robinson's will forbade his wife from marrying Branwell was incorrect.

Branwell Brontë to Francis H. Grundy, October 1845

I fear you will burn my present letter on recognising the handwriting; but if you will read it through, you will perhaps rather pity than spurn the distress of mind which could prompt my communication, after a silence of nearly three (to me) eventful years. While very ill and confined to my room, I wrote to you two months ago, hearing that you were resident engineer of the Skipton Railway, to the inn at Skipton. I never received any reply, and as my letter asked only for one day of your society, to ease a very weary mind in the company of a friend who <u>always</u> had what I always wanted, but most want now, <u>cheerfulness</u>, I am sure you never received my letter, or your heart would have prompted an answer.

Since I last shook hands with you in Halifax, two summers ago, my life till lately has been one of apparent happiness and indulgence. You will ask, 'Why does he complain, then?' I can only reply by showing the under-current of distress which bore my bark to a whirlpool, despite the surface waves of life that seemed floating me to peace. In a letter begun in the spring of [?1844 or 1845] and never finished owing to incessant attacks of illness, I tried to tell you that I was tutor to the son of [Revd. Edmund Robinson], a wealthy gentleman whose wife is sister to the wife of [William Evans], M.P. for the county of [Derbyshire], and the cousin of

Lord [?Goderich]. This lady (though her husband detested me) showed me a degree of kindness which, when I was deeply grieved one day at her husband's conduct, ripened into declarations of more than ordinary feeling. My admiration of her mental and personal attractions, my knowledge of her unselfish sincerity, her sweet temper, and unwearied care for others, with but unrequited return where most should have been given, ... although she is seventeen years my senior, all combined to an attachment on my part, and led to reciprocations which I had little looked for. During nearly three years I had daily 'troubled pleasure, soon chastised by fear.' Three months since I received a furious letter from my employer, threatening to shoot me if I returned from my vacation, which I was passing at home; and letters from her lady's-maid and physician informed me of the outbreak, only checked by her firm courage and resolution that whatever harm came to her, none should come to me . . . . I have lain during nine long weeks utterly shattered in body and broken down in mind. The probability of her becoming free to give me herself and estate never rose to drive away the prospect of her decline under her present grief. I dreaded, too, the wreck of my mind and body, which, God knows, during a short life have been severely tried. Eleven continuous nights of sleepless horror reduced me to almost blindness, and being taken into Wales to recover, the sweet scenery, the sea, the sound of music caused me fits of unspeakable distress. You will say,

'What a fool!' but if you knew the many causes I have for sorrow which I cannot even hint at here, you would perhaps pity as well as blame. At the kind request of Mr. Macaulay and Mr. Baines, I have striven to arouse my mind by writing something worthy of being read, but I really cannot do so. Of course you will despise the writer of all this. I can only answer that the writer does the same, and would not wish to live if he did not hope that work and change may yet restore him.
    —*The Letters of Charlotte Brontë*, v. 1, pp. 427–428

* * *

Branwell enclosed a copy of his poem "Penmaenmawr," which was published in the Halifax Guardian *20 December 1845, with this letter.*

Patrick Brontë to Joseph Leyland,
25 November 1845

'My dear Sir,
    'I send you the enclosed, — and I ought to tell you why I wished anything of so personal a nature to appear in print.

Patrick Branwell Brontë.

"I have seen Branwell's profile: it is what would be generally esteemed very handsome; the forehead is massive, the eye well set, and the expression of it fine and intellectual; the nose, too, is good; but there are coarse lines about the mouth, and the lips, though of handsome shape, are loose and thick, indicating self-indulgence, while the slightly retreating chin conveys an idea of weakness of will. His hair and complexion were sandy."—Mrs. Gaskell's "Life of Charlotte Brontë."
(Reproduced by kind permission of Mr. Clement K. Shorter.)

A medallion of Patrick Branwell Brontë made by his friend, sculptor Joseph Leyland (1811–1851) in 1845 (from The Bookman, *October 1904, Colorado College Library)*

A Brief Inquiry

Even after his dismissal from the railroad in 1842, Branwell sought employment there again. He wrote this letter to a solicitor associated with the railway company in late October 1845, when he was back in Haworth after he lost his position with the Robinsons.

Dear Sir,

    I respectfully beg leave to offer myself as candidate for the situation of Secretary to the Manchester and Hebden Bridge and Keighley and Carlisle Junction Railway.

    I trust to be able to produce full testimonials as to my qualifications and Securities, if required, to any probable amount.

                I am,
                    Dear Sir,
                        Your most respectful and
                        obdt Servt,
                            P. B. Brontë
    —*The Letters of Charlotte Brontë*, v. 1, p. 231

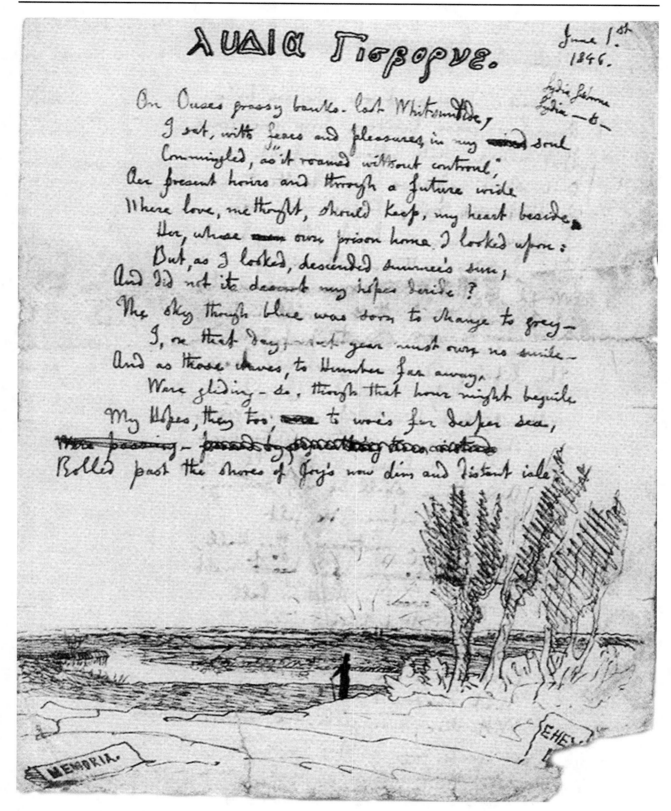

A poem Branwell wrote about his love for Mrs. Robinson. The Greek letters spell out Lydia Gisborne. Branwell frequently incorporated sketches into his letters and poems (Brontë Society, Brontë Parsonage Museum BS 128).

'I have no other way, not pregnant with danger, of communicating with one whom I cannot help loving. Printed lines, with my usual signature, "Northanger-land," could excite no suspicion–as my late unhappy employer shrank from the bare idea of my being able to write anything, and had a day's sickness after hearing that Macaulay had sent me a complimentary letter; so *he* won't know the name.

'I sent through a private channel one letter of comfort in her great and agonizing present afflictions, but I recalled it through dread of the consequences of a discovery.

'These lines have only one merit,–that of really expressing my feelings, while sailing under the Welsh mountain, when the band on board the steamer struck up, "Ye banks and braes!" God knows that, for many different reasons, those feelings were far enough from pleasure.

'I suffer very much from that mental exhaustion which arises from brooding on matters useless at present to think of, – and active employment would be my greatest cure and blessing,– for really, after hours of thoughts which business would have hushed, I have felt as if I could not live, and, if long continued, such a state will bring on permanent affection of the heart, which is already bothered with most uneasy palpitations.

'I should like extremely to have an hour's sitting with you, and, if I had the chance, I would promise to try not to look gloomy. You said you would be at Haworth ere long, but that "ere" has doubtless changed to "ne'er;" so I must wish to get to Halifax some time to see you.

'I saw Murray's monument praised in the papers, and I trust you are getting on well with Beckwith's, as well as with your own personal statue of living flesh and blood.

'Mine, like your Theseus, has lost its hands and feet, and I fear its head also, for it can neither move, write, nor think as it once could.

'I hope I shall hear from you on John Brown's return from Halifax, whither he has gone.

'I remain, &c.,

'P. B. Brontë'

– The Brontë Family with Special Reference to Patrick Branwell Brontë, v. 2, pp. 99–101

* * *

This excerpt is from a letter written after Reverend Robinson's death at Thorp Green on 26 May 1846. The "news from all hands" respecting Reverend Robinson's alteration of his will was evidently an inaccurate rumor.

Charlotte Brontë to Ellen Nussey, 17 June 1846

We–I am sorry to say have been somewhat more harrassed than usual lately–The death of Mr Robinson–which took place about three weeks or a month ago–served Branwell for a pretext to throw all about him into hubbub and confusion with his emotions–&c. &c. Shortly after came news from all hands that Mr Robinson had altered his will before he died and effectually prevented all chance of a marriage between his widow and Branwell by stipulating that she should not have a shilling if she ever ventured to reopen any communication with him–Of course he then became intolerable–to papa he allows rest neither day nor night and he is continually screwing money out of him sometimes threatening that he will kill himself if it is withheld from him–He says Mrs R–is now insane–that her mind is a complete wreck–owing to remorse for her conduct towards Mr R– (whose end it appears was hastened by distress of mind)–and grief for having lost him.

I do not know how much to believe of what he says but I fear she is very ill–Branwell declares now that he neither can nor will do anything for himself–good situations have been offered more than once–for which by a fortnight's work he might have qualified himself–but he will do nothing–except drink, and make us all wretched–

Do not say a word about this to any one dear Ellen–I know no one but yourself to whom I would communicate it–

– The Letters of Charlotte Brontë, v. 1, pp. 477–478

* * *

In the first edition of The Life of Charlotte Brontë, *Elizabeth Gaskell characterized the relationship between Branwell and Mrs. Robinson in such a vivid and judgmental way that Lydia Robinson (by this time remarried and known as Lady Scott) threatened to sue; as a result, lawyers for George Smith's firm published a retraction on page 5 of the 30 May 1857 issue of* The Times *alongside a letter from Lady Scott's lawyers stating that they "accept the apology" and understood that "the statements of Mrs. Gaskell were, as you say, made upon information which at the time Mrs. Gaskell believed to be well founded." In subsequent editions of the biography, portions of these descriptions were cut.*

This excerpt begins with a reference to the Brontë sisters' acknowledgment of the failure of their plan to start their own school.

"This Mature and Wicked Woman"
Elizabeth Gaskell

There were, probably, growing up in each sister's heart, secret unacknowledged feelings of relief,

Lydia Robinson, whom Mrs. Gaskell vilified in her biography of Charlotte (from Juliet Barker, The Brontës, *Thomas Cooper Library, University of South Carolina)*

no temporary remorse, however keen—could make him shake off the infatuation that bound him.

The story must be told. If I could, I would have avoided it; but not merely is it so well-known to many living as to be, in a manner, public property, but it is possible that, by revealing the misery, the gnawing, life-long misery, the degrading habits, the early death of her partner in guilt—the acute and long-enduring agony of his family—to the wretched woman, who not only survives, but passes about in the gay circles of London society, as a vivacious, well-dressed, flourishing widow, there may be awakened in her some feelings of repentance.

Branwell, I have mentioned, had obtained a situation as a private tutor. Full of available talent, a brilliant talker, a good writer, apt at drawing, ready of appreciation, and with a not unhandsome person, he took the fancy of a married woman, nearly twenty years older than himself. It is no excuse for him to say that she began the first advances, and "made love" to him. She was so bold and hardened, that she did it in the very presence of her children, fast approaching to maturity; and they would threaten her that, if she did not grant them such and such indulgences, they would tell their bed-ridden father "how she went on with Mr. Brontë." He was so beguiled by this mature and wicked woman, that he went home for his holidays reluctantly, stayed there as short a time as possible, perplexing and distressing them all by his extraordinary conduct—at one time in the highest spirits, at another, in the deepest depression—accusing himself of blackest guilt and treachery, without specifying what they were; and altogether evincing an irritability of disposition bordering on insanity.

Charlotte and her sister suffered acutely from his mysterious behaviour. He expressed himself more than satisfied with his situation; he was remaining in it for a longer time than he had ever done in any kind of employment before; so they could not conjecture that anything there made him so wilful, and restless, and full of both levity and misery. But a sense of something wrong connected with him, sickened and oppressed them. They began to lose all hope in his future career. He was no longer the family pride; an indistinct dread was creeping over their minds that he might turn out their deep disgrace. But, I believe, they shrank from any attempt to define their fears, and spoke of him to each other as little as possible. They could not help but think, and mourn, and wonder.

—*The Life of Charlotte Brontë,* v. 1, pp. 315–318

that their plan had not succeeded. Yes! a dull sense of relief that their cherished project had been tried and had failed. For that house, which was to be regarded as an occasional home for their brother, could hardly be a fitting residence for the children of strangers. They had, in all likelihood, become silently aware that his habits were such as to render his society at times most undesirable. Possibly, too, they had, by this time, heard distressing rumours concerning the cause of that remorse and agony of mind, which at times made him restless and unnaturally merry, at times rendered him moody and irritable.

In January, 1845, Charlotte says: —"Branwell has been quieter and less irritable, on the whole, this time than he was in summer. Anne is, as usual, always good, mild, and patient." The deep-seated pain which he was to occasion to his relations had now taken a decided form, and pressed heavily on Charlotte's health and spirits. Early in this year, she went to H. to bid good-bye to her dear friend Mary, who was leaving England for Australia. But a weight hung over her—the gloom preceding the full knowledge of sin in which her brother was an accomplice; which was dragging him down to confirmed habits of intemperance; yet by which he was so bewitched, that no remonstrance, however stern, on the part of others—

* * *

In the following excerpts, Leyland calls attention to the inconsistencies in the accounts Mrs. Gaskell relies upon, and offers his own view of what he calls Branwell's "strange passion." Leyland refers to T. Wemyss Reid's Charlotte Brontë *(1877), which used the letters and recollections supplied by Ellen Nussey.*

"Too Fond of Company"
Francis A. Leyland

The biographer of Charlotte, having obtained her information from the floating rumours of Haworth, formed an inconsiderate, erroneous, and hasty opinion on this affair and its supposed consequences. But she found many circumstances, in the proceedings of Branwell and his sisters which failed to corroborate her views, and that were, in fact, at variance with what would naturally have been expected had Branwell's misconduct really been of so deep a dye as she states. In order to bring out fully the force of what she here says, Mrs. Gaskell had, previously, as we have seen, in speaking of Charlotte's stay in Brussels eighteen months before, alluded to intelligence from home calculated to distress Charlotte exceedingly with fears respecting Branwell. Yet, in the January of 1844, shortly after her return from Brussels, Charlotte told her friend 'E' that Anne and Branwell were 'both wonderfully valued in their situations.' And again, writing of the year 1845, Mrs. Gaskell says: 'He was so beguiled by this mature and wicked woman, that he went home for his holidays reluctantly, stayed there as short a time as possible, perplexing and distressing them all by his extraordinary conduct—at one time in the highest spirits; at another, in the deepest depression—accusing himself of blackest guilt and treachery, without specifying what they were; and altogether evincing an irritability of disposition bordering on insanity. Charlotte and her sister suffered acutely from his mysterious behaviour . . . . an indistinct dread was creeping over their minds that he might turn out their deep disgrace." And it must be added that, when in the expurgated edition the opening of this passage was omitted, Mrs. Gaskell inserted—following where she ascribes to the sisters an ' indistinct dread,'— these words : 'caused partly by his own conduct, partly by expressions of agonizing suspicion in Anne's letters home.' But we know, from Charlotte's letter to her friend, that, when she had returned home and found Branwell ill, which she says he was often, she was not therefore shocked at first, but, when Anne informed her of the immediate cause of his present illness, she was very greatly shocked, showing clearly enough that Branwell's dismissal and its cause were a complete surprise to her

when she heard of them. How, then, could Anne's letters home have contained expressions of 'agonizing suspicion'?

Mrs. Gaskell found it necessary to summarize the portion of Charlotte's letter which contained these expressions of surprise, and, in her version, significantly enough, the obvious inconsistency is lost. The succeeding part also has suffered mutilation in Mrs. Gaskell's work, Charlotte's allusion to Branwell's 'frantic folly,' and the sentence, 'He promises amendment on his return,' being entirely omitted. Mr. Wemyss Reid, in publishing this letter, points out the circumstance, and says that 'Mrs. Gaskell could not bring herself to speak of such flagrant sins as those of which young Brontë had been guilty under the name of folly, nor could she conceive that there was any possibility of amendment on the part of one who had fallen so low in vice.' And, if we disregard Mrs. Gaskell's view of 'what *should have been*' Charlotte's feelings, and read the letter with the real state of the case before us, we shall at once see that, as Branwell had not fallen low in vice, the term 'frantic folly,' which his sister employed in speaking of his conduct, was precisely that which justly described it.

The simple truth respecting Branwell's conduct is this: he had been too fond of company and had not escaped its penalty. Doubtless Anne occasionally saw influences upon her brother which she would have wished entirely absent. Moreover he had, as we have seen, become wildly in love. Reluctantly at first, and, from what we know of him, he may, probably, in his latest vacation have accused himself of 'blackest guilt.' But there is reason to believe that on this episode, as on others connected with Branwell Brontë, we have been told not a little of what *must have ensued* from a standpoint of initial error.

Of the principal accusations which Mrs. Gaskell brings against Mrs. — I shall have to speak when I come to consider the consequences to Branwell of the final defeat of his hopes; but it may be said here that it is clear the lady never wrote letters to Branwell at all. She carefully avoided doing anything that might implicate her in the matter of Branwell's strange passion, and, so far as any provision of the husband's will, which was dated near the end the year, is concerned, Branwell Brontë might never have existed. Mrs. Gaskell cannot have seen the document.

—*The Brontë Family with Special Reference to Patrick Branwell Brontë, v. 2, pp. 64–68*

"The Sudden Early Obscure Close"

At the time of his death at the age of thirty-one on 24 September 1848, Branwell Brontë was probably suffering from pulmonary tuberculosis as well as the effects of his addictions. The official cause of death was listed as "Chronic bronchitis—Marasmus" (chronic wasting). He was buried in the vault in Haworth church.

Charlotte here writes of Branwell's death to the reader at Smith, Elder who first recognized her talent as a writer.

Charlotte Brontë to William Smith Williams, 2 October 1848

My dear Sir

"We have buried our dead out of our sight." A lull begins to succeed the gloomy tumult of last week. It is not permitted us to grieve for him who is gone as others grieve for those they lose; the removal of our only brother must necessarily be regarded by us rather in the light of a mercy than a chastisement. Branwell was his Father's and his sisters' pride and hope in boyhood, but since Manhood, the case has been otherwise. It has been our lot to see him take a wrong bent; to hope, expect, wait his return to the right path; to know the sickness of hope deferred, the dismay of prayer baffled, to experience despair at last; and now to behold the sudden early obscure close of what might have been a noble career.

I do not weep from a sense of bereavement—there is no prop withdrawn, no consolation torn away, no dear companion lost—but for the wreck of talent, the ruin of promise, the untimely, dreary extinction of what might have been a burning and a shining light. My brother was a year my junior; I had aspirations and ambitions for him once—long ago—they have perished mournfully— nothing remains of him but a memory of errors and sufferings—There is such a bitterness of pity for his life and death—such a yearning for the emptiness of his whole existence as I cannot describe—I trust time will allay these feelings.

My poor Father naturally thought more of his only son than of his daughters, and much and long as he had suffered on his account—he cried out for his loss like David for that of Absalom—My Son! My Son! And refused at first to be comforted—and then—when I ought to have been able to collect my strength, and be at hand to support him—I fell ill with an illness whose approaches I had felt for some time previously—and of which the crisis was hastened by the awe and trouble of the death-scene—the first I had ever witnessed. The past has seemed to me a strange week—Thank God—for my Father's sake—I am better now—though still feeble—I wish indeed I had more general physical strength—the

want of it is sadly in my way. I cannot do what I would do, for want of sustained animal spirits—and efficient bodily vigour.

My unhappy brother never knew what his sisters had done in literature—he was not aware that they had ever published a line; we could not tell him of our efforts for fear of causing him too deep a pang of remorse for his own time misspent, and talents misapplied—Now he will <u>never</u> know. I cannot dwell longer on the subject at present; it is too painful.

I thank you for your kind sympathy—and pray earnestly that your sons may all do well and that you may be spared the sufferings my Father has gone through.

Yours sincerely
C Brontë

—The Letters of Charlotte Brontë, v. 2, pp. 122–123

* * *

In this excerpt Charlotte reflects on the first death-scene she witnessed. In the moments right before Branwell died, he rose up to his feet.

Charlotte Brontë to William Smith Williams, 6 October 1848

When I looked on the noble face and forehead of my dead brother (Nature had favoured him with a fairer outside, as well as a finer constitution than his Sisters) and asked myself what had made him go ever wrong, tend ever downwards, when he had so many gifts to induce to, and aid in an upward course—I seemed to receive an oppressive revelation of the feebleness of humanity; of the inadequacy of even genius to lead to true greatness if unaided by religion and principle. In the value, or even the reality of these two things he would never believe till within a few days of his end, and then all at once he seemed to open his heart to a conviction of their existence and worth. The remembrance of this strange change now comforts my poor Father greatly. I myself, with painful, mournful joy, heard him praying softly in his dying moments, and to the last prayer which my father offered up at his bedside, he added "amen". How unusual that word appeared from his lips—of course you who did not know him, cannot conceive. Akin to this alteration was that in his feelings towards his relatives—all bitterness seemed gone.

When the struggle was over—and a marble calm began to succeed the last dread agony—I felt as I had never felt before that there was peace and forgiveness for him in Heaven. All his errors—to speak plainly—all his vices seemed nothing to me in that moment; every

A sketch Branwell sent to his friend Joseph Leyland in 1842. "Resurgam" translates as "I will rise again"; at the end of chapter 9 in Jane Eyre,
Jane notes that "Resurgam" is written on Helen Burns's gravestone (The Brotherton Collection, Leeds University Library;
from Christine Alexander and Jane Sellars, The Art of the Brontës, University of Colorado Libraries).

wrong he had done, every pain he had caused, vanished; his sufferings only were remembered; the wrench to the natural affections only was felt. If Man can thus experience total oblivion of his fellow's imperfection—how much more can the Eternal Being who made man, forgive his creature!

Had his sins been scarlet in their dye—I believe now they are white as wool—He is at rest—and that comforts us all long before he quitted this world—Life had no happiness for him.

—The Letters of Charlotte Brontë, v. 2, pp. 123–124

* * *

Charlotte recalled the pain caused by watching her brother destroy himself in these excerpts from a letter to publisher George Smith, who had sent her lectures by William Makepeace Thackeray.

Charlotte Brontë to George Smith, May 1853

The Lectures arrived safely; I have read them through twice. They must be studied to be appreciated. I thought well of them when I heard them delivered, but now I see their real power, and it is great. . . . Against his errors I protest, were it treason to do so. I was present at the Fielding lecture: the hour spent in listening to it was a painful hour. That Thackeray was

wrong in his way of treating Fielding's character and vices, my conscience told me. After reading that lecture, I trebly felt that he was wrong—dangerously wrong. Had Thackeray owned a son, grown, or growing up, and a son, brilliant but reckless—would he have spoken in that light way of courses that lead to disgrace and the grave? He speaks of it all as if he theorised; as if he had never been called on, in the course of his life, to witness the actual consequences of such failings; as if he had never stood by and seen the issue, the final result of it all. I believe, if only once the prospect of a promising life blasted on the outset by wild ways had passed close under his eyes, he never *could* have spoken with such levity of what led to its piteous destruction. Had I a brother yet living, I should tremble to let him read Thackeray's lecture on Fielding. I should hide it away from him. If, in spite of precaution, it should fall into his hands, I should earnestly pray him not to be misled by the voice of the charmer, let him charm never so wisely. Not that for a moment I would have had Thackeray to *abuse* Fielding, or even Pharisaically to condemn his life; but I do most deeply grieve that it never entered into his heart sadly and nearly to feel the peril of such a career, that he might have dedicated some of his great strength to a potent warning against its adoption by any young man. I believe temptation often assails the finest manly natures; as the pecking sparrow or destructive wasp attacks the sweetest and mellowest fruit, eschewing what is sour and crude. The true lover of his race ought to devote his vigour to guard and protect; he should sweep away every lure with a kind of rage at its treachery. You will think this far too serious, I dare say; but the subject is serious, and one cannot help feeling upon it earnestly.

— *The Life of Charlotte Brontë*, v. 2, pp. 292–293

* * *

This is the conclusion to Leyland's The Brontë Family with Special Reference to Patrick Branwell Brontë.

"Not Seldom Wronged"
Francis A. Leyland

The wild places of the earth, mountains and moorlands, where the storms raged, and the great winds blew, were nearest akin to the Titanic genius of Branwell and Emily. Thus, in the sonnet, the everlasting majesty of Black Comb was held up by Branwell as an example to man, and as a contrast to human feebleness; and later, when his woe was most acute, he was drawn into a 'communion of vague unity' with Penmaenmawr, comparing the living, beating heart of man with the stony hill, and begging,

'Let me, like it, arise o'er mortal care,
All woes sustain, yet never know despair,
Unshrinking face the griefs I now deplore,
And stand through storm and shine like moveless Penmaenmawr.'

And, lastly, in the 'Epistle from a Father to a Child in her Grave,' we find him comparing himself with one in the midst of wild mountains

'I, thy life's source, was like a wanderer breasting
Keen mountain winds, and on a summit resting,
Whose rough rocks rise above the grassy mead,
With sleet and north winds howling overhead.'

It will be seen from this short inquiry that the poetry of Branwell Brontë was entirely introspective, having, almost to the last line, some direct reference to his own thoughts or feelings; and that it may thus be read as an actual part of the story of his life. The disposition it reveals, though often hidden, as the readers of this book know, through the effects of folly and indulgence, was one of a singularly gentle, affectionate, and sympathetic character passionate and unstable, it is true, but a disposition, nevertheless, that has been frequently misunderstood, and not seldom wronged. One of the aims of this book has been to set Patrick Branwell Brontë right with the public; an attempt, not to clear him from follies and weaknesses that really were his— which the public, but for the mistakes of biographers, would never have known—but to show that, at any rate, his nature was one rather to be admired than condemned. It has aimed also, by the publication of his poetical writings, to demonstrate that his genius is not unworthy to be ranked with that which made his sisters famous. Yet it may, perhaps, be held that the poems here published contain more of rich promise than of real fulfilment, rather the earnest of literary success than the actual accomplishment of it. But, in reading the poetry of Branwell Brontë, which is so uniformly sad, it may be well to remember what Mr. Swinburne has said, in speaking of Mr. Browning, that 'to do justice to any book which deserves any other sort of justice than that of the fire or waste-paper basket, it is necessary to read it in a fit frame of mind.'

— *The Brontë Family with Special Reference to Patrick Branwell Brontë*, v. 2, pp. 300–302

Anne Brontë

Anne Brontë (1820–1849) was the youngest of the six Brontë children. Her mother died when she was only seventeen months old, and her mother's sister, "Aunt Branwell," who helped to raise the children until her own death in 1842, became a surrogate mother to her. Too young to attend the Clergy Daughters' School at Cowan Bridge, Anne was five years old when her two eldest sisters came home to die in 1825 after studying there. Like Charlotte and Emily, Anne was educated by her father and Aunt Branwell for much of her childhood. At age fifteen in October 1835, she took Emily's place as student at Miss Wooler's School at Roe Head and studied there until December 1837, when illness required her to return home for a period. In 1839 Anne began her career as a governess, which provided experiences that influenced her two novels, Agnes Grey *(1847) and* The Tenant of Wildfell Hall *(1848).*

During her brief life and writing career, Anne Brontë stood in the shadow of her older sisters, particularly of Charlotte, whose impressions of her youngest sister and estimation of what she regarded as her limited literary gifts defined critics' views of Anne throughout the nineteenth century. While Anne has remained "the other Brontë"—often ignored and held to be a writer of much less importance than either Charlotte or Emily—she is more highly esteemed in the twenty-first century for her nascent feminism and acute social observation than she was during her own time.

Anne on Her Own

In April 1839 Anne began the first of two positions as governess she held for most of her working life. Her initial post was for the Ingham family at Blake Hall, Mirfield, approximately eighteen miles to the southeast of Haworth. Charlotte described Anne's early experiences with the family in this excerpt. Anne left the Inghams in December 1839, having probably been dismissed by them for being unable to control the children sufficiently to educate them.

Charlotte Brontë to Ellen Nussey, 15 April 1839

I could not well write to you in the week you requested as about that time we were very busy in preparing for Anne's departure—poor child! She left us last Monday no one went with her—it was her

Anne Brontë, as portrayed by her sister Charlotte in a watercolor, 17 June 1834 (Brontë Parsonage Museum; from The Bookman, *October 1904, Colorado College Library)*

own wish that she might be allowed to go alone—as she thought she could manage better and summon more courage if thrown entirely upon her own ressources. We have had one letter from her since she went—she expressed herself very well satisfied—and says that Mrs. Ingham is extremely kind, the two eldest children alone are under her care, the rest are confined to the nursery—with which and its occupants she has nothing to do. both her pupils are desperate little dunces—neither of them can read and sometimes they even profess a profound ignorance of their alphabet. the worst of it is the little monkies are excessively indulged and she is not empowered to inflict any punishment. she is requested when they misbehave themselves to inform their Mamma—which she says is utterly out of the question as in that case she might be making complaints from morning till night—"So she alternately scolds, coaxes and threatens—sticks always to her first word and gets on as well as she can"—I hope she'll do, you would be astonished to see what a sensible, clever letter she writes—it is only the talking part that I fear—but I do seriously apprehend that Mrs Ingham will sometimes conclude that she has a natural impediment of speech.

—*The Letters of Charlotte Brontë*, v. 1, p. 189

* * *

Anne began working for her second family, the Robinsons of Thorp Green, near York, some seventy miles to the west of Haworth, in May 1840—a post she continued in for five years.

Anne and Emily had agreed to open their previous "diary paper," which they had written together in 1837, on Emily's birthday in 1841. As it happened, the sisters were separated at the time, as Anne was staying in the coastal resort of Scarborough with the Robinson family. She proceeded to write a new diary paper on her own. None of Anne's writings that she mentions have survived.

Diary Paper, 30 July 1841
Anne Brontë

This is Emily's birthday. She has now completed her 23rd year, and is, I believe, at home. Charlotte is a governess in the family of Mr. White. Branwell is a clerk in the railroad station at Luddenden Foot, and I am a governess in the family of Mr. Robinson. I dislike the situation and wish to change it for another. I am now at Scarborough. My pupils are gone to bed and I am hastening to finish this before I follow them.

We are thinking of setting up a school of our own, but nothing definite is settled about it yet, and we do not know whether we shall be able to or not. I hope we shall. And I wonder what will be our condition and how or where we shall all be on this day four years hence; at which time, if all be well, I shall be 25 years and 6 months old, Emily will be 27 years old, Branwell 28 years and 1 month, and Charlotte 29 years and a quarter. We are now all separate and not likely to meet again for many a weary week, but we are none of us ill that I know of and all are doing something for our own livelihood except Emily, who, however, is as busy as any of us, and in reality earns her food and raiment as much as we do.

A drawing by Anne, 13 November 1839 (Brontë Parsonage Museum; from Christine Alexander and Jane Sellars,
The Art of the Brontës, *University of Colorado Libraries)*

How little know we what we are
How less what we may be!

Four years ago I was at school. Since then I have
been a governess at Blake Hall, left it, come to
Thorp Green, and seen the sea and York Minster.
Emily has been a teacher at Miss Patchet's school,
and left it. Charlotte has left Miss Wooler's, been a
governess at Mrs. Sidgwick's, left her, and gone to
Mrs. White's. Branwell has given up painting, been
a tutor in Cumberland, left it, and become a clerk on
the railroad. Tabby has left us, Martha Brown has
come in her place. We have got Keeper, got a sweet
little cat and lost it, and also got a hawk. Got a wild
goose which has flown away, and three tame ones,
one of which has been killed. All these diversities,
with many others, are things we did not expect or
foresee in the July of 1837. What will the next four
years bring forth? Providence only knows. But we
ourselves have sustained very little alteration since
that time. I have the same faults that I had then,
only I have more wisdom and experience, and a little more self-possession than I then enjoyed. How
will it be when we open this paper and the one
Emily has written? I wonder whether the Gon-
dalian[s] will still be flourishing, and what will be
their condition. I am now engaged in writing the
fourth volume of *Solala Vernon's Life*.

For some time I have looked upon 25 as a sort
of era in my existence. It may prove a true presentiment, or it may be only a superstitious fancy; the latter seems most likely, but time will show.
  –*The Letters of Charlotte Brontë*, v. 1, pp. 264–265

* * *

Anne Brontë's Music Manuscript

*Anne Brontë's music manuscript copy book, into which she
began copying pieces in 1843 during the period she was governess to the Robinsons, shows the kinds of music she enjoyed;
twenty-four of the thirty-four pieces she copied into her book are
hymns and sacred songs. The other ten pieces include songs by
Robert Burns, and adaptations of pieces by Haydn, Handel,
Mozart, and Beethoven. Emily Brontë seems to have been more
accomplished as a pianist than Anne from what Charlotte and
Ellen Nussey indicate; and the editor of the facsimile of Anne's
manuscript indicates that the arrangements she copied into her
book "suggest a pianist of limited ability who expected to accompany her own singing, or perhaps that of a pupil" (Introduction,
Anne Brontë's Song Book [Clarabricken, Ireland: Boethius
Press Limited, 1980], no pagination).*

---

*In January 1843, Branwell Brontë joined Anne at
Thorp Green as tutor to the Robinsons' son; over the two
years that he worked for the Robinsons, Branwell fell in love
with the mother of the family, Mrs. Lydia Robinson, and possibly had an affair with her, though there is no proof of any
impropriety. Anne resigned from the Robinsons in June 1845;
Branwell was dismissed by them the same month.*

*In this diary paper Anne mentions family pets and writ-
ing that has not survived. The reference to having "begun the
third volume of passages in the life of an individual" may
indicate an early version of* Agnes Grey.

Diary Paper, 31 July 1845
Anne Brontë

Yesterday was Emily's birthday and the time
when we should have opened our 1845 [1841] paper
but by mistake we opened it to day instead. How
many things have happened since it was written–
some pleasant some far otherwise–Yet I was then at
Thorp Green and now I am only jt escaped from it. I
was wishing to leave [?it] then and if I had known
that I had four years longer to stay how wretched I
should have been–but during my stay I have had
some very unpleasant and undreamt of experience
of human nature–Others have seen more changes
Charlotte has left Mr White's and been twice to
Brussels where–she stayed each time nearly a year–
Emily has been there too and stayed nearly a year–
Branwell has left Luddendenfoot and been a Tutor
at Thorp Green and had much tribulation and ill
health he was very ill on Tuesday but he went with
John Brown to Liverpool where he now is I suppose
and we hope he will be better and do better in
future–This is a dismal cloudy wet evening we have
had so far a very cold wet summer–Charlotte has
lately been to Hathersage in Derbyshire on a visit of
three weeks to Ellen Nussy–she is now sitting sewing in the Dining-Room Emily is ironing upstairs I
am sitting in the Dining Room in the Rocking chair
before the fire with my feet on the fender Papa is in
the parlour Tabby and Martha are I think in the
Kitchen Keeper and Flossy are I do not know where
little Dick is hopping in his cage–When the last
paper was written we were thinking of setting up a
school–the scheem has been dropt and long after
taken up again and dropt again because we could
not get pupils–Charlotte is thinking about getting
another situation–she wishes to go to Paris–Will
she go? she has let Flossy in by the bye and he is
now lying on the sopha–Emily is engeaged in writing the Emperor Julius's life she has read some of it
and I want very much to hear the rest–she is writing

Pages from Anne's manuscript songbook (Brontë Parsonage Museum, Bonnell MS 133; from Anne Brontë's Song Book, *University of Houston Music Library)*

some poetry too I wonder what it is about—I have begun the third volume of passages in the life of an Individual. I wish I had finished it—This afternoon I began to set about making my grey figured silk frock that was dyed at Keigthley—What sort of a hand shall I make of it? E. and I have a great deal of work to do—when shall we sensibly diminish it? I want to get a habit of early rising shall I succeed? We have not yet finished our Gondal chronicles that we began three years and a half ago when will they be done?— The Gondals are at present in a sad state the Republicans are uppermost but the Royalists are not quite overcome—the young sovereigns with their brothers and sisters are still at the palace of Instruction—The Unique Society above half a year ago were wrecked on a dezart Island as they were returning from ?Gaaldin—they are still there but we have not played at them much yet—The Gondals in general are not yet in first rate playing condition—will they improve? I wonder how we shall all be and where and how situated on the thirtyeth of July 1848 when if we are all alive Emily will be just 30 I shall be in my 29th year Charlotte in her 33rd and Branwell in his 32nd and what changes shall we have seen and known and shall we be much chan[g]ed ourselves? I hope not— for the worse [a]t least—I for my part cannot well b[e] <u>flatter</u> or older in mind than I am n[o]w—Hoping for the best I conclude Anne Brontë

　　—*The Letters of Charlotte Brontë*, v. 1, pp. 409–411

* * *

The Robinson daughters sought to keep in touch with Anne after she left Thorp Green; however, Branwell was living at home in Haworth during this same period and still mourning his thwarted love for Mrs. Robinson and drinking. An excerpt from a letter from Charlotte to Ellen Nussey gives a glimpse of some of the Haworth parsonage dynamics at this point.

Charlotte Brontë to Ellen Nussey, 1 March 1847

. . . In summer—and in fine weather your visit here might be much better managed than in winter— we could go out more be more independent of the house and of one room—Branwell has been conducting himself very badly lately—I expect from the extravagance of his behaviour and from mysterious hints he drops—(for he never will speak out plainly) that we shall be hearing news of fresh debts contracted by him soon—

The Misses Robinson—who had entirely ceased their correspondence with Anne for half a

WEST FRONT.

York Minster, a cathedral that Anne loved, having seen it on trips while governess to the Robinson family. Anne took Emily on a special trip to York in June 1845. Anne saw it for the last time on 24 May 1849, en route to Scarborough, where she died five days later (from W. C. E. Newbolt, The Cathedrals of England, *University of Colorado Libraries).*

year after their father's death have lately recommenced it—for a fortnight they sent her a letter almost every day—crammed with warm protestation of endless esteem and gratitude—they speak with great affection too of their Mother—and never make any allusion intimating acquaintance with her errors—It is to be hoped they are and always will remain in ignorance on that point—especially since—I think—she has bitterly repented them. We take special care that Branwell does not know of their writing to Anne.

　　—*The Letters of Charlotte Brontë*, v. 1, pp. 517–519

Agnes Grey

Little is known of the composition of Agnes Grey—*no manuscript of either it or* The Tenant of Wildfell Hall *is known to have survived—but it is clear that Anne Brontë drew on her experiences as a governess, especially with the Ingham family, in writing her first novel. Published in December 1847 as the third volume of a three-volume work, with the first two volumes being devoted to Emily's* Wuthering Heights, Agnes Grey *was overshadowed in critical commentary by Emily's novel, and many critics ignored her volume entirely. Since it appeared some two months after Charlotte's* Jane Eyre, *a novel that also treated the life of a governess,* Agnes Grey *also suffered by the comparison to the work of Anne's eldest sister.*

This unsigned review appeared in a column in The Athenæum *titled "Our Library Table" on Christmas Day. H. F. Chorley, a frequent contributor to the periodical, is believed to have been the reviewer.*

"Eccentric and Unpleasant"
Review of *Wuthering Heights* and *Agnes Grey*

'Jane Eyre,' it will be recollected, was *edited* by Mr. Currer Bell. Here are two tales so nearly related to 'Jane Eyre' in cast of thought, incident and language as to excite some curiosity. All three might be the work of one hand,—but the first issued remains the best. In spite of much power and cleverness; in spite of its truth to life in the remote nooks and corners of England 'Wuthering Heights' is a disagreeable story. The Bells seem to affect painful and exceptional subjects:—the misdeeds and oppressions of tyranny—the eccentricities of "woman's fantasy." They do not turn away from dwelling on those physical acts of cruelty which we know to have their warrant in the real annals of crime and suffering,—but the contemplation of which taste rejects. The brutal master of the lonely house on "Wuthering

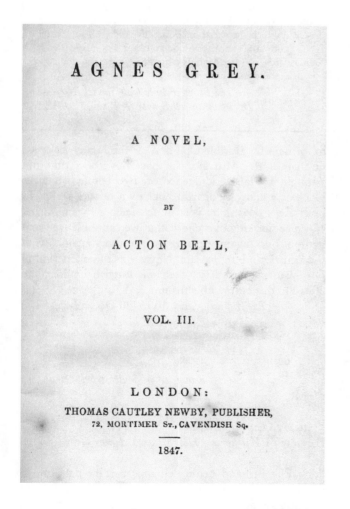

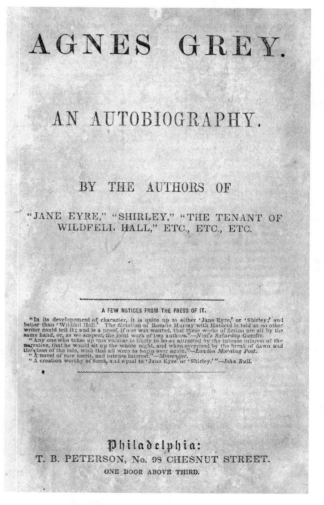

Title pages for the first English and American editions of Anne Brontë's first novel (Special Collections, Thomas Cooper Library, University of South Carolina)

"Under the Shadow of Her Brother's Disgrace"

After the publication of Elizabeth Gaskell's The Life of Charlotte Brontë *(1857), with its depiction of Branwell Brontë as a profligate, critics began to suggest that Branwell, with whom Anne had lived during the deepest phase of his addiction to alcohol (1845–1848), had inspired her depictions of dissolution. Brontë biographer Francis Leyland, who had known Branwell, disputed this interpretation of the siblings. Leyland refers to T. Wemyss Reid's* Charlotte Brontë: A Monograph *(1877) in this excerpt.*

'Agnes Grey' . . . is the picture of things its author had known, painted almost as she saw them. Anne's experience as a governess had made her acquainted with certain phases of life, which she could not but reproduce. Hence Agnes Grey is thrown into the sphere of the careless and selfish family of the Bloomfields; and afterwards, with the Murrays at Horton Lodge, she sees a kind of personal character and social life which, on account of its coldness and worldliness, greatly repelled Anne Brontë, with her warm and sympathetic nature. She teaches the same lesson of the folly of *mariages de convenance,* and of the wrong of subjecting the affections, and bartering happiness for the sake of worldly position, which she afterwards dwells upon more strongly in 'The Tenant of Wildfell Hall.' It is in this fictitious parallel of Anne Brontë's own experience, if anywhere in her writings, that we might expect to find some reflection of the recent history of her brother's fall. Mr. Reid has asserted that this formed the dark turning-point in her life, for 'living under the same roof with him when he went astray,' she 'was compelled to be a closer and more constant witness of his sins and his sufferings than either Charlotte or Emily.' Her letters home, it has been stated, conveyed the news of her dark forebodings. But, all the same, the story she wrote, almost under the shadow of her brother's disgrace, is the simple, straightforward, humorous narrative of the gentle and pious Anne Brontë, revealing not so much as a suspicion of vice or thought of evil; and, in this respect, it presents a contrast to her second work. There is evidence that when the sisters wrote their novels they had already attributed monomania to Branwell, and could thus explain his history for themselves. It was not in the nature of 'Agnes Grey' to be successful as a novel, but we find in it that Anne possessed a faculty which scarcely appears in Charlotte's writings,–that of humour. Look, for instance, at the way in which she sketches so forcibly, and with such droll perception, the character of the youthful Bloomfields, and, afterwards, of Miss Matilda Murray, with her equine propensities and masculine tastes.

–*The Brontë Family with Special Reference to Patrick Branwell Brontë,* v. 2, pp. 120–122

Heights"–a prison which might be pictured from life–has doubtless had his prototype in those ungenial and remote districts where human beings, like the trees, grow gnarled and dwarfed and distorted by the inclement climate; but he might have been indicated with far fewer touches, in place of so entirely filling the canvas that there is hardly a scene untainted by his presence. It was a like dreariness–a like unfortunate selection of objects–which cut short the popularity of Charlotte Smith's novels,–rich though they be in true pathos and faithful descriptions of Nature. Enough of what is mean and bitterly painful and degrading gathers round every one of us during the course of his pilgrimage through this vale of tears to absolve the Artist from choosing his incidents and characters out of such a dismal catalogue; and if the Bells, singly or collectively, are contemplating future or frequent utterances in Fiction, let us hope that they will spare us further interiors so gloomy as the one here elaborated with such dismal minuteness. In this respect 'Agnes Grey' is more acceptable to us, though less powerful. It is the tale of a governess who undergoes much that is the real bond of a governess's endurance:–but the new victim's trials are of a more ignoble quality than those which awaited 'Jane Eyre.' In the household of the Bloomfields the governess is subjected to torment by Terrible Children (as the French have it); in that of the Murrays she has to witness the ruin wrought by false indulgence on two coquettish girls, whose coquetries jeopardize her own heart's secret. In both these tales there is so much feeling for character, and nice marking of scenery, that we cannot leave them without once again warning their authors against what is eccentric and unpleasant. Never was there a period in our history of Society when we English could so ill afford to dispense with sunshine.

–*The Athenæum,* no. 1052 (25 December 1847): 1324–1325

* * *

This unsigned review was originally titled "Wuthering Heights."

"Utterly Opposed Modes"
Review of *Wuthering Heights* and *Agnes Grey*

Ellis Bell and Acton Bell appear in the light of two names borrowed to represent two totally different styles of composition and two utterly opposed modes of treatment of the novel, rather than to indicate two real personages.

They are names coupled together as mysteriously in the literary, as the sons of Leda are in the asterial world; and there is something at least gained by being mysterious at starting. "Wuthering Heights," by Ellis Bell, is a terrific story, associated with an equally fearful and repulsive spot. It should have been called *Withering* Heights, for any thing from which the mind and body would more instinctively shrink, than the mansion and its tenants, cannot be easily imagined. "Wuthering," however, as expressive in provincial phraseology of "the frequency of atmospheric tumults out of doors" must do, however much the said tumults may be surpassed in frequency and violence by the disturbances that occur in doors. Our novel reading experience does not enable us to refer to any thing to be compared with the personages we are introduced to at this desolate spot—a perfect misanthropist's heaven.

"Agnes Grey," by Acton Bell, is a story of quite a different character. It is a simple tale of a governess's experiences and trials of love, borne with that meekness, and met by that fortitude, that ensure a final triumph. It has one advantage over its predecessor, that while its language is less ambitious and less repulsive, it fills the mind with a lasting picture of love and happiness succeeding to scorn and affliction, and teaches us to put every trust in a supreme wisdom and goodness.

—*New Monthly Magazine*, 82 (January 1848): 140

* * *

This excerpt is from an unsigned review.

"A Tale Well Worth the Writing"
Review of *Agnes Grey*

Two of these volumes contain a tale by Mr. Ellis Bell, called "Wuthering Heights," and the third volume is devoted to another story, told in an autobiographical form, by Mr. Acton Bell, and is entitled "Agnes Grey."

Dissimilar as they are in many respects, there is a distinct family likeness between these two tales; and, if our organ of comparison be not out of order, we are not far wrong in asserting that they are not so much like each other, as they are both like a novel recently published under the editorship of Mr. Currer Bell, viz., "Jane Eyre." We do not mean to say that either of the tales now before us is equal in merit to that novel, but they have somewhat of the same fresh, original, and unconventional spirit; while the style of composition is, undoubtedly, of the same north-country, Doric school;

it is simple, energetic, and apparently disdainful of prettinesses and verbal display.

Of "Agnes Grey," much need not be said, further than this, that it is the autobiography of a young lady during the time she was a governess in two different families; neither of which is a favourable specimen of the advantages of home education. We do not actually assert that the author must have been a governess himself, to describe as he does the minute torments and incessant tediums of her life, but he must have bribed some governess very largely, either with love or money, to reveal to him the secrets of her prison-house, or, he must have devoted extraordinary powers of observation and discovery to the elucidation of the subject. In either case, "Agnes Grey" is a tale well worth the writing and the reading. The heroine is a sort of younger sister to "Jane Eyre;" but inferior to her in every way. . . .

—*Douglas Jerrold's Weekly Newspaper*
(15 January 1848): 77

The Tenant of Wildfell Hall

Anne became the first of the Brontë sisters to publish a second novel when The Tenant of Wildfell Hall *by Acton Bell was brought out in June 1848. The 10 June 1847 date at the end of the published work suggests that she finished drafting her novel a year before its publication. The* Tenant of Wildfell Hall *is a much more complex narrative than* Agnes Grey, *as Gilbert Markham's epistolary narrative frames the diary of Helen Huntingdon, whose disastrous marriage is the main focus of the novel—a structure that is similar to the double narration of* Wuthering Heights. *The novel offers a serious social critique in its portrayal of the profligate Arthur Huntingdon and the power he has over his wife.*

This excerpt is from an unsigned review to which Anne specifically responded in her preface to the second edition of her novel.

"A Morbid Love for the Coarse"
Review of *The Tenant of Wildfell Hall*

The volumes of fiction that some time since appeared under the name of Bell, with three several praenomens, had such a generic resemblance to one another that several reviewers remarked it. The first and most striking affinity was of substance. Each of the Bells selected the singular both in character and incident. The persons were such as are formed by a natural peculiarity of disposition, influenced by an equal peculiarity of circumstances, or produced by

THE TENANT

OF

WILDFELL HALL.

BY

ACTON BELL.

IN THREE VOLUMES.

VOL. I.

LONDON:

T. C. NEWBY, PUBLISHER,
72, MORTIMER STREET, CAVENDISH SQUARE.
1848.

Title page for Anne's second novel, published six months after Agnes
Grey *(The Parrish Collection, Princeton University Library)*

strong passions running their course unrestrained in the freedom of a remote country place, at a time which permitted greater liberty to individual will or caprice than is vouchsafed even to brutal and isolated squireens in these days. The composition—not mere diction, but the arrangement of the incidents and persons, as well as the style of the things themselves—was extreme and wild; seeking to base effects on the startling, without much regard either to probability or good taste. A rough vigour characterized the whole batch of Bells; but Currer Bell, the author or editor of *Jane Eyre,* exhibited rather the most cultivated taste and decidedly the most literary skill.

Nearly one half of *The Tenant of Wildfell Hall,* by Acton Bell, forms a sort of setting to the main story, and is pitched in a more natural key than the author's previous novel, though not without occa-

sional roughness. In escaping from his extreme and violent manner, however, he loses somewhat of his strength and interest. There is nature, undoubtedly; but it is of a common kind. The daily life of a young and self-sufficient gentleman farmer and his family, with the characters and gossip of his neighbourhood, are scarcely enough to sustain the reader for a volume, even with the addition of the aforesaid farmer's love for the mysterious tenant of Wildfell Hall.

The tale of this lady, which she has written down apparently for her lover to read, is a story of suffering in married life, arising from the licentiousness, drunkenness, and downright blackguardism of her husband and his associates. She is provoked by his profligacy, disgusted by his habits, and surrounded by tempting gallants; and scenes founded on such subjects form the narrative of the tale, till she secretly escapes, and takes refuge near her brother; whom Gilbert Markham, the farmer lover, has mistaken for a favoured swain, and ferociously assaulted. In due time Mr. Huntingdon the husband dies: his widow's possession of property causes a considerable delay in the denouement; but it comes at last.

The Tenant of Wildfell Hall, like its predecessor, suggests the idea of considerable abilities ill applied. There is power, effect, and even nature, though of an extreme kind, in its pages; but there seems in the writer a morbid love for the coarse, not to say the brutal; so that his level subjects are not very attractive, and the more forcible are displeasing or repulsive, from their gross, physical, or profligate substratum. He might reply, that such things are in life: and probably glimpses of such a set as Huntingdon and his friends are occasionally caught in Doctors Commons cases, and tradition pictures such doings as not very rare in the early part of George the Third's reign,—although Mr. Bell paints them as contemporary. Mere existence, however, as we have often had occasion to remark, is not a sufficient reason for a choice of subject: its general or typical character is a point to consider, and its power of pleasing must be regarded, as well as its mere capabilities of force or effect. It is not only the subject of this novel, however, that is objectionable, but the manner of treating it. There is a coarseness of tone throughout the writing of all these Bells, that puts an offensive subject in its worst point of view, and which generally contrives to dash indifferent things.

—*The Spectator,* no. 21 (8 July 1848): 662–663

* * *

This unsigned reviewer apparently also wrote the Christmas Day review of Wuthering Heights *and* Agnes Grey *for* The Athenæum.

An "Honest Recommendation"
Review of *The Tenant of Wildfell Hall*

The three Bells, as we took occasion to observe when reviewing "Wuthering Heights" [*Athenæum,* No. 1052] ring in a chime so harmonious as to prove that they have issued from the same mould. The resemblance borne by their novels to each other is curious. "The Tenant of Wildfell Hall" must not hope to gain the popularity of her elder sister "Jane Eyre,"—but the blood of the family is in her veins. A short extract will sufficiently prove this, even to such as require for proof of a likeness *data* somewhat more exact than those of Sterne's simile-maker—the

> —poor industrious man
> Who means no ill,
> But does the best he can
> With a quill, * *
> Just as a fisher shoots an owl
> Or a sea-fowl
> To make the likeness of a fly,
> To make a simile in no feature
> Resembling the creature
> That he has in his eye!

Acton Bell, like Ellis and Currer, knows the nooks of the north of England well. As the opening scene will sufficiently testify.—

"The day I last mentioned was a certain Sunday, the latest in the October of 1827. On the following Tuesday I was out with my dog and gun, in pursuit of such game as I could find within the territory of Linden-Car; but finding none at all, I turned my arms against the hawks and carrion crows, whose depredations, as I suspected, had deprived me of better prey. To this end, I left the more frequented regions, the wooded valleys, the corn-fields, and the meadow lands, and proceeded to mount the steep acclivity of Wildfell, the wildest and the loftiest eminence in our neighbourhood, where, as you ascend, the hedges, as well as the trees, become scanty and stunted, the former, at length, giving place to rough stone fences, partly greened over with ivy and moss, the latter to larches and Scotch fir-trees, or isolated blackthorns. The fields, being rough and stony and wholly unfit for the plough, were mostly devoted to the pasturing of sheep and cattle; the soil was thin and poor: bits of grey rock here and there peeped out from the grassy hillocks; bilberry plants and heather—relics of more savage wildness—grew under the walls; and in many of the enclosures, ragweeds and rushes usurped supremacy over the scanty herbage;—but these were not *my* property. Near the top of this hill, about

two miles from Linden-Car, stood Wildfell Hall, a superannuated mansion of the Elizabethan era, built of dark grey stone,—venerable and picturesque to look at, but doubtless, cold and gloomy enough to inhabit, with its thick stone mullions and little latticed panes, its time eaten airholes, and its too lonely, too unsheltered situation,—only shielded from the war of wind and weather by a group of Scotch firs, themselves half blighted with storms, and looking as stern and gloomy as the hall itself. . . ."

The reader is by this time curious to get a peep of "the tenant" of such a wild abode, being convinced that, since

Vague mystery hangs about these desert places,

she must be a Lady with "a history." But not a line or passage of this shall be divulged in the *Athenæum,*—however tempted to lengthen our lecture on family likeness. With regard to one point, however, we cannot remain silent:—The Bells must be warned against their fancy for dwelling upon what is disagreeable. The brutified estate of Mr. Huntingdon might have been displayed within a smaller compass in place of being elaborated with the fond minuteness of a Jan Steen. The position of the wife with regard to her husband's paramour is, on the other hand, treated with a sort of hard indifference,—natural enough, it may be, but not in harmony with the impressions of the Lady which we have been invited to entertain. Were the metal from this Bell foundry of baser quality than it is it would be lost time to point out flaws and take exceptions. As matters stand, our hints may not be without their use to future "castings:" nor will they be unpalatable, seeing that they are followed by our honest recommendation of "Wildfell Hall" as the most interesting novel which we have read for a month past.

—*The Athenæum* (July 8 1848): 670–671

* * *

Anne responded to critics who condemned the "coarseness" of the Bell writings in the preface she dated 22 July 1848.

Preface to the Second Edition
of *The Tenant of Wildfell Hall*
Acton Bell

While I acknowledge the success of the present work to have been greater than I anticipated, and the praises it has elicited from a few kind critics to have been greater than it deserved, I must also admit that from some other quarters it has been censured with an asperity which I was as little prepared to expect, and which my judgment, as well as my feelings, assures me is more bitter than just. It is scarcely the province of an author to refute the arguments of his censors and vindicate his own productions, but I may be allowed to make here a few observations with which I would have prefaced the first edition had I foreseen the necessity of such precautions against the misapprehensions of those who would read it with a prejudiced mind or be content to judge it by a hasty glance.

My object in writing the following pages, was not simply to amuse the Reader, neither was it to gratify my own taste, nor yet to ingratiate myself with the Press and the Public: I wished to tell the truth, for truth always conveys its own moral to those who are able to receive it. But as the priceless treasure too frequently hides at the bottom of a well, it needs some courage to dive for it, especially as he that does so will be likely to incur more scorn and obloquy for the mud and water into which he has ventured to plunge, than thanks for the jewel he procures; as, in like manner, she who undertakes the cleansing of a careless bachelor's apartment will be liable to more abuse for the dust she raises, than commendation for the clearance she effects. Let it not be imagined, however, that I consider myself competent to reform the errors and abuses of society, but only that I would fain contribute my humble quota towards so good an aim, and if I can gain the public ear at all, I would rather whisper a few wholesome truths therein than much soft nonsense.

As the story of "Agnes Grey" was accused of extravagant overcolouring in those very parts that were carefully copied from the life, with a most scrupulous avoidance of all exaggeration, so, in the present work, I find myself censured for depicting *con amore,* with 'a morbid love of the coarse, if not of the brutal,' those scenes which, I will venture to say, have not been more painful for the most fastidious of my critics to read, than they were for me to describe. I may have gone too far, in which case I shall be careful not to trouble myself or my readers in the same way again; but when we have to do with vice and vicious characters, I maintain it is better to depict them as they really are than as they would wish to appear. To represent a bad thing in its least offensive light is doubtless the most agreeable course for a writer of fiction to pursue; but is it the most honest, or the safest? Is it better to reveal the snares and pitfalls of life to the young and thoughtless traveller, or to cover them with branches and flowers? O Reader! if there were less of this delicate concealment of facts—this whispering 'Peace, peace,' when there is no peace—there would be less of sin and misery to the young of both sexes who are left to wring their bitter knowledge from experience.

I would not be understood to suppose that the proceedings of the unhappy scapegrace with his few profligate companions I have here introduced are a specimen of the common practices of society: the case is an extreme one, as I trusted none would fail to perceive; but I know that such characters do exist, and if I have warned one rash youth from following in their steps, or prevented one thoughtless girl from falling into the very natural error of my heroine, the book has not been written in vain. But, at the same time, if any honest reader shall have derived more pain than pleasure from its perusal, and have closed the last volume with a disagreeable impression on his mind, I humbly crave his pardon, for such was far from my intention; and I will endeavour to do better another time, for I love to give innocent pleasure. Yet, be it understood, I shall not limit my ambition to this,—or even to producing 'a perfect work of art:' time and talents so spent, I should consider wasted and misapplied. Such humble talents as God has given me I will endeavour to put to their greatest use; if I am able to amuse I will try to benefit too; and when I feel it my duty to speak an unpalatable truth, with the help of God, I *will* speak it, though it be to the prejudice of my name and to the detriment of my reader's immediate pleasure as well as my own.

One word more, and I have done. Respecting the author's identity, I would have it to be distinctly understood that Acton Bell is neither Currer nor Ellis Bell, and therefore, let not his faults be attributed to them. As to whether the name be real or fictitious, it cannot greatly signify to those who know him only by his works. As little, I should think, can it matter whether the writer so designated is a man, or a woman as one or two of my critics profess to have discovered. I take the imputation in good part, as a compliment to the just delineation of my female characters; and though I am bound to attribute much of the severity of my censors to this suspicion, I make no effort to refute it, because, in my own mind, I am satisfied that if a book is a good one, it is so whatever the sex of the author may be. All novels are or should be written for both men and women to read, and I am at a loss to conceive how a man should permit himself to write anything that would be really disgraceful to a woman, or why a woman should be censured for writing anything that would be proper and becoming for a man.

***

These excerpts are from an unsigned review.

"Faulty Construction"
Review of *The Tenant of Wildfell Hall*

The authors of 'Jane Eyre,' 'Wuthering Heights,' 'Agnes Grey' and 'The Tenant of Wildfell Hall' are evidently children of the same family. They derive their scenes from the same country; their associations are alike; their heroines are for the most part alike, three being thrown upon their own talents for self-support, and two of them being all-enduring governesses; and their heroes also resemble each other, in aspect, and temper, almost in habits. We have, once or twice, entertained a suspicion that all the books that we have enumerated might have issued from the same source; sent forth at different seasons, in different states of mind or humour, or at different periods or elevations of the intellect,–'Jane Eyre' having been achieved at the culminating point. At all events, the writers are of the same stock, have undoubted marks of family resemblance, and are, in fact,

> Matched in *mouth* like Bells,
> Each under each.

The Bells are of a hardy race. They do not lounge in drawing-rooms or boudoirs. The air they breathe is not that of the hot-house, or of perfumed apartments: but it whistles through the rugged thorns that shoot out their prickly arms on barren moors, or it ruffles the moss on the mountain tops. Rough characters, untamed by contact with towns or cities; wilful men, with the true stamp of the passions upon them; plain vigorous Saxon words, not spoiled nor weakened by bad French or school-boy Latin; rude habits; ancient residences–with Nature in her great loneliness all around;–these–with the gray skies or sunset glories above–are the elements of their stories, compounded and reduced to shape, in different moods and with different success.

From all this, it will be observed that Currer, Acton, and Ellis Bell, whatever may be their defects otherwise, are not common-place writers. Their characters are not faint or tawdry copies of other characters which have already wearied us, and which have oppressed the pages of novelists, month after month, for the last thirty years. They have bone and sinew about them; animal life peeps out in every form; and the phraseology, although sometimes tedious enough, is rarely conventional. On these accounts, we are disposed to give a full and overflowing measure of praise to writers, who in assuming to portray nature have been wise and sincere enough to go back to their original; and we earnestly recommend them as examples to other labourers in the same path.

The story called 'The Tenant of Wildfell Hall' is very inartificially constructed. The main part of the tale consists of a recital or journal made by a certain Mrs Graham, the mysterious tenant for the time being of the Hall, and the subject of innumerable slanderous hints and inuendos on the part of the restless gossips of a remote village. The lady herself, whose charms have disturbed the tranquillity of a very rough Cymon, by name Gilbert Markham, turns out to be a Mrs Huntingdon, and to be unhappily married; and it is not until the author very judiciously kills the first husband that the fortune of Gilbert the hero emerges out of the troubles which have hung about him, and his happiness is finally consummated.

There are two distinct series of character in the book: the one being the inhabitants of the village in the neighbourhood of Wildfell Hall; the other, less rural and far more ambitiously sketched, the friends and acquaintance who surround the heroine in her native county, and tend to illustrate her conduct in the earlier and later portions of her life. For she is 'Tenant of Wildfell Hall' during some months only, when she has been forced to fly from a drunken, vicious, and tyrannical husband; and there is in fact no connection whatever between the two sets of *dramatis personæ,* except the very slender link which the heroine herself presents, by passing from one place to the other.

To say the truth, there is no very intense excitement in any part of the book. Just at the time when we begin to feel some interest about Markham and the lady, we are thrown back upon her previous history, which occupies a full half of the three volumes before us. This is a fatal error: for, after so long and minute a history, we cannot go back and recover the enthusiasm which we have been obliged to dismiss a volume and half before.

Nevertheless, there are some distinct markings of character. In the village, besides the ordinary gabble of women who have nothing else to do but to slander their neighbour, there is an outline of a pompous parson, who seems drawn from life. The ladies are less original; and the general tone of all the conversations in this part of the story–except only when the wilfulness or ferocity of the hero intervenes–are tedious and commonplace. We are reminded occasionally of the minute gossip in which Miss Austin occasionally indulged, but with less of that particular quality which her dialogues invariably possessed, of illustrating the characters of the speakers.

Owing to the faulty construction of the tale, it is scarcely possible to analyze it, for the information of the reader. We must content ourselves with stating that Helen Lawrence (the heroine), a young lady of small fortune, but of considerable beauty and spirit, after having been persecuted by the adoration of two vulnerable lovers, casts herself into the arms of Mr Arthur Huntingdon, a person with no very attractive superfices, and a blackguard of undoubted quality. As this person is preceded by a tolerably bad reputation, and as his pretensions are discountenanced by the uncle and aunt of Helen, and supported simply by mean and impudent conduct on his own part, it is difficult to understand his success. But the lady is a little wilful, and has been worried and irritated by an old man's love; and, as we all know, it is sometimes the weakness of our adversary that enables us to conquer.

The following extracts will put the reader in possession of all that is necessary for him to know respecting Mr Arthur [sic] Huntingdon. . . .

She eventually marries this vulgar coxcomb, who introduces her to some of his associates,—a set of drunken savages, such as we do not remember to have heard of as having been tolerated for many years, within the pale of civilized society. Of these, Grimsby is a sordid blackleg; Hattersley, a wild beast (partially tamed at last by love and pity for a suffering wife); Lord Lowborough, the victim, and Hargrave, the Joseph Surface, of the party. There is something touching in the renovation of Lord Lowborough, who rises from his ruin, and abandons himself, heart and soul, to a heartless beauty, one Annabella Wilmot, who on her part despises and deserts him for the more ostentatious Huntingdon, already the husband of Helen. The infidelity of the parties is discovered by the heroine, who overhears a conversation between them, and who thereupon withdraws herself from the society of her husband (whose excesses of all sorts increase daily), and finally flies, with her child, from his residence, to seclude herself at Wildfell Hall, under the assumed name of Mrs Graham. . . .

The volumes afford few extracts. Here is a description, however, of Wildfell Hall, which is not very unlike the house inhabited by the wild people of *Wuthering Heights.* . . .

There is a drunken scene of considerable power in the second volume, but we do not know that we should edify any of our readers by extracting it. We therefore forbear, and turn to gentler matters. The husband of Helen dies, as we have said, but Markham is ignorant of the sentiments of the beautiful widow, respecting whom he has received no tidings; and therefore, restless and unhappy, he wanders about her residence—hears of her great wealth—and, poor himself, is too proud to announce himself to her. They meet, however, by accident, and, after a few of those little misunderstandings which only enhance the happiness that succeeds and clears them away, the lovers are united, and the narrative ends. Here is a short love passage; and with this we must conclude our extracts. . . .

—*The Examiner* (29 July 1848): 483–484

* * *

Anne Brontë's Poetry

As is the case with Emily's poetry, the earliest extant poem by Anne is from 1836; like Emily, Anne also wrote a mixture of explicitly Gondal-based pieces as well as more-general ones. Some of the fifty-nine poems believed to be written by Anne address themes of religious struggles and insights, at times in connection with the natural world. Other poems seem to be about William Weightman, Reverend Brontë's curate, who died in 1842 of cholera in Haworth at age twenty-nine. Charlotte had observed that Anne and Weightman appeared to have a mutual interest in each other.

THE THREE GUIDES.

SPIRIT of Earth! thy hand is chill;
  I've felt its icy clasp;
And, shuddering, I remember still
  That stony-hearted grasp.
Thine eye bids love and joy depart:
  Oh, turn its gaze from me!
It presses down my shrinking heart;
  I will not walk with thee!

'Wisdom is mine,' I've heard thee
    say:
  'Beneath my searching eye,
All mist and darkness melt away,
  Phantoms and fables fly.
Before me truth can stand alone,
  The naked, solid truth;
And man matured by worth will own,
  If I am shunned by youth.

Firm is my tread, and sure, though
    slow:
  My footsteps never slide;
And he that follows me shall know
  I am the surest guide.
Thy boast is vain; but were it true
  That thou couldst safely steer
Life's rough and devious pathway
    through,
  Such guidance I should fear.

How could I bear to walk for aye,
  With eyes to earthward prone,
O'er trampled weeds and miry clay,
  And sand and flinty stone;

Never the glorious view to greet
  Of hill, and dale, and sky;
To see that Nature's charms are
    sweet,
  Or feel that Heaven is nigh?

If in my heart arose a spring,
  A gush of thought divine,
At once stagnation thou wouldst
    bring
  With that cold touch of thine.
If glancing up I sought to snatch
  But one glimpse of the sky,
My baffled gaze would only catch
  Thy heartless, cold grey eye.

If to the breezes wandering near
  I listened eagerly,
And deemed an angel's tongue to hear
  That whispered hope to me,
That heavenly music would be
    drowned
  In thy harsh, droning voice;
Nor inward thought, nor sight, nor
    sound,
  Might my sad soul rejoice.

Dull is thine ear, unheard by thee
  The still small voice of Heaven;
Thine eyes are dim, and cannot see
  The helps that God has given.
There is a bridge o'er every flood
  Which thou canst not perceive;
A path through every tangled wood,
  But thou wilt not believe.

Pages from the August 1848 issue of Fraser's Magazine. *Anne contributed twenty-one poems to* Poems by Currer, Ellis, and Acton Bell *in 1846 (University of Colorado Libraries).*

These excerpts are from an unsigned review appearing in a periodical founded as "a journal of entertainment and instruction for general reading."

"Unfit for Perusal"
Review of *The Tenant of Wildfell Hall*

Several novels have lately appeared before the public, purporting to be written by three brothers, Currer, Ellis, and Acton Bell. Of these works, *Jane Eyre*, by Currer Bell, is the best known, and deservedly the most popular. We say deservedly, for though it has great faults, it has still greater merits. Such is by no means the

194   *The Three Guides.*   [August,

Striving to make thy way by force,
Toil-spent and bramble-torn,
Thou 'lt fell the tree that checks thy course,
And burst through brier and thorn;
And, pausing by the river's side,
Poor reasoner! thou wilt deem,
By casting pebbles in its tide,
To cross the swelling stream.

Right through the flinty rock thou'lt try
Thy toilsome way to bore,
Regardless of the pathway nigh
That would conduct thee o'er.
Not only art thou, then, unkind
And freezing cold to me,
But unbelieving, deaf, and blind;
I will not walk with thee!

Spirit of Pride! thy wings are strong,
Thine eyes like lightning shine;
Ecstatic joys to thee belong,
And powers almost divine.
But 't is a false, destructive blaze
Within those eyes I see;
Turn hence their fascinating gaze,
I will not follow thee!

'Coward and fool!' thou mayst reply,
'Walk on the common sod;
Go, trace with timid foot and eye
The steps by others trod.
'T is best the beaten path to keep,
The ancient faith to hold;
To pasture with thy fellow sheep,
And lie within the fold.

Cling to the earth, poor grovelling worm;
'Tis not for thee to soar
Against the fury of the storm,
Amid the thunder's roar!
There's glory in that daring strife
Unknown, undreamt by thee;
There's speechless rapture in the life
Of those who follow me.'

Yes, I have seen thy votaries oft,
Upheld by thee, their guide,
In strength and courage mount aloft
The steepy mountain-side;
I've seen them stand against the sky,
And, gazing from below,
Beheld thy lightning in their eye,
Thy triumph on their brow.

Oh, I have felt what glory, then,
What transport must be theirs!
So far above their fellow-men,
Above their toils and cares;

Inhaling Nature's purest breath,
Her riches round them spread,
The wide expanse of earth beneath,
Heaven's glories overhead!

But I have seen them helpless, dash'd,
Down to a bloody grave,
And still thy ruthless eye has flash'd,
Thy strong hand did not save;
I've seen o'er the mountain's brow
Sustain'd awhile by thee,
O'er rocks of ice and hills of snow
Bound fearless, wild, and free.

Bold and exultant was their mien,
While thou didst cheer them on;
But evening fell,—and then, I ween,
Their faithless guide was gone.
Alas! how fared thy favourites then,—
Lone, helpless, weary, cold?
Did ever wanderer find again
The path he left of old?

Where is their glory, where the pride
That swell'd their hearts before?
Where now the courage that defied
The mightiest tempest's roar?
What shall they do when night grows black,
When angry storms arise?
Who now will lead them to the track
Thou taught'st them to despise?

Spirit of Pride, it needs not this
To make me shun thy wiles,
Renounce thy triumph and thy bliss,
Thy honours and thy smiles!
Bright as thou art, and bold, and strong,
That fierce glance wins not me;
And I abhor thy scoffing tongue—
I will not follow thee!

Spirit of Faith! be thou my guide,
O clasp my hand in thine,
And let me never quit thy side;
Thy comforts are divine!
Earth calls thee blind, misguided one,—
But who can shew like thee
Forgotten things that have been done,
And things that are to be?

Secrets conceal'd from Nature's ken
Who like thee can declare?
Or who like thee to erring men
God's holy will can bear?
Pride scorns thee for thy lowly mien,—
But who like thee can rise
Above this toilsome, sordid scene,
Beyond the holy skies?

1848.]   *Yeast; or, the Thoughts, Sayings, &c.*   195

Meek is thine eye and soft thy voice,
But wondrous is thy might,
To make the wretched soul rejoice,
To give the simple light!
And still to all that seek thy way
This magic power is given,—
E'en while their footsteps press the clay,
Their souls ascend to heaven.

Danger surrounds them,—pain and woe
Their portion here must be,
But only they that trust thee know
What comfort dwells with thee;
Strength to sustain their drooping pow'rs,
And vigour to defend,—
Thou pole-star of my darkest hours,
Affliction's firmest friend!

Day does not always mark our way,
Night's shadows oft appal,
But lead me, and I cannot stray,—
Hold me, I shall not fall;
Sustain me, I shall never faint,
How rough soe'er may be
My upward road,—nor moan nor plaint
Shall mar my trust in thee.

Narrow the path by which we go,
And oft it turns aside
From pleasant meads where roses blow,
And peaceful waters glide;

Where flowery turf lies green and soft,
And gentle gales are sweet,
To where dark mountains frown aloft,
Hard rocks distress the feet,—

Deserts beyond lie bleak and bare,
And keen winds round us blow;
But if thy hand conducts me there,
The way is right, I know.
I have no wish to turn away;
My spirit does not quail,—
How can it while I hear thee say,
'Press forward and prevail!'

Even above the tempest's swell
I hear thy voice of love,—
Of hope and peace I hear thee tell,
And that blest home above;
Through pain and death I can rejoice,
If but thy strength be mine,—
Earth hath no music like thy voice,
Life owns no joy like thine!

Spirit of Faith, I'll go with thee!
Thou, if I hold thee fast,
Wilt guide, defend, and strengthen me,
And bear me home at last!
By thy help all things I can do,
In thy strength all things bear,—
Teach me, for thou art just and true,
Smile on me, thou art fair!
ACTON BELL.

YEAST; OR, THE THOUGHTS, SAYINGS, AND DOINGS OF LANCELOT SMITH, GENTLEMAN.

CHAP. III.—NEW ACTORS, AND A NEW STAGE.

WHEN Argemone rose in the morning, her first thought was of Lancelot. His face haunted her. The wild brilliance of his intellect struggling through foul smoke-clouds had haunted her still more. She had heard of his profligacy, his bursts of fierce Berserk-madness; and yet now these very faults, instead of repelling, seemed to attract her, and intensify her longing to save him. She would convert him; purify him; harmonise his discords. And that very wish gave her a peace she had never felt before. She had formed her idea; she had now a purpose for which to live, and she de-termined to concentrate herself for the work, and longed for the moment when she should meet Lancelot, and begin—how, she did not very clearly see.

It is an old jest—the fair devotee trying to convert the young rake. Men of the world laugh heartily at it; and so does the devil, no doubt. If any readers wish to be fellow-jesters with that personage, they may; but, as sure as old Saxon woman-worship remains for ever a blessed and healing law of life, the devotee may yet convert the rake, and, perhaps, herself into the bargain.

Argemone looked almost angrily

---

case with the work now before us; indeed, so revolting are many of the scenes, so coarse and disgusting the language put into the mouths of some of the characters, that the reviewer to whom we entrusted it returned it to us, saying it was unfit to be noticed in the pages of *Sharpe;* and we are so far of the same opinion, that our object in the present paper is to warn our readers, and more especially our lady-readers, against being induced to peruse it, either by the powerful interest of the story, or the talent with which it is written. Did we think less highly of it in these particulars, we should have left the book to its fate, and allowed it quietly to sink into the insignificance to which the good taste of the reading public speedily condemns works disfigured by the class of faults we have alluded to; but, like the fatal melody of the Syren's song, its very perfections render it more dangerous, and therefore more carefully to be avoided. Yet we consider the evils which render the work unfit for perusal (for we go that length in regard to it,) to arise from a perverted taste and an absence of mental refinement in the writer, together with a total ignorance of the usages of good society, rather than from any systematic design of opposing the cause of religion and morality. So far from any such intention being apparent, the moral of the tale is excellent, and the author we should imagine a religious character, though *he* (for, despite reports to the contrary, we *will* not believe any woman could have written such a work,) holds one doctrine, to which we shall more particularly allude hereafter, for which we fear he can find no sufficient authority in Scripture.

As we are unable to support our strictures by adducing extracts, (for we must not fall into a fault somewhat too common with reviewers, and, by polluting our pages with coarse quotations, commit the very sin we are inveighing against,) we will proceed to give a slight sketch of the story, and leave our readers to judge whether such scenes as we shall glance at, where each revolting detail is dwelt on with painful minuteness, each brutal or profane expression chronicled with hateful accuracy, can be fit subject matter for the pages of a work of fiction, a popular novel to be obtruded by every circulating library-keeper upon the notice of our sisters, wives, and daughters. . . .

Up to . . . more than two-thirds of the first volume, there is little to find fault with, much to praise. The character of Gilbert is cleverly drawn, original, yet perfectly true to nature; that of Helen, interesting in the extreme; and the scenes between them, though occasionally too warmly coloured, life-like and engrossing, while the description of village society is sufficiently amusing to afford relief to the more serious business of the novel. With the commencement of the journal, however, the faults we have already alluded to begin to develop themselves.

Fascinated by dazzling qualities, and an unusually handsome exterior, Helen, a headstrong girl of eighteen, bestows her heart and hand on an unprincipled profligate, ignoring with the blind willfulness of first love his evil propensities, or, where her good sense forbids her doing so entirely, trusting to her influence to eradicate them. The sequel is easily foreseen. Throwing off the slight restraint which his evanescent passion for Helen had placed him under, Mr. Huntingdon speedily resumes his dissipated habits; his absences from home become more and more protracted, the scenes on his return each time less endurable, till at length, losing all sense of decency and proper feeling, he fills his house with his profligate associates, and carries on a *liaison* with a married woman, beneath the roof which shelters his outraged wife. When we add, that the scenes which occur after the drinking bouts of these choice spirits are described with a disgustingly truthful minuteness, which shows the writer to be only too well acquainted with the revolting details of such evil revelry, we think we need scarcely produce further proof of the unreadableness of these volumes.

Let us turn from this hateful part of the subject to the character of Helen. The noble fortitude with which she endures the lot her self-willed rashness has brought upon her; the long suffering affection, induc-

ing her to hope against hope, as she tries in vain to reclaim her worthless husband; the brutal insults to which she is exposed while pursuing her labour of love; the bitterness of soul with which she perceives all her efforts to be unavailing, and the conviction of the hopeless depravity of the man she loves is forced upon her; the way in which (that love being at length extinguished and its place supplied by a mixed feeling of contempt and dislike,) she still remains with him from a sense of duty, are all beautifully delineated, and despite of ourselves, compel our admiration. . . .

The death of the profligate Huntingdon, the gay, the courted, the man of *pleasure*—oh, what a bitter mockery the name appears at such a time!—is one of the most powerfully drawn scenes of the whole work. . . .

The only thing which in the slightest degree affords Helen consolation under these harrowing circumstances, is her belief (which, from the way in which it is mentioned, we cannot but conclude to be that of the writer also,) in the doctrine of universal final salvation—the wicked are to pass through purifying penal fires, but all are to be saved at last. The dangerous tendency of such a belief must be apparent to any one who gives the subject a moment's consideration; and it becomes scarcely necessary, in order to convince our readers of the madness of trusting to such a forced distortion of the Divine attribute of mercy, to add that this doctrine is alike repugnant to Scripture, and in direct opposition to the teaching of the Anglican Church.

One word as to the authorship of this novel. At the first glance we should say, none but a man could have known so intimately each vile, dark fold of the civilized brute's corrupted nature; none but a man could make so daring an exhibition as this book presents to us. On the other hand, no man, we should imagine, would have written a work in which all the women, even the worst, are so far superior in every quality, moral and intellectual, to all the men; no man would have made his sex appear at once coarse, brutal, and contemptibly weak, at once disgusting and ridiculous. There are, besides, a thousand trifles which indicate a woman's mind, and several more important things which show a woman's peculiar virtues. Still there is a bold coarseness, a reckless freedom of language, and an apparent familiarity with the sayings and doings of the worst style of *fast* men, in their worst moments, which would induce us to believe it impossible that a woman could have written it. A possible solution of the enigma is, that it may be the production of an authoress assisted by her husband, or some other *male* friend: if this be not the case, we would rather decide on the whole, that it is a man's writing.

In taking leave of the work, we cannot but express our deep regret that a book in many respects eminently calculated to advance the cause of religion and right feeling, the moral of which is unimpeachable and most powerfully wrought out, should be rendered unfit for the perusal of the very class of persons to whom it would be most useful, (namely, imaginative girls likely to risk their happiness on the forlorn hope of marrying and reforming a captivating rake,) owing to the profane expressions, inconceivably coarse language, and revolting scenes and descriptions by which its pages are disfigured.

–*Sharpe's London Magazine*, 7 (August 1848): 181–184

* * *

These excerpts are from an unsigned review that appeared in a leading New York weekly. The reviewer seems to believe that Acton Bell is also the author of Wuthering Heights *and possibly of* Jane Eyre.

"Crude Though Powerful"
Review of *The Tenant of Wildfell Hall*

There is no longer a doubt that the public is threatened with an infinite series of novels of a new class, which will be strung on, like the knotted tail of a kite, to the popular work "Jane Eyre." That book has been already sufficiently discussed, and we purpose here confining our remarks to the crude though powerful production named at the head of this article. The mind that conceived them is one of great strength and fervor, but coarse almost to brutality. Its owner may be descended from a jarl or a sea-king; but though his name be written on the roll of Battle-Abbey, there is a leaven of intense vulgarity in his very fibre that no washings of heraldry can ever efface. But we mean not to be offensively severe on this trait—we only want his American readers to recognise it while doing just homage to his genius. The *reality* of these writings makes them seize upon the public mind; and already there is the liveliest discussion about their principles, when in fact the danger from their diffusion lies much nearer the surface. For good taste supplies the *antennæ* or feelers as to what is right with half the world, and if that be perverted the weaker part at least are sure to go wrong.

Let us illustrate. The delightful tales of Hogg, the Ettrick shepherd, are full of grossness; but these tell for nothing with the reader of education. 'Tis a man of genius whom he knows to have been originally low in his associations, describing scenes of social life through his own peculiar appointed medium of viewing them. But in the novels of Acton Bell the public mind is fixed as yet only upon the *genius* of the writer: his pictures of

"Secretly from My Own Heart"
Anne's Belief in Universal Salvation

In this excerpt from her 30 December 1848 letter to the Reverend David Thom, an advocate of the doctrine of universal salvation for all persons, Anne discusses her controversial belief and its treatment in The Tenant of Wildfell Hall.

. . . I have seen so little of controversial Theology that I was not aware the doctrine of Universal Salvation had so able and ardent an advocate as yourself, but I have cherished it from my very childhood—with a trembling hope at first, and afterwards with a firm and glad conviction of its truth. I drew it secretly from my own heart and from the word of God before I knew that any other held it. And since then it has ever been a source of true delight to me to find the same views either timidly suggested or boldly advocated by benevolent and thoughtful minds; and I now believe there are many more believers than professors in that consoling creed. Why good men should be so averse to admit it, I know not:—into their own hearts at least, however they might object to its promulgation among the bulk of mankind. But perhaps the World is not ripe for it yet. I have frequently thought that since it has pleased God to leave it in darkness so long respecting this particular truth, and often to use such doubtful language as to admit of such a general misconception thereupon, he must have some good reason for it. We see how liable men are to yield to the temptations of the passing hour; how little the dread of future punishment—how still less the promise of future reward can avail to make them forbear and wait; and if so many thousands rush into destruction with (as they suppose) the prospect of Eternal Death before their eyes,—what might not the consequence be, if that prospect were changed for one of a limited season of punishment, far distant and unseen,—however protracted and terrible it might be?

I thankfully cherish this belief; I honour those who hold it; and I would that all men had the same view of man's hopes and God's unbounded goodness as he has given to us, if it might be had with safety. But does not that <u>if</u> require some consideration? should we not remember the weak brother and the infatuated slave of satan, and beware of revealing these truths too hastily to those as yet unable to receive them?

But in these suggestions I am perhaps condemning myself, for in my late novel, "The Tenant of Wildfell Hall", I have given as many hints in support of the doctrine as I could venture to introduce into a work of that description. They are however <u>mere</u> suggestions, and as such I trust you will receive them, believing that I am well aware how much may be said in favour of boldly disseminating God's truth and leaving that to work its way. Only let our zeal be tempered with discretion, and while we labour, let us humbly look to God who is able and certain to bring his great work to perfection in his own good time and manner.

–*The Letters of Charlotte Brontë*, v. 2, pp. 160–161

Photo J. J. Stead.

Blake Hall, Mirfield (Grassdale Manor).

Where Anne Brontë was governess in 1837.

"My heart sank within me to behold that stately mansion in the midst of its expansive grounds. The park as beautiful now, in its wintry garb, as it could be in its summer glory: the majestic sweep, the undulating swell and fall, displayed to full advantage in that robe of dazzling purity, stainless and printless—save one long, winding track left by the trooping deer—the stately timber-trees with their heavy-laden branches gleaming white against the dull, grey sky; the deep encircling woods; the broad expanse of water sleeping in frozen quiet; and the weeping ash and willow drooping their snow-clad boughs above it—all presented a picture, striking indeed, and pleasing to an unencumbered mind, but by no means encouraging to me."—"The Tenant of Wildfell Hall."

The home where Anne served as governess for the Ingham family. It is believed to have been the basis for details of her descriptions of Wellwood, the Bloomfield family's house in Agnes Grey, *and of Arthur Huntingdon's Grassdale Manor in* The Tenant of Wildfell Hall *(from* The Bookman, *October 1904).*

nature are unsurpassed, and his pictures of life being almost equally vivid, we take his delineations of the better classes of society in the north of England with the same confidence that we accord to his delineations of scenery. And yet what a set of boorish cubs, nauseating profligates, and diabolical ruffians, does he present us, as specimens of the social life, whether immediately around him, or among the gay and far-descended, with whose habits and peculiarities he claims to be more or less familiar! In "Wuthering Heights," all his far-descended demi-noblesse of the north of England would be out of place in a decent American kitchen. And in his last book the beautiful tenant of Wildfell Hall, the heiress of parks and villas, and the belle of a London season, marries a boor, whom the writer describes as lacking either spirit, generosity, or language to make a full apology to her invalid brother, whom he has nearly beaten to death by mistake; and this caitiff ditcher, who should have been passed out of the window with a farm-yard fork, the writer makes his hero; because he can talk sentiment, and criticise pictures, loves poetry, and has something more than a peasant's meteorological observation of the influence of the weather on the landscape.

But it may be said, "there is a good deal of human nature about the whole thing." There is the blindness of the critic! It is the writer's genius which makes his incongruities appear natural. When or where was there such a state of society, such a jumble of character and manners as he describes. His London Buck, Mr. Huntingdon, belongs to the squire-archy period of Smollett and Fielding's novels—the wife of the profligate to the sentimental, progress women of the present era. His "Gilbert Markham" has the intelligence of a country gentleman that might have flourished in some pleasant hamlet on the North river; but he commits an assault and battery upon "the squire" that would have wrought an indict-ment wherever our country squires are to be found; while his very apology, if it did not provoke a call for pistols and coffee in the party outraged, would have insured his being set ashore from a Mississippi steam-boat as unfit to associate with the cabin passengers. Such gross incongruities of character do undoubtedly exist in individuals the world over; but can this sort of half-civilization, half-brutification, be characteristic of English society in any portion of that highly artifi-cial country? Is it customary to find the combination of the boor and the bravo (both male and female by the way) in hereditary possession of long-descended estates like Wuthering Heights? Is it characteristic of "English Respectabilities"—the landholders, common law men, or gig-keeping classes—to unite manners and principles like those of Huntingdon to property and position like his—or intelligence and taste like that of Markham to his clownishness?

We shrewdly suspect these books to be written by some gifted and retired woman, whose principal notions of men are derived from other books; or who, taking some walking automaton of her native village for a model, throws in certain touches of rascality, of uncouthness or boisterousness, to make her lay figures animated and, as she thinks, masculine. If any one chooses to study her male characters, it will be found that all that is good or attractive about them is or might be womanish, while all that is bad relishes either of the flash English novel, or of the melodramas of Kotzebue's day.

But what, then, do we leave this writer as the secret of her power?—It is comprised in vigor of thought, freshness and naturalness of expression, and remarkable reality of description. No matter how untrue to life her scene or character may be, the vivid-ness and fervor of her imagination is such that she instantly *realizes* it. And herein lies the undoubted test—the distinctive power—the often sad gift of genius, viz. the thorough sympathy with, the living in, the intense realization of the creations of its own fancy. There are many thoroughly matter of fact scenes in these books so literally depicted that we read them only as faithful transcripts of the writer's experience; yet these very scenes are not unlikely to originate just as much in the

conceptions of fancy as any others. You cannot detect the *jointing* on of the real to the unreal, in a writer of genius, from the simple fact that the images of the latter are often more vivid to his own mind than the actual pictures drawn by the former. But you may trace his identities through the medium of his tastes, natural or conventional. If these are coarse he will certainly betray himself at some time, like the cat who, endowed as a princess, instinctively betrayed the royal dignity, when a mouse at the foot of the throne called out her feline pro-pensities.

The work before us, although infinitely inferior to, yet in some respects greatly resembles *Jane Eyre:* not alone in manner of thinking, but in the execution. Like its predecessor, it is an autobiography. One-half of it consists of letters from Gilbert Markham to his brother-in-law, giving an account of his career; the remainder, of a journal kept by Helen Graham (we hate to give her any other name than the one we knew her by) of her own life. . . .

In all this the reader will discover a strong fam-ily likeness to the plot of *Jane Eyre,* which purports to be written by a brother of the author. It may be curi-ous to point out some few additional proofs of this resemblance. In both, the heroines, so soon as trou-bles thicken around them, take to the open country under an assumed name, like Rosalind and Celia, in the Forest of Arden, where they keep themselves con-cealed, and suffer hardships. Certainly, they ought to have had a legal adviser to show them the use of their country's laws. And so in style does this likeness exist. Every one remembers, in *Jane Eyre,* how beautifully, in a few words, a whole landscape is presented to the reader—aye, and more than that—how cunningly or how magically the author conveys the scene he (or she) describes to the mind's eye, so as not only to impress it with the mere view, but to speak, as it were, to the imagination, to the inner sense, as is ever the case with the Poetry as the Painting of real genius. This same mysterious word-painting is one of the fea-tures of the present tale. . . .

We have yet a few remarks to add before taking leave of these works. We have at the opening of this article expressed our sense of the author's views of life and society in sufficiently decided terms. But after placing him (or her) in about the same social position as the rarely endowed author of the Queen's Wake; and accounting for many coarsenesses upon the same score that every one excuses them in the prose tales of the Ettrick Shepherd, we do not believe one word in the charge of immorality so often brought against these books. An aberration of taste, an ignorance of society, must by no means be confounded with a departure from principle. But still further, while we hold the writer responsible at the bar of criticism for painting life and manners as they really exist—yet as to the correctness of his character in the abstract, we assuredly do not mean to hold him or any other author responsible.

We consider him here solely as an artist. . . . In tracing her career, the heroine tells truthfully everything that would interest the reader, however much the cool head of worldly calculation or of self-complacent inexperience may sneer at or condemn it. Who does not cry Amen to the indignant malison Jane Eyre denounces against her devilish aunt? Alas for poor human nature! who can justly discriminate between the glow of triumph at the ruin of Helen Graham's persecutors, and the recognition of the mysterious hand of Providence in their downfall? . . .

To pursue further the ideas that call forth the censure of some estimable judge of character against them. We are told that no woman, unless divested of all those finer sensibilities that constitute the chief graces of her heart, could possibly comport herself towards any man as do the heroines before us, Helen and Jane. Again we doubt all this. Utterly inexperienced as we are in the labyrinthine intricacies of the heart of woman, we may err in our conceptions of its nature. But still, we contend that it was not possible for Jane Eyre, loving as she did with all the nervous tension of which the heart is capable, to act otherwise than she did. The affections of a woman are like the tendrils of a vine; in their infancy they are tender and susceptible, but when for a time they have encircled the limb in their grasp, and have been exposed as well to the cold winds of Spring as to the hot suns of Summer, they become obdurate and hard; and then in the object of her affection "grappled to her soul with hooks of steel." It is contrary to the very spirit of Love to sit in judgment on every little peccadillo of his votaries. How could any one mould her heart to love one whom she had never seen, solely on grounds of esteem? If such were the case, if reason alone dictated in such matters, a man might marry his grandmother as likely as any one else. No, cold, deliberate calculation can never originate, though it may control love. The mariner who loosens his sails to the gale, may as well seek to make the wind blow from what quarter he listeth. . . .

It is sheer nonsense to say that because the ceremonials of society—that wholesome framework of conventionality which makes the common sense of the many in times past and present, the stay and support against which the weak and the bewildered may always lean with safety—it is sheer nonsense to say that these useful but arbitrary rules for discreet guid-

ance must always *inevitably* interfere between the earthly—perhaps the eternal happiness of two beings whose destiny is wound up in each other! Prims and Prudes may decry passages exhibiting the heart as it is, but as honest Jack Falstaff says, "Is not the truth the truth;" what more can we say? However objectionable these works may be to crude minds which cannot winnow the chaff of vulgarity from the rich grain of genius which burdens them, very many, while enjoying their freshness and vigor, will gladly hail their appearance, as boldly and eloquently developing blind places of wayward passion in the human heart, which it is far more interesting to trace than all the bustling lanes and murky alleys through which the will-o'-wisp genius of Dickens has so long led the public mind.

—*The Literary World,* no. 80 (12 August 1848): 544–546

* * *

This excerpt is from an unsigned article titled "Novels of the Season," believed to have been written by Edwin Percy Whipple, a leading American critic. Whipple identified Acton Bell as "the author of Wuthering Heights, The Tenant of Wildfell Hall, and if we mistake not, of certain offensive but powerful portions of Jane Eyre." His reference to the "immediate predecessor" of The Tenant of Wildfell Hall *is to* Wuthering Heights.

"No Enlarged View of Mankind"
Review of *The Tenant of Wildfell Hall*

The Tenant of Wildfell Hall is altogether a less unpleasing story than its immediate predecessor, though it resembles it in the excessive clumsiness with which the plot is arranged, and the prominence given to the brutal element of human nature. The work seems a convincing proof, that there is nothing kindly or genial in the author's powerful mind, and that, if he continues to write novels, he will introduce into the land of romance a larger number of hateful men and women than any other writer of the day. Gilbert, the hero, seems to be a favorite with the author, and to be intended as a specimen of manly character; but he would serve as the ruffian of any other novelist. His nature is fierce, proud, moody, jealous, revengeful, and sometimes brutal. We can see nothing good in him except a certain rude honesty; and that quality is seen chiefly in his bursts of hatred and his insults to women. Helen, the heroine, is doubtless a strong-minded woman, and passes bravely through a great deal of suffering; but if there be any lovable or feminine virtues in her composition, the author has managed to conceal them. She marries a profligate, thinking to reform him; but the gentleman, with a full knowledge of her purpose, declines reformation, goes deeper and deeper into vice, and becomes at last as fiendlike as a very limited stock of brains will allow. This is a reversal of the process carried on in Jane Eyre; but it must be admitted that the profligate in The Tenant of Wildfell Hall is no Rochester. He is never virtuously inclined, except in those periods of illness and feebleness which his debaucheries have occasioned, thus illustrating the old proverb,—

"When the devil was sick, the devil a monk would be,
When the devil was well, the devil a monk was he."

He has almost constantly by him a choice coterie of boon companions, ranging from the elegant libertine to the ferocious sensualist, and the reader is favored with exact accounts of their drunken orgies, and with numerous scraps of their profane conversation. All the characters are drawn with great power and precision of outline, and the scenes are as vivid as life itself. Everywhere is seen the tendency of the author to degrade passion into appetite, and to give prominence to the selfish and malignant elements of human nature; but while he succeeds in making profligacy disgusting, he fails in making virtue pleasing. His depravity is total depravity, and his hard and impudent debauchees seem to belong to that class of reprobates whom Dr. South considers "as not so much born as damned into the world." The reader of Acton Bell gains no enlarged view of mankind, giving a healthy action to his sympathies, but is confined to a narrow space of life, and held down, as it were, by main force, to witness the wolfish side of his nature literally and logically set forth. But the criminal courts are not the places in which to take a comprehensive view of humanity, and the novelist who confines his observation to them is not likely to produce any lasting impression, except of horror and disgust.

—North American Review, 67 (October 1848): 359–360

* * *

The author of this unsigned review from an article titled "Recent Novels" is believed to be Charles Kingsley, a clergyman, social reformer, and novelist. Toward the end of this excerpt the reviewer refers to the novelist as a she, giving the following explanation in a footnote: "We have spoken of the author in the feminine gender, because, of whatever sex the name 'Acton Bell' may be, a woman's pen seems to us indisputably discernible in every page. The very coarseness and vulgarity is just such as a woman, trying to write like a man, would invent,—second-hand and clumsy, and not such as men do use; the more honour to the writer's heart, if not to her taste."

"Vulgar and Improbable"
Review of *The Tenant of Wildfell Hall*

A people's novel of a very different school is *The Tenant of Wildfell Hall.* It is, taken altogether, a powerful and an interesting book. Not that it is a pleasant book to read; nor, as we fancy, has it been a pleasant book to write; still, less has it been a pleasant training which could teach an author such awful facts, or give courage to write them. The fault of the book is coarseness—not merely that coarseness of subject which will be the stumbling-block of most readers, and which makes it utterly unfit to be put into the hands of girls; of that we do not complain. There are foul and accursed undercurrents in plenty, in this same smug, respectable, whitewashed English society, which must be exposed now and then; and Society owes thanks, not sneers, to those who dare to shew her the image of her own ugly, hypocritical visage. We must not lay Juvenal's coarseness at Juvenal's door, but at that of the Roman world which he stereotyped in his fearful verses. But the world does not think so. It will revile Acton Bell for telling us, with painful circumstantiality, what the house of a profligate, uneducated country squire is like, perfectly careless whether or not the picture be true, only angry at having been disturbed from its own self-complacent doze. . . .

But taking this book as a satire, and an exposure of evils, still all unnecessary coarseness is a defect—a defect which injures the real usefulness and real worth of book. The author introduces, for instance, a long diary, kept by the noble and unhappy wife of a profligate squire: and would that every man in England might read and lay to heart that horrible record. But what greater mistake, to use mildest term, can there be than to fill such a diary with written oaths and curses, with details of drunken scenes which no wife, such as poor Helen is represented, would have the heart, not to say the common decency, to write down as they occurred? Dramatic probability and good feeling are equally outraged by such a method. The author, tempted naturally to indulge her full powers of artistic detail, seems to have forgotten that there are silences more pathetic than all words.

A cognate defect, too, struck us much; the splenetic and bitter tone in which certain personages in the novel are mentioned, when really, poor souls, no deeds of theirs are shewn which could warrant such wholesale appellations as 'brute' and 'demon.' One is inclined sometimes to suspect that they are caricatures from the life, against whom some private spite is being vented; though the author has a right to reply, that the whole novel being the autobiography of a young gentleman farmer, such ferocities are to be charged on him, not on

"A Character Utterly Distinct from Her Brother"

Francis A. Leyland argued strongly that Branwell was not the model for Arthur Huntingdon in The Tenant of Wildfell Hall.

Consumption and intemperance, the curses of our island and our climate, are found not the less in the West-Riding of Yorkshire. A cold and humid atmosphere, like poverty and want, begets a recourse to stimulants, and, with some natures, the bounds of moderation are soon passed. The prevalence of the latter evil had entered deeply into Anne's thoughts. Her brother's occasional indulgence had made it familiar to her; but we should clearly commit an error, as well as a great injustice to her, in supposing that, in the character of Huntingdon, she wished to present his failings to the public.

A careful study of the question has, indeed, convinced me, not only that Huntingdon is no portrait of Branwell Brontë, but that he is distinctly and designedly his very antitype. The author of 'Wildfell Hall' could scarcely have created a character so completely different from Branwell, unless she intended to do so; for, otherwise, writing under the influence of circumstances, and the inspiration of the moment, something of his strong personality must surely have found its way into the book. It is pleasant to be thus able to record, as an act of justice to Anne Brontë, that, though she had been compelled to witness the results of intemperance both in Branwell and in others, she purposely conveyed her lesson of these evils in the acts and thoughts of a character utterly distinct from her brother. Indeed, she was at considerable pains—which have unfortunately availed little—to prevent even a suspicion that her brother was the prototype of Huntingdon; for, to remove that impression, she has placed the hero of the story, Gilbert Markham, to a considerable extent, in Branwell's very circumstances. There is no resemblance between Markham's character and Branwell's, beyond that of an ardent and generous temperament; but it should be observed that—exactly as with Branwell—Markham is enamoured of a married woman, the death of whose husband he anxiously awaits; that this passion is attributed to him as a monomania—'A monomania,' says his brother Fergus, 'but don't mention it; all right but that;' and, lastly, that Markham, too, thinks, as Branwell did, that the deceased husband of the lady 'might have so constructed his will as to place restrictions upon her marrying again.'

It should likewise be observed that 'Wildfell Hall' is just as much a protest against *mariages de convenance,* as it is against intemperance; but what had this to do with the family circumstances of the Brontës? It had far more to do with such instances . . . where infelicity was combined with intemperance, as it is in the case of Arthur and Helen Huntingdon.

—The Brontë Family with Special Reference to Patrick Branwell Brontë, v. 2, pp. 226–228

her. True, but yet in his mouth as much as in any one's else they want cause for them to be shewn, according to all principles of fiction; and if none such exists on the face of the story, it only indicates a defect in the youth's character which makes his good fortune more improbable. For the book sets forth how the gallant Gilbert wins the heart, and after her husband's death, the hand of the rich squire's well-born and highly-cultivated wife.

Now we do not complain of the 'impossibility' of this. *Ne me dites jamais ce bête mot,* as Mirabeau said. Impossible? Society is full of wonders; our worst complaint against fiction-mongers is, that they are so tame, so common-place, so shamefully afraid of wonders, of ninety-nine hundredths of what a man may see every day of the week by putting his head out of his own window. . . . So much for improbabilities. But the novelist, especially when he invents a story, instead of merely giving dramatic life to one ready made, which is the Shakspearian, and, as we suspect, the higher path of art, must give some internal and spiritual probability to his outward miracles; and this, we think, Acton Bell has in this case failed to do. We cannot see any reason why Gilbert Markham, though no doubt highly attractive to young ladies of his own calibre, should excite such passionate love in Helen, with all her bitter experiences of life, her painting, and her poetry, her deep readings and deep thoughts—absolutely no reason at all, except the last one in the world, which either the author or she would have wished, namely, that there was no other man in the way for her to fall in love with. We want to see this strange intellectual superiority of his to the general run of his class (for we must suppose some such); and all the characteristics we do find, beyond the general dashing, manful spirit of a young farmer, is a very passionate and somewhat brutal temper, and, to say the least, a wanton rejection of a girl to whom he has been giving most palpable and somewhat rough proofs of affection, and whom he afterwards hates bitterly, simply because she rallies him on having jilted her for a woman against whose character there was every possible ground for suspicion. This is not to be counterbalanced by an occasional vein of high-flown sentimentalism in the young gentleman (and that, too, not often) when he comes in contact with his lady-love. If the author had intended to work out the noble old Cymon and Iphegenia myths, she ought to have let us see the gradual growth of the clown's mind under the influence of the accomplished woman; and this is just what she has not done. Gilbert Markham is not one character oscillating between his old low standard and his higher new one, according as he comes in contact with his own countrified friends or his new lady-love, but two different men, with no single root-idea of character to unite and explain the two opposite poles of his conduct. For instance, Mr. Markham is one day talking to Helen in the following high-flown vein:—

'It gives me little consolation to think that I shall next behold you as a disembodied spirit, or an altered being, with a frame perfect and glorious, but not like this; and a heart, perhaps, entirely estranged from me.'

'No, Gilbert, there is perfect love in heaven.'

'*So* perfect, I suppose, that it soars above distinctions, and you will have no closer sympathy with me than with any one of the ten thousand thousand angels, and the innumerable multitude of happy spirits round us.'

And so on; very fine indeed. But, lo! the same evening he goes to call upon an old and intimate friend, whom, after having brutally knocked him down and left him in a ditch, careless whether he died or not, on the supposition that he was, like himself, a lover of Helen, he has suddenly discovered to be neither more nor less than her brother; and after this fashion he makes his apology for having nearly killed him:—

My task must be performed at once, however, in some fashion; and so I plunged into it at once, and floundered through it as I could.

'The truth is, Lawrence, I have not acted quite correctly to you of late, especially on this last occasion; and I am come to—in short, to express my regret for what I've done, and to beg your pardon. If you don't choose to grant it,' I added, hastily, not liking the aspect of his face, 'it's no matter; only *I've* done *my* duty, that's all.'

To which *amende honorable* the knight of the broken head answering more sensibly than gratefully:—

'I forgot to tell you that it was in consequence of a mistake,' muttered I. 'I should have made a very handsome apology, but you have provoked me so confoundedly' (the young gentleman, like most characters in the book, is very fond of such expletives, and still stronger ones) 'with your—Well, I suppose it's all my fault. The fact is, I did n't know that you were Mrs. Graham's brother,' &c. &c.

Quantum mutates ab illo Hectore! To us, this and many other scenes seen as vulgar and improbable in conception, as they are weak and disgusting in execution. The puffs inform us that the book is very like *Jane Eyre*. To us it seems to have exaggerated all the faults of that remarkable book, and retained very few of its good points. The superior *religious* tone in which alone it surpasses *Jane Eyre* is, in our eyes, quite neutralised by the low *moral* tone which reigns throughout.

Altogether, as we said before, the book is painful. The dark side of every body and every thing is dilated on; we had almost said, revelled in. There are a very few quite perfect people in the book, but they are kept as far out of sight as possible; they are the 'accidentals,' the disagreeable people, the 'necessary' notes of the melody; and the 'timbre' of the notes themselves is harsh and rough. The author has not had the tact which enabled Mr. Thackeray, in *Vanity Fair*, to construct a pleasing whole out of most unpleasing materials by a harmonious unity of parts, and, above all, by a tone of tender grace and solemn ironic indignation; in the midst of all his humour, spreading over and softening down the whole;—that true poetic instinct, which gives to even the coarsest of Fielding's novels and Shakspeare's comedies, considered as wholes, a really pure and lofty beauty. The author has not seen that though it is quite fair to write in a melancholy, or even harsh key, and to introduce accidental discords or even sounds in themselves disagreeable, yet that this last must be done only to set off by contrast the background of harmony and melody and that the key of the whole must be a correct and a palpable one; it must not be buried beneath innumerable occasional flats and sharps; above all, we must not, as in *The Tenant of Wildfell Hall,* with its snappish fierceness, be tortured by a defective chord, in which one false note is perpetually recurring; or provoked by a certain flippant, rough, staccato movement throughout, without softness, without repose, and therefore, without dignity. We advise the author, before the next novel is taken in hand, to study Shakspeare somewhat more carefully, and see if she cannot discover the secret of the wonderful harmony with which he, like Raphael, transfigures the most painful, and, apparently, chaotic subjects.

—*Fraser's Magazine,* 39 (April 1849): 423–426

"A Slow Dark March"

Soon after Emily's death in December 1848 signs of pulmonary tuberculosis in Anne became too obvious to ignore. Charlotte reported on Anne's condition in these excerpts.

Charlotte Brontë to Ellen Nussey, 15 January 1849

I can scarcely say that Anne is worse, nor can I say she is better. She varies often in the course of a day yet each day is passed pretty much the same—the morning is usually the best time—the afternoon and evening the most feverish—Her cough is the most troublesome at night but it is rarely violent—the pain in her arm still disturbs her. She takes the cod-liver oil and the carbonate of iron regularly—she finds them both nauseous but especially the oil—her appetite is small indeed. Do not fear that I shall relax in my care of her—she is too precious to me not to be cherished with all the fostering strength I have. . . .

I avoid looking forward or backward and try to keep looking upward—this day is not the time to regret, dread or weep. What I have and ought to do is very dis-

tinctly laid out for me—what I want and pray for is strength to perform it. The days pass in a slow dark march—the nights are the test—the sudden wakings from restless sleep—the revived knowledge that one lies in her grave and another not at my side but in a separate and sick bed

However—God is over all.
—*The Letters of Charlotte Brontë*, v. 2, pp. 169–170

* * *

Charlotte's friend Ellen Nussey invited Anne to stay with the Nussey family in hopes that a change of scene would benefit her. Anne wrote to decline this offer but to press for a trip to the coast that shows she yet hoped to recover from her illness. Excerpt.

Anne Brontë to Ellen Nussey, 5 April 1849

. . . pray give my sincere thanks to your mother and sisters, but tell them I could not think of inflicting my presence upon them as I now am. It is very kind of them to make so light of the trouble, but still there must be more or less, and certainly no pleasure, from the

Tombstone in St. Mary's Churchyard, Scarborough, before and after its correction. Charlotte was dismayed by the errors she found when she visited Anne's grave a year after her death: Anne was twenty-nine when she died on 28 May 1849, but though the date of death was later corrected, her age at death was not (left, from Whiteley Turner, A Spring-Time Saunter: Round and About Brontë Land, *Sam Houston State University Library; right, photograph by Susan B. Taylor).*

society of a silent invalid stranger. I hope, however, that Charlotte will by some means make it possible to accompany me after all. She is certainly very delicate, and greatly needs a change of air and scene to renovate her constitution. And then your going with me before the end of May, is apparently out of the question, unless you are disappointed in your visitors; but I should be reluctant to wait till then, if the weather would at all permit an earlier departure. You say May is a trying month, and so say others. The earlier part is often cold enough, I acknowledge, but, according to my experience, we are almost certain of some fine warm days in the latter half, when the laburnums and lilacs are in bloom; whereas June is often cold, and July generally wet. But I have a more serious reason than this for my impatience of delay. The doctors say that change of air or removal to a better climate would hardly ever fail of success in consumptive cases, if the remedy were taken *in time;* but the reason why there are so many disappointments is, that it is generally deferred till it is too late. Now I would not commit this error; and, to say the truth, though I suffer much less from pain and fever than I did when you were with us, I am decidedly weaker, and very much thinner. My cough still troubles me a good deal, especially in the night, and, what seems worse than all, I am subject to great shortness of breath on going upstairs or any slight exertion. Under these circumstances, I think there is no time to be lost. I have no horror of death: if I thought it inevitable, I think I could quietly resign myself to the prospect, in the hope that you, dear Miss—, would give as much of your company as you possibly could to Charlotte, and be a sister to her in my stead. But I wish it would please God to spare me, not only for Papa's and Charlotte's sakes, but because I long to do some good in the world before I leave it. I have many schemes in my head for future practice—humble and limited indeed—but still I should not like them all to come to nothing, and myself to have lived to so little purpose. But God's will be done.

—*The Life of Charlotte Brontë*, v. 2, pp. 97–98

* * *

Excerpt.

Charlotte Brontë to Ellen Nussey, circa 12–14 May 1849

Anne was worse during the warm weather we had about a week ago—she grew weaker and both the pain in her side and her cough were worse—strange to say since it is colder, she has appeared rather to revive than sink. I still hope that if she gets over May she may last a long time.

A "Settled Longing to Be Gone"

Charlotte, who had lost one sister after the other, wrote of Anne's death in a 13 June 1849 letter to William Smith Williams.

. . . my Sister died happily; nothing dark, except the inevitable shadow of Death overclouded her hour of dissolution the doctor—a stranger—who was called in—wondered at her fixed tranquility of spirit and settled longing to be gone. He said in all his experience he had seen no such death-bed, and that it gave evidence of no common mind—Yet to speak the truth—it but half consoles to remember this calm—there is piercing pain in it. Anne had had enough of life such as it was—in her twenty-eighth year she laid it down as a burden. I hardly know whether it is sadder to think of that than of Emily turning her dying eyes reluctantly from the pleasant sun. Had I never believed in a future life before, my Sisters' fate would assure me of it.

—*The Letters of Charlotte Brontë*, v. 2, p. 220

We have engaged lodgings at Scarbro—We stipulated for a good sized sitting-room and an airy double-bedded lodging room—with a sea-view—and—if not deceived—have obtained these desiderata at No 2 Cliff—Anne says it is one of the best situations in the place—It would not have done to have taken lodgings either in the town or on the bleak, steep coast where Miss Wooler's house is situated—If Anne is to get any good she must have every advantage. Miss Outhwaite left her in her will a small legacy of 200£ and she cannot employ her money better than in obtaining what may prolong existence if it does not restore health—We hope to leave home on the 23rd. and I think it will be advisable to rest at York and stay all night there—I hope this arrangement will suit you. . . .

We reckon on your society—dear Ellen—as a real privilege and pleasure. We shall take little luggage and shall have to buy bonnets and dresses and several other things either at York or Scarbro' which place do you think would be best? Oh—if it would please God to strengthen and revive Anne how happy we might be together! His will—however—must be done—and if she is not to recover—it remains to pray for strength and patience . . .

. . . Anne was very ill yesterday. She had difficulty of breathing all day, Even when sitting perfectly still. Today she seems better again. I long for the moment to come when the experiment of the sea-air will be tried. Will it do her good? I cannot tell. I can only wish.

—*The Letters of Charlotte Brontë*, v. 2, pp. 208–209

Emily Brontë

Emily Brontë (1818–1848) is typically depicted as the most enigmatic of the Brontë sisters. Successive generations of critics have generally accepted Charlotte's characterizations of Emily and judged her as quirky, impassioned, antisocial, and intelligent. While these judgments may well be accurate, one should remember that the testimony of a single witness is necessarily subjective. But there is scarce evidence from others or from Emily herself on which to come to an understanding of such a complex personality. Beyond the drawings and paintings she left, her extant writings consist of four "diary papers," a few brief letters, some translations of classical writers, and nine "devoirs" (essays) from Brussels, as well as her poetry manuscripts, published poems, and a single novel. And yet the literary legacy of this reclusive young woman who lived almost her entire life in the remote village of Haworth endures. Many of her poems continue to be studied and admired; and her novel, Wuthering Heights (1847), while treated by many reviewers and nineteenth-century critics as an oddity, is now regarded as a masterpiece of both English and world literature.

At Home in Haworth

Emily Brontë spent more than twenty-five of her thirty years in the village of Haworth, where her family moved before her second birthday. She received little formal schooling: at age six, she briefly attended the Clergy Daughters' School at Cowan Bridge for less than half a year; at age seventeen, she went to Miss Wooler's School for three months, and at age twenty-three, she spent about eight months at the Pensionnat Héger in Belgium. Most of her education took place at the parsonage, where she studied under Aunt Branwell and Reverend Brontë, and then later with her sister Charlotte. Most important, she was an avid reader and studied on her own continuously.

Emily's four surviving "diary papers," written at approximately four-year intervals, indicate that she was happy with her life at the parsonage and her occupations, from caring for the animals and cooking to walking on the moors and writing. They also reveal her close relationship to Anne, who was her partner in creating the imaginary world of Gondal and in recording these brief glimpses of their lives.

This first paper, written by Emily but signed with both sisters' names, was headed "November the 24 1834 Mon-

Emily Jane Brontë, as painted by Branwell Brontë. This is the surviving fragment of a larger painting of Branwell, holding a long-barreled firearm, and his three sisters, the so-called Gun Group portrait (see p. 77). Arthur Bell Nicholls cut away and preserved the Emily portion of the painting sometime after the death of the Reverend Patrick Brontë (National Portrait Gallery; from Christine Alexander and Jane Sellars, The Art of the Brontës, University of Colorado Libraries).

day." Anne drew a ringlet down the side of the first page, which Emily labeled, "A bit of Lady Juliet's hair done by Anne."

122

Diary Paper, 24 November 1834
Emily and Anne Brontë

I fed Rainbow, Diamond, Snowflake Jasper phesant (alias this morning Branwell went down to Mr Drivers and brought news that Sir Robert peel was going to be invited to stand for Leeds Anne and I have been peeling Apples for Charlotte to make an apple pudding and for Aunts [?] and apple Charlotte said she made puddings perfectly and she was of a quick but lim[i]ted intellect[.] Taby said just now come Anne pillopatate (ie pill a potato Aunt has come into the Kitchen just now and said where are you feet Anne Anne answered on the floor Aunt papa opened the parlour Door and gave Branwell a Letter saying here Branwell read this and show it to your Aunt and Charlotte—The Gondals are discovering the interior of Gaaldine
Sally mosley is washing in the back Kitchin
It is past Twelve o'clock Anne and I have not tid[i]ed ourselvs, done our bed work or done our lessons and we want to go out to play We are going to have for Dinner Boiled Beef Turnips potato's and applepudding the Kitchin is in avery untidy state Anne and I have not Done our music excercise which consists of b majer Taby said on my putting a pen in her face Ya pitter pottering there instead of pilling a potate I answered O Dear, O Dear, O Dear I will derictly with that I get up, take a Knife and begin pilling (finished pilling the potatos papa going to walk Mr Sunderland expected
Anne and I say I wonder what we shall be like and what we shall be and where we shall be if all goes on well in the year 1874—in which year I shall be in my 57th year Anne will be going in her 55th year Branwell will be going in his 58th year And Charlotte in her 59th year hoping we shall all be well at that time We close our paper

—Juliet Barker, *The Brontës,* pp. 220–221

* * *

"The Breath of Emily's Nostrils"

In 1835, Emily went with Charlotte to Miss Wooler's School, where Charlotte was to teach and Emily to study. In this excerpt from her biography of Charlotte, Elizabeth Gaskell recounts how emotional distress combined with physical ailments led Emily to return home three months later in October 1835.

On the 29th of July, 1835, Charlotte, now little more than nineteen years old, went as teacher to Miss Wooler's. Emily accompanied her, as a pupil; but she became literally ill from home-sickness, and could not settle to anything, and after passing only three months at Roe Head, returned to the parsonage and the beloved moors.

Miss Brontë gives the following reasons as those which prevented Emily's remaining at school, and caused the substitution of her younger sister in her place at Miss Wooler's: —

"My sister Emily loved the moors. Flowers brighter than the rose bloomed in the blackest of the heath for her;—out of a sullen hollow in a livid hill-side, her mind could make an Eden. She found in the bleak solitude many and dear delights; and not the least and best-loved was—liberty. Liberty was the breath of Emily's nostrils; without it she perished. The change from her own home to a school, and from her own very noiseless, very secluded, but unrestricted and unartificial mode of life, to one of disciplined routine (though under the kindest auspices), was what she failed in enduring. Her nature proved here too strong for her fortitude. Every morning, when she woke, the vision of home and the moors rushed on her, and darkened and saddened the day that lay before her. Nobody knew what ailed her but me. I knew only too well. In this struggle her health was quickly broken: her white face, attenuated form, and failing strength, threatened rapid decline. I felt in my heart she would die, if she did not go home, and with this conviction obtained her recall. She had only been three months at school; and it was some years before the experiment of sending her from home was again ventured on."

This physical suffering on Emily's part when absent from Haworth, after recurring several times under similar circumstances, became at length so much an acknowledged fact, that whichever was obliged to leave home, the sisters decided that Emily must remain there, where alone she could enjoy anything like good health. She left it twice again in her life; once going as teacher to a school in Halifax for six months, and afterwards accompanying Charlotte to Brussels for ten. When at home, she took the principal part of the cooking upon herself, and did all the household ironing; and after Tabby grew old and infirm, it was Emily who made all the bread for the family; and any one passing by the kitchen-door, might have seen her studying German out of an open book, propped up before her, as she kneaded the dough; but no study, however interesting, interfered with the goodness of the bread, which was always light and excellent. Books were, indeed, a very common sight in that kitchen; the girls were taught by their father theoretically, and by their aunt practically, that to take an active part in all household work was, in their position, woman's simple duty; but, in their careful employment of time, they found many an odd five minutes for reading while watching the cakes, and managed by the union of two kinds of employment better than King Alfred.

—*The Life of Charlotte Brontë,* v. 1, pp. 149–151

First page of Emily's "Gondal Poems" manuscript notebook (Brontë Parsonage Museum; from Juliet Gardner,
The World Within: The Brontës at Haworth, *University of Colorado Libraries)*

Emily Brontë's Poetry

Emily's talent as a poet was recognized by the early critics of Poems by Currer, Ellis, and Acton Bell *(1846). In an unsigned review in the May 1857 issue of* Fraser's Magazine, *John Skelton remarked that some of Ellis's songs were "so perfect" that he could not "understand why they are not widely known; certainly modern poetry has produced few lyrics more felicitous either in sentiment or expression than 'Remembrance' ['Cold in the earth—and the deep snow piled above thee']." Arthur C. Benson in his introduction to* Brontë Poems *(1915) asserted, "It may be frankly confessed that the interest of the* Poems *is entirely centred on the work of Emily. If it had not been for the genius which her work unmistakably displays, the poetry of the other three would have sunk into oblivion."*

Twentieth-century scholars of Emily's poetry often examine her extant poems and fragments (numbering about two hundred) in terms of their placement in two categories, as labeled by Emily in the notebooks she set up in February 1844, one titled "Gondal Poems" and another labeled "E.J.B." Many critics have interpreted the distinction to mean that poems in the E.J.B. notebook refer to Emily's personal experiences and that the Gondal Poems should be read as poems that have their meanings within an unknown fictional world. Other critics question whether these categories should define the interpretations of her poetry.

Emily also copied poems into an earlier notebook, the Ashley Notebook (1837–1839), held at the British Library along with the Gondal Notebook. Other manuscripts and fragmentary poems are held in a variety of collections in Britain and the United States.

This second paper, written by Emily but again signed as a joint effort, was headed, "Monday evening June 26 1837."

Diary Paper, 26 June 1837
Emily and Anne Brontë

A bit past 4 o'Clock Charolotte working in Aunts room Branwell reading Eugene Aram to her Anne and I writing in the drawing room—Anne a poem beginning 'fair was the evening and brightly the sun—I Agustus Almedas life Ist vol—4th page from the last a fine rather coolish thin grey cloudy but Sunny day Aunt working in the little Room papa gone out. Tabby in the Kitchin—the Emperors and Empresses of Gondal and Gaaldine preparing to depart from Gaaldine to Gondal to prepare for the coranation which will be on the 12th of July Queen Victoria ascended the throne this month. Northangerland in Monceys Isle—Zamorna at Eversham. all tight and right in which condition it is to be hoped we shall all be on this day 4 years at which time Charollote will be 25 and 2 months—Branwell just 24 it being his birthday—myself 22 and 10 months and a peice Anne 21 and nearly a half I wonder where we shall be and how we shall be and what kind of a day it will be then let us hope for the best

Emily Jane Brontë —Anne Brontë

At the bottom of the diary note, Emily drew her and Anne sitting at the table where they were working. More text appeared below this sketch.

Aunt come Emily its past 4 o'clock Emily Yes Aunt
Anne Well do you intend to write in the evening
Emily well what think you
(we agreed to go out 1st to make sure if we get into a humor we may Stay [out? in?])

In the right margin Emily added this final note.

I guess that this day 4 years we shall all be in this drawing room comfortable I hope it may be so
    Anne guesses we shall all be gone somewhere together comfortable we hope it may be either
                    —Juliet Barker, *The Brontës,* pp. 271–272

* * *

Brontë scholar C. K. Shorter reported that the diary papers of 1841 and 1845 were found by Charlotte's husband in a little tin box: "Within were four little pieces of paper neatly folded to the size of a sixpence. These papers were covered with handwriting, two of them by Emily, and two by Anne Brontë. They revealed a pleasant if eccentric arrangement on the part of the sisters, which appears to have been settled upon even after they had passed their twentieth year. They had agreed to write a kind of reminiscence every four years, to be opened by Emily on her birthday." Shorter suggests that the writings about Gondal mentioned in the papers "were doubtless destroyed, with abundant other memorials of Emily, by the heart-broken sister who survived her." Several pets are referenced: "Victoria and Adelaide" are believed to be tame geese; "Keeper" was Emily's dog; "Nero" was a hawk.

This 1841 paper was headed "A Paper to be opened/ when Anne is / 25 years old / or my next birthday after—/ if / — all be well— / Emily Jane Brontë July the 30th 1841."

Diary Paper, 30 July 1841
Emily Brontë

It is Friday evening—near 9 o'clock—wild rainy weather I am seated in the dining room alone—having just concluded tidying our desk-boxes—writing this document—Papa is in the parlour. Aunt up stairs in her room—she has been reading Blackwood's Magazine to papa—Victoria and Adelaide are ensconced in the peat-house—Keeper is in the kitchen—Nero in his cage—We are all stout and hearty as I hope is the case with Charlotte, Branwell, and Anne, of whom the first is at John White Esq[re] upperwood House, Rawden The second is at Luddenden foot and the third is I beleive at—Scarborough—enditing perhaps a paper corresponding to this— A scheme is at present in agitation for setting us up in a school of our own as yet nothing is determined but

A manuscript poem by Emily beginning "The night of storms has past." This poem was not copied into Emily's notebooks. The speaker in the poem is believed to be a character from her Gondal stories (Morgan Library & Museum).

Emily's watercolor of her dog, Keeper. Charlotte wrote about the relationship between Emily and Keeper in Shirley, *depicting Shirley and her dog, Tartar (Brontë Parsonage Museum: E6; from Christine Alexander and Jane Sellars,* The Art of the Brontës, *University of Colorado Libraries).*

I hope and trust it may go on and prosper and answer our highest expectations. This day 4—years I wonder whether we shall still be dragging on in our present condition or established to our heart's content Time will show—

I guess that at the time appointed for the opening of this paper—we (i.e.) Charlotte, Anne and I—shall be all merrily seated in our own sitting-room in some pleasant and flourishing seminary having just ?gathered in for the midsummer holydays our debts will be paid off and we shall have cash in hand to a considerable amount. papa Aunt and Branwell will either have been—or be coming—to visit us—it will be a fine warm ?summery evening. very different from this bleak look-out Anne and I will perchance slip out into the garden a minutes to peruse our papers. I hope either this [o]r something better will be the case—

———

The ?Gondalians are at present in a threatening state but there is no open rupture as yet—all the princes and princesses of the ?royal royaltys are at the palace of In-struction—I have a good many books on hands but I am sorry to say that as usual I make small progress with any—however I have just made a new regularity paper! and I ?me[an] ?verb sap—to do great things—and now I close sending from far an ?exhortation of courage courage! to exiled and harassed Anne wishing she was here
—*The Letters of Charlotte Brontë*, v. 1, pp. 262–263

* * *

At Law Hill School

Emily left home in September 1838 to teach at Miss Patch-ett's school at Law Hill in Halifax. Charlotte reported on her life at the school in this excerpt from her 2 October 1838 letter to her friend Ellen Nussey.

My Sister Emily is gone into a Situation as teacher in a large school of near forty pupils near Halifax. I have had one letter from her since her departure it gives an appalling account of her duties—Hard labour from six in the morning until near eleven at night. with only one half hour of exercise between—this is slavery I fear she will never stand it—
—*The Letters of Charlotte Brontë*, v. 1, p. 182

Emily worked at the school until poor health required her to return home in late March 1839.

After Emily returned from teaching at Law Hill School in late March 1839, she remained at home until she and Charlotte traveled to Brussels to study at the Pensionnat Héger in February 1842. After their first term Emily was invited to teach music as payment for her own studies. Emily and Charlotte stayed at the pensionnat until Aunt Branwell's death at the end of October 1842. After they returned home, Emily took Aunt Branwell's place in running the parsonage for her father while Charlotte returned to Brussels alone in January 1843. Charlotte later used her experiences at the pensionnat in writing The Professor (1857) and Villette (1853).

This excerpt is from the first full biography of Emily Brontë, by A. Mary F. Robinson, which was published in 1883. Extrapolating from Charlotte's commentary in Gaskell's biography and in her letters to Ellen Nussey, Robinson enlarged on the meaning of the relatively few facts known of Emily's life while arguing for her genius.

At the Pensionnat Héger
A. Mary F. Robinson

The two Brontës were very different to the Belgian schoolgirls in Madame Héger's Pensionnat. They were, for one thing, ridiculously old to be at school—twenty-four and twenty-six—and they seemed to feel their position; their speech was strained and odd; all the "sceptical, wicked, immoral French novels, over forty of them, the best substitute for French conversation to be met with," which the girls had toiled through with so much singleness of spirit, had not cured the broadness of their accent nor the artificial idioms of their Yorkshire French. Monsieur Héger, indeed, considered that they knew no French at all. Their manners, even among English people, were stiff and prim; the hearty, vulgar, genial expansion of their Belgian

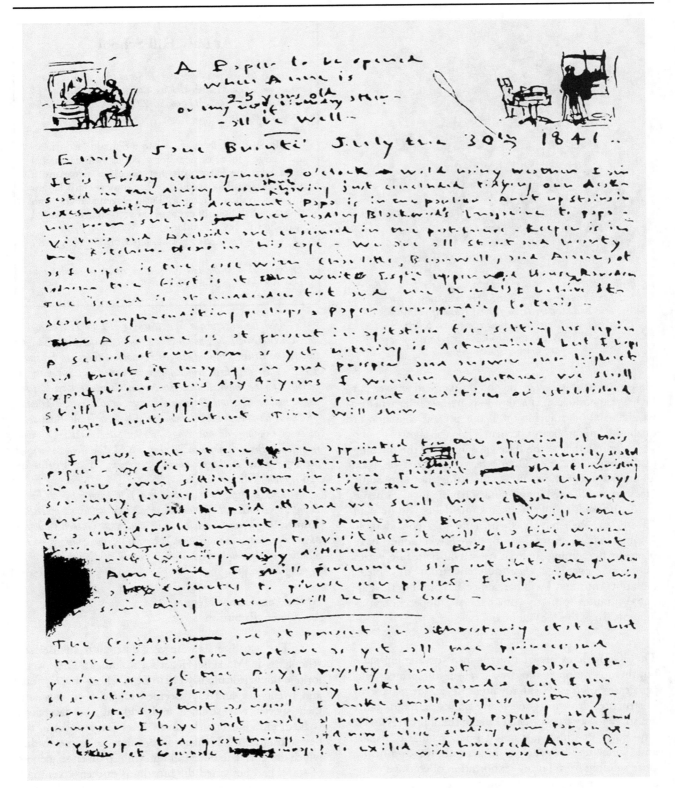

Emily's diary paper from 1841 (Brontë Parsonage Museum; from Clement K. Shorter, Charlotte Brontë and Her Circle, *University of Colorado Boulder Library)*

Emily's watercolor of Nero, a pet hawk. The hawk's name has often been mistranscribed as "Hero" by biographers (Brontë Parsonage Museum: Bonnell 34; from Christine Alexander and Jane Sellars, The Art of the Brontës, *University of Colorado Libraries).*

schoolfellows must have made them seem as lifeless as marionettes. Their dress—Haworth had permitted itself to wonder at the uncouthness of those amazing leg-of-mutton sleeves (Emily's pet whim in and out of fashion), at the ill-cut lankness of those skirts, clumsy enough on round little Charlotte, but a very caricature of mediaevalism on Emily's tall, thin, slender figure. They knew they were not in their element, and kept close together, rarely speaking. Yet Monsieur Héger, patiently watching, felt the presence of a strange power under those uncouth exteriors.

An odd little man of much penetration, this French schoolmaster. *"Homme de zèle et de conscience, il possède à un haut degré l'éloquence du bon sens et du coeur."* Fierce and despotic in the exaction of obedience, yet tender of heart, magnanimous and tyrannical, absurdly vain and absolutely unselfish. His wife's school was a kingdom to him; he brought to it an energy, a zeal, a faculty of administration worthy to rule a kingdom. It was with the delight of a botanist discovering a rare plant in his garden, of a politician detecting a future statesman in his nursery, that he perceived the unusual faculty which lifted his two English pupils above their schoolfellows. He watched them silently for some weeks. When he had made quite sure, he came forwards, and, so to speak, claimed them for his own.

Charlotte at once accepted the yoke. All that he set her to do she toiled to accomplish; she followed out his trains of thought; she adopted the style he recommended; she gave him in return for all his pains the most unflagging obedience, the affectionate comprehension of a large intelligence. She writes to Ellen of her delight in learning and serving: "It is very natural to me to submit, very unnatural to command."

Not so with Emily. The qualities which her sister understood and accepted, irritated her unspeakably. The masterfulness in little things, the irritability, the watchfulness, of the fiery little professor of rhetoric were utterly distasteful to her. She contradicted his theories to his face; she did her lessons well, but as she chose to do them. She was as indomitable, fierce, unappeasable, as Charlotte was ready and submissive. And yet it was Emily who had the larger share of Monsieur Héger's admiration. Egotistic and exacting he thought her, who never yielded to his petulant, harmless egoism, who never gave way to his benevolent tyranny; but he gave her credit for logical powers, for a capacity for argument unusual in a man, and rare, indeed, in a woman. She, not Charlotte, was the genius in his eyes, although he complained that her stubborn will rendered her deaf to all reason, when her own determination, or her own sense of right, was concerned. He fancied she might be a great historian, so he told Mrs. Gaskell. "Her faculty of imagination was such, her views of scenes and characters would have been so vivid and so powerfully expressed, and supported by such a show of argument, that it would have dominated over the reader, whatever might have been his previous opinions or his cooler perception of the truth. She should have been a man: a great navigator!" cried the little, dark, enthusiastic rhetorician. "Her powerful reason would have deduced new spheres of discovery from the knowledge of the old; and her strong imperious will would never have been daunted by opposition or difficulty; never have given way but with life!"

Yet they were never friends; though Monsieur Héger could speak so well of Emily at a time, be it remembered, when it was Charlotte's praises that were sought, when Emily's genius was set down as a lunatic's hobgoblin of nightmare potency. He and she were alike too imperious, too independent, too stubborn. A couple of swords, neither of which could serve to sheathe the other. . . .

The reader will already have recognized in the black, ugly, choleric little professor of rhetoric the one absolutely natural hero of a woman's novel, the beloved and whimsical figure of the immortal Monsieur Paul Emanuel.

"He and Emily," adds Charlotte, "don't draw well together at all. Emily works like a horse, and she has

"Le Chat"

In her preface to The Belgian Essays, *Sue Lonoff, editor and translator of Charlotte and Emily's devoirs, comments on Emily's approach to writing French: "In Emily's case, a literal translation can make sense of the original clearer because she often stuck to English rather than French syntax and thought of English rather than French idioms" (p. xv). Lonoff later comments specifically on Emily's "Le Chat," her first extant devoir: "If, as Charlotte alleges, Emily came to Belgium with only a rudimentary knowledge of French, she made all but incredible progress. She also learned while keeping compliance to a minimum, unlike her more submissive sibling. Manifest in almost every line here is resistance: to conventional notions about animals and humans, to the expectations of her sentimental teacher, and to the very language she was using" (p. 64).*

This is Lonoff's translation of "Le Chat," dated 15 May 1842.

I can say with sincerity that I like cats; also I can give very good reasons why those who despise them are wrong.

A cat is an animal who has more human feelings than almost any other being. We cannot sustain a comparison with the dog, it is indefinitely too good; but the cat, although it differs in some physical points, is extremely like us in disposition.

There may be people, in truth, who would say that this resemblance extends only to the most wicked men; that it is limited to their excessive hypocrisy, cruelty, and ingratitude; detestable vices in our race and equally odious in that of cats.

Without disputing the limits that those individuals set on our affinity, I answer that if hypocrisy, cruelty, and ingratitude are exclusively the domain of the wicked, that class comprises everyone. Our education develops one of those qualities in great perfection; the others flourish without nurture, and far from condemning them, we regard all three with great complacency. A cat, in its own interest, sometimes hides its misanthropy under the guise of amiable gentleness; instead of tearing what it desires from its master's hand, it approaches with a caressing air, rubs its pretty little head against him, and advances a paw whose touch is soft as down. When it has gained its end, it resumes its character of Timon; and that artfulness in it is called hypocrisy. In ourselves, we give it another name, politeness, and he who did not use it to hide his real feelings would soon be driven from society.

"But," says some delicate lady, who has murdered a half-dozen lapdogs through pure affection, "the cat is such a cruel beast, he is not content to kill his prey, he torments it before its death; you cannot make that accusation against us." More or less, Madame. Your husband, for example, likes hunting very much, but foxes being rare on his land, he would not have the means to pursue this amusement often, if he did not manage his supplies thus; once he has run an animal to its last breath, he snatches it from the jaws of the hounds and saves it to suffer the same infliction two or three more times, ending finally in death. You yourself avoid a bloody spectacle because it wounds your weak nerves. But I have seen you embrace your child in transports, when he came to show you a beautiful butterfly crushed between his cruel little fingers; and at that moment, I really wanted to have a cat, with the tail of a half-devoured rat hanging from its mouth, to present as the image, the true copy, of your angel. You could not refuse to kiss him, and if he scratched us both in revenge, so much the better. Little boys are rather liable to acknowledge their friends' caresses in that way, and the resemblance would be more perfect. The ingratitude of cats is another name for penetration. They know how to value our favors at their true price, because they guess the motives that prompt us to grant them, and if those motives might sometimes be good, undoubtedly they remember always that they owe all their misery and all their evil qualities to the great ancestor of humankind. For assuredly, the cat was not wicked in Paradise.

—Charlotte and Emily Brontë: The Belgian Essays,
pp. 56–59

had great difficulties to contend with, far greater than I have had."

Emily did indeed work hard. She was there to work, and not till she had learned a certain amount would her conscience permit her to return to Haworth. It was for dear liberty that she worked. She began German, a favorite study in after years, and of some purpose; since the style of Hoffmann left its impression on the author of 'Wuthering Heights.' She worked hard at music; and in half a year the stumbling schoolgirl became a brilliant and proficient musician. Her playing is said to have been singularly accurate, vivid, and full of fire. French, too, both in grammar and in literature, was a constant study.

Monsieur Héger recognized the fact that in dealing with the Brontës he had not to make the customary allowances for a schoolgirl's undeveloped inexperience. These were women of mature and remarkable intelligence. The method he adopted in teaching them was rather that of a University professor than such as usually is used in a pensionnat. He would choose some masterpiece of French style, some passage of eloquence or portraiture, read it to them with a brief lecture on its distinctive qualities, pointing out what was exaggerated, what apt, what false, what subtle in the author's conception or his mode of expressing it. They were then dismissed to make a similar composition, without the aid of grammar or dictionary, availing themselves as far as possible of the *nuances* of style and the

REMEMBRANCE

Facsimile MS. in Emily Brontë's handwriting

A version in Emily's hand of her poem that was titled "Remembrance" when it was published in Poems by Currer, Ellis and Acton Bell *(1846). One of Emily's best-known poems, it was included in her Gondal Poems notebook and is addressed from R[osina] Alcona to the dead J[ulius] Brenzaida. When it was published, the Gondal references were eliminated (from Arthur C. Benson,* Brontë Poems: Selections from the Poetry of Charlotte, Emily, Anne and Branwell Brontë, *University of Wyoming Library).*

peculiarities of method of the writer chosen as the model of the hour. In this way the girls became intimately acquainted with the literary *technique* of the best French masters. To Charlotte the lessons were of incalculable value, perfecting in her that clear and accurate style which makes her best work never wearisome, never old-fashioned. But the very thought of imitating any one, especially of imitating any French writer, was repulsive to Emily, "rustic all through, moorish, wild and knotty as a root of heath." When Monsieur Héger had explained his plan to them, "Emily spoke first; and said that she saw no good to be derived from it; and that by adopting it they would lose all originality of thought and expression. She would have entered into an argument on the subject, but for this Monsieur Héger had no time. Charlotte then spoke; she also doubted the success of the plan; but she would follow out Monsieur Héger's advice, because she was bound to obey him while she was his pupil." Charlotte soon found a keen enjoyment in this species of literary composition, yet Emily's *devoir* was the best. They are, alas, no longer to be seen, no longer in the keeping of so courteous and proud a guardian as Mrs. Gaskell had to deal with; but she and Monsieur Héger both have expressed their opinions that in genius, imagination, power, and force of language, Emily was the superior of the two sisters.

So great was the personality of this energetic, silent, brooding, ill-dressed young Englishwoman that all who knew her recognized in her the genius they were slow to perceive in her more sociable and vehement sister. Madame Héger, the worldly, cold-mannered *surveillante* of Villette, avowed the singular force of a nature most antipathetic to her own. Yet Emily had no companions; the only person of whom we hear, in even the most negative terms of friendliness, is one of the teachers, a certain Mademoiselle Marie, "talented and original, but of repulsive and arbitrary manners which have made the whole school, except Emily and myself, her bitter enemies." No less arbitrary and repulsive seemed poor Emily herself, a sprig of purple heath at discord with those bright, smooth geraniums and lobelias; Emily, of whom every surviving friend extols the never-failing, quiet unselfishness, the genial spirit ready to help, the timid but faithful affection. She was so completely *hors de son assiette* that even her virtues were misplaced.

There was always one thing she could do, one thing as natural as breath to Emily—determined labor. In that merciful engrossment she could forget her heartsick weariness and the jarring strangeness of things; every lesson conquered was another step taken on the long road home. And the days allowed ample space for work, although it was supported upon a somewhat slender diet.

—Emily Brontë, pp. 106–117

* * *

This final surviving diary paper by Emily was headed "Haworth—Thursday—July 30ᵗʰ 1845."

Diary Paper, 30 July 1845
Emily Brontë

My birthday—showery—breezy—coo[l]—I am twenty seven years old to day—this morning Anne and I opened the papers we wrote 4 years since on my twenty third birthday—this paper we intend, if all be well, to open on my 30ᵗʰ three years hence in 1848—since the 1841 paper, the following events have taken place

Our school-scheme has been abandoned and ?instead Charlotte and I went to Brussels on the 8ᵗʰ of Febrary 1842   Branwell left his place at Luddenden Foot C and I returned from Brussels November 8ᵗʰ 1842 in consequence of Aunt's death—Branwell went to Thorpgreen as a tutor where Anne still continued—January 1843 Charlotte returned to Brussels the same month and after staying a year came back again on new years day 1844 Anne left her situation at Thorp Green of her own accord—June 1845 Branwell ?left—July 1845 Anne and I went our first long Journey by ourselves together—leaving Home on the 30ᵗʰ of June—monday sleeping at York—returning to Keighley Tuesday evening sleeping there and walking home on Wedensday morning—though the weather was broken, we enjoyed ourselves very much except during a few hours at Bradford and during our excursion we were Ronald Macelgin, Henry Angora, Juliet Augusteena, Rosobelle ?Esualdar, Ella and Julian Egramon[t] Catherine Navarre and Cordelia Fitzaphnold escaping from the palaces of Instruction to join the Royalists who are hard driven at present by the victorious Republicans—The Gondals still flo[u]rish bright as ever   I am at present writing a work on the First Wars—Anne has been writing some articles on this and a book by Henry Sophona—We intend sticking firm by the rascals as long as they delight us which I am glad to say they do at present—I should have mentioned that last summer the school scheme was revived in full vigor—We had prospectuses printed. despatched letters to all aquaintances imparting our plans and did our little all—but it was found no go—now I dont desire a school at all and none of us have any great longing for it. We have cash enough for our present wants with a prospect of accumolation—we are all in decent health—only that papa has a complaint in his eyes and with the exception of B who I hope will be better and do better, hereafter. I am quite contented for myself—not as idle as formerly, altogether as hearty and having learnt to make the

A portion of Emily's diary paper from 1845 (Brontë Parsonage Museum; from Clement K. Shorter, Charlotte Brontë and Her Circle, University of Colorado Boulder Libraries)

most of the present and hope for the future with less fidget[i]ness that I cannot do all I wish—seldom or ever troubled with nothing to do ie and merely desiring that every body could be as comfortable as myself and as undesponding and then we should have a very tolerable world of it—

By mistake I find we have opened the paper on the 31st instead of the 30th Yesterday was much such a day as this but the morning was devine—

Tabby who was gone in our last paper is come back and has lived with us—two years and a half and is in good health—Martha who also departed is here too. We have got Flossey, got and lost Tiger—lost the Hawk. Nero which with the geese was given away and is doubtless dead for when I came back from Brussels I enquired on all hands and could hear nothing of him—Tiger died early last year—Keeper and Flossey are well also the canary acquired 4 years since

We are now all at home and likely to be there some time—Branwell went to Liverpool on Tuesday to stay a week. Tabby has just been teasing me to ?tu[r]n as formerly to—pilloputate. Anne and I should have picked the black currants if it had been fine and sunshiny. I must hurry off now to my turning and ironing I have plenty of work on hands and writing and am altogether full of buis[ness] with best wishes for the whole House till 1848 July 30th and as much longer as may be I conclude

E J Bronte
—The Letters of Charlotte Brontë, v. 1, pp. 407–409

* * *

Perspective on Emily's diary papers is provided in this excerpt from Lucasta Miller's chapter, "Interpreting Emily," in her book The Brontë Myth.

"To Reconstruct Emily Brontë's Own Story"
Lucasta Miller

From what we can reconstruct, it seems likely that this fiercely private woman would have resented biographers' attempts to pin her down. Above all, she seems to have loved liberty; freedom to think her own heterodox thoughts, freedom from social pressures, freedom from having to submit to the will of others. Although posterity has cast her as a wind-blown waif wafting across the moors in a fug of intuitive trance, the real Emily had both a razor-sharp intellect and a surprisingly down-to-earth imagination capable of taking delight in everyday objects. Her mental resistance to social conventionality meant that she could be infuriatingly difficult in company, reserved to the point of rudeness. It was only at

home in Haworth, where she could live unhindered in the world of her own imagination, that Emily was genuinely happy and relaxed.

"Happy" and "relaxed" are not words which one would easily associate with a novel as dark and tense as *Wuthering Heights*. But the impression we get from Emily's secret so-called diary papers is of a person with the capacity to feel at ease with herself. These four fragmentary papers are the only documents which give us anything like access into her personal world. As a result, they are like gold dust for the biographer. But the glimpses they give us are so fleeting, so provisional, so compromised by what they do not tell us, that they are as frustrating as they are fascinating. They invite us into Emily's private space only to warn us about the dangers inherent in biographical interpretation. She may have been at ease when she wrote them, but we cannot wholly relax while reading them because we are always straining to know more than they reveal.

Unlike Emily's carefully honed poetry or novel, her diary papers are spontaneous, unself-conscious scraps of prose in which she speaks in her own voice. They have a disarming realness about them which makes them uniquely attractive. But at the same time they remain slippery and incomplete. Written on small pieces of paper and hidden away, they were intended to be reread in future years, but only by Emily herself and her favorite sister, Anne. Emily was, as Charlotte put it, "not a person of demonstrative character, nor one, on the recesses of whose feelings, even those nearest and dearest to her could, with impunity, intrude unlicensed." Perusing her private diaries feels uncomfortably like trespassing, in the same way that reading Charlotte's Roe Head Journal makes you afraid you are committing a treacherous intrusion.

Yet the tone of these brief notes is much less pent-up than the Roe Head Journal. Emily did not use them for self-analysis or extended reverie, and as a result they are more tantalizing but less explicitly revealing of her innermost thoughts. They record the minute-by-minute occurrences of the day, capturing a moment and preserving it like an insect in amber. Snatches of conversation, accounts of the weather or of what the other members of the family were doing at that very instant, give tiny glimpses into the world of Haworth Parsonage which bring the dead momentarily to life. But it is only for a moment, and the fugitive, evanescent feel of Emily's unruly, dashed-off prose only underscores the transitoriness of time. They give us the illusion of recovering the past, but also show us what we've lost.

The 1837 diary ends with a snippet of recorded dialogue:

Aunt. Come Emily Its past 4 o'clock. Emily Yes Aunt
Anne well do you intend to write in the evening
Emily well what think you

The questions remain open-ended. We will never know whether the sisters did in fact spend the evening of June 26, 1837, writing. The passage concludes with a parenthesis, squashed up to the very edge of the sheet of paper, in which the closing bracket is omitted: "(we agreed to go out Ist to make sure if we get into a humor we may stay." In its incompleteness, the missing bracket symbolizes the absences with which the reader has to deal: the fact that we are not able to ascertain whether the sisters put their plans—either of writing in the evening or of going out—into action stresses the limits of interpretation. We simply cannot know what is the relation of these words to history, whether the future they project is real or purely speculative.

The diary papers are thus shifting, unstable indicators of reality. This seems only too appropriate when one considers what they tell us about Emily's habit of mind. What strikes most is the way in which, for her, the boundary between the real and the imaginary seems to have been unusually porous. The 1834 diary paper juxtaposes reality and fantasy as if there were no difference between them. Two consecutive sentences—"The Gondals are discovering the interior of Gaaldine Sally moseley is washing in the back-kitchin."—suggest that Emily is as comfortable in the invented kingdom of Gondal as she is in the actual world of the washerwoman. She can expand her imagination to fill vast tracts of unexplored land, or she can contract it to the cramped enclosure of the back kitchen. This combination of high-flown fantasy with the solidity of the everyday anticipates the style of *Wuthering Heights,* in which extremes of melodrama coexist with close attention to realist detail, such as the vast oak dresser with its pewter dishes and silver jugs which the narrator, Lockwood, notices as he enters the living room of Heathcliff's home.

Oddly enough, Emily's novel offers us an uncanny if unintended commentary on her diary papers and our own relationship to them as voyeurs and interpreters. Near the beginning of the novel, Lockwood is forced by the weather to spend the night at the Heights. In bed, he discovers Cathy's childhood journal, scribbled, as spontaneously as Emily's own, in the margins of her Bible. Like the diary papers it is both fragmentary and arrestingly immediate. Beginning *in*

medias res with the words "An awful Sunday!" it hauls the past right into the present, but remains only partially intelligible because, so far, neither we nor Lockwood have been introduced to all the characters involved.

As Lockwood puts it, Cathy's words are "faded hieroglyphics" which need to be "decyphered." They whet his appetite for knowledge—"an immediate interest kindled within me for the unknown Catherine"—but at the same time they fail fully to satisfy it. Like the 1837 diary paper, Cathy's journal ends unresolved, leaving the reader in a state of uncertainty. Cathy describes how she and Heathcliff are planning to borrow the dairywoman's cloak and go out for a scamper on the rain-swept moors. But neither Lockwood nor the reader are in a position as readers of the diary to know whether they eventually did so.

In poring over Emily's faded scraps of diary, we are like Lockwood. It is as well to remember that part of his function in the novel is to offer us a cautionary tale about the dangers of interpretation. A bumbling character, he is comically bad at reading signs and embarrasses himself by mistaking a pile of dead rabbits for his hostess's pet cats. His immediate reaction to Cathy's diary is to fall asleep and find himself in a dream about a crazy preacher performing a relentless and surreal exegesis on a scriptural text. This is meaning gone mad, but it shows how protean the written word can be and how dependent it is upon what the reader makes of it.

Wuthering Heights is in fact an intellectually complex work, conscious of its own literariness and aware of the philosophical problems inherent in the business of reading. Full of riddlesome texts which invite explication—such as the inscription over the door of the Heights or Cathy's graffiti on the windowsill—it alerts the reader to the dangers of misreading but also suggests that ambiguity and plurality are inescapable facts. This is a novel whose most famous phrase—Cathy's *"I am* Heathcliff"—undermines the very concept of individual identity. Uncannily, it seems to warn us against trying to make a single, stable, self-consistent entity out of the fragments of Emily Brontë which posterity has left us. We can read what we will into these literary scraps, but we run the risk, like the nightmare preacher Jabes Branderham, of shooting off into our own "private manner of interpreting" and missing the point altogether.

Cathy's diary fills Lockwood with such curiosity that he is determined to discover her story. He asks the housekeeper Ellen Dean to fill him in, and it is her account which becomes the central narrative of *Wuthering Heights.* Unlike Charlotte, whose best books are written in the first person, Emily constructed her single novel as a complex tale within a tale: the reader is held at a distance, through multiple narratives, from the main protagonists of the story, and has to rely on the narrators' versions of events.

Much the same is happening when the attempt is made to reconstruct Emily Brontë's own story. The biographer is as desperate to know it as Lockwood is to know Cathy's. But since there is so little direct access to her, it is necessary to rely on the testimonies of others, particularly of Charlotte, who famously remarked that an interpreter should have stood between Emily and the world.

As interpreter, Charlotte does indeed stand *between* posterity and Emily, beckoning us with one hand and waving us away with the other. Since she is almost the only source of biographical information, there is no option but to listen to what she says. But she is a slippery authority whose comments tell us more about her own attitude toward her sister than about the inner workings of Emily's mind. They betray ambivalent feelings: protectiveness tipping over into an urge to dominate, admiration tinged with condescension.

After Emily died, Charlotte took the reins and became the impresario of her posthumous reputation. Her attempts to rewrite her in fiction, criticism, and biography, and as an editor, are often as obfuscating as they are revealing. Quite possibly, Charlotte also destroyed many of the documents which might have given us a clearer picture of Emily's character and artistic development. Her actions—which grew out of her deep, complicated love for her sister, and the unbearable pain of bereavement—were not maliciously intended. Nevertheless, they have had an incalculable—and sometimes damaging—effect on posterity's perceptions, exacerbating the mystery which surrounds Emily to this day.

—The Brontë Myth, pp. 186–190

Wuthering Heights

No prepublication versions, in manuscript or type, of Wuthering Heights *exist. Emily probably finished much of the novel by April 1846 when Charlotte wrote to Aylott & Jones to inquire about publishing the three one-volume novels that she, Anne, and Emily were each preparing.* Wuthering Heights *was sent to an unknown number of publishers before being accepted by T. C. Newby in July 1847. It was published together with Anne's* Agnes Grey *in December 1847.*

Soon after Wuthering Heights *and* Agnes Grey *were published, Charlotte mentioned the novels in this excerpt from a letter to the reader for her own publisher, Smith, Elder. Charlotte's language describing the mind of Ellis, or Emily, anticipated some of the terms used by reviewers of* Wuthering Heights. *Her dissatisfaction with Newby later led Charlotte to bring out a new edition of her sisters' novels.*

Charlotte Brontë to William Smith Williams, 21 December 1847

You are not far wrong in your judgment respecting "Wuthering Heights" & "Agnes Grey". Ellis has a strong, original mind, full of strange though sombre power: when he writes poetry that power speaks in language at once condensed, elaborated and refined—but in prose it breaks forth in scenes which shock more than they attract—Ellis will improve, however, because he knows his defects. "Agnes Grey" is the mirror of the mind of the writer. The orthography & punctuation of the books are mortifying to a degree—almost all the errors that were corrected in the proof-sheets appear intact in what should have been the fair copies. If Mr. Newby always does business in this way, few authors would like to have him for their publisher a second time.

—The Letters of Charlotte Brontë, v. 1, p. 580

* * *

Upon Emily's death, five reviews of Wuthering Heights, *one of them unidentified, were found in her writing desk. Excerpts follow from the four identified reviews—all unsigned, all published in January 1848—which appeared in* The Examiner, Britannia, Douglas Jerrold's Weekly Newspaper, *and* The Atlas. *These reviews are characteristic of the range of critical responses* Wuthering Heights *elicited.*

"Fearlessly into the Moors" Review of *Wuthering Heights*

This is a strange book. It is not without evidences of considerable power: but, as a whole, it is wild, confused, disjointed, and improbable; and the people who make up the drama, which is tragic enough in its consequences, are savages ruder than those who lived before the days of Homer. With the exception of Heathcliff, the story is confined to the family of Earnshaw, who intermarry with the Lintons; and the scene of their exploits is a rude old-fashioned house, at the top of one of the high moors or fells in the north of England. Whoever has traversed the bleak heights of Hartside or Cross Fell, on his road from Westmoreland to the dales of Yorkshire, and has been welcomed there by the

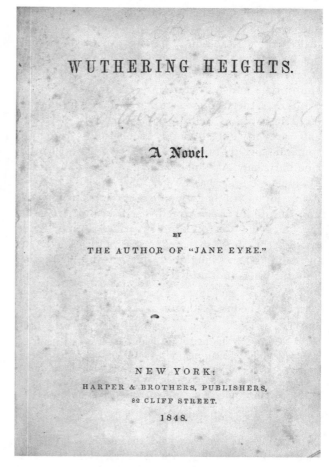

Title pages for the first English and American editions of Emily Brontë's only novel. The American edition misidentifies the author (Special Collections, Thomas Cooper Library, University of South Carolina).

winds and rain on a 'gusty day,' will know how to estimate the comforts of Wuthering Heights in wintry weather. But it may be as well to give the author's own sketch of the spot, taken, it should be observed, at a more genial season:

> "Wuthering Heights is the name of Mr Heathcliff's dwelling. 'Wuthering' being a significant provincial adjective, descriptive of the atmospheric tumult to which its station is exposed in stormy weather. . . ."

This Heathcliff may be considered as the hero of the book, if a hero there be. He is an incarnation of evil qualities; implacable hate, ingratitude, cruelty, falsehood, selfishness, and revenge. He exhibits, moreover, a certain stoical endurance in early life, which enables him to 'bide his time,' and nurse up his wrath till it becomes mature and terrible; and there is one portion of his nature, one only, wherein he appears to approxi-

mate to humanity. Like the Corsair, and other such melodramatic heroes, he is

> "Linked to one virtue and a thousand crimes;"

and it is with difficulty that we can prevail upon ourselves to believe in the appearance of such a phenomenon, so near our own dwellings as the summit of a Lancashire or Yorkshire moor.

It is not easy to disentangle the incidents and set them forth in chronological order. The tale is confused, as we have said, notwithstanding that the whole drama takes place in the house that we have described, and that the sole actors are the children of Earnshaw, by birth or adoption, and their servants. . . .

We are not disposed to ascribe any particular intention to the author in drawing the character of Heathcliff, nor can we perceive any very obvious moral in the story. There are certain good rough dashes at character; some of the incidents look like real events; and the book has the merit, which must not be undervalued, of avoiding commonplace and affectation. The language, however, is not always appropriate and we entertain great doubts as to the truth, or rather the *vraisemblance* of the main character. The hardness, selfishness, and cruelty of Heathcliff are in our opinion inconsistent with the romantic love that he is stated to have felt for Catherine Earnshaw. As Nelly Dean says, "he is as hard as a whinstone." He has no gratitude, no affection, no liking for anything human except for one person, and that liking is thoroughly selfish and ferocious. He hates the son of Hindley, which is intelligible enough; but he also hates and tyrannizes over his own son and the daughter of his beloved Catherine, and this we cannot understand.

We have said that there are some good dashes at character. The first Catherine is sketched thus:

> "Certainly, she had ways with her such as I never saw a child take up before; and she put all of us past our patience fifty times and oftener in a day: from the hour she came down stairs, till the hour she went to bed, we had not a minute's security that she wouldn't be in mischief. . . ."

From what we have said, the reader will imagine that the book is full of grim pictures. Here is one. It should be premised that Heathcliff has manifested symptoms of restlessness and trouble for some time past.

> "He turned abruptly to the fire, and continued, with what, for lack of a better word, I must call a smile—
>
> "'I'll tell you what I did yesterday! I got the sexton, who was digging Linton's grave, to remove the earth off her coffin lid, and I opened it. I thought, once, I would have stayed there, when I saw her face again—it is hers yet—he had hard work to stir me; but he said it would change, if the air blew on it, and so I struck one side of the coffin loose—and covered it up—. . ."

If this book be, as we apprehend it is, the first work of the author, we hope that he will produce a second,—giving himself more time in its composition than in the present case, developing his incidents more carefully, eschewing exaggeration and obscurity, and looking steadily at human life, under all its moods, for those pictures of the passions that he may desire to sketch for our public benefit. It may be well also to be sparing of certain oaths and phrases, which do not materially contribute to any character, and are by no means to be reckoned among the evidences of

a writer's genius. We detest the affectation and effeminate frippery which is but too frequent in the modern novel, and willingly trust ourselves with an author who goes at once fearlessly into the moors and desolate places, for his heroes; but we must at the same time stipulate with him that he shall not drag into light all that he discovers, of coarse and loathsome, in his wanderings, but simply so much good and ill as he may find necessary to elucidate his history—so much only as may be interwoven inextricably with the persons whom he professes to paint. It is the province of an artist to modify and in some cases refine what he beholds in the ordinary world. There never was a man whose daily life (that is to say, *all* his deeds and sayings, entire and without exception) constituted fit materials for a book of fiction. Even the figures of the Greeks (which are

> "In old marbles ever beautiful)"

were without doubt selected from the victors in the ancient games, and others, by Phidias and his scholars, and their forms and countenances made perfect before they were thought worthy to adorn the temple of the wise Athena.

The only book which occurs to us as resembling *Wuthering Heights* is a novel of the late Mr Hooton's,—a work of very great talent, in which the hero is a tramper or beggar, and the *dramatis personæ* all derived from humble and middle life; but which, notwithstanding its defects, we remember thinking better in its peculiar kind than anything that had been produced since the days of Fielding.

—The Examiner (January 1848): 21–22

* * *

"Much to Fascinate"
Review of *Wuthering Heights*

There are scenes of savage wildness in nature which, though they inspire no pleasurable sensation, we are yet well satisfied to have seen. In the rugged rock, the gnarled roots which cling to it, the dark screen of overhanging vegetation, the dank, moist ground and tangled network of weeds and bushes,—even in the harsh cry of solitary birds, the cries of wild animals, and the startling motion of the snake as it springs away scared by the intruder's foot,—there is an image of primeval rudeness which has much to fascinate, though nothing to charm, the mind. The elements of beauty are found in the midst of gloom and danger, and some forms are the more picturesque from their distorted growth amid so many obstacles. A tree clinging to the

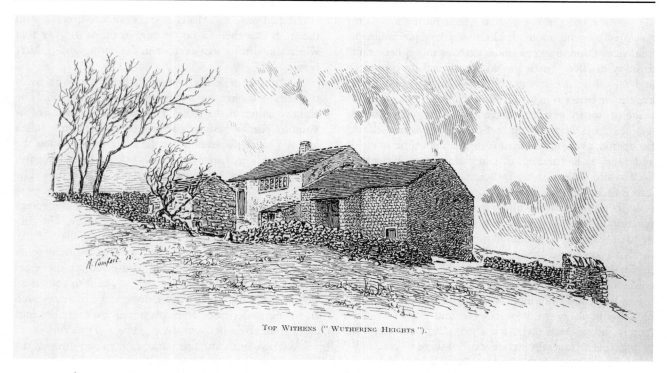

TOP WITHENS (" WUTHERING HEIGHTS ").

Top Withens, Haworth Moor, which may have been a model for Wuthering Heights. It was falling into ruin in the Brontës' era
(from Whiteley Turner, A Spring-Time Saunter: Round and About Brontë Land,
Sam Houston State University Library).

side of a precipice may more attract the eye than the pride of a plantation.

The principle may, to some extent, be applied to life. The uncultured freedom of native character presents more rugged aspects than we meet with in educated society. Its manners are not only more rough but its passions are more violent. It knows nothing of those breakwaters to the fury of tempest which civilized training establishes to subdue the harsher workings of the soul. Its wrath is unrestrained by reflection; the lips curse and the hand strikes with the first impulse of anger. It is more subject to brutal instinct than to divine reason.

It is humanity in this wild state that the author of *Wuthering Heights* essays to depict. His work is strangely original. It bears a resemblance to some of those irregular German tales in which the writers, giving the reins to their fancy, represent personages as swayed and impelled to evil by supernatural influences. But they give spiritual identity to evil impulses, while Mr. Bell more naturally shows them as the natural offspring of the unregulated heart. He displays a considerable power in his creations. They have all the angularity of misshapen growth, and form in this respect a striking contrast to those regular forms we are accustomed to meet with in English fiction. They exhibit nothing of the composite character. There is in them no trace of ideal models. They are so new, so wildly grotesque,

so entirely without art, that they strike us as proceeding from a mind of limited experience, but of original energy, and of a singular and distinctive cast.

In saying this we indicate both the merits and faults of the tale. It is in parts very unskilfully constructed: many passages in it display neither the grace of art nor the truth of nature, but only the vigour of one positive idea,—that of passionate ferocity. It blazes forth in the most unsuitable circumstances, and from persons the least likely to be animated by it. The author is a Salvator Rosa with his pen. He delineates forms of savage grandeur when he wishes to represent sylvan beauty. His Griseldas are furies, and his swains Polyphemi. For this reason his narrative leaves an unpleasant effect on the mind. There are no green spots in it on which the mind can linger with satisfaction. The story rushes onwards with impetuous force, but it is the force of a dark and sullen torrent, flowing between high and rugged rocks.

It is permitted to painting to seize one single aspect of nature, and, as the pleasure arising from its contemplation proceeds partly from love of imitation, objects unattractive in themselves may be made interesting on canvass. But in fiction this kind of isolation is not allowed. The exhibition of one quality or passion is not sufficient for it. So far as the design extends it must present a true image of life, and if it takes in many characters it must show them animated by many motives. There may be a predominant influence of one strong emotion, perhaps that is necessary to unity of effect, but it should be relieved by contrasts, and set off by accessories. *Wuthering Heights* would have been a far better romance if Heathcliff alone had been a being of stormy passions, instead of all the other characters being nearly as violent and destructive as himself. In fiction, too, as the imitation of nature can never be so vivid and exact as in painting, that imitation is insufficient of itself to afford pleasure, and when it deals with brutal subjects it becomes positively disgusting. It is of course impossible to prescribe rules for either the admission or the rejection of what is shocking and dreadful. It is nothing to say that reality is faithfully followed. The aim of fiction is to afford some sensation of delight. We admit we cannot rejoice in the triumph of goodness–that triumph which consists in the superiority of spirit to body–without knowing its trials and sufferings. But the end of fictitious writings should always be kept in view: and that end is not merely mental excitement, for a very bad book may be very exciting. Generally we are satisfied there is some radical defect in those fictions which leave behind them an impression of pain and horror. It would not be difficult to show why this is, and must be, the case, but it would lead us into deeper considerations than are appropriate to this article.

Mr. Ellis Bell's romance is illuminated by some gleams of sunshine towards the end which serve to cast a grateful light on the dreary path we have travelled. Flowers rise over the grave of buried horrors. The violent passions of two generations are closed in death, yet in the vision of peace with which the tale closes we almost fear their revival in the warped nature of the young survivors.

Heathcliff is the central character of the piece. He is a gipsy foundling, and has been adopted from a feeling of benevolence–though of a rough and eccentric kind–by a country gentleman. At the time the book opens, this Heathcliff, then past the middle of life, has the estate of his benefactor, together with a neighbouring property. . . .

It is difficult to pronounce any decisive judgment on a work in which there is so much rude ability displayed, yet in which there is so much matter for blame. The scenes of brutality are unnecessarily long and unnecessarily frequent; and as an imaginative writer the author has to learn the first principles of his art. But there is singular power in his portraiture of strong passion. He exhibits it as convulsing the whole frame of nature, distracting the intellect to madness, and snapping the heart-strings. The anguish of Heathcliff on the death of Catherine approaches to sublimity.

We do not know whether the author writes with any purpose; but we can speak of one effect of his production. It strongly shows the "brutalizing influence of

unchecked passion." His characters are a commentary on the truth that there is no tyranny in the world like that which thoughts of evil exercise in the daring and reckless breast.

Another reflection springing from the narrative is that temper is often spoiled in the years of childhood. 'The child is father of the man.' The pains and crosses of its youthful years are engrafted in its blood, and form a sullen and a violent disposition. Grooms know how often the tempers of horses are irremediably spoiled in training. But some parents are less wise regarding their children. The intellect in its growth has the faculty of accommodating itself to adverse circumstances. To violence it sometimes opposes violence, sometimes dogged obstinacy. The consequence in either case is fatal to the tranquillity of life. Young Catherine Linton is represented as a naturally sensitive, high-spirited, amiable girl; subjected to the cruel usage of her brutal stepfather, she is roused to resistance, and answers his curses with taunts, and his stripes with threatenings. Released from his tyranny, a more gracious spirit comes over her, and she is gentle and peaceful.

There are some fine passages scattered through the pages. Here is a thought on the tranquillity of death. . . .

Of Joseph, the old sullen servant of Heathcliff, it is quaintly said, that he was 'the sourest-hearted pharisee that ever searched a Bible to rake all the blessings to himself and fling all the curses to his neighbours.'

The third volume of the book is made up of a separate tale relating the fortunes of a governess. Some characters and scenes are nicely sketched in it, but it has nothing to call for special notice. The volumes abound in provincialisms. In many respects they remind us of the recent novel of *Jane Eyre*. We presume they proceed from one family, if not from one pen.

The tale to which we have more particularly alluded is but a fragment, yet of colossal proportion, and bearing evidence of some great design. With all its power and originality, it is so rude, so unfinished, and so careless, that we are perplexed to pronounce an opinion on it, or to hazard a conjecture on the future career of the author. As yet it belongs to the future to decide whether he will remain a rough hewer of marble or become a great and noble sculptor.

–*Britannia* (15 January 1848): 42–43

* * *

"Very Puzzling"
Review of *Wuthering Heights*

"Wuthering Heights" is a strange sort of book,– baffling all regular criticism; yet, it is impossible to begin and not finish it; and quite as impossible to lay it aside afterwards and say nothing about it. In the midst

Law Hill (Wuthering Heights).

"Wuthering Heights is the name of Mr. Heathcliff's dwelling, 'Wuthering' being a significant provincial adjective, descriptive of the atmospheric tumult to which its station is exposed in stormy weather. Pure, bracing ventilation they must have up there at all times, indeed; one may guess the power of the north wind blowing over the edge, by the excessive slant of a few stunted firs at the end of the house; and by a range of gaunt thorns all stretching their limbs one way, as if craving alms of the sun. Happily the architect had foresight to build it strong: the narrow windows are deeply set in the wall, and the corners defended with large jutting stones."

Ponden Hall (The Thrushcross Grange of "Wuthering Heights").

"I asked Mrs. Dean why Heathcliff let Thrushcross Grange, and preferred living in a situation and residence so much inferior. 'Is he not rich enough to keep the estate in good order?' I inquired.

"'Rich, sir!' she returned. 'He has nobody knows what money, and every year it increases. Yes, yes, he's rich enough to live in a finer house than this: but he's very near—close-handed; and, if he meant to flit to Thrushcross Grange, as soon as he heard of a good tenant he could not have borne to miss the chance of getting a few hundred more.'"

Settings that figured in Emily's conception of Wuthering Heights. *She used details from stories she heard about the original owner of Law Hill in her novel. Ponden Hall, the home of the Heaton family in Stanbury, was known to the Brontë children who may have used books from the Heatons' library (from* The Bookman, *October 1904, Colorado College Library).*

of the reader's perplexity the ideas predominant in his mind concerning this book are likely to be—brutal cruelty, and semi-savage love. What may be the moral which the author wishes the reader to deduce from his work, it is difficult to say; and we refrain from assigning any, because to speak honestly, we have discovered none but mere glimpses of hidden morals or secondary meanings. There seems to us great power in this book but a purposeless power, which we feel a great desire to see turned to a better account. We are quite confident that the writer of "Wuthering Heights" wants but the practiced skill to make a great artist; perhaps, a great dramatic artist. His qualities are, at present, excessive; a far more promising fault, let it be remembered, than if they were deficient. He may tone down, whereas the weak and inefficient writer, however carefully he may write by rule and line, will never work up his productions to the point of beauty in art. In "Wuthering Heights" the reader is shocked, disgusted, almost sickened by details of cruelty, inhumanity, and the most diabolical hate and vengeance, and anon come passages of powerful testimony to the supreme power of love—even over demons in the human form. The women in the book are of a strange fiendish-angelic nature, tantalizing, and terrible, and the men are indescribably out of the book itself. Yet, towards the close of the story occurs the following pretty, soft picture, which comes like the rainbow after a storm. . . .

We strongly recommend all our readers who love novelty to get this story, for we can promise them that they never have read anything like it before. It is very puzzling and very interesting, and if we had space we would willingly devote a little more time to the analysis of this remarkable story, but we must leave it to our readers to decide what sort of book it is.

—*Douglas Jerrold's Weekly Newspaper*
(15 January 1848): 77

* * *

This reviewer, while ranging over all the works by the Bells and briefly treating Anne's work, focuses on Wuthering Heights.

"Only a Promise"
Review of *Wuthering Heights* and *Agnes Grey*

About two years ago a small volume of poems by "Currer, Acton, and Ellis Bell" was given to the world. The poems were of varying excellence; those by Currer Bell, for the most part, exhibiting the highest order of merit; but, as a whole, the little work produced little or no sensation, and was speedily forgotten. Currer, Acton, and Ellis Bell have now all come before us as novelists, and all with so much success as to make their future career a matter of interesting speculation in the literary world.

Whether, as there is little reason to believe, the names which we have written are the genuine names of actual personages—whether they are, on the other hand, mere publishing names, as is our own private conviction—whether they represent three distinct individuals, or whether a single personage is the actual representative of the "three gentlemen at once" of the title-pages—whether authorship of the poems and the novels is to be assigned to one gentleman or to one lady, to three gentlemen or three ladies, or to a mixed male and female triad of authors—are questions over which the curious may puzzle themselves, but are matters really of little account. One thing is certain; as in the poems, so in the novels, the signature of "Currer Bell" is attached to pre-eminently the best performance. We were the first to welcome the author of *Jane Eyre* as a new writer of no ordinary power. A new edition of that singular work has been called for, and we do not doubt that its success has done much to ensure a favourable reception for the volumes which are now before us.

Wuthering Heights is a strange, inartistic story. There are evidences in every chapter of a sort of rugged power—an unconscious strength—which the possessor seems never to think of turning to the best advantage. The general effect is inexpressibly painful. We know nothing in the whole range of our fictitious literature which presents such shocking pictures of the worst forms of humanity. *Jane Eyre* is a book which affects the reader to tears; it touches the most hidden sources of emotion. *Wuthering Heights* casts a gloom over the mind not easily to be dispelled. It does not soften; it harasses, it extenterates. There are passages in it which remind us of the *Nowlans* of the late John Banim; but of all pre-existent works the one which it most recalls to our memory is the *History of Mathew Wald*. It has not, however, the unity and concentration of that fiction; but is a *sprawling* story, carrying us, with no mitigation of anguish, through two generations of sufferers—though one presiding evil genius sheds a grim shadow over the whole, and imparts a singleness of malignity to the somewhat disjointed tale. A more natural unnatural story we do not remember to have read. Inconceivable as are the combinations of human degradation which are here to be found moving within the circle of a few miles, the *vraisemblance* is so admirably preserved; there is so much truth in what we may call the *costumery* (not applying the word in its narrow acceptation)—the general mounting of the entire piece—that we readily identify the scenes and personages of the fiction; and when we lay aside the book it is some time before we can persuade ourselves that we have held nothing more than imaginary intercourse with the ideal creations of the brain. The reality of unreality has never been so aptly illustrated as in the scenes of almost savage life which Ellis Bell has brought so vividly before us.

The book sadly wants relief. A few glimpses of sunshine would have increased the reality of the picture and given strength rather than weakness to the whole. There is not in the entire *dramatis personæ,* a single character which is not utterly hateful or thoroughly contemptible. If you do not detest the person, you despise him; and if you do not despise him, you detest him with your whole heart. Hindley, the brutal, degraded sot, strong in the desire to work all mischief, but impotent in his degradation; Linton Heathcliff, the miserable, drivelling coward, in whom we see selfishness in its most abject form; and Heathcliff himself, the presiding evil genius of the piece, the tyrant father of an imbecile son, a creature in whom every evil passion seems to have reached a gigantic excess—form a group of deformities such as we have rarely seen gathered together on the same canvas. The author seems to have designed to throw some redeeming touches into the character of the brutal Heathcliff, by portraying him as one faithful to the "idol of his boyhood"—loving to the very last—long, long after death had divided them, the unhappy girl who had cheered and brightened up the early days of his wretched life. Here is the touch of nature which makes the whole world kin—but it fails of the intended effect. There is a selfishness—a ferocity in the love of Heathcliff, which scarcely suffer it, in spite of its rugged constancy, to relieve the darker parts of his nature. Even the female characters excite something of loathing and much of contempt. Beautiful and loveable in their childhood, they all, to use a vulgar expression, "turn out badly." Catherine the elder—wayward, impatient, impulsive—sacrifices herself and her lover to the pitiful ambition of becoming the wife of a gentleman of station. Hence her own misery—her early death—and something of the brutal wickedness of Heathcliff's character and conduct; though we cannot persuade ourselves that even a happy love would have tamed down the natural ferocity of the tiger. Catherine the younger is more sinned against than sinning, and in spite of her grave moral defects, we have some hope of her at the last.

Wuthering Heights is not a book the character of which it is very easy to set forth in extract; but the following scene in which Catherine and Heathcliff—the lovers of early days each wedded to another—are the actors, will afford a glimpse of Ellis Bell's power. Catherine, it must be premised, is dying; and, through the

"Your Next Novel"

Over the years there has been speculation that Emily Brontë was writing a second novel upon her death in December 1848. No evidence has emerged of an additional novel manuscript by Emily; however, the following brief letter, dated 15 February 1848, from publisher T. C. Newby addressed to Emily under her pseudonym Ellis Bell shows that Emily (and presumably Anne, whose second novel, The Tenant of Wildfell Hall, *was published by Newby in June 1848) were negotiating with him arrangements for any future work produced.*

Dear Sir,

I am much obliged by your kind note & shall have great pleasure in making arrangements for your next novel. I would not ?hurry its completion, for I think you are quite right not to let it go before the world until well satisfied with it, for much depends on your next work if it be an improvement on your first you will have established yourself as a first rate novelist, but if it fall short the Critics will be too apt to say that you have expended your talent in your first novel. I shall therefore, have pleasure in accepting it upon the understanding that its completion be at your own time.

Believe me
my dear Sir
Yrs. sincerely
T C Newby

—The Letters of Charlotte Brontë, v. 2, p. 26

agency of a servant, Heathcliff has obtained admittance to the sick chamber:– . . . .

This is at least forcible writing; but, to estimate it aright, the reader must have all the scenic accompaniments before him. He must not fancy himself in a London mansion; but in an old northcountry manor-house, situated on "the dreary, dreary moorland," far from the haunts of civilised men. There is, at all events, keeping in the book—the groups of figures and the scenery are in harmony with each other. There is a touch of Salvator-Rosa in all.

Agnes Grey is a story of very different stamp. It is a tale of every-day life, and though not wholly free from exaggeration (there are some detestable young ladies in it), does not offend by any startling improbabilities. It is more level and more sunny. Perhaps we shall best describe it as a somewhat coarse imitation of one of Miss Austin's [sic] charming stories. Like *Jane Eyre,* it sets forth some passages in the life of a governess; but the incidents, wound up with the heroine's marriage to a country clergyman, are such as might happen to anyone in that situation of life, and, doubtless, have happened to many. There is a want of distinctness in the character of Agnes, which prevents the reader from taking much interest in her

fate—but the story, though lacking the power and originality of *Wuthering Heights,* is infinitely more agreeable. It leaves no painful impression on the mind—some may think it leaves no impression at all. We are not quite sure that the next new novel will not efface it, but *Jane Eyre* and *Wuthering Heights* are not things to be forgotten. The work of Currer Bell is a great performance; that of Ellis Bell is only a promise, but it is a colossal one.

—The Atlas (22 January 1848): 59

* * *

"Charlotte reports reading to her sisters a review of Wuthering Heights *from a leading American periodical in a 22 November 1848 letter to William Smith Williams: "The North American Review is worth reading; there is no mincing the matter there. What a bad set the Bells must be! To-day, as Emily appeared a little easier, I thought the* Review *would amuse her, so I read it aloud to her and Anne. As I sat between them at our quiet but now somewhat melancholy fireside, I studied the two ferocious authors. Ellis, the 'man of uncommon talents, but dogged, brutal, and morose,' sat leaning back in his easy chair drawing his impeded breath as he best could, and looking, alas! piteously pale and wasted; it is not his wont to laugh, but he smiled half-amused and half in scorn as he listened. Acton was sewing, no emotion ever stirs him to loquacity, so he only smiled too, dropping at the same time a single word of calm amazement to hear his character so darkly portrayed. I wonder what the reviewer would have thought about his own sagacity could he have beheld the pair as I did" (Clement K. Shorter,* Charlotte Brontë and Her Sisters, *pp. 130–131). The unsigned reviewer, believed to be the respected critic Edwin Percy Whipple, mistakenly assumes that Acton Bell wrote* Wuthering Heights *and several parts of* Jane Eyre *and refers to Heathcliff erroneously as "Heathcote." This excerpt begins with the concluding observation of his treatment of* Jane Eyre.

"Power Thrown Away"
Review of *Wuthering Heights*

. . . The truth is, that the whole firm of Bell & Co. seem to have a sense of the depravity of human nature peculiarly their own. It is the yahoo, not the demon, that they select for representation; their Pandemonium is of mud rather than fire.

This is especially the case with Acton Bell, the author of Wuthering Heights, The Tenant of Wildfell Hall, and, if we mistake not, of certain offensive but powerful portions of Jane Eyre. Acton, when left altogether to his own imaginations, seems to take a morose satisfaction in developing a full and com-

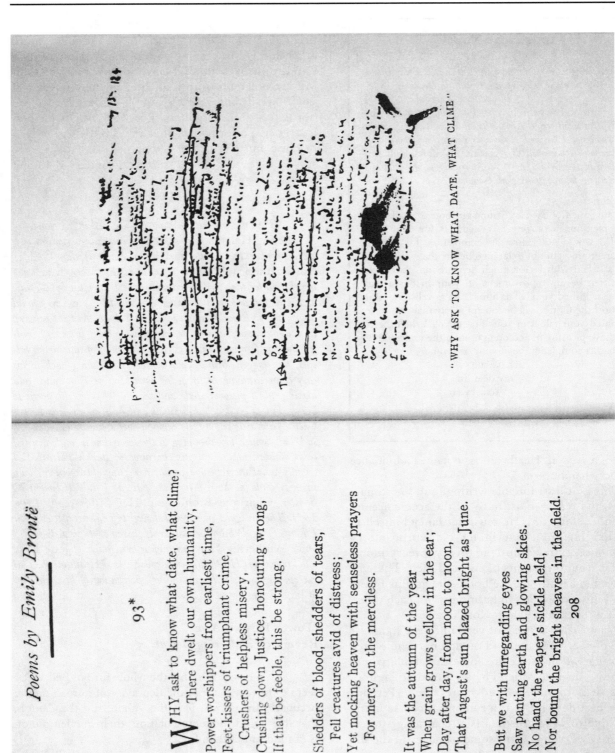

Pages from Brontë Poems showing published and manuscript versions of the last poem in Emily's Gondal manuscript–the last poem she is known to have written (from Arthur C. Benson, Brontë Poems: Selections from the Poetry of Charlotte, Emily, Anne and Branwell Brontë, University of Wyoming Library)

"WHY ASK TO KNOW WHAT DATE, WHAT CLIME"

Poems by Emily Brontë

93*

WHY ask to know what date, what clime?
   There dwelt our own humanity,
Power-worshippers from earliest time,
Feet-kissers of triumphant crime,
   Crushers of helpless misery,
Crushing down Justice, honouring wrong,
If that be feeble, this be strong.

Shedders of blood, shedders of tears,
   Fell creatures avid of distress;
Yet mocking heaven with senseless prayers
   For mercy on the merciless.

It was the autumn of the year
When grain grows yellow in the ear;
Day after day, from noon to noon,
That August's sun blazed bright as June.

But we with unregarding eyes
Saw panting earth and glowing skies.
No hand the reaper's sickle held,
Nor bound the bright sheaves in the field.

208

plete science of human brutality. In Wuthering Heights he has succeeded in reaching the summit of this laudable ambition. He appears to think that spiritual wickedness is a combination of animal ferocities, and has accordingly made a compendium of the most striking qualities of tiger, wolf, cur, and wild-cat, in the hope of framing out of such elements a suitable brute-demon to serve as the hero of his novel. Compared with Heathcote, Squeers is considerate and Quilp humane. He is a deformed monster, whom the Mephistopheles of Goethe would have nothing to say to, whom the Satan of Milton would consider as an object of simple disgust, and to whom Dante would hesitate in awarding the honor of place among those whom he has consigned to the burning pitch. This epitome of brutality, disavowed by man and devil, Mr. Acton Bell attempts in two whole volumes to delineate, and certainly he is to be congratulated on his success. As he is a man of uncommon talents, it is needless to say that it is to his subject and his dogged manner of handling it that we are to refer the burst of dislike with which the novel was received. His mode of delineating a bad character is to narrate every offensive act and repeat every vile expression which are characteristic. Hence, in Wuthering Heights, he details all the ingenuities of animal malignity, and exhausts the whole rhetoric of stupid blasphemy, in order that there may be no mistake as to the kind of person he intends to hold up to the popular gaze. Like all spendthrifts of malice and profanity, however, he overdoes the business. Though he scatters oaths as plentifully as sentimental writers do interjections, the comparative parsimony of the great novelists in this respect is productive of infinitely more effect. It must be confessed that this coarseness, though the prominent, is not the only characteristic of the writer. His attempt at originality does not stop with the conception of Heathcote, but he aims further to exhibit the action of the sentiment of love on the nature of the being whom his morbid imagination has created. This is by far the ablest and most subtile portion of his labors, and indicates that strong hold upon the elements of character, and that decision of touch in the delineation of the most evanescent qualities of emotion, which distinguish the mind of the whole family. For all practical purposes, however, the power evinced in Wuthering Heights is power thrown away. Nightmares and dreams, through which devils dance and wolves howl, make bad novels.

—*The North American Review,* 67 (October 1848): 358–359

"A Hard, Short Conflict"

Emily Brontë's symptoms of pulmonary tuberculosis became obvious soon after Branwell's death in September 1848. Through the brief course of her illness, Emily resisted any medical attention and even any commentary on her disease.

This excerpt indicates how Emily and her family were coping with the prospect of her approaching death.

Charlotte Brontë to William Smith Williams, 7 December 1848

I duly received Dr. Curie's work on Homœopathy, and ought to apologize for having forgotten to thank you for it. I will return it when I have given it a more attentive perusal than I have yet had leisure to do. My sister has read it, but as yet she remains unshaken in her former opinion: she will not admit there can be efficacy in such a system. Were I in her place it appears to me that I should be glad to give it a trial, confident that it can scarcely do harm and might do good.

I can give no favourable report of Emily's state. My Father is very despondent about her. Anne and I cherish hope as well as we can—but her appearance and her symptoms tend to crush that feeling. Yet I argue that the present emaciation, cough, weakness, shortness of breath are the results of inflammation now, I trust, subsided, and that with time, these ailments will gradually leave her, but my father shakes his head and speaks of others of our family once similarly afflicted, for whom he likewise persisted in hoping against hope, and who are now removed where hope and fear fluctuate no more. There were, however, differences between their case and hers—important differences I think—I <u>must</u> cling to the expectation of her recovery; I <u>cannot</u> renounce it.

Much would I give to have the opinion of a skilful professional man. It is easy, my dear sir, to say there is nothing in medicine and that physicians are useless but we naturally wish to procure aid for those we love when we see them suffer—most painful is it to sit still, look on and do nothing. Would that my sister added to her many great qualities the humble one of tractability! I have again and again incurred her displeasure by urging the necessity of seeking advice, and I fear I must yet incur it again and again. Let me leave the subject—I have no right thus to make you a sharer in our sorrows.

I am indeed surprised that Mr. Newby should say that he is to publish another work by Ellis and Acton Bell. Acton has had quite enough of him. I think I have before intimated that that author never more intends to have Mr. Newby for a publisher. Not only does he seem to forget that engagements made should be fulfilled—but by a system of petty and contemptible manœuvring he throws an air of charlatanry over the works of which he has the management: this does not suit the "Bells"; they have their own rude north-country ideas of what is delicate, honourable and gentlemanlike: Newby's conduct in no sort corresponds with these notions; they have found him—I will not say what they have found him; two words that would exactly suit him are at my pen point, but I shall not take the trouble to employ them.

Ellis Bell is at present in no condition to trouble himself with thoughts either of writing or publishing; should it please Heaven to restore his health and strength he reserves to himself the right of deciding whether or not Mr. Newby has forfeited every claim to his second work. . .

—The Letters of Charlotte Brontë, v. 2, pp. 147–148

* * *

Emily died at the age of thirty on 19 December 1848, of "Consumption—2 months duration," and was buried in Haworth Church 22 December. Excerpt.

Charlotte Brontë to Ellen Nussey, 23 December 1848

Emily suffers no more either from pain or weakness now. She never will suffer more in this world—she is gone after a hard, short conflict. She died on Tuesday, the very day I wrote to you. I thought it very possible then she might be with us still for weeks and a few hours afterwards she was in Eternity—Yes—there is no Emily in Time or on Earth now—yesterday, we put her poor, wasted mortal frame quietly under the Church pavement. We are very calm [a]t present, why should we be otherwise?—the anguish of seeing [he]r suffer is over—the spectacle of the pains of D[ea]th is gone by—the funeral day is past—we feel she is at peace—no need now to tremble for the hard frost and keen wind—Emily does not feel them. She has died in a time of promise—we saw her torn from life in its prime—but it is God's will—and the place where she is gone is better than that she has left.

—The Letters of Charlotte Brontë, v. 2, pp. 157–158

* * *

These excerpts are from a long article on Currer Bell that was published nearly two years after Emily's death. The unsigned critic, identified later as the poet Sydney Dobell, assumed that Currer was the single female author of the Bell novels, beginning with Wuthering Heights. *Charlotte was heartened by the article and in a 5 September 1850 letter to James Taylor referred to the remarks on Emily's novel: "they are true, they are discriminating, they are full of late justice."*

"The Stamp of High Genius" An Assessment of *Wuthering Heights* as Currer Bell's First Novel

Laying aside "Wildfell Hall," we open "Wuthering Heights," as at once the earlier in date and ruder in execution. We look upon it as the flight of an impatient fancy fluttering in the very exultation of young wings; sometimes beating against its solitary bars, but turning, rather to exhaust, in a circumscribed space, the energy and agility which it may not yet spend in the heavens—a youthful story, written for oneself in solitude, and thrown aside till other successes recall the eyes to it in hope. In this thought let the critic take up the book; lay it down in what thought he will, there are some things in it he can lay down no more.

That Catherine Earnshaw—at once so wonderfully fresh, so fearfully natural—new, "as if brought from other spheres," and familiar as the recollection of some woeful experience—what can surpass the strange compatibility of her simultaneous loves; the involuntary art with which her two natures are so made to co-exist, that in the very arms of her lover we dare not doubt her purity; the inevitable belief with which we watch the oscillations of the old and new elements in her mind, and the exquisite truth of the last victory of nature over education, when the past returns to her as a flood, sweeping every modern landmark from within her, and the soul of the child, expanding, fills the woman? Found at last, by her husband, insensible on the breast of her lover, and dying of the agony of their parting, one looks back upon her, like that husband, without one thought of accusation or absolution; her memory is chaste as the loyalty of love, pure as the air of the Heights on which she dwelt.

Heathcliff *might* have been as unique a creation. The conception in his case was as wonderfully strong and original, but he is spoilt in detail. The authoress has too often disgusted, where she should have terrified, and has allowed us a familiarity with her fiend which has ended in unequivocal contempt. If "Wuthering Heights" had been written as lately as "Jane Eyre," the figure of Heathcliff, symmetrised and elevated, might have been one of the most natural and most striking portraits in the gallery of fiction.

Not a subordinate place or person in this novel, but bears more or less the stamp of high genius. Ellen Dean is the ideal of the peasant playmate and servant of "the family." The substratum in which her mind moves is finely preserved. Josephus, as a specimen of the sixty years' servitor of "the house," is worthy a museum case. We feel that if Catherine Earnshaw bore her husband a child, it must be that Cathy Linton, and no other. The very Jane Eyre, of quiet satire, peeps out in such a paragraph as this: – "He told me to put on my cloak, and run to Gimmerton for the doctor and the parson. I went, through wind and rain, and brought one, the doctor, back with me: the other said, *he would come in the morning*." What terrible truth, what nicety of touch, what "uncanny" capacity for mental aberration in the first symptoms of Catherine's delirium. "I'm not wandering; you're mistaken, or else I should believe you really *were* that withered hag, and I should think I *was* under Penistone Crag: and I'm conscious it's night, and there are two candles on the table making the black press shine like jet." What an unobtrusive, unexpected sense of *keeping* in the hanging of Isabella's dog.

The book abounds in such things. But one looks back at the whole story as to a world of brilliant figures in an atmosphere of mist; shapes that come out upon the eye, and burn their colours into the brain, and depart into the enveloping fog. It is the unformed writing of a giant's hand; the "large utterance" of a baby god. In the sprawlings of the infant Hercules, however, there must have been attitudes from which the statuary might model. In the early efforts of unusual genius, there are not seldom unconscious felicities which maturer years may look back upon with envy. The child's hand wanders over the strings. It cannot combine them in the chords and melodies of manhood; but its separate notes are perfect in themselves, and perhaps sound all the sweeter for the Æolian discords from which they come.

We repeat, that there are passages in this book of "Wuthering Heights" of which any novelist, past or present, might be proud. Open the first volume at the fourteenth page, and read to the sixty-first. There are few things in modern prose to surpass these pages for native power. We cannot praise too warmly the brave simplicity, the unaffected air of intense belief, the admirable combination of extreme likelihood with the rarest originality, the nice provision of the possible even in the highest effects of the supernatural, the easy strength and instinct of keeping with which the accessory circumstances are grouped, the exquisite but unconscious art with which the chiaroscuro of the whole is managed, and the ungenial frigidity of place, time, weather, and persons, is made to heighten the unspeakable pathos of one ungovernable outburst.

The *thinking-out* of some of these pages—of pp. 52, 53, and 60—is the masterpiece of a poet, rather than the hybrid creation of the novelist. The mass of readers will probably yawn over the whole; but in the memory of those whose remembrance makes *fame,* the images in these pages will live—when every word that conveyed them is forgotten—as a recollection of *things heard and seen.* This is the highest triumph of description. . . .

. . . When Currer Bell writes her next novel, let her remember, as far as possible, the frame of mind in which she sat down to her first. She cannot now commit the faults of that early effort; it will be well for her if she be still capable of the virtues. She will never sin so much against consistent keeping as to draw another Heathcliff; she is too much *au fait* of her profession to make again those sacrifices to machinery which deprive her early picture of any claim to be ranked as a work of art. Happy she, if her next book demonstrate the unimpaired possession of those powers of insight that instinctive obedience to the nature within her, and those occurrences of infallible inspiration, which astound the critic in the young author of "Wuthering Heights." She will not let her next dark-haired hero babble away the respect of his reader and the awe of his antecedents; nor will she find another housekeeper who remembers two volumes *literatim*. Let her rejoice if she can again give us such an elaboration of a rare and fearful form of mental disease—so terribly strong, so exquisitely subtle—with such nicety in its transitions, such intimate symptomatic truth in its details, as to be at once a psychological and medical study. It has been said of Shakspeare, that he drew cases which the physician might study; Currer Bell has done no less. She will not, again, employ her wonderful pencil on a picture so destitute of moral beauty and human worth. Let her exult, if she can still invest such a picture with such interest. We stand painfully before the portraits; but our eyes are drawn to them by the irresistible ties of blood relationship. Let her exult, if she can still make us weep with the simple pathos of that fading face, which looked from the golden crocuses on her pillow to the hills which concealed the old home and the churchyard of Gimmerton. "These are the earliest flowers at the Heights," she exclaimed. "They remind me of thaw-winds, and warm sunshine, and nearly-melted snow. Edgar, is there not a south wind, and is not the snow almost gone?"–"The snow is quite gone down here, darling," replied her husband; "and I only see two white spots on the whole range of moors. The sky is blue, and the larks are singing, and the becks and brooks are all brimful. Catherine, last spring, at this time, I was longing to have you under this roof; now, I wish you were a mile or two up those hills:

13

Decr 25th 1848

My dear Sir

I will write to you more at length when my heart can find a little rest — now I can only thank you very briefly for your letter which seems to me eloquent in its sincerity.

Emily is nowhere here now — her wasted mortal remains are taken out of the house; we have laid her cherished head under the church = aisle beside my mother's my two sisters; dead long ago, and my poor, hapless brother's. But a small remnant of the race is left — so my poor father thinks.

Well — the loss is ours — not hers, and some sad comfort I take, as I hear the wind blow and feel the cutting keen —

*First page of Charlotte Brontë's letter to William Smith Williams, written Christmas Day 1848, seven days after Emily's death
(The British Library, c5689-06, Shelfmark Ashley 2452)*

the air blows so sweetly, I feel that it would cure you."–"I shall never be there but once more," said the invalid, "and then you'll leave me, and I shall remain for ever. Next spring, you'll long again to have me under this roof, and you'll look back, and think you were happy today." Let Currer Bell prize the young intuition of character which dictated Cathy's speech to Ellen. There is a deep, unconscious philosophy in it. There are minds, whose crimes and sorrows are not so much the result of intrinsic evil as of a false position in the scheme of things, which clashes their energies with the arrangements of surrounding life. It is difficult to cure such a soul from *within*. The point of view, not the eye or the landscape, is in fault. Move *that,* and, as at the changing of a stop, the mental machine assumes its proper relative place, and the powers of discord become, in the same measure, the instruments of harmony. It was a fine instinct which saw this. Let Currer Bell be passing glad if it is as vigorous now as then; and let her thank God if she can now draw the apparition of the "Wanderer of the Moor."

–*The Palladium* (September 1850): 165–166, 168–169

A New Edition of *Wuthering Heights*

In September 1850, Charlotte's publisher Smith, Elder offered to bring out a new edition of Wuthering Heights *and* Agnes Grey. *The 1847 edition published by T. C. Newby was out of print; Newby had published only 250 copies, instead of the 350 promised, and had never repaid Emily and Anne the £50 they invested in their novels' publication.*

Charlotte in this letter describes her plans for editing the volume.

Charlotte Brontë to William Smith Williams, 27 September 1850

My dear Sir

It is my intention to write a few lines of remark on "W. Heights" which however I proposed to place apart as a brief preface before the tale–I am likewise compelling myself to read it over for the first time of opening the book since my sister's death. Its power fills me with renewed admiration but yet I am oppressed– the reader is scarcely ever permitted a taste of unalloyed pleasure–every beam of sunshine is poured down through black bars of threatening cloud–every page is surcharged with a sort of moral electricity; and the writer was unconscious of all this–nothing could make her conscious of it. And this makes me reflect perhaps I

too am incapable of perceiving the faults and peculiarities of my own style.

I should wish to revise the proofs, if it be not too great an inconvenience to send them. It seems to me advisable to modify the orthography of the old servant Joseph's speeches–for though–as it stands–it exactly renders the Yorkshire accent to a Yorkshire ear–yet I am sure Southerns must find it unintelligible–and thus one of the most graphic characters in the book is lost on them.

What the probable quantity of new matter will be, I cannot say exactly–but I think it will not exceed thirty or, at the most forty pages–since it is so inconsiderable, would it not be better to place the title thus

Wuthering Heights & Agnes Grey
E & A Bell
With a Notice of the Authors by Currer Bell
and a Selection from their literary Remains?

I only suggest this–if there are reasons rendering the other title preferable–adopt it.

I will prepare and send some extracts from reviews.

I grieve to say that I possess no portrait of either of my sisters.

Believe me

Yours sincerely
C Brontë
–*The Letters of Charlotte Brontë*, v. 2, p. 479

* * *

In addition to the "Biographical Notice of Ellis and Acton Bell," published in the first chapter of this volume, Charlotte also wrote a brief introduction for Emily's novel.

Editor's Preface to *Wuthering Heights*
Currer Bell

I have just read over *Wuthering Heights,* and, for the first time, have obtained a clear glimpse of what are termed (and, perhaps, really are) its faults; have gained a definite notion of how it appears to other people–to strangers who knew nothing of the author; who are unacquainted with the locality where the scenes of the story are laid; to whom the inhabitants, the customs, the natural characteristics of the outlying hills and hamlets in the West-Riding of Yorkshire are things alien and unfamiliar.

To all such *Wuthering Heights* must appear a rude and strange production. The wild moors of the north of England can for them have no interest; the language, the manners, the very dwellings and household cus-

The Outcast Mother.

I'VE seen this dell in July's shine,
  As lovely as an angel's dream;
Above—Heaven's depth of blue divine,
  Around—the evening's golden beam.

I've seen the purple heather-bell
  Look out by many a storm-worn stone;
And, oh! I've known such music swell,—
  Such wild notes wake these passes lone—

So soft, yet so intensely felt;
  So low, yet so distinctly heard;
My breath would pause, my eyes would melt,
  And tears would dew the green heath-sward.

I'd linger here a summer day,
  Nor care how fast the hours flew by;
Nor mark the sun's departing ray
  Smile sadly from the dark'ning sky.

Then, then, I might have laid me down,
  And dreamed my sleep would gentle be;
I might have left thee, darling one,
  And thought thy God was guarding thee!

But now there is no wand'ring glow,
  No gleam to say that God is nigh;
And coldly spreads the couch of snow,
  And harshly sounds thy lullaby.

Forests of heather, dark and long,
  Wave their brown branching arms above;
And they must soothe thee with their song,
  And they must shield my child of love.

Alas! the flakes are heavily falling,
  They cover fast each guardian crest;
And chilly white their shroud is palling
  Thy frozen limbs and freezing breast.

Wakes up the storm more madly wild,
  The mountain drifts are tossed on high;
Farewell, unbless'd, unfriended child,
  I cannot bear to watch thee die!

                                    E. J. BRONTË.

HAWORTH, *July 12th,* 1839.

Poem by Emily Brontë published in the May 1860 issue of Cornhill Magazine. *Arthur Bell Nicholls selected and sent this poem to William Makepeace Thackeray, who was then the editor of the periodical. Of the 201 poems ascribed to Emily, only 21 were published during her lifetime (University of Colorado Libraries).*

toms of the scattered inhabitants of those districts, must be to such readers in a great measure unintelligible, and—where intelligible—repulsive. Men and women who, perhaps, naturally very calm, and with feelings moderate in degree, and little marked in kind, have been trained from their cradle to observe the utmost evenness of manner and guardedness of language, will hardly know what to make of the rough, strong utterance, the harshly manifested passions, the unbridled aversions, and headlong partialities of unlettered moorland hinds and rugged moorland squires, who have grown up untaught and unchecked, except by mentors as harsh as themselves. A large class of readers, likewise, will suffer greatly from the introduction into the pages of this work of words printed with all their letters, which it has become the custom to represent by the initial and final letter only—a blank line filling the interval. I may as well say at once that, for this circumstance, it is out of my power to apologize; deeming it, myself, a rational plan to write words at full length. The practice of hinting by single letters those expletives with which profane and violent people are wont to garnish their discourse, strikes me as a proceeding which, however well meant, is weak and futile. I cannot tell what good it does—what feeling it spares—what horror it conceals.

With regard to the rusticity of *Wuthering Heights,* I admit the charge, for I feel the quality. It is rustic all through. It is moorish, and wild, and knotty as the root of heath. Nor was it natural that it should be otherwise; the author being herself a native and nursling of the moors. Doubtless, had her lot been cast in a town, her writings, if she had written at all, would have possessed another character. Even had chance or taste led her to choose a similar subject, she would have treated it otherwise. Had Ellis Bell been a lady or a gentleman accustomed to what is called 'the world,' her view of a remote and unreclaimed region, as well as of the dwellers therein, would have differed greatly from that actually taken by the homebred country girl. Doubtless it would have been wider—more comprehensive: whether it would have been more original or more truthful is not so certain. As far as the scenery and locality are concerned, it could scarcely have been so sympathetic: Ellis Bell did not describe as one whose eye and taste alone found pleasure in the prospect; her native hills were far more to her than a spectacle; they were what she lived in, and by, as much as the wild birds, their tenants, or as the heather, their produce. Her descriptions, then, of natural scenery, are what they should be, and all they should be.

Where delineation of human character is concerned, the case is different. I am bound to avow that she had scarcely more practical knowledge of the peasantry amongst whom she lived, than a nun has of the country people who sometimes pass her convent gates. My sister's disposition was not naturally gregarious, circumstances favoured and fostered her tendency to seclusion; except to go to church or take a walk on the hills, she rarely crossed the threshold of home. Though her feeling for the people round was benevolent, intercourse with them she never sought; nor, with very few exceptions, ever experienced. And yet she knew them; knew their ways, their language, their family histories; she could hear of them with interest and talk of them with detail, minute, graphic, and accurate; but *with* them she rarely exchanged a word. Hence it ensued that what her mind had gathered of the real concerning them, was too exclusively confined to those tragic and terrible traits of which, in listening to the secret annals of every rude vicinage, the memory is sometimes compelled to receive the impress. Her imagination, which was a spirit more sombre than sunny, more powerful than sportive, found in such traits material whence it wrought creations like Heathcliff, like Earnshaw, like Catherine. Having formed these beings, she did not know what she had done. If the auditor of her work, when read in manuscript, shuddered under the grinding influence of natures so relentless and implacable, of spirits so lost and fallen; if it was complained that the mere hearing of certain vivid and fearful scenes banished sleep by night, and disturbed mental peace by day, Ellis Bell would wonder what was meant, and suspect the complainant of affectation. Had she but lived, her mind would of itself have grown like a strong tree; loftier, straighter, wider-spreading, and its matured fruits would have attained a mellower ripeness and sunnier bloom; but on that mind time and experience alone could work: to the influence of other intellects, it was not amenable.

Having avowed that over much of *Wuthering Heights* there broods 'a horror of great darkness'; that, in its storm-heated and electrical atmosphere, we seem at times to breathe lightning, let me point to those spots where clouded daylight and the eclipsed sun still attest their existence. For a specimen of true benevolence and homely fidelity, look at the character of Nelly Dean; for an example of constancy and tenderness, remark that of Edgar Linton. (Some people will think these qualities do not shine so well incarnate in a man as they would do in a woman, but Ellis Bell could never be brought to comprehend this notion: nothing moved her more than any insinuation that the faithfulness and clemency, the long-suffering and loving-kindness which are esteemed virtues in the daughters of Eve, become foibles in the sons of Adam. She held that mercy and forgiveness are the divinest attributes of the Great Being who made both man and woman, and that what clothes the Godhead in glory, can disgrace no form of feeble humanity.)

There is a dry saturnine humour in the delineation of old Joseph, and some glimpses of grace and gaiety animate the younger Catherine. Nor is even the first heroine of the name destitute of a certain strange beauty in her fierceness, or of honesty in the midst of perverted passion and passionate perversity.

Heathcliff, indeed, stands unredeemed; never once swerving in his arrow-straight course to perdition, from the time when 'the little black-haired, swarthy thing, as dark as if it came from the Devil,' was first unrolled out of the bundle and set on its feet in the farm-house kitchen, to the hour when Nelly Dean found the grim, stalwart corpse laid on its back in the panel-enclosed bed, with wide-gazing eyes that seemed 'to sneer at her attempt to close them, and parted lips and sharp white teeth that sneered too.'

Heathcliff betrays one solitary human feeling, and that is *not* his love for Catherine; which is a sentiment fierce and inhuman: a passion such as might boil and glow in the bad essence of some evil genius; a fire that might form the tormented centre—the ever-suffering soul of a magnate of the infernal world: and by its quenchless and ceaseless ravage effect the execution of the decree which dooms him to carry Hell with him wherever he wanders. No; the single link that connects Heathcliff with humanity is his rudely confessed regard for Hareton Earnshaw—the young man whom he has ruined; and then his half-implied esteem for Nelly Dean. These solitary traits omitted, we should say he was child neither of Lascar nor gipsy, but a man's shape animated by demon life—a Ghoul—an Afreet.

Whether it is right or advisable to create things like Heathcliff, I do not know: I scarcely think it is. But this I know; the writer who possesses the creative gift owns something of which he is not always master—something that at times strangely wills and works for itself. He may lay down rules and devise principles, and to rules and principles it will perhaps for years lie in subjection; and then, haply without any warning of revolt, there comes a time when it will no longer consent to 'harrow the vallies, or be bound with a band in the furrow'—when it 'laughs at the multitude of the city, and regards not the crying of the driver'—when, refusing absolutely to make ropes out of sea-sand any longer, it sets to work on statue-hewing, and you have a Pluto or a Jove, a Tisiphone or a Psyche, a Mermaid or a Madonna, as Fate or Inspiration direct. Be the work grim or glorious, dread or divine, you have little choice left but quiescent adoption. As for you—the nominal artist—your share in it has been to work passively under dictates you neither delivered nor could question—that would not be uttered at your prayer, nor suppressed nor changed at your caprice. If the result be attractive, the World will praise you, who little deserve praise; if it

be repulsive, the same World will blame you, who almost as little deserve blame.

Wuthering Heights was hewn in a wild workshop, with simple tools, out of homely materials. The statuary found a granite block on a solitary moor: gazing thereon, he saw how from the crag might be elicited the head, savage, swart, sinister; a form moulded with at least one element of grandeur—power. He wrought with a rude chisel, and from no model but the vision of his meditations. With time and labour, the crag took human shape; and there it stands colossal, dark, and frowning, half statue, half rock; in the former sense, terrible and goblin-like; in the latter, almost beautiful, for its colouring is of mellow grey, and moorland moss clothes it; and heath, with its blooming bells and balmy fragrance, grows faithfully close to the giant's foot.

* * *

Although Charlotte portrayed Emily as a writer who "did not know what she had done," later critics, especially those of the twentieth century, have seen her as a conscious artist and demonstrated that in fact Emily's writings can be traced to many sources and influences. This excerpt is from Miller's chapter titled "Interpreting Emily."

"Strands of Romantic Influence"
Lucasta Miller

She [Emily] frequently takes as her themes the imagination itself and the relationship between visible nature and the Unseen, constantly reformulating and questioning it. "A Day Dream" describes a visionary moment in which the poet's very breath seems "full of sparks divine" as she lies on a "sunny brae," though the vision is undercut in the final lines, "But Fancy, still, will sometimes deem / Her fond creation true." Similarly, in "To Imagination" she prizes "[t]he world within" for its "voice divine," but ends, again, on a questioning note, wondering whether to trust to its "phantom bliss." In "Stars," poet and nature, perceiver and perceived, become one in another visionary moment, though the epiphany is again impermanent, dissolved as it is by the sunrise.

Whether or not the influence was consciously acknowledged, Emily's visionary poetry shares its emphasis on nature and the imagination with Wordsworth, Coleridge, and the other Romantic writers to whom she had access through *Fraser's* and *Blackwood's*. The latter, for example, carried a lengthy review of *The Poetical Works of S. T. Coleridge,* when it was published in 1834. Some critics have suggested even closer verbal parallels between Emily's work and that of these poets. In addition, many of the Gondal lyrics of love and loss,

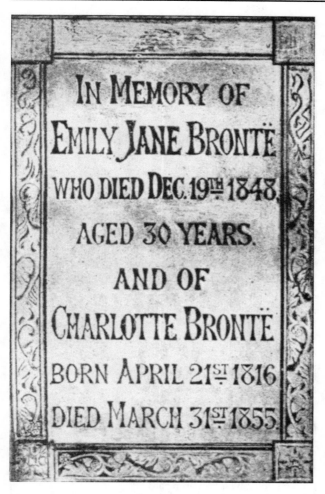

Brass plate over the Brontë vault in Haworth Church (from Whiteley Turner, A Spring-Time Saunter: Round and About Brontë Land, *Sam Houston State University Library)*

torment and despair, have been shown to contain verbal echoes of Byron's verse.

Wuthering Heights, too, is not without its literary forebears, even though it offers something completely different from the standard social realism of the period, which is why it baffled its first reviewers. Instead, Emily's novel harks back both to gothic and to the poetry and prose of the Romantic generation. Like Charlotte, she responded particularly to Byron and Walter Scott (chosen as one of the chief men for her island at the age of nine, and the inspiration behind Gondal's mountainous Scottish landscapes). The presence of both can be felt in her novel. The lullaby sung by Nelly Dean in chapter 9 directly quotes a ballad translated from the Danish which appeared in a note to Scott's poem *The Lady of the Lake,* while the names of Heathcliff and the Earnshaw family may derive from

Earncliff in Scott's *The Black Dwarf.* Like Lockwood in *Wuthering Heights,* Earncliff finds himself holed up in a solitary moorland dwelling with the eponymous dwarf, a piteous but horrifying character who has, like Heathcliff, turned misanthrope as a result of thwarted passion. More generally, the theme of family feud, particularly sexual and sibling rivalry, can be related to Scott's novels, as can Emily's use of dialect, and her narrative technique of the tale-within-a-tale.

Byron, who was such an influence on the young Charlotte, also made an impact on her sister. Even the diary papers, those apparently spontaneous records of the minute-to-minute occurrences of the day, show evidence of having been consciously composed in imitation of quotations from Byron's journal found in Moore's biography of the poet. Both Byron's life, as told by Moore, and his works can be traced in *Wuthering Heights.* In the biography, the sixteen-year-old Byron falls in love with a girl, Mary Chaworth, but overhears her scornfully telling the servant, "Do you think I could care anything for that lame boy?" Like Heathcliff, who overhears Catherine telling Nelly that it would degrade her to marry him, he then runs off into the night. Moore interprets this ur-rejection as the source of all Byron's subsequent sufferings and errors. He quotes as evidence a poem of 1811, "The Dream," which reads like a summary of Emily's plot, in which a spurned lover returns from abroad to find his beloved married to another and blames on her his future life of "deepening crimes," while she ends in madness.

It can be added that Moore's *Life* also provided a precursor for the literary representation of violent domestic quarrels, complete with pokers, tongs, and vicious dogs. A review in *Blackwood's* of 1830 contains the following, which is reminiscent of the marriage between Heathcliff and Isabella: "Had he not fired off pistols over his wife's head, as it lay on the pillow of their post-nuptial morn—and, as the smoke broke away, had he not, with the face of a fiend, whispered into her ear, delicately veiled in a lace night-cap, that he had married her from revenge and would break her heart?"

But it was in Byron's poetic romances, too, that Emily found the germ of the passion of Cathy and Heathcliff. With its overtones of sibling incest, theirs is a love of identity rather than difference. Her famous "I *am* Heathcliff" is echoed by his despair after her death, "I *cannot* live without my life! I *cannot* live without my soul!" In Byron's *Manfred* (1817), the fatal love between the hero and his spiritual twin and female doppelganger, Astarte, is a passion which is also mutual torture and ends destructively. She appears to him as a ghost, disappearing as soon as he tries to touch her, just as Heathcliff begs the ghost of Cathy to come back through the open window after she has appeared to

Lockwood in a dream. At the time of *Manfred's* publication it was common speculation in the press that Astarte represented Byron's half sister Augusta, with whom he was (accurately) rumored to have committed incest. In addition, Augusta was one of the names of Gondal's heroine, A. G. A., thought to be an early prototype of Catherine.

Along with these specific borrowings, Emily's art should be seen in the broader context of the Romanticism and sub-Romanticism which permeated the young Brontës' imaginations. The three strands of Romantic influence—Scott-ish, Byronic, and visionary—found in Emily's work can also be seen working together in, for example, a long verse romance by John Wilson which appeared in *Blackwood's* in 1831, *Unimore*. Wilson's setting, a Highland landscape of lochs and glens and gloomy castles, recalls Scott. His antihero, the chieftain Unimore of Morven, is Byronic. Victim of a "wicked love and fatal" for twin girls, his cousins and adoptive sisters, he is a "demon" who destroys them both and spends the rest of the poem "by misery crazed," eventually falling to his death as he chases after their ghosts. "Moody and wild, and with large restless eyes / Coal-black and lamping," he anticipates Heathcliff in looks. His period of disappearance from Morven, during which he visits an Indian isle and becomes a pirate and buccaneer, recalls both Heathcliff s mysterious absence from *Wuthering Heights* and Nelly Dean's orientalist fantasies about his mysterious origins. In addition to its references to Scott and Byron, Wilson's poem, divided into ten "Visions," draws on Coleridgean visionary poetics and pays Wordsworthian attention to nature. As in *Shirley,* the imagination is the active faculty which reveals the divine in the natural landscape.

In addition, another strand of influence on Emily may have come from her interest in German, which she studied while in Brussels. Her use of the uncanny and the supernatural in *Wuthering Heights,* as in Lockwood's dream of the ghostly Catherine, has been related to the stories of Hoffmann, but she is likely to have read more broadly among the German Romantics. As Stevie Davies has suggested in her account of Emily's intellectual context, she probably had contact with the philosophical German Romanticism which had influenced Coleridge and which was popularized in England during the 1820s and '30s by writers such as J. A. Heraud of *Fraser's,* De Quincey, and Thomas Carlyle. We can add for sure that Carlyle's *Sartor Resartus* made it into the Parsonage, as John Elliot Cairns noticed a copy on the shelves when he visited in 1858.

The visionary aspects of her poetry may thus have been informed by the idealist metaphysics (or "Visionary Theories," as they were known) ultimately derived from Kant and explained to the British public

---

Robert Bridges's Tribute

This is a poem by Robert Bridges, the poet laureate of England, that was published in the seventy-fifth year after Emily Brontë's death.

Emily Brontë
"Du hast Diamanten"

Thou hadst all Passion's splendor,
Thou hadst abounding store
Of heaven's eternal jewels,
Beloved; what wouldst thou more?

Thine was the frolic freedom
Of creatures coy and wild,
The melancholy of wisdom,
The innocence of a child,

The mail'd will of the warrior,
That buckled in thy breast
Humility as of Francis,
The Self-surrender of Christ;

And of God's cup thou drankest
The unmingled wine of Love,
Which makes poor mortals giddy
When they but sip thereof.

What was't to thee thy pathway
So rugged mean and hard,
Whereon when Death surprised thee
Thou gavest him no regard?

What was't to thee, enamour'd
As a red rose of the sun,
If of thy myriad lovers
Thou never sawest one?

Nor if of all thy lovers
That are and were to be
None ever had their vision,
O my belov'd, of thee,

Until thy silent glory
 Went forth from earth alone,
Where like a star thou gleamest
 From thine immortal throne.

—The London Mercury, 8 (June 1923): 120

---

by the antimaterialist Carlyle. Yet Emily's interest in philosophy, attested by poems such as "The Old Stoic" and "The Philosopher," may have gone all the way back to her early reading of Thomas Moore's life of Byron, which acknowledged its subject's religious skepticism and quoted his "detached thoughts" on such themes as the immortality of the soul and the nature of the mind. The image of the "chainless soul" in "The Old Stoic" has been recognized as deriving from the ancient philosopher Epictetus, who was popular in the late eighteenth and early nineteenth centuries; what has not been noted is that Moore quotes Byron alluding to it.

Tracing the influences Emily assimilated would not have acquired such significance if Charlotte had not misleadingly presented her as an untutored country girl. The effects of this portrayal are still with us, as can be seen in John Sutherland's essay "Heathcliff's Toothbrush," in his latest collection of wonderfully brainteasing literary conundrums. Sutherland sees literary parallels between *Wuthering Heights* and Bulwer-Lytton's novel, *Eugene Aram,* about a glamorous scholar murderer, originally published in 1832 but reissued in revised form in 1840 with a preface apologizing for the antihero's amorality. Sutherland hedges about, almost apologizing for speculating that the *Eugene Aram* controversy could have been picked up "even in remote Haworth."

In fact, Emily knew the novel. Her diary paper of June 26, 1837, paints the following scene—"A bit past 4 o'Clock Charlotte working in Aunts room Branwell reading Eugene Aram to her"—which proves not only that the book entered the Parsonage, but that it did so in its unexpurgated pre-1840 form. Sutherland has, it seems, been too eager to believe in the myth of Haworth's cultural remoteness which was first established by Charlotte in 1850.

What is in fact remarkable about *Wuthering Heights* is not that it borrows from literary sources (such intertextuality is arguably part of the definition of a literary text) but how it manages to use them as the basis for creating something entirely new. Like Charlotte, Emily transformed her Romantic legacy, and, in doing so, she created a fertile text which has outlived and overshadowed not only the turgid and derivative *Unimore* and the now unread works of Bulwer-Lytton, but the verse romances of Byron himself and even most of the novels of Walter Scott.

—The Brontë Myth, pp. 216–219

Charlotte Brontë

Charlotte Brontë (1816–1855)—the third Brontë daughter, who became the eldest child in the family with the deaths of her older sisters in 1825—is the Brontë about whom the most is known. The main source of information about Charlotte, her family, and her writings is the many letters she wrote, especially to Ellen Nussey, a lifelong friend she made at the school run by Margaret Wooler at Roe Head, and to her publisher George Smith and his reader William Smith Williams.

At Miss Wooler's School

Charlotte Brontë attended Miss Wooler's school as a student from January 1831 to June 1832, during which time she became friends with Ellen Nussey (1817–1897) and Mary Taylor. She served as a teacher for Miss Wooler from late July 1835 through December 1838.

This excerpt is from the article "Reminiscences of Charlotte Brontë," which was written for an American magazine more than fifteen years after Charlotte's death.

"First in Everything But Play"
School Days at Roe Head
Ellen Nussey

Arriving at school about a week after the general assembling of the pupils, I was not expected to accompany them when the time came for their daily exercise, but while they were out, I was led into the school-room, and quietly left to make my observations. I had come to the conclusion it was very nice and comfortable for a school-room, though I had little knowledge of school-rooms in general, when, turning to the window to observe the look-out I became aware for the first time that I was not alone; there was a silent, weeping, dark little figure in the large bay-window; she must, I thought, have risen from the floor. As soon as I had recovered from my surprise, I went from the far end of the room, where the book-shelves were, the contents of which I must have contemplated with a little awe in anticipation of coming studies. A crimson cloth covered the long table down the center of the room, which helped, no doubt, to hide the shrinking little figure from my view. I was touched and troubled at once to see her so sad and so tearful.

Charlotte Brontë, engraving based on a chalk drawing by George Richmond in 1850. Her publisher, George Smith, reported that the artist told him that Brontë had cried when she first saw the portrait because she found it so like her sister Anne, who had died the year before (from The Bookman, *October 1904, Colorado College Library).*

I said *shrinking*, because her attitude, when I saw her, was that of one who wished to hide both herself and her grief. She did not shrink, however, when spoken to, but in very few words confessed she was "homesick." After a little of such comfort as could be offered, it was suggested to her that there was a possibility of her too having to comfort the speaker by and by for the same cause. A faint quivering smile then lighted her face; the tear-drops fell; we silently took each other's hands, and at once we felt that genuine sympathy

Photo J. J. Stead.   **Miss Margaret Wooler**
                       (Mrs. Pryor of "Shirley").
" The lady had the clearest voice imaginable . . . . and a form decidedly
inclined to embonpoint."—" Shirley."

*Margaret Wooler (1792–1895), who maintained a connection with
Charlotte after her days as a student and teacher at Miss Wooler's school.
Miss Wooler gave Charlotte away at her wedding (from*
The Bookman, *October 1904).*

standard, and ready for the daily routine and arrangement of studies, and as quickly did she outstrip her companions, rising from the bottom of the classes to the top, a position which, when she had once gained, she never had to regain. She was first in everything but play, yet never was a word heard of envy or jealousy from her companions; every one felt she had won her laurels by an amount of diligence and hard labor of which they were incapable. She never exulted in her successes or seemed conscious of them; her mind was so wholly set on attaining knowledge that she apparently forgot all else.

Charlotte's appearance did not strike me at first as it did others. I saw her grief, not herself particularly, till afterwards. She never seemed to me the unattractive little person others designated her, but certainly she was at this time anything but *pretty;* even her good points were lost. Her naturally beautiful hair of soft silky brown being then dry and frizzy-looking, screwed up in tight little curls, showing features that were all the plainer from her exceeding thinness and want of complexion, she looked "dried in." A dark, rusty green stuff dress of old-fashioned make detracted still more from her appearance; but let her wear what she might, or do what she would, she had ever the demeanor of a born gentlewoman; vulgarity was an element that never won the slightest affinity with her nature. Some of the elder girls, who had been years at school, thought her ignorant. This was true in one sense; ignorant she was indeed in the elementary education which is given in schools, but she far surpassed her most advanced school-fellows in knowledge of what was passing in the world at large, and in the literature of her country. She knew a thousand things in these matters unknown to them.

She had taught herself a little French before she came to school; this little knowledge of the language was very useful to her when afterwards she was engaged in translation or dictation. She soon began to make a good figure in French lessons. Music she wished to acquire, for which she had both ear and taste, but her nearsightedness caused her to stoop so dreadfully in order to see her notes, she was dissuaded from persevering in the acquirement, especially as she had at this time an invincible objection to wearing glasses. Her very taper fingers, tipped with the most circular nails, did not seem very suited for instrumental execution; but when wielding the pen or the pencil, they appeared in the very office they were created for.

Her appetite was of the smallest; for years she had not tasted animal food; she had the greatest dislike to it; she always had something specially provided for her at our midday repast. Towards the close of the first half-year she was induced to take, by little and little,

which always consoles, even though it be unexpressed. We did not talk or stir till we heard the approaching footsteps of other pupils coming in from their play; it had been a game called "French and English," which was always very vigorously played, but in which Charlotte Brontë never could be induced to join. Perhaps the merry voices contesting for victory, which reached our ears in the school-room, jarred upon her then sensitive misery, and caused her ever after to dislike the game; but she was physically unequal to that exercise of muscle, which was keen enjoyment to strong, healthy girls, both older and younger than herself. Miss Wooler's system of education required that a good deal of her pupils' work should be done in classes, and to effect this, new pupils had generally a season of solitary study; but Charlotte's fervent application made this period a very short one to her,—she was quickly up to the needful meat gravy with vegetable, and in the second half-year she commenced taking a very small portion of animal food daily. She then grew a little bit plumper, looked younger and more animated, though she was never what is called lively at this period. She always seemed to feel that a deep responsibility rested upon her; that she was an object of expense to those at home, and that she must use every moment to attain the purpose for which she was sent to school, *i.e.,* to fit herself for governess life. She had almost too much opportunity for her conscientious diligence; we were so little restricted in our doings, the industrious might accomplish the appointed tasks of the day and enjoy a little leisure, but she chose in many things to do *double* lessons when not prevented by class arrangement or a companion. In two of her studies she was associated with her friend, and great was her distress if her companion failed to be ready, when she was, with the lesson of the day. She liked the stated task to be over, that she might be free to pursue her self-appointed ones. Such, however, was her conscientiousness that she never did what some girls think it generous to do; generous and unselfish though she was, she never whispered help to a companion in class (as she might have done), to rid herself of the trouble of having to appear again. All her school-fellows regarded her, I believe, as a model of high rectitude, close application, and great abilities. She did not play or amuse herself when others did. When her companions were merry round the fire, or otherwise enjoying themselves during the twilight, which was always a precious time of relaxation, she would be kneeling close to the window busy with her studies, and this would last so long that she was accused of seeing in the dark; yet though she did not play, as girls style play, she was ever ready to help with suggestions in those plays which required taste or arrangement.

When her companions formed the idea of having a coronation performance on a half-holiday, it was Charlotte Brontë who drew up the programme, arranged the titles to be adopted by her companions for the occasion, wrote the invitations to those who were to grace the ceremony, and selected for each a title, either for sound that pleased the ear or for historical association. The preparations for these extra half-holidays (which were very rare occurrences) sometimes occupied spare moments for weeks before the event. On this occasion Charlotte prepared a very elegant little speech for the one who was selected to present the crown. Miss W.'s younger sister consented after much entreaty to be crowned as our queen (a very noble, stately queen she made), and did her pupils all the honor she could by adapting herself to the role of the moment. The following exquisite little speech shows Charlotte's aptitude,

Ellen Nussey, who may have inspired the character Caroline Helstone in Brontë's novel Shirley *(from* The Bookman, *October 1904)*

even then, at giving fitting expression to her thoughts:—

"Powerful Queen! accept this Crown, the symbol of dominion, from the hands of your faithful and affectionate subjects! And if their earnest and united wishes have any efficacy, you will long be permitted to reign over this peaceful, though circumscribed, empire. [Signed, &c., &c.]

"Your loyal subjects."

The little fête finished off with what was called a ball; but for lack of numbers we had to content ourselves with one quadrille and two Scotch reels. Last of all there was a supper, which was considered very *recherché,* most of it having been coaxed out of yielding mammas and elder sisters, in addition to some wise expenditure of pocket-money. The grand feature, however, of the supper was the attendance of a mulatto servant. We descended for a moment from our assumed dignities to improvise this distinguishing appanage. The liveliest of our party, "Jessie York," volunteered this office, and surpassed our expectations. Charlotte evidently enjoyed the fun, in

The Rydings, Birstall,
At one time the home of Miss Ellen Nussey.

The Rydings, Birstall, a likely model for the exterior of Thornfield Hall in Jane Eyre. *Charlotte Brontë visited the home of Ellen Nussey, who lived there from 1826 to 1836, in fall 1832 (from* The Bookman, *October 1904).*

her own quiet way, as much as any one, and ever after with great zest helped, when with old school-fellows, to recall the performances of the exceptional half-holidays.

About a month after the assembling of the school, one of the pupils had an illness. There was great competition among the girls for permission to sit with the invalid, but Charlotte was never of the number, though she was as assiduous in kindness and attention as the rest in spare moments; but to sit with the patient was indulgence and leisure, and these she would not permit herself.

It was shortly after this illness that Charlotte caused such a panic of terror by her thrilling relations of the wanderings of a somnambulist. She brought together all the horrors her imagination could create, from surging seas, raging breakers, towering castle walls, high precipices, invisible chasms and dangers. Having wrought these materials to the highest pitch of effect, she brought out, in almost cloud-height, her

somnambulist, walking on shaking turrets,—all told in a voice that conveyed more than words alone can express. A shivering terror seized the recovered invalid; a pause ensued; then a subdued cry of pain came from Charlotte herself, with a terrified command to others to call for help. She was in bitter distress. Something like remorse seemed to linger in her mind after this incident; for weeks there was no prevailing upon her to resume her tales, and she never again created terrors for her listeners. Tales, however, were made again in time, till Miss W. discovered there was "late talking." That was forbidden; but understanding it was "late talk" only which was prohibited, we talked and listened to tales again, not expecting to hear Miss C. H. W. say, one morning, "All the ladies who talked last night must pay fines. I am sure Miss Brontë and Miss—were not of the number." Miss Brontë and Miss—were, however, transgressors like the rest, and rather enjoyed the fact of having to pay like them, till they saw Miss W.'s grieved and disappointed look. It was then a distress that they had failed where they were reckoned upon, though unintentionally. This was the only school-fine Charlotte ever incurred.

At the close of the first half-year, Charlotte bore off three prizes. For one she had to draw lots with her friend—a moment of painful suspense to both; for neither wished to deprive the other of her reward. Happily, Charlotte won it, and so had the gratifying pleasure of carrying home three tangible proofs of her goodness and industry. Miss W. had two badges of conduct for her pupils which were wonderfully effective, except with the most careless. A black ribbon, worn in the style of the Order of the Garter, which the pupils passed from one to another for any breach of rules, unlady-like manners, or incorrect grammar. Charlotte might, in her very earliest school-days, have worn "the mark," as we styled it, but I never remember her having it. The silver medal, which was the badge for the fulfillment of duties, she won the right to in her first half-year. This she never afterwards forfeited, and it was presented to her on leaving school. She was only three half-years at school. In this time she went through all the elementary teaching contained in our school-books. She was in the habit of committing long pieces of poetry to memory, and seemed to do so with real enjoyment and hardly any effort.

In these early days, whenever she was certain of being quite alone with her friend, she would talk much of her two dead sisters, Maria and Elizabeth. Her love for them was most intense; a kind of adoration dwelt in her feelings which, as she conversed, almost imparted itself to her listener.

She described Maria as a little mother among the rest, superhuman in goodness and cleverness. But the most touching of all were the revelations of her sufferings,—how she suffered with the sensibility of a grown-up person, and endured with a patience and fortitude that were Christ-like. Charlotte would still weep and suffer when thinking of her. She talked of Elizabeth also, but never with the anguish of expression which accompanied her recollections of Maria. When surprise was expressed that she should know so much about her sisters when they were so young, and she herself still younger, she said she began to analyze character when she was five years old, and instanced two guests who were at her home for a day or two, and of whom she had taken stock, and of whom after-knowledge confirmed first impressions.

The following lines, though not regarded of sufficient merit for publication in the volume of poems, yet have an interest as they depict her then desolated heart:—

MEMORY.

When the dead in their cold graves are lying
Asleep, to wake never again!
When past are their smiles and their sighing,
Oh, why should their memories remain?
Though sunshine and spring may have lightened
The wild flowers that blow on their graves,
Though summer their tombstones have brightened,
And autumn have palled them with leaves,
And winter have wildly bewailed them
With his dirge-wind as sad as a knell,
And the shroud of his snow-wreath have veiled them,
Still—how deep in our bosoms they dwell!

The shadow and sun-sparkle vanish,
The cloud and the light fleet away,
But man from his heart may not banish
Even thoughts that are torment to stay.
When quenched is the glow of the ember,
When the life-fire ceases to burn,
Oh! why should the spirit remember?
Oh! why should the parted return?

During one of our brief holidays Charlotte was guest in a family who had known her father when he was curate in their parish. They were naturally inclined to show kindness to his daughter, but the kindness here took a form which was little agreeable. They had had no opportunity of knowing her abilities or disposition, and they took her shyness and smallness as indications of extreme youth. She was slow, very slow, to express anything that bordered on ingratitude, but here she was mortified and hurt. "They took me for a child, and treated me just like one," she said. I can now recall the expression of that ever honest face as she added, "one tall lady *would* nurse me."

The tradition of a lady ghost who moved about in rustling silk in the upper stories of Roe Head had a great charm for Charlotte. She was a ready listener to any girl who could relate stories of others having seen her; but on Miss W. hearing us talk of our ghost, she adopted an effective measure for putting our belief in such an existence to the test, by selecting one or other from among us to ascend the stairs after the dimness of evening hours had set in, to bring something down which could easily be found. No ghost made herself visible even to the frightened imaginations of the foolish and the timid; the whitened face of apprehension soon disappeared, nerves were braced, and a general laugh soon set us all right again . . . I must not forget to state that no girl in the school was equal to Charlotte in Sunday lessons. Her acquaintance with Holy Writ surpassed others in this as in everything else.

Charlotte at Rydings

In this excerpt from "Reminiscences of Charlotte Brontë," Nussey recalls Charlotte's visit to her home at Birstall after completing her studies at Miss Wooler's school in June 1832.

Charlotte's first visit from Haworth was made about three months after she left school. She traveled in a two-wheeled gig, the only conveyance to be had in Haworth except the covered cart which brought her to school. Mr. Brontë sent Branwell as an escort; he was *then* a very dear brother, as dear to Charlotte as her own soul; they were in perfect accord of taste and feeling, and it was mutual delight to be together.

Branwell probably had never been far from home before; he was in wild ecstasy with everything. He walked about in unrestrained boyish enjoyment, taking views in every direction of the old turret-roofed house, the fine chestnut trees on the lawn (one tree especially interested him because it was "iron-garthed," having been split by storms, but still flourishing in great majesty), and a large rookery, which gave to the house a good background—all these he noted and commented upon with perfect enthusiasm. He told his sister he "was leaving her in Paradise, and if she were not intensely happy she never would be!" Happy, indeed, she then was, *in himself,* for she, with her own enthusiasms, looked forward to what her brother's great promise and talent might effect. He would at this time be between fifteen and sixteen years of age.

The visit passed without much to mark it (at this distance of time) except that we crept away together from household life as much as we could. Charlotte liked to pace the plantations or seek seclusion in the fruit-garden; she was safe from visitors in these retreats. She was so painfully shy she could not bear any special notice. One day, on being led in to dinner by a stranger, she trembled and nearly burst into tears; but notwithstanding her excessive shyness, which was often painful to others as well as herself, she won the respect and affection of all who had opportunity enough to become acquainted with her.

Charlotte's shyness did not arise, I am sure, either from vanity or self-consciousness, as some suppose shyness to arise; its source was (as Mr. Arthur Helps says very truly in one of his recent essays) in her "not being understood." She felt herself apart from others; they did not *understand* her, and she keenly felt the distance.

—*Scribner's Magazine,* 2 (May 1871): 24–25

At school she acquired that habit which she and her sisters kept up to the very last, that of pacing to and fro in the room. In days when out-of-door exercise was impracticable, Miss Wooler would join us in our evening hour of relaxation and converse (for which she had rare talent); her pupils used to hang about her as she walked up and down the room, delighted to listen to her, or have a chance of being nearest in the walk. The last day Charlotte was at school she seemed to realize what a sedate, hard-working season it had been to her. She said, "I should for once like to feel *out and out* a school-girl; I wish something would happen! Let us run round the fruit garden [running was what she never did]; perhaps we shall meet some one, or we may have a fine for trespass." She evidently was longing for some never-to-be-forgotten incident. Nothing, however, arose from her little enterprise. She had to leave school as calmly and quietly as she had there lived.

—*Scribner's Magazine,* 2 (May 1871): 18–24

* * *

This letter from Charlotte at Roe Head to Branwell, which may have been a school exercise, gives a sense of the ideas and interests that she shared with her brother at this point in their lives.

Charlotte Brontë to Branwell Brontë, 17 May 1832

Dear Branwell

As usual I address my weekly letter to you—because to you I find the most to say. I feel exceedingly anxious to know how, and in what state you, arrived at home after your long, and (I should think very fatiguing journey. I could perceive when you arrived at Roe-Head that you were very much tired though you refused to acknowledge it. After you were gone many questions and subjects of conversation recurred to me which I had intended to mention to you but quite forgot them in the agitation which I felt at the totally unexpected pleasure of seeing you. Lately I had begun to think that I had lost all the interest which I used formerly to take in politics but the extreme pleasure I felt at the news of the Reform-bill's being thrown out by the House of Lords and of the expulsion or resignation of Earl Grey' &c. &c. convinced me that I have not as yet lost all my penchant for politics. I am extremely glad that Aunt has consented to take in Frazer's Magazine for though I know from your description of its general contents it will be rather uninteresting when compared with "Blackwood" still it will be better than remaining the whole year without being able to obtain a sight of any periodical publication whatever, and such would assuredly be our case as in the little wild, moorland village where we reside there would be no possibility of borrowing, or obtaining a work of that description from a circulating library.

She was very familiar with all the sublimest passages, especially those in Isaiah, in which she took great delight. Her confirmation took place while she was at school, and in her preparation for that, as in all other studies, she distinguished herself by application and proficiency.

An enlarged page from one of Charlotte Brontë's Angrian tales, titled "The Secret and Lily Hart." The pages of the sixteen-page manuscript, dated 27 November 1833, each measured 11.4 x 9.2 centimeters (University of Missouri, Special Collections).

I hope with you that the present delightful weather may contribute to the perfect restoration of our dear Papa's health and that it may give Aunt pleasant reminiscences of the salubrious climate of her native place. With love to all believe [me] dear Branwell to remain

> Your affectionate sister
> Charlotte.
> *—The Letters of Charlotte Brontë, v. 1,*
> *pp. 112–113*

* * *

The extent of Charlotte's reading as a girl and young woman is indicated by this excerpt from a letter she wrote two years after she left Roe Head as a student.

Charlotte Brontë to Ellen Nussey, 4 July 1834

. . . You ask me to recommend some books for your perusal; I will do so in as few words as I can. If you like poetry let it be first rate, Milton, Shakespeare, Thomson; Goldsmith Pope (if you will though I don't admire him) Scott, Byron, Camp[b]ell, Wordsworth and Southey Now Ellen don't be startled at the names of Shakespeare, and Byron. Both these were great Men and their works are like themselves, You will know how to chuse the good and avoid the evil, the finest passages are always the purest, the bad are invariably revolting you will never wish to read them over twice, Omit the Comedies of Shakspeare and the Don Juan, perhaps the Cain of Byron though the latter is a magnificent Poem and read the rest fearlessly, that must indeed be a depraved mind which can gather evil from Henry the 8th from Richard 3d from Macbeth and Hamlet and Julius Cesar, Scott's sweet, wild, romantic Poetry can do you no harm nor can Wordsworth's nor Campbell's nor Southey's, the greatest part at least of his some is certainly exceptionable, For History read Hume, Rollin, and the Universal History if you *can* I never did. For Fiction—read Scott alone all novels after his are worthless. For Biography, read Johnson's lives of the Poets, Boswell's life of Johnson, Southey's life of Nelson Lockhart's life of Burns, Moore's life of Sheridan, Moore's life of Byron, Wolfe's remains. For Natural History read Bewick, and Audubon, and Goldsmith and White of Selborne For Divinity, but your brother Henry will advise you there I only say adhere to standard authors and don't run after novelty. If you can read this scrawl it will be to the credit of your patience.

> *—The Letters of Charlotte Brontë, v. 1,*
> *pp. 129–131*

* * *

Charlotte returned to Miss Wooler's school as teacher in July 1835, accompanied by Emily as student until October, when Anne came to take the ill Emily's place. Charlotte found teaching trying, especially compared to the pursuits she enjoyed at home with her family—in particular, writing about the imaginary kingdom of Angria and its evolving groups of characters. While at Roe Head, Charlotte in her miniscule script wrote sporadically about both the Angrian sagas and her experiences as teacher. The six manuscripts that survive, known now as the "Roe Head Journal," document her emotions and thoughts as she grappled with the responsibilities of being a teacher and the pull of her continuing creative desires.

The Roe Head Journal, 1836–1837
Charlotte Brontë

This edited transcription is based on the three-page untitled manuscript, 11.5 x 18.6 centimeters, in the Bonnell Collection, Pierpont Morgan Library.

Well, here I am at Roe Head. It is seven o'clock at night. The young ladies are all at their lessons; the schoolroom is quiet; the fire is low. A stormy day is at this moment passing off in a murmuring and bleak night. I now assume my own thoughts. My mind relaxes from the stretch on which it has been for the last twelve hours and falls back onto the rest which nobody in this house knows of but myself. I now, after a day of weary wandering, return to the ark which for me floats alone on the face of this world's desolate and boundless deluge. It is strange. I cannot get used to the ongoings that surround me. I fulfill my duties strictly and well. I must, so to speak. If the illustration be not profane—as God was not in the wind nor the fire nor the earthquake so neither is my heart in the task, the theme or the exercise. It is the still small voice alone that comes to me at eventide, that which like a breeze with a voice in it over the deeply blue hills and out of now leafless forests and from the cities on distant river banks of a far and bright continent. It is that which takes my spirit and engrosses all my living feelings, all my energies which are not merely mechanical and, like Haworth and home, wakes sensations which lie dormant elsewhere.

Last night, I did indeed lean upon the thunder-wakening wings of such a stormy blast as I have seldom heard blow, and it whirled me away like heath in the wilderness for five seconds of ecstasy. And as I sat by myself in the dining-room while all the rest were at tea, the trance seemed to descend on a sudden, and verily this foot trod the war-shaken shores of the Calabar, and these eyes saw the defiled and violated Adrianopolis, shedding its lights on the river from lattices whence the invader looked out and was not darkened. I went through a trodden garden whose groves were crushed down. I ascended a great terrace, the marble surface of which shone wet with rain where it was not darkened by the crowds of dead leaves, which were now showered on and now swept off by the vast and broken boughs which swung in the wind above them. Up I went to the wall of the palace, to the line of latticed arches which shimmered in light. Passing along quick as thought, I glanced at what the internal glare revealed through the crystal.

There was a room lined with mirrors, and with lamps on tripods, and very [?deserted] and splendid couches, and carpets, and large hall with vases white as snow, thickly embossed with whiter mouldings, [?and] one large picture in a frame of massive beauty representing a young man whose gorgeous and shining locks seemed as if they would wave on the breath and whose eyes were half hid by the hand, carved in ivory, that shaded them and supported the awful-looking raven head. A solitary picture, too great to admit of a companion. A likeness to be remembered, full of beauty not displayed, for it seemed as if the form had been copied so often in all imposing attitudes that at length the painter, satiated with its luxuriant perfection, had resolved to conceal half and make the imperial giant bend and hide, under his cloud-like tresses, the radiance he was grown tired of gazing on.

Often had I seen this room before and felt, as I looked at it, the simple and exceeding magnificence of its single picture, its five colossal cups of sculptured marble, its soft carpets of most deep and brilliant hues, and its mirrors broad, lofty and liquidly clear. I had seen it in the stillness of evening when the lamps so quietly and steadily burnt in the tranquil air and when their rays fell upon but one living figure: a young lady, who generally at that time appeared sitting on a low sofa, a book in her hand, her head bent over it as she read, her light brown hair dropping in loose and unwaving curls, her dress falling to the floor as she sat in sweeping folds of silk. All stirless about her, except her heart softly heaving under her dark satin bodice, and all silent, except her regular and very gentle respiration. The haughty sadness of grandeur beamed out of her intent, fixed, hazel eye, and, though so young, I always felt as if I dared not have spoken to her, for my life. How lovely were the lines of her straight, delicate features. How exquisite was her small and rosy mouth. But how very proud her white brow, spacious and wreathed with ringlets, and her neck, which though so slender had the superb curve of a queen's about the snowy throat. I knew why she chose to be alone at that hour and why she kept that shadow in the golden frame to gaze on her, and why she turned sometimes to her mirrors and looked to see if her loveliness and her adornments were quite perfect.

However, this night she was not visible—no—but neither was her bower void. The red ray of the fire flashed upon a table covered with wine flasks, some drained and some brimming with the crimson juice. The cushions of a voluptuous ottoman, which had often supported her slight fine form, were crushed by a dark bulk flung upon them in drunken prostration. Aye, where she had lain imperially robed and decked with pearls, every waft of her garments as she moved diffusing perfume, her beauty slumbering and still glowing as dreams of him for whom she kept herself in such hallowed and shrine-like separation wandered over her soul, on her own silken couch, a swarth and sinewy moor intoxicated to ferocious insensibility had stretched his athletic limbs, weary with wassail and stupified [sic] with drunken sleep. I knew it to be Quashia himself, and well could I guess why he had chosen the Queen of Angria's sanctuary for the scene of his solitary revelling. While he was full before my eyes, lying in his black dress on the disordered couch, his sable hair dishevelled on his forehead, his tusk-like teeth glancing vindictively through his parted lips, his brown complexion flushed with wine, and his broad chest heaving wildly as the breath issued in snorts from his distended nostrils, while I watched the fluttering of his white shirt ruffles, starting through the more than half-unbuttoned waistcoat, and beheld the expression of his Arabian countenance savagely exulting even in sleep—Quamina, triumphant lord in the halls of Zamorna! in the bower of Zamorna's lady!—while this apparition was before me, the dining-room door opened and Miss W[ooler] came in with a plate of butter in her hand. 'A very stormy night, my dear!' said she.

'It is, ma'am,' said I.

Feby the 4th 1836

. . . .

This edited transcription is based on a two-page manuscript, 11.5 x 18.6 centimeters, in the Bonnell Collection, Pierpont Morgan Library.

Friday afternoon

Now as I have a little bit of time, there being no French lessons this afternoon, I should like to write something. I can't enter into any continued narrative—my mind is not settled enough for that—but if I could call up some slight and pleasant sketch, I would amuse myself by jotting it down.

Let me consider the other day. I appeared to realize a delicious, hot day in the most burning height of summer. A gorgeous afternoon of idleness and enervation descending upon the hills of our Africa. An evening infolding a sky of profoundly deep blue and fiery gold about the earth.

Dear me! I keep heaping epithets together and I cannot describe what I mean. I mean a day whose rise, progress and decline seem made of sunshine. As you are travelling you see the wide road before you, the fields on each side and the hills far, far off, all smiling, glowing in the same amber light, and you feel such an intense heat, quite incapable of chilling damp, or even refreshing breeze. A day when fruits visibly ripen, when orchards appear suddenly to change from green to gold.

Such a day I saw flaming over the distant Sydenham Hills in Hawkscliffe Forest. I saw its sublime sunset pouring beams of crimson through the magnificent glades. It seemed to me that the war was over, that the trumpet had ceased but a short time since, and that its last tones had been pitched on a triumphant key. It seemed as if exciting events—tidings of battles, of victories, of treaties, of meetings of mighty powers—had diffused an enthusiasm over the land that made its pulses beat with feverish quickness. After months of bloody toil, a time of festal rest was now bestowed on Angria. The noblemen, the generals and the gentlemen were at their country seats, and the Duke, young but war-worn, was at Hawkscliffe.

A still influence stole out of the stupendous forest, whose calm was now more awful than the sea-like rushing that swept through its glades in time of storm. Groups of deer appeared and disappeared silently amongst the prodigious stems, and now and then a single roe glided down the savannah park, drank of the Arno and fleeted back again.

Two gentlemen in earnest conversation were walking in St Mary's Grove, and their deep commingling tones, very much subdued, softly broke the silence of the evening. Secret topics seemed to be implied in what they said, for the import of their words was concealed from every chance listener by the accents of a foreign tongue. All the soft vowels of Italian articulation flowed from their lips, as fluently as if they had been natives of the European Eden. 'Henrico' was the appellative by which the taller and the younger of the two addressed his companion, and the other replied by the less familiar title of 'Monsignore.' That young signore, or lord, often looked up at the Norman towers of Hawkscliffe, which rose even above the lofty elms of St Mary's Grove. The sun was shining on their battlements, kissing them with its last beam that rivalled in hue the fire-dyed banner hanging motionless above them.

'Henrico,' said he, speaking still in musical Tuscan, 'this is the 29th of June. Neither you nor I ever saw a fairer day. What does it remind you of? All such sunsets have associations.'

Henrico knitted his stern brow in thought and at the same time fixed his very penetrating black eye on the features of his noble comrade, which, invested by habit and nature with the aspect of command and pride, were at this sweet hour relaxing to the impassioned and fervid expression of romance. 'What does it remind <u>you</u> of, my lord?' said he, briefly.

'Ah! Many things, Henrico! Henrico! Ever since I can remember, the rays of the setting sun have acted on my heart, as they did on Memnon's wondrous statue. The strings always vibrate; sometimes the bones swell in harmony, sometimes in discord. They play a wild air just now—but sweet and ominously plaintive. Henrico, can you imagine what I feel when I look into the dim and gloomy vistas of this, my forest, and at yonder turrets which the might of my own hands has raised—not the halls of my ancestors, like hoary Mornington? Calm diffuses over this wide wood a power to stir and thrill the mind such as words can never express. Look at the red west! The sun is gone, and it is fading to gas and into those mighty groves, supernaturally still and full of gathering darkness. Listen how the Arno moans!'

. . . .

This edited transcription is based on the four-page untitled manuscript, 11.3 x 18.6 centimeters, in the Bonnell Collection, Brontë Parsonage Museum.

Friday August 11th—All this day I have been in a dream, half miserable and half ecstatic: miserable because I could not follow it out uninterruptedly; ecstatic because it shewed almost in the vivid light of reality the ongoings of the infernal world. I had been toiling for nearly an hour with Miss Lister, Miss Marriott and Ellen Cook, striving to teach them the distinction between an article and a substantive. The parsing lesson was completed, and dead silence had succeeded it in the schoolroom, and I sat sinking from irritation and weariness into a kind of lethargy.

The thought came over me: am I to spend all the best part of my life in this wretched bondage, forcibly suppressing my rage at the idleness, the apathy and the hyperbolical and most asinine stupidity of those fatheaded oafs, and on compulsion assuming an air of kindness, patience and assiduity? Must I from day to day sit chained to this chair prisoned within these four bare walls, while these glorious summer suns are burning in heaven and the year is revolving in its richest glow and declaring at the close of every summer day the time I am losing will never come again?

Stung to the heart with this reflection, I started up and mechanically walked to the window. A sweet August morning was smiling without. The dew was not yet dried off the field. The early shadows were stretching cool and dim from the haystack and the roots of the grand old oaks and thorns scattered along the sunk fence. All was still except the murmur of the scrubs about me over their tasks. I flung up the sash. An uncertain sound of inexpressible sweetness came on a dying gale from the south. I looked in that direction. Huddersfield and the hills beyond it were all veiled in blue mist; the woods of Hopton and Heaton Lodge were clouding the water's edge; and the Calder, silent but bright, was shooting among them like a silver arrow. I listened. The sound sailed full and liquid down the descent. It was the bells of Huddersfield parish church. I shut the window and went back to my seat.

Then came on me, rushing impetuously, all the mighty phantasm that this had conjured from nothing to a system strange as some religious creed. I felt as if I could have written gloriously. I longed to write. The spirit of all Verdopolis, of all the mountainous North, of all the woodland West, of all the river-watered East came crowding into my mind. If I had time to indulge it, I felt that the vague sensations of that moment would have settled down into some narrative better at least than anything I ever produced before. But just then a dolt came up with a lesson. I thought I should have vomited.

In the afternoon; Miss Ellen Lister was trigonometrically oecumenical about her French lessons. She nearly killed me between the violence of the irritation her horrid willfulness excited and the labour it took to subdue it to a moderate appearance of calmness. My fingers trembled as if I had had twenty-four hours' toothache, and my spirits felt worn down to a degree of desperate despondence. Miss Wooler tried to make me talk at tea time and was exceedingly kind to me, but I could not have roused if she had offered me worlds. After tea we took a long weary walk. I came back [?abime] to the last degree, for Miss L[ister] and Miss M[arriot]t had been boring me with their vulgar familiar trash all the time we were out. If those girls knew how I loathe their company, they would not seek mine so much as they do.

The sun had set nearly a quarter of an hour before we returned and it was getting dusk. The ladies went into the schoolroom to do their exercises and I crept up to the bedroom to be *alone* for the first time that day. Delicious was the sensation I experienced as I laid down on the spare bed and resigned myself to the luxury of twilight and solitude. The stream of thought, checked all day, came flowing free and calm along the channel. My ideas were too shattered to form any defined picture, as they would have done in such circumstances at home, but detached thoughts soothingly flitted round me, and unconnected scenes occurred and then vanished, producing an effect certainly strange but, to me, very pleasing.

The toil of the day, succeeded by this moment of divine leisure, had acted on me like opium and was coiling about me a disturbed but fascinating spell, such as I never felt before. What I imagined grew morbidly

vivid. I remember I quite seemed to see, with my bodily eyes, a lady standing in the hall of a gentleman's house, as if waiting for someone. It was dusk and there was the dim outline of antlers, with a hat and a rough greatcoat upon them. She had a flat candlestick in her hand and seemed coming from the kitchen or some such place. She was very handsome. It is not often we can form from pure idea faces so individually fine. She had black curls, hanging rather low on her neck, and very blooming skin and dark, anxious-looking eyes. I imagined it the sultry close of a summer's day, and she was dressed in muslin—not at all romantically—a flimsy, printed fabric with large sleeves and a full skirt.

As she waited, I most distinctly heard the front door open and saw the soft moonlight disclosed upon a lawn outside, and beyond the lawn at a distance I saw a town with lights twinkling through the gloaming. Two or three gentlemen entered, one of whom I knew by intuition to be called Dr Charles Brandon and another William Locksley Esqr. The doctor was a tall, handsomely built man, habited in cool, ample-looking white trowsers and a large straw hat, which being set on one side, shewed a great deal of dark hair and a sunburnt but smooth and oval cheek. Locksley and the other went into an inner room, but Brandon stayed a minute in the hall. There was a bason of water on a slab, and he went and washed his hands, while the lady held the light.

'How has Ryder borne the operation?' she asked.

'Very cleverly. He'll be well in three weeks.' was the reply. 'But Lucy won't do for a nurse at the hospital. You must take her for your head servant, to make my cambric fronts and handkerchiefs, and to wash and iron your lace aprons. Little silly thing, she fainted at the very sight of the instruments.'

Whilst Brandon spoke, a dim concatenation of ideas describing a passage in some individual's life, a varied scene in which persons and events, features and incidents, revolved in misty panorama, entered my mind. The mention of the hospital, of Ryder, of Lucy, each called up a certain set of reminiscences or rather fancies. It would be endless to tell all that was at that moment suggested.

Lucy first appeared before me as sitting at the door of a lone cottage on a kind of moorish waste, sorrowful and sickly; a young woman with those mild, regular features that always interest us, however poorly set off by the meanness of surrounding adjuncts. It was a calm afternoon. Her eyes were turned towards a road crossing the heath. A speck appeared on it far, far away. Lucy smiled to herself as it dawned into view, and while she did so there was something about her melancholy brow, her straight nose and faded bloom that reminded me of one who might, for anything I at that instant knew, be dead and buried under the newly plotted sod.

It was this likeness and the feeling of its existence that had called Dr Brandon so far from his bodily circle and that made him now, when he stood near his patient, regard her meek face, turned submissively and gratefully to him, with tenderer kindness than he bestowed on employers of aristocratic rank and wealth.

No more. I have not time to work out the vision. A thousand things were connected with it—a whole country, statesmen and kings, a revolution, thrones and princedoms subverted and reinstated.

Meantime, the tall man washing his bloody hands in a bason and the dark beauty standing by with a light remained pictured on my visual eye with irksome and alarming distinctness. I grew frightened at the vivid glow of the candle, at the reality of the lady's erect and symmetrical figure, of her spirited and handsome face, of her anxious eye watching Brandon's and seeking out its meaning, diving for its real expression through the semblance of severity that habit and suffering had given to his stern aspect.

I felt confounded and annoyed. I scarcely knew by what. At last I became aware of a feeling like a heavy weight laid across me. I knew I was wide awake and that it was dark, and that, moreover, the ladies were now come into the room to get their curl-papers. They perceived me lying on the bed and I heard them talking about me. I wanted to speak, to rise. It was impossible. I felt that this was a frightful predicament, that it would not do. The weight pressed me as if some huge animal had flung itself across me. A horrid apprehension quickened every pulse I had. 'I must get up,' I thought, and did so with a start. I have had enough of morbidly vivid realizations. Every advantage has its corresponding disadvantage. Tea's ready. Miss Wooler is impatient.

October 14th 1836

. . . .

This edited transcription is based on the two-page manuscript, 11.3 x 18.6 centimeters, in the Bonnell Collection, Brontë Parsonage Museum. It is believed to have been written in October 1836.

I'm just going to write because I cannot help it. Wiggins might indeed talk of scriblomania if he were to see me just now, encompassed by the bulls (query calves of Bashen), all wondering why I write with my eyes shut, staring, gaping. Hang their astonishment! A. C[oo]k on one side of me. E. L[iste]r on the other and Miss W[oole]r in the background. Stupidity the atmosphere. School-books the employment. Asses the society. What in all this is there to remind me of the divine, silent, unseen land of thought, dim now and indefinite as the dream of a dream, the shadow of a shade.

There is a voice, there is an impulse that wakens up that dormant power, which in its torpidity I sometimes think dead. That wind, pouring in impetuous current through the air, sounding wildly, unremittingly from hour to hour, deepening its tone as the night advances, coming not in gusts, but with a rapid gathering stormy swell. That wind I know is heard at this moment far away on the moors of Haworth. Branwell and Emily hear it, and as it sweeps over our house, down the churchyard and round the old church, they think perhaps of me and Anne.

Glorious! That blast was mighty. It reminded me of Northangerland. There was something so merciless in the heavier rush that made the very house groan as if it could scarce bear this acceleration of impetus. Oh, it has wakened a feeling that I cannot satisfy! A thousand wishes rose at its call which must die with me, for they will never be fulfilled. Now I should be agonized if I had not the dream to repose on. Its existences, its forms, its scenes do fill a little of the craving vacancy. Hohenlinden! Childe Harold! Flodden Field! The burial of Moore! Why cannot the blood rouse the heart, the heart wake the head, the head prompt the hand to do things like these? Stuff! Phd!

I wonder if Branwell has really killed the Duchess? Is she dead? Is she buried? Is she alone in the cold earth on this dreary night, with the ponderous, gold coffin-plate on her breast, under the black pavement of a church, in a vault closed up with lime mortar? Nobody near where she lies, she who was watched through months of suffering as she lay on her bed of state, now quite forsaken because her eyes are closed, her lips sealed and her limbs cold and rigid!—the stars, as they are fitfully revealed through severed clouds, looking in through the church windows on her monument.

A set of wretched thoughts are rising in my mind. I hope she's alive still, partly because I can't abide to think how hopelessly and cheerlessly she must have died, and partly because her removal, if it has taken place, must have been to North[angerland] like the quenching of the last spark that averted utter darkness.

What are Zenobia's thoughts among the stately solitudes of Ennerdale? She's by herself now in a large, lofty room that thirty years ago used nightly to look as bright and gay as it now looks lone and dreary. Her mother was one of the beauties of the West. She's sleeping in the dust of a past generation, and there is her portrait: a fine woman at her toilette. Vanity dictated that attitude. Paulina was noted for her profuse raven tresses, and the artist has shewn her combing them all out, the heavy locks uncurled and loose, falling over her white arms as she lifts them to arrange the dishev-

"Nothing But Nonsense"

The dating for this fragment of a letter from Charlotte to Ellen Nussey is uncertain, as Nussey was unsure whether it was written in 1836 or 1837. The references to the stupidity of her students and the stormy weather are similar to those in Brontë's journal of October 1836.

Weary with a day's hard work—during which an unusual degree of Stupidity has been displayed by my promising pupils I am sitting down to write a few hurried lines to my dear Ellen. Excuse me if I say nothing but nonsense, for my mind is exhausted, and dispirited. It is a Stormy evening and the wind is uttering a continual moaning sound that makes me feel very melancholy—At such times, in such moods as these Ellen it is my nature to seek repose in some calm, tranquil idea and I have now summoned up your image to give me rest There you sit, upright and still in your black dress and white scarf—your pale, marble-like face—looking so serene and kind—just like reality—I wish you would speak to me—. If we should be separated if it should be our lot to live at a great distance and never to see each other again. in old age how I should call up the memory of my youthful days and what a melancholy pleasure I should feel in dwelling on the recollection of my Early Friend Ellen Nussey!

If I like people it is my nature to tell them so and I am not afraid of offering incense to your vanity. It is from religion that you derive your chief charm and may its influence always preserve you as pure, as unassuming and as benevolent in thought and deed as you are now. What am I compared to you I feel my own utter worthlessness when I make the comparison. I'm a very coarse common-place wretch!

Ellen (I have some qualities that make me very miserable some feelings that you can have no participation in—that very few people in the world can at all understand I don't pride myself on these peculiarities, I strive to conceal and suppress them as much as I can. but they burst out sometimes and then those who see the explosion despise me and I hate myself for days afterwards). we are going to have prayers so I can write no more of this trash yet it is too true.

—*The Letters of Charlotte Brontë*, v. 1, pp. 152–153

This edited transcription is based on the seven-page manuscript, 11.2 x 18.6 centimeters, in the Bonnell Collection, Brontë Parsonage Museum. It is believed to have been written in March 1837. The first line, "My compliments to the weather. I wonder what" was written in a much larger script than the text that follows.

My compliments to the weather. I wonder what it would be at? Snow and sunshine? But, however, let me forget it. I've sat down for the purpose of calling up spirits from the vasty deep and holding half an hour's converse with them. Hush! there's a knock at the gates of thought and Memory ushers in the visitors. The visitors! There's only one: a tall gentleman with a presence, in a blue surtout and jaune trowsers.

'How do you do, sir? I'm glad to see you, take a seat. Very uncommon weather this, sir! How do you stand the changes?'

The gentleman, instead of answering, slowly divests his neck and chin of the folds of a large black silk handkerchief, deposits the light cane he carried in a corner, assumes a seat with a deliberate state and, bending his light-brown, beetling eye-brows over his lighter blue, menacing eyes, looks fixedly at me.

'Scarcely civil, sir. What's your name?'

'John of the Highlands,' answers the gentleman in a voice whose depth of base makes the furniture vibrate. 'John of the Highlands. You called me and I am come. Now what's your business?'

'Your servant Mʳ Saunderson,' says I. 'Beg your pardon for not recognizing you at once, but really you've grown so exceedingly mild-looking and unsaturnine since I saw you last, and you do look so sweet-tempered. How's Mʳˢ Saunderson, and how are the old people and the dear little hope of all the Saundersons?'

'Pretty well, thank ye. I'll take a little snuff, if ye have any. My box is empty.' So saying, Mʳ Saunderson held out his empty gold mull, which I speedily filled with black rappee. The conversation then proceeded.

'What news is stirring in your parts?' I asked.

'Nothing special,' was the answer. 'Only March has left the Angrians madder than ever.'

'What, they're fighting still are they?'

'Fighting! Aye and every man amongst them has sworn by his hilts that he'll continue fighting whilst he has two rags left stitched together upon his back.'

'In that case I should think peace would soon be restored,' said I.

Mʳ Saunderson winked. 'A very sensible remark,' said he. 'Mr Wellesley Senʳ made me the fellow to it last time I saw him.'

elled masses. There for nine and twenty years has that lovely Spaniard sat, looking down on the saloon that used to be her drawing-room. Can she see her descendant, a nobler edition of herself, the woman of a haughty and violent spirit, seated at that table meditating how to save her pride and crush her feelings? Zenobia is not easily warped by imagination. Yet she feels unconsciously the power of—[end of manuscript]

. . . .

'The sinews of war not particularly strong in the East?' I continued.

M^r S[aunderso]n winked again and asked for a pot of porter. I sent for the beverage to the Robin-Hood across the way, and when it was brought Mr Saunderson, after blowing off the froth, took a deep draught to the health of 'the brave and shirtless!' I added in a low voice 'to the vermined and victorious!' He heard me and remarked with a grave nod of approbation, 'very jocose.'

After soaking a little while, each in silence, Mr Saunderson spoke again—

Mr Saunderson did <u>not</u> speak again. He departed like the fantastic creation of a dream. I was called to hear a lesson, and when I returned to my desk again I found the mood which had suggested that allegorical whim was irrevocably gone. A fortnight has elapsed since I wrote the above. This is my first half hour's leisure since then and now, once more on a dull Saturday afternoon, I sit down to try to summon round me the dim shadows, not of coming events, but of incidents long departed, of feelings, of pleasures, whose exquisite relish I sometimes fear it will never be my lot again to taste.

How few would believe that from sources purely imaginary such happiness could be derived. Pen cannot pourtray the deep interest of the scenes, of the untimed trains of events, I have witnessed in that little room with the low, narrow bed and bare, white-washed walls, twenty miles away. What a treasure is thought! What a privilege is reverie. I am thankful that I have the power of solacing myself with the dream of creations whose reality I shall never behold. May I never lose that power! May I never feel it growing weaker! If I should, how little pleasure will life afford me—its lapses of shade are so wide, so gloomy, its gleams of sunshine so limited and dim!

Remembrance yields up many a fragment of past twilight hours spent in that little, unfurnished room. There have I sat on the low bedstead, my eyes fixed on the window, through which appeared no other landscape than a monotonous stretch of moorland, a grey church tower rising from the centre of a church-yard so filled with graves that the rank-weed and coarse grass scarce had room to shoot up between the monuments. Over these hangs in the eye of memory a sky of such grey clouds as often veil the chill close of an October day, and low on the horizon, glances at intervals through the rack the orb of a lurid and haloed moon.

Such was the picture that threw its reflection upon my eye, but communicated no impression to my heart. The mind knew but did not feel its existence. It was away. It had launched on a distant voyage. Haply it was nearing the shores of some far and unknown island, under whose cliffs no bark had ever before cast anchor. In other words, a long tale was perhaps then evolving itself in my mind, the history of an ancient and aristocratic family—the legendary records of its origin not preserved in writing, but delivered from the lips of old retainers, floating in tradition up and down the woods and vales of the earldom or dukedom or barony. The feeling of old oak avenues planted by the ancestors of three hundred years ago, of halls neglected by the present descendants, of galleries peopled with silent pictures, no longer loved and valued, for none now live who remember the substance of those shadows.

Then with a parting glance at the family-church, with a thought reverting to the wide, deep vault beneath its pavement, my dream shifted to some distant city, some huge, imperial metropolis, where the descendants of the last nobleman, the young lords and ladies, shine in gay circles of patricians. Dazzled with the brilliancy of courts, haply with the ambition of senates, sons and daughters have almost forgotten the groves where they were born and grew. As I saw them—stately and handsome, gliding through those saloons where many other well-known forms crossed my sight, where there were faces looking up, eyes smiling and lips moving in audible speech, that I knew better almost than my brother and sisters, yet whose voices had never woke an echo on this world, whose eyes had never gazed upon that day-light—what glorious associations crowded upon me, what excitement heated my face and made me clasp my hands in ecstasy!

I too forgot the ancient country seat. I forgot the great woods with their lonely glades peopled only by deer. I thought no more of the Gothic-chapel under whose floor mouldered the bones of a hundred barons. What then to me were the ballads of the grand-mothers, the tales of the grey-headed old men of that remote village on the Annesley Estate?

I looked at Lady Amelia, the eldest daughter, standing by a wide, lofty window, descending by marble steps on to a sunshiny lawn, amidst a flush of rose-trees in bloom, a lady of handsome features and full-growth. Just now she is exquisitely beautiful, though that extreme brightness which excitement and happiness are bestowing will soon pass away. I see the sweep of her light, summer dress, the fall and waving of her curled hair on her neck, the unaccustomed glow of her complexion and shine of her smiling eyes. I see them now. She is looking round at that ring of patricians. She is hearing her brother tell over the names and titles of many that are become the darlings of fame, the monarchs of mind. She has been introduced to some. As they pass, they speak to her.

I hear them speak as well as she does. I see distinctly their figures, and though alone I experience all the feelings of one admitted for the first time into a grand circle of classic beings, recognizing by tone, gesture and aspect hundreds whom I never saw before, but whom I have heard of and read of many a time. And is not this enjoyment? I am not accustomed to such magnificence as surrounds me, to the gleam of such large mirrors, to the beauty of marble figures, to soft, foreign carpets, to long, wide rooms, to lofty gilded ceilings. I know nothing of people of rank and distinction, yet there they are before me in throngs, in crowds. They come; they go; they speak; they beckon; and that not like airy phantoms but as noblemen and ladies of flesh and blood.

There is an aim in all. I know the house. I know the square it stands in. I passed through it this day. I ascended the steps leading to the vestibule. I saw the porter at the door. I went along hall and gallery till I reached this saloon. Is it not enjoyment to gaze around upon those changeful countenances, to mark the varied features of those highborn and celebrated guests, some gay and youthful, some proud, [?cold] and middle-aged, a few bent and venerable, here and there a head throwing the rest into shade, a bright, perfect face, with eyes and bloom and divine expression, whose realization thrills the heart to its core?

There is one just now crossing—a lady. I will not write her name, though I know it. No history is connected with her identity. She is not one of the transcendantly fair and inaccessibly sacred beings whose fates are interwoven with the highest of the high, beings I am not alluding to in this general picture. Far from home I cannot write of them, except in total solitude. I scarce dare think of them.

This nameless and casual visitant has crossed the drawing-room and is standing close by Lady Amelia. She is looking up and speaking to her. I wish I could trace the picture, so vivid, so obvious at this moment. She is a native of the East. I never saw a richer specimen of an Angrian lady, with all the characteristics of her country-woman in such perfection.

She is rather tall, well and roundly formed, with plump neck and shoulders as white as drift snow, profuse tresses in colour almost red, but fine as silk and lying in soft curls upon her cheeks and round her forehead. The sweetness of the features thus shaded is inexpressible: the beautiful little mouth, the oval chin and fine animated eyes, the frank, cheerful look, the clear skin with its pure healthy bloom. The dress of light blue satin, beautifully contrasting with her hair and complexion; the pearls circling her round, white wrist; the movements of her figure, not marked by the inceding grace of the West, but unstudied, prompt and natural; her laugh always ready; the sound of her voice—her rapid, rather abrupt, but sweet and clear utterance, possessing a charm of its own, very different from the rich, low, subdued melody that flows from the lips of Senegambia's daughters; the quick glances of her eye, indicating a warm and excitable temperament; the mingled expression of goodnature and pride, spirit and kindheartedness predominating in every feature. All these are as clearly before me as Ann's quiet image, sitting at her lessons on the opposite side of the table.

Jane Moore, that is her name, has long been celebrated as a beauty all over the province of Arundel, amongst whose green swells of pasture her father's handsome new mansion lies, with all its pleasant grounds and young plantations on this warm spring-day opening their delicate foliage as rapidly as the forests of Kentucky. George Moore Esqr is a rising man, one of those whose fortunes were made on the night Angria was declared a kingdom. He is a mercantile man moreover and has a huge warehouse down at Doverham, and a vessel or two lying in the docks, built by himself and christened the Lady Jane after his fair daughter. She is no petted only child. Moore, like a true Angrian, has given to the state some half dozen of stout youths and an equal number of well-grown girls, most of whom, now grave professional men and dignified young matrons, are married into the first families of the province, and each established in a hall of their own amongst the prairies.

But Jane is the youngest, the prettiest, the rose of the whole bouquet. She has been the most highly educated, and by nature she was one of those whose minds, manners and appearance must tend to elevate them wherever they go. Jane has ambition enough about her to scorn any offer that does not comprise a coronet—and it must be an Angrian coronet too. And there must be wealth and estates, and a noble mansion and servants and carriages and all the other means and appliances a dashing beauty can be supposed to require to set her off.

I am afraid Jane Moore, notwithstanding her natural quickness and high education, has none of the deep refined romance of the West. I am afraid she scarcely knows what it means. She is as matter of fact as any manufacturer of Edwardston and likes as well to receive her penny's-worth for her penny. With undisguised frankness, she acknowledges that this world would be nothing without a flash and glitter now and then. If Jane does any thing well, she eminently likes to be told so. She delights in society; not for worlds would she live alone. She has no idea even of playing a tune or singing a melancholy stanza to herself by twilight. Once or twice she has by some chance found herself alone in the evening, about dusk, in the large parlour at Kirkham-Wood, and she has gone to the window and looked out at the garden clustered over with dewy buds, and at the lawn carpeted with mossy verdure, and at the carriage walk winding down to the gate, and beyond that at the wide and sweeping swell of grazing country, all green, all opening with a smile to the moonlight beaming from the sky upon it. And as Jane looked, some unaccustomed feeling did seem to swell in her heart, but if you had asked her why her eyes glistened so, she would not have answered, 'the moonlight is so lovely', but 'Angria is such a glorious land!'

Then as Miss Moore turned from the window and looked round on the deserted room, with the restless firelight flickering over its walls and making the pictures seem to stir in their frames, as she rose and threw herself into her father's arm-chair and sat in silence listening for his tread, perhaps she might fall into abstracted reverie and begin to recall former days, to remember her eldest sister who died when she was a child, to think of the funeral-day, of the rigid and lengthened corpse laid in its coffin on the hall-table, of the servants pressing round to gaze on Miss Harriet for the last time, of the kiss that she herself was bidden to give the corpse, of the feeling which then first gushed into her childish and volatile heart that Harriet had left them for ever.

She recollects the contrast that struck upon her mind of her dead and of her living sister, the tall girl of eighteen who had left school, who was privileged always to be in the drawing-room when M^r and Mrs Kirkwall and Sir Frederic and Lady Fala came to pay their annual visit, who had her own dressing-room with her toilette table and her dressing case, who used so kindly to come into the nursery sometimes after dinner and bring them all down into the parlour, where she would sing for them and play marches and waltzes on the piano. Very lovely and a little awful did she then seem to the eye of Jane. Her superior stature, her handsome dress, her gold watch and chain, her powers of drawing and playing and reading French and Italian books, all tended to invest her with the character of a being of a superior order.

With these reminiscences comes one of a rumour Jane used to hear whispered by the house-maid to the nurse, that her sister was to be married to Mr Charles Kirkwall—and therewith steps in Charles's image: a tall, young man, who in those days was no unfrequent visitor at the Hall. He always attended Miss Moore in her walks and rides: often from the nursery window has Jane seen them both mounted on horseback and dashing down the avenue. She remembers her sister's figure as she bent over the neck of her beautiful mare, Jessy, her long curls and veil and her purple habit streaming in the wind. And she remembers Charles, too, his keen features and penetrating eye, always watching Miss Moore.

Then from those forms of life, from Harriet's mild and pleasing face as it was in health, never very blooming but lighted with soft, grey eyes of sweetest lustre, Jane's memory turns to the white, shrunk, sightless corpse. She starts and a tear falls on her silk frock. Ask her what she's crying for. 'Because I'm so low-spirited with being alone,' she will answer. Such is not Jane Moore's element; the inspiration of twilight, solitude, melancholy musing, is alien from her nature.

Step into this great assembly room full of Angrian grandees. A public ball is given in celebration of the third anniversary of independence. What light! What flashing of jewels and waxing of scarlet scarfe and plumes! What a tumultuous swell of melody! It is from a single instrument and the air is one of triumph. It proceeds from that recess. You cannot see the grand-piano for the ring of illustrissima crowding round it. Listen! A voice electrically sweet and thrilling in its tones. Angria's glorious song of victory, 'Sound the Loud Timbrel!'

Come nearer, lift up your eyes and look at the songstress. You know her, plumed, robed in vermilion, with glowing cheek and large blue eye eloquently telling what feelings the gales of Angria breathe into her daughters: Jane Moore. That feeling will not last. It will die away into oblivion as the echoes of those chords die away into silence. That expression too will leave your eye, that flush, your cheek. And you will look round and greet with a careless laugh the first word of flattery uttered by that dandy at your elbow. Yet your spirit can take a high tone. It can respond to an heroic call. You are not all selfish vanity, all empty shew. You are a handsome, generous, clever, flashy, proud, overbearing woman.

. . . .

This is an exact transcription, preserving errors, based on a single-page manuscript, 11.3 x 18.4 centimeters, in the Bonnell Collection, Brontë Parsonage Museum. It is believed to have been written in October 1837.

About a week since I got a letter from Branwell containing a most exquisitely, characteristic epistle from Northangerland to his daughter–It is astonishing what a soothing and delightful tone that letter seemed to speak–I lived on its contents for days. in every pause of employment–it came chiming in like some sweet bar of music–bringing with it agreeable thoughts such as I had for many weeks been a stranger to–Some representing scenes such as might arise in consequence of that unexpected letter some, unconnected with it referring to other–events, another set of feelings–these were not striking & stirring scenes of incident–no they were tranquil & retired in their character such as might every day be seen witnessed in the inmost circles of highest society–A curtain seemed to rise and discover to me the Duchess as she might appear when newly risen, and lightly dressed for the morning–discovering her fathers letter in the contents of the mail which lies on her breakfast-table–there seems nothing in such an idea as that–but the localities of the picture were so graphic–the room so distinct the clear fire–of morning–the window looking upon no object but a cold October sky except when you draw very near and look down on a terrace far beneath & at a still dizzier distance on a green court with a fountain and rows of stately limes–beyond a wide road & wider river and a vast metropolis–you feel it to be the Zamorna Palace for buildings on buildings piled round embosom this little verdant circle with its marble basin to receive the jet–and its grove of mellowing foliage–above fifty windows look upon the court admitting light into you know not what splendid and spacious chambers. The Duchess has read that letter–and she is following the steps of the writer–she knows not where–but with a vague idea that it is through no pleasant scenes–In strange situations her imagination places him–In the Inn of a Sea-port-Town sitting alone on a wet & gusty Autumn night–the wind bringing up the ceaseless roar of the sea–of the Atlantic to whose grim waves he will tomorrow commit himself in that Steamer–hissing amongst a crowd of masts in the harbor–She looks from the window and there is the high roof and lordly front of Northangerland-House–towering like some great Theatre above the Streets of Adrianopolis–The Owner of that Pile is a homeless Man.

–edited and transcribed by Christine Alexander,
Jane Eyre, Norton Critical Edition,
pp. 399–417

"For the Sake of Imaginative Pleasures"
The Desire To Be a Writer

While teaching at Miss Wooler's school Charlotte sent some of her poetry (it is not known exactly which pieces) to Robert Southey, then Poet Laureate of England, for his appraisal. Charlotte kept his response, recommending against a career as writer, within a wrapper on which she wrote "Southey's Advice/To be kept for ever/Roe-Head April 21/My twenty-first birthday 1837" (The Letters of Charlotte Brontë, v. 1, p. 170).

Robert Southey to Charlotte Brontë, 12 March 1837

Madam,

You will probably ere this have given up all expectation of receiving an answer to your letter of Decr. 29. I was on the borders of Cornwall when that letter was written. It found me a fortnight afterwards in Hampshire. During my subsequent movements in different parts of the country, & a tarriance of 3 busy weeks in London, I had no leisure for replying to it. And now that I am once more at home & am clearing the arrears of business wh had accumulated during a long absence, it has lain unanswered till the last of a numerous pile–not from disrespect or indifference to its contents, but in truth, because it is not an easy task to answer it, nor a pleasant one to cast a damp over the high spirits & the generous desires of youth.

What you are I can only infer from your letter, wh appears to be written in sincerity, tho' I may suspect that you have used a fictitious signature. Be that as it may, the letter & the verse bear the same stamp, & I can well understand the state of mind wh they indicate. What I am, you might have learnt by such of my publications as have come into your hands: but you live in a visionary world & seem to imagine that this is my case also, when you speak of my "stooping from a throne of light & glory." Had you happened to be acquainted with me, a little personal knowledge wd. have tempered your enthusiasm. You who so ardently desire "to be for ever known" as a poetess, might have had your ardour in some degree abated, by seeing a poet in the decline of life, & witnessing the effect wh age produces upon our hopes & aspirations. Yet I am neither a disappointed man, nor a discontented one, & you wd. never have heard from me any chilling sermonisings upon the text that all is vanity.

It is not my advice that you have asked as to the direction of your talents, but my opinion of them. 'and' Yet the opinion may be worth little, & the advice much. You evidently possess & in no inconsiderable degree what Wordsworth calls "the faculty of Verse." I am not depreciating it when I say that in these times it is not rare. Many volumes of poems are now published every year without attracting public attention, any one of wh, if it had appeared half a century ago, wd. have obtained a high reputation for its author. Whoever therefore is ambitious of distinction in this way, ought to be prepared for disappointment.

But it is not with a view to distinction that you shd. cultivate this talent, if you consult your own happiness. I who have made literature my profession, & devoted my life to it, & have never for a moment repented of the deliberate choice, think myself nevertheless bound in duty to caution every young man who applies as an aspirant to me for encouragement & advice, against taking so perilous a course. You will say that a woman has no need of such a caution, there can be no peril in it for her: & in a certain sense this is true. But there is a danger of wh I wd with all kindness & all earnestness warn you. The daydreams in wh you habitually indulge are likely to induce a distempered state of mind, & in proportion as all the "ordinary uses of the world" seem to you "flat & unprofitable", you will be unfitted for them, without becoming fitted for anything else. Literature cannot be the business of a woman's life: & it ought not to be. The more she is engaged in her proper duties, the less leisure will she have for it, even as an accomplishment & a recreation. To those duties you have not yet been called, & when you are you will be less eager for celebrity. You will then not seek in imagination for excitement, of wh the vicissitudes of this life & the anxieties, from wh you must not hope to be exempted (be your station what it may) will bring with them but too much.

But do not suppose that I disparage the gift wh you possess, nor that I wd. discourage you from exercising it, I only exhort you so to think of it & so to use it, as to render it conducive to your own permanent good. Write poetry for its own sake, not in a spirit of emulation, & not with a view to celebrity: the less you aim at <u>that</u>, the more likely you will be to deserve, & finally to obtain it. So written, it is wholesome both for the heart & soul. It may be made next to religion the surest means of soothing the mind & elevating it. You may embody in it your best thoughts & your wisest feelings, & in so doing discipline & strengthen them.

Farewell Madam! It is not because I have forgotten that I was once young myself that I write to you in this strain—but because I remember it. You will neither doubt my sincerity, nor my good will. And however ill what has been said may accord with your present views & temper, the longer you live the more reasonable it will appear to you. Tho' I may be but an ungracious adviser, you will allow me therefore to subscribe myself,

With the best wishes for your happiness, here & hereafter,

Your true friend
Robert Southey
–*The Letters of Charlotte Brontë*, v. 1,
pp. 165–167

* * *

Charlotte promptly wrote back to Southey, probably from Roe Head.

Charlotte Brontë to Robert Southey, 16 March 1837

Sir,

I cannot rest till I have answered your letter, even though by addressing you a second time I should appear a little intrusive; but I must thank you for the kind & wise advice you have condescended to give me. I had not ventured to hope for such a reply; so considerate in its tone, so noble in its spirit. I must suppress what I feel, or you will think me foolishly enthusiastic.

At the first perusal of your letter I felt only shame, and regret that I had ever ventured to trouble you with my crude rhapsody;—I felt a painful heat rise to my face, when I thought of the quires of paper I had covered with what once gave me so much delight, but which now was only a source of confusion; but, after I had thought a little and read it again and again, the prospect seemed to clear. You do not forbid me to write; you do not say that what I write is utterly destitute of merit. You only warn me against the folly of neglecting real duties, for the sake of imaginative pleasures; of writing for the love of fame; for the selfish excitement of emulation. You kindly allow me to write poetry for its own sake, provided I leave undone nothing which I ought to do, in order to pursue that single absorbing exquisite gratification. I am afraid, Sir, you think me very foolish. I know the first letter I wrote to you was all senseless trash from beginning to end; but I am not altogether the idle dreaming being it would seem to denote. My Father is a clergyman of limited, though competent, income, and I am the eldest of his children. He expended quite as much in my education as he could afford in justice to the rest. I thought it therefore my duty, when I left school, to become a governess. In that capacity, I find enough to occupy my thoughts all day long, and my head & hands too, without having a moment's time for one dream of the imagination. In the evenings, I confess, I do think, but I never trouble any one else with my thoughts. I carefully avoid any appearance of pre-occupation, and eccentricity, which might lead those I live amongst to suspect the nature of my pursuits. Following my Father's advice,—who from my childhood has counselled me just in the wise and friendly tone of your letter—I have endeavoured not only attentively to observe all the duties a woman ought to fulfil, but to feel deeply interested in them. I don't always succeed, for sometimes when I'm teaching or sewing I would rather be reading or writing; but I try to deny myself; and my Father's approbation amply rewarded me for the privation. Once more allow me to thank you with sincere gratitude. I trust I shall never

A First Proposal

Although Charlotte once described herself as "buried" in Haworth, she had opportunities to leave her father and the parsonage through marriage, turning down three men before accepting Arthur Bell Nicholls in 1854. This excerpt is from Charlotte's 12 March 1839 letter to Ellen Nussey, in which she discusses the proposal of Henry Nussey, Ellen's clergyman brother.

You ask me my dear Ellen whether I have received a letter from Henry–I have about a week since–The Contents I confess did a little surprise me, but I kept them to myself, and unless you had questioned me on the subject I would never have adverted to it–Henry says he is comfortably settled at Donnington in Sussex that his health is much improved & that it is his intention to take pupils after Easter–he then intimates that in due time he shall want a Wife to take care of his pupils and frankly asks me to be that Wife. Altogether the letter is written without cant or flattery–& in a common-sense style which does credit to his judgment–Now my dear Ellen there were in this proposal some things that might have proved a strong temptation–I thought if I were to marry so, Ellen could live with me and how happy I should be. but again I asked myself two questions–"Do I love Henry Nussey as much as a woman ought to love her husband? Am I the person best qualified to make him happy–?–Alas Ellen my Conscience answered "no" to both these questions. I felt that though I esteemed Henry–though I had a kindly leaning towards him because he is an aimiable–well-disposed man Yet I had not, and never could have that intense attachment which would make me willing to die for him–

and if ever I marry it must be in that light of adoration that I will regard my Husband ten to one I shall never have the chance again but n'importe. Moreover I was aware that Henry knew so little of me he could hardly be conscious to whom he was writing–why it would startle him to see me in my natural home-character he would think I was a wild, romantic enthusiast indeed–I could not sit all day long making a grave face before my husband–I would laugh and satirize and say whatever came into my head first–and if he were a clever man & loved me the whole world weighed in the balance against his smallest wish should be light as air–

Could I–knowing my mind to be such as that could I conscientiously say that I would take a grave quiet young man like Henry? No it would have been deceiving him–and deception of that sort is beneath me. So I wrote a long letter back in which I expressed my refusal as gently as I could and also candidly avowed my reasons for that refusal. I described to him too the sort of Character I thought would suit him for a wife–Good-bye my dear Ellen–write to me soon and say whether you are angry with me or not–.

–The Letters of Charlotte Brontë, v. 1, pp. 187–188

Later that same year Charlotte refused a Mr. Pryce, a young Irish curate, who proposed by letter soon after a single day's visit to the parsonage. Her third proposal came in 1851 from James Taylor, an employee of her publisher, who visited Haworth parsonage in 1851.

more feel ambitious to see my name in print; if the wish should rise, I'll look at Southey's letter, and suppress it. It is honour enough for me that I have written to him, and received an answer. That letter is consecrated; no one shall ever see it, but Papa and my brother and sisters. Again I thank you. This incident I suppose will be renewed no more; if I live to be an old woman I shall remember it thirty years hence as a bright dream. The signature which you suspected of being fictitious is my real name. Again, therefore, I must sign myself,

C. Brontë.

P.S.–Pray, Sir, excuse me for writing to you a second time; I could not help writing, partly to tell you how thankful I am for your kindness, and partly to let you know that your advice shall not be wasted; however sorrowfully and reluctantly it may be at first followed. C. B.

–The Letters of Charlotte Brontë, v. 1, pp. 168–169

* * *

Charlotte continued to write following her correspondence with Southey. As is indicated by the following fragment–believed to have been written in late 1839–she made a conscious decision to turn away from writing about the Angrian characters and histories that had been her focus for at least a dozen years. This resolution seems part of a trend in Charlotte's intellectual and creative development through the mid 1840s, influenced as well by the discipline of writing for M. Héger at the Pensionnat Héger in 1842–1843.

This edited transcription is of one-page untitled manuscript, 12.5 x 20 centimeters, in the Bonnell Collection at the Brontë Parsonage Museum.

Farewell to Angria
Charlotte Brontë

I have now written a great many books, and for a long time I have dwelt on the same characters and scenes and subjects. I have shewn my landscapes in every variety of shade and light, which morning, noon and evening–the rising, the meridian and the setting sun–can bestow upon them. Sometimes I have filled the air with the whitened tempest of winter: snow has embossed the dark arms of the beech and oak and filled with drifts the parks of the lowlands or the mountain-pass of wilder districts. Again, the same mansion with its woods, the same moor with its glens, has been softly coloured with the tints of moonlight in summer. And in the warmest June night the trees have clustered their full-plumed heads over glades flushed with flowers.

So it is with persons. My readers have been habituated to one set of features, which they have seen now in profile, now in full-face, now in outline, and again in finished painting, varied but by the change of feeling or temper or age; lit with love; flushed with passion; shaded with grief; kindled with ecstasy; in meditation and mirth, in sorrow and scorn and rapture; with the round outline of childhood; the beauty and fullness of youth; the strength of manhood and the furrow of thoughtful decline. But we must change, for the eye is tired of the picture so oft recurring and now so familiar.

Yet do not urge me too fast reader. It is no easy thing to dismiss from my imagination the images which have filled it so long. They were my friends and my intimate acquaintance, and I could with little labour describe to you the faces, the voices, the actions of those who peopled my thoughts by day and not seldom stole strangely even into my dreams by night. When I depart from these I feel almost as if I stood on the threshold of a home and were bidding farewell to its inmates. When I strive to conjure up new inmates, I feel as if I had got into a distant country where every face was unknown and the character of all the population an enigma which it would take much study to comprehend and much talent to expound. Still, I long to quit for a while that burning clime where we have sojourned too long—its skies flame; the glow of sunset is always upon it. The mind would cease from excitement and turn now to a cooler region, where the dawn breaks grey and sober and the coming day, for a time at least, is subdued in clouds.

—transcribed by Christine Alexander,
Jane Eyre, Norton Critical Edition,
pp. 424–425

Stonegappe, the home where Charlotte Brontë first worked as a governess. It is believed to have inspired Brontë's depiction of Gatehead Hall in Jane Eyre *(from* The Bookman, *October 1904).*

"Trials and Crosses"
Working as a Governess

Charlotte Brontë worked as governess for two families. She first worked for the Sidgwick family at Stonegappe, near Skipton, a town some ten miles north of Haworth, from May to mid July 1839. She also worked for John White's family, Upperwood House, Rawdon, some fifteen miles east of Haworth, from March to December 1841. In neither case did she find the occupation congenial.

This excerpt is from a letter written from Stonegappe.

Charlotte Brontë to Emily Brontë, 8 June 1839

I have striven hard to be pleased with my new situation. The country, the house, and the grounds are, as I have said, divine. But, alack-a-day! there is such a thing as seeing all beautiful around you—pleasant woods, winding white paths, green lawns, and blue sunshiny sky—and not having a free moment or a free thought left to enjoy them in. The children are constantly with me, and more riotous, perverse, unmanageable cubs never grew. As for correcting them, I soon quickly found that was entirely out of the question: they are to do as they like. A complaint to Mrs. Sidgwick brings only black looks upon oneself, and unjust, partial excuses to screen the children. I have tried that plan once. It succeeded so notably that I shall try it no more. I said in my last letter that Mrs. Sidgwick did not know me. I now begin to find that she does not intend to know me, that she cares nothing in the world about me except to contrive how the greatest possible quantity of labour may be squeezed out of me, and to that end she overwhelms me with oceans of needlework, yards of cambric to hem, muslin night-caps to make, and, above all things, dolls to dress. I do not think she likes me at all, because I can't help being shy in such an entirely novel scene, surrounded as I have hitherto been by strange and constantly changing faces. I see now more clearly than I have ever done before that a private governess has no existence, is not considered as a living and rational being except as connected with the wearisome duties she has to fulfil. While she is teaching the children, working for them, amusing them, it is all right. If she steals a moment for herself she is a nuisance. Nevertheless, Mrs. Sidgwick is universally considered an amiable woman. Her manners are fussily affable. She talks a great deal, but as it seems to me not much to the purpose. Perhaps I may like her better after a while. At present I have no call to her. Mr. Sidgwick is in my opinion a hundred times better—less profession, less

bustling condescension, but a far kinder heart. It is very seldom that he speaks to me, but when he does I always feel happier and more settled for some minutes after. He never asks me to wipe the children's smutty noses or tie their shoes or fetch their pinafores or set them a chair. One of the pleasantest afternoons I have spent here—indeed, the only one at all pleasant—was when Mr. Sidgwick walked out with his children, and I had orders to follow a little behind. As he strolled on through his fields with his magnificent Newfoundland dog at his side, he looked very like what a frank, wealthy, Conservative gentleman ought to be. He spoke freely and unaffectedly to the people he met, and though he indulged his children and allowed them to tease himself far too much, he would not suffer them grossly to insult others.

—Clement K. Shorter,
Charlotte Brontë and Her Circle,
pp. 80–81

* * *

In this excerpt, Charlotte mentions Mary Taylor's younger sister, Martha.

Charlotte Brontë to Ellen Nussey, 30 June 1839

My dearest Ellen

I am writing a letter to you with pencil because I cannot just now procure ink without going into the drawing-room—where I do not wish to go. I only received your letter yesterday for we are not now residing at Stonegappe but at Swarcliffe a summer residence of Mr Greenwood's Mrs Sidgwick's father. it is near Harrogate—& Ripon—a beautiful place in a beautiful country—rich and agricultural—

I should have written to you long since—and told you every detail of the utterly new scene into which I have lately been cast—had I not been daily expecting a letter from yourself—and wondering and lamenting that you did not write for you will remember it was your turn. I must not bother you too much with my sorrows Ellen, of which I fear you have heard an exaggerated account—if you were near me perhaps I might be tempted to tell you all—to grow egotistical and pour out the long history of a Private Governesse's trials and crosses in her first Situation—As it is I will only ask you to imagine the miseries of a reserved wretch like me—thrown at once into the midst of a large Family—proud as peacocks & wealthy as Jews—at a time when they were particularly gay—when the house was filled with Company—all Strangers people whose faces I had never seen before—in this state of things having the charge given me of a set of pampered spoilt & turbulent children—whom I was expected constantly to amuse as well as instruct—I soon found that the constant demand on my stock of animal spirits reduced them to the lowest state of exhaustion—at times I felt and I suppose seemed depressed—to my astonishment I was taken to task on the subject by Mrs Sidgwick with a stern[n]ess of manner & a harshness of language scarcely credible—like a fool I cried most bitterly—I could not help it my spirits quite failed me at first I thought I had done my best—strained every nerve to please her—and to be treated in that way merely because I was shy—and sometimes melancholy was too bad. at first I was for giving all up and going home—But after a little reflection I determined—to summon what energy I had and to weather the Storm—I said to myself I have never yet quitted a place without gaining a friend—Adversity is a good school—the Poor are born to labour and the Dependent to endure I resolved to be patient—to command my feelings and to take what came—the ordeal I reflected would not last many weeks—and I trusted it would do me good—. . .

She [Mrs. Sidgwick] behaves somewhat more civilly to me now than she did at first—and the children are a little more manageable—but she does not know my character & she does not wish to know it I have never had five minutes conversation with her since I came—except while she was scolding me—do not communicate the contents of this letter to any one—I have no wish to be pitied—except by yourself—do not even clatter with Martha Taylor about it—if I were talking to you I would tell you much more but I hope my term of bondage will soon be expired—and then I can go home and you can come to see me—

—The Letters of Charlotte Brontë, v. 1, pp. 193–194

* * *

Writing in this excerpt of Charlotte's second situation as a governess, Mrs. Gaskell contends that Charlotte was not suited for the work, though she writes that "no distaste, no suffering ever made her shrink from any course which she believed it to be her duty to engage in."

"Uncertain, Yet Perpetual Employment"
Elizabeth Gaskell

Early in March, 1841, Miss Brontë obtained her second and last situation as a governess. This time she esteemed herself fortunate in becoming a member of a kind-hearted and friendly household. The master of it,

"A Wearing, Wasting Existence"

In this excerpt from a 12 May 1848 letter to William Smith Williams, Charlotte writes about the difficulty of being a governess if one does not have "the great qualification."

Some remarks in your last letter on teaching commanded my attention. I suppose you never were engaged in tuition yourself, but if you had been, you could not have more exactly hit on the great qualification—I had almost said—the <u>one</u> great qualification necessary to the task: not merely of <u>acquiring</u> but of <u>imparting</u> knowledge; the power of influencing young minds; that natural fondness for—that innate sympathy with children, which, you say, Mrs. Williams is so happy as to possess. He or She who possesses this faculty, this sympathy—though perhaps not otherwise highly accomplished—need never fear failure in the career of instruction. Children will be docile with them, will improve under them; parents will consequently repose in them confidence; their task will be comparatively light, their path comparatively smooth. If the faculty be absent, the life of a teacher will be a struggle from beginning to end. No matter how amiable the disposition, how strong the sense of duty, how active the desire to please; no matter how brilliant and varied the accomplishments, if the governess has not the power to win her young charge, the secret to instill gently and surely her own knowledge into the growing mind entrusted to her, she will have a wearing, wasting existence of it. To <u>educate</u> a child as, I daresay Mrs. Williams has educated her children, probably with as much pleasure to herself as profit to them, will indeed be impossible to the teacher who lacks this qualification; but, I conceive, should circumstances—as in the case of your daughters—compel a young girl notwithstanding to adopt a governesse's profession, she may contrive to <u>instruct</u> and even to instruct well. That is—though she cannot form the child's mind, mould its character, influence its disposition and guide its conduct as she would wish, she may give lessons—even good, clear, clever lessons in the various branches of knowledge; she may earn and doubly earn her scanty salary; as a daily governess, or a school-teacher she may succeed, but as a resident governess she will never—(except under peculiar and exceptional circumstances) be happy. Her deficiency will harass her not so much in school-time as in play-hours; the moments that would be rest and recreation to the governess who understood and could adapt herself to children, will be almost torture to her who has not that power; many a time, when her charge turns unruly on her hands, when the responsibility which she would wish to discharge faithfully and perfectly, becomes unmanageable to her, she will wish herself a housemaid or kitchen-girl, rather than a baited, trampled, desolate, distracted governess.

—The Letters of Charlotte Brontë, v. 2, pp. 63–64

she especially regarded as a valuable friend, whose advice helped to guide her in one very important step of her life. But as her definite acquirements were few, she had to eke them out by employing her leisure time in needle-work; and altogether her position was that of "bonne" or nursery governess, liable to repeated and never-ending calls upon her time. This description of uncertain, yet perpetual employment, subject to the exercise of another person's will at all hours of the day, was peculiarly trying to one whose life at home had been full of abundant leisure. *Idle* she never was in any place, but of the multitude of small talks, plans, duties, pleasures, &c., that make up most people's days, her home life was nearly destitute. This made it possible for her to go through long and deep histories of feeling and imagination, for which others, odd as it sounds, have rarely time. This made it inevitable that—later on, in her too short career—the intensity of her feeling should wear out her physical health. The habit of "making out," which had grown with her growth, and strengthened with her strength, had become a part of her nature. Yet all exercise of her strongest and most characteristic faculties was now out of the question. She could not (as while she was at Miss Wooler's) feel amidst the occupations of the day, that when evening came, she might employ herself in more congenial ways. No doubt, all who enter upon the career of a governess have to relinquish much; no doubt, it must ever be a life of sacrifice; but to Charlotte Brontë it was a perpetual attempt to force all her faculties into a direction for which the whole of her previous life had unfitted them. Moreover, the little Brontës had been brought up motherless; and from knowing nothing of the gaiety and the sportiveness of childhood—from never having experienced caresses or fond attentions themselves—they were ignorant of the very nature of infancy, or how to call out its engaging qualities. Children were to them the troublesome necessities of humanity; they had never been drawn into contact with them in any other way. Years afterwards, when Miss Brontë came to stay with us, she watched our little girls perpetually; and I could not persuade her that they were only average specimens of well brought up children. She was surprised and touched by any sign of thoughtfulness for others, of kindness to animals, or of unselfishness on their part; and constantly maintained that she was in the right, and I in the wrong, when we differed on the point of their unusual excellence.

—The Life of Charlotte Brontë, v. 1,
pp. 224–226

Brussels and the Pensionnat Héger

To develop their language and music skills for the school the Brontë sisters hoped to open, Charlotte and Emily traveled to the Continent to attend school. They arrived at the Pensionnat Héger, Rue D'Isabelle, Brussels, on 15 February 1842. The most important influence on the sisters at the school was their French teacher, M. Constantin Héger (1809–1896), husband of Mme. Zoë Héger, who ran the pensionnat. M. Héger worked with Emily and Charlotte on their writing in French through "devoirs"—writing assignments on topics prompted by readings. Several scholars believe that Charlotte's prose style benefited from M. Héger's scrutiny and that his careful correction of her work was important to the maturation of her writing style.

In this excerpt Charlotte gives her early impressions of the school and her teacher.

Charlotte Brontë to Ellen Nussey, May 1842

I was twenty-six years old a week or two since—and at that ripe time of life I am a schoolgirl—a complete school-girl and on the whole very happy in that capacity It felt very strange at first to submit to authority instead of exercising it—to obey orders instead of giving them—but I like that state of things—I returned to it with the same avidity that a cow that has long been kept on dry hay returns to fresh grass—don't laugh at my simile—it is natural to me to submit and very unnatural to command

This is a large school in which there are about 40 externes or day-pupils and 12 pensionnaires or boarders—Madame Heger the head is a lady of precisely the same cast of mind degree of cultivation & quality of character as Miss Catherine Wooler—I think the severe points are a little softened because she has not been disappointed & consequently soured—in a word—she is a married instead of a maiden lady—. . .

All in the house are Catholics except ourselves one other girl and the gouvernante of Madam's children—an Englishwoman in rank something between a lady's maid and a nursery governess the difference in Country & religion makes a broad line of demarcation between us & all the rest we are completely isolated in the midst of numbers—yet I think I am never unhappy—my present life is so delightful so congenial to my nature compared to that of a Governess—my time constantly occupied passes too rapidly—hitherto both Emily and I have had good health & therefore we have been able to work well. There is one individual of whom I have not yet spoken Monsieur Heger the husband of Madame—he is professor of Rhetoric a man of power as to mind but very choleric & irritable in temperament—a little, black, ugly being with a face that varies in expression, sometimes he borrows the lineaments of an insane Tom-cat—sometimes those of a delirious Hyena—occasionally—but very seldom he discards these perilous attractions and assumes an air not above a hundred degrees removed from what you would call mild & gentleman-like he is very angry with me just at present because I have written a translation which—he chose to stigmatize as <u>peu correct</u>—not because it was particularly so in reality but because he happened to be in a bad humour when he read it—he did not tell me so—but wrote the accusation in the margin of my book and asked in brief stern phrase how it happened that my compositions were always better than my translations—adding that the thing seemed to him inexplicable the fact is some weeks ago in a high-flown humour he forbade me to use either dictionary or grammar—in translating the most difficult English compositions into French this makes the task rather arduous—& compels me every now and then to introduce an English word which nearly plucks the eyes out of his head when he sees it.

—*The Letters of Charlotte Brontë,*
v. 1, pp. 283–285

* * *

After studying one term at the pensionnat, Emily and Charlotte were offered teaching posts in exchange for continuing their education there. Excerpt.

Charlotte Brontë to Ellen Nussey, July? 1842

I consider it doubtful whether I shall come home in September or not—Madame Heger has made a proposal for both me and Emily to stay another half year—offering to dismiss her English master and take me as English teacher—also to employ Emily some part of each day in teaching music to a certain number of the pupils—for these services we are to be allowed to continue our studies in French and German—and to have board &c without paying for it—no salaries however are offered—the proposal is kind and in a great selfish city like Brussels and a great selfish school containing nearly ninety pupils (boarders & day-pupils included) implies a degree of interest which demands gratitude in return—I am inclined to accept it—what think you?

—*The Letters of Charlotte Brontë,*
v. 1, p. 289

* * *

The Protestant Cemetery

Martha Taylor, younger sister of Charlotte's friend Mary Taylor, was studying at the Château de Kockleberg in Brussels while Charlotte and Emily were at the pensionnat. On 12 October 1842, the twenty-three-year-old Martha died of cholera and was buried in the Protestant cemetery in Brussels. In her 1 November 1842 letter to Ellen Nussey, Mary Taylor writes of walking about six miles with Charlotte and Emily "to see the cemetery and the country round it. We then spent a pleasant evening with my cousins and in presence of my Uncle and Emily one not speaking at all; the other once or twice" (Mary Taylor: Friend of Charlotte Brontë, *p. 40).*

Charlotte used the memory of this experience in two of her novels. In The Professor—*the first novel she wrote, which was not published until 1857—she set a pivotal scene in the cemetery, which she describes thusly:*

The place was large enough to afford half an hour's strolling without the monotony of treading continually the same path; and, for those who love to peruse the annals of graveyards, here was variety of inscription enough to occupy the attention for double or treble that space of time. Hither people of many kindreds, tongues, and nations, had brought their dead for interment; and here, on pages of stone, of marble, and of brass, were written names, dates, last tributes of pomp or love, in English, in French, in German, and Latin. Here the Englishman had erected a marble monument over the remains of his Mary Smith or Jane Brown, and inscribed it only with her name. There the French widower had shaded the grave: of his Elmire or Celestine with a brilliant thicket of roses, amidst which a little tablet rising, bore an equally bright testimony to her countless virtues. Every nation, tribe, and kindred, mourned after its own fashion; and how soundless was the mourning of all!

—*The Professor,* chapter 19

When she wrote her second published novel, Shirley *(1849), she again invokes the experience:*

. . . This evening reminds me too forcibly of another evening some years ago: a howling, rainy autumn evening too—when certain who had that day performed a pilgrimage to a grave new-made in a heretic cemetery, sat near a wood-fire on the hearth of a foreign dwelling. They were merry and social, but they each knew that a gap, never to be filled, had been made in their circle. They knew they had lost something whose absence could never be quite atoned for so long as they lived: and they knew that heavy falling rain was soaking into the wet earth which covered their lost darling; and that the sad, sighing gale was mourning above her buried head. The fire warmed them; Life and Friendship yet blessed them; but Jessie lay cold, coffined, solitary—only the sod screening her from the storm.

—*Shirley,* volume 2, chapter 12

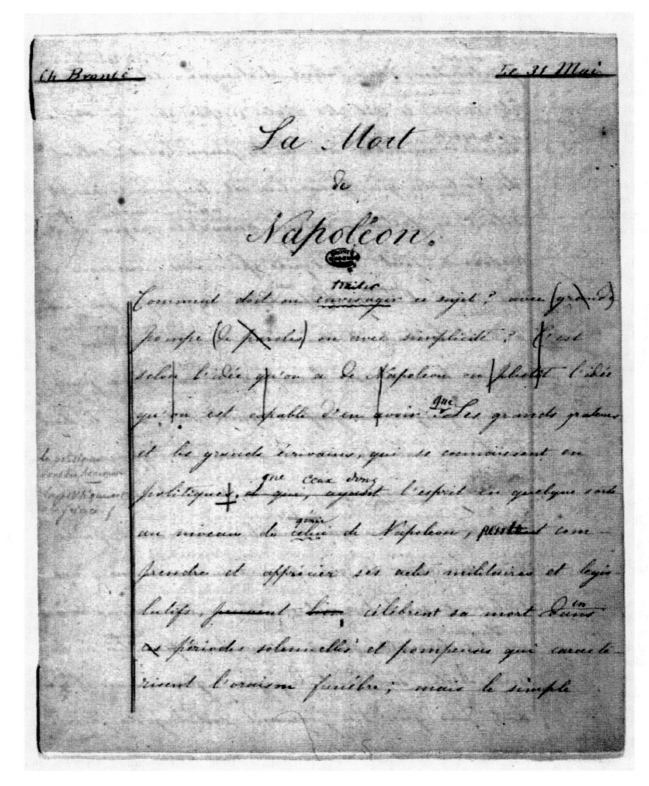

First page of one of Charlotte's devoirs writing assignments with editing marks by Constantin Héger (The Brontë Society)

On 29 October 1842, Aunt Branwell died in Haworth. Emily and Charlotte left Brussels, arriving in Haworth on 8 November. While Emily remained in Haworth from 1842 until her death in 1848, taking Aunt Branwell's place in running the household for Reverend Brontë, Charlotte returned alone to Brussels in January 1843 and worked and studied at the pensionnat until 31 December that year. The year Charlotte spent in Brussels without Emily was a different experience from their time there together, as this excerpt shows.

Charlotte Brontë to Emily Brontë, 29 May 1843

I have now the entire charge of the English lessons. I have given two lessons to the first class. Hortense Jannoy was a picture on these occasions, her face was black as a "blue-piled thunder-loft," and her two ears were red as raw beef. To all questions asked her reply was, *"je ne sais pas."* It is a pity but her friends could meet with a person qualified to cast out a devil. I am richly off for companionship in these parts. Of late days, M. and Mde. Héger rarely

ST. GUDULE'S CATHEDRAL, BRUSSELS

St. Gudule's Cathedral, Brussels, where Charlotte made confession during a time of emotional distress in August 1843. In Villette *Lucy Snowe, a Protestant, is drawn to the confessional in "an old solemn church, its pervading gloom not gilded but purpled by light shed through stained glass" (from* Life and Works of the Sisters Brontë, *University of Colorado Libraries).*

speak to me, and I really don't pretend to care a fig for any body else in the establishment. You are not to suppose by that expression that I am under the influence of warm affection for Mde. Héger. I am convinced she does not like me—why, I can't tell, nor do I think she herself has any definite reason for the aversion; but for one thing, she cannot comprehend why I do not make intimate friends of Mesdames Blanche, Sophie, and Haussé. M. Héger is wonderously influenced by Madame, and I should not wonder if he disapproves very much of my unamiable want of sociability. He has already given me a brief lecture on universal *bienveillance,* and, perceiving that I don't improve in consequence, I fancy he has taken to considering me as a person to be let alone—left to the error of her ways; and consequently he has in a great measure withdrawn the light of his countenance, and I get on from day to day in a Robinson-Crusoe-like condition—very lonely. That does not signify. In other respects I have nothing substantial to complain of, nor is even this a cause for complaint. Except the loss of M. Héger's goodwill (if I have lost it) I care for none of 'em.

—Clement K. Shorter, *Charlotte Brontë and Her Circle,*
pp. 114–115

* * *

Charlotte became increasingly isolated and lonely. She later incorporated much of her experience, including her confession in the cathedral of St. Gudule, into her 1853 novel Villette. *Excerpt.*

Charlotte Brontë to Emily Brontë, 2 September 1843

. . . The weather has been exceedingly fine during the last fortnight, and yet not so Asiatically hot as it was last year at this time. Consequently I have tramped about a great deal and tried to get a clearer acquaintance with the streets of Brussels. This week, as no teacher is here except Mdlle. Blanche, who is returned from Paris, I am always alone except at meal-times, for Mdlle. Blanche's character is so false and so contemptible I can't force myself to associate with her. She perceives my utter dislike and never now speaks to me—a great relief.

However, I should inevitably fall into the gulf of low spirits if I stayed always by myself here without a human being to speak to, so I go out and traverse the Boulevards and streets of Bruxelles sometimes for hours together. Yesterday I went on a pilgrimage to the cemetery, and far beyond it on to a hill where there was nothing but fields as far as the horizon. When I came back it was evening; but I had such a repugnance to return to the house, which contained nothing that I cared for, I still kept threading the streets in the neighbourhood of the Rue d'Isabelle and avoiding it. I found myself opposite to Ste. Gudule, and the bell, whose voice you know, began to toll for evening salut. I went in, quite alone (which procedure you will say is not much like me), wandered about the aisles where a few old women were saying their prayers, till vespers begun. I stayed till they were over. Still I could not leave the church or force myself to go home—to school I mean. An odd whim came into my head. In a solitary part of the Cathedral six or seven people still remained kneeling by the confessionals. In two confessionals I saw a priest. I felt as if I did not care what I did, provided it was not absolutely wrong, and that it served to vary my life and yield a moment's interest. I took a fancy to change myself into a Catholic and go and make a real confession to see what it was like. Knowing me as you do, you will think this odd, but when people are by themselves they have singular fancies. A penitent was occupied in confessing. They do not go into the sort of pew or cloister which the priest occupies, but kneel down on the steps and confess through a grating. Both the confessor and the penitent whisper very low, you can hardly hear their voices. After I had watched two or three penitents go and return I approached at last and knelt down in a niche which was just vacated. I had to kneel there ten minutes waiting, for on the other side was another penitent invisible to me. At last that went away and a little wooden door inside the grating opened, and I saw the priest leaning his ear towards me. I was obliged to begin, and yet I did not know a word of the formula with which they always commence their confessions. It was a funny position. I felt precisely as I did when alone on the Thames at midnight. I commenced with saying I was a foreigner and had been brought up a Protestant. The priest asked if I was a Protestant then. I somehow could not tell a lie and said "yes." He replied that in that case I could not *"jouir du bonheur de la confesse"*; but I was determined to confess, and at last he said he would allow me because it might be the first step towards returning to the true church. I actually did confess—a real confession. When I had done he told me his address, and said that every morning I was to go to the rue du Parc—to his house—and he would reason with me and try to convince me of the error and enormity of being a Protestant!!! I promised faithfully to go. Of course, however, the adventure stops there, and I hope I shall never see the priest again. I think you had better not tell papa of this. He will not understand that it was only a freak; and will perhaps think I am going to turn Catholic.

—Clement K. Shorter, *Charlotte Brontë and Her Circle,*

pp. 117–118

* * *

Over the course of 1842–1843, Charlotte fell in love with Constantin Héger. All evidence indicates that her love was not reciprocated. Nevertheless, after her return from Brussels in early 1844, Charlotte wrote to M. Héger periodically about her strong attachment to him.

This letter was written in French, translated here by Margaret Smith, while the postscript was added in English.

Charlotte Brontë to Constantin Héger, 18 November 1845

Monsieur,

The six months of silence have elapsed; to-day is the 18th November, my last letter was dated (I believe) the 18th May; therefore I can write to you again without breaking my promise.

The summer and autumn have seemed very long to me; to tell the truth I have had to make painful efforts to endure until now the privation I imposed on myself: you, Monsieur—you cannot conceive what that means—but imagine for a moment that one of your children is sepa-

---

"Governed by a Tragical Romantic Love"?

In the year following the Héger family's donation of four letters from Charlotte to Constantin to the British Museum, Frederika Macdonald published a book-length study, The Secret of Charlotte Brontë *(1914), in which she argued for the central importance of Charlotte Brontë's unrequited passion in understanding her life and work. She maintains that "with the knowledge of . . . these pathetic and beautiful Love-letters, the 'Problem of Charlotte Brontë,' as so many very clever but inattentive psychological critics have stated it, has lost all claim to serious attention."*

The basis of the 'Problem' was the alleged 'dissonance' between Charlotte's personality and her genius—between her dreary, desolate, dull, well-tamed existence, uncoloured, untroubled by romance (as Mrs. Gaskell painted it), and the passionate atmosphere of her novels, where all events and personages are seen through the medium of one sentiment—tragical romantic love.

We now know that the dissonance did not exist; that from her twenty-sixth year downwards, Charlotte's life was, not only coloured, but governed by a tragical romantic love: that, in its first stage, threw her into a hopeless conflict against the force of things and broke her heart: but that, because the battle was fought in the force, and in the cause, of noble emotions, saved her soul alive; and called her genius forth to life: so that it rose as an immortal spirit from the grave of personal hopes.

—*The Secret of Charlotte Brontë,* pp. 145–146

rated from you by a distance of 160 leagues, and that you have to let six months go by without writing to him, without receiving news of him, without hearing him spoken of, without knowing how he is, then you will easily understand what hardship there is in such an obligation. I will tell you candidly that during this time of waiting I have tried to forget you, for the memory of a person one believes one is never to see again, and whom one nevertheless greatly respects, torments the mind exceedingly and when one has suffered this kind of anxiety for one or two years, one is ready to do anything to regain peace of mind. I have done everything, I have sought occupations, I have absolutely forbidden myself the pleasure of speaking about you–even to Emily, but I have not been able to overcome either my regrets or my impatience–and that is truly humiliating–not to know how to get the mastery over one's own thoughts, to be the slave of a regret, a memory, the slave of a dominant and fixed idea which has become a tyrant over one's mind. Why cannot I have for you exactly as much friendship as you have for me–neither more nor less? Then I would be so tranquil, so free–I could keep silence for ten years without effort.

My father is well but his sight has almost gone, he can no longer read or write; nevertheless the doctors' advice is to wait a few months longer before attempting an operation–for him the winter will be nothing but a long night–he rarely complains, I admire his patience–If Providence ordains that the same calamity should be my own fate–may He at least grant me as much patience to endure it! It seems to me, Monsieur, that what is most bitterly painful in great bodily afflictions is that we are compelled to make all those who surround us sharers in our sufferings; we can hide the troubles of the soul, but those which attack the body and destroy its faculties cannot be hidden. My father now lets me read to him and write for him, he also shows more confidence in me than he has ever done before, and that is a great consolation.

Monsieur, I have a favour to ask you: when you reply to this letter, talk to me a little about yourself–not about me, for I know that if you talk to me about myself it will be to scold me, and this time I would like to see your kindly aspect; talk to me then about your children; your forehead never had a severe look when Louise and Claire and Prospère were near you. Tell me also something about the School, the pupils, the teachers–are Mesdemoiselles Blanche, Sophie and Justine still in Brussels? Tell me where you travelled during the holidays–haven't you been through the Rhineland? Haven't you visited Cologne or Coblenz? In a word, tell me what you will, my master, but tell me something. Writing to a former assistant teacher (no,–I don't want to remember my position as an assistant teacher, I disown it) well then, writing to an old pupil cannot be a very interesting occupation for you–I know that– but for me it is life itself. Your last letter has sustained me–

has nourished me for six months–now I need another and you will give it me–not because you have any friendship for me–you cannot have much–but because you have a compassionate soul and because you would not condemn anyone to undergo long suffering in order to spare yourself a few moments of tedium. To forbid me to write to you, to refuse to reply to me–that will be to tear from me the only joy I have on earth–to deprive me of my last remaining privilege–a privilege which I will never consent to renounce voluntarily. Believe me, my master, in writing to me you do a good deed–so long as I think you are fairly pleased with me, so long as I still have the hope of hearing from you, I can be tranquil and not too sad, but when a dreary and prolonged silence seems to warn me that my master is becoming estranged from me–when day after day I await a letter and day after day disappointment flings me down again into overwhelming misery, when the sweet delight of seeing your writing and reading your counsel flees from me like an empty vision–then I am in a fever–I lose my appetite and my sleep–I pine away.

May I write to you again next May? I would have liked to wait a full year–but it is impossible–it is too long–

C. Brontë

Portrait of the Héger family in 1847 by Ange Francois (Brontë Society; from Jane Sellars, Charlotte Brontë, *Colorado College Library)*

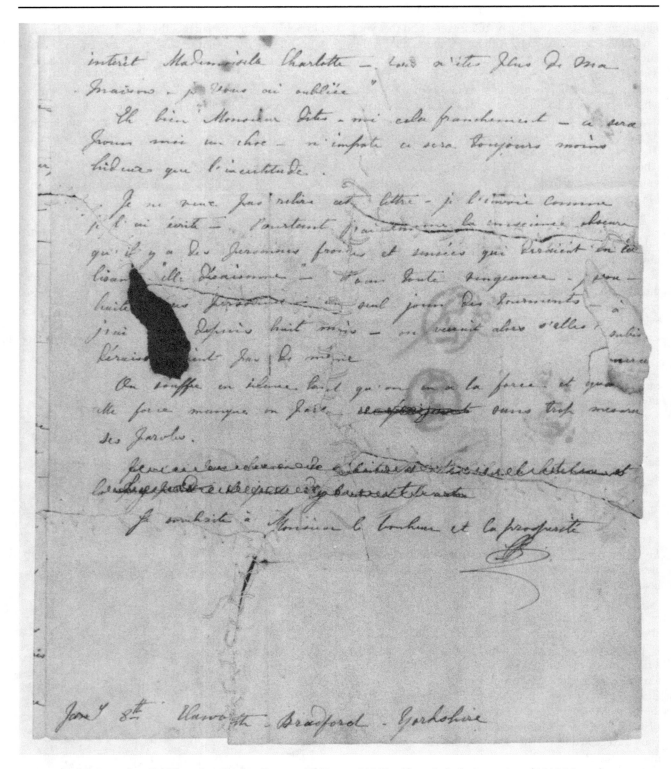

Last page of an 1845 letter from Charlotte Brontë to M. Héger, which his wife repaired after he tore it up (British Museum)

I must say one word to you in English—I wish I could write to you more cheerful letters, for when I read this over, I find it to be somewhat gloomy—but forgive me my dear master—do not be irritated at my sadness—according to the words of the Bible: "Out of the fullness of the heart, the mouth speaketh and truly I find it difficult to be cheerful so long as I think I shall never see you more. You will perceive by the defects in this letter that I am forgetting the French language—yet I read all the French books I can get, and learn daily a portion by heart—but I have never heard French spoken but once since I left Brussels—and then it sounded like music in my ears—every word was most precious to me because it reminded me of you—I love French for your sake with all my heart and soul.

Farewell my dear Master—may God protect you with special care and crown you with peculiar blessings

C B.
—The Letters of Charlotte Brontë, v. 1,
pp. 435–437

George Smith, the publisher of Jane Eyre *(The Brontë Society; from Jane Sellars,* Charlotte Brontë, *Colorado College Library)*

Jane Eyre

After the Brontë sisters gave up the idea of opening their own school, they began to think more seriously of authorship and were able to find a publisher for Poems by Currer, Ellis, and Acton Bell *(1846). Charlotte, like her sisters, was also trying to start a career as a novelist. She was unable to place her first effort,* The Professor, *which was rejected by several publishers, including Thomas Newby, who accepted Emily's* Wuthering Heights *(1847) and Anne's* Agnes Grey *(1847). In the meantime she had begun* Jane Eyre *while nursing her father after his August 1846 cataract removal operation.*

The first professional encouragement Charlotte received came from the publishing house Smith, Elder, which was headed by the twenty-three-year-old George Smith (1824–1901), who had taken over the firm upon his father's death in 1846. In this excerpt from his memoir of Charlotte Brontë, Smith recalls how he, with the support of his reader William Smith Williams (1800–1875), came to decide to publish Jane Eyre—a decision that helped to cement the firm's successful reputation.

"The Story Quickly Took Me Captive"
Smith, Elder and the Publication of *Jane Eyre*
George Smith

In July 1847 a parcel containing a MS. reached our office addressed to the firm, but bearing also the scored-out addresses of three or four other publishing houses; showing that the parcel had been previously submitted to other publishers. This was not calculated to prepossess us in favour of the MS. It was clear that we were offered what had been already rejected elsewhere.

A Plain Heroine

In her memoir of Charlotte Brontë, Harriet Martineau recalls the author's anecdote on the origin of her most famous character.

"Jane Eyre" was naturally and universally supposed to be Charlotte herself; but she always denied it calmly, cheerfully, and with the obvious sincerity which characterized all she said. She declared that there was no more ground for the assertion than this: she once told her sisters that they were wrong—even morally wrong—in making their heroines beautiful, as a matter of course. They replied that it was impossible to make a heroine interesting on other terms. Her answer was: "I will prove to you that you are wrong. I will show to you a heroine as small and as plain as myself, who shall be as interesting as any of yours." "Hence 'Jane Eyre,'" said she, in telling the anecdote: "but she is not myself any further than that."

—Daily News, 6 April 1855, p. 5

There was no possibility of taking a walk that day. We had been wandering indeed in the leafless shrubbery an hour in the morning, but since dinner (Mrs Reed, when there was no company, dined early) the cold winter wind had brought with it clouds so sombre, a rain so penetrating that further out-door exercise was now out of the question.

Photo J. J. Stead.   **A Portion of the MS. of "Jane Eyre."**

"Charlotte Brontë's method of writing was to take a piece of cardboard—the broken cover of a book, in fact—and a few sheets of notepaper, and write her first form of a story upon these sheets in a tiny handwriting in pencil. She would afterwards copy the whole out upon a quarto paper very neatly in ink. None of the original pencilled MSS. of her greater novels have been preserved. The extant manuscripts of 'Jane Eyre' and 'The Professor' are in ink."—Clement K. Shorter's "Charlotte Brontë and Her Circle."

The opening paragraph of the manuscript for Jane Eyre *(British Library; Shelfmark Add. 43474, f. 1, from* The Bookman, *October 1904)*

The parcel contained the MS. of 'The Professor,' by 'Currer Bell,' a book which was published after Charlotte Brontë's death. Mr. Williams, the 'reader' to the firm, read the MS., and said that it evinced great literary power, but he had doubts as to its being successful as a publication. We decided that he should write to 'Currer Bell' a letter of appreciative criticism declining the work, but expressing an opinion that he could produce a book which would command success. Before, however, our letter was despatched, there came a letter from 'Currer Bell' containing a postage-stamp for our reply, it having been hinted to the writer by 'an experienced friend' that publishers often refrained from answering communications unless a postage-stamp was furnished for the purpose! Charlotte Brontë herself has described the effect our letter had on her:

As a forlorn hope, he tried one publishing house more. Ere long, in a much shorter space than that on which experience had taught him to calculate, there came a letter, which he opened in the dreary anticipation of finding two hard hopeless lines, intimating that 'Messrs. Smith, Elder, & Co. were not disposed to publish the MS.,' and, instead, he took out of the envelope a letter of two pages. He read it trembling. It declined, indeed, to publish that tale for business reasons, but it discussed its merits and demerits so courteously, so considerately, in a spirit so rational, with a discrimination so enlightened, that this very refusal cheered the author better than a vulgarly expressed acceptance would have done. It was added, that a work in three volumes would meet with careful attention.

The writer of this letter was, as I have said, Mr. W. Smith Williams . . .

In reply to Mr. Williams's letter came a brief note from 'Currer Bell,' expressing grateful appreciation of the attention which had been given to the MS., and saying that the author was on the point of finishing another book, which would be sent to us as soon as completed.

The second MS. was 'Jane Eyre.' Here again 'Currer Bell's' suspicion as to the excessive parsimony of London publishers in regard to postage-stamps found expression in the letter accompanying the MS. She wrote:

I find I cannot prepay the carriage of the parcel, as money for that purpose is not received at the small station where it is left. If, when you acknowledge the receipt of the MS., you would have the goodness to

me strength to lead henceforth, a purer life than I have done
hitherto!"

Then he stretched his hand out to be led: I took that dear
hand, held it a moment to my lips, then let it pass round my
shoulder; being so much lower of stature than he, I served
both for his prop and guide. We entered the wood and
wended homeward.

Conclusion.

Reader — I married him. A quiet wedding we had: he and
I, the parson and clerk were alone present. When we got back
from church, I went into the kitchen of the Manor-house, where
Mary was cooking the dinner, and John, cleaning the knives — and
I said:

Mary — I have been married to Mr. Rochester this morning."
The housekeeper and her husband were both of that decent phleg-
matic order of people, to whom one may at any time safely
communicate a remarkable piece of news without incurring the
danger of having one's ears pierced by some shrill ejaculation, and
subsequently stunned by a torrent of wordy wonderment. Mary
did look up, and she did stare at me, the ladle with which
she was basting a pair of chickens roasting at the fire, did for
some three minutes hang suspended in air, and for the same

Page that began the last chapter of the Jane Eyre *manuscript (British Library, shelfmark Add. 43476, f. 239 from Jane Sellars,*
Charlotte Brontë, *Colorado College Library)*

mention the amount charged on delivery, I will immediately transmit it in postage-stamps.

The MS. of 'Jane Eyre' was read by Mr. Williams in due course. He brought it to me on a Saturday, and said that he would like me to read it. There were no Saturday half-holidays in those days, and, as was usual, I did not reach home until late. I had made an appointment with a friend for Sunday morning; I was to meet him about twelve o'clock, at a place some two or three miles from our house, and ride with him into the country.

After breakfast on Sunday morning I took the MS. of 'Jane Eyre' to my little study, and began to read it. The story quickly took me captive. Before twelve o'clock my horse came to the door, but I could not put the book down. I scribbled two or three lines to my friend, saying I was very sorry that circumstances had arisen to prevent my meeting him, sent the note off by my groom, and went on reading the MS. Presently the servant came to tell me that luncheon was ready; I asked him to bring me a sandwich and a glass of wine, and still went on with 'Jane Eyre.' Dinner came; for me the meal was a very hasty one, and before I went to bed that night I had finished reading the manuscript.

The next day we wrote to 'Currer Bell' accepting the book for publication. I need say nothing about the success which the book achieved, and the speculations as to whether it was written by a man or a woman. For my own part I never had much doubt on the subject of the writer's sex; but then I had the advantage over the general public of having the handwriting of the author before me. There were qualities of style, too, and turns of expression, which satisfied me that 'Currer Bell' was a woman, an opinion in which Mr. Williams concurred. We were bound, however, to respect the writer's anonymity, and our letters continued to be addressed to 'Currer Bell, Esq.'

–"Charlotte Brontë," *The Cornhill Magazine*, new series 9 (December 1900): 780, 782–783

* * *

Jane Eyre: An Autobiography was published on 19 October 1847, and reviews were generally strong. The first edition sold out in three months and further editions were published in January and April 1848.

This review was unsigned. Excerpts.

"A Book with a Great Heart"
Review of *Jane Eyre*

This is not merely a work of great promise; it is one of absolute performance. It is one of the most powerful domestic romances which have been published for many years. It has little or nothing of the old conventional stamp upon it; none of the jaded, exhausted attributes of a worn-out vein of imagination, reproducing old incidents and old characters in new combinations; but is full of youthful vigour, of freshness and originality, of nervous diction and concentrated interest. The incidents are sometimes melo-dramatic, and, it might be added, improbable; but these incidents, though striking, are subordinate to the main purpose of the piece, which depends not upon incident, but on the development of character; it is a tale of passion, not of intensity which is almost sublime. It is a book to make the pulses gallop and the heart beat, and to fill the eyes with tears.

Jane Eyre tells her own story. She is an orphan child, outwardly adopted but inwardly repudiated by a hard, unfeeling woman, her aunt, who outrages the affections of the child, and would fain crush her spirit. The little girl turns at times against her oppressor; and resistance strengthens the hatred and stimulates the cruelty of the bad woman. Jane is sent to a charitable institution, where she spends eight years of her life, emerging thence, at the age of eighteen, in the character of a governess. Here the interest of the story commences. The history of Jane's life at the Lowood institution is, perhaps, unnecessarily lengthened out. There is an air of truth about it; and we do not doubt that the character of Helen Burns— a youthful inmate of the asylum, who is the very incarnation of Christian charity and forbearance—is an especial favourite with the writer. Helen Burns is just one of those idealities in which young writers are fain to revel—conjuring up with the enchanter's wand beings who belong to a higher sphere and a purer atmosphere than this—dream-children, with the unspotted hearts of babyhood and the wisdom of adolescence. Creations such as these are very beautiful, but very untrue.

Jane obtains a situation as a governess in an old country house, ostensibly tenanted only by a venerable housekeeper, a few servants, and a little girl, the ward of the absent master. Mr. Rochester—such is his name— returns from abroad, and before long conceives a grand passion for the little teacher. Jane Eyre is not pretty, but she is very piquante. Her manner attracts Mr. Rochester—a man of forty, with strongly-marked and somewhat harsh lineaments both of countenance and character. His curiosity is excited; his interest awakened; he is charmed—fascinated. A bungler would certainly, under such circumstances, have painted the heroine in radiant colours. She would have been, in a novel of approved manufacture, a beauty of the first water. The author of Jane Eyre has too deep an insight into human character—too profound a knowledge of the sources of human passion, to commit any such mistake. It was precisely because Jane Eyre was not a beauty of the recognised stamp that Rochester, who had mixed

"Exceedingly Moved & Pleased" Thackeray Responds to *Jane Eyre*

On 23 October 1847, the established novelist William Make-peace Thackeray wrote to William Smith Williams, who had sent him a copy of the newly published Jane Eyre, *which Thackeray received while he was working on the serialization of his novel* Vanity Fair. *Williams forwarded Thackeray's praise to Charlotte Brontë.*

My dear Sir

    I wish you had not sent me Jane Eyre. It interested me so much that I have lost (or won if you like) a whole day in reading it at the busiest period, with the printers I know waiting for copy. Who the author can be I can't guess—if a woman she knows her language better than most ladies do, or has had a 'classical' education. It is a fine book though—the man & woman capital—the style very generous and upright so to speak. I thought it was Kinglake for some time. The plot of the story is one with wh. I am familiar. Some of the love passages made me cry—to the astonishment of John who came in with the coals. St. John the Missionary is a failure I think but a good failure there are parts excellent I dont know why I tell you this but that I have been exceedingly moved & pleased by Jane Eyre. It is a womans writing, but whose? Give my respects and thanks to the author—whose novel is the first English one (& the French are only romances now) that I've been able to read for many a day.

Very truly yours my dear Sir
W M Thackeray

—The Letters and Private Papers of William Makepeace
Thackeray, v. 2, pp. 318–319

largely with the world, who had tasted of satiety, who had been in his day almost a libertine—the libertine of circumstances, not of a corrupt heart—was stimulated into an intensity of love and desire. . . .

    We know not whether this powerful story is from the pen of a youthful writer; there is all the freshness and some of the crudeness of youth about it, but there is a knowledge of the profoundest springs of human emotion, such as is rarely acquired without long years of bitter experience in the troubled sea of life. The action of the tale is some times unnatural—but the passion is always true. It would be easy to point out incidental defects; but the merits of the work are so striking that it is a pleasure to recognise them without stint and qualification. It is a book with a great heart in it; not a mere sham—a counterfeit.

—*Atlas,* new series 6 (23 October 1847): 719

* * *

This excerpt is from an unsigned review. The reviewer finds fault with the novel's conclusion but instead of blaming the author faults the convention of the three-volume novel, a publishing practice encouraged in part by commercial lending libraries that allowed readers to check out only one volume at a time.

"A Story of Surpassing Interest" Review of *Jane Eyre*

    Our readers will probably remember a volume of poems, the joint production of three brothers, Bell, which, albeit little noticed by our critical brethren, took our fancy so much, as seeming to be freighted with promise, that we dedicated several columns to a review, and, as we are informed, thereby contributed mainly to establish for the authors a reputation which we hope was something more than nominal.

    The performance before us, by one of the brothers, proves the justice of those anticipations. Currer Bell can write prose as well as poetry. He has fertile invention, great power of description, and a happy faculty for conceiving and sketching character. *Jane Eyre* is a remarkable novel, in all respects very far indeed above the average of those which the literary journalist is doomed every season to peruse, and of which he can say nothing either in praise or condemnation, such is their tame monotony of mediocrity. It is a story of surpassing interest, riveting the attention from the very first chapter, and sustaining it by a copiousness of incident rare indeed in our modern English school of novelists, who seem to make it their endeavour to diffuse the smallest possible number of incidents over the largest possible number of pages. Currer Bell has even gone rather into the opposite extreme, and the incidents of his story are, if any thing, too much crowded. But this is a fault which readers, at least, will readily pardon.

    Jane Eyre is an orphan, dependant upon relations, who heap upon her all sorts of ill-treatment, until her spirit rebels instead of breaking, and as a punishment, or rather to be rid of her, she is sent to a Charitable Institution, whose wretched fare, exacting tyranny, puritanical pretension, and systematic hypocrisy are painted with a vividness which shews them to be no fiction, but a copy from the life, and it is evident that the author has aimed a well-directed blow at actually existing charities in more than one county, of which this one is a type.

    When this sort of slow torture can be endured no longer, she seeks a situation as governess, and finds it in the house of a gentleman, who entrusts to her care his *ward,* as she is called, but who is, in fact, the child of an opera-dancer. There is exquisite delicacy in the drawing of this young creature; it is a perfect picture of a little girl, such as we do not know where to parallel in the

J A N E   E Y R E.

An Autobiography.

EDITED BY

C U R R E R   B E L L

IN THREE VOLUMES.

VOL. I.

LONDON:
SMITH, ELDER, AND CO., CORNHILL.
1847.

Title page for the first edition of Charlotte's Brontë's first novel
(British Library)

whole range of literature—so rare it is to find childhood naturally depicted. If the author had done no more than this, he would have entitled himself to a high place among the novelists of his day. The mystery which attaches to Thornfield, so well preserved, is not so happily revealed. The *dénouement* is too abrupt, and there has been an evident effort to bring matters to a conclusion at a point prescribed rather by the printer than by the progress of the story.

This, however, is the consequence of our absurd three-volumed system, which compels improper curtailment as well as needless expansion. The character of Mr. Rochester is brought out with consummate skill, learned, as in real life, not by telling it but by shewing it, as events display the various features of his mind. Here the mystery is revealed, and the trials and troubles that follow thereupon, and the end of all, so entirely unexpected, and so different from the established usage of novelists, we leave the reader to explore, without marring the pleasure of the search by anticipating the plot. Among the per-

sonages most ably drawn are those who figure in the charity-school at Lowood, especially the patron, so pious and so hard-hearted, so firm in faith, so failing in worth, so good a Christian in precept, so bad an one in practice. The heroine also is very well sustained: she is not faultless, but human—a woman and not an angel; on which account we feel all the more interested in her fortunes.

Being such, we can cordially recommend *Jane Eyre* to our readers, as a novel to be placed at the top of the list to be borrowed, and to the circulating-library keeper as one which he may with safety order. It is sure to be in demand.

—*The Critic* (30 October 1847): 277–278

* * *

Charlotte Brontë believed that this unsigned review was written by the radical journalist Albany William Fonblanque, whom she regarded as an "able man." Excerpts.

"A Book of Decided Power"
Review of *Jane Eyre*

This book has just been sent to us by the publishers. An accident caused the delay, and is responsible for what might else have seemed a tardy notice of the first effort of an original writer.

There can be no question but that *Jane Eyre* is a very clever book. Indeed it is a book of decided power. The thoughts are true, sound, and original; and the style, though rude and uncultivated here and there, is resolute, straightforward, and to the purpose. There are faults, which we may advert to presently; but there are also many beauties, and the object and moral of the work is excellent. Without being professedly didactic, the writer's intention (amongst other things) seems to be, to show how intellect and unswerving integrity may win their way, although oppressed by that predominating influence in society which is a mere consequence of the accidents of birth or fortune. There are, it is true, in this autobiography (which though relating to a woman, we do not believe to have been written by a woman), struggles, and throes, and misgivings, such as must necessarily occur in a contest where the advantages are all on one side; but in the end, the honesty, kindness of heart, and perseverance of the heroine, are seen triumphant over every obstacle. We confess that we like an author who throws himself into the front of the battle, as the champion of the weaker party; and when this is followed up by bold and skilful soldiership, we are compelled to yield him our respect.

Whatever faults may be urged against the book, no one can assert that it is weak or vapid. It is anything but a fashionable novel. It has not a Lord Fanny for its hero, nor a Duchess for its pattern of nobility. The scene of action is never in Belgrave or Grosvenor Square. The pages are scant of French and void of Latin. We hear nothing of Madame Maradan; we scent nothing of the bouquet de la Reine. On the contrary, the heroine is cast amongst the thorns and brambles of life;–an orphan; without money, without beauty, without friends; thrust into a starving charity school; and fighting her way as governess, with few accomplishments. The hero, if so he may be called, is (or becomes) middle-aged, mutilated, blind, stern, and wilful. The sentences are of simple English; and the only fragrance that we encounter is that of the common garden flower, or the odour of Mr. Rochester's cigar.

Taken as a novel or history of events, the book is obviously defective; but as an analysis of a single mind, as an elucidation of its progress from childhood to full age, it may claim comparison with any work of the same species. It is not a book to be examined, page by page, with the fictions of Sir Walter Scott or Sir Edward Lytton or Mr Dickens, from which (except in passages of character where the instant impression reminds us often of the power of the latter writer) it differs altogether. It should rather be placed by the side of the autobiographies of Godwin and his successors, and its comparative value may be then reckoned up, without fear or favour. There is less eloquence, or rather there is less rhetoric, and perhaps less of that subtle analysis of the inner human history, than the author of *Fleetwood* and *Mandeville* was in the habit of exhibiting; but there is, at the same time, more graphic power, more earnest human purpose, and a more varied and vivid portraiture of men and things.

The danger, in a book of this kind, is that the author, from an extreme love of his subject, and interest in the investigation of human motives, may pursue his analysis beyond what is consistent with the truth and vitality of his characters. In every book of fiction, the reader expects to meet with animated beings, complete in their structure, and active and mingling with the world; and he will accordingly reject a tale as spurious if he finds that the author, in his love of scientific research, has been merely putting together a metaphysical puzzle, when he should have been breathing into the nostrils of a living man.

The writer of *Jane Eyre* has in a great measure steered clear of this error (by no means altogether avoiding it), and the book is the better for it. But it is time to introduce the reader a little into the secrets of the story. . . .

We like the few fashionable characters that are introduced into the book less than those of humble pretensions. Lady Ingram's deference and mode of address to her daughter, the proud Lady Blanche, strike us as improbable. The treatment, however, by the high-born ladies of the poor governess is cleverly described; and altogether we can consistently recommend the reader to consult the three volumes which comprise the autobiography of Jane Eyre, at his earliest leisure, and to place them among his choicest favourites.

    The Examiner (27 November 1847): 756–757

* * *

In a 17 November 1847 letter to Willams, Brontë wrote that this unsigned review "gave me much pleasure." Excerpts.

"No Woman's Writing" Review of *Jane Eyre*

This is an extraordinary book. Although a work of fiction, it is no mere novel, for there is nothing but nature and truth about it, and its interest is entirely domestic; neither is it like your familiar writings, that are too close to reality. There is nothing morbid, nothing vague, nothing improbable about the story of Jane Eyre; at the same time it lacks neither the odour of romance nor the hue of sentiment. On the other hand, we are not taken to vulgar scenes, and made acquainted with low mysteries. We have no high life glorified, caricatured, or libelled; nor low life elevated to an enviable state of bliss; neither have we vice made charming. The story is, therefore, unlike all that we have read, with very few exceptions; and for power of thought and expression, we do not know its rival among modern productions. Bulwer, James, D'Israeli, and all the serious novel writers of the day lose in comparison with Currer Bell, for we must presume the work to be his. It is no woman's writing. Although ladies have written histories, and travels, and warlike novels, to say nothing of books upon the different arts and sciences, no woman *could have* penned the 'Autobiography of Jane Eyre.' It is all that one of the other sex might invent, and much more, and reminds us of *Caleb Stukeley, Ten Thousand a Year,* and one or two domestic novels that have come out in strong relief within these few years. The tale is one of the heart, and the working out of a moral through the natural affections; it is the victory of mind over matter; the mastery of reason over feeling, without unnatural sacrifices. The writer dives deep into human life, and possesses the gift of being able to write as he thinks and feels. There is a vigour in all he says, a power which fixes the reader's attention, and a charm about his 'style and diction' which fascinates while it edifies. His pictures are like the Cartoons of Raphael. The figures are not elaborately executed, but true, bold, well-defined, and full of life—struck off by an artist who embodies his imaginings in a touch. . . .

The apt, eloquent, elegant, and yet easy mode by which the writer engages you, is something altogether out of the common way. He fixes you at the commencement, and there is no flagging on his part—no getting away on your's—till the end. You discover, in every chapter, that you are not simply amused, not only interested, not merely excited, but you are improved; you are receiving a delightful and comprehensible lesson, and you put down the volume with the consciousness of having benefited by its perusal. Such a work has no ordinary attractions, and it will be found that we have not overdrawn them. There is much to ponder over, rejoice over, and weep over, in its ably-written pages . . . The obvious moral thought is, that laws, both human and divine, approved in our calmer moments, are not to be disobeyed when our time of trial comes, however singular the 'circumstances' under which we are tempted to disregard them; that there is an immaterial world about us, one wherein disobedience is sure to bring punishment; and that although to be truly wise is not, as a certain and immediate consequence, to be truly happy, the practice of simple propriety, founded on strict morality and religious principles, is the sure road to ultimate bliss, and a means of securing many beautiful and encouraging prospects along its borders, however rugged be the journey.

—*Era* (14 November 1847): 9

* * *

George Henry Lewes (1817–1878), author and critic, was an early literary correspondent with Charlotte. In her biography of Brontë, Elizabeth Gaskell quotes Lewes's explanation of how their exchange about literary ideals began: "When 'Jane Eyre' first appeared, the publishers courteously sent me a copy. The enthusiasm with which I read it, made me go down to Mr. Parker, and propose to write a review of it for 'Frazer's Magazine.' He would not consent to an unknown novel—for the papers had not yet declared themselves—receiving such importance, but thought it might make one on Recent Novels: English and French—*which appeared in* Frazer, *December, 1847. Meanwhile I had written to Miss Brontë to tell her the delight with which her book filled me; and seem to have 'sermonized' her, to judge from her reply"* (The Life of Charlotte Brontë, *v. 2, pp. 41–42).*

**Charlotte Brontë to George Henry Lewes,
6 November 1847**

Dear Sir

Your letter reached me yesterday; I beg to assure you that I appreciate fully the intention with which it was written, and I thank you sincerely both for its cheering commendation and valuable advice.

You warn me to beware of Melodrame and you exhort me to adhere to the real. When I first began to write, so impressed was I with the truth of the principles you advocate that I determined to take Nature and Truth as my sole guides and to follow in their very footprints; I restrained imagination, eschewed romance, repressed excitement: over-bright colouring too I avoided, and sought to produce something which should be soft, grave and true.

My work (a tale in I vol.) being completed, I offered it to a publisher. He said it was original, faithful to Nature, but he did not feel warranted in accepting it, such a work would not sell. I tried six publishers in succession; they all told me it was deficient in "startling incident" and "thrilling excitement"; that it would never suit the circulating libraries, and as it was on those libraries the success of works of fiction mainly depended they could not undertake to publish what would be overlooked there—"Jane Eyre" was rather objected to at first [on] the same grounds—but finally found acceptance.

I mention this to you, not with a view of pleading exemption from censure, but in order to direct your attention to the root of certain literary evils—if in your forthcoming article in "Frazer" you would bestow a few words of enlightenment on the public who support the circulating libraries, you might, with your powers, do some good.

You advise me too, not to stray far from the ground of experience as I become weak when I enter the region of fiction; and you say "real experience is perennially interesting and to all men . ."

I feel that this also is true, but, dear Sir, is not the real experience of each individual very limited? and if a writer dwells upon that solely or principally is he not in danger of repeating himself, and also of becoming an egotist?

Then too, Imagination is a strong, restless faculty which claims to be heard and exercised, are we to be quite deaf to her cry and insensate to her struggles? When she shews us bright pictures are we never to look at them and try to reproduce them?—And when she is eloquent and speaks rapidly and urgently in our ear are we not to write to her dictation[?]

I shall anxiously search the next number of "Frazer" for your opinions on these points.

Believe me, dear Sir,
Yours gratefully
C Bell
—*The Letters of Charlotte Brontë*, v. 1,
pp. 559–560

* * *

Photos J. J. Stead.

Norton Conyers,
the Seat of Sir Reginald Graham.

The Rydings, Birstall, and Norton Conyers, near Ripon, make up the Thornfield Hall of "Jane Eyre." The description of the exterior is taken from the former, that of the interior from the latter.

Two views of the Norton Conyers mansion, near Ripon in North Yorkshire. Brontë visited the estate in 1839 and heard the legend of a mad woman who had been kept in its attics (top, frontispiece, J. A. Erskine Stuart, The Brontë Country, *Sam Houston State University; bottom, from* The Bookman, *October 1904).*

These excerpts are from Lewes's unsigned review article that treated Jane Eyre *among other French and English novels.*

"All That We Require in a Novelist"
Review of *Jane Eyre*

After laughing over the *Bachelor of the Albany,* we wept over *Jane Eyre.* This, indeed, is a book after our own heart; and, if its merits have not forced it into notice by the time this paper comes before our readers, let us, in all earnestness, bid them lose not a day in sending for it. The writer is evidently a woman, and, unless we are deceived, new in the world of literature. But, man or woman, young or old, be that as it may, no such book has gladdened our eyes for a long while. Almost all that we require in a novelist she has: perception of character, and power of delineating it; picturesqueness; passion; and knowledge of life. The story is not only of singular interest, naturally evolved, unflagging to the last, but it fastens itself upon your attention, and will not leave you. The book closed, the enchantment continues. With the disentanglement of the plot, and the final release of the heroine from her difficulties, your interest does not cease. You go back again in memory to the various scenes in which she has figured; you linger on the way and muse upon the several incidents in the life which has just been unrolled before you, affected by them as if they were the austere instructions drawn from a sorrowing existence, and not merely the cunning devices of an author's craft. Reality—deep, significant reality—is the great characteristic of the book. It *is* an autobiography,—not, perhaps, in the naked facts and circumstances, but in the actual suffering and experience. The form may be changed, and there some incidents invented; but the spirit remains such as it was. The machinery of the story may have been borrowed, but by means of this machinery, the authoress is unquestionably setting forth her own experience. This gives the book its charm: it is soul speaking to soul; it is an utterance from the depths of a struggling, suffering, much-enduring spirit: *suspiria de profundis!*

When we see a young writer exhibiting such remarkable power as there is in *Jane Eyre,* it is natural that we should ask, Is this experience drawn from an abundant source, or is it only the artistic mastery over small materials? Because, according as this question is answered, there are two suggestions to be made. Has the author seen much more and felt much more than what is here communicated? Then let new works continue to draw from that rich storehouse. Has the author led a quiet, secluded life, uninvolved in the great vortex of the world, undisturbed by varied passions, untried by strange calamities? Then let new works be planned and executed with excessive circumspection; for, unless a novel be built out of real experience, it can have no real success. To have vitality, it must spring from vitality. All the craft in the circulating-library will not make that seem true which is not true—will not affect the reader after his curiosity is satisfied. . . .

. . . we often hear professed novel-readers declare, that however stupid, trashy, and absurd the novel, they must finish it, "to see what becomes of the hero and heroine!" They are compelled to finish; but they never go back to it, never think of it afterwards. Whereas, if to that curiosity about the story there are added scenes which, being transcripts from the book of life, affect the reader as all truth of human nature must affect him, then the novel rises from the poor level of street-conjuring into the exalted regions of art.

Of this kind is *Jane Eyre.* There are some defects in it—defects which the excellence of the rest only brings into stronger relief. There is, indeed, too much melodrama and improbability, which smack of the circulating library,—we allude particularly to the mad wife and all that relates to her, and to the wanderings of Jane when she quits Thornfield; yet even those parts are powerfully executed. But the earlier parts—all those relating to Jane's childhood and her residence at Lowood, with much of the strange love story—are written with remarkable beauty and truth. The characters are few, and drawn with unusual mastery: even those that are but sketched—such as Mr Brockelhurst, Miss Temple, Mrs Fairfax, Rosamond, and Blanche—are sketched with a vividness which betrays a cunning hand: a few strokes, and the figure rises before you. Jane herself is a creation. The delicate handling of this figure alone implies a dramatic genius of no common order. We never lose sight of her plainness; no effort is made to throw romance about her—no extraordinary goodness or cleverness appeals to your admiration; but you admire, you love her,—love her for the strong will, honest mind, loving heart, and peculiar but fascinating person. A creature of flesh and blood, with very fleshly infirmities, and very mortal excellencies; a woman, not a pattern: that is the Jane Eyre here represented. Mr Rochester is also well drawn, and from the life; but it is the portrait of a man drawn by a woman, and is not comparable to the portrait of Jane. The way in which the authoress contrives to keep our interest in this imperfect character is a lesson to novelists. St. John Rivers, the missionary, has a touch of the circulating library, but not enough to spoil the truth of the delineation; there is both art and artifice in the handling, and, although true in the main, and very powerful in parts, one feels a certain misgiving about him; it is another example of the woman's pencil. Helen Burns is lovely and loveable; true, we believe, even in her exalted spirituality and her religious fervour: a character at once eminently ideal and accurately real.

The story is so simple in its outlines, yet so filled out—not spun out—with details, that we shall not do it the injustice of here setting down the mere plot. It is confined to few characters, and is easily, naturally evolved (with exceptions always for those melodramatic incidents before alluded to), carrying the reader on with it to the end. We have spoken of the reality stamped upon almost every part; and that reality is not confined to the characters and incidents, but is also striking in the descriptions of the various aspects of Nature, and of the houses, rooms, and furniture. The pictures stand out distinctly before you: they *are* pictures, and not mere bits of "fine writing." The writer is evidently painting by words a picture that she has in her mind, not "making up" from vague remembrances, and with the consecrated phrases of "poetic prose." It would be exceedingly easy to quote many examples, but we will content ourselves with this very brief passage, strongly characterized by the reality we speak of. It occurs in the third page:—

"Folds of scarlet drapery shut in my view to the right hand; to the left were the clear panes of glass, protecting, but not separating, me from the drear November day. At intervals, while turning over the leaves of my book, I studied the aspect of that winter afternoon. Afar, it offered a pale blank of mist and cloud; near, a scene of wet lawn and storm-beat shrub, with ceaseless rain sweeping away wildly before a long and lamentable blast."

Is not that vivid, real, picturesque? It reads like a page out of one's own life; and so do many other pages of the book.

In her delineation of country-houses and good society there is the ease and accuracy of one who has well known what she describes. We noticed but one slip of the pen, and that was giving to the door of Thornfield Hall a knocker; all the rest is not only accurate, but accurate in being represented from the governess point of view.

This faculty for objective representation is also united to a strange power of subjective representation. We do not simply mean the power over the passions—the psychological intuition of the artist, but the power also of connecting external appearances with internal effects—of representing the psychological interpretation of material phenomena. This is shewn in many a fine description; but we select that of the punished child shut up in the old bed-room, because it exhibits at the same time the power we speak of, and the power before-mentioned of representing the material aspects of things. The passage about the looking-glass, towards the close, strikes us as singularly fine:—

"The red room was a spare chamber, very seldom slept in; I might say never, indeed; unless when a chance influx of visitors to Gateshead Hall, rendered it necessary to turn to account all the accommodation it contained; yet it was one of the largest and stateliest chambers in the mansion. A bed, supported on massive pillars of mahogany, hung with curtains of deep red damask, stood out like a tabernacle in the centre; the two large windows, with their blinds always drawn down, were half shrouded in festoons and falls of similar drapery; the carpet was red; the table at the foot of the bed was covered with a crimson cloth; the walls were a soft fawn colour, with a blush of pink in it, the wardrobe, the toilet-table, the chairs, were of darkly polished old mahogany. Out of these surrounding shades rose high, and glared white, the piled-up mattresses and pillows of the bed, spread with a snowy Marseilles counterpane. Scarcely less prominent was an ample, cushioned, easy chair, near the head of the bed, also white, with a footstool before it, and looking, as I thought, like a pale throne.

"This room was chill, because it seldom had a fire; it was silent, because remote from the nursery and kitchens; solemn, because it was known to be so seldom entered. The housemaid alone came here on Saturdays, to wipe from the mirrors and the furniture a week's quiet dust; and Mrs. Reed herself at far intervals, visited it to review the contents of a certain secret drawer in the wardrobe, where were stored divers parchments, her jewel-casket, and a miniature of her deceased husband; and in those last words lies the secret of the red room; the spell which kept it so lonely in spite of its grandeur.

"Mr. Reed had been dead nine years; it was in this chamber he breathed his last; here he lay in state; hence his coffin was borne by the undertaker's men; and, since that day, a sense of dreary consecration had guarded it from frequent intrusion. My seat, to which Bessie and the bitter Miss Abbot had left me riveted, was a low ottoman near the marble chimneypiece; the bed rose before me; to my right hand there was the high, dark wardrobe, with subdued, broken reflexions varying the gloss of its panels; to my left were the muffled windows; a great looking-glass between them repeated the vacant majesty of the bed and room. I was not quite sure whether they had locked the door; and, when I dared to move, I got up, and went to see. Alas! yes: no jail was ever more secure. Returning, I had to cross before the looking-glass; my fascinated glance involuntarily explored the depth it revealed. All looked colder and darker in that visionary hollow than in reality; and the strange little figure there gazing at me, with a white face and arms specking the gloom, and glittering eyes of fear moving where all else was still, had the effect of a real spirit. I thought it like one of the tiny phantoms, half fairy, half imp, Bessie's evening stories represented as coming up out of lone, ferny dells in moors, and appearing before the eyes of belated travelers. I returned to my stool."

We have no space to go on quoting charming passages, though our pencil has been freely employed in marking them. We have already given enough to make both the authoress and the reader understand what we mean by our praise. To her we emphatically say, Persevere; keep reality distinctly before you, and paint it as accurately as you can: invention will never equal the effect of truth.

The style of *Jane Eyre* is peculiar; but, except that she admits too many Scotch or North-country phrases, we have no objection to make to it, and for this reason: although by no means a fine style, it has the capital point of all great styles in being *personal*,–the written speech of an individual, not the artificial language made up from all sorts of books. . . .

–*Fraser's Magazine*, 36 (December 1847): 690–693

* * *

For the second edition of Jane Eyre, *published in January 1848, Charlotte wrote a preface and dedicated the novel to William Makepeace Thackeray. At the time she did not know of the parallels between* Jane Eyre *and Thackeray's life—especially that, like her character Rochester, Thackeray had a mad wife—and did not foresee that readers might assume that the narrator of* Jane Eyre *was Thackeray's own governess. That Thackeray's novel* Vanity Fair *(1847–1848) also featured a governess, Becky Sharp, added to the unfortunate coincidences between the two writers. Thackeray was not disturbed by the rumors, but Charlotte was embarrassed to have unintentionally added to the gossip surrounding a writer she admired.*

Preface for the Second Edition of *Jane Eyre*
Charlotte Brontë

A preface to the first edition of "Jane Eyre" being unnecessary, I gave none: this second edition demands a few words both of acknowledgment and miscellaneous remark.

My thanks are due in three quarters.

To the Public, for the indulgent ear it has inclined to a plain tale with few pretensions.

To the Press, for the fair field its honest suffrage has opened to an obscure aspirant

To my Publishers, for the aid their tact, their energy, their practical sense, and frank liberality have afforded an unknown and unrecommended Author.

The Press and the Public are but vague personifications for me, and I must thank them in vague terms; but my Publishers are definite: so are certain generous critics who have encouraged me as only large-hearted

and high-minded men know how to encourage a struggling stranger; to them, *i.e.* to my Publishers and the select Reviewers, I say cordially, Gentlemen, I thank you from my heart.

Having thus acknowledged what I owe those who have aided and approved me, I turn to another class; a small one, so far as I know, but not, therefore, to be overlooked. I mean the timorous or carping few who doubt the tendency of such books as "Jane Eyre:" in whose eyes whatever is unusual is wrong; whose ears detect in each protest against bigotry–that parent of crime–an insult to piety, that regent of God on earth. I would suggest to such doubters certain obvious distinctions; I would remind them of certain simple truths.

Conventionality is not morality. Self-righteousness is not religion. To attack the first is not to assail the last. To pluck the mask from the face of the Pharisee, is not to lift an impious hand to the Crown of Thorns.

These things and deeds are diametrically opposed; they are as distinct as is vice from virtue. Men too often confound them; they should not be confounded: appearance should not be mistaken for truth; narrow human doctrines, that only tend to elate and magnify a few, should not be substituted for the world-redeeming creed of Christ. There is–I repeat it–a difference; and it is a good, and not a bad action to mark broadly and clearly the line of separation between them.

The world may not like to see these ideas dissevered, for it has been accustomed to blend them; finding it convenient to make external show pass for sterling worth– to let white-washed walls vouch for clean shrines. It may hate him who dares to scrutinize and expose–to rase the gilding, and show base metal under it–to penetrate the sepulchre, and reveal charnel relics: but hate as it will, it is indebted to him.

Ahab did not like Micaiah, because he never prophesied good concerning him, but evil: probably he liked the sycophant son of Chenaannah better; yet might Ahab have escaped a bloody death, had he but stopped his ears to flattery, and opened them to faithful counsel.

There is a man in our own days whose words are not framed to tickle delicate ears: who, to my thinking, comes before the great ones of society, much as the son of Imlah came before the throned Kings of Judah and Israel; and who speaks truth as deep, with a power as prophet-like and as vital–a mien as dauntless and as daring. Is the satirist of "Vanity Fair" admired in high places? I cannot tell; but I think if some of those amongst whom he hurls the Greek fire of his sarcasm, and over whom he flashes the levin-brand of his denunciation, were to take his warnings in time–they or their seed might yet escape a fatal Ramoth-Gilead.

Why have I alluded to this man? I have alluded to him, Reader, because I think I see in him an intellect pro-

THE VILLAGE OF HATHERSAGE (MORTON).

The likely Derbyshire model for the village of Morton in Jane Eyre. *Charlotte stayed with Ellen Nussey in the Hathersage vicarage in July 1845 and saw the "Eyre" and "Morton" names in the church. Ellen Nussey's brother Henry was vicar of Hathersage (from* Life and Works of the Sisters Brontë, *University of Northern Colorado).*

founder and more unique than his contemporaries have yet recognized; because I regard him as the first social regenerator of the day—as the very master of that working corps who would restore to rectitude the warped system of things; because I think no commentator on his writings has yet found the comparison that suits him, the terms which rightly characterize his talent. They say he is like Fielding: they talk, of his wit, humour, comic powers. He resembles Fielding as an eagle does a vulture: Fielding could stoop on carrion, but Thackeray never does. His wit is bright, his humour attractive, but both bear the same relation to his serious genius, that the mere lambent sheet-lightning playing under the edge of the summer-cloud, does to the electric death-spark hid in its womb. Finally; I have alluded to Mr Thackeray, because to him—if he will accept the tribute of a total stranger—I have dedicated this second edition of "Jane Eyre."

CURRER BELL.
Dec. 21st, 1847.
—pp. vii–xi

* * *

Charlotte corresponded frequently with William Smith Williams, the perceptive and kindly reader at Smith, Elder who first recognized her talent as a writer. Williams sent Charlotte many of the reviews of Jane Eyre *and her later works as they appeared.*

In this excerpt, Brontë refers to the private views expressed by the novelist Julia Kavanagh and the poet and essayist Leigh Hunt.

Charlotte Brontë to William Smith Williams, 4 January 1848

Miss Kavanagh's view of the Maniac coincides with Leigh Hunt's. I agree with them that the character is shocking, but I know that it is but too natural. There is a phase of insanity which may be called moral madness, in which all that is good or even human seems to disappear from the mind and a fiend-nature replaces it. The sole aim and desire of the being thus possessed is to exasperate, to molest, to destroy, and preternatural ingenuity and energy are often exercised to that dreadful end. The aspect in such cases, assimilates with the disposition; all seems demonized. It is true that profound pity ought to be the only sentiment elicited by the view of such degradation, and equally true is it that I have not sufficiently dwelt on that feeling; I have erred in making horror too predominant. Mrs. Rochester indeed lived a sinful life before she was insane, but sin is itself a species of insanity: the truly good behold and compassionate it as such.

"Jane Eyre" has got down into Yorkshire; a copy has even penetrated into this neighbourhood: I saw an elderly clergyman reading it the other day, and had the satisfaction of hearing him exclaim "Why–they have got––School, and Mr–here, I declare! and Miss–(naming the originals of Lowood, Mr. Brocklehurst and Miss Temple) He had known them all: I wondered whether he would recognize the portraits, and was gratified to find that he did and that moreover he pronounced them faithful and just– he said too that Mr–(Brocklehurst) "deserved the chastisement he had got."

He did not recognize "Currer Bell"–What author would be without the advantage of being able to walk invisible? One is thereby enabled to keep such a quiet mind. 'I make this small observation in confidence.'

–*The Letters of Charlotte Brontë*, v. 2, pp. 3–4

* * *

This unsigned review was written for The Christian Remembrancer, *an Anglican periodical that leaned toward the High Church. The reviewer, who begins by citing* Grantey Manor, *the second novel by Lady Georgiana Fullerton (1847), is mistaken in the assertion that other critics had not praised the power of* Jane Eyre. *Excerpts.*

"Moral Jacobinism"
Review of *Jane Eyre*

Since the publication of 'Grantley Manor,' no novel has created so much sensation as 'Jane Eyre.' Indeed, the public taste seems to have outstripped its guides in appreciating the remarkable power which this book displays. For no leading review has yet noticed it, and here we have before us the second edition. The name and sex of the writer are still a mystery. Currer Bell (which by a curious Hibernicism appears in the title-page as the name of a female autobiographer) is a mere *nom de guerre*–perhaps an anagram. However, we, for our part, cannot doubt that the book is written by a female, and, as certain provincialisms indicate, by one from the North of England. Who, indeed, but a woman

could have ventured, with the smallest prospect of success, to fill three octavo volumes with the history of a woman's heart? The hand which drew Juliet and Miranda would have shrunk from such a task. That the book is readable, is to us almost proof enough of the truth of our hypothesis. But we could accumulate evidences to the same effect. Mr. Rochester, the hero of the story, is as clearly the vision of a woman's fancy, as the heroine is the image of a woman's heart. Besides, there are many minor indications of a familiarity with all the mysteries of female life which no man can possess, or would dare to counterfeit. Those who have read Miss Edgeworth's Montem, and know how a lady paints the social nature of boys and the doings of boys' schools, may judge *e converso* what work a man would have made of the girls' school in the first volume of Jane Eyre. Yet we cannot wonder that the hypothesis of a male author should have been started, or that ladies especially should still be rather determined to uphold it. For a book more unfeminine, both in its excellences and defects, it would be hard to find in the annals of female authorship. Throughout there is masculine power, breadth and shrewdness, combined with masculine hardness, coarseness, and freedom of expression. Slang is not rare. The humour is frequently produced by a use of Scripture, at which one is rather sorry to have smiled. The love-scenes glow with a fire as fierce as that of Sappho, and somewhat more fuliginous. There is an intimate acquaintance with the worst parts of human nature, a practised sagacity in discovering the latent ulcer, and a ruthless rigour in exposing it, which must commend our admiration, but are almost startling in one of the softer sex. Jane Eyre professes to be an autobiography, and we think it likely that in some essential respects it is so. If the authoress has not been, like her heroine, an oppressed orphan, a starved and bullied charity-school girl, and a despised and slighted governess (and the intensity of feeling which she shows in speaking of the wrongs of this last class seems to prove that they have been her own), at all events we fear she is one to whom the world has not been kind. And, assuredly, never was unkindness more cordially repaid. Never was there a better hater. Every page burns with moral Jacobinism. 'Unjust, unjust,' is the burden of every reflection upon the things and powers that be. All virtue is but well masked vice, all religious profession and conduct is but the whitening of the sepulchre, all self-denial is but deeper selfishness. In the preface to the second edition, this temper rises to the transcendental pitch. There our authoress is Micaiah, and her generation Ahab; and the Ramoth Gilead, which is to be the reward of disregarding her denunciations, is looked forward to with at least as much of unction as of sorrow. . . .

WYCOLLER HALL (" FERNDEAN MANOR " OF *Jane Eyre*).

Wycoller Hall, Lancashire, eight miles from Haworth, a possible model for "Ferndean Manor" of Jane Eyre (*from Whiteley Turner,*
A Spring-Time Saunter: Round and About Brontë Land, *Sam Houston State University Library*)

We select the following extract as an illustration of our remarks—a specimen at once of extraordinary powers of analyzing character and moral painting, and of a certain want of feeling in their exercises which defeats the moral object and causes a reaction in the mind of the reader like that of a barbarous execution in the mind of the beholder. To render the passage intelligible, it is only necessary to premise that Jane Eyre, the heroine of the tale, is an orphan committed to the care of Mrs. Reed, her aunt, who after maltreating the child till she breaks out into a wild rebellion, sends her to a charity school to live or die as she may. Jane Eyre lives. Aunt Reed is dying, and Jane Eyre is at her bedside. . . .

Here we have a deathbed of unrepentant sin described with as deliberate a minuteness and as serene a tranquillity as a naturalist might display in recording the mortal orgasms of a jelly-fish. It is the despair of Beaufort—the 'He dies and makes no sign,' without the response, 'O God, forgive him!' All the expressions of tenderness and forgiveness, on the part of the injured Jane, are skilfully thrown in so as to set off to the utmost the unconquerable hardness

of the dying sinner's heart. They are the pleadings of the good angel, made audible, and rejected to the last. We are compelled to see and acknowledge beyond the possibility of doubt, that Mrs. Reed dies without remorse, without excuse, and without hope.

The plot is most extravagantly improbable, verging all along upon the supernatural, and at last running fairly into it. All the power is shown and all the interest lies in the characters. We have before intimated our belief, that in Jane Eyre, the heroine of the piece, we have, in some measure, a portrait of the writer. If not, it is a most skilful imitation of autobiography. The character embodied in it is precisely the same as that which pervades the whole book, and breaks out most signally in the Preface—a temper naturally harsh, made harsher by ill usage, and visiting both its defect and its wrongs upon the world—an understanding disturbed and perverted by cynicism, but still strong and penetrating—fierce love and fiercer hate—all this viewed from within and coloured by self-love. We only wish we could carry our hypothesis a step further, and suppose that the triumph which the loving and loveable element finally obtains over the unloving and unloveable in the fictitious character had also its parallel in the true. But we fear that few readers will rise from the book with that impression.

The character of Mr. Rochester, the hero, the lover, and eventually the husband, of Jane Eyre, we have already noticed as being, to our minds, the characteristic production of a female pen. Not an Adonis, but a Hercules in mind and body, with a frame of adamant, a brow of thunder and a lightning eye, a look and voice of command, all-knowing and all-discerning, fierce in love and hatred, rough in manner, rude in courtship, with a shade of Byronic gloom and appetizing mystery—add to this that when loved he is past middle age, and when wedded he is blind and fire-scarred, and you have such an Acis as no male writer would have given his Galatea, and yet what commends itself as a true embodiment of the visions of a female imagination. The subordinate characters almost all show proportionate power. Mr. Brocklehurst, the patron and bashaw of Lowood, a female orphan school, in which he practises self-denial, *alieno ventre,* and exercises a vicarious humility, is a sort of compound of Squeers and Pecksniff, but more probable than either, and drawn with as strong a hand. . . . Mrs. Reed is a good type of the 'strong-minded' and odious woman. Excellent too, in an artistic point of view, is the character of St. John Rivers, the Calvinist clergyman and missionary, with all its complex attributes and iridescent hues—self-denial strangely shot with selfishness—earthly pride and restless ambition blending and alternating with heaven-directed zeal, and resignation to the duties of a heavenly mission. The feeblest character in the book is that of Helen Burns, who is meant to be a perfect Christian, and is a simple seraph, conscious moreover of her own perfection. She dies early in the first volume, and our authoress might say of her saint, as Shakespeare said of his Mercutio, 'If I had not killed her, she would have killed me.' In her, however, the Christianity of Jane Eyre is concentrated, and with her it expires, leaving the world in a kind of Scandinavian gloom, which is hardly broken by the faint glimmerings of a 'doctrine of the equality of souls,' and some questionable streaks of that 'world-redeeming creed of Christ,' which being emancipated from 'narrow human doctrines, that only tend to elate and magnify a few,' is seldom invoked but for the purpose of showing that all Christian profession is bigotry and all Christian practice is hypocrisy.

In imaginative painting Jane Eyre is very good. Take the following—probably from the threshold of the lake country—the neighbourhood of Kirby Lonsdale. . . .

The rather ambitious descriptions of manners and social life which the book contains are, we are bound to say, a most decided failure. Their satire falls back with accumulated force upon the head of the satirist. It is 'high life below stairs' with a vengeance; the fashionable world seen through the area railings, and drawn with the black end of the kitchen poker. . . .

The Novelist is now completely lord of the domain of Fiction. Whatever good or evil is to be done in the present day through that medium, must be done by him. He is the only dramatist whose plays can now command an audience. He is the only troubadour who finds admittance into the carpeted and cushioned halls of our modern chivalry, and arrests the ear of the lords and ladies of the nineteenth century. His work is the mirror of our life. It is the Odyssey and the Niebelungen Lied under a strange form: but still it is them indeed. Man's appetites do not change, nor his faculties, but only the external conditions under which they act; and the same appetites, the same faculties, which under one set of external conditions gave birth to Achilles, under another set give birth to Waverley or Pelham; who is to the reading gentleman what the son of Thetis was to the listening Greek—himself made perfect. . . .

Our object in this somewhat rambling digression has been to show what responsibility rests upon the novelists of our day—a reflection which we beg to suggest to the authoress of Jane Eyre. With them it rests to determine, each for himself and according to the measure of his gifts, whether so powerful an instrument of moving men, as fiction is, shall be used to move them for good or evil. Are the poetic and artistic faculties given to man purely for his amusement? Are they alone of all his powers not subject in their exercise to the legislative or judicial conscience. Curiously enough, we believe no moral philosopher has yet given a complete scientific answer to this question. A philosophical account of that part of man's essence which is neither moral nor intellectual, but lies midway between the two, both in itself and in its relation to the moral and intellectual parts, would we believe still be an addition to Moral Science. . . . We do not mean to say that the writer of fiction is called upon to play the part of the preacher or theologian. Far from it. What he is called upon to do is to hold up a clear and faithful mirror to human nature—a mirror in which it shall see its good as good, its evil as evil. His pages must give back the true reflection of a world of which morality is the law, and into which Christianity has entered.

The tendency of English novelists seems happily to be at present in the right direction. Within the last fifteen years, common sense, at any rate, has achieved some victories in our literature. Shakespeare has shone forth again, and Byron labours in eclipse. No heads, we believe, but those of shopboys and farmers' daughters, are now in danger of being turned by Lytton Bulwer. *That* Upas tree is pretty well withered up by contempt and ridicule in this country, though it still flourishes with rank luxuriance in the congenial soil of France. Dumas, Sue, and George Sand are, indeed, read by us, as well as by their own countrymen; but then we read them for the story, and laugh at the sentiment, which a Frenchman swallows as the word of life. The belief that the pen of a west-end Adonis could regenerate society, without the tedious process of repentance and self-government, is passing away with the last great men of that heroic age which produced the National Gallery and the Reform Bill. The religion which teaches that to sin is the indifferent-best way to save your soul, and that to prostitution in the higher classes much will be forgiven, has day by day fewer symbolical writings and fewer prophets in the land. Whether another and a more fatal humbug may not succeed, and whether a certain phase of the religious novel may not prove that humbug, remains to be seen. But at present a better influence reigns in the whole world of fiction, poetry, and art; and everywhere men who work by the rules of sense and truth, the Christian architect and the Christian writer, are slowly gaining ground, and seem likely—unless their course is crossed by some convulsion of society such as the last month has taught us to consider possible—to make rubble of the chimney-potted Parthenon and waste paper of the Satanic novel.

What would be the fate of the authoress whose work we are now reviewing, should that happy consummation be brought to pass, must be considered as doubtful. To say that 'Jane Eyre' is positively immoral or antichristian, would be to do its writer an injustice. Still it wears a questionable aspect. The choice is still to be made, and he who should determine it aright would do literature and society some service. The authoress of 'Jane Eyre' will have power in her generation, whether she choose to exercise it for good or evil. She has depth and breadth of thought—she has something of that peculiar gift of genius, the faculty of discerning the wonderful in and through the commonplace—she has a painter's eye and hand—she has great satiric power, and, in spite of some exaggerated and morbid cynicism, a good fund of common sense. To this common sense we would appeal. Let her take care that while she detects and exposes humbug in other minds, she does not suffer it to gain dominion in her own. Let her take warning, if she will, from Mr. Thackeray, to whom she dedicates her second edition, whom she thinks 'the first social regenerator of the day,' and whose 'Greek-fire sarcasm' and 'levin-brand denunciation' she overwhelms with such extravagant panegyric. Let her mark how, while looking every where for 'Snobs' to denounce, he has himself fallen into one, and not the least vicious, phase of that very character which he denounces. Or let her seek a more signal and ominous example in the history of that far higher mind which, after demolishing innumerable 'shams,' has itself, for want of a real faith of its own, sunk into the mournfullest sham of all. Let her reconsider her preface, and see how conventional may be the denouncer of conventionality, how great an idol the iconoclast may leave unbroken in himself. Let her cease, if she can, to think of herself as Micaiah, and of society as Ahab. Let her be a little more trustful of the reality of human goodness, and a little less anxious to detect its alloy of evil. She will lose nothing in piquancy, and gain something in healthiness and truth. We shall look with some anxiety for that second effort which is proverbially decisive of a writer's talent, and which, in this case, will probably be decisive of the moral question also.

—*The Christian Remembrancer,* 15 (April 1848): 396–409

* * *

The confusion caused by three novels by the "Bell brothers" appearing within a few months of each other in the last three months of 1847 led to speculation that the Bells' names were in fact multiple pen names for just one writer. Charlotte asserted that she was the author only of Jane Eyre *in this note.*

Note to the Third Edition
Charlotte Brontë

I avail myself of the opportunity which a third edition of 'Jane Eyre' affords me, of again addressing a word to the public, to explain that my claim to the title of novelist rests on this one work alone. If, therefore, the authorship of other works of fiction has been attributed to me, an honour is awarded where it is not merited; and consequently, denied where it is justly due.

This explanation will serve to rectify mistakes which may already have been made, and to prevent future errors.

CURRER BELL.

April 13th, 1848.

* * *

Mary Taylor, who set up a shop in the settlement of Wellington, New Zealand, and made enough money to return to England in 1860 and live independently for the remainder of her life. Most of her correspondence with Charlotte was destroyed (from Juliet Barker, The Brontës, *Thomas Cooper Library, University of South Carolina).*

Mary Taylor (1817–1893), who was a correspondent of both Charlotte Brontë and Ellen Nussey after their friendship began at Miss Wooler's School, immigrated to New Zealand in March 1845. After teaching in Germany, she decided not to pursue the few options open to educated women who needed to support themselves in England. Excerpts.

Mary Taylor to Charlotte Brontë, June–24 July 1848

Dear Charlotte

About a month since I received and read *Jane Eyre*. It seemed to me incredible that you had actually written a book. Such events did not happen while I was in England. I begin to believe in your existence much as I do in Mr Rochester's. In a believing mood I don't doubt either of them. After I had read it I went on to the top of Mt. Victoria and looked for a ship to carry a letter to you. . . .

Your novel surprised me by being so perfect as a work of art. I expected something more changeable and unfinished. You have polished to some purpose. If I were to do so I should get tired and weary every one else in about two pages. No sign of this weariness is in your book—you must have had abundance, having kept it all to yourself!

You are very different from me in having no doctrine to preach. It is impossible to squeeze a moral out of your production. Has the world gone so well with you that you have no protest to make against its absurdities? Did you never sneer or declaim in your first sketches? I will scold you well when I see you.—I don't believe in Mr Rivers. There are no *good* men of the Brocklehurst species. A missionary either goes into his office for a piece of bread, or he goes from enthusiasm, and that is both too good and too bad a quality for St. John. It's a bit of your absurd charity to believe in such a man. You have done wisely in choosing to imagine a high class of readers. You never stop to explain or defend anything and never seem bothered with the idea—if Mrs Fairfax or any other well intentioned fool gets hold of this what will she think? And yet you know the world is made up of such, and worse. Once more, how have you written through 3 vols. without declaring war to the knife against a few dozen absurd do[ct]rines each of which is supported by "a large and respectable class of readers"? Emily seems to have had such a class in her eye when she wrote that strange thing Wuthering Heights. Ann too stops repeatedly to preach commonplace truths. She has had a still lower class in her mind's eye. Emily seems to have followed th[e b]ookseller's advice. As to the price you got it [was] certainly Jewish. But what could the people do? If they had asked you to fix it, do you know yourself how many cyphers your sum would have had? And how should they know better? And if they did, that's the knowledge they get their living by. If I were in your place the idea of being bound in the sale of 2! more would prevent from ever writing again. Yet you are probably now busy with another. It is curious to me to see among the old letters one from A. Sarah sending a *copy of* a *whole article* on the currency question written by Fonblanque! I exceedingly regret having burnt your letters in a fit of caution, and I've forgotten all the names. Was the reader Albert Smith? What do they all think of you? I perceive I've betrayed my habit of writing only on one side of the paper. Go on to the next page.

I mention the book to no one and hear no opinions. I lend it a good deal because it's a novel and it's *as good as another!* They say "it makes them cry." They are not literary enough to give an opinion. If ever I hear one I'll embalm it for you.

    —*Mary Taylor: Friend of Charlotte Brontë,* pp. 132–133

* * *

Rochester and Jane Eyre (from Life and Works of the Sisters Brontë, *University of Northern Colorado)*

The first American edition of Charlotte Brontë's Jane Eyre, *published in January 1848, was followed that year by American editions of two of her sisters' novels, Emily's* Wuthering Heights *in April and Anne's* The Tenant of Wildfell Hall *in July. This excerpt, from an unsigned article titled "Novels of the Season" that appeared in one of the most respected literary periodicals in the United States, provides an example of the speculation about the authorship of the Brontës' novels. The reviewer was the essayist and critic Edwin P. Whipple.*

"The Marks of More than One Mind and One Sex" Review of *Jane Eyre*

The first three novels on our list are those which have proceeded from the firm of Bell & Co. Not many months ago, the New England States were visited by a distressing mental epidemic, passing under the name of the "Jane Eyre fever," which defied all the usual nostrums of the established doctors of criticism. Its effects varied with different constitutions, in some producing a soft ethical sentimentality, which relaxed all the fibres of conscience, and in others exciting a general fever of moral and religious indignation. It was to no purpose that the public were solemnly assured, through the intelligent press, that the malady was not likely to have any permanent effect either on the intellectual or moral constitution. The book which caused the distemper would probably have been inoffensive, had not some sly manufacturer of mischief hinted that it was a book which no respectable man should bring into his family circle. Of course, every family soon had a copy of it, and one edition after another found eager purchasers. The hero, Mr. Rochester, (not the same person who comes to so edifying an end in the pages of Dr. Gilbert

Burnet,) became a great favorite in the boarding-schools and in the worshipful society of governesses. That portion of Young America known as ladies' men began to swagger and swear in the presence of the gentler sex, and to allude darkly to events in their lives which excused impudence and profanity.

While fathers and mothers were much distressed at this strange conduct of their innocents, and with a pardonable despair were looking for the dissolution of all the bonds of society, the publishers of Jane Eyre announced Wuthering Heights, by the same author. When it came, it was purchased and read with universal eagerness; but, alas! it created disappointment almost as universal. It was a panacea for all the sufferers under the epidemic. Society returned to its old condition, parents were blessed in hearing once more their children talk common sense, and rakes and battered profligates of high and low degree fell instantly to their proper level. Thus ended the last desperate attempt to corrupt the virtue of the sturdy descendants of the Puritans.

The novel of Jane Eyre, which caused this great excitement, purports to have been edited by Currer Bell, and the said Currer divides the authorship, if we are not misinformed, with a brother and sister. The work bears the marks of more than one mind and one sex, and has more variety than either of the novels which claim to have been written by Acton Bell. The family mind is strikingly peculiar, giving a strong impression of unity, but it is still male and female. From the masculine tone of Jane Eyre, it might pass altogether as the composition of a man, were it not for some unconscious feminine peculiarities, which the strongest-minded woman that ever aspired after manhood cannot suppress. These peculiarities refer not only to elaborate descriptions of dress, and the minutiae of the sick-chamber, but to various superficial refinements of feeling in regard to the external relations of the sex. It is true that the noblest and best representations of female character have been produced by men; but there are niceties of thought and emotion in a woman's mind which no man can delineate, but which often escape unawares from a female writer. There are numerous examples of these in Jane Eyre. The leading characteristic of the novel, however, and the secret of its charm, is the clear, distinct, decisive style of its representation of character, manners, and scenery; and this continually suggests a male mind. In the earlier chapters, there is little, perhaps, to break the impression that we are reading the autobiography of a powerful and peculiar female intellect; but when the admirable Mr. Rochester appears, and the profanity, brutality, and slang of the misanthropic profligate give their torpedo shocks to the nervous system,—and especially when we are favored with more than one scene given to the exhibition of mere animal appetites,

and to courtship after the manner of kangaroos and the heroes of Dryden's plays,—we are gallant enough to detect the hand of a gentleman in the composition. There are also scenes of passion, so hot, emphatic, and condensed in expression, and so sternly masculine in feeling, that we are almost sure we observe the mind of the author of Wuthering Heights at work in the text.

—*The North American Review,* 67 (October 1848): pp. 355–357

* * *

This excerpt from an article titled "Vanity Fair—and Jane Eyre" *is preceded by a plot summary of Brontë's novel. The anonymous reviewer is Elizabeth Rigby, who as Lady Eastlake became the first woman to serve as regular contributor to* The Quarterly Review. *She compares Thackeray's heroine Becky Sharpe to Jane Eyre. According to her publisher George Smith, Brontë was quite unconscious that her novel should be considered immoral and "was as much surprised as affronted" by this review.*

"An Anti-Christian Composition"
Review of *Jane Eyre*

Such is the outline of a tale in which, combined with great materials for power and feeling, the reader may trace gross inconsistencies and improbabilities, and chief and foremost that highest moral offence a novel writer can commit, that of making an unworthy character interesting in the eyes of the reader. Mr. Rochester is a man who deliberately and secretly seeks to violate the laws both of God and man, and yet we will be bound half our lady readers are enchanted with him for a model of generosity and honour. We would have thought that such a hero had had no chance, in the purer taste of the present day; but the popularity of Jane Eyre is a proof how deeply the love for illegitimate romance is implanted in our nature. Not that the author is strictly responsible for this. Mr. Rochester's character is tolerably consistent. He is made as coarse and as brutal as can in all conscience be required to keep our sympathies at a distance. In point of literary consistency the hero is at all events impugnable, though we cannot say as much for the heroine.

As to Jane's character—there is none of that harmonious unity about it which made little Becky so grateful a subject of analysis—nor are the discrepancies of that kind which have their excuse and their response in our nature. The inconsistencies of Jane's character lie mainly not in her own imperfections, though of course she has her share, but in the author's. There is that confusion in the relations between cause and effect, which is not so much untrue to human nature as to human art. The error in Jane Eyre is, not that her character is this or that, but that she is made one thing in the eyes of her imaginary companions, and another in that of the actual reader. There is a perpetual disparity between the account she herself gives of the effect she produces, and the means shown us by which she brings that effect about. We hear nothing but self-eulogiums on the perfect tact and wondrous penetration with which she is gifted, and yet almost every word she utters offends us, not only with the absence of these qualities, but with the positive contrasts of them, in either her pedantry, stupidity, or gross vulgarity. She is one of those ladies who put us in the unpleasant predicament of undervaluing their very virtues for dislike of the person in whom they are represented. One feels provoked as Jane Eyre stands before us—for in the wonderful reality of her thoughts and descriptions, she seems accountable for all done in her name—with principles you must approve in the main, and yet with language and manners that offend you in every particular. Even in that *chef-d'oeuvre* of brilliant retrospective sketching, the description of her early life, it is the childhood and not the child that interests you. The little Jane, with her sharp eyes and dogmatic speeches, is a being you neither could fondle nor love. There is a hardness in her infantine earnestness, and a spiteful precocity in her reasoning, which repulses all our sympathy. One sees that she is of a nature to dwell upon and treasure up every slight and unkindness, real or fancied, and such natures we know are surer than any others to meet with plenty of this sort of thing. As the child, so also the woman—an uninteresting, sententious, pedantic thing; with no experience of the world, and yet with no simplicity or freshness in its stead. . . .

. . . Coarse as Mr. Rochester is, one winces for him under the infliction of this housemaid *beau idéal* of the arts of coquetry. A little more, and we should have flung the book aside to lie for ever among the trumpery with which such scenes ally it; but it were a pity to have halted here, for wonderful things lie beyond—scenes of suppressed feeling, more fearful to witness than the most violent tornados of passion—struggles with such intense sorrow and suffering as it is sufficient misery to know that any one should have conceived, far less passed through; and yet with that stamp of truth which takes precedence in the human heart before actual experience. The flippant, fifth-rate, plebeian actress has vanished, and only a noble, high-souled woman, bound to us by the reality of her sorrow, and yet raised above us by the strength of her will, stands in actual life before us. If this be Jane Eyre, the author has done her injustice hitherto, not we. Let us look at her in the first recognition of her sorrow after the discomfiture of the marriage. True, it is not the attitude of a Christian, who

From a Drawing by J. H. Bacon.   **Jane Eyre and St. John Rivers.**
"'Young woman, rise, and pass before me into the house.'
"With difficulty I obeyed him. Presently I stood within that clean, bright kitchen—on the very hearth—trembling, sickening; conscious of an aspect in the last degree ghastly, wild, and weather-beaten. The two ladies, their brother, Mr. St. John, the old servant, were all gazing at me.
"'St. John, who is it?' I heard one ask."—"Jane Eyre."
(Reproduced from "Jane Eyre," by kind permission of Messrs. Blackie and Son, Ltd.)

(from The Bookman, *October 1904)*

knows that all things work together for good to those who love God, but it is a splendidly drawn picture of a natural heart, of high power, intense feeling, and fine religious instinct, falling prostrate, but not grovelling, before the tremendous blast of sudden affliction. . . .

We have said that this was the picture of a natural heart. This, to our view, is the great and crying mischief of the book. Jane Eyre is throughout the personification of an unregenerate and undisciplined spirit, the more dangerous to exhibit from that prestige of principle and self-control which is liable to dazzle the eye too much for it to observe the inefficient and unsound foundation on which it rests. It is true Jane does right, and exerts great moral strength, but it is the strength of a mere heathen mind which is a law unto itself. No Christian grace is perceptible upon her. She has inherited in fullest mea-

than it is repudiated by her heart. It is by her own talents, virtues, and courage that she is made to attain the summit of human happiness, and, as far as Jane Eyre's own statement is concerned, no one would think that she owed anything either to God above or to man below. She flees from Mr. Rochester, and has not a being to turn to. Why was this? The excellence of the present institution at Casterton, which succeeded that of Cowan Bridge near Kirkby Lonsdale—these being distinctly, as we hear, the original and the reformed Lowoods of the book—is pretty generally known. Jane had lived there for eight years with 110 girls and fifteen teachers. Why had she formed no friendships among them? Other orphans have left the same and similar institutions, furnished with friends for life, and puzzled with homes to choose from. How comes it that Jane had acquired neither? Among that number of associates there were surely some exceptions to what she so presumptuously stigmatises as 'the society of inferior minds.' Of course it suited the author's end to represent the heroine as utterly destitute of the common means of assistance, in order to exhibit both her trials and her powers of self-support—the whole book rests on this assumption—but it is one which, under the circumstances, is very unnatural and very unjust.

Altogether the auto-biography of Jane Eyre is pre-eminently an anti-Christian composition. There is throughout it a murmuring against the comforts of the rich and against the privations of the poor, which, as far as each individual is concerned, is a murmuring against God's appointment—there is a proud and perpetual assertion of the rights of man, for which we find no authority either in God's word or in God's providence—there is that pervading tone of ungodly discontent which is at once the most prominent and the most subtle evil which the law and the pulpit, which all civilized society in fact has at the present day to contend with. We do not hesitate to say that the tone of mind and thought which has overthrown authority and violated every code human and divine abroad, and fostered Chartism and rebellion at home, is the same which has also written Jane Eyre.

Still we say again this is a very remarkable book. We are painfully alive to the moral, religious, and literary deficiencies of the picture, and such passages of beauty and power as we have quoted cannot redeem it, but it is impossible not to be spellbound with the freedom of the touch. It would be mere hackneyed courtesy to call it 'fine writing.' It bears no impress of being written at all, but is poured out rather in the heat and hurry of an instinct, which flows ungovernably on to its object, indifferent by what means it reaches it, and unconscious too. As regards the author's chief object, however, it is a failure—that, namely, of making a plain, odd woman, desti-

sure the worst sin of our fallen nature—the sin of pride. Jane Eyre is proud, and therefore she is ungrateful too. It pleased God to make her an orphan, friendless, and penniless—yet she thanks nobody, and least of all Him, for the food and raiment, the friends, companions, and instructors of her helpless youth—for the care and education vouchsafed to her till she was capable in mind as fitted in years to provide for herself. On the contrary, she looks upon all that has been done for her not only as her undoubted right, but as falling far short of it. The doctrine of humility is not more foreign to her mind

tute of all the conventional features of feminine attraction, interesting in our sight. We deny that he has succeeded in this. Jane Eyre, in spite of some grand things about her, is a being totally uncongenial to our feelings from beginning to end. We acknowledge her firmness—we respect her determination—we feel for her struggles; but, for all that, and setting aside higher considerations, the impression she leaves on our mind is that of a decidedly vulgar-minded woman—one whom we should not care for as an acquaintance, whom we should not seek as a friend, whom we should not desire for a relation, and whom we should scrupulously avoid for a governess.

There seem to have arisen in the novel-reading world some doubts as to who really wrote this book; and various rumours, more or less romantic, have been current in Mayfair, the metropolis of gossip, as to the authorship. For example, Jane Eyre is sentimentally assumed to have proceeded from the pen of Mr. Thackeray's governess, whom he had himself chosen as his model of Becky, and who, in mingled love and revenge, personified him in return as Mr. Rochester. In this case, it is evident that the author of 'Vanity Fair,' whose own pencil makes him grey-haired, has had the best of it, though his children may have had the worst, having, at all events, succeeded in hitting that vulnerable point in the Becky bosom, which it is our firm belief no man born of woman, from her Soho to her Ostend days, had ever so much as grazed. To this ingenious rumour the coincidence of the second edition of Jane Eyre being dedicated to Mr. Thackeray has probably given rise. For our parts, we see no great interest in the question at all. The first edition of Jane Eyre purports to be edited by Currer Bell, one of a trio of brothers, or sisters, or cousins, by names Currer, Acton, and Ellis Bell, already known as the joint-authors of a volume of poems. The second edition the same—dedicated, however, 'by the author,' to Mr. Thackeray; and the dedication (itself an indubitable *chip* of Jane Eyre) signed Currer Bell. Author and editor therefore are one, and we are as much satisfied to accept this double individual under the name of 'Currer Bell,' as under any other, more or less euphonious. Whoever it be, it is a person who, with great mental powers, combines a total ignorance of the habits of society, a great coarseness of taste, and a heathenish doctrine of religion. And as these characteristics appear more or less in the writings of all three, Currer, Acton, and Ellis alike, for their poems differ less in degree of power than in kind, we are ready to accept the fact of their identity or of their relationship with equal satisfaction. At all events there can be no interest attached to the writer of 'Wuthering Heights'—a novel succeeding 'Jane Eyre,' and purporting to be written by Ellis Bell—unless it were for the sake of more individual reprobation. For though there is a decided family likeness between the two, yet the aspect of the Jane and Rochester

animals in their native state, as Catherine and Heathfield, is too odiously and abominably pagan to be palatable even to the most vitiated class of English readers. With all the unscrupulousness of the French school of novels it combines that repulsive vulgarity in the choice of its vice which supplies its own antidote. The question of authorship, therefore, can deserve a moment's curiosity only as far as 'Jane Eyre' is concerned, and though we cannot pronounce that it appertains to a real Mr. Currer Bell and to no other, yet that it appertains to a man, and not, as many assert, to a woman, we are strongly inclined to affirm. Without entering into the question whether the power of the writing be above her, or the vulgarity below her, there are, we believe, minutiae of circumstantial evidence which at once acquit the feminine hand. No woman—a lady friend, whom we are always happy to consult, assures us—makes mistakes in her own *métier*—no woman *trusses game* and garnishes dessert-dishes with the same hands, or talks of so doing in the same breath. Above all, no woman attires another in such fancy dresses as Jane's ladies assume—Miss Ingram coming down, irresistible, 'in a *morning* robe of sky-blue crape, a gauze azure scarf twisted in her hair!!' No lady, we understand, when suddenly roused in the night, would think of hurrying on '*a frock.*' They have garments more convenient for such occasions, and more becoming too. This evidence seems incontrovertible. Even granting that these incongruities were purposely assumed; for the sake of disguising the female pen, there is nothing gained; for if we ascribe the book to a woman at all, we have no alternative but to ascribe it to one who has, for some sufficient reason, long forfeited the society of her own sex.

And if by no woman, it is certainly also by no artist. The Thackeray eye has had no part there. There is not more disparity between the art of drawing Jane assumes and her evident total ignorance of its first principles, than between the report she gives of her own character and the conclusions we form for ourselves. Not but what, in another sense, the author may be classed as an artist of very high grade. Let him describe the simplest things in nature—a rainy landscape, a cloudy sky, or a bare moorside, and he shows the hand of a master; but the moment he talks of the art itself, it is obvious that he is a complete ignoramus.

We cannot help feeling that this work must be far from beneficial to that class of ladies whose cause it affects to advocate. Jane Eyre is not precisely the mouthpiece one would select to plead the cause of governesses, and it is therefore the greater pity that she has chosen it. . . .

—The Quarterly Review, 84 (December 1848): 166–176

Shirley

Charlotte Brontë began writing Shirley *in early 1848, after Smith, Elder rejected her idea to revise* The Professor *into three volumes. Set in 1811–1812,* Shirley *incorporated political and cultural events, especially the destruction of labor-saving machinery by workers—the so-called Luddite protest—in Yorkshire, that Charlotte researched in back issues of the* Leeds Mercury. *With a host of characters and several subplots, the novel focuses primarily on four persons: two brothers, Robert Gerard Moore, a mill owner, and Louis Moore, a tutor, and two female main characters, the rector's daughter Caroline Helstone and the wealthy heiress Shirley Keeldar, who moves to the area to take over a family property. The independent and energetic Shirley contrasts with the more conventional Caroline; the novel concludes with the marriages of Caroline and Robert Moore and Shirley and Louis Moore. As in all of her writing, Charlotte also drew on her own experience—for example, using members of Mary Taylor's family, whom she had visited when she and Mary were students together, for the Yorkes of the novel.*

In this excerpt Nussey traces the origins of Charlotte's second novel back to her school days at Miss Wooler's school at Roe Head.

"The Germ" of *Shirley*
Ellen Nussey

It was while Charlotte was at school that she imbibed the germ of many of those characters which she afterwards produced in *Shirley;* but no one could have imagined that, in the unceasing industry of her daily applications, she was receiving any kind of impress external to her school-life.

She was particularly impressed with the goodness and saintliness of one of Miss W.'s guests,—the Miss Ainley of *Shirley,* long since gone to her rest. The character is not of course a literal portrait, for the very reasons Charlotte herself gave. She said, "You are not to suppose any of the characters in *Shirley* intended as literal portraits. It would not suit the rules of art nor of my own feelings to write in that style. We only suffer reality to *suggest,* never to *dictate.* Qualities I have seen, loved, and admired, are here and there put in as decorative gems, to be preserved in that setting." I may remark here that nothing angered Charlotte more, than for any one to suppose they could not be in her society without incurring the risk of "being put in her books." She always stoutly maintained she never thought of persons in this light when she was with them.

In the seldom recurring holidays Charlotte made sometimes short visits with those of her companions whose homes were within reach of school. Here she made acquaintance with the scenes and

---

"Something about the 'Condition of Women'"

In the postscript to her 12 May 1848 letter to William Smith Williams, Charlotte Brontë discussed what developed into a major theme in Shirley—*the lack of useful occupations for women.*

I must, after all, add a morsel of paper—for I find—on glancing over yours that I have forgotten to answer a question you ask respecting my next work—I have not therein so far treated of governesses, as I do not wish it to resemble its predecessor. I often wish to say something about the "condition of women" question—but it is one respecting which so much "cant" has been talked, that one feels a sort of repugnance to approach it. It is true enough that the present market for female labour is quite overstocked—but where or how could another be opened? Many say that the professions now filled only by men should be open to women also—but are not their present occupants and candidates more than numerous enough to answer every demand? Is there any room for female lawyers, female doctors, female engravers, for more female artists, more authoresses? One can see where the evil lies—but who can point out the remedy? When a woman has a little family to rear and educate and a houshold to conduct, her hands are full, her vocation is evident—when her destiny isolates her—I suppose she must do what she can—live as she can—complain as little—bear as much—work as well as possible. This is not high theory—but I believe it is sound practice—good to put into execution while philosophers and legislators ponder over the better ordering of the Social System. At the same time, I conceive that when Patience has done its utmost and Industry its best, whether in the case of Women or Operatives, and when both are baffled and Pain and Want triumphant—the Sufferer is free—is entitled—at last to send up to Heaven any piercing cry for relief—if by that cry he can hope to obtain succour.

—The Letters of Charlotte Brontë, v. 2, p. 66

---

prominent characters of the Luddite period; her father materially helped to fix her impressions, for he had held more than one curacy in the very neighborhood which she describes in *Shirley.* He was present in some of the scenes, an active participator as far as his position permitted. Sometimes on the defensive, sometimes aiding the sufferers, uniting his strength and influence with the Mr. Helstone of *Shirley.* Between these two men there seems to have been in some respects a striking affinity of character which Charlotte was not slow to perceive, and she blended the two into one, though she never personally beheld the original of Mr. Helstone, except once when she was ten years old. He was a man of remarkable vigor and energy, both of mind and will. An absolute disci-

Shirley

Vol. I.

*Chap 1*ˢᵗ

Levitical.

Of late years an abundant shower of curates has fallen upon the North of England: they lie very thick on the hills; every parish has one or more of them; they are young enough to be very active and ought to be doing a great deal of good. But not of late years are we about to speak; we are going back to the beginning of this century; late years — present years are dusty, sunburnt, hot, arid; we will evade the noon, forget it in siesta, pass the midDay in slumber and dream of Dawn.

If you think, from this prelude, that anything like a romance is preparing for you — reader — you never were more mistaken Do you anticipate sentiment and poetry and reverie? Do you expect passion and stimulus and melo-drama? It is

First page of the manuscript for Charlotte Brontë's second novel (from Jane Sellars, Charlotte Brontë, *British Library)*

plinarian, he was sometimes called "Duke Ecclesiastic," a very Wellington in the Church.

Mr. Brontë used to delight in recalling the days he spent in the vicinity of this man. Many a breakfast hour he enlivened by his animated relations of his friend's unflinching courage and dauntless self-reliance,—and how the ignorant and prejudiced population around misunderstood and misrepresented his worthiest deeds. In depicting the Luddite period Charlotte had the power of giving an almost literal description of the scenes then enacted, for, in addition to her father's personal acquaintance with what occurred, she had likewise the aid of authentic records of the eventful time, courteously lent to her by the editors of the *Leeds Mercury.*

—*Scribner's Magazine,* 2 (May 1871): 23–24

* * *

"Stripped and Bereaved"

The deaths of Branwell, Emily, and Anne interrupted Charlotte's work on Shirley. *After Anne's death in Scarborough on 29 May 1849, Charlotte and Ellen Nussey traveled down the western coast to Filey, from where she wrote to William Smith Williams on 13 June 1849. Excerpt.*

You have been kind enough to take a certain interest in my afflictions, and I feel it a sort of duty to tell you how I am enabled to sustain them. The burden is lightened far beyond what I could expect by more circumstances than one. Papa is resigned and his health is not shaken. An immediate change of scene has done me good—All I meet are kind—my friend Ellen is affectionately so. You—on whom I have no claim—write to me in the strain best tending to consolation.

Then—my Sister died happily; nothing dark, except the inevitable shadow of Death overclouded her hour of dissolution the doctor—a stranger—who was called in—wondered at her fixed tranquility of spirit and settled longing to be gone. He said in all his experience he had seen no such death-bed, and that it gave evidence of no common mind—Yet to speak the truth—it but half consoles to remember this calm—there is piercing pain in it. Anne had had enough of life such as it was—in her twenty-eighth year she laid it down as a burden. I hardly know whether it is sadder to think of that than of Emily turning her dying eyes reluctantly from the pleasant sun. Had I never believed in a future life before, my Sisters' fate would assure me of it.

There must be Heaven or we must despair—for life seems bitter, brief—blank. To me—these two have left in their memories a noble legacy. Were I quite solitary in the world—bereft even of Papa—there is something in the past I can love intensely and honour deeply—and it is something which cannot change—which cannot decay—which immortality guarantees from corruption.

They have died comparatively young—but their short lives were spotless their brief career was honourable—their untimely death befel amidst all associations that can hallow, and not one that can desecrate.

A year ago—had a prophet warned me how I should stand in June 1849—how stripped and bereaved—had he foretold the autumn—the winter, the spring of sickness and suffering to be gone through—I should have thought—this can never be endured. It is over. Branwell—Emily—Anne are gone like dreams—gone as Maria and Elizabeth went twenty years ago. One by one I have watched them fall asleep on my arm—and closed their glazed eyes—I have seen them buried one by one—and—thus far—God has upheld me. from my heart I thank Him.

—*The Letters of Charlotte Brontë*, v. 2, p. 220

A month after Anne's death, at the end of June 1849 Charlotte returned to her novel, beginning again with the first chapter of her third volume, titled "The Valley of the Shadow of Death." She finished the work by 8 September, when James Taylor, her publisher's clerk, arrived at the parsonage to pick up the manuscript. Shirley *was published 26 October 1849, to mixed reviews.*

This review was anonymous. Excerpts.

"Not Another *Jane Eyre*"
Review of *Shirley*

Not for many years has a second appearance been looked for so eagerly as the second appearance of the author of *Jane Eyre*. The public waited long and anxiously for it; but in spite of the tardy advent of the new claimant we never forgot the piquant Jane, with her plain black gown, her insignificant stature, her irregular features, her somewhat brusque style of address, and her wonderful fascinations. More than two years have passed since *Jane Eyre* was published; but it has never ceased to be a constant object of inquiry wherever the English language is read, and never has the third volume of that indescribable fiction been laid down without a longing after more fruit from the same tree and a singular interest in its development. But for the causes of delay, we should have rejoiced that the second appearance of Currer Bell has been so long retarded. It has left full time for *Jane Eyre* to be appreciated. The new has not come too soon to supersede the old, even if the new work were another *Jane Eyre*. But it is not another *Jane Eyre*. In some respects it is superior; but we do not like it half as well—or, we should say, we do not succumb to it half as much. *Shirley* we have quite in our power. In *Jane Eyre* there was an irresistible spell; one was not, for some time, the same as before after reading it. It would take a great many *Shirleys* to put *Jane Eyre* out of our heads.

Now *Jane Eyre* has taken a high, a very high, place among English novels; but whether Currer Bell could take a high place among English novelists remained to be proved—nay, it still remains to be proved. We will not admit that *Shirley* settles the question. If we thought it did, our decision would be against the claims of Currer Bell. We should be obliged to confess that the author of *Shirley* is singularly destitute of invention. The leading idea of this new story is the same as the leading idea of the old. The sexes are only reversed. Instead of a gentleman of property and a governess, we have a lady of property and a tutor. *Mutatis mutandis,* Shirley (such is the lady's somewhat masculine baptismal name) and Louis Moore are but a reproduction of Rochester and Jane Eyre. The points of resemblance are so many that we cannot venture to particularise them. The scenery and costume of the story are very much the same as we have in the preceding fictions of the Bell family. There is a wild north-country landscape—an old manorial house, of which the proprietor comes to take possession—and a somewhat rude state of society obtaining in all the neighbourhood. "Remote from towns," the people run a rather godless and very uncivilised race; and, to our southern visions, the entire environments of the piece seem somewhat strange and uncouth, but not without a possible reality, which, though one's experience cannot, one's imagination can readily embrace.

There is one thing which may be said, without any misgivings, after even a careless perusal of *Shirley*. It sets at rest now and for ever all question of the sex of the writer. For our own parts, we could never acknowledge that there was any question about it; but it was pertinaciously raised and volubly discussed, in the face of the strongest possible evidence of female workmanship. The reasons for the entertainment of an opposite faith, put forth by the *Quarterly Review* and other grave authorities, always appeared to us of the weakest: and we were not less certain that the writer of *Jane Eyre* had a woman's heart in her breast, than that the writer of *Shirley* is so endowed. But now the most sceptical will cease to doubt. There is woman stamped on every page of the present fiction.

In spite of even more deplorable evidences of bad taste than disfigure the former work of Currer Bell, *Shirley* is a more womanly book than *Jane Eyre*, and on the whole more pleasing. The charm of the story lies in its exquisitely truthful delineation of female character. There is nothing to our taste so piquante—nothing to our mind so interesting—as dear Jane Eyre; but Caroline Helstone, the real heroine of *Shirley*, is a sweeter, gentler creature; more of a "young lady"—fitter for every-day life and genteel society—and will, peradventure, have the suffrages of the many. The progress of an attachment, fluctuating between hopelessness and full assurance, through all the varying grades of pleasing and painful doubt, has seldom been traced with more delicacy and truth. The reader who wants strong stimulants will probably be disappointed. There is very little action in *Shirley*. The story is but a slender one. The *dramatis personae* do little; but they feel much. It is the deep under-current of womanly emotion, whose windings he must be content to follow. The narrative, indeed, is throughout rather psychological than dramatic; although in form it is

more dramatic than *Jane Eyre*, and it is written almost wholly in dialogue. It is the inner rather than the outer world, that is set forth; and the effort to impart something more of social life to the story is singularly unsuccessful. And it is not a mere negative failure. The minor characters are, for the most part, extraordinarily unreal and repulsive. There is, for example, a batch of curates, who act as a sort of *chorus* to the piece; but there is no dramatic fitness in their introduction; they are in harmony with nothing; what they have been obtruded upon us for it is very difficult to say. They occupy the stage at the first drawing up of the curtain, like a bevy of goblins in a pantomime; and are almost as much out of place as if such an introduction were to usher in the romantic love-drama of *Romeo and Juliet*.

The first chapter of *Shirley* is enough to deter many a reader from advancing a step further than the

SHIRLEY.

A Tale.

BY

CURRER BELL,

AUTHOR OF "JANE EYRE."

IN THREE VOLUMES.

VOL. I.

LONDON:
SMITH, ELDER AND CO., 65, CORNHILL.
—
1849.

Title page for Charlotte's second novel, written during a period in which she endured the deaths of her siblings (Special Collections, Thomas Cooper Library, University of South Carolina)

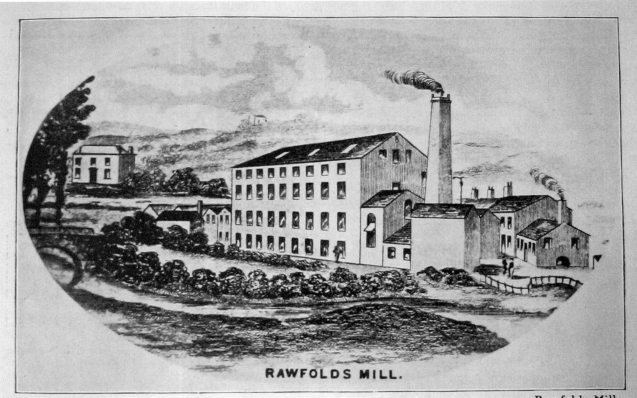

RAWFOLDS MILL.

Photo J. J. Stead.   Rawfolds Mill.
The mill, now no longer in existence, where the attack of rioters actually took place. The description of Hollows Mill in " Shirley " was taken
from Hunsworth Mill.

" A crash—smash—shiver—stopped their whispers. A simultaneously-hurled volley of stones had saluted the broad front of the mill, with all its
windows ; and now every pane of every lattice lay in shattered and pounded fragments. A yell followed this demonstration—a rioters' yell—a North-of-
England—a Yorkshire—a West-Riding—a West-Riding-clothing-district-of-Yorkshire rioters' yell. You never heard that sound, perhaps, reader? So
much the better for your ears—perhaps for your heart ; since, if it rends the air in hate to yourself, or to the men or principles you approve, the interests
to which you wish well, Wrath wakens to the cry of Hate: the Lion shakes his mane, and rises to the howl of the Hyena: Caste stands up, ireful
against Caste ; and the indignant, wronged spirit of the Middle Rank bears down in zeal and scorn on the famished and furious mass of the Operative class. It is difficult to be tolerant—difficult to be just—in such moments."—" Shirley."

*Rawfolds Mill, near Liversedge, where Luddite rioters attacked in April 1812. Reverend Brontë was curate at the neighboring town of
Hartshead (from* The Bookman, *October 1904).*

threshold. It required all the remembered fascinations of "Jane Eyre" to keep down the feelings of dis-satisfaction (we had nearly written another word with the same commencement) which the first chapter of *Shirley* raised up within us. All this is very coarse–very irreverential. And there is besides, discernible in other parts, an unseemly mode of allusion to solemn topics, a jesting with scriptural names, and a light usage of scriptural expressions, which will grate painfully upon the feelings of a considerable number of Currer Bell's many-minded readers. . . . *Shirley* is better written than *Jane Eyre;* but there is less power in it. There is nothing like the originality of the little governess in these pages–nothing that will be so remembered. Still it is a very noticeable book. It has the stamp of genius upon it.

–*Atlas* (3 November 1849): 696–697

* * *

Brontë believed this unsigned review was written by Albany Fonblanque. In a 5 November letter to Williams, she wrote: "Fonblanque has power, he has discernment—I bend to his censorship; I am grateful for his praise; his blame deserves consideration; when he approves I permit myself a modest emotion of pride" (The Letters of Charlotte Brontë, *v. 2, p. 278). Excerpts.*

"The Proof of Genius"
Review of *Shirley*

The peculiar power which was so greatly admired in *Jane Eyre* is not absent from this book. Indeed it is repeated, if we may so speak of anything so admirable, with too close and vivid a resemblance. The position of Shirley and her tutor is that of Jane and her master reversed. Robert and Louis Moore are not quite such social savages, externally, as Mr. Rochester; but in trifling with women's affections they are hardly less harsh or selfish, and they are just as strong in will and giant in limb. The heroines are of the family of Jane, though with charming differences, having wilful as well as gentle ways, and greatly desiderating "masters." The expression of motive by means of dialogue is again indulged to such minute and tedious extremes, that what ought to be developments of character in the speaker become mere exercitations of will and intellect in the author. And finally the old theme of tutors and governesses is pushed here and there to the tiresome point. The lesson intended is excellent; but works of art should be something more than moral parables, and should certainly embody more truths than one.

While we thus freely indicate the defects of *Shirley,* let us at the same time express, what we very strongly feel, that the freshness and lively interest which the author has contrived to impart to a repetition of the same sort of figures, grouped in nearly the same social relations, as in her former work, is really wonderful. It is the proof of genius. It is the expression of that intellectual faculty, or quality, which feels the beautiful, the grand, the humorous, the characteristic, as vividly after the thousandth repetition as when it first met the sense. We formerly compared the writer to Godwin, in the taste manifested for mental analysis as opposed to the dealing with events; and might have taken Lord Byron within the range of the comparison. As in *Jane Eyre,* so in *Shirley,* the characters, imagery, and incidents are not impressed from without, but elaborated from within. They are the reflex of the writer's peculiar feelings and wishes. In this respect alone, however, does she resemble the two authors named. She does not, like Godwin, subordinate human interests to moral theories, nor, like Byron, waste her strength in impetuous passion. Keen, intellectual analysis is her forte; and she seems to be, in the main, content with the existing structure of society, and would have everybody make the most of it.

As well in remarking on *Jane Eyre,* as in noticing other books from the same family, if not from the same hand, we have directed attention to an excess of the repulsive qualities not seldom rather coarsely indulged. We have it in a less degree in *Shirley,* but here it is. With a most delicate and intense perception of the beautiful, the writer combines a craving for stronger and rougher stimulants. She goes once again to the dales and fells of the north for her scenery, erects her "confessionals" on a Yorkshire moor, and lingers with evident liking amid society as rough and stern as the forms of nature which surround them. She has a manifest pleasure in dwelling even on the purely repulsive in human character. We do not remember the same taste to the same extent in any really admirable writer, or so little in the way of playful or tender humour to soften and relieve the habit of harsh delineation. Plainly she is deficient in humour. In

the book before us, what is stern and hard about Louis Moore is meant to be atoned by a dash of that genial quality. But while the disagreeable ingredient is powerfully portrayed in action, the fascinating play of fancy is no more than talked about.

Is there, indeed, in either of these books, or any of the writings which bear the name of "Bell," one really natural, and no more than natural, character—a character, we mean, in which the natural is kept within its simple and right proportions? We suspect it would be hardly an exaggeration to answer this question in the negative. The personages to whom Currer Bell introduces us are created by intellect, and are creatures of intellect. Habits, actions, conduct are attributed to them, such as we really witness in human beings; but the reflections and language which accompany these actions, are those of intelligence fully developed, and entirely self-conscious. Now in real men and women such clear knowledge of self is rarely developed at all, and then only after long trials. We see it rarely in the very young—seldom or ever on the mere threshold of the world. The sentient and impulsive preponderates, at least in this stage of existence: at the utmost the intellectual only struggles to emerge from it. It is impossible to imagine that Shirley and her lover could have refined into each other's feelings with such keen intellectual clearness as in the dialogues and interviews detailed, yet remained ignorant so long of what it most behoved them both to know. But even in the children described in this book we find the intellectual predominant and supreme. The young Yorkes, ranging from twelve years down to six, talk like Scotch professors of metaphysics, and argue, scheme, vituperate, and discriminate, like grown up men and women.

Yet in spite of this, and of the very limited number of characters and incidents in this tale as in the former, the book before us possesses deep interest, and an irresistible grasp of reality. There is a vividness and distinctness of conception in it quite marvellous. The power of graphic delineation and expression is intense. There are scenes which for strength and delicacy of emotion are not transcended in the range of English fiction. There is an art of creating sudden interest in a few pages worth volumes of common-place description. Shirley does not enter till the last chapter in the first volume, but at once takes the heroine's place. Louis Moore does not enter till the last chapter of the second volume, yet no one would dream of disputing with him the character of hero.

Story there is none in *Shirley.* The principal continuous interest of the book attaches to two brothers, and two girls with whom they are in love. . . . But the women will be the favourites with all readers. Both are charming. Caroline is a gentle, loving nature, who long loves hopelessly, and "never tells her love," though she lets it be seen. Shirley is, as the "wildly witty" Rosalind, clear, decisive, wilful, self-dependant, yet also most womanly and

Photo J. J. Stead.
Red House, Gomersal (The Briarmains of "Shirley").
The residence of Mr. Joshua Taylor (Hiram Yorke of "Shirley").
" But if Briar Chapel seemed alive, so also did Briarmains, though certainly the mansion appeared to enjoy a quieter phase of existence than the temple ; some of its windows, too, were aglow. The lower casements opened upon the lawn, curtains concealed the interior, and partly obscured the ray of the candles which lit it, but they did not entirely muffle the sound of voice and laughter.—Shirley."
(Reproduced from the Haworth Edition of "Shirley," by kind permission of Messrs. Smith, Elder and Co.)

Red House, Gomersal, West Yorkshire, where Charlotte visited Mary Taylor during her days at Miss Wooler's school
(from The Bookman, *October 1904)*

affectionate; too proud to woo her inferior in station, whom she nevertheless wishes to woo her. The staple of the three volumes is made up of the thinkings, sayings, and doings of these four persons; presented to us less in the manner of a continuous tale, in which incidents spring from character, and reflections are suggested by incidents, than in a series of detached and independent pictures, dialogues, and soliloquies, written or spoken. So instinct with life, however, are these pictures, dialogues, and soliloquies; so replete with power, with beauty, and with subtle reflections; that the want of continuity in the tale is pardoned. Tediousness is felt before the author's purpose comes distinctly in view; but when it does, the interest becomes enchaining. We could not lay down the third volume.

We may single out two of its chapters more especially—the "Valley of the Shadow of Death," and the "Rushedge Confessional." In the first, Caroline is nursed through a dangerous fever by Shirley's governess, Mrs. Pryor, in whom she discovers the parent whom her father had maltreated and deserted. . . .

In the "Rushedge" chapter, Robert Moore makes confession to a friend—a sturdy, Yorkshire, radical, manufacturer, who has had a love disappointment in his youth—of the indignation with which Shirley had rejected his proposal of his hand. . . . This introduction of Yorke may remind us of a host of subordinate characters yet undescribed, who figure round the principal persons, and appear or disappear as it suits the author's whim or convenience. Indeed by no means the least charm of the book consists in the vigour and felicity with which these accessories are sketched. They are hit off, mentally and bodily, with a startling force and reality. Sometimes the mood they are conceived in is delightfully tender and tolerant (as with the old maids, Miss Mann and Miss Ainley), sometimes placidly just (as with Hortense Moore, and those capital operative sketches, Joe Scott and William Farren), but more often sarcastic to the utmost extreme of the merciless (as with the Sympson family, hardly redeemed by their gentle invalid boy, the wife and children of Yorke, the wooden-legged Barraclough, and the curates of Whin-bury, Briarfield, and Nunnely).

The Rev. Mr. Mathewson Helstone, rector of Briarfield, one of the most happily conceived and exe-cuted pictures in the book, claims mention at more length. We wish we could give his first introduction, "straight as a ramrod, keen as a kite," interrupting a noisy dispute of three curates rather like a veteran officer than a venerable priest. . . . Wherever the rector makes his appearance, he is striking, characteristic, con-sistent. At home, cold, silent, and unsympathising; in company, brilliant and vivacious; eager to seek out dan-ger, in high spirits when brought face to face with it, and making less powerful natures bend to his strong will; nothing can be better done throughout. . . .

Very characteristic is Yorke, too, in his way; and the contrast of Helstone and Yorke with Robert Moore, so dif-ferent, yet with so much in common, all three so fearless, so strong in will, yet each so individual, so marked out by his temper and the influence of his position and pursuits, is among the cleverest things in the book.

We can give little in the way of extract to illustrate the character of Shirley. The minute, delicate, and bril-liant traits would lose too much in the transfer. We can-not show her calm resolve in danger, her prompt decision in difficulty, her fearless defiance of injustice, her quiet self-command in sorrow, her generally willful, charming, loving, petulant ways. . . .

Nevertheless in the predilection and general con-clusions of the author of Shirley we will not pretend to concur. There is a large and liberal tolerance in them, and a rational acquiescence in the inevitable tendencies of society. But this acquiescence we suspect to be reluc-tant. There is a hankering, not to be suppressed, after the fleshpots of Egypt—a strong sympathy with Toryism and High Church. The writer sees clearly that they are things of the past, but cannot help regretting them. The tone assumed to the dissenters and manufacturers is hardly fair. Their high qualities are not denied, but there is a disposition to deepen the shadows in delineat-ing them. There is cordiality when the foibles of rectors and squires are laughed at, but when the defects of the commercial class are touched there is bitterness. The independence and manlier qualities of even that class are nevertheless appreciated, and some truths are told, though told too sharply, by which they may benefit. The views of human nature which pervade the vol-umes, notwithstanding the taste for dwelling on its harsher features already adverted to, are healthy, toler-ant, and encouraging. A sharp relish for the beauties of external nature, no mean power of reproducing them, and occasional glimpses of ideal imagination of a high order, are visible throughout. The writer works upon a very limited range of rather homely materials, yet

inspires them with a power of exciting, elevating, pleas-ing, and instructing, which belongs only to genius of the most unquestionable kind.

We have not hesitated to speak of the writer as a woman. We doubted this, in reading *Jane Eyre;* but the internal evidence of *Shirley* places the matter beyond a doubt.

          —*The Examiner* (3 November 1849): 692–694

* * *

These excerpts are from an unsigned review.

"Ingrained Rudeness"
Review of *Shirley*

In several respects this "tale" exhibits a consider-able improvement upon the novels that under the name of Bell with several prefixes have excited so much atten-tion. There is less coarseness than was displayed in all of them, somewhat less questionable propriety than appeared in the best of them, *Jane Eyre,* and nothing of the low and almost disgusting characters and circum-stances that disfigured the rest. *Shirley* has more variety of persons, and in a certain sense more of actual life than was found in *Jane Eyre;* but in essentials we observe little difference. That part which forms the *story* of the novel still depends less upon incidents than upon metaphysical delineation of character, executed with more power than skill or naturalness; a sort of ingrained rudeness—an absence of delicacy and refine-ment of feeling—pervades the book; and above all, we have small sympathy with either the principal or the subordinate characters. It would seem as if the writer's mind had a peculiarity which defeated its genius, com-pelling it to drop something distasteful into every idio-syncracy, that increases in proportion to the importance of the character to the fiction. The only exceptions to this are two old maids and a clergyman, who rarely appear, and who do nothing. These faults coexist with great clearness of conception, very remarkable powers of delineation both of internal emotion and outward scenes, much freshness of topic, scenery, and composi-tion, with a species of vigour, which rather resembles the galvanic motions of a "subject" than the natural movements of life. But Currer Bell has yet to learn, that in art the agreeable is as essential as the powerful, and that the reader's attention must be attracted, not forced.

The scene of *Shirley* is laid in Yorkshire, towards the close of the war against Napoleon, when the Imperial Decrees and the British Orders in Council were creating apprehension amongst the clothiers, distress among the workmen, and Jacobinical principles generally. To paint this state of society is one object of the tale, and, we think, the most successfully attained; though the generality of the characters have so strong a dash of the repelling, as well as of a literal provincial coarseness, that the attractive effect is partly marred by the ill-conditioned nature of the persons, whether it be the author's fault or Yorkshire's. The sketches of the workmen, the masters, the dignified clergy, the curates, the Dissenters, and the various persons who forty years ago went to make up the society of an obscure place in Yorkshire, are done with a somewhat exaggerated style, and coloured too much by the writer's own mind, but possessing rude vigour and harsh truth. The darkest part of the political night, immediately preceding the dawn, had raised peace-at-any-price people then, and enables the writer to give a present interest to the past in some of the general remarks. The following observations, indeed, are more applicable now than they would have been some forty years ago. The war against Napoleon was on the whole popular even among the trading classes. . . .

The mode by which life and continuous interest is given to what would otherwise have been a series of provincial sketches, is by two love tales; but neither of a sufficiently large or pleasing kind. . . .

Whether broad cloth and bankruptcy, or the marriage of a poor lover to a rich wife, are proper moving elements of fiction, may be doubted. Trade, in its money-making aspect, appeals to no lofty emotion, if it does not rather suggest the reverse. A bankruptcy or a legacy may be a means of inducing ill or good fortune, but it is only to be mentioned and dismissed. The meanness attaching to a fortune-hunter seems to have established as an unalterable canon that the hero's wealth should precede his formal declaration of love: he achieves greatness, but comes into property by luck or succession towards the "finis." This ill choice of subjects in *Shirley* is not counterbalanced by felicity of treatment. Robert Moore, out of the factory, is a self-satisfied melodramatic coxcomb "half soft and half savage"; in the factory, he is a hard and mercenary man, his objects being too much sunk and his means too much presented. Caroline Helstone is marred by weakness and by an unfeminine display of her feelings. Louis Moore, though well drawn, and well sustained up to a certain point, flags at the critical moment, and, to make a bad thing worse, writes down the whole account of his wooing autobiographically. Indeed, this part is a sort of reverse of Mr. Rochester and Jane Eyre, and that of Caroline and Robert is a repetition of what is rarely attractive itself–a metaphysical love tale.

These circumstances render the incidental sketches, or scenes that are not directly connected with the love affairs, the most agreeable parts of the book.

–*The Spectator*, 22 (3 November 1849): 1043–1045

* * *

This unsigned review is unusual in its linking of Brontë the poet and Brontë the novelist. The poem discussed in the first paragraph is "Gilbert." Excerpts.

"Originality of Mind"
Review of *Shirley*

Some years ago there appeared in most modest guise a small volume of poems by Ellis, Currer, and Acton Bell. They were generally overlooked on their publication, yet they had a kind of merit of an uncommon kind, and contained some passages well calculated to fix themselves on the mind. The principal pieces bore the signature of Currer Bell, and, though the versification was none of the smoothest, evinced wonderful power in raising images before the eye and in picturing scenes. One of these poems, we remember, consisted of several tableaux . . . As a poem the piece had faults, but for power of portraiture and for that rare faculty of exhibiting in words the shadowy images of mental agony, confused yet clear, undeveloped yet fully conceived, a thought without sensible embodiment, it was almost unequalled. Less finished than some similar pieces by Hood, it had a deeper significance and more impressive mystery. . . .

In *Shirley* there is striking and delightful evidence of the same talent. Shirley Keeldar is a young lady, a Yorkshire heiress, with very independent notions, and a somewhat masculine style of thought, though her face and figure are delicate in the extreme. She has been named Shirley from the failure of male issue, and it is her whim sometimes to assume mannish airs. Mr. Bell has exerted all his ability to render this character at once original and attractive, and he has perfectly succeeded. She is like no other heroine of romance ever drawn. Wilful, obstinate, proud, pettish, provoking, she has a soul capable of the purest and deepest passion, and all her singularities of manner and expression only serve to set off her genius. In contrast . . . is another young girl, Caroline, of a softer and gentler nature. For a time the reader is left to suppose that their affections are fixed on the same man, Robert Moore, a Yorkshire manufacturer. We do not get an inkling of the truth, or of the real aim, of the book until the middle of the third volume . . .

More than one half of the work has little or no connection with the main story, and, though we can never read long together without coming upon some vigorous passage, yet we have the disagreeable feeling that much of the matter we are wading through is purposeless, and had better have been omitted. It is probable that Mr. Bell will hereafter compose with more art. But, were his faults infinitely greater than they are, his originality of mind, and the triumphant beauty of his

heroine's character, would at once secure for his book great and deserved popularity.
                    —*Britannia* (10 November 1849): 714–715

* * *

These excerpts are from an unsigned review article titled "New Novels." The reviewer is believed to have been W. G. Clark, a Shakespearean scholar at Trinity College, Cambridge.

"A Good Novel"
Review of *Shirley*

Well do we remember how we took up *Jane Eyre* one winter's evening, somewhat piqued at the extravagant commendations we had heard, and sternly resolved to be as critical as Croker. But as we read on we forgot both commendations and criticism, identified ourselves with Jane in all her troubles and finally married Mr. Rochester about four in the morning. So to us the announcement of another novel by the same hand was exciting. We refused an invitation for the 31st October, and shut ourselves up with *Shirley*—there were four of us, three volumes and the present writer—determined on a sleepless night. But, no, about eleven o'clock we began our habitual series of yawns, then lighted the bed-candle, went to bed, fell asleep, and did not resume *Shirley* even in our dreams. It was three days before we finished it. Not that it is a dull book by any means—indeed nearly every page contains something worth reading; but the story is deficient in connexion and interest. In *Jane Eyre* the reader accompanied the heroine throughout, saw with her eyes, heard with her ears, in short, lived over again in one life, and regarded other persons and things from *one* point of view—the heroine's personality. On this ground an autobiography well done is sure of creating the most absorbing interest. But a story in the narrative form requires much more artistic skill in its construction. It is required to concentrate the interest upon one person or one group, while regarding that person or group, as well as the subordinate groups, *ab extra*. The threads of intrigue must be so crossed and interlaced as to form but one pattern. Otherwise, the reader's mind will have to make a painful effort (a sort of squint) to see two or more distinct things at once. Again care must be taken lest by too great elaboration in the details you diminish the prominence of your central group—like Maclise in his pictures. On that foot halts Sir Walter Scott himself. Who cares for Waverley, though the author does call him our hero? *Our* hero is the Baron of Bradwardine. Now in the book before us there are characters that occupy much more space than the eponymous of the tale. It might as well have been called *Caroline,* or *Helstone,* as

far as that goes. Shirley, the heroine—for masculine as that name sounds, Shirley is a woman—does not appear at all till the end of the first volume and the hero only drops in at the end of the second. Besides, the stage is overcrowded with characters too insignificant to be named in the bills, some, mere scene-shifters and candle-snuffers, have no business to be there at all. Let us count up the *dramatis personae,* those who are actually named, and have a *rôle* in the play. Over and above the four young people whose marriage, somehow or other, is the object of the book, we have the Yorke family, seven; the Sympsons, five; the Nunnelys, four; the Sykeses, eight (we believe); three vicars; three curates; three Methodist preachers; three old maids; one governess; one patiently suffering operative and family; five or six riotous ditto; besides gardeners, grooms, housekeepers, housemaids, &c. Nearly a hundred characters to be disposed of! It could not be done, even with the 'resources' of Covent Garden. . . .

The scene of *Shirley* is laid in the West Riding of Yorkshire, in the years 1811–12, amidst the frame-breaking and bank-breaking performed by operatives and masters respectively, and caused by the improvements in machinery and the Orders in Council. We think, by the way, that the author exaggerates the distress and alarm of those times, though she does not make them tell with much effect on her story. All the results would have come about, we are sure, without the rioters.

The first volume will be unintelligible to most people, for it is half in French and half in broad Yorkshire. There are many who know 'Yorkshire,' and don't know French; and others, we fear, who know French and don't know Yorkshire. For our own part, we possess a decent knowledge of both, and we venture to pronounce that the French and the Yorkshire are both excellent. Most writers seem to imagine that they can produce a genuine Yorkshireman by cutting off the final consonant of every word he utters. Currer Bell's Yorkshiremen are not such Cockneyfied automata. Their thoughts are as provincial as their speech. We would bet a trifle that the author is a Yorkshirewoman;–Yorkshire we are sure; woman, we think. Why not Miss Currer Bell as well as Miss Shirley Keldar? She knows women by their brains and hearts, men by their foreheads and chests. She (we cannot help begging the question) depicts women often quaint and odd, but never unnatural, while the men are not unfrequently ranting mountebanks, who, instead of the toleration and applause the author claims for them, would infallibly, in real life, be 'cut' or kicked, or shut up in a madhouse. The author, then, is a woman. Moreover she is, or has been, a governess. She is always good on the topic of governesses, their rights and wrongs. Jane Eyre was (as all the world knows) a governess, so (we beg to inform the world) is Mrs. Pryor, and Caroline Helstone wants to be one. Again, she has a sympathy with the cognate class of private tutors. As in her former book she made the governess marry her 'master,' so, in the present, the tutor has a love affair with his lady pupil (we are not going to tell how it ends). . . .

With regard to the male characters, it is not so much of the original conception as of the working out of that conception, that we wish to complain. The rough sketch is often as correct as it is daring–psychologically faultless. Take, for example, Robert Gerard Moore, as the author first presents him to us, half English, half French, a bankrupt mill-owner and a thorough gentleman, a furious Radical who detests the mob, a man of taste and refinement with his heart and

soul in the dyeing-vats, lavishly generous, yet ready to sell his love for gold. The author deserves credit for not common skill in combining, out of such dissonant elements, a harmonious whole. But would this being ever have spoken as he does in chap. v.? Would he have carried on a colloquy with Joe Scott, his foreman, in that Alexander-the-Great style? Surely not. . . .

We could point out many other instances of violence and exaggeration; the little Yorkes, lads in their early teens, talk like Master Betterton on the stage. The little Miss Yorkes, too, have an Ossianic style of their own, and a marvelous acquaintance with Johnson's *Dictionary*. We rather suspect that the author is planning another novel on the fate and fortunes of the Yorke family. For all their ranting, we should like to hear more of them. But we are drawing near the end of our paper. We sat down fully resolved to mete out praise and blame according to the most approved recipe of enlightened criticism, and lo! we have done nothing but censure. We may have led our readers to suppose that this is but a mediocre novel, a thing which *our* columns join gods and men in prohibiting. But, in truth, it is a good novel, dashed with a fair human alloy of bad; and we, with the amiable instinct of our craft, have fixed on the weak part.

After all, it is not easy to give *extracts* for admiration. We like the book as a whole. On the whole, we like its spirit. The author does not, after the manner of some we could name, plead the cause of the poor by indiscriminate slander of the rich, nor advocate religious tolerance by a display of the bitterest sectarian hatred.

The character of Shirley is excellently conceived and well sustained. And how touching is the story of Caroline; an old story, by the way, which reminds one of the poor Hartley Coleridge's mournful music:–

Say, what is worse than blank despair?
'Tis that sick hope too weak for flying,
Which plays at fast and loose with care,
And wastes a weary life in dying.

We sympathize with the author's general charity, with her special love for the old country, the old Church, and the old Duke; we kindle with her fervid bursts of eloquence, and recognize the truth of her pictures from life.

As to the morality, it must be a very precise prude, indeed, who could ferret out an innuendo in *Shirley*.

–*Fraser's Magazine,* 40 (December 1849): 692–694

* * *

Brontë regarded this unsigned review by George Henry Lewes as a betrayal of the friendship they had developed since the publication of Jane Eyre. *The two writers continued their relationship, but the pace of their correspondence slackened after their disagreement. In these excerpts, Lewes evidently refers to Elizabeth Rigby's review of* Jane Eyre *in* The Quarterly Review, *misremembering her as citing "irresistible evidence" that Currer Bell is a woman.*

"An Artisan, Not an Artist"
Review of *Shirley*

Men in general, when serious and *not* gallant, are slow to admit woman even to an equality with themselves; and the prevalent opinion certainly is that women are inferior in respect of intellect. This opinion may be correct. The question is a delicate one. We very much doubt, however, whether sufficient *data* exist for any safe or confident decision. For the position of women in society has never yet been—perhaps never can be—such as to give fair play to their capabilities. It is true, no doubt, that none of them have yet attained to the highest eminence in the highest departments of intellect. They have had no Shakespeare, no Bacon, no Newton, no Milton, no Raphael, no Mozart, no Watt, no Burke. But while this is admitted, it is surely not to be forgotten that these are the *few* who have carried off the high prizes to which millions of Men were equally qualified by their training and education to aspire, and for which, by their actual pursuits, they may be held to have been contending; while the number of *Women* who have had either the benefit of such training, or the incitement of such pursuits, has been comparatively insignificant. When the bearded competitors were numbered by thousands, and the smooth-chinned by scores, what was the chance of the latter? Or with what reason could their failure be ascribed to their inferiority as a class?

Nevertheless, with this consideration distinctly borne in mind, we must confess our doubts whether women will ever rival men in *some* departments of intellectual exertion; and especially in those which demand either a long preparation, or a protracted effort of pure thought. But we do not, by this, prejudge the question of superiority. We assume no general organic inferiority; we simply assert an organic *difference*. Women, we are entirely disposed to admit, are substantially *equal* in the aggregate worth of their endowments: But equality does not imply identity. They may be equal, but not exactly alike. Many of their endowments are specifically different. Mentally as well as bodily there seem to be organic diversities; and these must make themselves felt, whenever the two sexes come into competition.

The grand function of woman, it must always be recollected, is, and ever must be, *Maternity:* and this we regard not only as her distinctive characteristic, and most endearing charm, but as a high and holy office—the prolific source, not only of the best affections and virtues of which our nature is capable, but also of the wisest thoughtfulness, and most useful habits of observation, by which that nature can be elevated and adorned. But with all this, we think it impossible to deny, that it must essentially interfere both with that steady and unbroken application, without which no proud eminence in science can be gained—and with the discharge of all official or professional functions that do not admit of long or frequent postponement. All women are intended by Nature to be mothers; and by far the greater number—not less, we suppose, than nine tenths—are called upon to act in that sacred character; and, consequently for twenty years of the best years of their lives—those very years in which men either rear the grand fabric or lay the solid foundations of their fame and fortune—women are mainly occupied by the cares, the duties, the enjoyments and the sufferings of maternity. During large parts of these years, too, their bodily health is generally so broken and precarious as to incapacitate them for any strenuous exertion; and, health apart, the greater portion of their time, thoughts, interests, and anxieties ought to be, and generally are, centered in the care and the training of their children. But how could such occupations consort with the intense and unremitting studies which seared the eyeballs of Milton, and for a time unsettled even the powerful brain of Newton? High art and science always require the whole man; and never yield their great prizes but to the devotion of a life. But the life of a woman, from her cradle upwards, is otherwise devoted: and those whose lot it is to expend their best energies, from the age of twenty to the age of forty, in the cares and duties of maternity, have but slender chances of carrying off these great prizes. It is the same with the high functions of statesmanship, legislation, generalship, judgeship, and other elevated stations and pursuits, to which some women, we believe, have recently asserted the equal pretensions of their sex. Their still higher and *indispensably* functions of maternity afford the answer to all such claims. What should we do with a leader of opposition in the seventh month of her pregnancy? or a general in chief who at the opening of a campaign was 'doing as well as could be expected'? or a chief justice with twins?

If it be said that these considerations only apply to wives and mothers, and ought not to carry along with them any disqualification of virgins or childless widows, the answer is, that as Nature qualifies and apparently designs *all* women to be mothers, it is impossible to know who are to escape that destiny, till it is too late to begin the training necessary for artists, scholars, or politicians. On the other hand, too much stress has, we think, been laid on man's superiority in physical strength—as if that, in itself, were sufficient to account for the differences in intellectual power. It should be remembered that, in the great contentions of man with man, it has not been physical strength which has generally carried the day; and it should further be remembered, that it is precisely in *that* art, which demands least employment of physical force, viz.—music, that the apparent inferiority of women is most marked and unaccountable. . . .

It is in literature, however, that women have most distinguished themselves; and probably because hundreds have cultivated literature, for one that has cultivated science or art. Their list of names in this department is a list that would rank high even among literary males. Madame de Stael was certainly as powerful a writer as any man of her age or country; and whatever may be the errors of George Sand's opinions, she is almost without a rival in eloquence, power, and invention. Mrs. Hemans, Miss Edgeworth, Miss Baillie, Miss Austen, Mrs. Norton, Miss Mitford, Miss Landon, are second only to the first-rate men of their day; and would probably have ranked even higher, had they not been too solicitous about male excellence,—had they not often written from the man's point of view, instead of from the woman's. That which irretrievably condemns the whole literature of Rome to the second rank,—viz. imitation,—has also kept down the literature of women. The Roman only thought of rivalling a Greek,—not of mirroring life in his own nationality; and so women have too often thought but of rivalling men. It is their boast to be mistaken for men,—instead of speaking sincerely and energetically as women. So true is this, that in the department where they have least followed men, and spoken more as women,—we mean in Fiction,—their success has been greatest. Not to mention other names, surely no man has surpassed Miss Austen as a delineator of common life? Her range, to be sure, is limited; but her art is perfect. She does not touch those profounder and more impassioned chords which vibrate to the heart's core—never ascends to its grand or heroic movements, nor descends to its deeper throes and agonies; but in all she attempts is she is uniformly and completely successful.

It is curious too, and worthy of a passing remark, that women have achieved success in every department of fiction but that of *humour*. They deal, no doubt, in sly humorous touches often enough; but the broad provinces of that great domain are almost uninvaded by them; beyond the outskirts, and open borders, they have never ventured to pass. Compare Miss Austen,

Miss Ferriar, and Miss Edgeworth, with the lusty mirth and riotous humour of Shakespeare, Rabelais, Butler, Swift, Fielding, Smollett, or Dickens and Thackeray. It is like comparing a quiet smile with the 'inextinguishable laughter' of the Homeric gods! So also on the stage,—there have been comic actresses of incomparable merit, lively, pleasant, humorous women, gladdening the scene with their airy brightness and gladsome presence; but they have no comic energy. There has been no female Munden, Liston, Matthews, or Keeley. To be sure, our drama has no female parts, the representation of which after such a fashion would not have been a caricature.

But we must pursue this topic no further; and fear our readers may have been wondering how we have wandered away to it, from the theme which seemed to be suggested by the title of the work now before us. The explanation and apology is, that we take Currer Bell to be one of the most remarkable of female writers; and believe it is now scarcely a secret that Currer Bell is the pseudonym of a woman. An eminent contemporary, indeed, has employed the sharp vivacity of a female pen to prove 'upon irresistible evidence' that 'Jane Eyre' must be the work of a man. But all that 'irresistible evidence' is set aside by the simple fact that Currer Bell is a woman. We never, for our own parts, had a moment's doubt on the subject. That Jane herself was drawn by a woman's delicate hand, and that Rochester equally betrayed the sex of the artist, was to our minds so obvious, as absolutely to shut our ears to all the evidence which could be adduced by the erudition even of a *marchande des modes* [fashion merchant]; and that, simply because we knew that there were women profoundly ignorant of the mysteries of the toilette, and the terminology of fashion (independent of the obvious solution, that such ignorance might be counterfeited to mislead), and felt that there was no man who *could so* have delineated a woman—or *would so* have delineated a man. The fair and ingenious critic was misled by her own acuteness in the perception of details; and misled also in some other way, and more uncharitably, in concluding that the *author* of 'Jane Eyre' was a heathen educated among heathens,—the *fact* being, that the *authoress* is the daughter of a clergyman!

This question of authorship, which was somewhat hotly debated a little while ago, helped to keep up the excitement about 'Jane Eyre;' but, independently of that title to notoriety, it is certain that, for many years, there had been no work of such power, piquancy, and originality. Its very faults were faults on the side of vigour; and its beauties were all original. The grand secret of its success, however,—as of all genuine and lasting success,—was its *reality*. From out the depths of a sorrowing experience, here was a voice speaking to the experience of thousands. The aspects of external nature, too, were painted with equal fidelity,–the long cheerless winter days, chilled with rolling mists occasionally gathering into the strength of rains,–the bright spring mornings,–the clear solemn nights,–were all painted to your *soul* as well as to your eye, by a pencil dipped into a soul's experience for its colours. Faults enough the book has undoubtedly: faults of conception, faults of taste, faults of ignorance, but in spite of all, it remains a book of singular fascination. A more masculine book, in the sense of vigour, was never written. Indeed that vigour often amounts to coarseness,–and is certainly the very antipode to 'lady like.'

This same over-masculine vigour is even more prominent in 'Shirley,' and does not increase the pleasantness of the book. A pleasant book, indeed, we are not sure that we can style it. Power it has unquestionably, and interest too, of a peculiar sort; but not the agreeableness of a work of art. . . . Nature speaks to us distinctly enough, but she does not speak sweetly. She is in her stern and sombre mood, and we see only her dreary aspects.

'Shirley' is inferior to 'Jane Eyre' in several important points. It is not quite so true; and it is not so fascinating. It does not so rivet the reader's attention, nor hurry him through all obstacles of improbability, with so keen a sympathy in its reality. It is even coarser in texture, too, and not unfrequently flippant; while the characters are almost all disagreeable, and exhibit intolerable rudeness of manner. In 'Jane Eyre' life was viewed from the standing point of individual experience; in 'Shirley' that standing point is frequently abandoned, and the artist paints only a panorama of which she, as well as you, are but spectators. Hence the unity of 'Jane Eyre' in spite of its clumsy and improbable contrivances, was great and effective: the fire of one passion fused the discordant materials into one mould. But in 'Shirley' all unity, in consequence of defective art, is wanting. There is no passionate link; nor is there any artistic fusion, or intergrowth, by which one part evolves itself from another. Hence its falling-off in interest, coherent movement, and life. The book may be laid down at any chapter, and almost any chapter might be omitted. The various scenes are gathered up into three volumes,–they have not grown into a work. The characters often need a justification for their introduction; as in the case of the three Curates, who are offensive, uninstructive, and unamusing. That they are not *inventions,* however, we feel persuaded. For nothing but a strong sense of their reality could have seduced the authoress into such a mistake as admitting them at all. We are confident she has seen them, known them, despised them; and *therefore* she paints them! although they have no relation with the story, have no interest in themselves, and cannot be accepted as types of a class,–for they are not *Curates* but *boors:* and although not

inventions, we must be permitted to say that they are *not true.* Some such objections the authoress seems indeed to have anticipated; and thus towards the close of her work defends herself against it. 'Note well! wherever you present *the actual simple truth, it is somehow always denounced as a lie:* they disown it, cast it off, throw it on the parish; whereas the product of your imagination, the mere figment, the sheer fiction, is adopted, petted, proper, sweetly natural.' Now Currer Bell, we fear, has here fallen into a vulgar error. It is one, indeed, into which even Miss Edgeworth has also fallen: who conceived that she justified the introduction of an improbable anecdote in her text, by averring in a note that it was a 'fact.' But, the intrusion is not less an error for all that. Truth is never rejected, unless it be truth so exceptional as to stagger our belief; and in that case the artist is wrong to employ it, without so *preparing* our minds that we might receive it unquestioned. The coinage of imagination, on the other hand, is not accepted *because* it departs from the actual truth, but only because it presents the recognised attributes of our nature in new and striking combinations. If it falsify these attributes, or the known laws of their associations, the fiction is at once pronounced to be *monstrous,* and is rejected. Art, in short, deals with the broad principles of human nature, not with idiosyncracies: and, although it requires an experience of life both comprehensive and profound, to enable us to say with confidence, that '*this* motive is unnatural,' or '*that* passion is untrue,' it requires no great experience to say 'this character has not the air of reality; it may be copied from nature, but it does not *look* so.' Were Currer Bell's defence allowable, all criticism must be silenced at once. An author has only to say that his characters *are copied from nature,* and the discussion is closed. But though the portraits may be like the oddities from whom they are copied, they are faulty as works of art, if they strike all who never met with these oddities, as unnatural. . . .

Again we say that 'Shirley' cannot be received as a work of art. It is not a picture; but a portfolio of random sketches for one or more pictures. The authoress never seems distinctly to have made up her mind as to what she was to do; whether to describe the habits and manners of Yorkshire and its social aspects in the days of King Lud, or to paint a character, or to tell a love story. All are by turns attempted and abandoned; and the book consequently moves slowly, and by starts–leaving behind it no distinct or satisfactory impression. Power is stamped on various parts of it; power unmistakeable, but often misapplied. Currer Bell has much yet to learn,–and, especially, the discipline of her own tumultuous energies. She must learn also to sacrifice a little of her Yorkshire roughness to the demands of good taste: neither saturating her writings with such rudeness and offensive harshness, nor suffering her

Charlotte Brontë's 9 January 1850 letter to her publisher's mother. Charlotte stayed with Mrs. Smith and the Smith family during her visits to London in December 1849, May 1850, May 1851, and January 1853 (from Life and Works of the Sisters Brontë, *Fort Lewis College).*

whether he would be true to us; I
will tell you, who would better espouse
and defend our cause; the very
men who attacks us; in Mr— Thacker
ay's nature as a good angel and a
bad, and I would match the one
against the other.

Will you ask Mr— Smith whether
the 2 vols of "Violet" reached him safely,
I returned them by post as I remembered he said they were borrowed.
Give my kind regards to all your
family circle, tell little Bell to be sure
and not wear out her eyes with too
much reading or she will repent it
when she is grown a woman Believe
me, my dear Mrs— Smith
         Yours sincerely
              C Brontë

You demand a bulletin respecting the "little
books"; I am sorry I cannot issue a
more favourable one; they continue much
the same. Should they ever be finished,

style to wander into such vulgarities as would be inexcusable—even in a man. . . .

But, to quit this tone of remonstrance,—which after all is a compliment, for it shows how seriously we treat the great talents of the writer,—let us cordially praise the real freshness, vividness, and fidelity, with which most of the characters and scenes are depicted.

Similar power is manifested in the delineation of character: her eye is quick, her hand certain. With a few brief vigorous touches the picture starts into distinctness. Old Helstone, the copper-faced little Cossack parson, straight as a ramrod, keen as a kite; Yorke, the hard, queer, clever, parson-hating, radical-Gentleman; the benevolent Hall; the fluttering, good, irresolute Mrs Pryor; the patient, frugal, beneficent old maid, Miss Ainley; Hortense and Moore, and the Sympson family,—are all set with so much life before us, that we seem to see them moving through the rooms and across the moor. . . .

The two heroes of the book, however,—for there are two—are not agreeable characters; nor are they felicitously drawn. They have both something sordid in their minds, and repulsive in their demeanour. Louis Moore is talked about as if he were something greater than our ordinary humanity; but, when he shows himself, turns out to be a very small person indeed. Robert, more energetic, and more decisively standing out from the canvas, is disgraced by a sordid love of money, and a shameless setting aside of an affection for Caroline in favour of the rich heiress. . . . A hero may be faulty, erring, imperfect; but he must not be sordid, mean, wanting in the statelier virtues of our kind. Rochester was far more to be respected than this Robert Moore! Nor is Louis Moore much better. On any generous view of life there is almost as much sordidness in his exaggerated notions of Shirley's wealth, and of the *distance* it creates between his soul and hers, as there is in Robert's direct and positive greed of the money. . . .

The heroines are more lovable. Shirley, if she did not occasionally use language one would rather not hear from the lips of a lady, and did not occasionally display something in her behaviour, which, with every allowance for Yorkshire plainness, does imply want of breeding,—Shirley, we say, would be irresistible. So buoyant, free, airy, and healthy in her nature, so fascinating in her manner, she is prettily enough described by her lover as a 'Peri too mutinous for heaven, too innocent for hell.' But if Shirley is, on the whole, a happy creation, Caroline Helstone, though sometimes remarkably sweet and engaging, is—if we may venture to say so—a failure. Currer Bell is exceedingly scornful on the chapter of heroines drawn by men. The cleverest and acutest of our sex, she says, are often under the strangest illusions about women—

we do not read them in their true light; we constantly misapprehend them, both for good and evil. Very possibly. But we suspect that female artists are by no means exempt from mistakes quite as egregious when *they* delineate their sex; nay, we venture to say, that Mrs. Pryor and Caroline Helstone are as untrue to the universal laws of our common nature as if they had been drawn by the clumsy hand of a male: though we willingly admit that in both there are little touches which at once betray the more exquisite workmanship of a woman's lighter pencil.

Mrs. Pryor, in the capital event of her life—at least as far as regards this story—belies, the most indisputable laws of our nature, in becoming an unnatural mother,—from some absurd prepossession that her child *must* be bad, wicked, and the cause of anguish to her, because it is pretty! . . . Really this is midsummer madness! Before the child had shown whether its beauty *did* conceal perversity, the mother shuts her heart against it! Currer Bell! if under your heart had ever stirred a child, if to your bosom a babe had ever been pressed,—that mysterious part of your being, towards which all the rest of it was drawn, in which your whole soul was transported and absorbed,—never could you have *imagined* such a falsehood as that! It is indeed conceivable—under some peculiar circumstances, and with peculiar dispositions—that the loathing of the wife for the husband, might extend to the child, because it was the husband's child; the horror and hate being so intense as to turn back the natural current of maternal instincts; but to suppose that the mere beauty and 'aristocratic' air of an infant could so wrest out of its place a woman's heart,—supposing her not irretrievably insane,—and for eighteen years keep a mother from her child, is to outrage all that we know of human nature.

Not quite so glaring, and yet very glaring, is the want of truth in Caroline. There are traits about this character quite charming; and we doubt not she will be a favourite with the majority of readers. But any one examining 'Shirley' as a work of art, must be struck with want of keeping in making the gentle, shy, not highly cultivated Caroline *talk* from time to time in the strain of Currer Bell herself rather than in the strain of Helstone's little niece. We could cite several examples: the most striking perhaps is that long soliloquy at pages 269–274 of the second volume, upon the condition of women,—in which Caroline takes a leaf out of Miss Martineau's book. The whole passage, though full both of thought and of eloquence, is almost ludicrously out of place. The apostrophes to the King of Israel, to the fathers of Yorkshire, and to the men of England, might have rounded a period in one of the authoress's own perorations; but to introduce them into a soliloquy by

If Fieldhead had few other merits as a building, it might at least be termed picturesque: its irregular architecture, and the grey and mossy colouring communicated by time, gave it a just claim to this epithet. The old latticed windows, the stone porch, the walls, the roof, the chimney-stacks, were rich in crayon touches and sepia lights and shades. The trees behind were fine, bold, and spreading; the cedar on the lawn in front was grand, and the granite urns on the garden wall, the fretted arch of the gateway, were, for an artist, as the very desire of the eye.

—*Shirley,* book 1, chapter 11

Two views of Oakwell Hall, Birstall, the model for Fieldhead in Shirley. *When Charlotte saw it in the 1830s, it was in use as a school run by a relative of Ellen Nussey (from* The Bookman, *October 1904).*

Caroline Helstone is an offence at once against art and against nature.

This, however, is but one point in the faulty treatment of the character. A graver error,—one implying greater forgetfulness of dramatic reality and probability,—is the conduct of Caroline in her love for Moore. The mystery kept up between the two girls is the trick of a vulgar novelist. Shirley must have set Caroline's mind at rest; *must* have said, 'Don't be unhappy about Moore and me; I have no love for him—nor he for me.' Instead of this, she is allowed to encourage the delusion which she cannot but perceive in Caroline's mind; but what is more incredible still, Caroline—who believes that Moore loves Shirley and will marry her—never once feels the sharp and terrible pang of jealousy! Now, unless we are to be put out of court as men, and consequently incompetent to apprehend the true nature of woman, we should say that this entire absence of jealous feelings on Caroline's part, is an omission, which, conscious or unconscious, we cannot reconcile with any thing we have ever seen, heard, or read of about the sex. That a girl like Caroline might be willing to resign her claims, might be willing even to submit in silence to the torture of her disappointment, is conceivable enough; and a fine theme might this have afforded for some profound psychological probings, laying open the terrible conflict of irrepressible instincts with more generous feelings,—the conflict of jealousy with reason. But Caroline Helstone merely bows her head in meekness, and loves and clings to Shirley all the more; never has even a moment's rebellion against her, and behaves like pattern young ladies in 'good' books! . . .

. . . The attack on the Mill, too, instead of being described in the natural course of the narrative, is told us in snatches of dialogue between the two girls; who, in utter defiance of all *vraisemblance,* are calm spectators of that which they could not have seen. It is scarcely worth while to point out the several details in this scene, which betray a female and inexperienced hand. Incident is not the *forte* of Currer Bell. If her invention were in any degree equal to her powers of execution, (with a little more judgment and practice,) she would stand alone among novelists; but in invention she is as yet only an artisan, not an artist. . . .

Our closing word shall be one of exhortation. Schiller, writing to Goethe about Madame de Stael's 'Corinne,' says, 'This person wants every thing that is graceful in a woman; and, nevertheless, the faults of her book are altogether womanly faults. She steps out of her sex—without elevating herself above it.' This brief and pregnant criticism is quite as applicable to Currer Bell: For she, too, has genius enough to create a great name for herself; and if we seem to have insisted too gravely on her faults, it is only because we are ourselves sufficiently her admirers to be most desirous to see her remove these blemishes from her writings, and take the rank within her reach. She has extraordinary power—but let her remember that '*on tombe du côté où l'on penche!*' [*one falls in the direction in which one leans!*]

—*The Edinburgh Review,* 91 (January 1850): 153–173

* * *

"An *Author* Not as a Woman" Currer Bell Responds to Lewes's Review

Brontë's first response to Lewes was a single line that was probably sent around 10 January 1850.

I can be on my guard against my enemies, but God deliver me from my friends!

Currer Bell

She sent a more detailed explanation of her objections to his review on 19 January 1850.

My dear Sir

I will tell you why I was so hurt by that review in the Edinburgh; not because its criticism was keen or its blame sometimes severe; not because its praise was stinted (for indeed I think you give me quite as much praise as I deserve) but because, after I had said earnestly that I wished critics would judge me as an *author* not as a woman, you so roughly—I even thought—so cruelly handled the question of sex. I daresay you meant no harm, and perhaps you will not now be able to understand why I was so grieved at, what you will probably deem, such a trifle; but grieved I was, and indignant too.

There was a passage or two which you did quite wrong to write.

However I will not bear malice against you for it: I know what your nature is; it is not a bad or an unkind one, though you would often jar terribly on some feelings with whose recoil and quiver you could not possibly sympathize. I imagine you are both enthusiastic and implacable, as you are at once sagacious and careless. You know much and discover much, but you are in such a hurry to tell it all, you never give yourself time to think how your reckless eloquence may affect others, and, what is more, if you knew how it did affect them you would not much care.

However I shake hands with you: you have excellent points; you can be generous: I still feel angry and think I do well to be angry, but it is the anger one experiences for rough play rather than for foul play.

I am yours with a certain respect and some chagrin

Currer Bell

—*The Letters of Charlotte Brontë,* v. 2, pp. 330, 332–333

This unsigned review compares Brontë's novel to Elizabeth Gaskell's Mary Barton *(1848), a work that had been attacked as being biased against employers.*

"A Feeble Effort"
Review of *Shirley*

'Shirley' is a novel which has floated into circulation on the popularity of its predecessors. 'Jane Eyre' was a remarkable production. There was originality in its construction, skill in the delineation of character, and great artistic power in the development of a plot—in itself a simple one, but wrought up to scenes of breathless interest. Moreover, it touched, although with great delicacy, upon certain ethical problems which were certain to lead to controversy, and which at once compelled every one to read the book who would take any part in the evening discussions of a lady's drawing-room. 'Shirley' is nothing of this: it has a merit of its own; but must be regarded as a feeble effort—the effort, however, of a writer who shows in every page that she could do better if she would, but has been only half inspired by her subject. She tells us, in her preface, that we are not to expect a thrilling narrative, and she keeps her word. The character and incidents of the first volume fade from the memory before we have fairly got to the end; and, what is more provoking, in the third, when our attention ought to be at least fairly aroused, we can lay down the book in the middle of a chapter,—and go to sleep. This failure arises from the interest being too much diffused. The *dramatis personae* are numerous, and many of them of no assistance to the plot; while in 'Jane Eyre' the interest was concentrated upon the heroine and Mrs Rochester. 'Shirley' begins with an extravagant portraiture of three young curates (very much in the nature of a caricature, but without bitterness), who, after supplying the materials of a few chapters, are quietly dropped, as of no further use to the author. Then we have two heroines where one would suffice—sweetness and gentleness in the person of Caroline Helston, and fire and animation in the person of Shirley—the latter a clever heiress, cleverly drawn. Both these ladies are

Drawings of the title character by F. H. Townsend for an 1897 edition of Shirley *published in London by Service & Paton: left, from the chapter titled "Mr. Donne's Exodus"; right, from "The First Blue-Stocking" (from* The Bookman, *October 1904)*

in love with two brothers, without knowing it. One of the brothers is in the same predicament; and the other, who is intended as the soul of honour, only just escapes the condemnation of the reader as a bashful blockhead. When, in the *dénouement,* they all get comfortably married, we are glad that they have at last found out the state of each other's minds, but wonder they did not sooner make the same discovery, 'Shirley' is to some extent a reminiscence of 'Mary Barton.' The tale, like 'Mary Barton,' is laid in the manufacturing districts, and the wrongs and rights of mill-owners and their operatives form the subsidiary parts of the story. In treating of these questions, a discriminating and a kindly spirit is evinced, with a manifold desire to heal the antagonism of classes; and we are glad to notice generally this great improvement in modern works of fiction.
—*The Westminster Review,* 52 (January 1850): pp. 418–419

* * *

By early 1850, rumors were widespread in the Haworth area that Charlotte was in fact the famed author Currer Bell. On 28 February 1850 the Bradford Observer *reported: "It is understood that the only daughter of the Rev P Brontë, incumbent of Haworth is the authoress of* Jane Eyre *and* Shirley, *two of the most popular novels of the day, which have appeared under the name of 'Currer Bell.'" In this excerpt Brontë remarks on the response of the curates she caricatured in her novel.*

Charlotte Brontë to William Smith Williams, 3 April 1850

. . . it may be that annoying remarks, if made, are not suffered to reach my ear, but certainly, while I have heard little condemnatory of "Shirley"—more than once have I been deeply moved by manifestations of even enthusiastic approbation. I deem it unwise to dwell much on these matters, but for once I must permit myself to remark that the generous pride many of the Yorkshire people have taken in the matter has been such as to awake and claim my gratitude—especially since it has afforded a source of reviving pleasure to my Father in his old age. The very Curates—poor fellows! shew no resentment; each characteristically finds solace for his own wounds in crowing over his brethren. Mr. Donne was—at first, a little disturbed; for a week or two he fidgetted about the neighbourhood in some disquietude—but he is now soothed down, only yesterday I had pleasure of making him a comfortable cup of tea and seeing him sip it with revived complacency. It is a curious fact that since he read "Shirley" he has come to the house oftener than ever and been

Thackeray's house, No. 13 Young Street, Kensington, where he lived from 1846 to 1853 (from Lewis Melville, William Makepeace Thackeray: A Biography, *University of Colorado Libraries)*

remarkably meek and assiduous to please.—Some people's natures are veritable enigmas—I quite expected to have one good scene at the least with him, but as yet nothing of the sort has occurred—and if the other curates do not tease him into irritation, he will remain quiet now.
—*The Letters of Charlotte Brontë,* v. 2, pp. 375–376

* * *

In New Zealand, Mary Taylor, a single woman supporting herself, was passionate in her response to what she had learned of Charlotte's treatment of her theme. Excerpts.

Mary Taylor to Charlotte Brontë, April 1850

I have set up shop! I am delighted with it it *[sic]* as a whole—that is it is as pleasant or as little disagreeable as you can expect an employment to be that you earn your living by. The best of it is that your labour has some return and you are not forced to work on hopelessly without result. . . .

The Brontë-Thackeray Relationship

Charlotte Brontë again visited London in May 1850 and stayed with the Smiths at Gloucester Terrace, Hyde Park Gardens. She went to the opera, the Royal Academy, the Zoological Gardens, the Ladies' Gallery in the House of Commons, and saw her longtime hero the Duke of Wellington in the Chapel Royal. Charlotte also had dinner at Thackeray's house on Young Street, beginning a relationship that George Smith recounts.

On an occasion when I took her to dine with Mr. Thackeray the excitement with which Charlotte Brontë's visit was expected is portrayed by Miss Thackeray, who was then a mere child:

I can still see the scene quite plainly!—the hot summer evening, the open windows, the carriage driving to the door as we all sat silent and expectant; my father, who rarely waited, waiting with us: our governess, my sister, and I all in a row, and prepared for the great event. We saw the carriage stop, and out of it sprang the active, well-knit figure of young Mr. George Smith, who was bringing Miss Brontë to see our father. My father, who had been walking up and down the room, goes out into the hall to meet his guests, and then after a moment's delay the door opens wide, and the two gentlemen come in, leading a tiny, delicate, serious, little lady, pale, with fair straight hair, and steady eyes. She may be a little over thirty; she is dressed in a little *barège* dress with a pattern of faint green moss. She enters in mittens, in silence, in seriousness; our hearts are beating with wild excitement.

Charlotte Brontë's intense interest in Thackeray, to whom she had dedicated the second edition of 'Jane Eyre,' is graphically described by Miss Thackeray:

She sat gazing at him with kindling eyes of interest, lighting up with a sort of illumination every now and then as she answered him. I can see her bending forward over the table, not eating, but listening to what he said as he carved the dish before him.

Thackeray himself has drawn a touching picture of Charlotte Brontë as he first saw her:

'I saw her first' he says, 'just as I rose out of an illness from which I had never thought to recover. I remember the trembling little frame, the little hand, the great honest eyes. An impetuous honesty seemed to me to characterise the woman.'

Smith later relates how Thackeray offended Brontë "by failing to respect the anonymity behind which, at that time, she was very anxious to screen herself."

. . . On another occasion Thackeray roused the hidden fire in Charlotte Brontë's soul, and was badly scorched himself as the result. My mother and I had taken her to one of Thackeray's lectures on 'The English Humourists.' After the lecture Thackeray came down from the platform and shook hands with many of the audience, receiving their congratulations and compliments. He was in high spirits, and rather thoughtlessly said to his mother—Mrs. Carmichael Smyth—'Mother, you must allow me to introduce you to Jane Eyre.' This was uttered in a loud voice, audible over half the room. Everybody near turned round and stared at the disconcerted little lady, who grew confused and angry when she realised that every eye was fixed upon her. My mother got her away as quickly as possible.

On the next afternoon Thackeray called. I arrived at home shortly afterwards, and when I entered the drawing-room found a scene in full progress. Only these two were in the room. Thackeray was standing on the hearthrug, looking anything but happy. Charlotte Brontë stood close to him, with head thrown back and face white with anger. The first words I heard were, 'No, Sir ! If *you* had come to our part of the country in Yorkshire, what would you have thought of me if I had introduced you to my father, before a mixed company of strangers, as "Mr. Warrington"?' Thackeray replied, 'No, you mean "Arthur Pendennis."' 'No, I *don't* mean Arthur Pendennis!' retorted Miss Brontë; 'I mean Mr. Warrington, and Mr. Warrington would not have behaved as you behaved to me yesterday.' The spectacle of this little woman, hardly reaching to Thackeray's elbow, but, somehow, looking stronger and fiercer than himself, and casting her incisive words at his head, resembled the dropping of shells into a fortress.

By this time I had recovered my presence of mind, and hastened to interpose. Thackeray made the necessary and half-humorous apologies, and the parting was a friendly one.

Thackeray shocked Charlotte Brontë sadly by the fashion of his talk on literary subjects. The truth is, Charlotte Brontë's heroics roused Thackeray's antagonism. He declined to pose on a pedestal for her admiration, and with characteristic contrariety of nature he seemed to be tempted to say the very things that set Charlotte Brontë's teeth, so to speak, on edge, and affronted all her ideals. He insisted on discussing his books very much as a clerk in a bank would discuss the ledgers he had to keep for a salary. But all this was, on Thackeray's part, an affectation; an affectation into which he was provoked by what he considered Charlotte Brontë's high falutin'. Miss Brontë wanted to persuade him that he was a great man with a 'mission'; and Thackeray, with many wicked jests, declined to recognise the 'mission.'

But, despite all this, Charlotte Brontë, much as she scolded Thackeray, never doubted his greatness. He was, she once said, 'a Titan in mind.'

—"Charlotte Brontë," *The Cornhill Magazine*, new series 9 (December 1900): 788–789, 790–791

I have seen some extracts from Shirley in which you talk of women working. And this first duty, this great necessity you seem to think that *some* women may indulge in—if they give up marriage and don't make themselves too disagreeable to the other sex. You are a coward and a traitor. A woman who works is by that alone better than one who does not and a woman who does not happen to be rich and who *still* earns no money and does not wish to do so, is guilty of a great fault—almost a crime—A dereliction of duty which leads rapidly and almost certainly to all manner of degradation. It is very wrong of you to *plead* for toleration for workers on the ground of their being in peculiar circumstances and few in number or singular in disposition. Work or degradation is the lot of all except the very small number born to wealth.

—*Mary Taylor: Friend of Charlotte Brontë*, pp. 92–94

* * *

Mary was the basis for Rose Yorke in Shirley.

Mary Taylor to Charlotte Brontë, 13 August 1850

Dear Charlotte

After waiting about six months we have just got Shirley. It was landed from the Constantinople one Monday afternoon just in the thick of our preparations for a "small party" for the next day. . . . On Wednesday I began Shirley and continued in a curious confusion of mind till now principally abt the handsome foreigner who was nursed in our house when I was a little girl.—By the way you've put him in the servant's bedroom. You make us all talk much as I think we shd have done if we'd ventured to speak at all—What a little lump of perfection you've made me! There is a strange feeling in reading it of hearing us all talking. I have not seen the matted hall and painted parlour windows so plain these 5 years. But my Father is not like. He hates well enough and perhaps loves too but he is not honest enough. It was from my father I learnt not to marry for money nor to tolerate any one who did and he never wd advise any one to do so or fail to speak with contempt of those who did. Shirley is much more interesting than J. Eyre—who indeed never interests you at all until she has something to suffer. All through this last novel there is so much more life and stir—that it leaves you far more to remember than the other.

—*Mary Taylor: Friend of Charlotte Brontë*, pp. 96–98

At the Crystal Palace

In May 1851, Charlotte traveled to London to stay with the Smiths again. During her visit, she saw plays at the French Theatre and the picture galleries at Somerset House, Grosvenor House, and Bridgewater House. With George Smith (under the aliases Mr. and Miss Fraser) she went to the phrenologist Dr. Brown to have their personalities read.

Brontë was fascinated by the Great Exhibition, or Crystal Palace, which she visited five times. This excerpt is from her 7 June 1851 letter to her father.

Yesterday I went for the second time to the Crystal Palace—we remained in it about three hours—and I must say I was more struck with it on this occasion tha[n] at my first visit. It is a wonderful place—vast—strange new and impossible to describe. Its grandeur does not consist in one thing but in the unique assemblage of all things—Whatever human industry has created—you find there—from the great compartments filled with Railway Engines and boilers, with Mill-machinery in full work—with splendid carriages of all kinds—with harness of every description—to the glass-covered and velvet spread stands loaded with the most gorgeous work of the goldsmith and silversmith—and the carefully guarded caskets full of real diamonds and pearls worth hundreds of thousands of pounds. It may be called a Bazaar or a Fair—but it is such a Bazaar or Fair as eastern Genii might have created. It seems as if magic only could have gathered this mass of wealth from all the ends of the Earth—as if none but supernatural hands could have arranged it thus—with such a blaze and contrast of colours and marvellous power of effect. The multitude filling the great aisles seems ruled and subdued by some invisible influence—Amongst the thirty thousand souls that peopled it the day I was there, not one loud noise was to be heard—not one irregular movement seen—the living tide rolls on quietly with a deep hum like the sea heard from a distance.

—*The Letters of Charlotte Brontë*, v. 2, pp. 630–631

"Against the Grain"

Charlotte had first met the prolific writer Harriet Martineau (1802–1876) in December 1849. This excerpt is from a letter to Martineau that Brontë probably wrote in early October 1850.

. . . were I dependent on my exertions for my daily bread, I think I would rather hire myself out again as a governess than write against the grain or out of the mood. I am not like you, who have no bad days. I have bad days, bad weeks, aye! and bad months.

—*The Letters of Charlotte Brontë*, v. 2, pp. 480–481

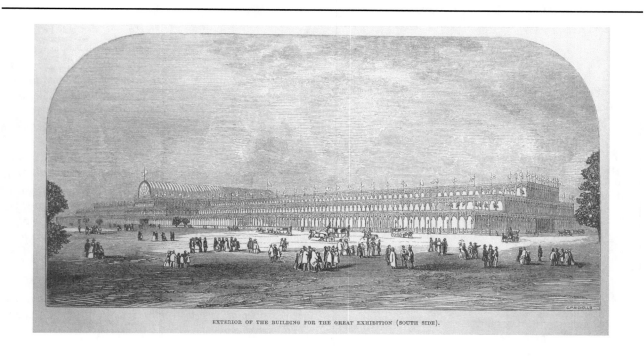

EXTERIOR OF THE BUILDING FOR THE GREAT EXHIBITION (SOUTH SIDE).

THE MAIN AVENUE—EAST.

Two views of the Great Exhibition, which Charlotte Brontë visited often during her spring 1851 London stay (from The Art Journal
Illustrated Catalogue: The Industry of All Nations, *University of Colorado Libraries)*

"A Lion out of Judah"

George Smith recalls his mother's story of taking Brontë to see Samuel Laurence's portrait of Thackeray.

Before Thackeray went to America in the autumn of 1852 I had a portrait of him made by Mr. Samuel Laurence as a present to his daughters. My mother took Charlotte Brontë to see it at the artist's studio. It was a very fine and expressive rendering of Thackeray's powerful head. Charlotte Brontë stood looking long upon it in silence; and then, as if quoting the words unconsciously, she said: 'There came up a lion out of Judah.'

–"Charlotte Brontë," *The Cornhill Magazine,*
new series 9 (December 1900): 791

WILLIAM MAKEPEACE THACKERAY
From a painting by Samuel Laurence in the National Portrait Gallery

William Makepeace Thackeray, as painted by Samuel Laurence (National Portrait Gallery, from Lewis Melville, William Makepeace Thackeray: A Biography, *University of Colorado Libraries)*

Villette

Some critics and scholars believe that Villette *is Charlotte Brontë's best novel. Her transposition of her own Brussels experiences to the imaginary city of Villette includes the pain of her unrequited love for Constantin Héger, the model for Paul Emmanuel. Her heroine, Lucy Snowe, is often compared with Jane Eyre in her appearance and demeanor.*

Charlotte began writing Villette *in February 1852, after a bout of illness from December 1851 to January 1852 that was worsened by the "blue pills" she was prescribed. By the end of March 1852, Charlotte had drafted the first volume of* Villette; *the second volume took Charlotte until the end of October 1852 to finish. She then sent the first two volumes of what was to be a three-volume work to Smith, Elder for comment.*

In this letter Brontë contrasts her work to Harriet Beecher Stowe's Uncle Tom's Cabin *(1852), which had become a sensation in the United States by treating the important issue of slavery. Excerpts.*

Charlotte Brontë to George Smith, 30 October 1852

You must notify honestly what you think of "Villette" when you have read it. I can hardly tell you how much I hunger to have some opinion besides my own, and how I have sometimes desponded and almost despaired because there was no one to whom to read a line–or of whom to ask a counsel. "Jane Eyre" was not written under such circumstances, nor were two-thirds of "Shirley". I got so miserable about it, I could bear no allusion to the book–it is not finished yet, but now–I hope.

As to the anonymous publication–I have this to say. If the witholding of the author's name should tend materially to injure the publisher's interest–to interfere with booksellers' orders &c. I would not press the point; but if no such detriment is contingent–I should be most thankful for the sheltering shadow of an incognito. I seem to dread the advertisements–the large lettered "Currer Bell's New Novel" or "New Work by the Author of 'Jane Eyre'". These, however, I feel well enough are the transcendentalisms of a retired wretch–and must not be intruded in the way of solid considerations; so you must speak frankly. . . .

You will see that "Villette" touches on no matter of public interest. I cannot write books handling the topics of the day–it is of no use trying. Nor can I write a book for its moral–Nor can I take up a philanthropic scheme though I honour Philanthropy–And voluntarily and sincerely veil my face before such a mighty subject as that handled in Mrs. Beecher Stowe's work–"Uncle Tom's Cabin".

Blue Pills

Charlotte Brontë suffered from various illnesses and symptoms over the course of her life. She was subject to frequent headaches and to bouts of depression; additionally, she had "bilious" complaints in which her liver functions seemed impaired. The medical science of her day could offer little to ameliorate the state of her health—and on at least one occasion seriously undermined her health.

In late 1851 and early 1852, before beginning work on Villette, she had a particularly disabling set of complaints for which she was prescribed "blue pills"—a remedy that contained the powerful neurotoxin mercury, which ingested in too great quantities can result in serious complications. In an undated January letter she reported her condition to Ellen Nussey:

I have certainly been ill enough since I wrote to you—but do not be alarmed or uneasy—I believe my sufferings have been partly perhaps in a great measure owing to the medicine—the pills given me—they were alterative and contained a mixture of Mercury—this did not suit me—I was brought to a sad state . . .

Charlotte was evidently able to recover fully after she stopped taking the pills, but she had become very ill indeed, as she admitted in a letter to Ellen dated 16 January:

I am better—to-day—much better—but you can have little idea of the sort of condition into which Mercury throws people to ask me to go from home anywhere in close or open carriage—and as to talking—four days since I could not well have articulated three sentences—my mouth and tongue were ulcerated—for a week I took no sustenance except half-a-tea-cupful of liquid administered by tea-spoonfuls in the course of the day—yet I did not need nursing—and I kept out of bed. It was enough to burden myself—it would have been misery to me to have annoyed another.

—*The Letters of Charlotte Brontë*, v. 3, p. 7

To manage these great matters rightly they must be long and practically studied—their bearings known intimately and their evils felt genuinely—they must not be taken up as a business-matter and a trading-speculation. I doubt not Mrs. Stowe had felt the iron of slavery enter into her heart from childhood upwards long before she ever thought of writing books. The feeling throughout her work is sincere and not got up.

Remember to be an honest critic of "Villette" and tell Mr. Williams to be unsparing—not that I am likely to alter anything—but I want to know his impressions and yours.

—*The Letters of Charlotte Brontë*, v. 3, pp. 74–75

* * *

Smith wrote back with encouragement, criticism, and publishing concerns, to which Charlotte responded in this excerpt.

Charlotte Brontë to George Smith, 3 November 1852

I feel very grateful for your letter: it relieved me much for I was a good deal harassed by doubts as to how "Villette" might appear in other eyes than my own. I feel in some degree authorized to rely on your favourable impressions, because you are quite right where you hint disapprobation; you have exactly hit two points at least where I was conscious of defect: the discrepancy, the want of perfect harmony between Graham's boyhood and manhood; the angular abruptness of his change of sentiment towards Miss Fanshawe. You must remember though that in secret he had for some time appreciated that young lady at a somewhat depressed standard—held her as a *little* lower than the angels, but still—the reader ought to have been better made to feel this preparation towards a change of mood.

As for the publishing arrangements—I leave them to Cornhill. There is undoubtedly a certain force in what you say about the inexpediency of affecting a mystery which cannot be sustained—so you must act as you think is for the best. I submit also to the advertisements and large letters—but under protest, and with a kind of Ostrich-longing for concealment.

Most of the 3rd. Vol. is given to the development of the "crabbed Professor's" character. Lucy must not marry Dr. John; he is far too youthful, handsome, bright-spirited and sweet-tempered; he is a "curled darling" of Nature and of Fortune; he must draw a prize in Life's Lottery; his wife must be young, rich and pretty; he must be made very happy indeed. If Lucy marries anybody—it must be the Professor—a man in whom there is much to forgive—much to "put up with." But I am not leniently disposed towards Miss Frost—from the beginning I never intended to appoint her lines in pleasant places.

The conclusion of this 3rd. Vol. is still a matter of some anxiety. I can but do my best, however; it would speedily be finished—could I but ward off certain obnoxious headaches which—whenever I get into the spirit of my work, are apt to seize and prostrate me.

—*The Letters of Charlotte Brontë*, v. 3, pp. 77–78

* * *

Writing about Imagined Experience

Elizabeth Gaskell reports Charlotte's description of how she wrote about experience of which she had no firsthand knowledge.

I asked her whether she had ever taken opium, as the description given of its effects in "Villette" was so exactly like what I had experienced,—vivid and exaggerated presence of objects, of which the outlines were indistinct, or lost in golden mist, &c. She replied, that she had never, to her knowledge, taken a grain of it in any shape, but that she had followed the process she always adopted when she had to describe anything which had not fallen within her own experience; she had thought intently on it for many and many a night before falling to sleep, —wondering what it was like, or how it would be, —till at length, sometimes after the progress of her story had been arrested at this one point for weeks, she wakened up in the morning with all clear before her, as if she had in reality gone through the experience, and then could describe it, word for word, as it had happened. I cannot account for this psychologically; I only am sure that it was so, because she said it.

—The Life of Charlotte Brontë,
v. 2, p. 301

Charlotte Brontë to William Smith Williams, 6 November 1852

My dear Sir

I must not delay thanking you for your kind letter with its candid and able commentary on "Villette". With many of your strictures—I concur. The 3rd. Vol. may perhaps do away with some of the objections—others will remain in force. I do not think the interest of the story culminates anywhere to the degree you would wish. What climax there is—does not come on till near the conclusion—and even then—I doubt whether the regular novel-reader will consider "the agony piled sufficiently high"—(as the Americans say) or the colours dashed on to the Canvass with the proper amount of daring. Still—I fear they must be satisfied with what is offered: my palette affords no brighter tints—were I to attempt to deepen the reds or burnish the yellows—I should but botch.

Unless I am mistaken—the emotion of the book will be found to be kept throughout in tolerable subjection.

As to the name of the heroine—I can hardly express what subtility of thought made me decide upon giving her a cold name; but—at first—I called her "Lucy Snowe" (spelt with an e) which "Snowe" I afterward changed to "Frost". Subsequently—I rather regretted the change and wished it "Snowe" again: if not too late—I should like the alteration to be made now throughout the M.S. A <u>cold</u> name she must have—partly—perhaps—on the "lucus a non

lucendo"—principle—partly on that of the "fitness of things"—for she has about her an external coldness.

You say that she may be thought morbid and weak unless the history of her life be more fully given. I consider that she <u>is</u> both morbid and weak at times—the character sets up no pretensions to unmixed strength—and anybody living her life would necessarily become morbid. It was no impetus of healthy feeling which urged her to the confessional for instance—it was the semi-delirium of solitary grief and sickness. If, however, the book does not express all this—there must be a great fault somewhere—

I might explain away a few other points but it would be too much like drawing a picture and then writing underneath the name of the object intended to be represented. We know what sort of a pencil that is which needs an ally in the pen.

Thanking you again for the clearness and fulness with which you have responded to my request for a statement of impressions—I am, my dear Sir

Yours very sincerely
C Brontë

I trust the work will be seen in M.S. by no one except Mr. Smith and yourself.

—The Letters of Charlotte Brontë, v. 3, p. 80

* * *

Brontë finished the third volume by 20 November 1852, and Smith, Elder published Villette *28 January 1853. Smith was able to note many details from Brontë's third novel that he and his family had experienced.*

Villette and "Miss Brontë's Visits"
George Smith

'Villette' is full of scenes which one can trace to incidents which occurred during Miss Brontë's visits to us.

The scene at the theatre, at Brussels in that book, and the description of the actress, were suggested by Rachel, whom we took her to see more than once. The scene of the fire comes from a slight accident to the scenery at Devonshire House, where Charles Dickens, Mr. Forster, and other men of letters gave a performance. I took Charlotte Brontë and one of my sisters to Devonshire House, and when the performance, which was for a charity, was repeated, I took another of my sisters, who had been too unwell to go on the first occasion, and a Miss D. At one stage of the second performance the scenery caught fire. There was some risk of a general panic, and I took my sister and Miss D. each by the wrist, and held them down till the panic had ceased. I seem to have written a description of the occurrence to Miss Brontë, for I find that she refers to it in one of her letters, saying, 'It is easy to realise the scene.'

In 'Villette' my mother was the original of 'Mrs. Bretton;' several of her expressions are given *verbatim*. I myself, as I discovered, stood for 'Dr. John.' Charlotte Brontë admitted this to Mrs. Gaskell, to whom she wrote: ' I was kept waiting longer than usual for Mr. Smith's opinion of the book, and I was rather uneasy, for I was afraid he had found me out, and was offended.'

–"Charlotte Brontë," *The Cornhill Magazine,*
new series 9 (December 1900): 793

* * *

Reviews of Villette *were generally positive. Many reviewers found the novel more powerfully and effectively written than* Shirley; *some ranked* Villette *above* Jane Eyre.

This unsigned review was by Harriet Martineau, who had written much to the same effect in a personal letter to Charlotte. It was among the most critical responses to the novel and led to the estrangement of the two authors.

"Almost Intolerably Painful"
Review of *Villette*

Everything written by 'Currer Bell' is remarkable. She can touch nothing without leaving on it the stamp of originality. Of her three books, this is perhaps the strangest, the most astonishing, though not the best. The sustained ability is perhaps greater in *Villette* than in its two predecessors, there being no intervals of weakness, except in the form of a few passages, chiefly episodical, of over-wrought writing, which, though evidently a sincere endeavour to express real feeling, are not felt to be congenial, or very intelligible, in the midst of so much that is strong and clear. In regard to interest, we think that this book will be pronounced inferior to *Jane Eyre* and superior to *Shirley*. In point of construction it is superior to both; and this is a vast gain and a great encouragement to hope for future benefits from the same hand which shall surpass any yet given. The whole three volumes are crowded with beauties–with the good things for which we look to the clear sight, deep feeling and singular, though not extensive, experience of life which we associate with the name of 'Currer Bell'. But under all, through all, over all, is felt a drawback, of which we were anxious before, but which is terribly aggravated here–the book is almost intolerably painful. We are wont to say, when we read narratives which are made up of the external woes of life, such as may and do happen every day, but are never congregated in one experience–that the

Harriet Martineau, essayist, short-story writer, and novelist, who became Charlotte Brontë's friend and correspondent. Charlotte visited Martineau's home at Ambleside in December 1850 but was later offended by the older writer's criticism of Villette.

author has no right to make readers so miserable. We do not know whether the right will be admitted in the present case, on the ground of the woes not being external; but certainly we ourselves have felt inclined to rebel against the pain, and, perhaps on account of protraction, are disposed to deny its necessity and truth. With all her objectivity, 'Currer Bell' here afflicts us with an amount of subjective misery which we may fairly remonstrate against; and she allows us no respite–even while treating us with humour, with charming description and the presence of those whom she herself regards as the good and gay. In truth, there is scarcely anybody that is good–serenely and cheerfully good, and the gaiety has pain in it. An atmosphere of pain hangs about the whole, forbidding that repose which we hold to be essential to the true presentment of any large portion of life and experience. In this pervading pain, the book reminds us of Balzac; and so it does in the prevalence

VILLETTE.

BY CURRER BELL,

AUTHOR OF "JANE EYRE," "SHIRLEY," ETC.

IN THREE VOLUMES.

VOL. I.

LONDON:
SMITH, ELDER & CO., 65, CORNHILL.

SMITH, TAYLOR & CO., BOMBAY.
—
1853.
The Author of this work reserves the right of translating it.

Title page for Charlotte Bronte's third novel (Thomas Cooper Library, University of South Carolina)

A Last London Visit

Charlotte resisted visiting London for several years, believing she needed to produce another novel before she deserved such a trip. On what would turn out to be her last trip to London in January 1853, Charlotte stayed with the Smiths while correcting the proofs of Villette; *during this visit she decided to see another side of London, which she describes in this excerpt from her 19 January letter to Ellen Nussey.*

I still continue to get on very comfortably and quietly in London—in the way I like—seeing rather things than persons—. Being allowed to have my own choice of sights this time—I selected rather the real than the decorative side of Life—I have been over two prisons ancient & modern—Newgate and Pentonville—also the Bank, the Exchange 'the Foundling Hospital,'—and to-day if all be well—I go with Dr. Forbes to see Bethlehem Hospital. Mrs. S[mith] and her daughters are—I believe—a little amazed at my gloomy tastes, but I take no notice. . . .
—*The Letters of Charlotte Brontë,* v. 3, p. 108

George Smith recalled Charlotte's behavior at Newgate prison.

. . . At Newgate she rapidly fixed her attention on an individual prisoner. There was a poor girl with an interesting face, and an expression of the deepest misery. She had, I believe, killed her illegitimate child. Miss Brontë walked up to her, took her hand, and began to talk to her. She was, of course, quickly interrupted by the prison warder with the formula, 'Visitors are not allowed to speak to the prisoners.'
—"Charlotte Brontë," *The Cornhill Magazine,* new series 9 (December 1900): 785

Elizabeth Gaskell comments on the effect of this last visit on the author.

The power of vast yet minute organisation, always called out her respect and admiration. She appreciated it more fully than most women are able to do. All that she saw during this last visit to London impressed her deeply—so much so as to render her incapable of the immediate expression of her feelings, or of reasoning upon her impressions while they were so vivid. If she had lived, her deep heart would sooner or later have spoken out on these things.
—*The Life of Charlotte Brontë,* v. 2, pp. 277–278

---

of one tendency, or one idea, throughout the whole conception and action. All the female characters, in all their thoughts and lives, are full of one thing, or are regarded by the reader in the light of that one thought—love. It begins with the child of six years old, at the opening—a charming picture—and it closes with it at the last page; and, so dominant is this idea—so incessant is the writer's tendency to describe the need of being loved, that the heroine, who tells her own story, leaves the reader at last under the uncomfortable impression of her having either entertained a double love, or allowed one to supersede another without notification of the transition. It is not thus in real life. There are substantial, heartfelt interests for women of all ages, and under ordinary circumstances, quite apart from love: there is an absence of introspection, an unconsciousness, a repose in women's lives—unless under peculiarly unfortunate circumstances—of which we find no admission in this book; and to the absence of it, may be attributed some of the criticism which the book will meet from readers who are not prudes, but whose reason and taste will reject the assumption that events and characters are to be regarded through the medium of one passion only.

And here ends all demur. We have thought it right to indicate clearly the two faults in the book, which it is scarcely probable that anyone will deny. Abstractions made of these, all else is power, skill and interest. The freshness will be complete to readers who know none but English novels. Those who are familiar with Balzac may be reminded, by the sharp distinction of the pictured life, place and circumstance, of some of the best of his tales: but there is nothing borrowed; nothing that we might not as well have had if 'Currer Bell' had never read a line of Balzac—which may very likely be the case. As far as we know, the life of a foreign *pension* (Belgian, evidently) and of a third-rate capital, with its half provincial population and proceedings, is new in purely English literature; and most lifelike and spirited it is. The humour which peeps out in the names—the court of Labassecour, with its heir-apparent, the Duc of Dindoneau—the Professors Boissec and Rochemorte—and so forth—is felt throughout, though there is not a touch of lightheartedness from end to end. The presence of the heroine in that capital and *pension* is strangely managed; and so is the gathering of her British friends around her there; but, that strangeness surmounted, the picture of their lives is admirable. The reader must go to the book for it; for it fills two volumes and a half out of the three. The heroine, Lucy Snowe, tells her own story. Every reader of *Jane Eyre* will be glad to see the autobiographical form returned to. Lucy may be thought a younger, feebler sister of Jane. There is just enough resemblance for that—but she has not Jane's charm of mental and moral health, and consequent repose. She is in a state of chronic nervous fever for the most part; is usually silent and suffering; when she speaks, speaks in enigmas or in raillery, and now and then breaks out under the torture of passion; but she acts admirably—with readiness, sense, conscience and kindliness. Still we do not wonder that she loved more than she was beloved, and the love at last would be surprising enough, if love could ever be so. Perhaps Pauline and her father are the best-drawn characters in the book, where all are more or less admirably delineated. We are not aware that there is one failure.

A striking peculiarity comes out in the third volume, striking from one so large and liberal, so removed from ordinary social prejudices as we have been accustomed to think 'Currer Bell'. She goes out of her way to express a passionate hatred of Romanism. It is not the calm disapproval of a ritual religion, such as we should have expected from her, ensuing upon a presentment of her own better faith. The religion she envokes is itself but a dark and doubtful refuge from the pain which

---

"Always Engaged in Observing and Analysing"

George Smith recalls the effect of Charlotte's several visits on his family.

Her letters show that she enjoyed the recollection of these visits, and the society at our house; but my mother and sisters found her a somewhat difficult guest, and I am afraid she was never perfectly at her ease with them. Strangers used to say that they were afraid of her. She was very quiet and self-absorbed, and gave the impression that she was always engaged in observing and analysing the people she met. She was sometimes tempted to confide her analysis to the victim. Here is an extract from a letter which she wrote to myself:

I will tell you a thing to be noted often in your letters and almost always in your conversation, a psychological thing, and not a matter pertaining to style or intellect—I mean an undercurrent of quiet raillery, an inaudible laugh to yourself, a not unkindly, but somewhat subtle playing on your correspondent or companion for the time being—in short a sly touch of a Mephistopheles with the fiend extracted. In the present instance this speciality is perceptible only in the slightest degree, but it is there, and more or less you have it always. I by no means mention this as a *fault*. I merely tell you you have it, and I can make the accusation with comfortable impunity, guessing pretty surely that you are too busy just now to deny this or any other charge.

For my own part, I found her conversation most interesting; her quick and clear intelligence was delightful. When she became excited on any subject she was really eloquent, and it was a pleasure to listen to her.
—"Charlotte Brontë," *The Cornhill Magazine*, new series 9 (December 1900): 787–788

---

impels the invocation; while the Catholicism on which she enlarges is even virulently reprobated. We do not exactly see the moral necessity for this (there is no artistical necessity) and we are rather sorry for it, occurring as it does at a time when catholics and protestants hate each other quite sufficiently; and in a mode which will not affect conversion. A better advocacy of protestantism would have been to show that it can give rest to the weary and heavy laden; whereas it seems to yield no comfort in return for every variety of sorrowful invocation. . . .

We cannot help looking forward still to other and higher gifts from this singular mind and powerful pen. When we feel that there is no decay of power here and think what an accession there will be when the cheerfulness of health comes in with its bracing influence, we trust we have only to wait to have such a boon as *Jane Eyre* gives us warrant to expect, and which 'Currer Bell' alone can, give.

—*Daily News* (3 February 1853): 2

* * *

These excerpts are from an unsigned review written by George Henry Lewes for a periodical, The Leader, *that he founded with Thornton Hunt in 1850.*

"The Triumph of What Is Sterling"
Review of *Villette*

In Passion and Power—those noble twins of Genius—Currer Bell has no living rival, except George Sand. Hers is the passionate heart to feel, and the powerful brain to give feeling shape; and that is why she is so original, so fascinating. Faults she has, in abundance; they are so obvious, they lie so legible on the surface, that to notice them with more insistance than a passing allusion is the very wantonness of criticism. On a former occasion, and in another place, we remonstrated with her on these said faults, but we now feel that the lecture was idle. Why wander delighted among the craggy clefts and snowy solitudes of the Alps, complaining at the want of verdure and of flowers? In the presence of real Power why object to its not having the

quiet lineaments of Grace? There is Strength clothed with Gentleness, but there may also be Strength rugged, vehement—careless of Beauty. . . .

One may say of Currer Bell that her genius finds a fitting illustration in her heroes and heroines—her Rochesters and Jane Eyres. They are men and women of deep feelings, clear intellects, vehement tempers, bad manners, ungraceful, yet loveable persons. Their address is brusque, unpleasant, yet individual, direct, free from shams and conventions of all kinds. They outrage "good taste," yet they fascinate. You dislike them at first, yet you learn to love them. The power that is in them makes its vehement way right to your heart. Propriety, ideal outline, good manners, good features, ordinary thought, ordinary speech, are not to be demanded of them. They are the Mirabeaus of romance; and the idolatry of a nation follows the great gifts of a Mirabeau, let "Propriety" look never so "shocked." It is the triumph of what is sterling over what is tinsel, of what is essential to human worth over what is collateral. Place a perfectly well-bred, well-featured, graceful considerate gentleman—a hero of romance, vague and ideal—beside one who is imperious, coarse, ill-tempered, ill-featured, but who, under this husk of manner and of temper contains the kernel of what is noble, generous, loving, powerful, and see how in the long run human sympathies will detach themselves from the unsatisfying hero, and cling to the man whose brain and heart are powerful! It is like placing a clever agreeable novel beside *Jane Eyre*.

**The Forbidden Alley
at the Pensionnat.**

"An alley which ran parallel with the very high wall on that side the garden, was forbidden to be entered by the pupils. It was called indeed 'l'allée défendue,' and any girl setting foot there would have rendered herself liable to 'as severe a penalty as the mild rules of Madame Beck's establishment permitted. Teachers might indeed go there with impunity; but as the walk was narrow, and the neglected shrubs were grown very thick and close on each side, weaving overhead a roof of branch and leaf, which the sun's rays penetrated but in rare chequers, this alley was seldom entered even during day, and after dusk was carefully shunned."—"Villette."

(Reproduced from the Haworth Edition of Mrs. Gaskell's Life, by kind permission of Messrs. Smith, Elder and Co.)

**The Pensionnat in the Rue D'Isabelle
(Rue Fossette of "Villette")**

Where Charlotte and Emily Brontë went as pupils in February, 1842.

"In a very quiet and comparatively clean and well-paved street I saw a light burning over the door of a rather large house, loftier by a story than those round it. *This* might be the inn at last. I hastened on: my knees now trembled under me: I was getting quite exhausted.

"No inn was this. A brass-plate embellished the great porte-cochère: 'Pensionnat de Demoiselles' was the inscription; and beneath, a name, 'Madame Beck.' "—"Villette."

(Reproduced from the Haworth Edition of "Villette," by kind permission of Messrs. Smith, Elder and Co.)

Two settings in Villette *(from* The Bookman, *October 1904)*

Janet captured all our hearts; not because she was lovely, ladylike, good, but because she was direct, clear, upright, capable of deep affections, and of bravely enduring great affliction. If any one pointed out her faults, we admitted them, but never swerved a line from our admiration. We never thought her perfect, we loved her for what was loveable, and left the rest to be set down to human imperfection.

And so of this story we have just read. *Villette* has assuredly many faults, and novel readers, no less than critics, will have much to say thereon. More adroit "construction," more breathless suspense, more thrilling incidents, and a more moving story, might easily have been manufactured by a far less active, inventive, passionate writer; but not such a book. Here, at any rate, is an *original* book. Every page, every paragraph, is sharp with *individuality*. It is Currer Bell speaking to you, not the Circulating Library reverberating echos. How *she* has looked at life, with a saddened, yet not vanquished soul; what *she* has thought, and felt, not what she thinks others will expect her to have thought and felt; *this* it is we read of here, and this it is which makes her writing welcome above almost every other writing. It has held us spell-bound.

Descending from generals to particulars, let us say that, considered in the light of a novel, it is a less interesting story than even "Shirley." It wants the unity and progression of interest which made "Jane Eyre" *so* fascinating; but it is the book of a mind more conscious of its power. *Villette* is meant for Brussels. The greater part of the scenes pass in the Netherlands, not unhappily designated as *Labassecour*. People will wonder why this transparent disguise was adopted. We conjecture that it was to prevent personal applications on the reader's part, and also to allow the writer a greater freedom as to details. The point is, however, very unimportant.

The story begins in England. Charming, indeed, is the picture of Mrs. Bretton's house, and the little love-affair between Polly, a quaint child of six, and Graham, a youth of sixteen, who pets her as boys sometimes pet children. We hear this child objected to, and called "unnatural." To our experience, the child's character is perfectly consonant, and the only thing we could wish in the delineation is that which we miss in *all* portraits of quaint precocious children,–viz., a more vivid recollection on the artist's part of the childlike nonsense and whimsicality which *accompany* the demonstrations of feeling and intelligence. Children do frequently think and say things, the wisdom and maturity of which are startling–children constantly rival genius in the bright originality of their remarks–but these very children *also* say childish foolish things, and to convey a true

picture of the child, both the foolishness and the "old fashioned" remarks must be contemporaneous. There is no true pudding made only of plums. . . .

It is surely unnecessary to say that all the scenes in this book are presented with wonderful distinctness before the reader's eye; and that the characters, though not drawn with equal truth, are all made to live and move across the scene as in few other novels. Not their persons alone, but their souls are revealed to us; the mental analysis is equal to the pictorial power. We could say something on Madame Beck and John Bretton, but to do so we should be forced to touch upon the story, and we prefer silence. . . .

The poetry scattered through these volumes, hidden though it be in the folds of prose, will escape no poetic reader; sometimes it lies in an epithet, at other times in an image; here–to take one example– is a description we beg you to read with proper cadence:–

"Her eyes were the eyes of one who can remember; one whose childhood does not fade like a dream, nor whose youth vanish like a sunbeam. She would not take life, loosely and incoherently, in parts, and let one season slip as she entered on another; she would retain and add; often review from the commencement, and so grow in harmony and consistency as she grew in years."

The Leader (12 February 1853): 163–164

* * *

Lewes commented on Brontë's novel a second time in an unsigned article in which he also considered Elizabeth Gaskell's novel Ruth. *In one of the omitted passages in this review, Lewes cited what he had written in* The Leader, *agreeing with "what a contemporary has already said" about Currer Bell's "Rochesters" and "Jane Eyres" being the "Mirabeaus of Romance."*

"Contempt of Conventions"
Review of *Villette*

Turning from "Ruth" to "Villette," the contrasts meet us on all sides. Never were two women's books more unlike each other. There is a moral too in "Villette," or rather many morals, but not so distinctly a *morale en action*. It is a work of astonishing power and passion. From its pages there issues an influence of truth as healthful as a mountain breeze. Contempt of conventions in all things, in style, in thought, even in the art of story-telling, here visibly springs from the independent originality of a strong mind nurtured in solitude. As a novel, in the ordinary sense of the word, "Villette" has few claims; as a *book,* it is one which, having read, you will not easily forget. It is quite true that the episode of Miss Marchmont, early in the first volume, is unnecessary, having no obvious connexion with the plot or the characters; but with what wonderful imagination is it painted! Where shall we find such writing as in that description of her last night, wherein the memories of bygone years come trooping in upon her with a vividness partaking of the last energy of life? It is true also that the visit to London is unnecessary, and has many unreal details. Much of the book seems to be brought in merely that the writer may express something in her mind; but at any rate she *has* something in her mind, and expresses it as no other can. We have objected to Mrs. Gaskell's portraiture of a child's feelings as unnatural, and we have heard Currer Bell's portrait of little Polly also objected to, but we cannot agree in this latter objection. Polly's quaintness and primness are not more than the experience of many people will guarantee. Where the defect lies is in an occasional 'over-ageing' of her feelings and emotions, such as at page 13, where her nurse says, "Be a good child, missy," and she replies, "I am good, but I ache here," putting her hand on her heart, and moaning, while she reiterated "papa! papa!" Now that is not the language of a child of six years old; children have no such anatomical knowledge; and to make it credible, it would be necessary to surround it, and the other "old-fashioned things" she says, with the prattle of childhood and nonsense which is best sense to it and to parents, in order that the reader might feel he had a child before him, and not a little idealism. The want of attention to reality is certainly not the complaint we can make against Currer Bell, and therefore were we the more surprised to find her saying, for instance, that John Bretton was accustomed to take up the Greek dramatists, and read off a translation of them for the benefit of the family circle. To any one who has ever read a Greek dramatist, the supposition of this feat will be extremely amusing. It would be a large demand upon our credulity, to imagine a man reading off in that way a French or German dramatist, without terribly fatiguing his audience, but considering the difficulty of reading the Greek with all appurtenances, the idea of "improvising" a translation is preposterous. In the same way Currer Bell makes M. Paul read aloud novels and plays to the young ladies, and whenever he comes upon any passage not very well adapted to young ladies' reading, (which must be very often one would think) we are told, that he improvised passages to supply their places, and that these were often better than the original. She gives us sufficient evidence of M. Paul's vigour of intellect without having recourse to such a weak expedient. While we are thus hinting at defects in a book for which we can scarcely find mea-

sured language to express our admiration, let us further note the melodramatic character of Madame Beck, who passes into unreality simply from the want of a little light and shade, and the occasional indistinctness in the drawing of John Bretton. Currer Bell has also the fault of running metaphors to death sometimes, and is oppressively fond of the allegorical expression of emotions; thus making passages look mechanical and forced, which if more directly put before us would be very powerful. . . .

We could go on quoting and commenting through several pages, for indeed it is as a book that "Villette" most affects us, and every chapter contains or suggests matter for discourse. We say emphatically, a book; meaning by a book the utterance of an original mind. In this world, as Goethe tells us, "there are so few voices, and so many echoes;" there are so few books, and so many volumes—so few persons thinking and speaking for themselves, so many reverberating the vague noises of others. Among the few stands "Villette." In it we read the actual thoughts and feelings of a strong, struggling soul; we hear the cry of pain from one who has loved passionately, and who has sorrowed sorely. Indeed, no more distinct characteristic of Currer Bell's genius can be named, than the depth of her capacity for all passionate emotions. Comparing "Villette" with "Ruth," in this respect, we are comparing sunlight with moonlight, passion with affection; and there is no writer of our day, except George Sand, who possesses the glory and the power which light up the writings of Currer Bell. She has not the humour, so strong and so genial, of Mrs. Gaskell. There are, occasionally, touches approaching to the comic in "Villette," but they spring mostly from fierce sarcasm, not from genial laughter. Ginevra Fanshaw is "shown up" in all her affectations and careless coquetry, but there is something contemptuous in the laugh, nothing sympathetic. Nor has Currer Bell any tendency towards the graceful, playful, or fanciful. There is more of Michael Angelo than of Raffaelle in her drawing; more of Backhuysen than of Cuyp; more of Salvator Rosa than of Claude. . . .

If, as critics, we have one thing to say with regard to the future, it is, that Currer Bell, in her next effort, should bestow more pains on her story. With so much passion, with so much power of transmitting experience into forms of enduring fiction, she only needs the vehicle of an interesting story to surpass the popularity of "Jane Eyre."

—The Westminster Review, 60 (April 1853): 251–254

* * *

The Gateway to the Garden of the Pensionnat in the Rue D'Isabelle (Rue Fossette of "Villette").

"Behind the house at the Rue Fossette there was a garden—large, considering that it lay in the heart of a city, and to my recollection at this day it seems pleasant: but time, like distance, lends to certain scenes an influence so softening; and when all is stone around, blank wall and hot pavement, how precious seems one shrub, how lovely an enclosed and planted spot of ground!"—"Villette."

(Reproduced from the Haworth Edition of "Villette," by kind permission of Messrs. Smith, Elder and Co.)

A setting in Villette *(from* The Bookman, *October 1904)*

These excerpts are from a forty-three-page, unsigned article by Anne Mozley that treated a novel by the Catholic writer Lady Georgiana Fullerton as well as Currer Bell's Villette. *The sister of the editor of* The Christian Remembrancer; *Mozley was a frequent contributor to the periodical.*

"The Novelist of the Schoolroom"
Review of *Villette*

Currer Bell, the Protestant, takes an opposite line. She boldly says, that if ever she forsakes the true God, it will be to worship reason. She declares against calling things by wrong names. Suffering is suffering; do not call it a privilege or a blessing; and get away from it if you lawfully can. The 'Bible and the Bible only,' is her religion; and with its pages she is so famil-iar, in every sense, that little awe or reverence remains, and she incorporates its phrases and idea into her ordinary language with no more pause or apology than if she were quoting Shakspeare or Bacon. As for forms and ceremonies, they are not likely to gain much respect where the Bible fails. Nor is she tolerant of controversies, on what she is pleased to consider minor points, amongst which a great many grave questions are included. Only against 'the Pope and all his works' is she fiercely zealous. In opposing him you can only be secure of not fighting shadows. . . .

After threading the maze of harrowing perplexities thus set forth by Lady Georgiana . . . it is, we own, a relief to turn to the work-day world of 'Villette.' The rough winds of common life make a better atmosphere for fiction than the stove heat of the 'higher circles.' Currer Bell, by hardly *earning* her experience, has, at least, won her knowledge in a field of action where more can sympathise; though we cannot speak of sympathy, or of ourselves as in any sense sharing in it, without a protest against the outrages on decorum, the moral perversity, the toleration of, nay, indifference to vice which deform her first powerful picture of a desolate woman's trials and sufferings—faults which make Jane Eyre a dangerous book, and which must leave a permanent mistrust of the author on all thoughtful and scrupulous minds. But however alloyed with blame this sympathy has necessarily been, there are indications of its having cheered her and done her good. Perhaps . . . she has been the better for a little happiness and success, for in many important moral points 'Villette' is an improvement on its predecessors. The author has gained both in amiability and propriety since she first presented herself to the world,—soured, coarse, and grumbling; an alien, it might seem, from society, and amenable to none of its laws.

We have said that Currer Bell has found life not a home, but a school; and this is more than a figure, as we gather from all her works. She may, indeed, be considered the novelist of the schoolroom, not, we need scarcely explain, for any peculiar fitness for the pure youthful mind, her best efforts exhibit, but because, as the scholastic world would seem to have been the main theatre of her experience—as here have been excited, in herself, many a vivid thought and keen interest—she chooses that others shall enter it with her. She will not condescend to shift the scene; she will not stoop to her reader's prejudices—they must overcome them; what has interested her, she means shall interest them: nor are we losers by the obligation. It cannot be denied that hitherto the art of teaching has cast a suspicion of coldness and dryness over its professors: it should not be so; it is unfair to an honourable profession, which should at least be cheered by sympathy in its irksome labours. In these days of educational enthusiasm the prejudice ought to be done away. Currer Bell seems to regard it as the mission of her genius to effect this: her clear, forcible, picturesque style gives life to what our fancies thought but a vegetating existence. Not that she wishes to represent life in the schoolroom as happy; far from it; but she shows us that life does not stagnate there in an eternal round of grammar and dictionary—in a perpetual infusion of elementary knowledge; and wherever it can be shown to flow freely and vigorously, wherever the mind has scope and the heart and emotions free play, there we can find interest and excitement. 'Villette' must be considered the most scholastic of the series. In 'Jane Eyre' we have the melancholy experience of the Clergy-daughters' school, and her own subsequent position as governess; in 'Shirley' we have the heart-enthralling tutor, and the heiress falling in love as she learns her French and writes her copy-books under the assumed austerity of his rule,—a wrong state of things, we need not say: but in 'Villette' almost the whole corps of the drama is furnished for the *Pensionnat de Demoiselles*. The flirting beauty of a school-girl; the grave, thoughtful young English teacher, with her purely intellectual attractions; Madame, the directress, the presiding genius; the little French professor of *Belleslettres,* for the hero, and the classes and large school-garden for the scenes. Even the outer-world hero, Graham, comes in as the physician of the establishment, and is entangled by the school-girl beauty; though it is his business to introduce us sometimes to the world beyond the walls, which now and then affords a refreshing change.

Nor does she gain the point of interesting us by ignoring any professional peculiarity which belongs to the science of teaching. Even the writer (for it is an autobiography) is, we see clearly, in look and air the 'teacher' she describes herself: her manner affected and influenced by her position. The consciousness of being undervalued, the longings for some one to care for her leading to some undignified results, the necessary self-reliance, the demure air, the intellect held in check, but indemnifying itself for the world's neglect and indifference by the secret indulgence of an arrow-like penetration,—all are portrayed; and for the hero—what can be more like a professor and less like a standard hero than M. Paul Emanuel? a character in the highest degree fresh and original, but in no sense calculated to attract a lady's fancy except in scenes where the world of male society is shut out as it is in large female assemblies,—in schools, convents, and, according to the satirist, old maid coteries,—in all of which a very small amount of heroic qualities are often found enough to constitute a man a hero. . . .

M. Paul takes no prominent part, however, at first. Madame Beck's establishment and system have to be described,—a very fair scene for this author's peculiar habits of observation; for her favourite point of view is not the

received one, and quite the reverse of that pedestal and harmonious arrangement of lights, which some clever women have thought the only fair site from which they are to be contemplated. We have, on the contrary, the *deshabille* of every character when free from the restraints that society imposes. Thus the beautiful flirt that fascinates in the ball-room, is seen with all her careless, rude, rough, schoolroom selfishness, where there are no men to keep her in order; girlhood, in general, is stripped of its poetical illusions; Madame Beck, whose public career is so useful and respectable, sinks into a spy. It is the same in Currer Bell's former works. She is jealous of the dress-side of life:—being, for some reason, cut off from, and by her peculiar class of faults and deficiencies ill adapted to it, she is not in its interests. She describes gay scenes well and vividly; but solely as a spectator, not as an assistant and component part, which is the element of pleasure in all festal scenes. A feeling is always conveyed which it would be unjust to call envy, implying rather a kind of yearning, a sense of isolation, which may not belong wholly to situation, and perhaps is inseparable from keen penetration, but which, as we have said, fits in exactly with the position and the character assumed in the story.

Madame Beck's establishment is conducted on the system of surveillance which some have thought necessary to good education,—a system of which she is complete mistress, being addicted to arts which are usually supposed to be practised only by the detective police of some tyrannical power, but which the present writer traces to the influence of Roman Catholicism in the countries where it prevails.

There is probably prejudice, but there may be also valuable information, in her picture of even a good foreign school. . . .

We have left the Professor for the duties of the story; it is fit now to return to him. While indulging in these unreasonable cravings for Graham's sympathy, she [Lucy Snowe] has become an object of real interest to M. Paul, though of a very particular sort. Alive to her talent, and decidedly jealous of it, his attentions often assume the most unpleasant, obtrusive, and inconvenient forms—critical, authoritative, querulous, he is perpetually interfering with her. He has a peculiar view of her character—that it needs being kept down: he thinks it his mission to do this. . . .

We do not wonder, with such skill in turning this fiery little temper, that Miss Lucy found herself attracted towards the possessor of it. It diverted her to hear his strictures on herself. . . . [S]he can still afford to take it all with the most edifying serenity of temper, for she has her indemnity in the pleasure of watching and appreciating his singularities, national and individual. . . .

For success in society, and to be its match and equal, a person should not be too deep a student

SHIRLEY: A TALE.

BY THE AUTHOR OF "JANE EYRE."

LIBRARY EDITION, 12MO, MUSLIN, $1 00. 8VO, PAPER, 37½ CENTS.

A book which, like its predecessor, indicates exquisite feeling, and very great power of mind in the writer.—*London Daily News.*

The book embraces grand character, grand scenes, grand thoughts; it proves, conclusively, that the writer is a wonderful creature, a phenomenon of mind.—*Boston Post.*

It is strongly marked by the peculiar characteristics of "Jane Eyre," indicating exquisite feeling and remarkable power of mind in the writer.—*Boston Rambler.*

Very ably written, and interesting.—*Philadelphia Saturday Evening Post.*

It is marked by originality of style, and displays command of language, and ability at framing and developing a plot.—*Literary American.*

* * * But we must stop here with a general and hearty approval of the book, which is as healthy in tone as it is pleasing in style—*New York Mirror.*

The women in "Shirley" are marvelously real.—*Albion.*

The book possesses deep interest, and an irresistible grasp of reality. There is a vividness and distinctness of conception in it quite marvelous. There are scenes which for strength and delicacy of emotion are not transcended in the range of English fiction.—*London Examiner.*

"Shirley" produces a highly favorable impression. The power of its author is felt throughout. The work is strongly individual. There is a racy novelty in its style, in its minute analysis of character, in its descriptions of natural scenery, and in its combinations of conflicting passions.—*Eclectic Review.*

We like the book as a whole: we like its spirit. We sympathize with the author's general charity with her special love for the old country, the old church, and the Old Duke; we kindle with her fervid bursts of eloquence, and recognize the truth of her pictures from life.—*Frazer's Magazine.*

There is great ability in this work; it is full of eloquence. The descriptive passages have seldom been surpassed in beauty and picturesqueness. The presence of a searching power and a lofty genius is visible.—*Bentley's Miscellany.*

There is human life as it is in England, in the thoughtful and toiling classes, with the women and clergy thereto appurtenant.—*Globe.*

JANE EYRE: AN AUTOBIOGRAPHY.

EDITED BY CURRER BELL.

LIBRARY EDITION, 12MO, MUSLIN, $1 00. 8VO, PAPER, 25 CENTS.

Since the time when Scott was used to astonish the world no novel has had such success or attracted so much attention.—*Daily Times.*

This novel has excited a deeper and more wide-spread interest than any other book that has been issued from the press for years.—*Brattleborough Eagle.*

A book of decided power. The thoughts are true, sound, and original; and the style is resolute, straightforward, and to the purpose. The object and moral of the work are excellent.—*London Examiner.*

The most extraordinary production that has issued from the press for years. We know no author who possesses such power. From the first page to the last it is stamped with vitality.—*Weekly Chronicle.*

One of the most powerful domestic romances which have been published for many years; full of youthful vigor, of freshness and originality, of nervous diction and consecrated interest. It is a book with a great heart in it.—*Atlas.*

Of all the novels we have read for years, this is the most striking, and, we may add, the most interesting. Its style, as well as its characters, are unhackneyed, perfectly fresh and life-like. It is thoroughly English.—*London Economist.*

The reading of such a book as this is a healthful exercise.—*Tablet.*

It is written with the most exquisite art of composition: the author is as plausible as Defoe, and as good a master of English prose as Bulwer.—*Philadelphia Dollar Newspaper.*

It is a book to make the heart beat, and to fill the eyes with tears.—*London Atlas.*

"Jane Eyre" is the truest and best romance we have ever read, except those of Fielding.—*Standard*

Original, vigorous, edifying, and absorbingly interesting.—*Douglas Jerrold's Paper.*

HARPER & BROTHERS, PUBLISHERS, NEW YORK.

Page from an inserted catalogue in the first American edition of Villette *(Special Collections, Thomas Cooper Library, University of South Carolina)*

either of himself or others. With all his absurdities, M. Paul is a man of great ability, almost of genius. We are conscious of his real power while we laugh at him. It is a sort of simplicity and humility, an avowed contempt for his own dignity, which shows so prominently his vanity and other weak points. We are disposed in the end to adopt the writer's conclusion, that it is his nerves that are irritable, not his temper. His religion, too, after the fashion of his country, is a very real and genuine feature. We quite acquiesce in her content to have him as he is, without any attempt to make him like herself. He had been educated by a Jesuit, and is still most dutiful at confession, having to go through some tribulations on account of his predilection for the English heretic, whom he endeavours in vain to convert by laying persuasive *brochures* in her way, which she treats with true Protestant contempt. Childlike in his faith, he is also pure in life, and the soul of honour; in all these points being in happy contrast with his brother professors. Some romantic acts of generosity and self-denial, which come out towards the end of the story, have not truth enough about them to match with his very true character; and in the same way the scenes of love-making in the end, between him and Lucy, have a very apocryphal air, unrelieved by those felicitous traits of nature which brighten the more comic representations of his character, and from which we have derived so much amusement, that we would not exchange one of his foibles for all the perfections of the stereotyped hero. . . . Whether they *are* married, or whether he is drowned in a storm, described in very windy fashion, is a moot point, but happily one which in no way affects the spirits, and scarcely arouses the curiosity, of the reader: an indifference which leads to the true conclusion—that the merit of the book lies in its scenes, and not in its plot.

The moral purpose of this work seems to be to demand for a certain class of minds a degree of sympathy not hitherto accorded to them; a class of which Lucy Snowe is the type, who must be supposed to embody much of the authoress's own feelings and experience, all going one way to express a character which finds itself unworthily represented by person and manner, conscious of power, equally and painfully conscious of certain drawbacks, which throw this superiority into shade and almost hopeless disadvantage. For such she demands room to expand, love, tenderness, and a place in happy domestic life. But in truth she draws a character unfit for this home which she yearns for. We want a woman at our hearth; and her impersonations are without the feminine element, infringers of modest restraints, despisers of bashful fears, self-reliant, contemptuous of prescriptive deco-

rum; their own unaided reason, their individual opinion of right and wrong, discreet or imprudent, sole guides of conduct and rules of manners,—the whole hedge of immemorial scruple and habit broken down and trampled upon. We will sympathise with Lucy Snowe as being fatherless and penniless, and are ready, if this were all, to wish her a husband and a fire-side less trying than M. Paul's must be, unless reformed out of all identity; but we cannot offer even the affections of our fancy (right and due of every legitimate heroine) to her unscrupulous, and self-dependent intellect—to that whole habit of mind which, because it feels no reverence, can never inspire for itself that one important, we may say, indispensable element of man's true love.

One suggestion we would make in parting with these two ladies—a question applicable to other scrutinizers of the female bosom—whether, indeed, they are consulting the interests of the sex, for which they contend so earnestly, by betraying—what gallantry is slow to credit—that women give away their hearts unsought as often as they would have us believe? So long as men wrote romance, that heart was described as an all-but-impregnable fortress . . . But now that our fair rivals wield the pen, the tables are turned. These spies within the walls reveal a wholly different state of things. They show us the invader greeted from afar—invited, indeed, within the walls. They betray the castle to have been all the while wanting a commander, the heart an owner. If it were indeed so, would the prize won on such easy terms be thought so much worth the having? Would this 'more than willingness' satisfy the inherent love of difficulty and of achievement in man's nature? But, happily, the question need not seriously be asked. A restless heart and vagrant imagination, though owned by woman, can have no sympathy or true insight into the really feminine nature. Such cannot appreciate the hold which a daily round of simple duties and pure pleasures has on those who are content to practise and enjoy them. They do not know the power of home over the heart—how it asserts its sway against new and more enthralling interests. Those who own such influences will still be difficult to win. Nor can we promise the aspirant to their favour any such eloquent, unsought avowals as the maidens of modern romance succeed so well in. He must be content to wait for the genial influences of a new home, to unthaw reserve; for trial, to prove constancy; and time and sorrow, to develop the full force, the boundless resources, of a pure, unselfish affection.

—*Christian Remembrancer,* new series 25 (April 1853): 402, 423–425, 431–432, 436, 439–443

* * *

"Hunger, Rebellion, and Rage"
Matthew Arnold on Brontë's Flaw

In a 14 April 1853 letter to his sister Jane Martha Arnold Foster, poet and critic Matthew Arnold commented on Brontë's novel.

Why is *Villette* disagreeable? Because the writer's mind contains nothing but hunger, rebellion, and rage, and therefore that is all she can, in fact, put into her book. No fine writing can hide this thoroughly, and it will be fatal to her in the long run.
— *Letters of Matthew Arnold, 1848–88*, p. 34

These excerpts are from an unsigned article titled "Recent Novels."

"Admirable Portraits"
Review of *Villette*

We were disposed to entertain some doubts whether the fame so justly acquired by the author of "Jane Eyre" and "Shirley," would be sustained by the work we now proceed to notice; but the interest with which we opened these volumes increased as we went on, and however high the test by which the critic might be disposed to subject a new *brochure* by this distinguished author, we think there can hardly be a doubt, that in "Villette" her reputation will be amply sustained. The novel is not only constructed with great care, but there is displayed throughout so abundant a variety of resources, such a perfect mastery of the springs of character, and such graphic pictures of external life, which are all used with art admirably directed to the end in view, that whatever the casual reader may think of the degree of success with which the latter is worked out, he will not be likely to deem the canon of criticism applied by Goldsmith at all applicable, "that the picture would have been better if the painter had taken more pains."

The story takes its shape after the fashion of former models. It is in the form of an autobiography, a certain Lucy Snowe being the narrator. . . . We have now said enough to enable our readers to understand what we conceive to be the great merits, as well as the no less remarkable defects of this tale. In the delineation of the character of the heroine, we cannot help thinking there is displayed some inconsistency. The qualities with which she is endowed can scarcely be called natural, although, like Jane

Eyre, she has that intense longing after affection, that strong devotion to the duties of her daily life, and those other qualities which would indicate a high moral tone of character; all these are in some degree marred and defaced by a species of morbid sensibility which seems strangely at variance with such attributes, while the aim of the book would seem to be the utterance of a further complaint against the destiny of such of the softer sex as are reduced by necessity to look for their living by the most irksome of all occupations—viz., that of teaching. The moral it would inculcate is, that there can be no real happiness to a woman, at least independently of the exercise of those affections with which nature has endowed her. We shall not stop to argue the metaphysical question which such an inquiry would necessarily involve. We shall only say that the doctrine is an unwise one, and likely to lead to most disastrous results, which would establish the necessity of indulgence in such feelings as indispensable to a calm enjoyment of life and an honourable and useful employment of it. We have each of us to bear our burden of sorrow; there is no house, however blessed with social advantages, which has not a skeleton hanging up in some quiet corner, and the philosophy which would inculcate the necessity of the indulgence of morbid feeling of any kind is obviously unsound in its conclusions. We will quote one passage of the book, as illustrative of our observations:—

> "'I shudder at the thought of being liable to such an illusion, it seemed so real. Is there no cure?—no preventative?'
>
> "'Happiness is the cure, a cheerful mind the preventative; cultivate both.'
>
> "'No mockery in this world ever sounds to me so hollow as that of being told to *cultivate* happiness. What does such advice mean? Happiness is a glory shining far down upon us out of Heaven: it is a divine dew which the soul, on certain of its summer mornings, feels dropping upon it from the amaranth bloom and golden fruitage of Paradise.'
>
> "'Cultivate happiness,' I said, briefly, to the doctor. 'Do you cultivate happiness? How do you manage?'
>
> "'I am a cheerful fellow by nature; and then ill-luck has never dogged me. Adversity gave me and my mother one passing scowl and brush; but we despised her, or rather, laughed at her, and she went by.'"

In this passage is contained the point of the philosophy, upon the unsatisfactory nature of which

"An Unjust Literary and Historical Method"

In her study of Charlotte's Brontë's relationship with the Hégers, Frederika Macdonald—who had attended the Pensionnat Héger in the late 1850s and early 1860s, about twenty years after Charlotte—examines what she regards as the license Brontë took in distorting fact in the service of fiction.

When we study Charlotte Brontë's masterpiece *Villette* in comparison with what we now know about the romance in her own life, we recognise two facts: the first is that, *in this work especially,* she has painted with such power the emotions she has undergone that her words become feelings that lift and ennoble the reader's sensibility: and thus serve him—in the way that it belongs to Romantics to serve mankind.

But the second fact we discover is that,—again, *in this book particularly,*—historical personages and real events are used as the materials for an imaginary story, in a way that has produced critical confusion: and what is graver still—has caused false and injurious opinions to be formed about historical people. And the difficulty we have to face is, not what amount of blame belongs to Charlotte for misrepresenting historical facts, nor even need we ask ourselves what reason she had for thus misrepresenting them. Because the reason becomes plain when we take the trouble to realise that the motive the writer of this work of genius had in view was one that concerned her own personal liberation from haunting memories, rather than any motive concerning the impressions she might produce.

There can be no doubt that Charlotte's motive in *Villette,* judged as a method of personal salvation, was not only a permissible, but a noble one. It is the one that Pater attributed to Michael Angelo: *'the effort of a strong nature to attune itself, to tranquillise vehement emotions by withdrawing them into the region of ideal senti-*ments':—*'an effort to throw off the clutch of cruel and humiliating facts by translating them into the imaginative realm, where the artist, the author, the dreamer even, has things as he wills, because the hold of outward things'* (such a stern and merciless one in the case of Charlotte Brontë!) *'is thrown off at pleasure.'*

But, judged as a literary and historical method, was Charlotte Brontë's manner of treating the real Director and Directress of the Pensionnat in the Rue d'Isabelle a justifiable or fair one? Can she be held without fault in this; that in Paul Emanuel and in Madame Beck she painted Monsieur and Madame Heger in a way that rendered them visible to every one who knew them; and then placed them in fictitious circumstances that altered the character of their actions and feelings, in such a way as to misrepresent their true behaviour? It seems to me that we must admit that the authoress of the *Professor* and of *Villette* adopted an unjust literary and historical method in so far as these real people are concerned: and that in the case of Madame Heger especially, passion and prejudice betrayed her: and rendered her guilty of a fault that must be recognised as a very grave one. But when this fault has been recognised and admitted, it seems to me a conscientious critic's duty does not compel him to scold this woman of genius for having the passions of her kind. A great Romantic is not an angel: and in this case the main facts about Charlotte are not her shortcomings as a celestial being, but her transcendent merits as an interpreter of the human heart. For my own part, I confess that after reading Charlotte's Love-letters, I am in no mood to look for faults in her, nor even to lend much attention to some faults that, without looking for them, one is bound to recognise.

—*The Secret of Charlotte Brontë,*
pp. 146–149

we would most strenuously insist. If happiness be only a glory shining down out of Heaven, it is a blessing servile to the skiey influences, and as much out of our own control as the weather. To teaching such as this we object. In the sedulous performance of all life's daily duties; in the meek endurance of its cares and troubles; in the strength of will which it is necessary to call into exercise in order to subdue them; in all these, and in the exertion necessary to practise them, we believe true happiness will most frequently be found; it is, therefore, more or less within the reach of every man who prefers a life of active labour in whatever vocation it has pleased Providence to assign him, to a life of sluggish despondency. To forget sorrow is by no means necessary; all that we would insist upon is, that it is wisest and safest to have it put aside, and kept carefully out of sight, that its remembrance should not be suffered to impede the more active operations of the mind; if this be done, all will go on well. We would incline to think that another rather prevailing defect in the book is the somewhat too elaborate analysis of characters with which we are occasionally presented, who have but little claim upon our sympathy or regard. An instance of this occurs in the case of Paul Emanuel, the singularly unattractive teacher in

Madame Beck's seminary. We point to this, because the fault is one which appears to be rapidly spreading among our modern writers of fiction; whole pages are now not infrequently filled with broken dialogue, in which the point to be discovered is but slowly evolved, and by which not only the progress of the story, but the interest of the reader are very materially retarded. Of the characters both of Lucy and Jane Eyre, the elements are, in some degree at least, the same;—strong and deep natural affections, great sensibility, and great independence, softened down by adversity, and constrained to self-control by the hard pressure of misfortune. Like the other heroines of the former works, both of these are almost destitute of personal attractions, captivating their admirers entirely through the power of a similar influence. But though the elements in each nature are almost identical, the character becomes differently developed by the operation of different circumstances; and it is in the skilful application of these, so as to bring out the points upon which the authoress wishes to dwell with the most stress, that the great charm of this story consists. We must not, in the enumeration of portrait, forget that of the warm hearted professor of languages, Monsieur Paul Emanuel, upon whom the charms of Miss Lucy work such sad havoc. It is drawn with singular force and completeness. . . .

We would gladly, did our space admit, present our readers with many more of these admirable portraits. We had marked several other passages for extract—that of the inimitable Madame Beck, who rules her school upon the principles of continental politics, espionage—with that of her companion, the French tragic actress, Vashti; but we must refrain—the novel is a pleasant and an admirably written one. We can so seriously recommend it to the notice of our readers, that it is perhaps of less consequence we should illustrate our opinion by further specimens. Indeed, so closely is the narrative woven and matted together, it would by no means be easy to convey, by means of mere isolated passages, any adequate idea of its originality and genius. It must be read continuously to be either understood or appreciated; and that it will be so read, not only thus, but with avidity, by a large circle of readers, we entertain no manner of doubt.

—*Dublin University Magazine,* 42 (November 1853): 612–615

A Marriage of 276 Days

The negotiation of the marriage of Charlotte Brontë and Reverend Arthur Bell Nicholls lasted longer than the marriage itself. More than a year and a half passed between Nicholls's proposal and the couple's wedding, while the marriage lasted less than a year, cut short when Charlotte died of what was diagnosed as pthisis—a general term often used for tuberculosis.

In this excerpt, Charlotte relates the story of the surprising proposal she received from Mr. Nicholls, the man who had been serving as her father's curate for some seven years. The mentioned note from Nicholls has not been located.

Charlotte Brontë to Ellen Nussey, 15 December 1852

I enclose another note which—taken in conjunction with the incident immediately preceding it—and with a long series of indications whose meaning I scarce ventured hitherto to interpret to myself—much less hint to any other—has left on my mind a feeling of deep concern.

This note—you will see—is from Mr. Nicholls. I know not whether you have ever observed him specially—when staying here—: your perception in these matters is generally quick enough—<u>too</u> quick—I have sometimes thought—yet as you never said anything—I restrained my own dim misgivings—which could not claim the sure guide of vision. What Papa has seen or guessed—I will not inquire—though I may conjecture. He has minutely noticed all Mr. Nicholls' low spirits—all his threats of expatriation—all his symptoms of impaired health—noticed them with little sympathy and much indirect sarcasm.

On Monday evening—Mr. N—was here to tea. I vaguely felt—without clearly seeing—as without seeing, I have felt for some time—the meaning of his constant looks—and strange, feverish restraint.

After tea—I withdrew to the dining-room as usual. As usual—Mr. N. sat with Papa till between eight & nine o'clock. I then heard him open the parlour door as if going. I expected the dash of the front-door—He stopped in the passage: he tapped: like lightning it flashed on me what was coming. He entered—he stood before me. What his words were you can guess; his manner—you can hardly realize—nor can I forget it—Shaking from hea[d] to foot, looking deadly pale, speaking low, vehemently yet with difficulty—he made me for the first time feel what it costs a man to declare affection where he doubts response.

The spectacle of one ordinarily so statue-like—thus trembling, stirred, and overcome gave me a kind of strange shock. He spoke of sufferings he had borne for months—of sufferings he could endure no longer—and craved leave for some hope. I could only entreat him to leave me then and promise a reply on the morrow. I asked if he had spoken to Papa. He said—he dared not—I think I half-led, half put him out of the room. When he was gone I immediately went to Papa—and told him what had taken place. Agitation and Anger disproportionate to the occasion ensued—if I had <u>loved</u> Mr. N—and had heard such epithets applied to him as were used—it would have transported me past my patience—as it was—my blood boiled with a sense of injustice—but Papa worked himself into a state not to be trifled with—the veins on his temples started up like whip-cord—and his eyes became suddenly blood-shot—I made haste to promise that Mr. Nicholls should on the morrow have a distinct refusal.

I wrote yesterday and got this note. There is no need to add to this statement any comment—Papa's vehement antipathy to the bare thought of any one thinking of me as a wife—and Mr. Nicholls' distress—both give me pain. Attachment to Mr. N—you are aware I never entertained but the poignant pity

inspired by his state on Monday evening—by the hurried revelation of his sufferings for many months is something galling and irksome. That he cared something for me—and wanted me to care for him—I have long suspected—but I did not know the degree or strength of his feelings

—The Letters of Charlotte Brontë, v. 3, pp. 92–93

* * *

With Reverend Brontë's seemingly unalterable opposition to the match, Nicholls left Haworth for a post in Kirk Smeaton about forty miles southeast of Haworth. In summer 1853, Charlotte and Arthur began to correspond secretly. Charlotte in this letter explains how her relationship with Arthur Nicholls was sustained and her father's objection overcome, leading to the couple's engagement on 3 April 1854.

Charlotte Brontë to Ellen Nussey, 11 April 1854

My dear Ellen

Thank you for the collar—It is very pretty, and I <u>will</u> wear it for the sake of her who made and gave it.

Mr Nicholls came on Monday 3rd. and was here all last week.

Matters have progressed thus since last July. He renewed his visit in Septr—but then matters so fell out that I saw little of him. He continued to write. The correspondence pressed on my mind. I grew very miserable in keeping it from Papa. At last sheer pain made me gather courage to break it—I told all. It was very hard and rough work at the time—but the issue after a few days was that I obtained leave to continue the communication. Mr. N. came in Jany he was ten days in the neighbourhood. I saw much of him—I had stipulated with Papa for opportunity to become better acquainted—I had it and all I learnt inclined me to esteem and, if not love—at least affection—Still Papa was very—<u>very</u> hostile—bitterly unjust. I told Mr. Nicholls the great obstacles that lay in his way. He has persevered—The result of this his last visit is—that Papa's consent is gained—that his respect, I believe is won for Mr. Nicholls has in all things proved himself disinterested and forbearing. He has shewn too that while his feelings are exquisitely keen—he can freely forgive. Certainly I must respect him—nor can I withold from him more than mere cool respect. In fact, dear Ellen, I am engaged.

Mr. Nicholls in the course of a few months will return to the curacy of Haworth. I stipulated that I would not leave Papa—and to Papa himself I proposed a plan of residence—which should maintain his seclusion and convenience uninvaded and in a pecuniary sense bring him gain instead of loss. What

Photo J. J. Stead.

The Rev. Arthur Bell Nicholls about 1854.

Charlotte Brontë was married to Mr. Nicholls on June 29th, 1854.

The Reverend Arthur Bell Nicholls, circa 1854
(*from* The Bookman, *October 1904*)

seemed at one time—impossible—is now arranged—and Papa begins really to take a pleasure in the prospect.

For myself—dear Ellen—while thankful to One who seems to have guided me through much difficulty, much and deep distress and perplexity of mind—I am still very calm—<u>very</u>—inexpectant. What I taste of happiness is of the soberest order. I trust to love my husband—I am grateful for his tender love to me—I believe him to be an affectionate—a conscientious—a high-principled man—and if with all this, I should yield to regrets—that fine talents, congenial tastes and thoughts are not added—it seems to me I should be most presumptuous and thankless.

Providence offers me this destiny. Doubtless then it is the best for me—Nor do I shrink from wishing those dear to me one not less happy.

It is possible that our marriage may take place in the course of the Summer. Mr. Nicholls wishes it to be in July. He spoke of you with great kindness and said he hoped you would be at our wedding. I said I thought of having no other bridesmaid. Did I say right? I mean the marriage to be literally <u>as quiet as possible</u>.

Do not mention these things just yet. I mean to write to Miss Wooler shortly. Good-bye—There is a strange—half-sad feeling in making these announcements—The whole thing is something other than imagination paints it beforehand: cares—fears—come mixed inextricably with hopes. I trust yet to talk the matter over with you—Often last week I wished for your presence and said so to Mr. Nicholls—Arthur—as I now call him—but he said it was the only time and place when he could not have wished to see you.

Good bye
Yours affectionately
C Brontë
—*The Letters of Charlotte Brontë*, v. 3,
pp. 239–240

* * *

This letter was written some seven weeks before Charlotte Brontë's marriage to Arthur Nicholls on 26 June 1854. Charlotte had first met Catherine Winkworth in April 1853 in Manchester at the home of their mutual friend "Lily" Gaskell, as Mrs. Gaskell was known to her closest friends. Catherine here writes to her sister Emily about seeing Charlotte during the writer's early May visit to Manchester. Excerpts.

Catherine Winkworth to Emma Shaen, 8 May 1854

I meant to have written to you last week, but finding that I was to see Miss Brontë this week I determined to wait till I could write about her, and her *marriage*. . . . Lily drew me directly to the room, whispering: "Say something about her marriage." . . . When she was summoned away I began: "I was very glad to hear something Mrs. Gaskell told me about you." "What was it?" "That you are not going to be alone any more." She leant her head on her hand and said very quickly "Yes, I am going to be married in June." "It will be a great happiness for you to have some one to care for, and make happy." "Yes; and it is a great thing to be the first object with any one." "And you must be very sure of that with Mr. Nicholls; he has known you and wished for this so long, I hear." "Yes, he has more than once refused preferment since he left my father, because he knew he never could marry me unless he could return to

84 PLYMOUTH GROVE

Plymouth Grove, the home of Elizabeth Gaskell's family in Manchester, where Charlotte Brontë visited in June 1851, spring 1853, and May 1854 (from Ellis H. Chadwick, Mrs. Gaskell: Haunts, Homes, and Stories, *Colorado College Library)*

Haworth; he knew I could not leave my father." She stopped, and then went on: "But, Katie, it has cost me a good deal to come to this." "You will have to care for his things, instead of his caring for yours, is that it?" "Yes, I can see that beforehand." "But you have been together so long already that you know what his things are, very well. He is very devoted to his duties, is he not?—and you can and would like to help him in those?" "I have always been used to those, and it is one great pleasure to me that he is so much beloved by all the people in the parish; there is quite a rejoicing over his return. But those are not everything, and I cannot conceal from myself that he is *not* intellectual; there are many places into which he could not follow me intellectually." "Well; of course every one has their own tastes. For myself; if a man had a firm, constant, affectionate, reliable nature, with tolerable practical sense, I should be much better satisfied with him than if he had an intellect far beyond mine, and brilliant gifts without that trustworthiness. I care most for a calm, equable, atmosphere at home." "I do believe Mr. Nicholls is as reliable as you say, or I wouldn't marry him." . . .

What I hear from Lily of Mr. Nicholls is all good. She [Miss Brontë] knew him well all those eight years, and has the greatest trust in his temper and principles. He loved her, but she refused him; he went on, but her father discovered it, went into a rage, and sent him away. He wrote to her very miserably; wrote six times, and then she answered him—a letter exhorting him to heroic submission to his lot, &c. He sent word it had comforted him so much that he must have a little more, and so she came to write to him several times. Then her father wanted a curate, and never liked any one so well as Mr. Nicholls, but did not at first like to have him; sent for him, however, after a time. This was about Christmas. Miss Brontë had not then made up her mind; but when she saw him again, she decided that she could make him happy, and that his love was too good to be thrown away by one so lonely as she is; and so they are to be married. He thinks her intellectually superior to himself, and admires her gifts, and likes her the better, which sounds as though he were generous. And he has very good family connections, and he gets on with her father, and all the parishioners adore him; but they will be very poor, for the living is only £250 a year. If only he is not altogether far too narrow for her, one can fancy her much more really happy with such a man than with one who might have made her more in love, and I am sure she will be really good to him. But I *guess* the true love was Paul Emanuel after all, and is dead; but I don't know, and don't think that Lily knows.

–Margaret J. Shaen, *Memorials of Two Sisters: Susanna and Catherine Winkworth,* pp. 111–115

* * *

This letter was written while Charlotte and her husband were still on their honeymoon trip to Ireland.

Charlotte Brontë Nicholls to Catherine Winkworth, 30 July 1854

Dear Katie,–It was at a little wild spot on the southwest coast of Ireland that your letter reached me. I did not at first recognize the handwriting, and when I saw the signature and afterwards read the full and interesting communication, I was touched;–you are very good, Katie, very thoughtful for others.

Yes! I am married. A month ago this very day (July 27th) I changed my name. The same day we went to Conway; stayed a few days in Wales; then crossed from Holyhead to Dublin. After a short sojourn in the capital we went to the coast. Such a wild rock-bound coast: with such an ocean view as I had not yet seen, and such battling of waves with rocks as I had never imagined!

My husband is not a poet or a poetical man, and one of my grand doubts before marriage was about "congenial tastes" and so on. The first morning we went out on to the cliffs and saw the Atlantic coming in, all white foam, I did not know whether I should get leave or time to take the matter in my own way. I did not want to talk, but I *did* want to look and be silent.

Having hinted a petition, license was not refused; covered with a rug to keep off the spray, I was allowed to sit where I chose, and he only interrupted me when he thought I crept too near the edge of the cliff. So far, he is always good in this way, and this protection which does not interfere or pretend, is, I believe, a thousand times better than any half sort of pseudosympathy. I will try with God's help to be as indulgent to him whenever indulgence is needed.

We have been to Killarney. I will not describe it a bit. We saw and went through the Gap of Dunloe. A sudden glimpse of a very grim phantom came on us in the Gap. The guide had warned me to alight from my horse, as the path was now very broken and dangerous; I did not feel afraid and declined. We passed the dangerous part, the horse trembled in every limb and slipped once, but did not fall. Soon after, she started and was unruly for a minute; however I kept my seat, my husband went to her head and led her. Suddenly, without any apparent cause, she seemed to go mad–reared, plunged–I was thrown on the stones right under her. My husband did not see that I had fallen–he still held on: I saw and felt her kick, plunge, trample round me. I had my thoughts about the moment–its consequences, my husband, my father. When my plight was seen, the struggling creature was let loose, and she sprang over me. I was lifted off the stones, neither bruised by the fall nor touched by the mare's hoofs! Of course the only feeling left was gratitude for more sakes than my own.

I go home soon; good-bye, dear Katie, I direct this to Plymouth Grove, not being sure of your address.

C.B. Nicholls
–Margaret J. Shaen, *Memorials of Two Sisters: Susanna and Catherine Winkworth,* pp. 115–117

* * *

This letter was written from the Haworth parsonage, where the newlyweds had returned to live with Reverend Brontë.

Charlotte Brontë to Margaret Wooler, 22 August 1854

My dear Miss Wooler
I found your letter with Many others awaiting me on my return home from Ireland. I thought to answer it immediately, but I reckoned without my host. Marriage certainly makes a difference in some things and amongst others the disposition and consumption of time. I really seem to have had scarcely a spare moment since that dim quiet June Morning when you, E. Nussey and myself all walked down to Haworth Church–. Not that I have been hurried or oppressed–but the fact is my time is not my own now; Somebody else wants a

Marriage record of Charlotte Brontë and Arthur Bell Nicholls (Haworth Church; photograph by Susan B. Taylor)

good portion of it—and says we must do so and so. We do "so and so" accordingly, and it generally seems the right thing—only I sometimes wish that I could have written the letter as well as taken the walk.

We have had many callers too—from a distance—and latterly some little occupation in the way of preparing for a small village entertainment. Both Mr. Nicholls and myself wished much to make some response for the hearty welcome and general good-will shewn by the parishioners on his return; accordingly the Sunday and day-Scholars and Teachers—the church ringers, singers &c. to the number of 500 were asked to Tea and Supper in the schoolroom—. They seemed to enjoy it much, and it was very pleasant to see their happiness. One of the villagers in proposing my husband's health described him as "a consistent Christian and a kind gentleman." I own the words touched me—and I thought—(as I know you would have thought—had you been present)—that to merit and win such a character was better than to earn either Wealth or Fame or Power. I am disposed to echo that high but simple eulogium now. If I can do so with sincerity and conviction seven years—or even a year hence—I shall esteem myself a happy woman. Faultless my husband is not—faultless no human being is; but as you well know—I did not expect perfection.

My dear Father was not well when we returned from Ireland—I am however most thankful to say that he is better now—May God preserve him to us yet for some years! The wish for his continued life—together with a certain solicitude for his happiness and health seems—I scarcely know why—stronger in me now than before I was married. So far the understanding between Papa and Mr. Nicholls seems excellent—if it only continues thus I shall be truly grateful. Papa has taken no duty since we returned—and each time I see Mr. Nicholls put on gown or surplice—

I feel comforted to think that this marriage has secured Papa good aid in his old age.

Are you at Richmond alone my dear Miss Wooler? Are you well and enjoying some share of that happiness you so thoroughly deserve? I wonder when I shall see you again—now you are once at Richmond you will stay there a long time I fear. As I do not know your address I enclose this under cover to Mr. Carter, answering his kind note at the same time Yours always with true respect and warm affection

C. B. Nicholls.
—*The Letters of Charlotte Brontë*, v. 3, pp. 286–287

* * *

By January 1855, less than six months after her wedding, Charlotte was feeling ill. In February, as she continued to decline, suffering from extreme nausea likely caused by early pregnancy, she revised her will. In March, as she grew ever weaker, Charlotte, Arthur, and Reverend Brontë confronted the likelihood of her death.

Patrick Brontë to Ellen Nussey, 30 March 1855

My Dear Madam,

We are all in great trouble, and Mr. Nicholls so much so, that he is not so sufficiently strong, and composed as to be able to write—

I therefore devote a few moments, to tell you, that my Dear Daughter is very ill, and apparently on the verge of the grave—

If she could speak, she would no doubt dictate to us whilst answering your kind letter, but we are left to ourselves, to give what answer we can—The Doctors have no hope of her case, and fondly as we a long time, cherished hope, that hope is now gone, and we [have] only to look forward to the solemn event, with prayer to God, that he will give us grace and Strength sufficient unto our day—

Will you be so kind as to write to Miss Wooler, and Mrs. Joe Taylor, and inform them that we requested you to do so—telling them of our present condition.—

Ever truly and
respectfully Yours,
P Brontë

—The Letters of Charlotte Brontë, v. 3, pp. 329–330

* * *

Charlotte Brontë was not yet thirty-nine when she died 31 March 1855. Her death prompted a series of elegiac responses to her life and work—among them this appreciation by Harriet Martineau. Excerpts.

Charlotte Brontë ("Currer Bell")
Harriet Martineau

"CURRER BELL" is dead! The early death of the large family of whom she was the sole survivor, prepared all who knew the circumstances to expect the loss of this gifted creature at any time; but not the less deep will be the grief of society that her genius will yield us nothing more. We have three works from her, which will hold their place in the literature of our century; and but for her frail health, there might have been three times three, for she was under forty, and her genius was not of an exhaustible kind. If it had been exhaustible, it would have been exhausted some time since. She had every inducement that could have availed with one less high-minded to publish two or three novels a year. Fame waited upon all she did; and she might have enriched herself by very slight exertion; but her steady conviction was that the publication of a book is a solemn act of conscience; in the case of a novel as much as any other kind of book. She was not fond of speaking of herself and her conscience; but she now and then uttered to her very few friends things which may, alas! be told now, without fear of hurting her sensitive nature,—things which ought to be told in her honor. Among these sayings was one which explains the long interval between her works. She said that she thought every serious delineation of life ought to be the product of personal experience and observation,—experience naturally occurring, and observation of a normal, and not of a forced or special kind. "I have not accumulated, since I published 'Shirley,'" she said, "what makes it needful for me to speak again; and, till I do, may God give me grace to be dumb!" She had a conscientiousness which could not be relaxed by praise or even sympathy—dear as sympathy was to keen affections. She had no vanity which praise could aggravate or censure mortify. She calmly read all adverse reviews of her books for the sake of instruction; and when she could not recognize the aptness of the criticism, she was more puzzled than hurt or angry. The common flatteries which wait upon literary success she quizzed with charming grace; and any occasional severity, such as literary women are favored with at the beginning of their course, she accepted with a humility which was full of dignity and charm. From her feeble constitution of body, her sufferings by the death of her whole family, and the secluded and monotonous life she led, she became morbidly sensitive in some respects; but in her high vocation she had, in addition to the deep intuitions of a gifted woman, the strength of a man, the patience of a hero, and the conscientiousness of a saint. In the points in which women are usually most weak—in regard to opinion, to appreciation, to applause—her moral strength fell not a whit behind the intellectual force manifested in her works. Though passion occupies too prominent a place in her pictures of Life, though women have to complain that she represents Love as the whole and sole concern of their lives, and though governesses especially have reason to remonstrate, and do remonstrate, that their share of human conflict is laid open somewhat rudely and inconsiderately, and with enormous exaggeration, to social observation, it is a true social blessing that we have had a female writer who has discountenanced sentimentalism and feeble egotism with such practical force as is apparent in the works of "Currer Bell." Her heroines love too readily, too vehemently, and sometimes after a fashion which their female readers may resent; but they do their duty through everything, and are healthy in action, however morbid in passion. . . .

. . . We all remember how long it was before we could learn who wrote it, and any particulars of the writer, when the name was revealed. She was living among the wild Yorkshire hills, with a father who was too much absorbed in his studies to notice her occupations: in a place where newspapers were never seen (or where she never saw any), and in a house where the servants knew nothing about books, manuscripts, proofs, or the post. When she told her secret to her father, she carried her book in one hand and an adverse review in the other, to save his simple and unworldly mind from rash expectations of a fame and fortune which she was determined should never be the aims of her life. That we have had only two novels since, shows how deeply grounded was this resolve.

"Shirley" was conceived and wrought out in the midst of fearful domestic griefs. Her only brother, a young man of once splendid promise, which was early blighted, and both her remaining sisters, died in one year. There was something inexpressibly affecting in the aspect of the frail little creature who had done such wonderful things, and who was able to bear up, with so bright an eye and so composed a countenance, under not only such a weight of sorrow, but such an prospect of solitude. In her deep mourning dress (neat as a Quaker's), with her beautiful hair, smooth and brown, her fine eyes, and her sensible face indicating a habit of self-control, she seemed a perfect household image—irresistibly recalling Wordsworth's description of that domestic treasure. And she was this. She was as able at the needle as at the pen. The household knew the excellence of her cookery before they heard of that of her books. In so utter a seclusion as she lived in—in those dreary wilds where she was not strong enough to roam over the hills; in that retreat where her studious father rarely broke the silence—and there was no one else to do it; in that forlorn house, planted on the very clay of the churchyard, where the graves of her sisters were before her window; in such a living sepulchre, her mind could not but prey upon itself; and how it did suffer, we see in the more painful portions of her last novel, "Villette." She said, with a change in her steady countenance, that she should feel very lonely when her aged father died. But she formed new ties after that. She married; and it is the old father who survives to mourn her. He knows, to his comfort, that it is not for long. Others now mourn her, in a domestic sense; and as for the public, there can be no doubt that a pang will be felt, in the midst of the strongest interests of the day, through the length and breadth of the land, and in the very heart of Germany (where her works are singularly appreciated), France, and America, that the "Currer Bell" who so lately stole as a shadow into the field of contemporary literature has already become a shadow again—vanished from our view, and henceforth haunting only the memory of the multitude whose expectation was fixed upon her.

–*Daily News,* 6 April 1855, p. 5

* * *

Mrs. Gaskell wrote of Charlotte's funeral in the last pages of her biography.

Charlotte Brontë's Funeral
Elizabeth Gaskell

Few beyond that circle of hills knew that she, whom the nations praised far off, lay dead that Easter morning. Of kith and kin she had more in the grave to which she was soon to be borne, than among the living. The two mourners, stunned with their great grief, desired not the sympathy of strangers. One member out of most of the families in the

parish was bidden to the funeral; and it became an act of self-denial in many a poor household to give up to another the privilege of paying their last homage to her; and those who were excluded from the formal train of mourners thronged the churchyard and church, to see carried forth, and laid beside her own people, her whom, not many months ago, they had looked at as a pale white bride, entering on a new life with trembling happy hope.

Among those humble friends who passionately grieved over the dead, was a village girl who had been seduced some little time before, but who had found a holy sister in Charlotte. She had sheltered her with her help, her counsel, her strengthening words; had ministered to her needs in her time of trial. Bitter, bitter was the grief of this poor young woman, when she heard that her friend was sick unto death, and deep is her mourning until this day. A blind girl, living some four miles from Haworth, loved Mrs. Nicholls so dearly that, with many cries and entreaties, she implored those about her to lead her along the roads, and over the moor-paths, that she might hear the last solemn words, "Earth to earth, ashes to ashes, dust to dust; in sure and certain hope of the resurrection to eternal life, through our Lord Jesus Christ."

Such were the mourners over Charlotte Brontë's grave.

I have little more to say. If my readers find that I have not said enough, I have said too much. I cannot measure or judge of such a character as hers. I cannot map out vices, and virtues, and debateable land. One who knew her long and well,—the "Mary" of this Life—writes thus of her dead friend:—

"As Good as She Was Gifted"

This excerpt is from an 11 April 1855 letter written by Arthur Bell Nicholls. He wrote to "My dear Madam"; the recipient is not definitely known.

Mr. Brontë & myself thank you very sincerely for your sympathy with us in our sad bereavement—our loss is indeed great—the loss of one as good as she was gifted—Altho' she had been ill from the beginning of January, it was only a few days previous to her death that we became alarmed for her safety—On [the] whole she had not much suffering—she spoke little during the last few days, but continued quite conscious—

–*The Letters of Charlotte Brontë,*
v. 3, p. 336

"She thought much of her duty, and had loftier and clearer notions of it than most people, and held fast to them with more success. It was done, it seems to me, with much more difficulty than people have of stronger nerves, and better fortunes. All her life was but labour and pain; and she never threw down the burden for the sake of present pleasure. I don't know what use you can make of all I have said. I have written it with the strong desire to obtain appreciation for her. Yet, what does it matter? She herself appealed to the world's judgment for her use of some of the faculties she had,—not the best,—but still the only ones she could turn to strangers' benefit. They heartily, greedily enjoyed the fruits of her labours, and then found out she was much to be blamed for possessing such faculties. Why ask for a judgment on her from such a world?"

But I turn from the critical, unsympathetic public,—inclined to judge harshly because they have only seen superficially and not thought deeply. I appeal to that larger and more solemn public, who know how to look with tender humility at faults and errors; how to admire generously extraordinary genius, and how to reverence with warm, full hearts all noble virtue. To that Public I commit the memory of Charlotte Brontë.

—The Life of Charlotte Brontë, v. 2, pp. 325–327

The Professor

On several occasions Charlotte Brontë asked if Smith, Elder were interested in having her rework her first novel for publication. Although not interested in such a project while Charlotte lived, the firm decided to bring out the novel after her death. Arthur Bell Nicholls edited the manuscript and Smith, Elder published The Professor *in two volumes in early June, 1857.*

Preface for *The Professor: A Tale*
Charlotte Brontë and Arthur Bell Nicholls

This little book was written before either "Jane Eyre" or "Shirley," and yet no indulgence can be solicited for it on the plea of a first attempt. A first attempt it certainly was not, as the pen which wrote it had been previously worn a good deal in a practice of some years. I had not indeed published anything before I commenced "The Professor," but in many a crude effort, destroyed almost as soon as composed, I had got over any such taste as I might once have had for ornamented and redundant composition, and come to prefer what was plain and homely. At the same time I had adopted a set of principles on the subject of incident, &c., such as would be generally approved in theory, but the result of which, when carried out into practice, often procures for an author more surprise than pleasure.

I said to myself that my hero should work his way through life as I had seen real living men work theirs—

"A New View of a Grade, an Occupation, and a Class of Characters"

After it was clear that Jane Eyre *was a success, Charlotte began to consider her second novel. In a 14 December 1847 letter to William Smith Williams, she rejected the idea of a serialized work, preferring to "make another venture in the 3 vol. novel form." She then proceeded to assess the weaknesses and strengths of* The Professor—*without convincing Williams that she should return to her former work.*

Respecting the plan of such a work, I have pondered it, but as yet with very unsatisfactory results. Three commencements have I essayed, but all three displease me. A few days since I looked over "The Professor." I found the beginning very feeble, the whole narrative deficient in incident and in general attractiveness; yet the middle and latter portion of the work, all that relates to Brussels, the Belgian school &c. is as good as I can write; it contains more pith, more substance, more reality, in my judgment, than much of "Jane Eyre." It gives, I think, a new view of a grade, an occupation, and a class of characters—all very common-place, very insignificant in themselves, but not more so than the materials composing that portion of "Jane Eyre" which seems to please most generally—.

My wish is to recast "the Professor," add as well as I can, what is deficient, retrench some parts, develop others—and make of it a 3-vol. work; no easy task, I know, yet I trust not an impracticable one.

I have not forgotten that "the Professor" was set aside in my agreement with Messrs. Smith & Elder—therefore before I take any step to execute the plan I have sketched, I should wish to have your judgment on its wisdom. You read or looked over the M.S.—what impression have you now respecting its worth? And what confidence have you that I can make it better than it is?

—The Letters of Charlotte Brontë, v. 1, pp. 574

that he should never get a shilling he had not earned—that no sudden turns should lift him in a moment to wealth and high station; that whatever small competency he might gain, should be won by the sweat of his brow; that, before he could find so much as an arbour to sit down in, he should master at least half the ascent of "the Hill of Difficulty;" that he should not even marry a beautiful girl or a lady of rank. As Adam's son he should share Adam's doom, and drain throughout life a mixed and moderate cup of enjoyment.

In the sequel, however, I found that publishers in general scarcely approved of this system, but would have liked something more imaginative and poetical—something more consonant with a highly wrought fancy, with a taste for pathos, with sentiments more tender, elevated, unworldly. Indeed until an author has tried to dispose of a manuscript of this kind, he can never know what stores of romance and sensibility lie hidden in breasts he would not have suspected of casketing such treasures. Men in business are usually thought to prefer the real; on trial the idea will be often found fallacious: a passionate preference for the wild, wonderful, and thrilling—the strange, startling, and harrowing—agitates divers souls that show a calm and sober surface.

Such being the case, the reader will comprehend that to have reached him in the form of a printed book, this brief narrative must have gone through some struggles—which indeed it has. And after all, its worst struggle and strongest ordeal is yet to come; but it takes comfort—subdues fear—leans on the staff of a moderate expectation—and mutters under its breath, while lifting its eye to that of the public,

"He that is low need fear no fall."

CURRER BELL.

The foregoing preface was written by my wife with a view to the publication of "The Professor," shortly after the appearance of "Shirley." Being dissuaded from her intention, the authoress made some use of the materials in a subsequent work—"Villette." As, however, these two stories are in most respects unlike, it has been represented to me that I ought not to withhold "The Professor" from the public. I have therefore consented to its publication.

A. B. NICHOLLS.
Haworth Parsonage,
September 22nd, 1856.
—pp. v–viii

* * *

THE PROFESSOR,

A Tale.

BY

CURRER BELL,

AUTHOR OF "JANE EYRE," "SHIRLEY," "VILLETTE," &c.

IN TWO VOLUMES.
VOL. II.

LONDON:
SMITH, ELDER & CO., 65, CORNHILL.
——
1857.

[*The right of Translation is reserved.*]

Title page for Charlotte's last novel (Special Collections, Thomas Cooper Library, University of South Carolina)

Reviewers tended to find the novel flawed but nonetheless interesting as an early work by the famous writer. These excerpts are from an unsigned review.

"A New Trial"
Review of *The Professor*

After nine years—the fitting Horatian interval—Currer Bell's rejected novel makes its posthumous appearance in print. The wondrous story of 'Jane Eyre' has so much gratified, and the more wondrous, "ower true," and over-tragic life-drama of Charlotte Brontë so much amazed the world, that it feels disposed rather to err on the side of gentleness than rigour, and to question the justice of the criticism which refused, rather than the constructive power which was latent in the earlier tale. Accordingly friends, lovers, and biographer have moved for a new trial, and 'The Professor' comes before the public with every advantage of typography, and with the best prospects of a hearing. Whether the counsel which prompted, or the love which consented, to publication was wise or considerate, is as fairly open to doubt as the friendship which is disinclined to consider a dog Diamond as on some occasions providential. The world has not gained greatly by 'The Prelude,' and perhaps we ought to be resigned to the loss of a few sheets more of 'The Opium-Eater.' That the work before us will be read and discussed by all who have read the 'Life of Charlotte Brontë' is certain enough, but the interest excited will be rather curious than deep, and the impression left on the reader one of pain and incompleteness. It is a mere study for 'Jane Eyre' or 'Shirley,'—certainly displaying effects of the same force, the same characteristic keenness of perception, the same rough, bold, coarse truthfulness of expression, the same compressed style, offence of dialogue, preference for forbidden topics, and pre-Raphaelitish contempt for grace,—but with scarcely any relief or shadow, and with fewer descriptive or womanly touches. Unity or arrangement there is none. The sketches are carelessly left loose for the reader to connect or not, as he chooses,—a carelessness the result of a deliberate intention, as is clear enough from the Preface. . . .

The incidents of the story are few; the principal parts are sustained by an unnatural brother, a rough manufacturer, of the type of Mr. Helstone, who interposes *ex machinâ* and rescues the hero, an obstinate but well-regulated character in difficulties. The hero, a younger son of a Yorkshire blue-dyer, is of patrician race by the mother's side, but though educated at Eton he declines to adopt the church and the opinions of his titled uncles, and in preference offers himself as a clerk to his brother, a rich Yorkshire manufacturer, the husband of a childish-looking, *red-haired* lady, whom he terrifies by driving a restive quadruped,—"only opening his lips to damn his horse." . . .

Miss Brontë does not exhibit her characters in critical action, or under strong temptation. Low chicane, astuteness, sensuality, and tyranny, are keenly and observantly drawn; but throughout the novel the quietness is unnatural, the level of fact too uniform, the restraint and the theory of life too plain. The principles and the art of the writer, though true, excite no corresponding sympathy on the part of the reader,—few demands being made on his softer or gentler nature. There is no Helen Burns that we can watch or weep over,—no sprightly little Adele that we

can sport with. Frances may possibly be the mother of Lucy Snow, and Mdlle. Reuter and M. Pelet the coefficients of Madame Modeste and Paul Emanuel. Similarities of opinion respecting marriage may be traced, not as a crime, but an imbecility. Now and then there is a touch of grandiloquence that astonishes us. Words and events are utilized in a way that now, knowing the author's opportunities, appear to us remarkable. On the whole, this tale bears to Currer Bell's later works the relation which a pre-Shakspearian story does to the drama,—it is curious to an artist or psychologist. On closing this posthumous chapter, and ending Charlotte Brontë's strange literary history, we are reminded of a saying of Jean Paul's—"God deals with poets as we do with nightingales, hanging a dark cloth round the cage until they sing the right tune."

—*The Athenæum* (13 June 1857): 755, 757

* * *

This review was unsigned.

"The Unripe Mind"
Review of *The Professor*

Miss Brontë had proposed that this her first novel—originally rejected by the publishers—should follow *Shirley* in the order of publication, and in pursuance of that wish she wrote a preface for it. Being, however, dissuaded from her purpose, she considered the work finally suppressed, and drew upon it for some of the matter used in writing her last book, *Villette*. The main topic of the 'Professor,' as of 'Villette,' is the Brussels school, but the difference of detail to be found in the two novels, and again the difference between each story and the truth on which it had been founded, is very worthy of remark.

That Miss Brontë's earlier impressions of life were unhappy, partly by accident, chiefly because of a want of health in her own mind, the recent publication of her Life makes evident. In that book we have read under what circumstances of domestic anxiety the tale now published was written, and have learnt how much of reference to her own history the author put into her narrative. But the plan of the book shows, in this first novel even more distinctly than in her later works, that Miss Brontë considered her invention free, and never thought that anybody would apply to the events in her story-books a test of comparison with incidents in her own comfortless history. As the case stands, we may regret that in the 'Professor' even more bitterly than in 'Villette,' experience of kindness in a Brussels school has furnished matter for a sketch, vivid as if drawn from life, of treacherous school directors and of children who are all detestable. Miss Brontë meant no personality and no untruth; she wove the threads of fiction, and she coloured them with tints which she thought well chosen as a match to the prevailing hues of life. The world she saw was, indeed, but a shadow of the truth, while her perception of the shadow was so vivid, that when she described it she could bring it home to us, by the mere substance of her words, as something more distinct than the reality itself as shadowed in the words of nine-tenths of her neighbours. Her thoughts were very real to her, and she had taught herself to put the force of her genius not into the ornaments, but into the essentials of speech, to give her whole mind to her meaning. She did this in the 'Professor,' as she did it afterwards in 'Jane Eyre' and in 'Shirley.' Her very merit may thus lay her open to the accusation of a fault; innocent fiction passing for hard truth itself, or for truth harshly perverted, because the active fancy that has broken up and recombined in its own way the few materials a lonely girl's life could afford, was truth itself to the possessor of it.

Sad truth it was in the first instance. 'Villette' showed how the experience of generous appreciation and a nearer intimacy with the world had tended towards the cure of some of those morbid impressions which kept out the sun from Charlotte Brontë's early life. Her last book was the healthiest, and had she lived we do not doubt that out of her perfect happiness to which she had but just attained before she died, there would have come a book like this her first book in distinctness of expression, but entirely differing from it in tone. The lesson might have been the same,—that obstacles to success or happiness in this world are to be overcome mainly by the force of hard, determined work; but there would have been an end to the delusion that such work has to be done in the midst of buffetings from nearly all the people who stand round about. After all, though Miss Brontë gave intensity to the expression of it, this is but a delusion common in the unripe mind. Young writers usually dig their scalpels into the world and declare it heartless, but their anatomy improves as they grow older. That in Miss Brontë's case time did its work any one may feel who will read the 'Professor' and compare it with 'Villette,' as one may compare the bud closed tightly on itself in June with the expanding blossom of July.

The story of the 'Professor' begins rather clumsily (the first chapter being the only clumsy part of it), with a letter from the hero, giving all preliminary information to a dear Charles, who is supposed for the occasion and then summarily dismissed. The hero, William Crimsworth, left early an orphan dependent upon the goodwill of his maternal uncles, is sent by them to Eton, because if they neglect him it is threatened by somebody that their neglect will be made to tell against them in a contested election. Old enough to understand that they were unkind to his mother, William Crimsworth refuses further help from them, breaks with them,—one is a lord, and the other is an "honourable John,"—and betakes himself to a mill-owning brother Edward, ten years older than himself. The brother is a master, and a hard one. His temper is represented by his private exclamation, after he had been twitted in the Town hall with domestic subjects: "I wish you were a dog! I'd set to this minute and never stir from the spot till I'd cut every strip of flesh from your bones with this whip."

Discharged from his hard brother's service, William Crimsworth forsakes trade and seeks new fortune at Brussels, helped by a letter of recommendation from a young manufacturer named Hunsden; one of the very few persons in the book who is shown dealing kindly with his neighbours, and whose saving peculiarity it is to do generous things in a way that stings the person whom he favours, while it is the peculiarity of Crimsworth's humour to receive him as a friend, and never thank him for his favours. In Brussels William Crimsworth promptly obtains the place as Professor—which means simply teacher—of English and Latin, in the school of M. Pelet. Now M. Pelet has "a false glance and insinuating smile," and very soon, says William "the sense of insult and treachery lived in me like a kindling, though as yet smothered, coal." William is introduced as Professor of English to the girls' school of Mdlle Reuter, next door. Mdlle with her pleasant garden, her fair form, her quiet manner, with the dove in her that makes her dangerous to others, and the serpent in her that may bring her to the dust, is represented as distinctly as if she had been taken alive out of the world and set down in the middle of the story, yet she is unnaturally bad. The Professor is at first attracted by her, and then treats her with scorn, whereupon she is in turn herself attracted.

The fact is, that as it was her nature to doubt the reality and undervalue the worth of modesty, affection, disinterestedness—to regard these qualities as foibles of character—so it was equally her tendency to consider pride, hardness, selfishness, as proofs of strength. She would trample on the neck of humility, she would kneel at the feet of disdain; she would meet tenderness with secret contempt, indifference she would woo with ceaseless assiduities. Benevo-

CHARLOTTE BRONTË.
(By special permission of Mr. John Grant, Publisher, Edinburgh).

Charlotte Brontë, portrait by J. H. Thompson (from Whiteley Turner,
A Spring-Time Saunter: Round and About Brontë Land,
Sam Houston State University Library)

that was vicious and repulsive."–"These girls," we are told, "belonged to what are called the respectable ranks of society; they had all been carefully brought up, yet was the mass of them mentally depraved." Then we have individual recollections of them: a first, filthy in person and impure in mind; a second–"suspicion, sullen ill-temper were on her forehead, vicious propensities in her eye, envy and panther-like deceit about her mouth;" a third–"narrow as was her brow, it presented space for the legible graving of two words, Mutiny and Hate." These girls are sketched in detail, and having sketched them the Professor adds that "these three pictures are from the life." From it, no doubt, and also, no doubt, far from it, since there are certainly no children born to any race under the sun which may be represented fairly by such types as these. Children are here described as "deaf to reason, and for the most part insensate to persuasion," while after much kindness received by

lence, devotedness, enthusiasm, were her antipathies; for dissimulation and self interest she had a preference–they were real wisdom in her eyes; moral and physical degradation, mental and bodily inferiority, she regarded with indulgence; they were foils capable of being turned to good account as set-offs for her own endowments. To violence, injustice, tyranny, she succumbed–they were her natural masters; she had no propensity to hate, no impulse to resist them; the indignation their behests awake in some hearts was unknown in hers. From all this it resulted that the false and selfish called her wise, the vulgar and debased termed her charitable, the insolent and unjust dubbed her amiable, the conscientious and benevolent generally at first accepted as valid her claim to be considered one of themselves; but ere long the plating of pretension wore off, the real material appeared below, and they laid her aside as a deception.

She also is vanity: and so are all the girls who go to school in Belgium. Her school was an "assemblage of all that was insignificant and defective, much

---

"All overgrown by cunning moss"

Emily Dickinson's poem about Charlotte Brontë was first published in 1896, with a title "Charlotte Brontë's Grave" added by the volume's editor. Some later editors have published stanzas 1, 4, and 5 as a three-stanza poem (omitting stanzas 2 and 3 below) based on Dickinson's notation of "Or" between stanzas 3 and 4.

All overgrown by cunning moss,
All interspersed with weed,
The little cage of 'Currer Bell,'
In quiet Haworth laid.

This bird, observing others,
When frosts too sharp became,
Retire to other latitudes,
Quietly did the same,

But differed in returning;
Since Yorkshire hills are green,
Yet not in all the nests I meet
Can nightingale be seen.

Gathered from many wanderings,
Gethsemane can tell
Through what transporting anguish
She reached the asphodel!

Soft fall the sounds of Eden
Upon her puzzled ear,
Oh, what an afternoon for heaven
When 'Brontë' entered there!

–Poems by Emily Dickinson, pp. 193–194

herself from the heads of a Roman Catholic school in Brussels, Miss Brontë was so far from having learnt to repose trust in kindness that she here defines every such school as "a building with porous walls, a hollow floor, and a false ceiling," and adds, "what the house is, the inhabitants are, very treacherous; they all think it lawful to tell lies; they all call it politeness to profess friendship where they feel hatred."

But if the book which contains these views of life, shows how the mists gathered about Miss Brontë's path, while yet the sun of her short day was creeping up to the horizon, it at least shows also, that she was not walking far astray. Into the character of the Professor himself the writer has transferred much from her own nature, and in the second volume she develops for him a fit mate, in Mdlle Henri, a poor Anglo-Swiss governess whose powers and graces expand under the genial influence of sympathy. This also is essentially a Brontë, and most worthy of respect does, in each case, the Brontë nature show itself to be. Something is here to be learnt of the strong will, the earnest mind, the heart with its unsounded depths that belonged to a woman who, after all, so fed upon the past as to create out of it nerve and sinew for the future. Against physical infirmities of body and of mind, Miss Brontë worked, and against views of life begotten by them that would only lead weak natures to despair she battled on, winning more strength and better health of mind by the exertion. There is a touching significance in two or three pages of this novel which represent the Professor in the first days of his greatest happiness, after he has won to himself his Frances, suddenly cast down by Hypochondria. Once before, he says, for the space of a whole year, "I had her to myself in secret; she lay with me, she ate with me, she walked out with me, showing me nooks in woods, hollows in hills, where we could sit together, and where she could drop her dark veil over me, and so hide sky and sun, grass and green tree; taking me entirely to her death-cold bosom, and holding me with arms of bone. What tales she would tell me at such hours! What songs she would recite in my ears!"

—The Examiner (20 June 1857): 388

The Cultural Legacy of the Brontës

In the more than 150 years since the deaths of the Brontë siblings, thousands of articles and books on the family have been published. In the latter half of the nineteenth century and through the founding of the Brontë Society and the Brontë Museum at Haworth in the 1890s, Charlotte was regarded as the greatest writer of the family. However, in the twentieth century, as scholarship and criticism on all of the Brontës proliferated, Emily's reputation rose to equal or surpass that of her older sister. Both Charlotte and Emily are established as canonical Victorian novelists, and their most famous creations, Jane Eyre *(1847) and* Wuthering Heights *(1847), continue to interest literary scholars and to hold sway over the popular imagination.*

Mrs. Gaskell's *Life of Charlotte Brontë*

The first full-length biography to treat the Brontë family was Elizabeth Gaskell's The Life of Charlotte Brontë *(1857), which was written at the request of Reverend Brontë following Charlotte's death in 1855. Although controversial for its negative depiction of Reverend Brontë, Branwell, and the Cowan Bridge School, Gaskell's work was seen at the time as a model biography because of her diligent research and extensive interviews with persons who had known Charlotte. In her quest for a thorough understanding of her subject, Gaskell traveled to Brussels to meet with Constantin Héger and copy down portions of Charlotte's letters to him, though she avoided any mention of Charlotte's romantic attachment to Héger in her biography. Ellen Nussey also cooperated with Gaskell, allowing her access to many of the five hundred letters she had received from Charlotte. Reverend Brontë, despite the unflattering portrayal of him, praised the biography in a 30 July 1857 letter to the author: "And my opinion, and the reading World's opinion of the 'Memoir,' is that it is every way worthy of what one great Woman should have written of Another, and that it ought to stand, and will stand, in the first rank of Biographies till the end of time" (John and Canon W. T. Dixon,* A Man of Sorrow: The Life, Letters and Times of the Revd. Patrick Brontë, 1877–1861, *p. 509). Later scholars and critics have noted biases and omissions in Gaskell's biography, often following from her desire to emphasize Charlotte's reputation as an admirable, dutiful daughter, sister, and wife. But all serious subsequent biographers of the Brontës have had to reckon with Mrs. Gaskell's research.*

As is clear in this excerpt from The Life of Charlotte Brontë, *Gaskell saw Charlotte's writing as at odds with her*

Elizabeth Gaskell, friend and biographer of Charlotte Brontë, by George Richmond (from Esther Alice Chadwick, Mrs. Gaskell: Haunts, Homes, and Stories, *Colorado College Library*)

domestic role. In her emphasis on the domestic expectations of women (and Charlotte's fulfillment of these), Gaskell always assured readers that Charlotte followed the "Angel in the House" model of womanhood despite her writing talent and ambitions.

"Two Parallel Currents"
Elizabeth Gaskell

I remember . . . many little particulars which Miss Brontë gave me, in answer to my inquiries respecting her mode of composition, &c. She said, that it was not

1855.]
527

HAWORTH CHURCHYARD,

April, 1855.

WHERE, under Loughrigg, the stream
　　Of Rotha sparkles, the fields
Are green, in the house of one
Friendly and gentle, now dead,
Wordsworth's son-in-law, friend—
Four years since, on a mark'd
Evening, a meeting I saw.

Two friends met there, two fam'd
Gifted women. The one,
Brilliant with recent renown,
Young, unpractis'd, had told
With a Master's accent her feign'd
History of passionate life :
The other, maturer in fame,
Earning, she too, her praise
First in Fiction, had since
Widen'd her sweep, and survey'd
History, Politics, Mind.

They met, held converse : they wrote
In a book which of glorious souls
Held memorial : Bard,
Warrior, Statesman, had left
Their names :—chief treasure of all,
Scott had consign'd there his last
Breathings of song, with a pen
Tottering, a death-stricken hand.

I beheld ; the obscure
Saw the famous. Alas !
Years in number, it seem'd,
Lay before both, and a fame
Heighten'd, and multiplied power.
Behold ! The elder, to-day,
Lies expecting from Death,
In mortal weakness, a last
Summons : the younger is dead.

First to the living we pay
Mournful homage : the Muse
Gains not an earth-deafen'd ear.

Hail to the stedfast soul,
Which, unflinching and keen,
Wrought to erase from its depth
Mist, and illusion, and fear !
Hail to the spirit which dar'd
Trust its own thoughts, before yet
Echoed her back by the crowd !
Hail to the courage which gave
Voice to its creed, ere the creed
Won consecration from Time !

Haworth Churchyard, April, 1855.　　　[May,

Turn, O Death, on the vile,
Turn on the foolish the stroke
Hanging now o'er a head
Active, beneficent, pure !
But, if the prayer be in vain—
But, if the stroke must fall—
Her, whom we cannot save,
What might we say to console ?

She will not see her country lose
Its greatness, nor the reign of fools prolong'd.
She will behold no more
This ignominious spectacle,
Power dropping from the hand
Of paralytic factions, and no soul
To snatch and wield it : will not see
Her fellow-people sit
Helplessly gazing on their own decline.

Myrtle and rose fit the young,
Laurel and oak the mature.
Private affections, for these,
Have run their circle, and left
Space for things far from themselves,
Thoughts of the general weal,
Country, and public cares :
Public cares, which move
Seldom and faintly the depth
Of younger passionate souls
Plung'd in themselves, who demand
Only to live by the heart,
Only to love and be lov'd.

How shall we honour the young,
The ardent, the gifted ? how mourn ?
Console we cannot ; her ear
Is deaf. Far northward from here,
In a churchyard high mid the moors
Of Yorkshire, a little earth
Stops it for ever to praise.

Where, behind Keighley, the road
Up to the heart of the moors
Between heath-clad showery hills
Runs, and colliers' carts
Poach the deep ways coming down,
And a rough, grim'd race have their homes—
There, on its slope, is built
The moorland town. But the church
Stands on the crest of the hill,
Lonely and bleak ; at its side
The parsonage-house and the graves.

See ! in the desolate house
The childless father ! Alas—
Age, whom the most of us chide,
Chide, and put back, and delay—
Come, unupbraided for once !
Lay thy benumbing hand,
Gratefully cold, on this brow !

Matthew Arnold's tribute to the Brontës, as published in Fraser's Magazine *two months after Charlotte Brontë's death. Arnold met Charlotte in December 1850. He begins by praising Harriet Martineau and Charlotte, before turning to the other Brontës, mistakenly assuming their graves were in the churchyard (University of Colorado Libraries).*

every day that she could write. Sometimes weeks or even months elapsed before she felt that she had anything to add to that portion of her story which was already written. Then, some morning, she would waken up, and the progress of her tale lay clear and bright before her, in distinct vision. When this was the case, all her care was to discharge her household and filial duties, so as to obtain leisure to sit down and write out the incidents and consequent thoughts, which were, in fact, more present to her mind at such times than her actual life itself. Yet notwithstanding this "possession" (as it were), those who survive, of her daily and household companions, are clear in their testimony, that never was the claim of any duty, never was the call of another for help, neglected for an instant. It had become necessary to give Tabby—now nearly eighty years of age—the assistance of a girl. Tabby relinquished any of her work with jealous reluctance, and could not bear to be reminded, though ever so delicately, that the acuteness of her senses was dulled by age. The other servant might not interfere with what she chose to consider her exclusive work. Among other things, she reserved to herself the right of peeling the potatoes for

1855.]   *Haworth Churchyard, April, 1855.*

Shut out the grief, the despair!
Weaken the sense of his loss!
Deaden the infinite pain!

Another grief I see,
Younger: but this the Muse,
In pity and silent awe
Revering what she cannot soothe,
With veil'd face and bow'd head,
Salutes, and passes by.

Strew with roses the grave
Of the early-dying. Alas!
Early she goes on the path
To the Silent Country, and leaves
Half her laurels unwon,
Dying too soon: yet green
Laurels she had, and a course
Short, yet redoubled by Fame.

For him who must live many years
That life is best which slips away
Out of the light, and mutely; which avoids
Fame, and her less-fair followers, Envy, Strife,
Stupid Detraction, Jealousy, Cabal,
Insincere Praises:—which descends
The mossy quiet track to Age.

But, when immature Death
Beckons too early the guest
From the half-tried Banquet of Life,
Young, in the bloom of his days;
Leaves no leisure to press,
Slow and surely, the sweet
Of a tranquil life in the shade—
Fuller for him be the hours!
Give him emotion, though pain!
Let him live, let him feel, *I have liv'd.*
Heap up his moments with life!
Quicken his pulses with Fame!

And not friendless, nor yet
Only with strangers to meet,
Faces ungreeting and cold,
Thou, O Mourn'd One, to-day
Enterest the House of the Grave.
Those of thy blood, whom thou lov'dst,
Have preceded thee; young,
Loving, a sisterly band:
Some in gift, some in art
Inferior; all in fame.
They, like friends, shall receive
This comer, greet her with joy;
Welcome the Sister, the Friend;
Hear with delight of thy fame.

Round thee they lie; the grass
Blows from their graves toward thine.
She, whose genius, though not
Puissant like thine, was yet
Sweet and graceful: and She—

Haworth Churchyard, April, 1855.   [May,

(How shall I sing her?)—whose soul
Knew no fellow for might,
Passion, vehemence, grief,
Daring, since Byron died,
That world-fam'd Son of Fire; She, who sank
Baffled, unknown, self-consum'd;
Whose too-bold dying song
Shook, like a clarion-blast, my soul.

Of one too I have heard,
A Brother—sleeps he here?—
Of all his gifted race
Not the least-gifted; young,
Unhappy, beautiful; the cause
Of many hopes, of many tears.
O Boy, if here thou sleep'st, sleep well!
On thee too did the Muse
Bright in thy cradle smile:
But some dark Shadow came
(I know not what) and interpos'd.

Sleep, O cluster of friends,
Sleep! or only, when May,
Brought by the West Wind, returns
Back to your native heaths,
And the plover is heard on the moors,
Yearly awake, to behold
The opening summer, the sky,
The shining moorland; to hear
The drowsy bee, as of old,
Hum o'er the thyme, the grouse
Call from the heather in bloom:

Sleep; or only for this
Break your united repose.

         A.

---

dinner; but as she was growing blind, she often left in those black specks, which we in the North call the "eyes" of the potato. Miss Brontë was too dainty a housekeeper to put up with this; yet she could not bear to hurt the faithful old servant, by bidding the younger maiden go over the potatoes again, and so reminding Tabby that her work was less effectual than formerly. Accordingly she would steal into the kitchen, and quietly carry off the bowl of vegetables, without Tabby's being aware, and breaking off in the full flow of interest and inspiration in her writing, carefully cut out the specks in the potatoes, and noiselessly carry them back to their place. This little proceeding may show how orderly and fully she accomplished her duties, even at those times when the "possession" was upon her.

Any one who has studied her writings,—whether in print or in her letters; any one who has enjoyed the rare privilege of listening to her talk, must have noticed her singular felicity in the choice of words. She herself, in writing her books, was solicitous on this point. One set of words was the truthful mirror of her thoughts; no others, however apparently identical in meaning, would do. She had that strong practical regard for the simple holy truth of expression, which Mr. Trench has enforced, as a duty too often neglected. She would wait patiently searching for the right term, until it presented itself to her. It might be provincial, it might be derived from the Latin; so that it accurately represented her idea, she did not mind whence it came; but this care makes her style present the finish of a piece of mosaic. Each component part, however small, has been dropped into the right place. She never wrote down a sentence until she clearly understood what she wanted to say, had deliberately chosen the words, and arranged them in their right order. Hence it comes that, in the scraps of paper covered with her pencil writing which I have seen, there will occasionally be a sentence scored out, but seldom, if ever, a word or an expression. She wrote on these bits of paper in a minute hand, holding each against a piece of board, such as is used in binding books, for a desk. This plan was necessary for one so short-sighted as she was; and, besides, it enabled her to use pencil and paper, as she sat near the fire in the twilight hours, or if (as was too often the case) she was wakeful for hours in the night. Her finished manuscripts were copied from these pencil scraps, in clear, legible, delicate traced writing, almost as easy to read as print.

The sisters retained the old habit, which was begun in their aunt's life-time, of putting away their work at nine o'clock, and beginning their study, pacing up and down the sitting room. At this time, they talked over the stories they were engaged upon, and described their plots. Once or twice a week, each read to the others what she had written, and heard what they had to say about it. Charlotte told me, that the remarks made had seldom any effect in inducing her to alter her work, so possessed was she with the feeling that she had described reality; but the readings were of great and stirring interest to all, taking them out of the gnawing pressure of daily-recurring cares, and setting them in a free place. It was on one of these occasions, that Charlotte determined to make her heroine plain, small, and unattractive, in defiance of the accepted canon. . . .

Whether justly or unjustly, the productions of the two younger Miss Brontës were not received with much favour at the time of their publication. . . .

Henceforward Charlotte Brontë's existence becomes divided into two parallel currents—her life as Currer Bell, the author; her life as Charlotte Brontë, the woman. There were separate duties belonging to each character—not opposing each other; not impossible, but difficult to be reconciled. When a man becomes an author, it is probably merely a change of employment to him. He takes a portion of that time which has hitherto been devoted to some other study or pursuit; he gives up something of the legal or medical profession, in which he has hitherto endeavoured to serve others, or

relinquishes part of the trade or business by which he has been striving to gain a livelihood; and another merchant or lawyer, or doctor, steps into his vacant place, and probably does as well as he. But no other can take up the quiet, regular duties of the daughter, the wife, or the mother, as well as she whom God has appointed to fill that particular place: a woman's principal work in life is hardly left to her own choice; nor can she drop the domestic charges devolving on her as an individual, for the exercise of the most splendid talents that were ever bestowed. And yet she must not shrink from the extra responsibility implied by the very fact of her possessing such talents. She must not hide her gift in a napkin; it was meant for the use and service of others. In an humble and faithful spirit must she labour to do what is not impossible, or God would not have set her to do it.

—*The Life of Charlotte Brontë*, v. 2, pp. 8–12, 49–50

* * *

After the publication of The Life of Charlotte Brontë, *reviewers tended not only to review the biography but also to assess the Brontës' novels in light of the context Gaskell provided, often echoing her admiration of Charlotte's "womanly" qualities. These excerpts are from John Skelton's unsigned assessment, titled "Charlotte Brontë," in which he also treats Emily's* Wuthering Heights.

"A Remarkable Race"
Review of *The Life of Charlotte Brontë*

After passing through much uncongenial drudgery as teachers, both at home and on the Continent, the sisters, in 1844, find themselves once more united in the quiet home among the hills. Throughout the intervening period, Charlotte has been silently amassing materials for future work. Nothing comes amiss to that observant and inventive brain. She notices every one with whom she is brought into contact—dissects and analyses. The result is, that when she begins to write, her life is transcribed into her novels. The one is a daguerreotype of the other. The scenes reviewers condemn as exaggerated, the characters they pronounce unnatural, are taken from personal experience. When you read her life, you read *Jane Eyre, Shirley, Villette,* in fragments. The separate parts have simply to be taken out, arranged, riveted together, and you have the romance. But what in the life is fragmentary and incomplete—for we live bit by bit, and never contrive to act out our play uninterruptedly at one sitting—is by the artist's insight cast into dramatic sequence. . . . But no explanation can ever be quite exhaustive. The experi-

"Wasp Nest"

In these excerpts from a spring 1856 letter to Ellen Nussey, Mary Taylor wrote of the difficult task of writing truthfully of Charlotte's life.

Your letter is most interesting concerning poor Charlotte's *life*. If for the sake of those who behaved ill to her the truth cannot be spoken, still people should not tell lies. The fact reached me even here that Mr Brontë did not chuse his daughter should marry–she wrote to me that she once dismissed Mr Nichols because he (papa) was so angry that she was frightened,–frightened for *him*. It was long after, years I think that she told him that she had determined to see Mr N. again, and without positively saying yes to retract her refusal. I can never think without gloomy anger of Charlotte's sacrifices to the selfish old man–how well we know that, had she left him entirely and succeeded in gaining wealth and name and influence she would have had all the world lauding her to the skies for any trivial act of generosity that wd cost her nothing! But how on earth is all this to be set straight! Mrs Gaskell seems far too able a woman to put her head into such a wasp nest as she wd raise about her by speaking the truth of living people. How she will get through with it I can't imagine. . . .

. . . I wish I could set the world right on many points all respecting Charlotte. It would do said world good to know her and be forced to revere her in spite of their contempt for poverty and helplessness. No one ever gave up more than she did and with full consciousness of what she sacrificed. I don't think myself that women are justified in sacrificing themselves for others, but since the world generally expects it of them they should at least acknowledge it. But where much is given we are all wonderfully given to gra[sp] at more. If Charlotte had left home and made a favor of returning she wd have got thanks instead of tyranny–wherefore take care of yourself Ell[en] and if you chose to give a small modicum of attention to other people, *grumble hard.*

–Mary Taylor: Friend of Charlotte Brontë: Letters from New Zealand & Elsewhere,
pp. 126, 128–129

ence can never entirely explain the work. For between lies the mystery of Genius. . . .

Shortly after the arrival of the book of Poems at Haworth, *Wuthering Heights,* by *Ellis Bell,* or Emily Brontë, is sent to the printer.

Emily Brontë–the finer, we are afraid we must say the ideal, side of whose character is sketched in *Shirley*–is, I think, the most powerful of the Brontë family. They are a remarkable race, all of them. Branwell, even, whose life was wrecked at the outset, meets death Mirabeau-like. He holds an old theory, that the Will can be supreme to the end; and so, when he feels the last agony approaching, he desires to be raised to his feet, and dies standing. But Emily is a Titan. Charlotte loved her with her whole heart; to her the implacable sister is 'mine bonnie love;' but Emily never responds. She is stern, taciturn, untameable. Her logic is rigorous; but when she once forms an opinion, however extreme it may be, no logic can move her. She clings to it with stubborn tenacity. Her affections, such as they are, are spent on her moorland home, and the wild animals she cherishes. The tawny bull-dog 'Keeper' is her special friend. But even 'Keeper' must be taught to obey that iron will, and he is taught in a way that he never forgets. On her death-bed she accepts no assistance–does not admit that she suffers even. Her death, Charlotte said afterwards, 'was very terrible. She was torn, conscious, panting, reluctant, yet resolute, out of a happy life.'

Wuthering Heights is not unworthy of its grim parentage. Emily's novel is not, perhaps, more powerful than her sister's; but we meet in it, I think, with more subtle diversities of character than we do in any of them. Charlotte Brontë's heroes are all broad and emphatic; marked types, not delicate suggestions. They are strong, passionate, generous, vindictive, as the case may be; but no attempt is made to explain conflicting motives, to assimilate complex passions. There is a certain immobility and hardness in the outline. They want the delicate tendernesses of the imagination, the gleams of barbaric poetry which lie deep buried under the swart brow of the Moor, or flash from the blue eyes of the Northman. Masculine, independent, impatient of the prose of life, they are, yet they are not poetic. There is nothing of the gipsy nature in them. They remain broad-featured, broad-shouldered Anglo-Saxons, even in their moments of dreariest independence. In Emily's we are conscious of something more. A volcano is beneath the flowers where we stand, and we cannot tell where it may burst. There is a refrain of fierce poetry in the men and women she draws–gleams of the gipsy savageness and of the gipsy tenderness. A strange fire, inherited from an Eastern kindred, lighted among Norland moors, burns in their eyes. They flutter on the confines between our love and our hate. Their caprice, their sullenness, their mercilessness, hurt and revolt us; but we cannot abandon them to perdition without a prayer that they may be saved. Heathcliff, the boy, is ferocious, vindictive, wolfish; but we understand the chain of fire that binds Cathy to him. There stands the brawny young Titan, with his blackened visage and unwashed hands and unkempt hair, as though he had come in hot haste from the infernal forge, sullen, resentful, no Christian virtue implanted in his heathenish soul, no English grace softening his obdurate visage;

> ## "Unwonted Anxieties"
> ## The Suppression of *The Life*
> ## *of Charlotte Brontë*
>
> *After George Smith's death, Sidney Lee wrote a "Memoir of George Smith" giving credit to Charlotte Brontë for introducing Smith to several writers he later published, including William Makepeace Thackeray, Harriet Martineau, and Elizabeth Gaskell. Excerpt.*
>
> At the same period as he became Miss Martineau's publisher there began Smith's interesting connection with Mrs. Gaskell; which was likewise due to Charlotte Brontë. Late in 1855 Mrs. Gaskell set to work, at the request of Charlotte Brontë's father, on his daughter's life. She gleaned many particulars from Smith and his mother, and naturally requested him to publish the book, which proved to be one of the best biographies in the language. But its publication (in 1857) involved him in unwonted anxieties. Mrs. Gaskell deemed it a point of conscience to attribute, for reasons that she gave in detail, the ruin of Miss Brontë's brother Branwell to the machinations of a lady, to whose children he had acted as tutor. As soon as Smith learned Mrs. Gaskell's intention he warned her of the possible consequences. The warning passed unheeded. The offensive particulars appeared in the biography, and, as soon as it was published, an action for libel was threatened: Mrs. Gaskell was travelling in France at the moment, and her address was unknown. Smith investigated the matter for himself, and, perceiving that Mrs. Gaskell's statements were not legally justifiable, withdrew the book from circulation. In later editions the offending passages were suppressed. Sir James Stephen, on behalf of friends of the lady whose character was aspersed, took part in the negotiations, and on their conclusion handsomely commended Smith's conduct.
>
> —*Dictionary of National Biography,* supplement,
> volume I (1901), p. xxvi

and yet, as he stands moodily in the presence of his fastidious, courtly, and well-bred rival, we feel that though his soul is the fouler, he is the greater, the more loveable of the two. He may be an imp of darkness at bottom—as is indeed most probable, considering his parentage—but he has come direct from the affluent heart of nature, and the hardy charm of her bleak hill-sides and savage moorlands rests upon the boy. On the boy only, however for the man develops and degenerates; it is then a tiger-cat's passion, a ghoul's vindictiveness, a devil's remorse.

The elder Cathy, too, is very subtlely conceived in her fire, and tenderness, and vanity, and perversity, and the untutored grace of her free moorland nature. The hardy half savage child, with her mocking spirit, and bleeding feet, and swart companion-imp, 'as dark

almost as if it came from the devil,' scampering across the hills in gipsy-fashion, and scaring the meek maidens of the village with her elfish laughter; the wilful little vagrant who, in her dream of Heaven, breaks her heart with weeping to come back to earth, and wakens sobbing for joy because 'the angry angels have cast her out into the middle of the heath on the top of Wuthering Heights;' the perverse, fervent, untamed coquette, alternating between love and pride, hell and heaven, our admiration and our dread—unplummed depths of passion convulsing her soul, but with nothing mean or meagre in the whole of her burning heart,—excites a wonderful interest, retains it to the last, and gives to the *Catherine Linton* scrawled upon the nursery panel an eerie and fitful pathos. Her childish delight in arranging on her death-bed the lapwing, the mallard, and the moor-fowl's feathers—the wild birds she had followed with Heathcliff in their childish rambles across the moorland,—is sad and true as the 'coronet flowers' of Ophelia. In that idle forgetfulness and tender confusion there is a genuine reminiscence of the Shaksperian madness. This richness and affluence of poetic life in which Emily invests the creations of her brain, these delicacies and subtleties of insight, are all the more striking, from the grave, sombre, and resolutely homely form in which her tale is narrated. She may describe abnormal characters; but, whatever they are, she describes them with startling genuineness.

This was the only romance Emily ever wrote: a year after its publication she died. These very grand and impressive lines were her last:—

> No coward soul is mine,
> No trembler in the world's storm-troubled sphere;
> I see Heaven's glories shine,
> And faith shines equal, arming me from fear.
>
> O God, within my breast,
> Almighty, ever-present Deity!
> Life—that in me has rest
> As I—undying Life—have power in thee!
>
> Vain are the thousand creeds
> That move men's hearts; unutterably vain;
> Worthless as withered weeds,
> Or idlest froth amid the boundless main,
>
> To waken doubt in one
> Holding so fast by thine infinity;
> So surely anchored on
> The steadfast rock of immortality.
>
> With all-embracing love
> Thy spirit animates eternal years,
> Pervades and broods above;
> Changes, sustains, dissolves, creates, and rears.

Though earth and man were gone,
And suns and universes ceased to be,
And Thou were left alone,
Every existence would exist in Thee.

There is not room for Death,
Nor atom that his might could render void;
Thou—THOU art Being and Breath,
And what THOU art may never be destroyed.

While *Wuthering Heights* was being slowly printed, Charlotte, after many disappointments, had at length found a publisher for *Jane Eyre,* and the former was still in the press when the latter appeared. The book spread like wildfire. . . .

Emily and Anne Brontë died soon after the publication of *Jane Eyre;* but they lived long enough to know that their sister had become famous. To that sister, however, fame was but a sorry exchange for affection; and with the exception of her aged father, Charlotte was now left utterly alone. When I read the letters she wrote at that time, I wonder how she contrived to live through these dreary winters:—

> Sometimes when I wake in the morning (she writes), and know that Solitude, Remembrance, and Longing are to be almost my sole companions all day through, that at night I shall go to bed with them, that they will long keep me sleepless, that next morning I shall wake to them again, sometimes, Nell, I have a heavy heart of it. I miss familiar voices commenting mirthfully and pleasantly; the room seems very still, very empty. Happiness quite unshared can scarcely be called happiness; it has no taste.

Mrs. Gaskell has chosen a few lines from *Aurora Leigh* for the motto to her book:—

>   Oh! my God,
> —Thou hast knowledge, only Thou,
> How dreary 'tis for women to sit still
> On winter nights by solitary fires,
>   And hear the nations praising them far off.

So Charlotte Brontë felt at that desolate hearthstone among the hills.

But her father still lives, and she lives for him. It is long before the old gentleman can realize that this woman of whom all England is talking, is his daughter Charlotte; but when at length convinced, and when Yorkshire people begin to honour, in their rough way, the little woman who had drawn their hard features so faithfully, and make pilgrimages to the rude parsonage as to a shrine, he becomes gladly and proudly interested in his child's fame. And Charlotte is the most faithful and docile of children; is bound up in the old man's happiness, obeys his slightest wish,—nay, will not

allow 'Paul Emmanuel' to die, because her father asks her to spare him; and so—though with her mind's eye she has seen her hero perish in that wild storm on the Atlantic, and *knows* that he is dead—leaves his fate unexplained and enigmatical. As the years went by, life brightened upon her. She paid an occasional visit to the metropolis, where she beheld the great soldier of her childish romance; and Thackeray, who, of all men, after 'the Duke,' she honoured most; and Rachel, whose performances inspired her with the critical admiration and womanly antipathy she has described in one of her novels. *Shirley* and *Villette* followed each other rapidly; they were received with acclamation; 'Currer Bell' became a fixed star in contemporary literature. One vivid streak of sunlight broke across her life at its close; but the frail frame was unused to happiness; it wore grief better; and the joy of a new life killed her. She died on Easter Eve, 1855.

Mrs. Gaskell has done her work well. Her narrative is simple, direct, intelligible, unaffected. Her descriptions of the Yorkshire uplands and of the people who live there are vivid and picturesque. She dwells on her friend's character with womanly tact, thorough understanding, and delicate sisterly tenderness. Once or twice there is a burst of uncontrollable indignation against those who blunderingly misunderstood or wilfully maligned. The extracts from the letters are excellently selected. And they are remarkable letters—as the letters of the most remarkable woman of her age could not fail to be; but we own that we were not prepared for the fine sense and temperate strength they disclose. Many parts of the book cannot be read without deep, even painful, emotion. That life-long sickness, bourne meekly, uncomplainingly, with quiet courage, and which yet at times pressed tears, as though they were drops of blood, out of the heart, is sadder than any story. Still, we feel as we read, that though trying and distressing im many ways, it is a life always womanly. And we are thankful that such a life—the life of the authoress of *Villette*—should have been written by the writer of *Ruth*. No one else could have paid so tender and discerning a tribute to the memory of Charlotte Brontë.

Such was the life and the character,—we have a few 'last words' on the works and the genius.

Jane Eyre has been austerely condemned by austere critics. It is said that in it the interest depends on the terrible and the immoral,—two elements of interest which cannot be rightly appropriated by fiction. Admitting that the charge is true, we inquire—why not?

The old dramatists, at least, did not judge so; and their result was that they evoked 'high passions and high actions' which stir our hearts to the core. . . . They looked terror and death, the momentous issues of life, fearlessly in the face; wherever the true tragic came out, there we find them. And they succeeded in impressing on us a sense of its greatness, its reality, its infinite capacities for grief or gladness, such as we now seldom obtain. Seldom, because we have become afraid of its sternness, and gloss it over; because very few of our poets dare to gauge boldly the perilous pains of the spirit, the great majority contenting themselves with saying pretty things at their fastidious leisure about sorrows which are as genuine as a pasteboard doll's; because, when a woman like Charlotte Brontë does try to evoke that mighty spirit of tragedy which lurks in the heart of every man, she is told that she is creating the horrible, and breaking artistic statutes more immutable than those of the Medes and Persians.

The charge of immorality is one easily made—still more easily repeated. According to certain scrupulous zealots, everything is immoral in our present art—from *Marie* and *La Traviata,* to *Ruth, Jane Eyre,* and *Aurora Leigh*—which presumes to assert that society is not a mass of respectabilities, and that there are certain waifs and strays scattered about, who, as they have contrived to get into the world, require at least to be looked after till they leave it. . . . But if *Aurora Leigh* is such a book, then *Jane Eyre* may be included in the class. For it speaks freely of many questionable matters on which our sanctimonious society closes its eyes or passes by on the other side; and it exhibits a freedom and latitude in discussing difficult questions which have struck many pious souls with consternation. Wiser critics there are, however, who may judge more leniently. They may hold that rudeness, indelicacy, masculine directness, are words that have been somewhat loosely applied to describe a fine and peculiar insight into the heart of man. They may even go the length of inquiring, as we do—Why should not holy hypocrisy be unmasked and scarified? Why should not the struggle between virtue and vice be chronicled? Why should it not be said—She was tempted, and she overcame; nay, even—She was tempted, and she fell? . . .

But while we aver without hesitation that *Jane Eyre* is not an immoral book, we are ready to admit that those parts which have been censured are by no means blameless, when considered artistically. The confidence between Jane Eyre and Rochester is much too sudden and excessive. There is too little attractiveness in the heroine to account for a violent passion in such a man. The explanation is inadequate. Why should so much fondness be lavished upon this demure, keen-eyed little woman? Why should it be? we ask; and the reply is, It would not be so with us; and a feeling of contempt for the infatuation of this otherwise astute and daring man of the world is the result.

The characters, also, though drawn with mastery, are too strongly marked. Rochester is the type of one order of mind; St. John Rivers of another; and the features in each case are exaggerated to produce an effective contrast. . . .

Shirley presents a notable contrast to Miss Brontë's other novels. In them there is a profound and frequently overmastering sense of the intense dreariness of existence to certain classes. The creative spirit of poetry and romance breaks at times through the dull and stagnant life; but as a rule it is different; and *Villette,* especially, becomes monotonous from the curb maintained upon the imagination. But *Shirley* is a Holiday of the Heart. It is glad, buoyant, sunshiny. The imagination is liberated, and revels in its liberty. It is the pleasant summer-time, and the worker is idling among the hills. The world of toil and suffering lies behind, but ever so far away. True, it must be again encountered, its sores probed; the hard and obstinate war again waged manfully; but in the mean time the burn foams and sparkles through the glen; there is sunshine among the purple harebells; and the leaves in the birken glade dance merrily in the summer wind.

> Surely, surely slumber is more sweet than toil, the shore
> Than labour in the deep mid ocean, wind, and wave, and oar;
> O, rest ye, brother mariners, we will not wander more.

In *Villette* Miss Brontë returns to the realities of life; but with power more conscious and sustained. She is less absorbed, and more comprehensive. There is the same passionate force; but the horizon is wider.

Villette is by no means a cheerful book; on the contrary, it is often very painful, especially where the central figure—the heroine—is involved. *Her* pain—her tearless pain—is intense and protracted. And in this connexion *Villette* may be regarded as an elaborate psychological examination—the anatomy of a powerful but pained intellect—of exuberant emotions watchfully and vigilantly curbed. The character of this woman is peculiar, but drawn with a masterly hand. She *endures* much in a certain Pagan strength, not defiantly, but coldly and without submission. Over her heart and her intellect she exercises an incessant restraint—a restraint whose vigilant activity curbs every feeling, controls every speculation, becomes as it were engrained into her very nature. *She,* at least, will by all means look at the world as it is—a hard, dry, practical world, not wholly devoid of certain compensating elements—and she will not be cajoled into seeing it, or making others see it, under any other light. For herself, she will live honestly upon the earth, and invite or suffer no delusions; strong, composed, self-reliant, sedate in the sustaining sense of inde-

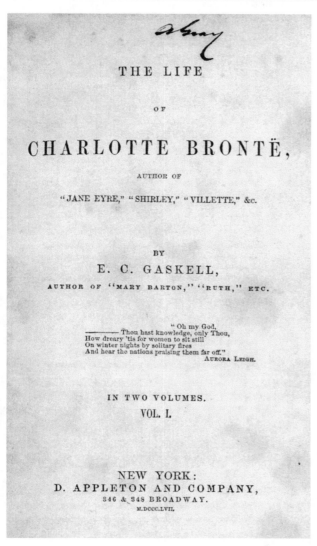

Title page for the first volume of the American edition of Gaskell's biography, which included the statements that publisher George Smith believed might be considered libelous. The offending passages are included in the Branwell chapter under the title "This Mature and Wicked Woman" (Special Collections, Thomas Cooper Library, University of South Carolina).

pendence. But cold and reserved as she may appear, she is not without imagination—rich, even, and affluent as a poet's. This is in a measure, however, the root of her peculiar misery. The dull and cheerless routine of homely life is not in her case relieved and penetrated by the creative intellect, but on the contrary, acquires through its aid a subtle and sensitive energy to hurt, to afflict, and to annoy. Thus she is not always strong; her imagination sometimes becomes loaded and surcharged; but she is always passionately ashamed of weakness. And through all this torture she is very solitary: her heart is very empty; she bears her own burden. There are cheerful hearths, and the pleasant firelight plays on the purple drapery that shuts out the inhospitable night; but none are here who can convey to her the profound sympathy her heart needs pitifully, and so she passes on, pale and unrelenting, into the night. Undoubtedly, there is a very subtle, some may say obnoxious, charm in this pale, watchful, lynx-like woman—a charm, certainly, but for our own part we have an ancient prejudice in behalf of 'Shirley's' piquant and charming ferocity.

Miss Brontë always wrote earnestly, and in *Villette* she is peremptorily honest. In it she shows no mercy for any of the engaging *ruses* and artifices of life: with her it is something too real, earnest, and even tragic, to be wantonly trifled with or foolishly disguised. She will therefore tolerate no hypocrisy, however decent or fastidious; and her subdued and direct insight goes at once to the root of the matter. She carried this perhaps too far—it may be she lacks a measure of charity and toleration, not for what is bad—for *that* there must be no toleration—but for what is humanly weak and insufficient. Graham Bretton, for instance, with his light hair and kind heart and pleasant sensitiveness, is ultimately treated with a certain implied contempt; and this solely because he happens to be what God made him, and not something deeper and more devout, the incarnation of another and more vivid kind of goodness, which it is not in his nature to be, and to which he makes no claim. . . .

Villette excels Miss Brontë's other fictions in the artistic skill with which the characters are—I use the word advisedly—*developed*. She brings us into contact with certain men and women with whom she wishes to make us acquainted. She writes no formal biography; there is no elaborate introduction; the characters appear incidently during the course of the narrative, and by degrees are worked into the heart of the every-day life with which the story is concerned. But the dissection goes on patiently all the time—so leisurely and yet so ruthlessly—one homely trait accumulated upon another with such steady, untiring pertinacity, that the man grows upon us line by line, feature by feature, until his idiosyncrasy is stamped and branded upon the brain. Probably the most genuine power is manifested in the mode in which the interest is shifted from Graham Bretton to the ill-favoured little despot—Paul Emmanuel. No essential change takes place in *their* characters, *they* remain the same, the colours in which they were originally painted were quite faithful, perfectly accurate—not by any means exaggerated for subsequent effect and contrast. It is only that a deeper insight has been gained by *us*, and if our original judgment undergoes modification, it is not because any new or inconsistent element has been introduced, but because, the conditions remaining the same, *we* see further. . . .

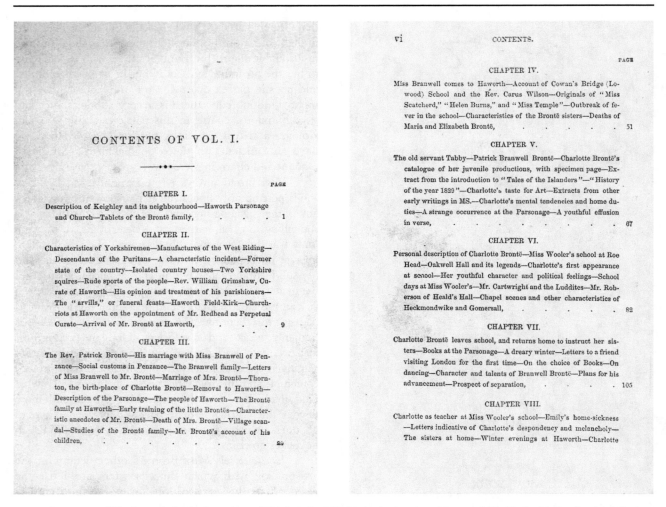

Table of contents for the first volume of Elizabeth Gaskell's biography that shaped Brontë scholarship for decades (Special Collections, Thomas Cooper Library, University of South Carolina)

To ourselves, one of the most surprising gifts of the authoress of these volumes is the racy and inimitable English she writes. No other English-woman ever commanded such language—terse and compact, and yet fiercely eloquent. We have already had occasion to notice the absence of comparison or metaphor in her poetry; the same is true of her prose. The lava is at white heat; it pours down clear, silent, pitiless; there are no bright bubbles nor gleaming foam. A mind of this order—tempered, and which cuts like steel—uses none of the pretty dexteri-ties of the imagination; for to use these infers a pause of satisfied reflection and conscious enjoy-ment which it seldom or never experiences. Its rigor-ous intellect seeks no trappings of pearl or gold. It is content to abide in its white veil of marble—naked and chaste, like 'Death' in the Vatican. Yet, the still severity is more effective than any paint could make it. The chisel has been held by a Greek, the marble hewed from Pentelicus.

–*Fraser's Magazine*, 55 (May 1857): 570, 574–582

* * *

This unsigned review article, representative of the kind of response Gaskell's work elicited, appeared in one of the leading literary periodicals in the United States. The reviewer was Margaret Sweat, who early in the article suggests that knowledge of an author's life aids a critic's insight: "When we criticise a work with no personal knowledge of the writer, we obtain an impartiality of judgment in some respects, at the expense of thorough and sympathetic understanding of his point of view, his qualifying circumstances and his personal enthusiasms and prejudices. The blunders of inference which follow upon letting loose the astuteness of professed critics over an unknown country, are often ludicrous, sometimes disastrous." Excerpts.

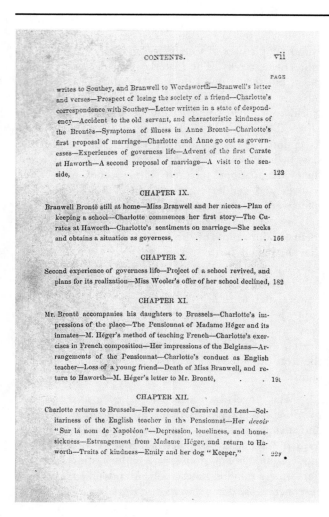

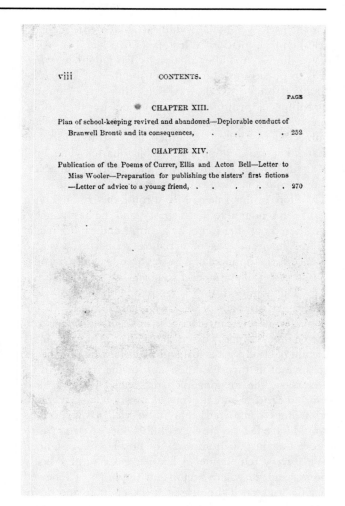

Charlotte Brontë and the Brontë Novels
Review of *The Life of Charlotte Brontë*

In the search for information concerning an author, we are fortunate when we come upon a biography like that which Mrs. Gaskell gives us of Miss Brontë. We find in it, not only the satisfaction of an urgent curiosity upon many points of personal history, but a key to Currer Bell's fictions, which sends us to their reperusal with a new and more tender interest. And in the glimpses given of the sisters Emily and Anne,—those strange mental organizations in which peculiarities were carried almost into deformities,—we learn to account for the strange elements present in their works. We find the atmosphere of the novels predominating in the "Life,"—the "counterfeit present-ment" of persons and incidents known personally or by tradition, placed before us in the romances. This is

especially true in Charlotte's case; for her mind was less narrow by nature, and her life more varied in feeling and in action, than that of either of her sisters. The most repulsive and the most contradictory of her ficti-tious characters prove to be but the careful elaboration of outlines sketched from her own circle of experience. In the vivid description which Mrs. Gaskell gives of Charlotte Brontë's life, we are surprised to find how lit-tle the novelist strained her privilege of coloring and intensifying the elements of character about her. . . .

Mrs. Gaskell has not only given us a graphic delineation of the incidents in the life of her friend, and a clear and delicately outlined portrait of her personal-ity, but in the very doing of this she has nobly fulfilled her own desire to vindicate and to honor the memory of Currer Bell. Without flattery, or violent declamation, she has eulogized her friend in the most fitting and effectual manner, by simply permitting facts to speak for themselves. The best vindication of a true life is to tell the plain, unadorned history of that life. The world has a shrewd, and after all a pretty fair judgment, when it is in possession of a sufficient number of facts. The unavoidable distortion which the circumstances attending a prominent position before the public receive, from the great amount of handling they are subjected to, is best remedied by a straightforward statement from some responsible quarter. The final judgment of the community is almost always in accordance with the dictates of generosity and truth. . . . Therefore in this Life of Miss Brontë the truest service has been rendered to her memory, and the best panegyric uttered over her tomb, by a simple and candid recital of the environments of a nature so peculiar, yet so noble, the endurances of a heart so tender, yet so strong, the struggles of an intellect so powerful, yet so susceptible. The literary history is a rare one, in this age when intellectual strength of all kinds rushes eagerly to the arena, when even mediocrity is unwilling to sit silent in the chimney-corner. The inner record is as strange, in its picture of steady self-denial and struggle, when the heart, sensible of its own weakness and of the strength of its adversary, the imagination, still waged battle against morbid fancies and nervous depression, and, though sometimes conquered, refused to yield. Few persons would have felt the pressure of filial duty so strong as to prevail against such an array of hostile circumstances. With every temptation to leave a desolate and sickly home, and go where honor and the hope of renewed health brightened the prospect, the courage and devotion which could sustain Charlotte Brontë through those long years upon the Yorkshire moors was no small virtue. We learn from her works, even better than from the occasional outbreaks in her private correspondence, how varied and how eager were her longings and her capabilities. The thirst for action, the yearning for change, the power of emotional enjoyment, the intelligent desire to travel, are all revealed to us in her fictions, though jealously guarded and conscientiously repressed in her daily life.

Few who read the Brontë novels when they first appeared could have suspected, in ever so faint a degree, the strangeness of the private history which lay concealed behind the friendly shelter of those oracular names. It is questionable whether the criticism which attacked them from some quarters so ferociously and so blindly did not, in the end, prove a benefit to them. It drew the more attention to the defects indisputably existing, in the works of the younger sisters especially, but with that attention has come a more impartial judgment and a higher award of praise; for the knowledge that the authors painted life as it lay around them in their daily path is sufficient refutation of the charge,

that they revelled in coarseness, for coarseness' sake, and drew pictures of vice in accordance with their own inherent depravity. The materials were not selected by them, but thrust upon them by circumstances clamorous for utterance. The narrowness of their general world-knowledge could hardly be suspected by themselves. They probably did not regard their sphere as an exceptional one, but supposed that in their circle they saw, in little, what the world was in large, and when their imaginations pictured fairer scenes and softer natures and gentler emotions, then, they fancied that they were straying into realms of impossibility. And looking at these novels in the strong daylight cast upon them by our study of the hearts and brains in which they had their birth,—no longer mere creations of an imagination which leaves a cheery social circle at its will, to retire to the study and indulge its untrammelled powers, able to return at any moment to healthful and happy influences from without,—they come to us as the very outpouring of pent-up passion, the cry of fettered hearts, the panting of hungry intellects, restrained by the iron despotism of adverse and unconquerable circumstance.

Few novels have called forth, even in these days of violent literary sensations, such decided opinions and such contradictory criticisms as "Jane Eyre." Upon its first reading no one seemed able to pronounce a moderate judgment. Some were enthusiastic in admiration, others rabid in detestation. All possible merits and all conceivable defects were discovered in it. Immorality, coarseness, and unnaturalness were seen by some, while others beheld only a brilliantly colored picture of the human heart. Critics fell upon it, for it challenged criticism; sagacity speculated upon it, for it defied surmise; explanations were hazarded without contradiction, for the author remained silent, and apparently undisturbed by the commotion awakened. Some readers traced only the bold, broad strokes of a masculine hand; others discerned the touch of a woman's delicate fingers; and the wise ones declared it the production of a brother and a sister, not the effort of any single mind. Like a meteor, it swept across the literary heavens, drawing towards it the gaze of thousands.

The public judgment still remains somewhat undecided as to the tendency of *Jane Eyre,* viewed simply in its moral aspect, and this is, perhaps, so long as the majority is on the side of a favorable judgment, no small testimonial to the general truthfulness and power of the story. . . . To those who track "little Jane" over the stony road of her temptation, and go forth with her as she goes into the desolate world, impelled by the unerring instinct of her conscience, no further search for moral power will be necessary.

The book has been too universally read and too fully criticised to need more than a passing notice from us in regard to its literary merit. But there are several points wherein our present knowledge of the author decidedly modifies, and others in which it totally changes, opinions passed upon it in the absence of such knowledge. Not long after the publication of the work, the world outside concluded that it was in great measure autobiographic; but this, so far from uniting the different opinions, only placed the battle upon a new ground, and the writer became as fruitful a topic for discussion as the work itself, while the point where truth blended with fiction was decided at the pleasure of the critic. We now know it to have been autobiographic chiefly in that sense in which true genius throws its very self into its work, pours its lifeblood through its creation, making it throb with vitality, and then, by right of kingship, calls its conquered territory by its own name. The first part of "Jane Eyre," the child-life of the heroine, deserves a more special notice than it is apt to receive; for the more rapid and tumultuous play of passion that succeeds obliterates the impression made by it. It is, however, artistic in the highest degree, and, viewed as a prelude to the main plot, is almost unequalled in its preparatory movement. Every stroke of the pencil which paints the heroine as formed by nature and influenced by circumstance, is of value in sketching the precise outline which is afterwards filled up. There are no waste lines or uncertain etchings, and the fidelity with which the first conception of character is clung to is quite marvellous. The childhood of Jane, with its embryo qualities, its nascent strength, its nervous imaginings, and its strong antagonisms, develops in steady preparation for the fervid passion-life of the woman. The strong but long-repressed impulse, the passionate heart, the conscience and right principle dominant over both by virtue of native vigor alone, take us into regions of struggle, and unveil to us a conflict which romance-writers have usually left untouched, or but weakly portrayed. It is somewhat singular that this new and fascinating field of romance should have been selected by one living far from all literary competition, and with only her own judgment to decide upon its fitness. It was a kind of literary clairvoyance which enabled Currer Bell to see that the time was ripe for such utterances. Novel-readers now-a-days are not satisfied with pictures of external and social life, however brilliantly colored they may be, or however various in style. The demand—to speak in mercantile parlance—is for a better article. We ask for deeper insight into character, for the features of the mind and heart rather than of the face and figure. Heroines cease to be miracles of beauty, yet prove themselves still powerful to charm; heroes are no longer of necessity stalwart and Her-

culean, yet they are still victors in the life-arena. The author plays the part of anatomist, and dissects heart, brain, and nerve, to lay them before the reader for examination and analysis. Perhaps Thackeray may be regarded as the most skilful in this dissection, though he enjoys the work more as if he were pulling an enemy to pieces with malice aforethought, than as a surgeon regarding the result only in a scientific light. Currer Bell is more genial than Thackeray, and never loses her faith in the heroic element of humanity. She delights and interests us in persons who are neither magnificently handsome nor superlatively magnanimous, but who have warm human hearts and active minds, and the battle of whose life is no ignoble struggle, though it may be a silent and single-handed one. It is this single-handed conflict, indeed, that she delights in, and depicts with greatest power, believing, as she says herself, that "Men and women never struggle so hard as when they struggle alone, without witness, counsellor, or confidant; unencouraged, unadvised, and unpitied." The reader of Miss Brontë's life may judge whether or not she knew what such a lonely life-battle really was.

In "Jane Eyre," as the first positive outburst of long-repressed vitality, we might excuse much more violent demonstrations than we find. The reticence so evident in Currer Bell's personal character often asserts itself in her writings, and although at times the volcano bursts forth, and hot lava-streams scorch the air, yet we feel that but a small portion of the internal fire finds its way to the surface. We hardly need to be told that a large part of "Jane Eyre" was written in a wonderfully short time. The whole movement of the Thornfield life betokens an irrepressible impulse in the author, and establishes in the mind of the reader a confidence similar to that we acquire in a great musician, whom we have heard successfully surmounting difficult passages of his art; breathing freely once more, we lay aside all anxiety for the future, certain that the power will be equal to the strain made upon it. The characters in "Jane Eyre" are stronger than most of the surrounding circumstances, to which, with consummate skill, they are made to seem to yield. It is in the accumulation of circumstances tending in one direction, and the indomitable will of the heroine which breaks this linked chain when the crisis comes, that we find the moral of the tale. Her moral strength and her unswerving instinct are out of the range of ordinary minds, as the sphere of her conflict is removed from commonplace environments. Isolated alike from restraint and from assistance, from praise and from blame, she is clothed in a God-given armor of proof, and wins the victory in the very strength of her woman's weakness. Natures like hers present extremes and approach paradox; strength and vigor of action in a crisis are balanced by impres-

"Not So Gloomy as the Truth"

This excerpt is from Mary Taylor's 30 July 1857 letter to Elizabeth Gaskell.

I am unaccountably in receipt by post of two vols containing the 'Life of C. Brontë.' I have pleasure in attributing this compliment to you; I beg, therefore, to thank you for them. The book is a perfect success, in giving a true picture of a melancholy life, and you have practically answered my puzzle as to how you would give an account of her, not being at liberty to give a true description of those around. Though not so gloomy as the truth, it is perhaps as much so as people will accept without calling it exaggerated, and feeling the desire to doubt and contradict it. I have seen two reviews of it. One of them sums it up as 'a life of poverty and self-suppression,' the other has nothing to the purpose at all. Neither of them seems to think it a strange or wrong state of things that a woman of first-rate talents, industry, and integrity should live all her life in a walking nightmare of 'poverty and self-suppression.' I doubt whether any of them will.
—*Mary Taylor: Friend of Charlotte Brontë: Letters from New Zealand & Elsewhere,*
pp. 132–133

sionableness and superior receptivity for the magnetic force in others, producing a sort of fascinated submission to a certain point, at which the tremendous revulsive power is awakened. In Rochester a study of another kind is placed before us, as successfully managed, though less admirable in itself. Indeed, he makes no attempt to win our admiration, but he gains from us the somewhat surly liking which would suit him best were he aware of it. We can even understand how he managed to "suit little Jane" "to the inmost fibre of her being." Knowing the difficulties of his position, and the original and acquired faults of his character, we judge his short-comings rather as we do those of our own prodigal sons, for whom our hearts yearn and our lips frame excuses, than as judges on the bench do those of criminals whose antecedents are nothing to them. This may be wrong, but it is true to human nature, which never can divest itself of these warpings of judgment, or fail to discover the under-tone in the Rochester nature, and believe in its nobility while it condemns its errors. The predominant feeling is, that the nature is bent out of its true course by adverse influences, not that it loves best of itself a distorted growth, and we keep hoping for calmer airs to allow it to rise erect once more. In St. John, the third type of character, self-denial soars (paradoxical as it may seem) into an intense selfishness; and in laying aside all the humanizing and pleasurable influences within and around him, he immolates others at the shrine of self as remorselessly as Rochester's eager and impulsive selfishness would do. Jane in both instances enjoys the struggle with their iron wills; ultimate victory we are sure must be with her, and we watch the contest with faith in our chosen champion. Like David with the Philistine, she takes no sword too large for her handling, nor tries to wield a lance too heavy for her strength, but with the small stone in the sling she slays her adversary, she herself hardly knows how. There is no bravado in her onset, no panoply of war, and her nerves tremble though her heart is strong, when the Goliath of her battle shakes the ground with his terrible tread. Like David also, she can return to the tending of her sheep, no whit puffed up by the great deed she has done. She has mounted no stilts upon which she cannot remain, yet from which it is mortifying to descend, and ordinary mortals are not afraid of her, though she has fought with and slain giants.

The most prominent artistic defects in the work are, in our opinion, the too highly colored pictures of the physical distress endured by Jane after leaving Thornfield, and the somewhat hackneyed melodrama of the discovery of her cousins in the persons of her chance benefactors, and her subsequent acquisition of a fortune. The former removes our interest to a new range of antagonistic experiences without relieving the tension, for the introduction of starvation and physical exposure as additional suffering for the lacerated nature does not harmonize with the general effect, or add force to the *dénouement;* and the latter detracts from the generally unique management of the characters and the plot.

Miss Brontë was always keenly alive to the attacks made upon "Jane Eyre," and it is certain that any trenching upon the limits of delicacy or of morality was far from her thought, and that, in telling her story as it arose in her imagination, her obedience to the truth of her perceptions of humanity is as complete when she paints its sins as when she dwells upon its virtues. If the alternative is to be true to the life-picture she tries to paint, even by confounding our perceptions with our sympathies, as she sees them constantly confounded in those around her and in her own self, or to sacrifice the fidelity of her coloring in order to throw into stronger relief the line between wrong and right, her decision as an artist may be different from that of a political economist. The public voice has declared in favor of retaining the faithful picture, and there are those who do not despair of finding in it profitable study. It is not always in those works which make the loudest claims as moral utterances, that the most searching truth and the keenest strength are to be found.

The general tone of "Shirley" is somewhat unlike that of its predecessor; the characters are more numerous, the scenes more varied, the interest less concentrated. It lacks the impetuous impulse, the passionate glow, the lava-rush towards a single point, and gives us instead, more changing tableaux, more general friction, wider varieties of emotion. It retains the spiciness of seasoning however; the viands are still of racy flavor and delicate concoction, but we detect more common and familiar ingredients in them. We still have vivacious conversations sparkling with repartee, descriptions quite Turner-like in their brilliancy of painting, and touches of deep pathos side by side with sunny and gleeful scenes. In the opening chapters we have a rough "charcoal sketch" of characters, a bold outline of coarseness quite unlike the usual efforts of the feminine pen in such directions. We are glad to learn from the "Life" that the curates did not originate in the imagination of Miss Brontë, or derive their absurdities from any desire on her part to cast a slur upon the profession to which they belong. The characters in "Shirley" are nearly all of them drawn from life, and their behavior under the circumstances created for them by the author is in perfect keeping with the tendencies which her analysis of their characteristics enabled her to discover and set in motion.

It is pleasant to trace the delicate revelations of Miss Brontë's own tastes and habits in her writings. We find her love of nature, her keen perception of the changing moods of earth and sky, and all her atmospheric susceptibilities, continually peeping out. She sets it down against one of her characters in "Shirley," that he "was not a man given to close observation of nature, he could walk miles on the most varying April day, and never see the beautiful dallying of earth and heaven, never mark when a sunbeam kissed the hill-tops, making them smile clear in green light, or when a shower wept over them, hiding their crests with the low-hanging, dishevelled tresses of a cloud"; and we feel directly that Currer Bell neither likes, nor means that her readers shall like, that man. The heroine in "Shirley" was intended as an impersonation of Emily Brontë, as her sister fancied she would have shown herself under more genial circumstances than those which surrounded her in reality. We detect the touch of a loving finger in the arrangement of the drapery around this peculiar figure. That incident in the romance which has been condemned as too melodramatic,—the bite of the mad dog,—is an exact transcript of a similar experience on the part of Emily Brontë. Caroline Helstone represents a much-loved friend of Charlotte, and is evidently a favorite with the author, though a stronger contrast than that between such a disposition and her own Jane Eyre-ish nature cannot well be imagined. She gives us in the two Moores men nearly as selfish as Rochester and St. John, and endowed with the power which selfish men almost always possess when they are shrewd and energetic. They obtain that which they really set their hearts upon having. It is undeniable that Currer Bell's heroes love themselves very much even in loving their mistresses. Having acknowledged this, or any other element of character in her creations, she never avoids for them any legitimate consequence of its existence, never shrinks from any situation into which it brings them, from fear of jarring upon the prepossessions of the reader. Inexorable as Nemesis, she forces upon them the mortifications and the disasters which are their due. Few writers would have dared the strain upon our liking given in the mercenary love-making of Robert Moore to Shirley, since Robert is intended to win our respect on the whole; but this was the natural consequence of the premises established in Robert himself, and we have to go through it as we may, and get over it as he did. In the delicately painful descriptions of illness we trace the experience of Charlotte Brontë by the bedside of her dying sisters; and there is a frequent tone of sadness in "Shirley," which tells us that the author is by no means sitting in unclouded sunshine. The characters arrive at conclusions which we feel that the writer herself has reached, and in passages like the following, we feel that she speaks her own carefully wrought-out philosophy.

> "I believe—I daily find it proved—that we can get nothing in this world worth keeping, not so much as a principle or a conviction, except out of purifying flame, or through strengthening peril. We err; we fall; we are humbled,—then we walk more carefully. We greedily eat and drink poison out of the gilded cup of vice, or from the beggar's wallet of avarice; we are sickened, degraded; everything good in us rebels against us; our souls rise bitterly indignant against our bodies; there is a period of civil war; *if the soul has strength, it conquers and rules thereafter.*"

In this conflict of life within itself in which Currer Bell finds the secret of progression, the labor of the soul upon itself and the fulfilment of its appointed work, she is very skilful to interest us and powerful to reveal its movement. We feel that the hard discipline of her men and women is like that which we make for ourselves, and that the process by which they struggle into greater freedom is that by which we must ourselves emerge from bondage. "Shirley" excited nearly as much attention as "Jane Eyre," and its admirable portraiture of

Yorkshire people and scenery led to the detection of its author's identity.

In 1852 "Villette," Currer Bell's last work, was published. In this novel the scene of action is removed from England to the Continent, it being, as we have seen, a transcript of her own residence in Belgium. In some respects "Villette" is her most remarkable work. It possesses a more classic elegance of outline and a more delicate finish of detail than either "Jane Eyre" or "Shirley." In its analysis of character it is absolutely clairvoyant. The heart of Lucy Snowe,—that name so rightly chosen,—a volcano white with drifts without, glowing with molten heat within,—is laid bare before us, and we may watch every flicker of the flame, every surging of the fiery billows. No anatomist could more clearly describe the physical vitality, than she has sketched this weird and wild, yet hushed and still nature. She plays in the romance a part similar to that of Charlotte Brontë herself in the world,—that of a silent, unsuspected analyzer of others. Miss Brontë says of her: "I was not leniently disposed towards Lucy Snowe; from the beginning, I never meant to appoint her lines in pleasant places";—and we feel that ordinary sources of happiness were necessarily closed to such a one. In eloquence of language, also, "Villette" bears the palm, rich as the others were in choice diction and fitting phrases. Certain passages in "Villette" rise to a height of sublimity or reach a depth of pathos which moves the very soul. Sadness is its prevailing tone, the hand of Fate casts its shadow from the beginning, and we know that it will fall upon us at the last.

There are, however, certain defects in "Villette" which Miss Brontë herself acknowledged, though she felt powerless to remedy them. She writes to her publisher: "I must pronounce you right again, in your complaint of the transfer of interest, in the third volume, from one set of characters to another. It is not pleasant, and it will probably be found as unwelcome to the reader, as it was, in a sense, compulsory upon the writer." The childhood of Paulina, also, promises more than it performs. She is much more of a woman when she is a child in years, than when she is fairly grown up. The queer little girl impresses us as "quite a character," and we are disappointed when she degenerates into a mere pretty woman. The giddy, shrewd-witted Ginevra is decidedly more entertaining; her whimsicalities amuse and her absurdities provoke us as they did Lucy, while she manages to keep the same place in our liking. Paul Emanuel is a personage apparently after Miss Brontë's own heart, and she evidently enjoys dwelling upon the dark-complexioned, irascible little man. He is strangely effective in the pages of "Villette," and our admiration for him grows with the progressive development of the story, till our affections twine about him

whether we will or no. In regard to his fate as set forth in the last paragraph, the meaning of which has been often disputed, we have now the confirmation of its tragic import from Miss Brontë's own lips. Indeed, the romance would have been imperfect without it, every stroke of the pen prepared us for it, and the author would have been false to "all the unities" had she forced a different *dénouement*. The oracular style of its announcement was merely out of deference to her father's request, that she would "make them happy at last."

From these three works we must make up our estimate of Currer Bell's genius; for "The Professor," written first, but not published till the halo of an assured reputation surrounded the name of its author, hardly influences our judgment either way. Its faults, which are many, were redeemed in her subsequent works; its crudeness, which is great, gave place to exquisite finish both of plot and of character; and its choice of material, which reminds us of her sisters rather than of herself as we now know her, was replaced by more genial and more natural specimens of humanity. Its best portions are developed in "Villette" with more power and richer charm, and, so far as Currer Bell is concerned, the publication of "The Professor" might still have been omitted; but viewed by itself, and compared with most of the romances issuing from the prolific and not over-fastidious press of the day, we confess some surprise that the occasional flashes of talent in its details, and the unquestionable strength of its conception, should not have won the attention of some one of the publishers to whose inspection it was submitted. One inference we may certainly draw from its perusal now; if "The Professor" was destined to be followed by such works as "Jane Eyre," "Shirley," and "Villette," we might fairly have expected a rich harvest from the minds that in their first efforts could originate "Wuthering Heights" and "The Tenant of Wildfell Hall." Had the two sisters been spared, "the Brontë novels" might have become a long and illustrious list of noble fictions.

In one respect Currer Bell is not altogether unlike her favorite, Thackeray; for she selects for her *dramatis personæ* no impossible abstractions, but warm human hearts with a fair share of imperfections, and presents us with characters which neither awe nor astonish, but which we make welcome in our family circle. But she does not, like Thackeray, become jocosely bitter over the natures she evokes, nor abuse them till the reader is roused in their defence. Sarcasm with her does not dip its arrow in poison. There is more of good than of evil in her characters; and we feel confidence in their latent heroism, draw strength from the contemplation of their struggles, and rise from the perusal of her works without bitterness. The charge of coarseness has occasionally reappeared; but, after the vindication of Mrs. Gaskell, we think it must take rank with those suggestions which recommend a "Shakespeare for the use of private families" and a mantilla for the Venus de' Medici.

We have room for but a brief notice of Emily and Anne and their works, but the public is familiar with their history. Emily seems to have been a very Titaness with her imperious will and her uncompromising ways, though Charlotte declares, in her delineation of her as Shirley, her faith in her capacity for more genial development. The best criticism of her novel, "Wuthering Heights," is by Charlotte, and that is an explanation rather than a criticism; for it is only in the author that the key to such an extraordinary story can be found. She described human nature as it appeared to her distorted fancy, and it bore the same resemblance to healthful humanity, that a faithful description of an eclipse of the sun, as seen through smoked glass, would bear to the usual appearance of that luminary. Charlotte says:–

"What her mind gathered of the real, was too exclusively confined to those tragic and terrible traits, of which, in listening to the secret annals of every rude vicinage, the memory is sometimes compelled to receive the impress. Her imagination, which was a spirit more sombre than sunny, more powerful than sportive, found in such traits materials whence it wrought creations like Heathcliffe, like Earnshaw, like Catherine. Having formed these beings, she did not know what she had done. If the auditor of her work, when read in manuscript, shuddered under the grinding influence of natures so relentless and implacable, of spirits so lost and fallen,–if it was complained that the mere hearing of certain vivid and fearful scenes banished sleep by night, and disturbed mental peace by day,–Ellis Bell would wonder what was meant, and suspect the complainant of affectation."

This would naturally be the case with a mind capable of creating such monsters, and marshalling them coolly through all the movements of a romance; the shrinking from them must have been on their first appearance to the imagination, or not at all. The power of the creations is as great as it is grotesque, and there is, after all, a fearful fascination in turning over the pages of "Wuthering Heights." It calls for no harsh judgment as a moral utterance; for its monstrosity removes it from the range of moralities altogether, and can no more be reduced to any practical application than the fancies which perplex a brain in a paroxysm of nightmare.

Anne, the younger and more gentle sister, was of a different mould; yet some passages of her "Tenant of Wildfell Hall" would lead us to suppose that she was gentle chiefly through contrast with her Spartan sister, and that the savage elements about her found an occasional echo from within. "Agnes Grey," which appeared with "Wuthering Heights," made little impression; her reputation rests upon her second and last work, "The Tenant of Wildfell Hall." For a criticism of this, we turn again to Charlotte; for though different in scope and style from "Wuthering Heights," it is nearly as inexplicable at a first glance.

"She had," says her sister, "in the course of her life, been called on to contemplate near at hand, and for a long time, the terrible effects of talents misused and faculties abused; what she saw sunk very deeply into her mind. She brooded over it till she believed it to be a duty to reproduce every detail (of course with fictitious characters, incidents, and situations), as a warning to others. She hated her work, but would pursue it. She must be honest; she must not varnish, soften, or conceal."

It must be owned that she did not "varnish" the horrors which she painted, and which her first readers did not suspect of causing the artist so much suffering. We can now trace the quiverings of a sister's heart through the hateful details of a vicious manhood; and if the book fail somewhat in its attempt to become a warning, it may at least claim the merit of a well-meant effort.

The history of the Brontë family is a tragedy throughout. Seldom have we been allowed to unveil such peculiar natures acting upon each other in one home-circle, and emerging from profound isolation into brief but dazzling publicity. With the death of Charlotte ends the sad history, and we have now only the memory of what they were. The world will not soon forget them, and would gladly offer them a more kindly tribute than it could conscientiously have given while ignorant of so much which now reveals the virtues, the struggles, and the sufferings of the sisters in that desolate Haworth parsonage. We once more thank Mrs. Gaskell for her labor of love, so gracefully executed, and echo to the letter the indignant language with which she condemns the too hastily uttered comments of ignorant criticism.

"It is well that the thoughtless critics, who spoke of the sad and gloomy views of life presented by the Brontës in their tales, should know how such words were wrung out of them by the living recollection of the long agony they suffered. It is well, too, that they who have objected to the representation of coarseness, and shrank from it with repugnance, as if such conceptions arose out of the writers, should learn, that not from the imagination, not from internal conception, but from the hard, cruel facts, pressed down, by

Watching and Wishing.

Oh, would I were the golden light
　That shines around thee now,
As slumber shades the spotless white
　Of that unclouded brow!
It watches through each changeful dream
　Thy features' varied play;
It meets thy waking eyes' soft gleam
　By dawn—by op'ning day.

Oh, would I were the crimson veil
　Above thy couch of snow,
To dye that cheek so soft, so pale,
　With my reflected glow!
Oh, would I were the cord of gold
　Whose tassel set with pearls
Just meets the silken cov'ring's fold
　And rests upon thy curls,

Dishevell'd in thy rosy sleep,
　And shading soft thy dreams;
Across their bright and raven sweep
　The golden tassel gleams!
I would be anything for thee,
　My love—my radiant love—
A flower, a bird, for sympathy,
　A watchful star above.

CHARLOTTE BRONTË.

A previously unpublished poem that George Smith included in the December 1860 issue of his recently established literary periodical,
The Cornhill Magazine. *Earlier in the year Smith had published Charlotte's "Emma," a novel fragment*
that William Makepeace Thackeray introduced (University of Colorado Libraries).

external life, upon their very senses, for long months and years together, did they write out what they saw, obeying the stern dictates of their consciences. They might be mistaken. They might err in writing at all, when their afflictions were so great that they could not write otherwise than they did of life. It is possible that it would have been better to have described only good and pleasant people, doing only good and pleasant things (in which case they could hardly have written at any time). All I say is, that never, I believe, did

women, possessed of such wonderful gifts, exercise them with a fuller feeling of responsibility for their use. As to mistakes, they stand now—as authors as well as women—before the judgment-seat of God."

—*The North American Review*, 85 (October 1857):
294–296, 314–329

Nineteenth-Century Assessments

Nearly a decade after the publication of The Life of Charlotte Brontë, *critic Susan M. Waring argued for the greatness of the heroine of* Villette. *She ends her article with a footnote: "It will serve me to state in a note that I would not be supposed to advance the idea that Lucy Snowe and Charlotte Brontë are coincident. This would be inexcusable shallowness. I have merely theorized that, as artists who would deepest read mankind by the axiom 'Know thyself,' Charlotte Brontë has made Lucy Snowe the medium for expressing her own experience and temperament further than perhaps any reader is aware."*

Charlotte Brontë's Lucy Snowe
Susan M. Waring

"I said I disliked Lucy Snowe," relates the biographer of Charlotte Brontë in allusion to a certain conversation held with her, who had conceived the essence in question—called by a "cold name" according to the nice law of contrasts—I suppose.

One can imagine a small quiet smile lightening the deep eyes of the listener at that bit of information, for Charlotte Brontë well knew that her creation christened thus coldly would reveal herself to the few—never to the many. Yet the keen, incisive reader who looks to the core of things, and who knows by instinct a creation palpitating with heart-life from one galvanized into a semblance of being, will feel that the Brontë has distilled into the character which missed of Mrs Gaskell's approbation a meaning more profound and far-reaching, a pathos more personal than will readily be found within the range of modern art.

Out of the four women therefore—Jane Eyre, Shirley, Caroline Helstone, and Lucy Snowe—the essential heroines of her novels, that with a touch unrivaled for sweep, matchless for delicacy, were patiently chiseled into being by those small child-fingers which Shakespeare himself would not disdain to clasp in his majestic palm, I choose the woman—Lucy Snowe, and entreat your attention.

I choose her for several reasons. Because she has never been truly recognized by any critic; because she represents a type of woman before unknown to the realms of novel-land; because she is most minutely informed with Charlotte Brontë's own experience, and is therefore the fittest exponent of her consummate genius.

Like most of the great masters throughout the range of Art—and in the term "Art" I include Music, Poetry, and the rest—like all indeed who live long enough to fitly develop their genius, the Brontë's style passed through three gradations.

Her intense nature had with touching patience striven to find expression through the medium of the pencil, and the pilgrim to the heaths of Haworth will find hanging upon the wall of the small stone parsonage copies of engravings wrought out line by line with minute fidelity. But the pencil proved too slow and tame—therefore she would make verses next. But poetry was with this unique nature a bird of too wild a wing to bear imprisonment in any cage of rhyme—it would break bounds and be lost in illimitable space, or dash itself to death in the endeavor.

The book "Jane Eyre" therefore, was the first adequate expression of the feeling which wrestled within her, and the heart of Charlotte Brontë found in words only, uncontrolled by any rules of rhythm, the joy of expression, the right of recognition. It is therefore that Jane Eyre may not be too strictly judged, for it was an outburst, a great surging heart bursting its bounds and finding outlet for its accumulated passion.

In "Shirley" we have the second style, rarely apt to be the best. The author says of it, with childlike humility: "I took great pains with 'Shirley,' I did not hurry. I tried to do my best." But weariness and watching had diminished the spontaneity of the ardent nature, the fire of inspiration burned less brightly, tears had quenched it, and its loss had yet scarcely been replaced by the serene light of that crowning grace which is the final reward of those who wrestle faithfully for great prizes. It therefore chances that "Shirley," full as it is of grand philosophy and pure religion, does not awaken the sympathy so entirely, or more to such fond liking as the first-born (I say first-born, "The Professor" being merely a book in embryo) of Charlotte Brontë's genius.

"Villette" shows us the third style of the master-genius. In the Brontë case at all events it is the perfected development of ripened power. Patience has wrought her "perfect work," suffering terrible and almost unremitting fulfilled her divinest mission, and calm with the repose of power, majestic almost to austerity, yet with a trembling about the mouth which tells of tears that are ended, "Villette" stands upon its pedestal the master-piece of its author. Palmer's White Captive renders this feeling—pathetic almost beyond words—perfectly: a faint quiver in the marble, tears past, the destiny accepted. The antique has nothing that compares with the statue in this point.

In cool, quiet phrases intended to give the reader the impression that she is rather a narrator of than an actor in the scenes about to transpire, Lucy Snowe opens the book. The reader—especially if he be superficial—takes her at her word, and becomes absorbed in the quaint childhood of Polly Home, intertwining itself with the boyhood of Graham Bretton. Suddenly the *dramatis personae* are swept from the boards, and we are left alone with Lucy Snowe. This is not quite relishable at first, and turning your head you look wistfully after him of the "tawny locks" and little Paulina.

The fourth chapter opens with two paragraphs which for terse bitterness and condensed description are both amazing and admirable, and these comprise all we are to know of Lucy Snowe's antecedents. After the decease of Miss Marchmont, to whom Lucy Snowe has been companion, friend, and nurse, we follow her in her desperate journey to France, still somewhat doubtful of her, still not quite sure that she entirely enlists our sympathies; and then begins the record of her life in "Villette"—a life which is double-sided, and to which these two sentences furnish the key.

"In catalepsy and dead trance I studiously held the quick of my nature.......It is on the surface only the common gaze will fall."

Like all women, therefore, who are sensitive, impassioned, imaginative, yet withheld by the seemingly despotic hand of circumstance—which means Providence assuredly, moulding the soul to higher ends while seeming to suppress—Lucy Snowe led two lives, the outer one neutral-tinted, divested of saliency for the "common gaze;" the other surging, yearning, wild with ungratified longings and clamorous desires for sustenance withheld.

As a foil to this struggling two-sided existence walks on the stage Miss Ginevra Fanshawe, a creature so tiny of soul, so infinitesimal of heart, that fingers possessing the microscopic delicacy of the Brontës alone could ever have taken her to bits. This Ginevra Fanshawe is an embodiment of the genus Young Lady—an organization in this instance incapable of ever converting to any thing like womanhood. She is the type *par excellence* of that to which the shallow tenuities of life at a boarding-school may reduce the human soul—that soul a woman's, meant for all noble possibilities. Do you not read and shiver to think of all the "Finishing-Schools" that shall turn you out just such shallow-hearted, graceless, graceful—according to Madame Fricfrac—specimen young ladies whom you are entreated to accept for daughters, sisters, wives, mothers?

Lucy Snowe, starving for recognition, sympathy, affection, circumscribed to arid wastes where flowers are forbidden to bloom, sees this bit of feminity, yclept Ginevra Fanshawe, embowered in delights, fed on sweetest flatteries, the treasure of a "good man's love" laid at her feet, and all these gifts of fortune vouchsafed because this waft of thistledown possesses the—comparatively—trivial gift of beauty. In the meantime the "little man," M. Paul, careers occasionally across the field of vision—eccentric, meteoric, evoking what is best of Charlotte Brontë's humor.

This humor of hers is by no means her least peculiar and individual gift. Its irony is scathing, its sarcasm more intense than that of Thackeray, because more impulsive, less studied—an accident, and not a specialty of style—a blade keen and fine, yet wielded only when truth calls upon its earnest champion. Indeed, sincerity stamps its signet upon every word ever written by the Brontë. Dickens sometimes falls into clap-trap, and we applaud him; Thackeray—let us speak most gently here, for flowers bloom above him, now, tears in their chalices!—condescended to it rarely; Kingsley does not disdain it; Charles Reade unblushingly abounds in the same. She alone, of all the brilliant company, is always and inevitably sincere. This humor of Brontë's is at times infiltrated by something which we can not call wit, for this quality, in its usual and superficial acceptation, she certainly had not. The diamond of wit *adamantine,* "unconquerable" as it may be, fused beneath the rays of a genius so intense, yet is it not lost. It sparkles in the quick, trenchant sentences, its white light penetrates into unexplored recesses of the heart, its vivid flashes render the opaque luminous; so that which we are wont to term wit doffs its usual garb and becomes a character of style.

This humor, however, generally kept in abeyance, or else apt to reveal itself as almost pure sarcasm, whatever its qualities on other occasions, shows all it possesses of sweet and genial whenever it is brought into contact with M. Paul. And so magical does it render the atmosphere surrounding him that of all the Brontës' creations scarce one takes the fancy more irresistibly or touches the heart more nearly than this "magnificent-minded, grand-hearted, dear, faulty little man—Paul Carlos David Emanuel." He, in common with Rochester, shares a wonderful gift—a gift that makes any man or woman great however faulty besides. I mean the power of piercing beneath surfaces, sweeping away externals and conventionalities, and estimating the soul beneath them at its intrinsic value. That this highest instinct of character, this invaluable touchstone for all things, is possessed but by the few only renders it the more precious and desirable.

Opposed to M. Paul in vivid contrast—for the Brontë had a nice eye here—Michael Angelo, Reubens, Rembrandt, no painter of them all a keener vision—is Graham Bretton, who figures in the scenes of Madame Beck's pensionnat as "Dr. John;" also, as Isidore, the lover of that "dear angel," Ginevra Fanshawe. He who is "in visage, in shape, in hue, as unlike the dark, acerb, and caustic little Professor as the fruit of the Hesperides might be unlike the sloe in the wild thicket."

I have spoken of Lucy Snowe as minutely informed with Charlotte Brontë's own experience. This is not a mere assumption grounded in fancy, but an undoubted truth: the record of her life—as contained in the two volumes of her biography—needs a scarcely careful perusal to pronounce it so.

Just a few words here regarding this biography. We may call it unsatisfactory, nay, at times insist that its narrowness of feeling wounds us to the quick. But as its author declares, "The family with whom I have now to do shoot their roots down deeper than I can penetrate," we must acknowledge. I suppose, that a deficiency admitted is half-atoned for. But what is to be said of the passage beginning, "I do not deny for myself the existence of coarseness here and there in her works, otherwise so entirely noble," in which charity is absolutely asked for Charlotte Brontë, much as a hat is extended for alms.—Charity for the great pre-Raphaelite among women, who was not ashamed or afraid to utter what God had shown her, and was too single-hearted of aim to swerve one hair-breadth in duplicating Nature's outlines? When charity is needed for dauntless courage, for fidelity to one's own convictions (the pith and marrow of the bona fide artist), then it will be time to ask it for Charlotte Brontë! Charity is indeed too rare a virtue to be squandered—use it not then to "gild refined gold." No; let us be brave and confess that Truth is too dazzling to be looked upon unveiled; but let us place the fault, where it belongs, in the cowardly weakness of our vision, not charge it to the hand of her who is strong enough and pure enough to thrust aside illusions and show the goddess in her awful splendor!

But to return to the main point, which is, that the biography in question, however faulty, can not help revealing its subject as she really was. And her profound shyness, her proud humility, her spasmodic fits of impulse, the frequent prostration of spirits to which she was liable, will all be found duplicated in Lucy Snowe. Furthermore, most of the Brontë's own habits and moods of mind are illustrated by this character. See the chapter entitled "M. Paul," where Lucy Snowe is made to declare her "creative impulse" to be the "most intractable, the most capricious, the most maddening of masters......yielding its significance sordidly, as though each word were a drop of the dark ichor of its own deathless veins." Can it be that the perfect sentences of "Villette," each word imbedded in its place in obedience to a decree as immutable as that of the Medes and Persians, were at times actually wrenched from their author?—were the offspring born of intolerable agony?

Turning from Charlotte Brontë to Lucy Snowe—easy transition, where one blends so naturally into the other—we find the latter living on this complex,

---

The Brontës' Novels in the Nineteenth Century

Editions of the Brontës' novels proliferated in the decades that followed their initial publication. In addition to cheaper editions of the novels that appeared in the 1850s and later, collected editions were produced beginning in the later part of the nineteenth century. Smith, Elder published a seven-volume edition, The Life and Works of Charlotte Brontë and her Sisters *(1889–1895) with illustrations by Edmund Morison Wimperis and a later seven-volume Haworth Edition of the works under the same title but illustrated with photographs (1899–1900); Mrs. Humphry Ward wrote introductions for the novels in this collection.*

---

two-sided life of hers, sedulously cultivating suppression until it almost kills her. This is the difficulty with natures whose intensity is riveted by pride. They hold feeling and emotion in a leash until, irritated to frenzy, feeling and emotion turn and rend their oppressor. Lucy Snowe knows this, but can not, rather will not, remedy it; it is the misfortune of such that "you must love them ere to you they will seem worthy of your love." They will not reveal themselves, but wait for destiny. But God, who takes care of us all, manages for these souls; they shall not go away from His great table, which is the universe, ahungered!

But in the mean time Lucy Snowe drinks in solitude of the cup that is forced to her lips—"black, strong, strange, drawn from no well, but filled up seething from a bottomless and boundless sea." What awful words are these! how more than awful must have been the anguish that taught a mortal woman to compress in human phrase a meaning so deep and direful! At length driven to extremes, unable longer to quell craving for sympathy, she seeks it at the altar of an alien faith, and demands it from the confessional, impelled thither by the semi-delirium of solitary grief and physical suffering.

These last are the forerunners of fever and insensibility. Her return to consciousness is marked by one of the most masterly and ingenious transitions in the range of Charlotte Brontë's works. I mean that chapter wherein the presence of "phantoms of chairs," "wraiths of looking-glasses," "tea-urns," "tea-cups," etc., once familiar furniture of Bretton, are made to return the reader into the company with which the book opens, viz., that of Mrs. Bretton, Lucy Snowe's godmother, and her son, "Dr. John." This last finally recognizes in Madame Beck's English teacher the old acquaintance of his boyhood; *she* had known him long before, but it had not "suited" her "habits of thought or system of feeling to hint at the discovery."

And now occurs one of those curious experiences which occasionally arise out of the relations existing between men and women—an experience possible only, I suppose, to natures ardent yet chaste as Sabrina, rising cool and lily-crowned from a mist of waters. I allude to the curious, one-sided friendship which was "half marble, half life" existing between "Dr. John" and Lucy Snowe.

The emotion involved here is very fine, deep as well, pathetic also. Shelley only has expressed any thing like it in his delicate verses, beginning, "One word is too often profaned for me to profane it." Lucy Snowe is, of course, the sufferer in this "one-sided friendship," yet indignantly repels the accusation of "warmer feelings." It would be worth our while to see where the grievance lay.

Here is a woman cabin'd, cribb'd, confin'd, leading what aspiration declares to be a halting, stammering, imperfect life. Here is a man gifted with all the graces which had been denied the woman— "handsome, bright-spirited, and sweet-tempered, a curled darling of Nature and of Fortune," possessing the power of action and a sphere wherein to exercise the power, holding what we term the "winning" qualities in the race of life—"born a conqueror as some are born conquered." From this man the woman asks recognition, friendship, and obtains the kindness of a philanthropist and humanitarian— entreats for bread and receives a stone.

Lucy Snowe, brave at heart as all intense persons are, will not waste puerile regrets over the inevitable, but with the quiet benediction, "Goodnight, Dr. John, you are good, you are beautiful, but you are not mine;" resigns for aye that sweet consolation of friendship her hungry soul had craved.

It would seem that Charlotte Brontë had been entreated to make fate more propitious to Lucy Snowe, to which she returns answer—a sad meaning underlying the words—"From the beginning I never meant to appoint her lines in pleasant places." So she gives her a "cold name on the *lucus a non lucendo* principle, for she has about her an external coldness" and relentlessly sends her forth. But we are not to be cheated by any thing "external," so we recognize the fiery soul, the exquisite power of sympathy veiled beneath indifference, and will dearly like and fondly cherish her in spite of all.

Little Polly Home—now transformed into Paulina De Bassompierre and a countess—by means of an accident requiring the medical services of "Dr. John," reappears, and the group with which the book opens is complete. Of this "airy fairy thing" Paulina, that "pleases almost to pain," Charlotte

Brontë thus speaks: "I felt that this character lacked substance; I fear the reader will feel the same."

It is true that Paulina lacks the strong flavor of our common humanity with which the rest are impregnated. But what matters it when the conception is consistent with itself from beginning to end? Does not the very daintiness and ideality of "little Polly" enhance the vivid reality of the others and throw it out in stronger relief? And does not the rose-leaf-lined existence of the little countess, side by side with the tortured life of Lucy Snowe, invest this last with a most appealing pathos? and was not this a part of the original design?

We watch Dr. John's courtship of Paulina, and for the nonce forget the narrator. But she complains not, she is reserving her hour of triumph. In the course of this wooing De Bassompierre's "little girl" develops a character for delicate finesse quite in accordance with her possibilities, but which Charlotte Brontë's women, simple, direct, impulsive, are not apt to possess. Witness the description given by her, Paulina, to Lucy Snowe of her answer to her lover's letter. "Having confected it until it seemed to me to resemble a morsel of ice flavored with ever so slight a zest of fruit or sugar, I ventured to seal and dispatch it."

We learn that these two marry and are "blessed." Then read the touching paragraph wherein a parallel is drawn between "those whom sorrow rarely visits, or if she does comes only in her most gracious aspect," and those "other travelers who encounter weather fitful and gusty, wild and variable, breast adverse winds, are belated, and overtaken by the early closing winter-night"—we read, and bowing our heads, bewail that she who thus wrote was the prophet of her own sad destiny.

If "Dr. John" made no effort to comprehend Lucy Snowe, his antithesis, M. Paul, was far from exhibiting a similar indifference. If in regard to the first she was obliged to complain, "had Lucy Snowe been intrinsically the same, but possessing the additional advantages of wealth and station, would your manner to her, your value for her have been quite what they actually were?"—if these considerations carried weight with "Dr. John," they mattered not a little to him of the "bonnet-grec and paletot." "Dr. John" might regard Lucy Snowe in the light of "a being as inoffensive as a shadow," but for M. Paul she bristled with salient points and aggravating peculiarities. She was the woman whom one man alone finds piquant, attractive, in the end irresistible.

It has been said that whatever is best of Charlotte Brontë's humor is evoked by the "little man in his cherished and ink-stained paletot." Caustic astringent, merciless, as it often is elsewhere, in dealing with him it becomes most gentle and childlike–precious as the royal spice which the Queen of Sheba presented to King Solomon.

Seen in the mellow magical light of this humor most loving and tender, we are fain to sympathize with that lady who vowed she would "either find the duplicate of Professor Emanuel or remain forever single." So that if grudgeful fate bestows upon Lucy Snowe but one admirer, it may be questioned whether he be not more than equal to the half-a-dozen lovers that kneel at the feet of other heroines.

Finally, the cobwebs of machination woven by Madame Beck and her coadjutor, Père Silas, are swept away, and we learn that Lucy Snowe loves and is loved by that "guileless Napoleon," Paul Emanuel. Not with the love "born of beauty," of which she is "sensitively jealous," but with the love that touches the most "inner springs of life."

Ere this consummation is reached, however, her hour of triumph with the reader is arrived. In the whirl of that description, showing the keen anguish of a faithful heart riven by suspense, we know that Paulina, "Dr. John," and the rest are inconsequent, and we realize at last that Lucy Snowe is the book.

Paul Emanuel gives the last proof of his unselfish love, and installing "Mees Lucie" in the dearest wish of her heart–a school of her own, departs upon his voyage. We read of "storm and shrieking winds that strew the sea with wrecks," yet striving to smile say, "Surely, surely he came back again," while tears fast-dropping declare the sad finality–Paul Emanuel is seen of Lucy Snowe no more.

The wonderful tale is told, the unprecedented book, full of human nature as any play of Shakspeare's, ended. Take it, search it thoroughly, it was meant to bear close and stern inspection. Hold it in the strongest light, try it by the severest tests, and know this "Vilette" of Charlotte Brontë's is, as far as human art can make it, a diamond without a flaw, one entire and perfect chrysolite. May no other woman ever write so well, may none other ever suffer so acutely!

I lay this flower, O Charlotte Brontë! upon the altar of your memory. I know it's scarce worthy of so high a resting-place, and that blooms richer and fairer a thousand times shall shame it there. But I claim it pure rosemary at least–the flower of loving memory, and its breath is fragrant. So whomever may disdain, your deep heart would not despise it.

–*Harper's New Monthly Magazine*, 32 (February 1866): 368–371

* * *

Leslie Stephen, an eminent Victorian man of letters and the father of novelist Virginia Woolf, wrote about Charlotte Brontë in his Hours in a Library *series for* Cornhill Magazine, *a periodical for which Stephen served as editor. These excerpts are from an unsigned article in which he set out to "approximately decide" Charlotte Brontë's "place in the great hierarchy of imaginative thinkers." He believed that it was "undeniable" that her position was "very high."*

Charlotte Brontë
Leslie Stephen

Putting aside living writers, the only female novelist whom one can put distinctly above her is George Sand; for Miss Austen, whom some fanatics place upon a still higher level, differs so widely in every way that "comparison" is absurd. It is almost silly to draw a parallel between writers when every great quality in one is "conspicuous by its absence" in the other.

The most obvious of all remarks about Miss Brontë is the close connection between her life and her writings. Nobody ever put so much of themselves into their work. She is the heroine of her two most powerful novels; for Lucy Snowe is avowedly her own likeness, and Lucy Snowe differs only by accidents from Jane Eyre; whilst her sister is the heroine of the third. All the minor characters, with scarcely an exception, are simply portraits, and the more successful in proportion to their fidelity. The scenery and even the incidents are, for the most part, equally direct transcripts from reality. And, as this is almost too palpable a peculiarity to be expressly mentioned, it seems to be an identical proposition that the study of her life is the study of her novels. More or less true of all imaginable writers, this must be pre-eminently true of Miss Brontë. Her experience, we would say, has been scarcely transformed in passing through her mind. She has written down not only her feelings, but the more superficial accidents of her life. She has simply given fictitious names and dates, with a more or less imaginary thread of narrative, to her own experience at school, as a governess, at home and in Brussels. *Shirley* contains a continuous series of photographs of Haworth and its neighbourhood; as *Villette* does of Brussels: and if *Jane Eyre* is not so literal, except in the opening account of the school-life, much of it is almost as strictly autobiographical. It is one of the oddest cases of an author's self-delusion that Miss Brontë should have imagined that she could remain anonymous after the publication of *Shirley,* and the introduction of such whole-length portraits from the life as the Yorke family. She does not appear to have been herself conscious of the closeness of her adherence to facts. "You are not to suppose," she says in a letter given by Mrs. Gaskell, "any of the characters in *Shirley* intended

INTERIOR OF HAWORTH CHURCH.

Two views inside the Haworth Church as the Brontës knew it. Reverend Brontë's successor had the old church–apart from the tower–demolished in 1879 (from Ellen Nussey, "Reminiscences of Charlotte Brontë," Scribner's Monthly, May 1871, Colorado College Library).

as real portraits. It would not suit the rules of art, nor of my own feelings, to write in that style. We only suffer reality to *suggest,* never to *dictate.*" She seems to be thinking chiefly of her "heroes and heroines," and would perhaps have admitted that the minor personages were less idealised. But we must suppose also that she failed to appreciate fully the singularity of characters which, in her seclusion, she had taken for average specimens of the world at large. If I take my village for the world, I cannot distinguish the particular from the universal; and must assume that the most distinctive peculiarities are unnoticeably commonplace. The amazing vividness of her portrait-painting is the quality which more than any other makes her work unique amongst modern fiction. Her realism is something peculiar to herself; and only the crudest of critics could depreciate its merits on

the ground of its fidelity to facts. The hardest of all feats is to see what is before our eyes. What is called the creative power of genius is much more the power of insight into commonplace things and characters. The realism of the De Foe variety produces an illusion, by describing the most obvious aspects of everyday life, and introducing the irrelevant and accidental. A finer kind of realism is that which, like Miss Austen's, combines exquisite powers of minute perception with a skill which can light up the most delicate miniatures with a delicate play of humour. A more impressive kind is that of Balzac, where the most detailed reproduction of realities is used to give additional force to the social tragedies which are being enacted at our doors. The specific peculiarity of Miss Brontë seems to be the power of revealing to us the potentiality of intense passions lurk-

THE ORGAN LOFT, OVER THE BRONTE TABLET AND PEW.

ing behind the scenery of everyday life. Except in the most melodramatic—which is also the weakest—part of *Jane Eyre,* we have lives almost as uneventful as those of Miss Austen, and yet charged to the utmost with latent power. A parson at the head of a school-feast somehow shows himself as a "Cromwell, guiltless of his country's blood;" a professor lecturing a governess on composition is revealed as a potential Napoleon; a mischievous schoolboy is obviously capable of developing into a Columbus or a Nelson; even the most commonplace natural objects, such as a row of beds in a dormitory, are associated and naturally associated with the most intense emotions. Miss Austen makes you feel that a tea-party in a country parsonage may be as amusing as the most brilliant meeting of cosmopolitan celebrities; and Miss Brontë that it may display characters capable

of shaking empires and discovering new worlds. The whole machinery is in a state of the highest electric tension, though there is no display of thunder and lightning to amaze us.

The power of producing this effect without stepping one hand's-breadth beyond the most literal and unmistakable fidelity to ordinary facts is explicable, one would say, so far as genius is explicable at all, only in one way. A mind of extraordinary activity within a narrow sphere has been brooding constantly upon a small stock of materials, and a sensitive nature has been enforced to an unusual pressure from the hard facts of life. The surroundings must surely have been exceptional, and the receptive faculties impressible even to morbidness, to produce so startling a result, and the key seemed to be given by Mrs. Gaskell's touching biography, which, with certain minor faults, is still one of the most pathetic records of a heroic life in our literature. Charlotte Brontë and her sister, according to this account, resembled the sensitive plant exposed to the cutting breezes of the West Riding moors. Their writings were the cry of pain and of only half-triumphant faith, produced by a life-long martyrdom, tempered by mutual sympathy, but embittered by family sorrows and the trials of a dependent life. It is one more exemplification of the common theory, that great art is produced by taking an exceptionally delicate nature and mangling it slowly under the grinding wheels of the world.

A recent biographer has given us to understand that this is in great part a misconception, and, whilst paying high compliments to Mrs. Gaskell, he virtually accuses her of unintentionally substituting a fiction for a biography. Mr. Wemyss Reid's intention is excellent; and one can well believe that Mrs. Gaskell did in fact err by carrying into the earlier period the gloom of later years. Most certainly one would gladly believe this to be the case. . . . The plain truth is, that Miss Brontë's letters, read without reference to the disputes of rival biographers, are disappointing. The most striking thing about them is that they are young-ladyish. Here and there a passage revealing the writer's literary power shines through the more commonplace matter, but, as a whole, they give a curious impression of immaturity. The explanation seems to be, in the first place, that Miss Brontë, with all her genius, was still a young lady. Her mind, with its exceptional powers in certain directions, never broke the fetters by which the parson's daughter of the last generation was restricted. Trifling indications of this are common in her novels. . . . The letters may dissipate some of Mrs. Gaskell's romantic gloom, but they do not persuade us that the Brontës were ever like their neighbours. The doctrine that the people of Haworth were really commonplace mortals, may be accepted with a similar reserve. . . .

Sensitive natures brought into contact with those of coarser grain may relieve themselves in various ways. Some might have been driven into revolt against the proprieties which found so harsh an expression. Poor Branwell Brontë took the unluckily commonplace path of escape from a too frigid code of external morality which leads to the public-house. His sisters followed the more characteristically feminine method. They learnt to be proud of the fetters by which they were bound. Instead of fretting against the stern law of repression, they identified it with the eternal code of duty, and rejoiced in trampling on their own weakness. The current thus restrained ran all the more powerfully in its narrow channel. What might have been bright and genial sentiment was transformed and chastened into a kind of austere enthusiasm. They became recluses in spirit, sternly enforcing a self-imposed rule, though, in their case, the convent walls were invisible and the objects of their devotion not those which dominate the ascetic imagination. . . .

The sisters, indeed, differed widely, though with a strong resemblance. The iron had not entered so deeply into Charlotte's nature. Emily's naturally subjective mode of thought—to use the unpleasant technical phrase—found its most appropriate utterance in lyrical poetry. She represents, that is, the mood of pure passion, and is rather encumbered than otherwise by the necessity of using the more indirect method of concrete symbols. She feels, rather than observes; whereas Charlotte feels in observing. Charlotte had not that strange self-concentration which made the external world unreal to her sister. Her powers of observation, though restricted by circumstances and narrowed by limitations of her intellect, showed amazing penetration within her proper province. The greatest of all her triumphs in this direction is the character of Paul Emanuel, which has tasked Mr. Swinburne's powers of expressing admiration, and which one feels to be, in its way, inimitable. A more charming hero was never drawn, or one whose reality is more vivid and unmistakable. We know him as we know a familiar friend, or rather as we should know a friend whose character had been explained for us by a common acquaintance of unusual acuteness and opportunity of observation. Perhaps we might venture to add, that it is hardly explicable, except as a portrait drawn by a skilful hand guided by love, and by love intensified by the consciousness of some impassable barrier. . . .

Although the secret of Miss Brontë's power lies, to a great extent, in the singular force with which she can reproduce acute observations of character from without, her most esoteric teaching, the most accurate reflex from her familiar idiosyncrasy, is of course to be found in the characters painted from within. We may infer her personality more or less accurately from the mode in which she contemplates her neighbours, but it is directly manifested in various avatars of her own spirit. Among the characters who are more or less mouthpieces of her peculiar sentiment we may reckon not only Lucy Snowe and Jane Eyre, but, to some extent, Shirley, and, even more decidedly, Rochester. When they speak we are really listening to her own voice, though it is more or less disguised in conformity to dramatic necessity. There are great differences between them; but they are such differences as would exist between members of the same family, or might be explained by change of health or internal circumstances. Jane Eyre has not had such bitter experience as Lucy Snowe; Shirley is generally Jane Eyre in high spirits, and freed from harassing anxiety; and Rochester is really a spirited sister of Shirley's, though he does his very best to be a man, and even an unusually masculine specimen of his sex.

Mr. Rochester, indeed, has imposed upon a good many people; and he is probably responsible in part for some of the muscular heroes who have appeared since his time in the world of fiction. I must, however, admit that, in spite of some opposing authority, he does not appear to me to be a real character at all, except as a reflection of a certain side of his creator. He is in reality the personification of a true woman's longing (may one say it now?) for a strong master. But the knowledge is wanting. He is a very bold but necessarily unsuccessful attempt at an impossibility. The parson's daughter did not really know anything about the class of which he is supposed to be a type, and he remains vague and inconsistent in spite of all his vigour. . . .

. . . To gather up into a single formula the meaning of such a character as Lucy Snowe, or in other words, of Charlotte Brontë, is, of course, impossible. But at least such utterances always give us the impression of a fiery soul imprisoned in too narrow and too frail a tenement. The fire is pure and intense. It is kindled in a nature intensely emotional, and yet aided by a heroic sense of duty. The imprisonment is not merely that of a feeble body in uncongenial regions, but that of a narrow circle of thought, and consequently of a mind which has never worked itself clear by reflection, or developed a harmonious and consistent view of life. There is a certain feverish disquiet which is marked by the peculiar mannerism of the style. At its best, we have admirable flashes of vivid expression, where the material of language is the incarnation of keen intuitive thought. At its worst, it is strangely contorted, crowded by rather awkward personifications, and degenerates towards a rather unpleasant Ossianesque. More severity of taste would increase the power by restraining the abuse. We feel an aspiration after more than can be accomplished, an unsatisfied yearning for potent excitement, which is sometimes more fretful than forcible. . . .

This is the unhappy discord which runs through Miss Brontë's conceptions of life, and, whilst it gives an indescribable pathos to many pages, leaves us with a sense of something morbid and unsatisfactory. She seems to be turning for relief alternately to different teachers, to the promptings of her own heart, to the precepts of those whom she has been taught to revere, and occasionally, though timidly and tentatively, to alien schools of thought. The attitude of mind is, indeed, best indicated by the story (a true story, like most of her incidents) of her visit to the confessional in Brussels. Had she been a Catholic, or a Positivist, or a rebel against all the creeds, she might have reached some consistency of

doctrine, and therefore some harmony of design. As it is, she seems to be under a desire which makes her restless and unhappy, because her best impulses are continually warring against each other. She is between the opposite poles of duty and happiness, and cannot see how to reconcile their claims, or even—for perhaps no one can solve that, or any other great problem exhaustively—how distinctly to state the question at issue. She pursues one path energetically, till she feels her self to be in danger, and then shrinks with a kind of instinctive dread, and resolves not only that life is a mystery, but that happiness must be sought by courting misery. Undoubtedly such a position speaks of a mind diseased, and a more powerful intellect would even under her conditions have worked out some more comprehensible and harmonious solutions.

—*The Cornhill Magazine* (December 1877): 726–739

* * *

The poet and critic Algernon Charles Swinburne (1837–1909) wrote several pieces about the Brontës that contributed to the increasing respect and interest Emily's work garnered in the later nineteenth century. This wide-ranging essay, originally titled "Emily Brontë," was written after the 1883 publication of Mary Robinson's biography, the only book-length treatment of the author's life published in the nineteenth century. Swinburne alludes to Reverend Sabine Baring-Gould's novel Mehalah: A Story of the Salt Marshes *(1880) as well as to many other authors then believed superior to Emily Brontë.*

"Troubled and Taintless"
Review of *Emily Brontë*
Algernon Charles Swinburne

To the England of our own time, it has often enough been remarked, the novel is what the drama was to the England of Shakespeare's. The same general interest produces the same incessant demand for the same inexhaustible supply of imaginative produce, in a shape more suited to the genius of a later day and the conditions of a changed society. Assuming this simple explanation to be sufficient for the obvious fact that in the modern world of English letters the novel is everywhere and the drama is nowhere, we may remark one radical point of difference between the taste of playgoers in the age of Shakespeare and the taste of novel-readers in our own. Tragedy was then at least as popular as either romantic or realistic comedy; whereas nothing would seem to be more unpopular with the run of modern readers than the threatening shadow of tragedy projected across the whole length of a story, inevitable and unmistakable from the lurid harshness of its dawn to the fiery softness of its sunset. The objection to

HAWORTH OLD CHURCH, SCHOOL AND PARSONAGE, AS IN THE BRONTË DAYS.
(By kind permission of Mr. J. H. Widdop, Haworth).

A view of the locus of the Brontë family. The church, including the tower that still stands, dates back to the fifteenth century; forty thousand people are estimated to be buried in the graveyard (from Whiteley Turner, A Spring-Time Saunter: Round and About Brontë Land, *Sam Houston State University Library).*

a novel in which the tragic element has an air of incongruity and caprice–in which a tragic surprise is, as it were, sprung upon the reader, with a jarring shock such as might be given by the actual news of some unforeseen and grievous accident–this objection seems to me thoroughly reasonable, grounded on a true critical sense of fitness and unfitness; but the distaste for high and pure tragedy, where the close is in perfect and simple harmony with the opening, seems not less thoroughly pitiable and irrational.

A recent work of singular and admirable power, in which the freshness of humour is as real and vital as the fervour of passion, was at once on its appearance compared with Emily Brontë's now famous story. And certainly not without good cause; for in point of local colour 'Mehalah' is, as far as I know, the one other book which can bear and may challenge the comparison. Its pages, for one thing, reflect the sterile glitter and desolate fascination of the salt marshes, their minute splendours and barren beauties and multitudinous

monotony of measureless expanse, with the same instinctive and unlaborious accuracy which brings all the moorland before us in a breath when we open any chapter of 'Wuthering Heights.' And the humour is even better; and the passion is not less genuine. But the accumulated horrors of the close, however possible in fact, are wanting in the one quality which justifies and ennobles all admissible horror in fiction: they hardly seem inevitable; they lack the impression of logical and moral certitude. All the realism in the world will not suffice to convey this impression; and a work of art which wants it wants the one final and irreplaceable requisite of inner harmony. Now in 'Wuthering Heights' this one thing needful is as perfectly and triumphantly attained as in 'King Lear' or 'The Duchess of Malfi,' in 'The Bride of Lammermoor' or 'Notre-Dame de Paris.' From the first we breathe the fresh dark air of tragic passion and presage; and to the last the changing wind and flying sunlight are in keeping with the stormy promise of the dawn. There is no monotony, there is no repetition, but there is no discord. This is the first and last necessity, the foundation of all labour and the crown of all success, for a poem worthy of the name; and this it is that distinguishes the hand of Emily from the hand of Charlotte Brontë. All the works of the elder sister are rich in poetic spirit, poetic feeling, and poetic detail; but the younger sister's work is essentially and definitely a poem in the fullest and most positive sense of the term. It was therefore all the more proper that the honour of raising a biographical and critical monument to the author of 'Wuthering Heights' should have been reserved for a poetess of the next generation to her own. And those who had already in their mind's eye the clearest and most definite conception of Emily Brontë will be the readiest to acknowledge their obligation and express their gratitude to Miss Robinson for the additional light which she has been enabled to throw upon a great and singular character. It is true that when all has been said the main features of that character stand out before us unchanged. The sweet and noble genius of Mrs. Gaskell did not enable her to see far into so strange and sublime a problem; but, after all, the main difference between the biographer of Emily and the biographer of Charlotte is that Miss Robinson has been interested and attracted where Mrs. Gaskell was scared and perplexed. On one point, however, the new light afforded us is of the very utmost value and interest. We all knew how great was Emily Brontë's tenderness for the lower animals; we find, with surprise as well as admiration, that the range of this charity was so vast as to include even her own miserable brother. Of that lamentable and contemptible caitiff—contemptible not so much for his commonplace debauchery as for his abject selfishness, his lying pretension, and his nerveless cowardice—there is far too much in this memoir: it is inconceivable how any one can have put into a lady's hand such a letter as one which defaces two pages of the volume, and it may be permissible to regret that a lady should have made it public; but this error is almost atoned for by the revelation that of all the three sisters in that silent home "it was the silent Emily who had ever a cheering word for Branwell; it was Emily who still remembered that he was her brother, without that remembrance freezing her heart to numbness." That she saved his life from fire, and hid from their father the knowledge of her heroism, no one who knows anything of Emily Brontë will learn with any mixture of surprise in his sense of admiration; but it gives a new tone and colour to our sympathetic and reverent regard for her noble memory when we find in the depth of that self-reliant and stoic nature a fountain so inexhaustible of such Christlike longsuffering and compassion.

I cannot however but think that Miss Robinson makes a little too much of the influence exercised on Emily Brontë's work by the bitter, narrow, and ignoble misery of the life which she had watched burn down into such pitiful ruin that its memory is hardly redeemed by the last strange and inconsistent flash of expiring manhood which forbids us to regard with unmixed contempt the sufferer who had resolution enough to die standing if he had lived prostrate, and so make at the very last a manful end of an abject history. The impression of this miserable experience is visible only in Anne Brontë's second work, 'The Tenant of Wildfell Hall'; which deserves perhaps a little more notice and recognition than it has ever received. It is ludicrously weak, palpably unreal, and apparently imitative, whenever it reminds the reader that it was written by a sister of Charlotte and Emily Brontë; but as a study of utterly flaccid and invertebrate immorality it bears signs of more faithful transcription from life than anything in 'Jane Eyre' or 'Wuthering Heights.' On the other hand, the intelligent reader of 'Wuthering Heights' cannot fail to recognize that what he is reading is a tragedy simply because it is the work of a writer whose genius is essentially tragic. Those who believe that Heathcliff was called into existence by the accident that his creator had witnessed the agonies of a violent weakling in love and in disgrace might believe that Shakespeare wrote 'King Lear' because he had witnessed the bad effects of parental indulgence, and that Æschylus wrote the 'Eumenides' because he had witnessed the uncomfortable results of matricide. The book is what it is because the author was what she was; this is the main and central fact to be remembered. Circumstances have modified the details; they have not implanted the conception. If there were any need for explanation there would be no room for apology. As it is, the few faults of design or execution leap to sight at a first glance, and vanish in the final effect and unimpaired impression of the whole; while those who object to the violent illegalities of conduct with regard to real or personal property on which the progress of the story does undeniably depend—"a senseless piece of glaring folly," it was once called by some critic learned in the law—might as well complain, in Carlylesque phrase, that the manners are quite other than Belgravian.

It is a fine and accurate instinct that has inevitably led Miss Robinson to cite in chosen illustration of the book's quality at its highest those two incomparable pictures of dreamland and delirium which no poet that ever lived has ever surpassed or equalled for passionate and lifelike beauty of imaginative truth. But it is even somewhat less than exact to say that the latter scene "is given with a masterly pathos that Webster need not have made more strong, nor Fletcher more lovely and appealing." Fletcher could not have made it as lovely and appealing it is; he would have made it exquisitely pretty and effectively theatrical; but the depth, the force, the sincerity, recalling here so vividly the "several forms of distraction" through which Webster's Cornelia passes after the murder of her son by his brother, excel everything else of the kind in imaginative art; not excepting, if truth may be spoken on such a subject, the madness of Ophelia or even of Madge Wildfire. It is hardly ever safe to say dogmatically what can or cannot be done by the rarest and highest genius; yet it must surely be borne in upon us all that these two crowning passages could never have been written by any one to whom the motherhood of earth was less than the brotherhood of man—to whom the anguish, the intolerable and mortal yearning, of insatiate and insuppressible homesickness, was less than the bitterest of all other sufferings endurable or conceivable in youth. But in Emily Brontë this passion was twin-born with the passion for truth and rectitude. The stale and futile epithet of Titaness has in this instance a deeper meaning than appears; her goddess mother was in both senses the same who gave birth to the divine martyr of Æschylean legend: Earth under one aspect and one name, but under the other Righteousness. And therefore was the first and last word uttered out of the depth of her nature a cry for that one thing needful without which all virtue is as worthless as all pleasure is vile, all hope as shameful as all faith is abject—a cry for liberty.

And therefore too, perhaps we may say, it is that any seeming confusion or incoherence in her work is merely external and accidental, not inward and spiritual. Belief in the personal or positive immortality of the individual and indivisible spirit was not apparently, in her case, swallowed up or nullified or made nebulous by any doctrine or dream of simple reabsorption into some indefinite infinity of eternal life. So at least it seems to me that her last ardent confession of dauntless and triumphant faith should properly be read, however capable certain phrases in it may seem of the vaguer and more impersonal interpretation. For surely no scornfuller or stronger comment on the "unutterable" vanity of creeds could pass more naturally into a chant expressive of more profound and potent faith; a song of spiritual trust more grave and deep and passionate in the solemn ardour of its appeal than the Hymn to God of Cleanthes. Her infrangible self-reliance and lonely sublimity of spirit she had in common with him and his fellows of the Porch; it was much more than "some shy ostrich prompting" which bade her assign to an old Stoic the most personal and characteristic utterance in all her previous poems; but the double current of imaginative passion and practical compassion which made her a tragic poet and proved her a perfect woman gives as it were a living warmth and sweetness to her memory, such as might well have seemed incompatible with that sterner and colder venera-

tion so long reserved for her spiritual kinsmen of the past. As a woman we never knew her so well as now that we have to welcome this worthy record of her life, with deeper thanks and warmer congratulations to the writer than can often be due even to the best of biographers and critics. As an author she has not perhaps even yet received her full due or taken her final place. Again and again has the same obvious objection been taken to that awkwardness of construction or presentation which no reader of 'Wuthering Heights' can undertake to deny. But, to judge by the vigour with which this objection is urged, it might be supposed that the rules of narrative observed by all great novelists were of an almost legal or logical strictness and exactitude with regard to probability of detail. Now most assuredly the indirect method of relation through which the story of Heathcliff is conveyed, however unlikely or clumsy it may seem from the realistic point of view, does not make this narrative more liable to the charge of actual impossibility than others of the kind. Defoe still remains the one writer of narrative in the first person who has always kept the stringent law of possibilities before the eye of his invention. Even the admirable ingenuity and the singular painstaking which distinguish the method of Mr. Wilkie Collins can only give external and transient plausibility to the record of long conversations overheard or shared in by the narrator only a few hours before the supposed date of the report drawn up from memory. The very greatest masters in their kind, Walter Scott and Charles Dickens, are of all narrators the most superbly regardless of this objection. From 'Rob Roy' and 'Redgauntlet,' from 'David Copperfield' and 'Bleak House,' we might select at almost any stage of the autobiographic record some instance of detail in which the violation of plausibility, probability, or even possibility, is at least as daring and as glaring as any to be found in the narrative of Nelly Dean. Even when that narrative is removed, so to speak, yet one degree further back—even when we are supposed to be reading a minute detail of incident and dialogue transcribed by the hand of the lay figure Mr. Lockwood from Nelly Dean's report of the account conveyed to her years ago by Heathcliff's fugitive wife or gadding servant, each invested for the nonce with the peculiar force and distinctive style of the author—even then we are not asked to put such an overwhelming strain on our faculty of imaginative belief as is exacted by the great writer who invites us to accept the report drawn up by Mr. Pendennis of everything that takes place—down even to the minutest points of dialogue, accent, and gesture—in the household of the Newcomes or the Firmins during the absence no less than in the presence of their friend the reporter. Yet all this we gladly and gratefully admit, without demur or cavil, to be thoroughly authentic and credible, because the whole matter of the report, however we get at it, is found when we do get at it to be vivid and lifelike as an actual experience of living fact. Here, if ever anywhere, the attainment of the end justifies the employment of the means. If we are to enjoy imaginative work at all, we must "assume the virtue" of imagination, even if we have it not; we must, as children say, "pretend" or make believe a little as a very condition of the game.

A graver and perhaps a somewhat more plausible charge is brought against the author of 'Wuthering Heights' by those who find here and there in her book the savage note or the sickly symptom of a morbid ferocity. Twice or thrice especially the details of deliberate or passionate brutality in Heathcliff's treatment of his victims make the reader feel for a moment as though he were reading a police report or even a novel by some French "naturalist" of the latest and brutallest order. But the pervading atmosphere of the book is so high and healthy that the effect even of those "vivid and fearful scenes" which impaired the rest of Charlotte Brontë is almost at once neutralized—we may hardly say softened, but sweetened, dispersed, and transfigured—by the general impression of noble purity and passionate straightforwardness, which removes it at once and for ever from any such ugly possibility of association or comparison. The whole work is not more incomparable in the effect of its atmosphere or landscape than in the peculiar note of its wild and bitter pathos; but most of all is it unique in the special and distinctive character of its passion. The love which devours life itself, which devastates the present and desolates the future with unquenchable and raging fire, has nothing less pure in it than flame or sunlight. And this passionate and ardent chastity is utterly and unmistakably spontaneous and unconscious. Not till the story is ended, not till the effect of it has been thoroughly absorbed and digested, does the reader even perceive the simple and natural absence of any grosser element, any hint or suggestion of a baser alloy in the ingredients of its human emotion than in the splendour of lightning or the roll of a gathered wave. Then, as on issuing sometimes from the tumult of charging waters, he finds with something of wonder how absolutely pure and sweet was the element of living storm with which his own nature has been for a while made one; not a grain in it of soiling sand, not a waif of clogging weed. As was the author's life, so is her book in all things: troubled and taintless, with little of rest in it, and nothing of reproach. It may be true that not many will ever take it to their hearts; it is certain that those who do like it will like nothing very much better in the whole world of poetry or prose.

—*The Athenæum*, no. 2903 (16 June 1883): 762–763

* * *

This excerpt—the conclusion of a fifteen-page article on Emily Brontë that was published two years before the turn of the century—is representative of a growing number of critics who recognized and were willing to proclaim her genius.

"Shakespeare's Younger Sister"
An Assessment of Emily Brontë
Angus M. Mackay

. . . But, as I have already said, Emily Brontë's rank as a poet is to be measured, not by her verse, but by her single romance. The quantity as well as the quality of work must needs be taken into account in estimating the genius of a writer, and it may seem that a beginner's first volume forms a slender foundation for a claim to high rank. But if we look only to the *quality* of the imagination displayed in *Wuthering Heights*—its power, its intensity, its absolute originality—it is scarcely too much to say of Emily that she might have been Shakespeare's younger sister. To the many, of course, this will seem merely fantastic; but the few who have really learnt to appreciate *Wuthering Heights* will see no exaggeration in the title. Putting aside the clumsiness of the framework—the only mark of the prentice-hand in the whole book—what is there comparable to this romance except the greater tragedies of Shakespeare? The single peasant in the story, Joseph, is of the kin of Shakespeare's clowns, and yet is quite distinct from them. Heathcliffe is one of the most vivid creations in all literature; he fascinates the imagination, and in some scenes almost paralyses us with horror, and yet that subtle human touch is added which wrings from us pity and almost respect. He reminds us of Shylock and Iago—not, indeed, by any likeness to their characters, but by the sense of wonder he awakens in us at the power that could create such a being. Catharine Earnshaw, again, and Catharine Linton—are not these by their piquancy and winsomeness almost worthy of a place in Shakespeare's gallery of fair women? The whole story has something of the pathos of *King Lear* and much of the tragic force of *Macbeth,* and yet both characters and story are, perhaps, as absolutely original as any that can be named in English literature. It is not, of course, meant that Emily Brontë achieved anything comparable to Shakespeare's greatest work: Shakespeare lived to become a great artist, while Emily only once tried her prentice-hand; Shakespeare knew the world in all its phases, while Emily passed her life in the seclusion of a remote village: but the material out of which the two wrought their work, the protoplasm of their creations, so to speak, was the same. Suppose Shakespeare had died, as Emily did, after completing his first work—*Love's Labours Lost*—would he have lived in men's memories at all? Or suppose the great dramatist's career to have closed at the same age as Emily's—twenty-nine: he would then have written a group

THE

BRONTË COUNTRY:

ITS TOPOGRAPHY, ANTIQUITIES,
AND HISTORY.

BY

J. A. ERSKINE STUART,
L.R.C.S., Edin.

"Thank God for the green earth."—KARL VON LINNÉ.

"Pan is the embodiment of the universe, and Echo is the
mere talker about the universe. Let us go, therefore, to Pan
himself, if we wish truly to know the universe; and to Echo, if
we wish only to hear about it."—LORD BACON.

LONDON:
LONGMANS, GREEN & CO.
1888.

*Title page for a study that examines how the Brontë family became
deeply associated with their part of Yorkshire (Sam Houston
State University Library)*

of five complete plays, many of them comparatively immature, and none of them of the first rank as showing the real supremacy of his genius. Thus considered, the claim that Emily Brontë's creative power had something of the nature of Shakespeare's will not appear extravagant to those who can justly estimate what she has accomplished in *Wuthering Heights.*

It would be profitless, perhaps, to speculate on the work which this powerful imagination might have achieved had time been granted; let us rather be grateful for the imperishable work with which she has enriched our literature, and cherish the careless preludes which show how great a poet was lost to the world when Emily Brontë died.

—*The Westminster Review,* 150 (August 1898): 217–218

The Brontës' Enduring Reputation

The first Brontë pilgrims began making their way to Haworth while Charlotte Brontë was still alive. The tourist industry that developed rapidly within a few years of her death eventually led to the establishment in May 1895 of the first Brontë Museum, which opened at Haworth on an upper floor of the Yorkshire Penny Bank, close to the church and parsonage. Visitors could view some of the Brontë manuscripts, drawings, personal effects, paintings, and information about the family. In the first summer the museum was open, ten thousand visitors came to see the Brontë exhibits. In 1928 the collection was moved to its current home in the Brontë Parsonage.

This account was first published in the scholarly journal produced by The Brontë Society, one of the largest and oldest literary societies in the world, which was organized in 1893. W. T. Field of Bradford served as the corresponding secretary for the society.

Account of the Opening of the
Brontë Museum at Haworth, May 18th, 1895
W. T. Field

The little hill-town in the valley of the Worth, the place of pilgrimage for so many lovers of literature, drawing to itself as by magnetic force visitors from all parts of the United Kingdom, as well as from across the broad Atlantic, never looked gayer than it did on Saturday, when the long-talked-of museum was opened. The weather had been lovely and sunny. Spring had fled the kingdom for a time before the icy gales of a once more threatening winter, but on the afternoon of that day those gales ceased to blow. Again there was a return of the goddess, and all nature looked fresh and beautiful. The air was clear, the far distant landscape open to the view, and all the beauties of Yorkshire moorland scenery were before the visitors. Yes, Haworth was gay; no other word so well expresses its appearance on the auspicious occasion. There were flags here and there—the "Union Jack of old England," many times repeated, floated in the breeze from house top or other prominent position, and flags floated here and there in the little High Street, which was as clean as the proverbial new pin. Each of its very paving stones was as free from soil and stain as if each had been duly scrubbed and cleaned and then guarded with jealous care. It was evident the local governing body had had an eye to what was required. And the houses and other buildings that lined the old thoroughfare! Each was spotlessly clean, and as for the substantial-looking folk, the inhabitants, they were decked out in their best, the evident desire being to welcome the numerous visitors, and to show the interest felt in the new institution just being established in their midst. Yes, and the visitors were gay too.

The original Brontë Museum, located on the second floor of this bank building in Haworth
(*from* The Bookman, *October 1904, Colorado College Library*)

A long and well freighted special train had discharged its passengers, at the little station in the valley, and so had the preceding ordinary trains. Most of the new comers were from Bradford, others from the Spen Valley and the Dewsbury district, wherein reminiscences of the Brontës cluster thickly; several came from Leeds and neighbourhood; Lancashire sent a contingent, London a few, and so did Bonnie Scotland; and there were with them in spirit, if not in flesh, kindred hearts, in America and Australia. A love of the writings and the characters of the three Brontë sisters had drawn all there; love and sympathy we should say, and love, too, for their erring talented brother, and sympathy with him also, had compelled them, and so had love for the only half understood man, their father, the vicar. These visitors were as diverse in rank and occupation, perhaps, as any crowd ever drawn together, yet all so much in accord in their purpose that day. The man of leisure rubbed shoulders with the busy manufacturer, the doctor, the lawyer, and the German professor; and they with the parson, the journalist, the merchant, the clerk, the operative. So much for the sterner sex of the large party. The sisters, may we call them, of the Brontë girls, were from the mansion, the villa, and the cottage; from

quiet vale or hill top, and from stirring manufacturing town and village; wives, mothers, and daughters, and sisters all eager to do honour to the memory of the immortal trio, and to look upon what had once been theirs—the written page, the simple trinket, the half skilful drawing, or bit of needlework. Families, and parts of families, had come together, but there were no children—so marked a feature in ordinary English crowds.

Emerging from the railway station the strangers were surprised at seeing the Haworth Band in the roadway, surrounded by a large body of people, and came to the conclusion, most of them, that the musicians were about to board the train on its return, to take part at a contest or other celebration at a distance. But no, the bandsmen had come to do honour to the visitors, and to lead the way to their ancient town, and this they did with ardour, and in the course of the afternoon discoursed sweet music at the top of the High Street. Their spontaneous services were much appreciated alike by the committee of the Brontë Society and the visitors at large. It had been expected that Sir T. Wemyss Reid, the author of the well-known monograph on Charlotte Brontë, would have been present to open the museum, as announced, but he was ill, and therefore unable to

The Brontë Fascination

The great interest in the Brontës led at times to scholarship that was less than scrupulous, as critic Angus Mackay indicates in this excerpt from his review of The Brontës in Ireland; or, Facts Stranger Than Fiction *(1893).*

More than a year ago Dr. William Wright issued a book in which he professed not only to trace the history of four generations of Irish Brontës, but to prove that the plot of *Wuthering Heights* was founded on family history, and that the other Brontë novels had likewise an Irish origin. As a Brontë enthusiast I was naturally interested; but when review after review came to hand, all speaking of Dr. Wright's book in laudatory terms, and declaring that he had established his thesis, my curiosity died down, and I accepted this verdict as final. Recently I procured his volume for the purpose of keeping my Brontë knowledge up to date. Imagine my surprise to find it a mass of absurdities and inconsistencies, bearing its own refutation on every page for any reader who, with adequate knowledge, would examine its statements. It reminds me of nothing so much as of that prophetical literature which once undertook to prove that Napoleon III was Antichrist, and which still is prepared to fix the date of the end of the world. There is the same absence of all critical faculty, the same unreasoning acceptance of every alleged fact which can serve the end in view, the same substitution of faith for proof.

–"A Crop of Brontë Myths,"
The Westminister Review, 144
(October 1895): 424

Mackay addressed the question of why so many readers are drawn to the Brontës in this excerpt from an article published five years later.

The interest felt by a considerable section of the reading public in all that concerns the Brontë sisters seems to broaden and intensify as time goes on. Every trivial object, every scrap of material that once belonged to the Brontës or their friends, is religiously stored up in the Museum at Haworth, and pilgrims, singly or in troops, resort year by year to every spot with which the sisters were even remotely connected. No doubt all this has its ludicrous side, and it is easy for anyone who has not come under the spell to jeer at such enthusiasm. But while it may be conceded that the fanatical devotees of a cult are not always its most intelligent adherents, on the other hand it must be granted that when relics are highly venerated and shrines thronged, there must be connected with them some idea or some truth worthy of admiration. And in the case of the Brontës we cannot argue that the greatness of their popularity points to the commonplace nature of their achievements. Those writers who have estimated their genius most highly have been the *élite* of the critics, from Lockhart to Matthew Arnold; and of Emily Brontë's work we may say that it appeals exclusively to minds appreciative of the finer and subtler qualities of literature; it is to such poets as Sydney Dobell and Swinburne that we owe its full recognition.

But indeed the existence of what has been called the Brontë cult ought not to surprise us. If the interest evinced is unique, so is that which calls it forth. The works of Emily and Charlotte Brontë, whatever other merits or demerits, have in a very high degree that indefinable quality which is best described by the word *fascination:* other, perhaps greater novels are read, admired, and forgotten; but the Brontë stories lure us back after an interval to re-peruse them with an increasing appreciation. This is eminently true of Emily Brontë's masterpiece, "Wuthering Heights," and it is true also in a lesser degree of Charlotte's novels. And the attraction is not due only to the writings. A further spell is laid upon the imagination by the history of the various members of that strange Haworth household, told so admirably and with such wealth of detail by Mrs. Gaskell and in the more recent books of Mr. Clement Shorter, and commented upon with so much charm by Augustine Birrell, Wemyss Reid, Mary L. Robinson, and others. And then the curiosity of the reader is piqued and his imagination roused by the insolvable problems arising out of the story: how came the union of a simple Cornish lady with the eccentric but intellectually commonplace Irish Prunty to produce so remarkable a group of persons and how could the environment of the bleak and lonely parsonage supply these girls with the material and the experience of which they made such remarkable use in their novels? When these various lines of interest are focused we are no longer at a loss to account for the potency of the Brontë spell.

–"The Brontës: Their Fascination and Genius,"
The Bookman, 27 (October 1904): 9

attend. Mr. W. S. Cameron, editor of the *Leeds Mercury,* read Sir T. Wemyss Reid's address in his stead, and the opening ceremony was fittingly performed in his absence by Alderman John Brigg, of Kildwick Hall, the Chairman of the Brontë Committee.

The opening ceremony was announced for half-past three, but long before that hour people clustered round the entrance to the building, and at the time appointed there were several hundred people present. As the opening ceremony was in progress the sun broke out, and brightened the scene. Amongst those present were Alderman Brigg; the Rev. Dr. Wm Wright, author of "The Brontës in Ireland," of London; Mr. W. S. Cameron, of the *Leeds Mercury;* the Rev. J. T. Slugg, Haworth; Mr. Alfred Merrall, chairman of the Haworth School Board; Mr. F. Harper, chairman of the

Haworth District Council; Mr. Swire Smith, Keighley; Mr. Butler Wood and Mr. W. T. Field, secretaries of the Brontë Society; Mr. J. Horsfall Turner; Mr. F. C. Galloway (treasurer) and Mrs. Galloway; Mr. J. Rawlinson Ford, Mr. Washington Teasdale, Mr. John Bowling, and Mr. W. Howgate, Leeds; Mr. H. S. Green, Manchester; Mr. W. E. B. Priestley, Mr. John Popplewell, Mr. W. Scruton, Mr. Edmund Lee, Prof. C. A. Federer, and Mr. J. A. Clapham, Bradford; the Rev. J. W. Dunne, vicar of Laisterdyke; Mr. Dunlop, Kilmarnock; Mr. John Waugh, C. E., Baildon; Mr. S. P. Unwin, Shipley; Mr. W. Law, Littleborough, &c. Those who attended the ceremony from the Heavy Woollen District were as follows: The Rev. Canon Lowther Clarke, M.A., Alderman and Mrs. Richards, Mr. W. W. Yates, Miss Yates, Mr. Walter Walker, Mr. and Mrs. Wilson Hemingway, Mr. John Ingram, Mr. P. F. Lee, Mr. and Mrs. J. Chadwick, Mr. T. Brown, Miss James (Head Mistress of the Girls' High School), Mr. and Mrs. Fred Wilson, and Mr. F. Green, Dewsbury; the Rev. J. G. and Mrs. Henderson, Mr. J. J. Stead, Mr. Frank Peel and Miss Peel, Heckmondwike; Dr Erskine Stuart (author of the "Brontë Country," Staincliffe) and Mrs. Stuart; Mr. J. I. Wilson and Miss Blackburn, of Batley; Mr. and Mrs. G. H. Oldroyd, of Gomersal; the Misses Fearnsides, Earlsheaton; Mrs. Scatcherd, Morley; Miss Clay, Ossett; the Misses Walker, Huddersfield.

Alderman JOHN BRIGG, addressing the gathering, announced the inability of Sir T. Wemyss Reid, Sir Isaac Holden, M.P, the Mayor of Bradford (Alderman W. Willis Wood), the Rev. W. H. Keeling (Head Master of the Bradford Grammar School), and Mr. Claude Meeker (American Consul at Bradford) to attend. Continuing, he said the position he occupied that day was a very important one, and not only in the eyes of the people of Haworth and its neighbourhood. The function had a far wider interest than that. There were people all over Europe and in the United States who were taking an active interest in that which now concerned them, and though they had not their bodily presence, they all knew they had their sympathy and good-will. He congratulated the General Committee on having obtained the assistance of a good local committee to look after the interests of the museum, and he should like to congratulate the people of Haworth on the fact that it had been established in their midst. As they were aware, there were very good claims put forward on behalf of other towns, but the friends in Haworth made such promises and gave such undertakings, that it was seen that Haworth was clearly the proper place for the museum, and there was practically no opposition when the proposal was made.

Mr. W. S. CAMERON said that though Sir Wemyss Reid was far away from them, his thoughts were with them, and his words were with them. He then read the address which Sir Wemyss Reid had prepared for delivery before his doctor's orders came imperatively urging him to cease all work and engagements, and to take a long sea voyage. The address was as follows:

"The object with which we have met here to-day does not call for any detailed or lengthened explanation on my part. We are met as Yorkshiremen, or as those who feel themselves closely identified with the interests of this great county, to pay a mark of affectionate respect to the memory of a family whose fortune it has been to give to Yorkshire her highest claim to an abiding literary distinction. For this act in itself no justification can be needed. Our place to-day is, indeed, that of debtors who come to acknowledge, and in a certain measure to relieve themselves of a heavy burden of obligation. We owe the Brontës much, and we come to pay a fraction of the debt. We owe them as individuals many an hour of happiest literary enjoyment, in which we have feasted upon the work of their brains and their pens. We owe them as a community an everlasting debt of gratitude for the keen insight, the sympathetic analysis, and the brilliant artistic skill with which they placed on record for ever the salient features of life in our West Riding towns and vales, and real meaning and nature of our West Riding character. Not altogether prepossessing at the first superficial glance, this life and this character need to be interpreted with wisdom and with love, with humour and with tolerance, if they are to be appreciated by the stranger. It was this interpretation which they met with at the hands of Charlotte Brontë, and to her we owe it more than to any other human being that those outside our gates have learned to understand something of what lies beneath the surface of our West Riding life, something of the heart which beats beneath the rugged West Riding exterior. By her genius and skill this particular district of England has ceased to be provincial, and has secured an established place in the great world of letters. Above all, we, as Yorkshiremen, owe to Charlotte Brontë and her sister that which is beyond doubt the chief literary glory of our shire. It is they who have set in our midst, in this little valley of the Worth, a shrine of genius which draws to itself pilgrims from every quarter of the world; it is they who have gilded the substantial triumphs of our people with the rays of intellectual light, and who, to the material achievements in commerce and in science in which our county is so rich, have added the crowning honour which a noble artistic faculty alone can furnish. We stand within a stone's throw of the modest house where the Brontës lived and died. To us it is for their sake a sacred place; but it should be not less sacred to all to whom our English literature is dear, for it was the home during all their years of work of two of the greatest of all Englishwomen. Mr. Swinburne has told us that "the perfect trinity of highest female fame for England" is made up by Mrs. Browning and Charlotte and Emily Brontë. In other words, two of the three greatest women this country, in her long and glorious history, has produced were the two sisters who dwelt together in this village where we are now met, who lived and worked side by side in yonder parsonage. We need not bind ourselves absolutely to the proposition laid down by the great poet in order to feel that Haworth was at least the home of two women who must always enjoy a foremost place in the annals of English literature, and whose names must always fill a glorious niche in the splendid roll of illustrious Englishwomen. But it is not merely a commanding intellect and a magnificent genius that we wish to honour. There is no need to assert the claims of Charlotte and Emily Brontë, and in a lesser degree of their gentle, younger sister Anne, to that fame which is the reward of brilliant intellectual powers. The world at large has made full acknowledgment of those claims; and the years of neglect and obscurity which fell to the lot of the Brontës when they lived amongst us have been atoned for by the glory which now surrounds their name. But in the case of Charlotte, at all events, we know now that the woman was greater than the writer, and that by her life, even more than by her printed pages, the author of *Jane Eyre* has taught us not a few of the lessons which our poor humanity needs so constantly to learn. We honour Haworth parsonage as having once been the home of a wonderful genius. We love and reverence it still more as having been the scene of the life of patient endurance, unmurmuring submission, and steadfast devotion to duty of one of the noblest and purest of her sex. The lamp of her genius burns with a splendid radiancy; but brighter and clearer still is the lamp of her soul, the lamp which makes visible to us her love, her faith, her courage, her constancy, her unswerving persistence in well-doing. Thanks to the heart and the brain of another great woman, Mrs. Gaskell, we have been enabled to see that life as it really was. There is no need to dwell upon the story here; for here, at least, one may rest assured that none is ignorant of it. We have all followed with quickly beating hearts, and eyes that were sometimes dim, the history of the three sisters who lived among these hills, and two of whom now rest beneath the shadow of the old tower. We have all followed Branwell, and Charlotte, and Emily, and Anne through their troubled, though not altogether joyless youth, with its brilliant flashes of promise for the future. There is none among us who does not know something of the governess days of the three sisters, with their bitter pains, their sordid cares; none who has not followed the two elder to the boarding-school at Brussels, where Charlotte was destined to drink so deep of the bitter cup of knowledge; and there can be no one who has not watched them in those dark hours before the dawn, when in sorrow and sadness, and sickness of heart, they worked together with their pens in the little sitting-room in the parsonage, producing the first, and, in the case of Emily, the last also of their wonderful romances. No need is laid upon me to speak of the brilliant triumph of Charlotte when *Jane Eyre* was given to the world; nor can it be necessary to remind you how in the very midst of that triumph Emily was suddenly laid low by death, and went to her grave uncheered by the faintest sign of recognition on the part of her contemporaries.

Nor need I dwell upon those after-days in which Charlotte was left alone with her old father in the house that echoed no more with the voice of sisters or brother, alone with the sombre memories of bereavement assailing her on every side; and how she faced the empty world with the courage of a hero and the resignation of a saint, and in those saddest hours of life brought forth her brightest and ripest works, the brilliant story of *Shirley* and the noble study of *Villette*. It is the story of that life as it has been told us by Mrs. Gaskell, that life which lay so constantly in the shadow, and which yet was never without a light of its own, that has made the name of Charlotte Brontë a cherished one in thousands of households; it is the memory of that life to which we now seek to do honour; it is its lesson that we wish to emphasise and perpetuate. Nor let us forget that amid the other debts we owe to Charlotte Brontë is one for which this generation ought to feel profoundly grateful. It was her lot to be one of the pioneers in that noble band of thinkers and writers to whom we owe the breaking of those bonds of a narrow conventionalism which so long fettered our English thought. She was as fearless as she was pure; and at a time when old traditions were still paramount in literature and theology, she did not hesitate to take her own course without regard to the cost. "To tear the mask from the face of the Pharisee," she once declared, in words that burn themselves into the heart, "is not to lift an impious hand to the Crown of Thorns." And so, "like an austere little Joan of Arc," as Thackeray once described her, she rode into the great market place of Vanity Fair, and preached her own sermon and pursued her own crusade, regardless of the anger of those whose hypocrisies and follies she unveiled. But the time would fail me if I were to attempt anything like a complete characterisation of Charlotte Brontë and of her work in life. Still less would it be possible or fitting to attempt an analysis of the lives of her two sisters, or of their place in literature. We must accept them as they are, and we must acknowledge with thankfulness the glory they have conferred upon Haworth, upon Yorkshire, upon England. They stand before us, no longer unknown, as when they walked through these streets and lanes. They have taken their place for ever in the great gallery of noble English women, and there is no one now to dispute their claim to the admiration and affection of the world. The little oddities, the eccentricities of speech and manner, the homeliness of dress and appearance that marked them when they lived, are now of no account. It is true women who stand revealed to us in their books, and in the story of their life, and of them we can say, as was said of Charlotte's idol, the great Duke. "Whatever record leap to light they never shall be shamed." It is in part as an atonement for the comparative failure of the generation that went before us to see these great women as they really were, that we of to-day have sought to bring to a focus the world-wide Brontë cult by establishing this modest institution, within a few yards of the spot where they worked and suffered, and died. If it serves no other purpose, it will at least convince the world in future days that the Brontës were not without honour in their own country: that they touched the hearts and won the love of their fellow Yorkshire people, and were not left, as great geniuses too often have been, to the cold homage of the stranger and the alien. And may we not hope that this Brontë Museum, with all its proofs of loving reverence for the genius and the character of the great sisters, will help to stimulate the interest of all classes in their story, and to impress still more deeply upon our hearts the lesson of their lives, the one true lesson, which, I think can best be summed up in the quaint verses of Holy George Herbert, when he sang of a day in spring:—

Sweet day, so cool, so calm, so bright;
The bridal of the earth and sky;
Sweet dews shall weep thy fall to-night;
For thou must die.

Sweet rose, whose hue, angry and brave,
Bids the rash gazer wipe his eye,
Thy root is ever in its grave,
And thou must die.

Sweet spring, full of sweet days and roses,
A box where sweets compacted lie,
My music shows ye have your closes,
And all must die.

Only the sweet and virtuous soul
Like seasoned timber never gives,
But when the whole world turns to coal,
Then chiefly lives.

Fame, even the highest literary fame, like riches may take wings and disappear, but virtue will endure. We believe that the fame of the Brontës, as stars in the firmament of our literature, will long abide; but whatever may be the actual result so far as their place among the writers of our tongue is concerned, we know that the heroic example of their lives will remain an inspiration and encouragement for ever."

Alderman BRIGG next read the following telegram from Mr. Charles Brontë Morgan, barrister, London:—"Felicitations to the Brontëites present at the opening of the Brontë Museum, from one proud of his connection with the Brontë family." He then unlocked the door and formally declared the museum open.

During the afternoon and evening a large number of people visited the museum. Owing to the crush people were kept waiting for hours before they could be admitted.

After the ceremony, many of the visitors were conducted to places of special interest in the village by members of the Brontë Committee, who are well acquainted with the locality.

After tea, the committee and officers of the Brontë Society were photographed.

PUBLIC MEETING.

At six o'clock, a public meeting took place in the Wesleyan Chapel, at Haworth, and there was a large attendance. Alderman Brigg presided, and was supported by a large number of the gentlemen whose names have been given in connection with the opening proceedings.

Mr. W. T. FIELD read a letter from the Rev. A. B. Nicholls (Charlotte Brontë's husband), who wrote from Ireland—

"While duly appreciating the kindness of your committee, I regret I could not possibly be present at the ceremony referred to in your letter of the 1st, as the journey would be too fatiguing for me at my advanced age."

The CHAIRMAN said that for many years people from America and other parts of the world were in the habit of visiting Haworth, and it was thought the time had arrived when a place should be found where some of the relics of the famous family could be kept, and seen by those who admired the Brontës. Mr. Yates, of Dewsbury, was the first to take action in this matter. He came over to Bradford to see a few of those who were likely to sympathise with his views, and the movement owed much to Mr. Yates's energetic and devoted advocacy. On December 16th, 1893, a resolution was moved by Mr. Yates in favour of a Brontë Society being established, and since then the efforts of the promoters had been attended with marked success.

The Rev. Canon LOWTHER CLARKE, M.A., was first called upon to address the meeting. He said they had assembled in order to listen to the speeches of gentlemen who were deeply interested in the famous Brontë family, and which it was hoped would stimulate many present in the work which had been inaugurated under most auspicious circumstances that day. He was sure of this, that the inaugural gathering gave encouragement to those who had promoted the establishment of the museum. He would like to commence his remarks by congratulating the parish of Haworth on the fact that it had obtained possession of the newly-established museum. The people of Dewsbury would all have been glad to have had the interesting museum in their midst, for they had an anxiety not to miss what others would give them. They, like the Bradford people, made an offer of a very suitable place for the establishment of a museum of the Brontë relics; but he was not prepared to contend for one moment that the claim of the people of the Dewsbury district to have the museum in their midst compared with the claim which the people of the parish of Haworth possessed;

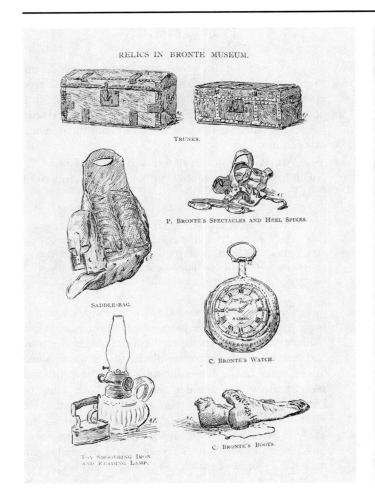

RELICS IN BRONTË MUSEUM.

TRUNKS.

SADDLE-BAG.

P. BRONTË'S SPECTACLES AND HEEL SPIKES.

C. BRONTË'S WATCH.

TOY SMOOTHING IRON AND READING LAMP.

C. BRONTË'S BOOTS.

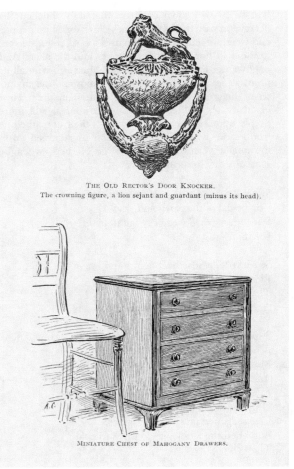

THE OLD RECTOR'S DOOR KNOCKER.
The crowning figure, a lion sejant and guardant (minus its head).

MINIATURE CHEST OF MAHOGANY DRAWERS.

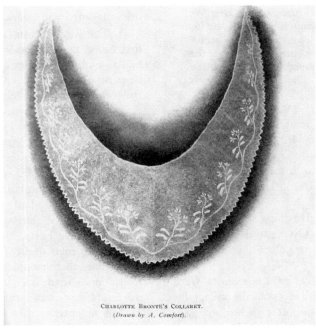

CHARLOTTE BRONTË'S COLLARET.
(Drawn by A. Comfort).

Articles preserved in the Brontë Museum in Haworth (from Whiteley Turner, A Spring-Time Saunter: Round and About Brontë Land, *Sam Houston State University Library)*

and therefore he most heartily congratulated the Haworth residents upon the fact that they had secured the museum in a place which was so closely associated with the gifted sisters whose lives had made the place famous, not only in England, but in all parts of the world. As they had heard, people who were admirers of the Brontë family came from America and other distant places, year after year to see the church, the parsonage, and the wild moors behind, and they would continue to come, having now the additional attraction of the museum, where so many things connected with that most talented family were collected. He felt in the first place that he had an official position there, because as vicar of Dewsbury the Brontës were linked with him in a certain way. At the church under his charge the Rev. Patrick Brontë was curate for a time. His signature could be found scores of times in the registers kept at the Parish Church of Dewsbury, and one of his predecessors appointed the Rev. Patrick Brontë to the first vicarage he held, which was at Hartshead. In addition to that, Charlotte Brontë was for a number of years a teacher at Dewsbury Moor, and many of her most intimate friends lived in the town and neighbourhood where he came from, and therefore as vicar of Dewsbury he felt much obliged to the committee for allowing him to be present and take some part in their proceedings. In addition to his official connection he had a deep personal interest in the proceedings. He had been strolling on the moors with a few friends, and the scenes that met his eye reminded him of his childish days. He was brought up in a place similar to Haworth, but he hoped he would be allowed to say, with pardonable pride, a place a little more beautiful—the English Lake district. Another reason he had for being glad to be present was because he felt they had been paying a tribute of respect to a talented family. They could not have had such a society as had been formed, they could not have had such a gathering as that to-day in Haworth unless there had been a general and prevailing sentiment with regard to the Brontë family, and their noble talents and genius had been recognised. He had heard people express compassion for the sad suffering life that Charlotte Brontë lived, and say it was a pity she was not rescued from her surroundings and brought away into some literary company, where her talents might have been developed and where she might have spent happy instead of miserable days. He was inclined to think that persons who spoke in that way did not take a sufficiently wide view of the conditions under which genius always worked, and of the necessary accompaniment of suffering for the perfection of character, and for the development of the talents a person possessed. And yet the true poet or writer is not so wholly dependent upon external aid as we imagine. Truth is verily stranger than

fiction, and the materials for both tragedy and comedy are to be found in every parish. What is wanted is someone with the divine power to see these things, the heart to understand them, and finally, the pen to write them down. He was not, therefore, disposed to regret very much either that she was condemned to spend her life upon those dreary moors, or that part of her life was a very suffering life, because that suffering reacted upon her character, and had produced those powers we were now paying a tribute of respect to. He contended that Charlotte Brontë found in her surroundings much that was useful to her in her works, and declared that the great novelist, by the study of people, by the pictures she had drawn of that district, had done for it what Wordsworth had done for the Lake District, and Sir Walter Scott for the Highlands. Let us not lament that Charlotte Brontë and her sisters did so little and died so young. They lived where the providence of God placed them, and looking out upon the life around them they wove it into their stories. He said it was the privilege of genius to see and imagine where others could observe nothing. The difference was in the eye, and not in the external object. Genius, however, was not to be denied the right of imagination. When people asked where Charlotte Brontë could have learnt some of the most thrilling scenes in *Jane Eyre* they forgot that genius was creative, and that whilst it very often took facts for its foundations the final fabric bore the impress of the master hand alone. In conclusion Canon Clarke said he thought the establishment of a museum ought to increase the people's interest, especially of that locality, in the talented family. It was a great privilege to have had such a family in their midst, and, in order to increase the interest, and keep green the memory of the gifted family, the museum had been established. He hoped the people would take a pride in the institution, and that it would be kept in such a condition as the committee wished it should be.

Mr. W. W. YATES who was next called upon by the Chairman, said it was highly gratifying to notice the success which the movement had met since its inception. He took no credit upon himself for suggesting the establishment of a museum in honour of the talented Brontë family. The scheme had been suggested before, but at that time it was not ripe, and when it came to be named again public feeling had so far ripened that it was accepted, and the grand demonstration of that day was an indication that the committee had taken a proper step in providing the visitors to Haworth with a place for a collection of the personal relics of the wonderful family with which the district was so closely identified. He desired to say that the promoters of the museum owed a debt of gratitude to the chairman (Alderman Brigg.) When this matter was first taken up by himself he received strong support from the newspapers of the West Riding, for which he was very grateful, and his next step was to cast about for somebody in the neighbourhood of Haworth who would be able to launch the scheme, and by more than one the name of Alderman Brigg, of Kildwick Hall, was given. Knowing that Alderman Brigg was connected with the County Council he went to a friend of his, who was a member of the same body, Mr. T. B. Fox, of Dewsbury, and who, he deeply deplored, had passed away within the last few days, and asked him to give him a letter of introduction to Alderman Brigg. He did so very readily, and after a little correspondence had passed between them, he (the speaker) went over to Bradford and then met Alderman Brigg, his son, Mr. Swire Smith, and a number of other gentlemen from the district where they were assembled. The movement for the establishment of a society and museum was taken up with great warmth, and from that day to the present time everything had gone on smoothly.

Dr. WM. WRIGHT, of London, in the course of a lengthy address, referred to the claim which it is said Branwell Brontë had put forward as to the authorship of *Wuthering Heights,* and said that in the course of a few weeks it would be proved beyond the shadow of a doubt that Branwell never knew that the story had been published, and that therefore he never could have made the statement that he had himself written it. Referring to the pleasure with which he found himself in Yorkshire, Dr. Wright claimed for himself a Yorkshire descent, though he had been introduced to the audience as an Irishman, and remarked that Yorkshire people were said to be a very hard-hearted, sour kind of people. He thought them, however, a very soft-hearted people, and that assembly was proof positive of the fact, for they had met in honour of an Irish family who had come unknown into their midst, and whom they had accepted as their own. From the time he himself had been three or four years of age he had heard in his nursery scarcely any tales which were not in connection with the Brontës in Ireland, and his eyes had shone at the stories at which other eyes had since shone. He had penned most of his book when he was about sixteen years of age; then it was put aside until recently, when, through the urgency of his friends, he decided to publish the story. A very large number of those from whom he had received the information had died in the meantime. He knew that many of his statements would be challenged, and so he had had to set to work anew to gather oral evidence from people still living that he might fall back upon. He thought he had demonstrated that many of the incidents which the daughters had introduced into their novels were those they had heard from their father with regard to the Brontës in Ireland.

Mr. JOSEPH NORMINGTON moved a resolution congratulating the Brontë Society on the establishment of their museum, and commending the institution to the sympathy and support of all classes.

The Rev. J. T. SLUGG, in seconding the proposition, said the committee need have no fear as to the care or interest the Haworth people would have with the museum, as the residents in that parish were civilized—(laughter)—and they did not go about with stones in their pockets. They had seen a museum before, and they had seen pictures and their treasures, but at the same time he had to confess that the people of Haworth were not so enthusiastic as they ought to be, one reason being the publication of Mrs. Gaskell's book, which he had heard spoken of by the Haworth people as being crammed full of misstatements as anything could be.

Mr. J. F. HARPER, Mr. J. HORSFALL TURNER, Mr. JOHN POPPLEWELL, Dr. ERSKINE STUART, and Mrs. SCATCHERD also addressed the meeting.

Votes of thanks to the Chairman, speakers, and the Haworth Brass Band were proposed by Messrs. BUTLER WOOD, REGISTRAR LEE, and SWIRE SMITH, were duly seconded and carried, and the proceedings then terminated.

Mr. CLAUDE MEEKER, the United States Consul, Bradford, who was invited as a representative American to the opening ceremony at Haworth was unable, through sudden illness, to be present. He sent, however, an interesting letter, which is herewith reprinted for the benefit of the members.

May 18th, 1895.

To the Secretary, Brontë Society,

Dear Sir,—I am fully aware that it is the accident of position alone that has caused me to be invited as the representative of the people of the United States on this occasion. It would be more fitting that someone distinguished in letters, or a critic whose name has gone abroad, should occupy the place assigned to me at this time. I may be excused, however, for suggesting that what I lack in this respect is partially compensated by the enthusiasm of a layman who comes from the heart of the people. As the representative of that commonwealth of nearly *seventy million souls,* where the Brontë works have had such a wonderful circulation, and where they are still so popular, I congratulate you upon the work you have done and the enterprise you inaugurate to-day. It has been said that neither Charlotte Brontë nor her sisters have a memorial in bronze or marble; no towering columns to commemorate their achievements. Lord Byron said he wanted none of these, all he asked, all he wished, was a tear. What living relative, what devoted admirer of the Brontë family could ask for more than is demonstrated at this moment? We can all form an estimate of the tears that have been shed from our own experience in reading their life's story, of the battle so bravely fought, and how they conquered all obstacles save the one to which we must all in time submit. But what tribute more endearing could be rendered than this voluntary association of a succeeding generation which, upon the very ground rendered historic by them, rear memory's monuments to the departed great, and is joined in spirit in that loving labour by almost countless millions from across the seas.

I have been frequently asked to explain the admiration for the Brontë works in the United States, an admiration so early manifested and so long maintained. Wonder has been expressed that a people so far separated by distance of land and water, so dissimilar in habits, occupation, temperament and customs should be so attracted towards and so steadfast in their loyalty to the Brontë works. I can answer the question in but one way: The genius of nature is imprinted on every page, and we know that "one touch of nature makes the whole world kin." In addition to this fact no great or permanent success is ever attained that has not a background of grand human endeavour, and the American people, quick in action and keen in perception, knew that a new light had dawned when the entrancing pages of *Jane Eyre* were spread before them.

Figures are never interesting, but I know you will allow me a few words to show the enormous circulation of the Brontë works in the United States. The *Nineteenth Century* magazine for May, 1894, is authority for the statement that there are 6000 Public Free Libraries in the United States. As there are as many more connected with churches, societies, and various institutions, there would be a grand total of 12,000 libraries in that country of a public and semi-public character in which one or several sets of the Brontë works are constantly in demand. This is in addition to the thousands of libraries, large and small, of private ownership in which the Brontë works are to be found. I recently read in a newspaper statistics from several libraries showing the popularity of different authors of fiction, as instanced by calls for their works. I am sorry I have not the exact figures at hand, but Charles Dickens stood first, and high up in the list were the names of the Brontës.

Amongst those people who read books at all (and their name is legion) I personally know very few who have not read one or more of the Brontë novels. And with an average daily attendance of over 15,000,000 pupils at our public and private schools it is not likely that the supply of readers will soon run out. When my fellow countrymen or countrywomen come to see me at Bradford, no matter what their station in life, one of their first questions is: "How far is it to Haworth, the home of the Brontës?"

Since the days of Charlotte Brontë many stars have been added to the azure field in the flag of the country I represent to-day. Great states and proud cities exist, with church libraries, schools, and other concomitants of a high civilisation, and her works are read by thousands where fifty years ago there were only scattered settlements.

I regret that I was unable to come to dear old Haworth, as I had fully intended, but allow me to say that I appreciate your courtesy in inviting an American to be present; that all my fellow-countrymen will join with you in spirit in paying tribute to the gifted family, and claim with you an equal share in the delightful inheritance the Brontë family have left to posterity.– Yours truly,

Claude Meeker.

Mr. W. T Field, Hon. Sec. Brontë Society.
–*Brontë Society Transactions*, 1 part 3
(December 1895): 19–32

* * *

Virginia Stephen, who as Virginia Woolf became a celebrated writer, visited Haworth in 1904 and described her reactions upon seeing the museum, the church, and the parsonage. This was her first published essay, appearing unsigned in a Church of England periodical.

Haworth, November 1904

I do not know whether pilgrimages to the shrines of famous men ought not to be condemned as sentimental journeys. It is better to read Carlyle in your own study chair than to visit the sound-proof room and pore over the manuscripts at Chelsea. I should be inclined to set an examination on Frederick the Great in place of entrance fee; only, in that case, the house would soon have to be shut up. The curiosity is only legitimate when the house of a great writer or the country in which it is set adds something to our understanding of his books. This justification you have for a pilgrimage to the home and country of Charlotte Brontë and her sisters.

The *Life,* by Mrs. Gaskell, gives you the impression that Haworth and the Brontës are somehow inextricably mixed. Haworth expresses the Brontës; the Brontës express Haworth; they fit like a snail to its shell. How far surroundings radically affect people's minds, it is not for me to ask: superficially, the influence is great, but it is worth asking if the famous parsonage had been placed in a London slum, the dens of Whitechapel would not have had the same result as the lonely Yorkshire moors. However, I am taking away my only excuse for visiting Haworth. Unreasonable or not, one of the chief points of a recent visit to Yorkshire was that an expedition to Haworth could be accomplished. The necessary arrangements were made, and we determined to take advantage of the first fine day for our expedition. A real northern snowstorm had been doing the honours of the moors. It was rash to wait fine weather, and it was also cowardly. I understand that the sun very seldom shone on the Brontë family, and if we chose a really fine day we should have to make allowance for the fact that fifty years ago there were few fine days at Haworth, and that we were, therefore, for sake of comfort, rubbing out half the shadows in the picture. However, it would be interesting to see what impression Haworth could make upon the brilliant weather of Settle. We certainly passed through a very cheerful land, which might be likened to a vast wedding cake, of which the icing was slightly undulating; the earth was bridal in its virgin snow, which helped to suggest the comparison.

Keighley—pronounced Keethly—is often mentioned in the *Life;* it was the big town four miles from Haworth in which Charlotte walked to make her more important purchases—her wedding gown, perhaps, and the thin little cloth boots which we examined under glass in the Brontë Museum. It is a big manufacturing town, hard and stony, and clattering with business, in the way of these northern towns. They make small provision for the sentimental traveller, and our only occupation was to picture the slight figure of Charlotte trotting along the streets in her thin mantle, hustled into the gutter by more burly passers-by. It was the Keighley of her day, and that was some comfort. Our excitement as we neared Haworth had in it an element of suspense that was really painful, as though we were to meet some long-separated friend, who might have changed in the interval—so clear an image of Haworth had we from print and picture. At a certain point we entered the valley, up both sides of which the village climbs, and right on the hill-top, looking down over its parish, we saw the famous oblong tower of the church. This marked the shrine at which we were to do homage.

It may have been the effect of a sympathetic imagination, but I think that there were good reasons why Haworth did certainly strike one not exactly as gloomy, but, what is worse for artistic purposes, as dingy and commonplace. The houses, built of yellow-brown stone, date from the early nineteenth century. They climb the moor step by step in little detached strips, some distance apart, so that the town instead of making one compact blot on the landscape has contrived to get a whole stretch into its clutches. There is a long line of houses up the moor-side, which clusters round the church and parsonage with a little clump of trees. At the top the interest for a Brontë lover becomes suddenly intense. The church, the parsonage, the Brontë Museum, the school where Charlotte taught, and the Bull Inn where Branwell drank are all within a stone's throw of each other. The museum is certainly rather a pallid and inanimate collection of objects. An effort ought to be made to keep things out of these mausoleums, but the choice often

lies between them and destruction, so that we must be grateful for the care which has preserved much that is, under any circumstances, of deep interest. Here are many autograph letters, pencil drawings, and other documents. But the most touching case—so touching that one hardly feels reverent in one's gaze—is that which contains the little personal relics, the dresses and shoes of the dead woman. The natural fate of such things is to die before the body that wore them, and because these, trifling and transient though they are, have survived, Charlotte Brontë the woman comes to life, and one forgets the chiefly memorable fact that she was a great writer. Her shoes and her thin muslin dress have outlived her. One other object gives a thrill; the little oak stool which Emily carried with her on her solitary moorland tramps, and on which she sat, if not to write, as they say, to think what was probably better than her writing.

The church, of course, save part of the tower, is renewed since Brontë days; but that remarkable churchyard remains. The old edition of the *Life* had on its title-page a little print which struck the keynote of the book; it seemed to be all graves—gravestones stood ranked all round; you walked on a pavement lettered with dead names; the graves had solemnly invaded the garden of the parsonage itself, which was as a little oasis of life in the midst of the dead. This is no exaggeration of the artist's, as we found; the stones seem to start out of the ground at you in tall, upright lines, like an army of silent soldiers. There is no hand's breadth untenanted; indeed, the economy of space is somewhat irreverent. In old days a flagged path, which suggested the slabs of graves, led from the front door of the parsonage to the churchyard without interruption of wall or hedge; the garden was practically the graveyard too; the successors of the Brontës, however, wishing a little space between life and death, planted a hedge and several tall trees, which now cut off the parsonage garden completely. The house itself is precisely the same as it was in Charlotte's day, save that one new wing has been added. It is easy to shut the eye to this, and then you have the square, boxlike parsonage, built of the ugly, yellow-brown stone which they quarry from the moors behind, precisely as it was when Charlotte lived and died there. Inside, of course, the changes are many, though not such as to obscure the original shape of the rooms. There is nothing remarkable in a mid-Victorian parsonage, though tenanted by genius, and the only room which awakens curiosity is the kitchen, now used as an ante-room, in which the girls tramped as they conceived their work. One other spot has a certain grim interest—the oblong recess beside the staircase into which Emily drove her bulldog during the famous fight, and pinned him while she pommelled him. It is

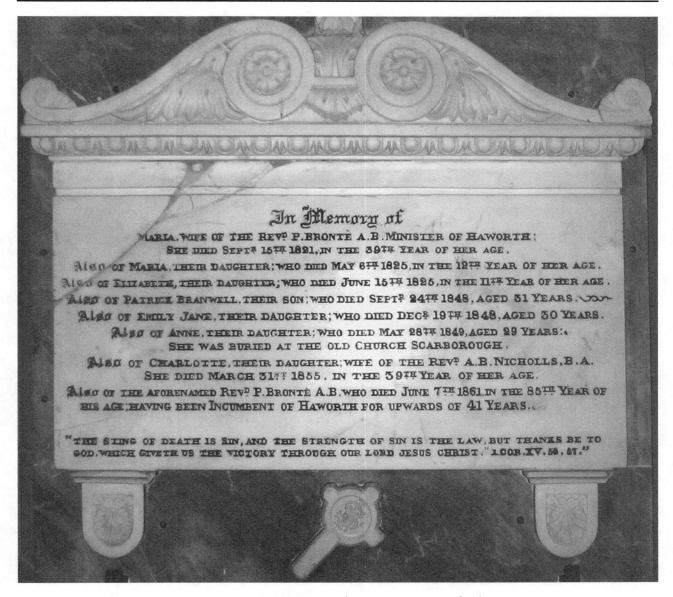

Memorial at the Haworth Church (photograph by Susan B. Taylor)

otherwise a little sparse parsonage, much like others of its kind. It was due to the courtesy of the present incumbent that we were allowed to inspect it; in his place I should often feel inclined to exorcise the three famous ghosts.

One thing only remained: the church in which Charlotte worshipped, was married, and lies buried. The circumference of her life was very narrow. Here, though much is altered, a few things remain to tell of her. The slab which bears the names of the succession of children and of their parents—their births and deaths—strikes the eye first. Name follows name; at very short intervals they died—Maria the mother, Maria the daughter, Elizabeth, Branwell, Emily, Anne, Charlotte, and lastly the old father, who outlived them all. Emily was only thirty years old, and Charlotte but nine years older. "The sting of death is sin, and the strength of sin is the law, but thanks be to God which giveth us the victory through our Lord Jesus Christ." That is the inscription which has been placed beneath their names, and with reason; for however harsh the struggle, Emily, and Charlotte above all, fought to victory.

—The Guardian, 21 December 1904, p. 2159

* * *

Woolf, who had published her first novel the year before, wrote this essay in 1916 and included it in her first essay collection, The Common Reader (1925).

Jane Eyre and *Wuthering Heights*
Virginia Woolf

Of the hundred years that have passed since Charlotte Brontë was born, she, the centre now of so much legend, devotion, and literature, lived but thirty-nine. It is strange to reflect how different those legends might have been had her life reached the ordinary human span. She might have become, like some of her famous contemporaries, a figure familiarly met with in London and elsewhere, the subject of pictures and anecdotes innumerable, the writer of many novels, of memoirs possibly, removed from us well within the memory of the middle-aged in all the splendour of established fame. She might have been wealthy, she might have been prosperous. But it is not so. When we think of her we have to imagine some one who had no lot in our modern world; we have to cast our minds back to the 'fifties of the last century, to a remote parsonage upon the wild Yorkshire moors. In that parsonage, and on those moors, unhappy and lonely, in her poverty and her exaltation, she remains for ever.

These circumstances, as they affected her character, may have left their traces on her work. A novelist, we reflect, is bound to build up his structure with much very perishable material which begins by lending it reality and ends by cumbering it with rubbish. As we open *Jane Eyre* once more we cannot stifle the suspicion that we shall find her world of imagination as antiquated, mid-Victorian, and out of date as the parsonage on the moor, a place only to be visited by the curious, only preserved by the pious. So we open *Jane Eyre;* and in two pages every doubt is swept clean from our minds.

> Folds of scarlet drapery shut in my view to the right hand; to the left were the clear panes of glass, protecting, but not separating me from the drear November day. At intervals, while turning over the leaves of my book, I studied the aspect of that winter afternoon. Afar, it offered a pale blank of mist and cloud; near, a scene of wet lawn and storm-beat shrub, with ceaseless rain sweeping away wildly before a long and lamentable blast.

There is nothing there more perishable than the moor itself, or more subject to the sway of fashion than the "long and lamentable blast". Nor is this exhilaration short-lived. It rushes us through the entire volume, without giving us time to think, without letting us lift our eyes from the page. So intense is our absorption that if some one moves in the room the movement seems to take place not there but up in Yorkshire. The writer has us by the hand, forces us along her road, makes us see what she sees, never leaves us for a moment or allows us to forget her. At the end we are steeped through and through with the genius, the vehemence, the indignation of Charlotte Brontë. Remarkable faces, figures of strong outline and gnarled feature have flashed upon us in passing; but it is through her eyes that we have seen them. Once she is gone, we seek for them in vain. Think of Rochester and we have to think of Jane Eyre. Think of the moor, and again, there is Jane Eyre. Think of the drawing-room, even, those "white carpets on which seemed laid brilliant garlands of flowers", that "pale Parian mantelpiece" with its Bohemia glass of "ruby red" and the "general blending of snow and fire"—what is all that except Jane Eyre?

The drawbacks of being Jane Eyre are not far to seek. Always to be a governess and always to be in love is a serious limitation in a world which is full, after all, of people who are neither one nor the other. The characters of a Jane Austen or of a Tolstoi have a million facets compared with these. They live and are complex by means of their effect upon many different people who serve to mirror them in the round. They move hither and thither whether their creators watch them or not, and the world in which they live seems to us an independent world which we can visit, now that they have created it, by ourselves. Thomas Hardy is more akin to Charlotte Brontë in the power of his personality and the narrowness of his vision. But the differences are vast. As we read *Jude the Obscure* we are not rushed to a finish; we brood and ponder and drift away from the text in plethoric trains of thought which build up round the characters an atmosphere of question and suggestion of which they are themselves, as often as not, unconscious. Simple peasants as they are, we are forced to confront them with destinies and questionings of the hugest import, so that often it seems as if the most important characters in a Hardy novel are those which have no names. Of this power, of this speculative curiosity, Charlotte Brontë has no trace. She does not attempt to solve the problems of human life; she is even unaware that such problems exist; all her force, and it is the more tremendous for being constricted, goes into the assertion, "I love", "I hate", "I suffer".

For the self-centered and self-limited writers have a power denied the more catholic and broad-minded. Their impressions are close packed and strongly stamped between their narrow walls. Nothing issues from their minds which has not been marked with their own impress. They learn little from other writers, and what they adopt they cannot assimilate. Both Hardy and Charlotte Brontë appear to have founded their styles upon a stiff and decorous journalism. The staple of their prose is awkward and unyielding. But both

Charlotte Brontë on the First Dramatic Production of *Jane Eyre*

The expanding interest in the Brontës in the twentieth century is demonstrated by the proliferation of stage, radio, movie, and television productions, as well as art and music, based on their lives and works. In particular, Jane Eyre *and* Wuthering Heights *have been produced for various media many times.*

Charlotte was the only Brontë who lived to consider the possibility of a dramatic production of one of her novels. Some three months after the publication of Jane Eyre, *a drama titled* Jane Eyre or The Secrets of Thornfield Manor *was produced in London, premiering at the end of January 1848. This excerpt is from her 5 February 1848 letter to William Smith Williams, from whom she learned of the play.*

A representation of "Jane Eyre" at a Minor Theatre would no doubt be a rather afflicting spectacle to the author of that work: I suppose all would be woefully exaggerated and painfully vulgarized by the actors and actresses on such a stage. What—I cannot help asking myself—would they make of Mr. Rochester? And the picture my fancy conjures up by way of reply is a somewhat humiliating one. What would they make of Jane Eyre? I see something very pert and very affected as the answer to that query.

Still—were it in my power, I should certainly make a point of being myself a witness to the exhibition—Could I go quietly and alone, I undoubtedly should go; I should endeavour to endure both rant and whine, strut and grimace for the sake of the useful observations to be collected in such a scene.

As to whether I wish <u>you</u> to go—that is another question. I am afraid I have hardly fortitude enough really to wish it. One can endure being disgusted with one's own work, but that a friend should share the repugnance is unpleasant.

Still, I know it would interest me to hear both your account of the exhibition and any ideas which the effect of the various parts on the spectators, might suggest to you. In short, I should like to know what you would think, and to hear what you would say on the subject.— But you must not go merely to satisfy my curiosity; you must do as you think proper: whatever you decide on will content me: if you do <u>not</u> go, you will be spared a vulgarizing impression of the book; if you <u>do</u> go, I shall perhaps gain a little information: either alternative has its advantage.

The Letters of Charlotte Brontë, v. 2, pp. 25–26

Charlotte responded to Williams's report of a performance in her letter dated 15 February 1848.

Your letter, as you may fancy, has given me something to think about—it has presented to my mind a curious picture, for the description you give is so vivid, I seem to realize it all. I wanted information and I have got it: you have raised the veil from a corner of your great world—your London—and have shewn me a glimpse of what I might call—<u>loathsome</u>, but which I prefer calling <u>strange</u>. Such then is a sample of what amuses the Metropolitan populace! Such is a view of one of their haunts!

Did I not say that I would have gone to this theatre and witnessed the exhibition if it had been in my power? What absurdities people utter when they speak of they know not what!

You must try now to forget entirely what you saw. . . .

—*The Letters of Charlotte Brontë,* v. 2, pp. 27–28

with labour and the most obstinate integrity by thinking every thought until it has subdued words to itself, have forged for themselves a prose which takes the mould of their minds entire; which has, into the bargain, a beauty, a power, a swiftness of its own. Charlotte Brontë, at least, owed nothing to the reading of many books. She never learnt the smoothness of the professional writer, or acquired his ability to stuff and sway his language as he chooses. "I could never rest in communication with strong, discreet, and refined minds, whether male or female," she writes, as any leader-writer in a provincial journal might have written; but gathering fire and speed goes on in her own authentic voice "till I had passed the outworks of conventional reserve and crossed the threshold of confidence, and won a place by their hearts' very hearthstone". It is there that she takes her seat; it is the red and fitful glow of the heart's fire which illumines her page. In other words, we read Charlotte Brontë not for exquisite

observation of character—her characters are vigorous and elementary; not for comedy—hers is grim and crude; not for a philosophic view of life—hers is that of a country parson's daughter; but for her poetry. Probably that is so with all writers who have, as she has, an overpowering personality, who, as we should say in real life, have only to open the door to make themselves felt. There is in them some untamed ferocity perpetually at war with the accepted order of things which makes them desire to create instantly rather than to observe patiently. This very ardour, rejecting half shades and other minor impediments, wings its way past the daily conduct of ordinary people and allies itself with their more inarticulate passions. It makes them poets, or, if they choose to write in prose, intolerant of its restrictions. Hence it is that both Emily and Charlotte are always invoking the help of nature. They both feel the need of some more powerful symbol of the vast and slumbering passions in human nature than

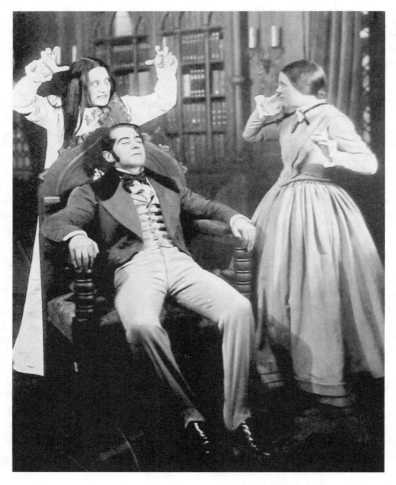

A scene from the 1936 production of Helen Jerome's play Jane Eyre *at the Queen's Theatre in London: Dorothy Hamilton*
as the mad Bertha, Reginald Tate as Rochester, and Curigwen Lewis as Jane
(from Play Pictorial, *University of Colorado Libraries)*

words or actions can convey. It is with a description of a storm that Charlotte ends her finest novel *Villette*. "The skies hang full and dark—a wrack sails from the west; the clouds cast themselves into strange forms." So she calls in nature to describe a state of mind which could not otherwise be expressed. But neither of the sisters observed nature accurately as Dorothy Wordsworth observed it, or painted it minutely as Tennyson painted it. They seized those aspects of the earth which were most akin to what they themselves felt or imputed to their characters, and so their storms, their moors, their lovely spaces of summer weather are not ornaments applied to decorate a dull page or display the writer's powers of observation—they carry on the emotion and light up the meaning of the book.

The meaning of a book, which lies so often apart from what happens and what is said and consists rather in some connection which things in themselves different have had for the writer, is necessarily hard to grasp. Espe-

cially this is so when, like the Brontës, the writer is poetic, and his meaning inseparable from his language, and itself rather a mood than a particular observation. *Wuthering Heights* is a more difficult book to understand than *Jane Eyre,* because Emily was a greater poet than Charlotte. When Charlotte wrote she said with eloquence and splendour and passion "I love", "I hate", "I suffer". Her experience, though more intense, is on a level with our own. But there is no "I" in *Wuthering Heights*. There are no governesses. There are no employers. There is love, but it is not the love of men and women. Emily was inspired by some more general conception. The impulse which urged her to create was not her own suffering or her own injuries. She looked out upon a world cleft into gigantic disorder and felt within her the power to unite it in a book. That gigantic ambition is to be felt throughout the novel—a struggle, half thwarted but of superb conviction, to say something through the mouths of her characters which is not merely "I love" or "I hate", but "we, the whole human race" and "you, the eternal powers . . ." the sentence remains unfinished. It is not strange that it should be so; rather it is astonishing that she can make us feel what she had it in her to say at all. It surges up in the half-articulate words of Catherine Earnshaw, "If all else perished and *he* remained, I should still continue to be; and if all else remained and he were annihilated, the universe would turn to a mighty stranger; I should not seem part of it". It breaks out again in the presence of the dead. "I see a repose that neither earth nor hell can break, and I feel an assurance of the endless and shadowless hereafter—the eternity they have entered—where life is boundless in its duration, and love in its sympathy and joy in its fulness." It is this suggestion of power underlying the apparitions of human nature, and lifting them up into the presence of greatness that gives the book its huge stature among other novels. But it was not enough for Emily Brontë to write a few lyrics, to utter a cry, to express a creed. In her poems she did this once and for all, and her poems will perhaps outlast her novel. But she was novelist as well as poet. She must take upon herself a more laborious and a more ungrateful task. She must face the fact of other existences, grapple with the mechanism of external things, build up, in recognisable shape, farms and houses and report the speeches of men and women who existed independently of herself. And so we reach these summits of emotion not by rant or rhapsody but by hearing a girl sing old songs to herself as she rocks in the branches of a tree; by watching the moor sheep crop the turf; by listening to the soft wind breathing through the grass. The life at the farm with all its absurdities and its improbability is laid open to us. We are given every opportunity of comparing *Wuthering Heights* with a real farm and Heathcliff with a real man. How, we are allowed to ask, can there be truth or insight or the finer shades of emotion in men and women who so little resemble what we have seen ourselves? But even as we ask it we see in Heathcliff the brother that a sister of genius might have seen; he is impossible we say, but nevertheless no boy in literature has so vivid an existence as his. So it is with the two Catherines; never could women feel as they do or act in their manner, we say. All the same, they are the most lovable women in English fiction. It is as if she could tear up all that we know human beings by, and fill these unrecognisable transparences with such a gust of life that they transcend reality. Hers, then, is the rarest of all powers. She could free life from its dependence on facts; with a few touches indicate the spirit of a face so that it needs no body; by speaking of the moor make the wind blow and the thunder roar.

—*The Common Reader,* pp. 219–227

* * *

Wuthering Heights was first made into a movie in 1920; no copy of this silent version survives. The most famous and influential movie based on the novel was the 1939 version, which takes many liberties with Emily Brontë's story, eliminating all second-generation characters.

"A Masterly Translation"
Review of *Wuthering Heights*
Howard Barnes

"Wuthering Heights," a screen drama by Ben Hecht and Charles MacArthur from the novel by Emily Bronte, directed by William Wyler and presented by Samuel Goldwyn at the Rivioli Theater with the following cast:

Cathy	Merle Oberon
Heathcliff	Laurence Olivier
Edgar	David Niven
Ellen Dean	Flora Robson
Dr. Kenneth	Donald Crisp
Isabella	Geraldine Fitzgerald
Hindley	Hugh Williams
Joseph	Leo G. Carroll
Judge Linton	Cecil Humphreys
Lockwood	Miles Mander
Robert	Romaine Callender
Earnshaw	Cecil Kellaway
Heathcliff (as a child)	Rex Downing
Cathy (as a child)	Sarita Wooton
Hindley (as a child)	Douglas Scott
Harpsichordist	Mme. Alice Ehlera

Emily Brontë's somber story of passion, hatred and revenge has been brought to the screen with great courage and skill in "Wuthering Heights." It is at once a fine film and a masterly translation of a literary classic. The characters are presented with all the relentless vigor of the original; the mood remains one of brooding violence, and the romantic tragedy is given powerful and poignant statement. There is shrewd showmanship in this Samuel Goldwyn production, but it is also marked by a rare integrity. In a brilliant and balanced collaboration scenarists, director, cast and technicians have succeeded in holding the film to a straight, tragic line. It is a moving and notable motion picture in its own right; it is also a challenging example of how effective an honest treatment can be.

The temptation must have been great to soften the harsh outlines of the Bronte novel, endow its figures with sympathy and relieve the bitter burden of the plot. Fortunately, none of these things have been done. The Ben Hecht-Charles MacArthur script has reshaped the tale to a fluent screen pattern, without losing any of its implacable intensity. The portrayals, from Laurence Olivier's

Page from the pressbook for the 1939 production of Emily Brontë's novel (Pacific Film Archive Library, University of California, Berkeley Art Museum)

Dust jacket for a movie tie-in edition, published by Triangle in 1940 (Pandora Books)

furies-driven Heathcliff to Merle Oberon's wilful Cathy, are grimly substantial and the backgrounds of the Yorkshire moors are such as to continually heighten the action. The result is an uncompromising and absorbing photoplay, which has all of the strange, haunting quality of the original.

While the production has been remarkably successful in conjuring up the bleak English countryside of a century ago and an early Victorian atmosphere, it never takes refuge in period trappings. It is concerned with thwarted love and terrible vengeance and it has dramatic authority because of its emotional conviction. The tortured love affair between Cathy and Heathcliff, the stablehand; her escape by marriage to Edgar Linton and Heathcliff's savage retaliation unfold in an inexorable continuity. "Wuthering Heights" on the screen has the same common idiom of human experience which was employed by the rector's spinster daughter when she poured all her repressed passion into a book and died before she knew that she had written imperishably.

That the film seldom falters emotionally is largely due to the actors' fine performances. Mr. Olivier is splendid as the beaten and jilted stable boy who bides his time before exacting a terrifying vengeance. He plays with a restrained passion which always sustains the key of romantic melodrama. Miss Oberon gives an immensely versatile characterization of Cathy and rises to a fine pitch of intensity in her final death scene. There there are such solid and compelling portrayals of minor parts as Hugh Williams's ill-starred Hindley, Flora Robson's Ellen Dean, David Niven's Edgar, Geraldine Fitzgerald's Isabella and Donald Crisp's Dr. Kenneth. The child actors of the early sequences leave something to be desired, but they at least succeed in foreshadowing the ultimate tragedy.

In his staging William Wyler has not always kept the narrative in true motion picture terms. On the other hand he has been extraordinarily adept at achieving a subjective approach to the material. Meanwhile, the dramatically revealing incident and dialogue of the Messrs. Hecht and MacArthur recapture the full mood of the original book. Honesty and first-rate craftsmanship have gone into "Wuthering Heights" and the result is a distinguished and engrossing screen tragedy.

–*New York Herald Tribune*, 14 April 1939

* * *

A Boxed Set of Classic Novels

In 1943 the Book-of-the-Month Club offered new illustrated editions of Jane Eyre *and* Wuthering Heights *as dividend books for its members. New members received this boxed set, illustrated by Fritz Eichenberg, upon joining in November or December that year. In the advertisement for the Book-of-the-Month Club editions that appeared in the 12 December 1943 issue of* The New York Times *Emily Brontë is identified as the outstanding writer in the family:* "Jane Eyre *and* Wuthering Heights *rank among the greatest love stories in English literature; and the author of one of them, Emily Brontë, is considered by many to be the foremost of all English women writers. First published in 1847,* Jane Eyre *was an immediate and sensational success.* Wuthering Heights, *published some time later, by no means met with the same instantaneous acclaim as the older sister's novel, but today, with the true perspective of the years, we know it surely as 'one of the greatest stories ever written by man, woman or angel.'"*

In a 1979 interview Eichenberg explained why he decided to use wood engraving or lithography to illustrate literature.

Any medium where I could work from dark into light, or from black into white, with all the gradations—which is also symbolic procedure: a process which makes it possible for you to create life out of a void. As you face the blank woodblock or the darkened surface of a lithographic stone, you create life out of it by throwing with your first touch of the graver—the first touch of your etching needle, or razor blade. You create a source of life that spreads over the whole scene and picks out the main actors and the main emphasis on the certain interrelationship, usually, between two human beings. . . .

It's always a kind of a dialogue between two people as you have when you read the novel, too. When you read Dostoyevsky you have a dialogue between the two individuals—you and the author. No matter what. If you read the Bible you have the same kind of thing. To bring this out in my work, to make the dialogue clear so that it becomes a kind of a touchstone for the effectiveness of my representation. Does it unmistakably carry my message and the message of the author, or doesn't it? Somehow, without manipulation it comes to me naturally. Over the years I have paid very little attention to it. But

now that I am getting old I see all these reactions coming back.

I get letters from people I will never see, from all over the world—as you know when you look at my correspondence—who have seen my work and have been touched by it—moved by it—and have learned to love that particular literature in which I'm also interested. And since I have been lucky enough to be commissioned to do the imagery accompanying the works of great writers, it makes me a kind of a mediator—a kind of interpreter—a visual interpreter—and has helped many people to read Dostoyevsky who've never read Dostoyevsky before. Or the Brontes. *Jane Eyre* and *Wuthering Heights* are probably the most popular books I have done. Wherever I go people say, "I grew up with Heathcliff, you know, under the tree" and "I grew up with Jane Eyre." Hundreds of people, after I give talks, come up to me and they always mention *Wuthering Heights* and *Jane Eyre.*

Eichenberg later discussed how he tries to capture "the spirit" of the writer and her book.

Well, this is the marvelous thing about being an illustrator of my connotation—that you have a tremendous opportunity to create life, to create a person, to create a character, to create a situation. You are the director of a scene, let's say. In a film or on the stage it would be the same kind of thing. Here I'm all alone with a little woodblock with my imagination and with a book. Between the three of us we solve the problem of making it touching, convincing in the spirit of the writer. This is to me very important, that I don't violate any of the writer's intentions. . . . You either get it or you don't. And not all of my work is that successful, you know. Sometimes it falls flat; it's not always possible to catch what you want. But in those examples that I show, I naturally try to show the successful conclusion or creation of a scene that corresponds to the spirit of the book.

—Interview conducted by Robert Brown, 14 May 1979 and 7 December 1979, Archives of American Art, Smithsonian Institution

Produced in 1944, the classic Hollywood movie version of Jane Eyre *truncated the story, omitting Jane's flight from Rochester and her relationship with the Rivers family.*

"Cleverly Distilled"
Review of *Jane Eyre*
Howard Barnes

"Jane Eyre" a screen play by Aldous Huxley, Robert Stevenson and John Houseman, from the novel by Charlotte Bronte, directed by Mr. Stevenson, produced by William Goets, presented by Twentieth Cen-

tury-Fox Pictures at Radio City Music Hall with the following cast:

Jane Eyre	Joan Fontaine
Edward Rochester	Orson Welles
Adele Varens	Margaret O'Brien
Jane (as a child)	Peggy Ann Garner
Dr. Rivers	John Sutton
Bessie	Sara Allgood
Brocklehurst	Henry Daniell
Mrs. Reed	Agnes Moorehead
Colonel Dent	Aubrey Mather

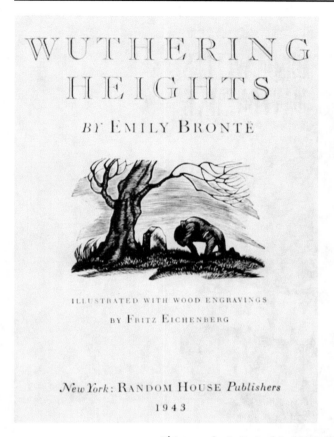

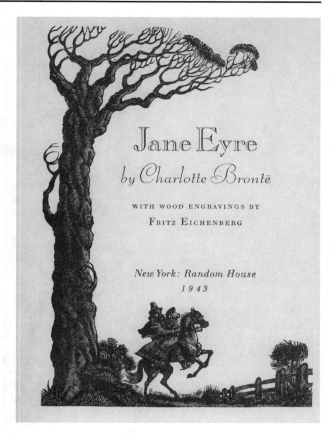

Title pages for the Book-of-the-Month Club boxed set of works by the Brontë sisters
(left, Colorado College Tutt library; right, Colorado State University, Fort Collins)

Mrs. Fairfax...Edith Barrett
Lady Ingram ....Barbara Everest
Blanche Ingram.....................................Hillary Brooke
Grace Poole ....Ethel Griffies
Leah...Mae Marsh
Miss Scatcherd ....Eily Malyon
Mrs. Eshton...Mary Forbes
Sir George Lynn ....Thomas Loudon
Mason..John Abbott
John ....Ronald Harris
Auctioneer ....Charles Irwin

The essential quality of "Jane Eyre" has been cleverly distilled in the current screen version of the Charlotte Brontë novel at the Music Hall. Without taking undue liberties with the original, the production has heightened every dramatic aspect of an early Victorian romantic tragedy. The subject matter of the film is about as remote as Mars, but it has been given an engrossing melodramatic outline in staging, script and acting. With Robert Stevenson as director and co-author and Joan Fontaine in the all-important title role,

the picture has a brooding intensity which is sustained artfully through to the final climax.

It was wise of the producers to give Stevenson the key job in the offering. The brilliant English film-maker has understood both the naivete and the depth of passion in the Brontë work. On the one hand he has achieved an archaic, grand guignol atmosphere which is remarkably effective on the screen. On the other he has articulated a desperate love affair with remarkable force. The early years passed by Jane in a charity school, under the sadistic eye of a clergyman, are sketched in briefly but unerringly. Her term as governess to the wealthy Edward Rochester makes up the body of the show, and it is filled with violence, frustrated love and moral scruples.

Only an Englishman, I think, could have established some sort of affinity with a century-old book, so bound up in conventions and improbabilities as "Jane Eyre." Stevenson has done a masterly job in making the romance between a shy, unhappy governess and her employer, who has a mad wife locked up in the tower of his castle, a bit valid. Only Miss Fontaine could have

Poster for the 1944 American movie version of Jane Eyre, *dubbed into Spanish and retitled "Rebellious Soul"*
(Rare Book School at the University of Virginia)

made the title role so luminous and appealing that her plight is understandable. Between them, director and star have resurrected a dated classic with sense and considerable feeling.

Orson Welles plays Rochester a bit too dramatically for complete comfort. He pitches his performance too high at the start and has a hard time making it stand up when he is coping with his crazy wife, trying to marry his governess and finally finding happiness through ultimate physical misfortune. The supporting players are invariably excellent at creating atmosphere or dramatic embellishments to the continuity. Sara Allgood, Henry Daniell, Agnes Moorehead, Ethel Griffies, and the others are interesting as well as being early Victorian. "Jane Eyre" is interesting, sometimes chilling and even moving. As genuine escapist drama, it should be a highly successful entertainment.

—*New York Herald Tribune,* 4 February 1944

* * *

In 1948 at the suggestion of the American publisher John C. Winston, novelist W. Somerset Maugham selected and edited the ten best novels in world literature. Emily Brontë's only novel made Maughm's list along with Leo Tolstoy's War and Peace, *Honoré de Balzac's* Old Man Goriot, *Henry Fielding's* Tom Jones, *Jane Austen's* Pride and Prejudice, *Stendhal's* The Red and the Black, *Gustave Flaubert's* Madame Bovary, *Charles Dickens's* David Copperfield, *Fyodor Dostoevsky's* The Brothers Karamazov, *and Herman Melville's* Moby-Dick. *In the first two sections of this essay, here omitted, Maugham provided an account of the Brontë family.*

The Ten Best Novels: *Wuthering Heights*
W. Somerset Maugham

3

It is not without intention that in writing about Emily Brontë's *Wuthering Heights* I have said so much about her father, her brother, and her sister Charlotte, for in the books written about the family it is of them

THE BRONTË SISTERS

Card made from the painting by Branwell Brontë for the National Portrait Gallery's "Famous Faces" deck (Collection of Joan Ray)

that we hear most. Emily and Anne hardly come into the picture; Anne was a gentle, pretty little thing, but insignificant, and her talent was small. Emily was very different. She is a strange, mysterious, and shadowy figure. She is never seen directly but reflected, as it were, in a moorland pool. You have to guess what sort of woman she was from an allusion here and there and from scattered anecdotes. She was aloof, a harsh, uncomfortable creature and when you hear of her giving over to unrestrained gaiety, as she sometimes did on walks over the moors, it makes you uneasy. Charlotte had friends, Anne had friends, Emily had none.

Mary Robinson describes her at fifteen as "a tall, long-armed girl, full grown, elastic as to tread; with a slight figure that looked queenly in her best dresses, but loose and boyish when she slouched over the moors, whistling to the dogs, and taking long strides over the rough earth. A tall, thin, loose-jointed girl—not ugly, but with irregular features and a pallid thick complexion." Like her father, her brother, and her sisters she wore spectacles. She had an aquiline nose and a large, expressive prominent mouth. She dressed regardless of fashion, with leg-of-mutton sleeves long after they had ceased to be worn; in straight long skirts clinging to her lanky figure.

She hated Brussels and was miserable there. She stayed only by an effort of will. Friends tried to be nice to the two girls and asked them to spend Sundays and holidays with them, but they were so shy that to go was an agony for them, and after a while their hosts thought it kinder not to invite them. It was natural that they should be shy; they had been brought up in seclusion and had had little experience of social life; but shyness is a somewhat complicated state of mind, there is diffidence in it, but also conceit, and from this Emily at least was not free.

During the hours of recreation at school the two sisters always walked together and generally in silence. When they were spoken to, Charlotte answered. Emily rarely spoke to anyone. Monsieur Héger thought her intelligent, but so stubborn that she would listen to no reason when it interfered with her wishes or beliefs. He found her egotistical, exacting, and with Charlotte tyrannical. But he recognized that there was something unusual in her. She should have been a man, he said, "her strong imperious will would never have been daunted by opposition or difficulty; never have given way but with life."

When Emily went back to Haworth after her aunt's death it was for good. She never left it again.

She got up in the morning before anybody else and did the roughest part of the day's work before Tabby, the maid, who was old and frail, came down. She did the household ironing and most of the cooking. She made the bread and the bread was good. While she kneaded the dough she would glance at the book propped up before her. "Those who worked with her in the kitchen, young girls called in to help in stress of business, remember how she would keep a scrap of paper, a pencil at her side, and how when the moment came that she could pause in her cooking or her ironing, she would jot down some impatient thought and then resume her work."

With these girls she was always friendly and hearty—"pleasant, sometimes quite jovial like a boy." "So genial and kind, a little masculine," say my informants, "but of strangers she was exceedingly timid, and if the butcher's boy or the baker's man came to the kitchen door she would be off like a bird into the hall or the parlour till she heard their hobnails clumping down the path." I think that much in her behavior that was strange to her contemporaries would be clear to a psychiatrist today.

4

It is evident that Charlotte did not quite know what to make of *Wuthering Heights;* she had no notion that her sister had produced a book of astonishing originality and one compared with which her own were

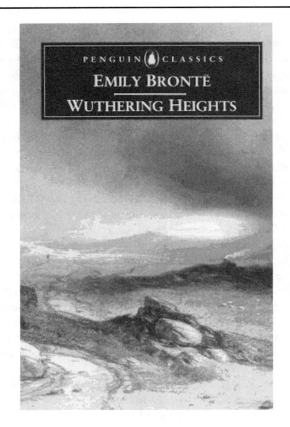

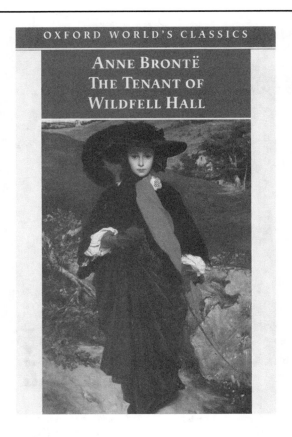

Covers for paperback editions of Wuthering Heights *(1996),* The Tenant of Wildfell Hall *(1998), and* Jane Eyre *(2006)*

commonplace. She felt compelled to apologize for it. When it was proposed to republish it she undertook to edit it. "I am likewise compelling myself to read it over, for the first time of opening the book since my sister's death. Its power fills me with renewed admiration; but yet I am oppressed: the reader is scarcely ever permitted a taste of unalloyed pleasure; every beam of sunshine is poured down through black bars of threatening cloud; every page is surcharged with a sort of moral electricity; and the writer was unconscious of all this—nothing could make her conscious of it."

One is inclined to think that she little knew her sister. *Wuthering Heights* is an extraordinary book. It is a very bad one. It is a very fine one. It is ugly. It has beauty. It is a terrible, an agonizing, a passionate book. Some have thought it impossible that a clergyman's daughter who led a retired, humdrum life and knew few people and nothing of the world could have written it. This seems to me absurd. *Wuthering Heights* is wildly romantic: now romanticism eschews the patient observation of realism, it revels in the unbridled flight of the imagination and indulges, sometimes with gusto, sometimes with gloom, in horror, mystery, fearful passions, and deeds of violence. It is an escape from reality. Given Emily Brontë's character, of which I have tried to give some indication, and fierce, repressed passions, which what we know of her suggests, *Wuthering Heights* is just the sort of book one would have expected her to write. But on the face of it, it is much more the sort of book that her scapegrace brother Branwell might have written and a number of people have been able to persuade themselves that he had either in whole or in part done so.

Some of his friends were convinced of it. Francis Grundy wrote: "Patrick Brontë declared to me, and what his sister said bore out the assertion, that he wrote a great part of *Wuthering Heights* himself. . . . The weird fancies of diseased genius with which he used to entertain me in our long talks at Luddendenfoot, reappear in the pages of the novel, and I am inclined to believe that the very plot was his invention rather than his sister's." On one occasion two of Branwell's friends, Dearden and Leyland by name, arranged to meet him at an inn on the road to Keighley to read their poetical effusions to one another and this is what Dearden some twenty years later wrote to the *Halifax Guardian:* "I read the first act of *The Demon Queen;* but when Branwell dived into his hat—the usual receptacle of his fugitive scraps—where he supposed he had deposited his manuscript poem, he found he had by mistake placed there a number of stray leaves of a novel on which he had been trying his 'prentice hand.' Chagrined at the disappointment he had caused, he was about to return the papers to his hat, when both friends earnestly pressed him to read them, as they felt a curiosity to see how he could wield the pen of a novelist. After some hesitation, he complied with the request, and riveted our attention for about an hour, dropping each sheet, when read, into his hat. The story broke off abruptly in the middle of a sentence, and he gave us the sequel, *viva voce,* together with the real names of the prototypes of his characters; but, as some of these persons are still living, I refrain from pointing them out to the public. He said he had not yet fixed upon a title for his production, and was afraid he would never be able to meet with a publisher who would have the hardihood to usher it into the world. The scene of the fragment which Branwell read, and the characters introduced in it—so far as they developed—were the same as those in *Wuthering Heights,* which Charlotte Brontë confidently asserts was the production of her sister Emily."

Now this is either a tissue of lies or it is true. Charlotte despised and within the bounds of Christian charity hated her brother, but as we know, Christian charity has always been able to make allowances for a lot of good honest hatred, and Charlotte's unsupported word cannot be accepted. She may, as people often do, have persuaded herself to believe what she wanted to believe. The story is circumstantial and it is odd that anyone for no particular reason should have invented it.

What is the explanation? There is none. It has been suggested that Branwell wrote the first four chapters, and then, drunk and doped as he was, gave it up, whereupon Emily took it over. The argument adduced is that these chapters are written in a more stilted style than the rest of the novel. That I cannot see. The whole book is very badly written in the bogus literary manner that the amateur is apt to affect. When the amateur, and it must be remembered that Emily Brontë had never written a book before, sits down to write he thinks he must use grand words rather than ordinary ones. It is only by practice that he learns to write naturally.

The main part of the story is told by a Yorkshire servant and she expresses herself in a way that no human being could. Emily Brontë was perhaps aware that she was putting words into Mrs. Dean's mouth that she could hardly have known and, to explain it, makes her say that she has in the course of her service had the opportunity to read a number of books, but even at that the pretentiousness of her discourse is appalling. She never *tries* to do a thing, but *endeavors* or *essays,* she never *leaves* a room but *quits* it, she never *meets* anybody but *encounters* him. I should have said that whoever wrote the first chapters wrote the rest, and if in the early ones there is somewhat more pomposity in the writing I surmise that this is owing to a not unsuccessful attempt on Emily's part to show that Lockwood was a silly, conceited young man.

Cover for the Broadway musical adapted from Charlotte Brontë's novel that opened in December 2000. Marla Schaffel played Jane, and James Barbour played Rochester in the original cast (Collection of Joan Ray).

Cover for the DVD of a 2003 television production of Emily Brontë's novel

I have read somewhere the conjecture that if it was Branwell who wrote the beginning of the novel his intention was to make Lockwood take a much greater part in the action. There is indeed a hint that he was attracted by the younger Catherine and it is obvious that if he had fallen in love with her a complication would have been added to the intrigue. As it is, Lockwood is merely a nuisance. The novel is very clumsily constructed. But is this surprising? Emily Brontë had a complicated story to tell dealing with two generations. This is always a difficult thing to do because the author has to give some sort of unity to a narrative that concerns two sets of characters and two sets of events; and

he must be careful not to allow the interest of one set to overshadow the interest of the other. He has also to compress the passage of years into a period of time that can be accepted by the reader with a comprehensive glance as one seizes in a single view the whole of a vast fresco.

I do not suppose that Emily Brontë deliberately thought out how to get a unity of impression into a straggling story, but I think she must have wondered how to make it coherent and it occurred to her that she could best do this by making one character narrate the long succession of events to another. It is a convenient way of telling the story and she did not invent it.

Set of the 2005 Royal Mint stamps issued to commemorate the 150th anniversary of Charlotte Brontë's death. The lithographs by Paula Rego illustrate scenes from Jane Eyre *(Collection of Susan B. Taylor).*

Its disadvantage is, as I pointed out just now, that it is almost impossible to maintain a conversational manner when the narrator has to tell a number of things, descriptions of scenery for instance, which no sane person would think of doing. An experienced novelist might have found a better way of telling a story of *Wuthering Heights,* but I cannot persuade myself that Emily Brontë was working on a foundation of someone else's invention.

5

I think that Emily Brontë's method might have been expected of her when you consider her extreme, her morbid, shyness and reticence. What were the alternatives? One was to write the novel from the standpoint of omniscience, as for instance *Middlemarch* and *Madame Bovary* were written. I think it would have shocked her harsh, uncompromising virtue to tell the outrageous story as a creation of her own; and if she had, moreover, she could hardly have avoided giving some account of Heathcliff during the years he spent away from Wuthering Heights when he managed to acquire an education and make money. She couldn't do this because she simply didn't know how he had done it. The fact the reader is asked to accept is hard to believe and she was content to state it and leave it at that.

Another alternative was to have the story narrated to her by Mrs. Dean, say, and telling it then in the first person, but I suspect that too would have brought her into a contact with the reader too close for her quivering sensibility. By having the story in its beginning told by Lockwood and unfolded to Lockwood by Mrs. Dean she hid herself behind as it were a double mask.

And why did Emily need to hide herself when she wrote this powerful, terrible book? I think because she disclosed in it her innermost instincts. She looked deep into the well of loneliness of her heart and saw there undisclosable secrets which, notwithstanding, her impulse as a writer drove her to unburden herself of. It is said that her imagination was kindled by the weird stories her father used to tell of the Ireland of his youth and by the tales of Hoffmann which she learned to read when she went to school in Belgium and which she continued to read, we are told, back at the parsonage seated on a hearthrug by the fire with her arm round her dog's neck.

Charlotte was at pains to state that Emily, whatever she had heard of them, had no communication with the people round her who might be supposed to have suggested the characters of her novel. I am willing to believe that this is true and I am willing to believe that she found in the stories of mystery and horror of the German romantic writers something that appealed to her own fierce nature; but I think she found Heathcliff and Catherine Earnshaw in the hidden depths of her own soul. It may be that in the lesser characters—Linton and his sister, Earnshaw's wife and Heathcliff's—objects of her disdain for their weakness and frailty, she found hints in persons she had known, but readers seldom give an author credit for a power of invention and it is just as likely that she created them out of her own overbearing and contemptuous imagination.

I think she was herself Catherine Earnshaw, wild, tempestuous, passionate; and I think she was Heathcliff. Is it strange that she should have put herself into the two chief characters of her book? Not at all. We are none of us all of a piece; more than one person dwells within us, often in uneasy companionship with his fellows. And the peculiarity of the writer of fiction is that he has the power to objectify the diverse persons of which he is compounded into individual characters: his misfortune is that he cannot bring to life characters, however necessary to his story they may be, in which there is no part of himself. It is not only not uncommon for an author writing his first novel, as *Wuthering Heights* was, to make himself his principal character, it is not uncommon either that in his theme there will be something of wish-fulfillment. It becomes then a confession of the reveries, on solitary walks or in wakeful hours at night, in which he has imagined himself saint or sinner, great lover or great statesman, heroic general or cold-blooded murderer; and it is because there is a lot of absurdity in most people's reveries that there is a great deal of nonsense in most writers' first novels. I think *Wuthering Heights* is just such a confession.

I think Emily Brontë put the whole of herself into Heathcliff. She gave him, I think, her violent rage, her sexuality, vehement but frustrated, her passion of unsatisfied love, her jealousy, her hatred and contempt of human beings, her cruelty, her sadism. There is a curious incident related by Charlotte's friend, Ellen Nussey: "She enjoyed leading Charlotte where she would not dare go of her own free will. Charlotte had a mortal dread of unknown animals, and it was Emily's pleasure to lead her into close vicinity, and then tell her of how and what she had done, laughing at her horror with great amusement."

I think Emily loved Catherine Earnshaw with Heathcliff's masculine, purely animal love, and I think she laughed, as she had at Charlotte's fears, when as Heathcliff she kicked and trampled on Earnshaw and dashed his head repeatedly against the stone flags, and I think she laughed when, as Heathcliff, she hit the younger Catherine in the face and heaped humiliations upon her; I think it gave her a thrill of release when she bullied, reviled, and browbeat the persons of her invention because in real life she suffered such bitter mortification in the company of her fellow creatures. And I think as Catherine, doubling the roles, as it were, though she fought Heathcliff, though she despised him, though she knew him for the evil thing he was, she loved him with her body and soul, she exulted in her power over him, she felt they were kin (as indeed they were if I am right in supposing they were both Emily Brontë) and since there is in the sadist often something of the masochist too, she was fascinated by his violence, his brutality, his untamed nature.

But I have said enough. *Wuthering Heights* is not a book to talk about: it is a book to read. It is easy to find fault with it; it is very imperfect; and yet it has what few novelists can give you, power. I do not know a novel in which the pain, the ecstasy, the ruthlessness, the obsessiveness of love have been so wonderfully described. *Wuthering Heights* reminds me of one of those great pictures of El Greco in which a somber, arid landscape under dark clouds heavy with thunder, long, emaciated figures in contorted attitudes, spellbound by an unearthly emotion, hold their breath. A streak of lightning flitting across the leaden sky gives a final touch of mysterious terror to the scene.

—The Atlantic Monthly, 181 (February 1948):
89–94

Selected Secondary Works Cited

This listing of sources cited in the volume does not include periodicals.

Alexander, Christine. "Charlotte Brontë at Roe Head" in *Jane Eyre,* by Charlotte Brontë, Norton Critical Edition, edited by Richard J. Dunn. New York: Norton, 2001, pp. 394–425.

Alexander. *The Early Writings of Charlotte Brontë.* Oxford: Blackwell, 1983.

Alexander and Jane Sellars. *The Art of the Brontës.* Cambridge & New York: Cambridge University Press, 1995.

The Art Journal Illustrated Catalogue: The Industry of All Nations. London: George Vertue, ca. 1851.

Barker, Juliet. *The Brontës.* New York: St. Martin's Press, 1995.

Brontë, Patrick. *The Rural Minstrel: A Miscellany of Descriptive Poems.* Halifax, U.K.: P. K. Holden, 1813.

The Brontës: The Critical Heritage, edited by Miriam Allott. London & Boston: Routledge & Kegan Paul, 1974.

Chadwick, Esther Alice. *Mrs. Gaskell: Haunts, Homes, and Stories.* London: Pitman, 1910.

De Quincey Memorials, 2 volumes, edited by Alexander H. Japp. New York: United States Book Company, 1891.

Dickinson, Emily. "All overgrown by cunning moss," in *Poems by Emily Dickinson,* third series, edited by Mabel Loomis Todd. Boston: Roberts, 1896, pp. 193–194.

Drinkwater, John. *A Book for Bookmen: Being Edited Manuscripts & Marginalia with Essays on Several Occasions.* London: Dulau, 1926.

Finding the North Pole, edited by Charles Morris. Philadelphia, ca. 1909.

Gardner, Juliet. *The World Within: The Brontës at Haworth.* London: Collins & Brown, 1992.

Gaskell, Elizabeth. *The Life of Charlotte Brontë,* 2 volumes. London: Smith, Elder, 1857.

Gérin, Winifred. *Branwell Brontë.* London & New York: Thomas Nelson, 1961.

Godfrey, Walter H. *A History of Architecture in London.* London: B. T. Balsford, 1911.

Graham, Thomas John. *Modern Domestic Medicine.* London: Simpkin & Marshall, 1827.

Home, Gordon. *Yorkshire: Painted & Described.* London: Adam & Charles Black, 1908.

Hubbard, Elbert. *Little Journeys to the Homes of Famous Women.* New York: Putnam, 1897.

Hutchinson, Robert. *1800 Woodcuts by Thomas Bewick and His School.* New York: Dover, 1962.

Latimer, Elizabeth Wormeley. *England in the Nineteenth Century,* fourth edition. Chicago: McClurg, 1897.

The Letters and Private Papers of William Makepeace Thackeray, edited by Gordon N. Ray, 4 volumes (London: Oxford University Press, 1945–1946.

Letters of Matthew Arnold 1848–1888, edited by G. W. E. Russell. New York & London: Macmillan, 1895.

Leyland, Francis A. *The Brontë Family with Special Reference to Patrick Branwell Brontë,* 2 volumes. London: Hurst & Blackett, 1886.

Macdonald, Frederika. *The Secret of Charlotte Brontë Followed by Some Reminiscences of the Real Monsieur and Madame Heger.* London & Edinburgh: T. C. & E. C. Jack, 1914.

Martineau, Harriet. "Charlotte Brontë," in her *Biographical Sketches.* New York: Leypoldt & Holt, 1869, pp. 43–50.

Mary Taylor: Friend of Charlotte Brontë: Letters from New Zealand & Elsewhere, edited by Joan Stevens. Auckland, New Zealand: Auckland University Press, 1972.

Melville, Lewis. *William Makepeace Thackeray: A Biography Including Hitherto Uncollected Letters & Speeches & a Bibliography of 1300 Items,* 2 volumes. London: John Lane, Bodley Head, 1910)

Miller, Lucasta. *The Brontë Myth.* New York: Knopf, 2003.

Newbolt, W. C. E. *The Cathedrals of England,* second series. New York: Thomas Whittaker, 1898.

The Oxford Companion to the Brontës, edited by Christine Alexander and Margaret Smith. New York: Oxford University Press, 2003.

Patrick Brontë: Cottage Poems and *The Rural Minstrel,* edited by Donald H. Reiman. New York: Garland, 1977.

Robinson, A. Mary F. *Emily Brontë.* Boston: Roberts, 1883.

Sellars, Jane. *Charlotte Brontë.* London: British Library, 1997.

Shaen, Margaret J. *Memorials of Two Sisters: Susanna and Catherine Winkworth.* London & New York: Longmans, Green, 1908.

Shorter, Clement K. *Charlotte Brontë and Her Circle.* London: Hodder & Stoughton, 1896.

Stuart, J. A. Erskine. *The Brontë Country: Its Topography, Antiquities, and History.* London: Longmans, Green, 1888.

Towle, Eleanor A. *A Poet's Children: Hartley and Sara Coleridge.* London: Methuen, 1912.

Turner, J. Horsfall. *Brontëana: The Rev. Patrick Brontë, A.B., His Collected Works and Life.* Bingley: T. Harrison, 1898.

Turner. *Haworth—Past and Present.* Brighouse: J. S. Jowett, "News" Office, 1879.

Turner, Whiteley. *A Spring-Time Saunter: Round and About Brontë Land.* Halifax: Halifax Courier, 1913.

White, Walter. *A Month in Yorkshire.* London: Chapman & Hall, 1858.

Wilson, W. Carus. *Thoughts Suggested to the Superintendent and Ladies of the School at Casterton, on Their Re-Assembling.* N.p.: T. Butler, 1858.

Wilson. *Youthful Memoirs.* Philadelphia: American Sunday School Union, 1829.

Woolf, Virginia. "Jane Eyre and *Wuthering Heights,*" in her *The Common Reader.* New York: Harcourt, Brace, 1925, pp. 219–224.

The Works of Lord Byron with His Letters and Journals and His Life, 14 volumes, edited by Thomas Moore. London: Murray, 1832.

Checklist for Further Reading

In addition to the primary and secondary works cited in this volume, the following sources are recommended.

Alexander, Christine. *A Bibliography of the Manuscripts of Charlotte Brontë*. Haworth: The Brontë Society/Meckler, 1982.

Allott, Miriam, ed. *The Brontës: The Critical Heritage*. London: Routledge & Kegan Paul, 1974.

Barker, Juliet. *Sixty Treasures*. Haworth: The Brontë Society, 1988.

Boumelha, Penny. *Charlotte Brontë*. Bloomington: Indiana University Press, 1990.

Chitham, Edward. *The Birth of 'Wuthering Heights': Emily Brontë at Work*. London: Macmillan, 1998.

Chitham. *The Brontës' Irish Background*. London: Macmillan, 1986.

Chitham. *A Life of Anne Brontë*. Oxford: Oxford University Press, 1991.

Chitham. *A Life of Emily Brontë*. Oxford: Blackwell, 1987.

Christian, Mildred G. *A Census of Brontë Manuscripts in the United States*. N.p., 1947–1948. Reprinted from *Trollopian*, 3 (December 1947); 4 (March 1948); 1 (June 1948); 2 (September 1948); 3 (December 1948).

Crump, R. W. *Charlotte and Emily Brontë, A Reference Guide*, 3 volumes. Boston: G. K. Hall, 1982, 1985, and 1986.

Dane, Clemence. *Wild Decembers*. London: Heinemann, 1932.

Davies, Stevie. *Emily Brontë*. Bloomington: Indiana University Press, 1988.

du Maurier, Daphne. *The Infernal World of Branwell Brontë*. London: Gollancz, 1960.

Eagleton, Terry. *Myths of Power: A Marxist Study of the Brontës*. London: Macmillan, 1975.

Elmes, James. *Metropolitan Improvements; or London in the Nineteenth Century*. London: Jones, 1827.

Frank, Katherine. *A Chainless Soul: A Life of Emily Brontë*. Boston: Houghton Mifflin, 1990.

Fraser, Rebecca. *The Brontës: Charlotte Brontë and Her Family*. New York: Crown, 1988.

Frawley, Maria H. *Anne Brontë*. New York: Twayne, 1996.

Gérin, Winifred. *Anne Brontë*. London: Allen Lane, 1976.

Gérin. *Charlotte Brontë: The Evolution of Genius*. Oxford: Clarendon Press, 1967.

Gérin. *Emily Brontë: A Biography*. Oxford: Oxford University Press, 1971.

Gezari, Janet. *Charlotte Brontë and Defensive Conduct: The Author and the Body at Risk*. Philadelphia: University of Pennsylvania Press, 1992.

Gezari. *Last Things: Emily Brontë's Poems*. Oxford: Oxford University Press, 2007.

Gilbert, Sandra, and Susan Gubar. *The Madwoman in the Attic: The Woman Writer and the Nineteenth-Century Imagination*. New Haven: Yale University Press, 1976.

Glen, Heather. *Charlotte Brontë: The Imagination in History*. Oxford: Oxford University Press, 2002.

Glen, ed. *The Cambridge Companion to the Brontës*. Cambridge: Cambridge University Press, 2002.

Gordon, Lyndall. *Charlotte Brontë: A Passionate Life*. London: Chatto & Windus, 1994.

Homans, Margaret. *Women Writers and Poetic Identity: Dorothy Wordsworth, Emily Brontë, and Emily Dickinson*. Princeton: Princeton University Press, 1980.

Ingham, Patricia. *The Brontës*. New York: Oxford University Press, 2006.

Kim, Jin-Ok. *Charlotte Brontë and Female Desire*. New York: Peter Lang, 2003.

Lamonica, Drew. *"We Are Three Sisters": Self and Family in the Writing of the Brontës*. Columbia: University of Missouri Press, 2003.

Langland, Elizabeth. *Anne Brontë: The Other One*. Totowa, N.J.: Barnes & Noble, 1989.

Lock, John, and Canon W. T. Dixon. *A Man of Sorrow: The Life, Letters and Times of the Revd. Patrick Brontë, 1777–1861*. London: Thomas Nelson, 1965.

Mackay, Angus M. "A Crop of Brontë Myths." *Westminster Review*, 144 (October 1895): 424–437.

Maynard, John. *Charlotte Brontë and Sexuality*. Cambridge & New York: Cambridge University Press, 1984.

McNees, Eleanor. *The Brontë Sisters: Critical Assessments*. 4 volumes. Mountfield, Westfield, Hastings, U.K.: Helm Information, 1996.

Meyer, Susan. *Imperialism at Home: Race and Victorian Women's Fiction*. Ithaca, N.Y.: Cornell University Press, 1996.

Matus, Jill L., ed. *The Cambridge Companion to Elizabeth Gaskell*. New York: Cambridge University Press, 2007.

Nash, Julie, and Barbara A. Suess, eds. *New Approaches to the Literary Art of Anne Brontë*. Hampshire, U.K.: Ashgate, 2001.

Nestor, Pauline. *Charlotte Brontë*. Totowa, N.J.: Barnes & Noble, 1987.

Palmer, Geoffrey. *The Brontës Day by Day*. Haworth: The Brontë Society, 2002.

Peters, Margot. *Charlotte Brontë: Style in the Novel*. Madison: University of Wisconsin Press, 1973.

Pykett, Lyn. *Emily Brontë*. Savage, Md.: Barnes & Noble, 1989.

Ratchford, Fannie E. *The Brontës' Web of Childhood*. New York: Columbia University Press, 1941.

Raymond, Ernest. *In the Steps of the Brontës*. London: Rich & Cowan, 1948.

Shorter, Clement K. *The Brontës and their Circle*. London: Dent, 1914.

Shuttleworth, Sally. *Charlotte Brontë and Victorian Psychology*. Cambridge: Cambridge University Press, 1996.

Sinclair, May. *The Three Brontës*. London: Hutchinson, 1914.

Stoneman, Patsy. *Brontë Transformations: The Cultural Dissemination of* Jane Eyre *and* Wuthering Heights. New York: Prentice Hall, 1996.

Tayler, Irene. *Holy Ghosts: The Male Muses of Emily and Charlotte Brontë*. New York: Columbia University Press, 1990.

Thormählen, Marianne. *The Brontës and Religion*. Cambridge: & New York: Cambridge University Press, 1999.

Wheat, Patricia H. *The Adytum of the Heart: The Literary Criticism of Charlotte Brontë*. Rutherford, N.J.: Fairleigh Dickinson University Press, 1992.

Wilks, Brian. *The Brontës of Haworth*. New York: Facts on File, 1986.

Winnifrith, Tom. *The Brontës and Their Background, Romance and Reality*. London: Macmillan, 1973.

Winnifrith and Edward Chitham. *Charlotte and Emily Brontë*. New York: St. Martin's Press, 1989.

Cumulative Index

Dictionary of Literary Biography, Volumes 1-340
Dictionary of Literary Biography Yearbook, 1980-2002
Dictionary of Literary Biography Documentary Series, Volumes 1-19
Concise Dictionary of American Literary Biography, Volumes 1-7
Concise Dictionary of British Literary Biography, Volumes 1-8
Concise Dictionary of World Literary Biography, Volumes 1-4

Cumulative Index

DLB before number: *Dictionary of Literary Biography*, Volumes 1-340
Y before number: *Dictionary of Literary Biography Yearbook*, 1980-2002
DS before number: *Dictionary of Literary Biography Documentary Series*, Volumes 1-19
CDALB before number: *Concise Dictionary of American Literary Biography*, Volumes 1-7
CDBLB before number: *Concise Dictionary of British Literary Biography*, Volumes 1-8
CDWLB before number: *Concise Dictionary of World Literary Biography*, Volumes 1-4

Best-Seller Lists
    An Assessment Y-84

    What's Really Wrong With
        Bestseller Lists Y-84

Bestuzhev, Aleksandr Aleksandrovich
    (Marlinsky) 1797-1837 . . . . .DLB-198

Bestuzhev, Nikolai Aleksandrovich
    1791-1855 . . . . .DLB-198

Betham-Edwards, Matilda Barbara
    (see Edwards, Matilda Barbara Betham-)

Betjeman, John
    1906-1984 . . . . .DLB-20; Y-84; CDBLB-7

Betocchi, Carlo 1899-1986. . . . . .DLB-128

Bettarini, Mariella 1942- DLB-128

Betts, Doris 1932- DLB-218; Y-82

Beveridge, Albert J. 1862-1927. . . . . .DLB-17

Beveridge, Judith 1956- DLB-325

Beverley, Robert circa 1673-1722 . . . . . .DLB-24, 30

Bevilacqua, Alberto 1934- DLB-196

Bevington, Louisa Sarah 1845-1895 . . . . .DLB-199

Beyle, Marie-Henri (see Stendhal)

Bèze, Théodore de (Theodore Beza)
    1519-1605 . . . . .DLB-327

Bhatt, Sujata 1956- DLB-323

Białoszewski, Miron 1922-1983 . . . . .DLB-232

Bianco, Margery Williams 1881-1944 . . . .DLB-160

Bibaud, Adèle 1854-1941. . . . . .DLB-92

Bibaud, Michel 1782-1857 . . . . .DLB-99

Bibliography
    Bibliographical and Textual Scholarship
        Since World War II. Y-89

    Center for Bibliographical Studies and
        Research at the University of
        California, Riverside. Y-91

    The Great Bibliographers Series Y-93

    Primary Bibliography: A Retrospective. . . .Y-95

Bichsel, Peter 1935- DLB-75

Bickerstaff, Isaac John 1733-circa 1808 . . . .DLB-89

Drexel Biddle [publishing house] DLB-49

Bidermann, Jacob
    1577 or 1578-1639 . . . . .DLB-164

Bidwell, Walter Hilliard 1798-1881 . . . . . . .DLB-79

Biehl, Charlotta Dorothea 1731-1788. . . . .DLB-300

Bienek, Horst 1930-1990 . . . . .DLB-75

Bierbaum, Otto Julius 1865-1910. . . . . . . .DLB-66

Bierce, Ambrose 1842-1914?
    . . . . . . DLB-11, 12, 23, 71, 74, 186; CDALB-3

Bigelow, William F. 1879-1966. . . . . .DLB-91

Biggers, Earl Derr 1884-1933 . . . . .DLB-306

Biggle, Lloyd, Jr. 1923-2002. . . . . .DLB-8

Bigiaretti, Libero 1905-1993 . . . . .DLB-177

Bigland, Eileen 1898-1970 . . . . .DLB-195

Biglow, Hosea (see Lowell, James Russell)

Bigongiari, Piero 1914-1997. . . . . .DLB-128

Bilac, Olavo 1865-1918 . . . . .DLB-307

Bilenchi, Romano 1909-1989. . . . . .DLB-264

Billinger, Richard 1890-1965 . . . . .DLB-124

Billings, Hammatt 1818-1874. . . . . .DLB-188

Billings, John Shaw 1898-1975 . . . . .DLB-137

Billings, Josh (see Shaw, Henry Wheeler)

Binchy, Maeve 1940- DLB-319

Binding, Rudolf G. 1867-1938 . . . . .DLB-66

Bing Xin 1900-1999. . . . . .DLB-328

Bingay, Malcolm 1884-1953 . . . . .DLB-241

Bingham, Caleb 1757-1817 . . . . .DLB-42

Bingham, George Barry 1906-1988 . . . . . .DLB-127

Bingham, Sallie 1937- DLB-234

William Bingley [publishing house] DLB-154

Binyon, Laurence 1869-1943 . . . . .DLB-19

Biographia Brittanica DLB-142

Biography
    Biographical Documents Y-84, 85

    A Celebration of Literary Biography Y-98

    Conference on Modern Biography Y-85

    The Cult of Biography
        Excerpts from the Second Folio Debate:
        "Biographies are generally a disease of
        English Literature" Y-86

    New Approaches to Biography: Challenges
        from Critical Theory, USC Conference
        on Literary Studies, 1990 . . . . .Y-90

    "The New Biography," by Virginia Woolf,
        New York Herald Tribune,
        30 October 1927. . . . . .DLB-149

    "The Practice of Biography," in *The English
        Sense of Humour and Other Essays,* by
        Harold Nicolson DLB-149

    "Principles of Biography," in *Elizabethan
        and Other Essays,* by Sidney Lee . . .DLB-149

    Remarks at the Opening of "The Biographical
        Part of Literature" Exhibition, by
        William R. Cagle Y-98

    Survey of Literary Biographies. Y-00

    A Transit of Poets and Others: American
        Biography in 1982 . . . . .Y-82

    The Year in Literary
        Biography. Y-83–01

Biography, The Practice of:
    An Interview with B. L. Reid Y-83

    An Interview with David Herbert Donald . . .Y-87

    An Interview with Humphrey Carpenter. . . .Y-84

    An Interview with Joan Mellen Y-94

    An Interview with John Caldwell Guilds Y-92

    An Interview with William Manchester . . .Y-85

John Bioren [publishing house] DLB-49

Bioy Casares, Adolfo 1914-1999 . . . . .DLB-113

Birch, Thomas 1705-1766 . . . . .DLB-336

Bird, Isabella Lucy 1831-1904 . . . . .DLB-166

Bird, Robert Montgomery 1806-1854 . . . .DLB-202

Bird, William 1888-1963 . . . . .DLB-4; DS-15

    The Cost of the *Cantos:* William Bird
        to Ezra Pound. Y-01

Birdsell, Sandra 1942- DLB-334

Birken, Sigmund von 1626-1681 . . . . .DLB-164

Birney, Earle 1904-1995. . . . . .DLB-88

Birrell, Augustine 1850-1933 . . . . .DLB-98

Bisher, Furman 1918- DLB-171

Bishop, Elizabeth
    1911-1979 . . . . .DLB-5, 169; CDALB-6

    The Elizabeth Bishop Society Y-01

Bishop, John Peale 1892-1944 . . . . . .DLB-4, 9, 45

Bismarck, Otto von 1815-1898 . . . . .DLB-129

Bisset, Robert 1759-1805 . . . . .DLB-142

Bissett, Bill 1939- DLB-53

Bitov, Andrei Georgievich 1937- DLB-302

Bitzius, Albert (see Gotthelf, Jeremias)

Bjørnboe, Jens 1920-1976. . . . . .DLB-297

Bjørnson, Bjørnstjerne 1832-1910 . . . . . . .DLB-329

Bjørnvig, Thorkild 1918-2004 . . . . .DLB-214

Black, David (D. M.) 1941- DLB-40

Black, Gavin (Oswald Morris Wynd)
    1913-1998 . . . . .DLB-276

Black, Lionel (Dudley Barker)
    1910-1980 . . . . .DLB-276

Black, Winifred 1863-1936 . . . . .DLB-25

Walter J. Black [publishing house] DLB-46

Blackamore, Arthur 1679-? DLB-24, 39

Blackburn, Alexander L. 1929- Y-85

Blackburn, John 1923-1993 . . . . .DLB-261

Blackburn, Paul 1926-1971 . . . . DLB-16; Y-81

Blackburn, Thomas 1916-1977 . . . . .DLB-27

Blacker, Terence 1948- DLB-271

Blackmore, R. D. 1825-1900 . . . . .DLB-18

Blackmore, Sir Richard 1654-1729. . . . . . .DLB-131

Blackmur, R. P. 1904-1965 . . . . .DLB-63

Blackwell, Alice Stone 1857-1950. . . . . . .DLB-303

Basil Blackwell, Publisher DLB-106

Blackstone, William 1723-1780 . . . . .DLB-336

Blackwood, Algernon Henry
    1869-1951 . . . . DLB-153, 156, 178

Blackwood, Caroline 1931-1996 . . . . .DLB-14, 207

William Blackwood and Sons, Ltd. DLB-154

Blackwood's Edinburgh Magazine
    1817-1980 . . . . .DLB-110

Blades, William 1824-1890 . . . . .DLB-184

Blaga, Lucian 1895-1961 . . . . .DLB-220

Blagden, Isabella 1817?-1873 . . . . .DLB-199

Blair, Eric Arthur (see Orwell, George)

Blair, Francis Preston 1791-1876. . . . . .DLB-43

Blair, Hugh
    Lectures on Rhetoric and Belles Lettres (1783),
        [excerpts] .DLB-31

Blair, James circa 1655-1743 . . . . .DLB-24

Blair, John Durburrow 1759-1823 . . . . .DLB-37

Blais, Marie-Claire 1939- DLB-53

Blaise, Clark 1940- DLB-53

G

H

K

N

O

Q

R

U

ISBN-13: 978-0-7876-8158-6
ISBN-10: 0-7876-8158-X

90000